Lecture Notes in Computer Science 1939
Edited by G. Goos, J. Hartmanis and J. van Leeuwen

Springer
Berlin
Heidelberg
New York
Barcelona
Hong Kong
London
Milan
Paris
Singapore
Tokyo

Andy Evans Stuart Kent
Bran Selic (Eds.)

«UML» 2000 – The Unified Modeling Language

Advancing the Standard

Third International Conference
York, UK, October 2-6, 2000
Proceedings

Series Editors

Gerhard Goos, Karlsruhe University, Germany
Juris Hartmanis, Cornell University, NY, USA
Jan van Leeuwen, Utrecht University, The Netherlands

Volume Editors

Andy Evans
University of York
Department of Computer Science
Heslington, York, Y010 5DD UK
E-mail: andye@cs.york.ac.uk

Stuart Kent
University of Kent
Computing Laboratory
Canterbury, Kent, UK
E-mail: s.j.h.kent@ukc.ac.uk

Bran Selic
Rational Software Inc.
340 March Road, Kanata, Ontario, K2K, 2E4, Canada
E-mail: bselic@rational.com

Cataloging-in-Publication Data applied for

Die Deutsche Bibliothek - CIP-Einheitsaufnahme

The unified modeling language : advancing the standard ; third international conference ; proceedings / UML 2000, York, UK, October 2 - 6, 2000. Andy Evans . . . (ed.). - Berlin ; Heidelberg ; New York ; Barcelona ; Hong Kong ; London ; Milan ; Paris ; Singapore ; Tokyo : Springer, 2000
(Lecture notes in computer science ; Vol. 1939)
ISBN 3-540-41133-X

CR Subject Classification (1998): D.2, D.3

ISSN 0302-9743
ISBN 3-540-41133-X Springer-Verlag Berlin Heidelberg New York

Springer-Verlag Berlin Heidelberg New York
a member of BertelsmannSpringer Science+Business Media GmbH

Printed in Germany

Typesetting: Camera-ready by author
Printed on acid-free paper SPIN 10780937 06/3142 5 4 3 2 1 0

Preface

Shall I go off to South America?
Shall I put out in my ship to sea?
Or get in my cage and be lions and tigers?
Or – shall I be only Me?

A. A. Milne, When We Were Very Young

The Unified Modeling Language (UML) is a language for specifying, visualising, constructing and documenting the artifacts of software systems. The UML originated from the wave of object-oriented analysis and design methods (OOA & D) that appeared in the early 1980's and 1990's. It's formation came about in direct response to a call for a standard OOA & D method by the Object Management Group (OMG) in 1996/7.

Since then, the UML has arguably become the lingua franca of the software engineering community – it is rare to find a new CASE tool, software engineering text, course or method that does not support UML in some way. This success can be attributed to many factors. The most important of these has been UML's capitalization of a general move in the software industry towards open standards. This has demonstrated that industry is more interested in a common, standardised modelling approach than in the particular philosophies that distinguished the earlier approaches to OOA & D. In addition, the UML standard has clearly benefited from its association with the OMG, which has provided an excellent open forum for its development. Currently, the OMG/UML standard is at version 1.4. However, at the time of writing, UML is on the verge of a lengthy period of major review and revision, which will result in version 2.0.

Version 2.0 of the UML represents an opportunity to realise many exciting and visionary ideas that are emerging in the field of object modelling. The first of these is the opportunity to develop a generally applicable standard modelling language, whose semantics and notation can be adapted to suit a wide variety of application domains. Such a language has a clear advantage over fixed definition languages, in that new variants can be quickly developed to meet different modelling requirements. In terms of UML, this means being able to view UML as a family of languages, i.e. a set of variations within the confines of a common core semantic base. The term that has emerged to describe these variations is a 'profile'. A profile is a UML semantic definition which extends and tailors the UML meta-model to a specific domain, process or application. Already, many examples of UML profiles are emerging (some of which are described in these proceedings). These include, user interaction, common warehouse data, software process engineering and real-time profiles, among many others.

Currently, UML 1.3 and, in particular, UML 1.4 provide a number of extension mechanisms which support profile design. However, significant work is being done to understand how version 2.0 can build on and extend these facilities. In particular, it seems important that the core part of UML that forms the root of all profiles be clearly delineated and precisely defined. Furthermore, UML 2.0 needs to provide the methodologies and tools necessary to support the difficult task of profile building. Ideally, some sort of profile building facility is required, which combines powerful meta-modelling tools, a meta-modelling language (itself a profile), appropriate meta-modelling patterns and tool generators.

Tools are another vital component of the UML 2.0 vision. Until recently, UML tools mainly offered diagram editors, design repositories and basic checking facilities. However, tools are now emerging that support sophisticated analysis and checking of UML models. This includes support for the Object Constraint Language (OCL), UML's standard language for describing constraints. These tools (a number of which are described in these proceedings) are examples of the first of a new breed of industrial strength software modelling tools. As the UML continues to develop, we fully expect that these types of tools will offer the modeller with increasingly powerful means of checking, interacting with and testing models. This will include the ability to analyse incomplete, non-executable and under-determined models, thus greatly improving confidence in the correctness of abstract specifications.

Underlying the development of profiles, tools and notations for UML is the need for greater precision within the next version of the standard. At present, the informal nature of the UML semantics means that there is significant scope for misinterpretation and misuse of the language. Much work being carried out in academia aims to address this problem by developing formal specifications of the UML semantics. However, it is increasingly apparent that formal specifications alone do not address the needs of the UML community. Industrial practitioners require a semantics that it is readily understandable, that can be interacted with using tools, and which is scalable and adaptable to the needs of profile definition. To this end, it appears likely that OO technologies (object modelling, patterns, reflection, component-based development, frameworks, product lines, and so on) have a key role to play in the production of such a semantic definition.

Finally, the widespread application of UML is leading to further refinements of the language's notations and supporting methodologies. Practical experiences in many other fields, including architectural design, data modelling, real-time systems and user interaction are significantly contributing to the development of the language. As such, this is where the true worth of UML will be determined and reflected in future versions of the standard. For only if a component of UML is effective in practice will it continue to flourish. Understanding the importance of practicality, and the experiences of other disciplines, is a vital step towards recognising the primary reason for UML's success in the first place.

The objective of ≪UML≫2000, in line with the ≪UML≫'99 and ≪UML≫'98 conferences, is to bring together researchers and developers from both academia and industry, to present and discuss *their* visions of the future of the UML standard.

In total 102 abstracts and 82 papers were submitted to the conference, of which 36 were selected by the programme committee for presentation. Previous ≪UML≫ conferences have been primarily structured around paper presentations and discussion panels. However, this year's conference also included a two-day tutorial and workshop session, in which 6 tutorials and 6 workshops were scheduled. These were selected from 20 tutorial and 12 workshop submissions. The primary purpose of these sessions was to provide a more informal forum for discussing state-of-the-art research in UML. Topics included: real-time UML, web applications, the OCL, interactive systems, tool support, extreme modelling and component-based development. Links to the workshops can be found at the conference web site: http://www.cs.york.ac.uk/uml2000.

We would like to express our deepest appreciation to the authors of submitted papers, tutorials, workshops and panels, and the programme committee members and the additional referees. In particular, Jaelson Castro and Stephen Mellor did an excellent job of managing the workshop and tutorial submissions. We would also like to thank Steve Cook, Ivar Jacobson and Cris Kobryn for agreeing to present invited talks at the conference. James Willans and Sara-Jayne Farmer at the University of York are also thanked for their contribution to setting up the conference web site and in organising and handling the electronic submission process. The START program (http://www.cs.umd.edu/~rich/start.html) was used to gather and organise submitted papers and reviews, and was extended to deal with an online voting process. We would also like to thank the ≪UML≫ steering committee for their advice, Jean-Michel Bruel and Robert France for maintaining the mailing list, and Kathy Krell for agreeing to act as on-site meeting organiser.

August 2000

Andy Evans
Stuart Kent
Bran Selic

Organisation

≪UML≫2000 was organised by Andy Evans from the Department of Computer Science at the University of York, UK, by Stuart Kent from the Computing Laboratory at the University of Kent, UK, and by Bran Selic from Rational Software Inc., Canada, under the auspices of the IEEE Technical Council on Complexity in Computing, and in cooperation with ACM SIGSOFT.

Executive Commitee

General Chair:	Bran Selic (Rational Software Inc., Canada)
Conference Chair:	Stuart Kent (University of Kent, UK)
Programme Chair:	Andy Evans (University of York, UK)
Tutorial Chair:	Stephen Mellor (Project Technology Inc., USA)
Workshop Chair:	Jaelson Castro, (Universidade Federal de Pernambuco, Brazil)

Organising Team

On-site Coordinator:	Kathy Krell
Web Programming :	James Willans and Sara-Jayne Farmer
Publicity Chair (Europe) :	Jean-Michel Bruel
Publicity Chair (Americas):	Robert France

Programme Committee

Colin Atkinson (Germany)
Jean Bezivin (France)
Grady Booch (USA)
Alan Brown (USA)
Jean-Michel Bruel (France)
David Bustard (UK)
Jaelson Castro (Brazil)
Betty Cheng (USA)
Derek Coleman (UK)
Steve Cook (UK)
John Daniels (UK)
Desmond D'Souza (USA)
Gregor Engels (Germany)
Eduardo. B. Fernandez (USA)
Robert France (USA)
Martin Gogolla (Germany)
Brian Henderson-Sellers (Australia)
Heinrich Hussmann (Germany)
Pavel Hruby (Denmark)
Peter Hrushchka (Germany)
Jean-Marc Jezequel (France)
Haim Kilov (USA)
Cris Kobryn (USA)
Craig Larman (USA)
Peter Linnington (UK)
Ian Maung (USA)
Stephen Mellor (USA)
Richard Mitchell (UK)
Ana Moreira (Portugal)
Pierre-Alain Muller (France)
John Mylopoulos (US)
Gunnar Overgaard (Sweden)
Niall Ross (UK)
James Rumbaugh (USA)
Bernhard Rumpe (Germany)
Andy Schuerr (Germany)
Keng Siau (USA)
Ed Seidewitz (USA)
Perdita Stevens (UK)
Jos Warmer (Netherlands)
Anthony Wasserman (USA)
Alan Cameron Wills (UK).

Additional Referees

Joao Araujo
Mohammed Benattou
Lutz Bichler
Jim Bieman
Alan Birchenough
Christian Bunse
Luis Caires
Laura Campbell
Robert Clark
Tony Clark
Ralph Depke
Mike Fischer
Falk Fünfstück
Emanuel Grant
Luuk Groenewegen
Reiko Heckel
Wolfram Kahl
Manuel Kolp
Thomas Kuehne
Jiahne Liao
Katharina Mehner
Wai Ming Ho
Ansgar Radermacher
Aamod Sane
Stefan Sauer
Anne Thomas

Sponsoring Association

IEEE Technical Council on Complexity in Computing,
http://www.computer.org

Cooperating and Supporting Associations

ACM SIGSOFT (Association for Computing Machinery, Special Interest Group for Software Engineering), http://www.acm.org/sigsoft/

OMG (The Object Management Group), http://www.omg.org.
UML and ≪UML≫ are trademarks of the OMG.

Sponsoring Companies

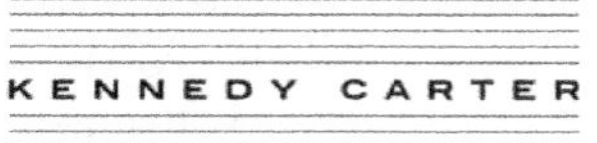

Kennedy-Carter, UK. http://www.kc.com/

Project Technology Inc. USA. http://www.projtech.com/

Rational Software Inc. Canada. http://www.rational.com

Table of Contents

Use Cases

Enterprise Applications

Panel 1

Interactive Systems

Applications

Roles

Knowledge Bases

Invited Talk

OCL Tools

Meta-modelling

Panel 2

Behavioural Modelling

Methodology

Actions and Constraints

Patterns

Invited Talk

Architecture

State Charts

Panel 3

From Use Cases to System Operation Specifications

Shane Sendall and Alfred Strohmeier

Swiss Federal Institute of Technology Lausanne
Department of Computer Science
Software Engineering Laboratory
1015 Lausanne EPFL, Switzerland

email: {Shane.Sendall, Alfred.Strohmeier}@epfl.ch

ABSTRACT The purpose of this paper is to first showcase the concept of an operation schema—a precise form of system-level operation specification—and secondly show how operation schemas enhance development when they are used as a supplement to use case descriptions. An operation schema declaratively describes the effects of a system operation by pre- and postconditions using the Object Constraint Language (OCL), as defined by the Unified Modeling Language (UML). In particular, the paper highlights techniques to map use cases to operation schemas and discusses the advantages of doing so in terms of clarifying the granularity and purpose of use cases and providing a precise specification of system behavior.

KEYWORDS Unified Modeling Language, Use Cases, Object Constraint Language, Operation Specification, Object-Oriented Software Development.

1 Introduction

The invasion of software-intensive systems into nearly every domain of our life has seen the practice of software development stretched to combat the ever-increasing complexity of such systems and to meet the increased demand. In such a development environment, the transformation from concept to running implementation needs to rapidly meet the market demand, but at the same time the software should exhibit the necessary qualities of robustness, maintainability, and meet other requirements, such as usability and performance demands. Currently, software is often lacking quality—as observed by the US President's IT Advisory Committee [10],

> "We have become dangerously dependent on large software systems whose behavior is not well understood and which often fail in unpredicted ways."

They continue further on, pin-pointing one of the deficiencies in current software development,

> "Having meaningful and standardized behavioral specifications would make it feasible to determine the properties of a software system and enable more thorough and less costly testing. Unfortunately such specifications are rarely used. Even less frequently is there a correspondence between a specification and the software itself."

Currently in industry much of what would be loosely classified as system specification is performed with use cases. Use cases are an excellent tool for capturing behavioral requirements of software systems. They are informal descriptions, almost always written in natural language, and consequently they lack rigor and a basis to reason about system properties.

A. Evans, S. Kent and B. Selic (Eds.): «UML» 2000, LNCS 1939, pp. 1-15, 2000.

In this paper, we look at bringing the benefits of behavioral specification techniques to main-stream software development by proposing the use of operation schemas as a supplement to use cases. An operation schema declaratively describes the effects of a system operation by pre- and postconditions using the Object Constraint Language (OCL) [15], as defined by the Unified Modeling Language (UML) [9]. We illustrate the advantages of complementing use cases with operation schemas by an example of a multi-cabin elevator control system. Moreover, we look at how one gets from use cases to operation schemas, and thus propose a mapping from use cases to operation schemas.

This paper is composed in the following way: section 2 gives an introduction to use cases; section 3 describes the elevator control system example that is used throughout the paper; section 4 gives some motivation for supplementing use cases with operation schemas; section 5 provides an introduction to operation schemas and OCL; section 6 proposes a mapping from a use case to operation schemas and demonstrates it for the elevator control system example; section 7 discusses related work; and finally section 8 concludes the paper and proposes possible future work.

2 Use Cases

Use cases are used to capture behavioral requirements of software systems. Use cases are popular because of their informal, easy to use and to understand style which caters to technical as well as non-technical stakeholders of the software under development. Use cases can be decomposed into further use cases, and therefore they are scalable to any system size. Moreover, it is possible to trace between subordinate use cases and the "parent" use case. Also, use cases have a wide spectrum of applicability: they can be used in many different ways, in many different domains, even non-software domains, making them a very versatile tool to have in one's development toolkit.

Contrary to popular belief, use cases are primarily textual descriptions, the graphical appearance, called a use case diagram in UML, tells nothing more than the names of the use cases and their relationships to actors. This graphical appearance is just used to give an overview of the use cases in focus, from which allocation of work can be partitioned, for example.

UML also defines three relationships that can be used to structure use cases: "extends", "includes", and "specialization". These relationships help to avoid duplication of work and try to direct one towards a more object-oriented view of the world rather than towards functional decomposition. UML, however, does not go into detail about what content a use case description consists in and how it is structured. UML states that textual descriptions can be used, but that activity and state diagrams might be another alternative.

In practice, use cases can have varying degrees of formality depending on how much and what kind of information is recorded. Some will be just a casual story-telling description, others will be fully-dressed use cases that include an assortment of secondary information and that are possibly even described using pre- and postconditions. The type of template and style one chooses reflects how and where one is going to model with use cases.

On the one hand, the loose guidelines governing the general form of use cases has seen use cases used in new and imaginative ways, allowing many flavors of use cases to grow and diversify, but on the other hand, the lack of strict guidelines/style in the original definition has led to confusion among inexperienced users as to what the structure and purpose of a use case should be.

We use and advocate a style of use case proposed by Cockburn [1]. This style elaborates on the original work on use cases by Ivar Jacobson. Jacobson's definition of a use case introduces the notion of transaction [6]:

> "A use case is a sequence of transactions performed by a system, which yields an observable result of value for a particular actor."

where he defines a transaction as:

> "A transaction consists of a set of actions performed by a system. A transaction is invoked by a stimulus from an actor to the system, or by a timed trigger within the system."

Cockburn's definition [1] highlights that effective use cases are goal-based:

> "A use case is a description of the possible sequences of interaction between the system under discussion and external actors, related to the goal of one particular actor."

Cockburn also clarifies Jacobson's notion of transaction. He states that it consists of 4 steps [1]:

> "1. The primary actor sends request and data to the system; 2. The system validates the request and the data; 3. The system alters its internal state; 4. The system replies to the actor with the result".

A use case describes every possible situation that can arise when a user has a particular goal against the system. Each "possible situation" that arises is referred to as a scenario, and a use case can be considered as a collection of related scenarios.

Cockburn [1] provides some suggestions for defining granularity levels in use cases. He identified three different abstraction levels, in terms of the view of the system: summary level is the 50,000 feet perspective, user-goal level is the sea-level perspective, sub-function is the underwater perspective. Summary level use cases show the life-cycle sequencing of related goals; they act as a table of contents for lower-level use cases. User-goal level use cases describe the goal that the primary actor has in trying to do something. A user-goal level use case is usually done by one person, in one place, at one time, and the actor can normally go away happy as soon as this goal is completed. Subfunction level use cases are those required to carry out user goals, they are low-level and are generally the level of operation schemas or below. Therefore, as a general rule of thumb, we do not normally deal with sub-function use cases, we use operation schemas instead. User-goal level use cases are of greatest interest to us, and we will illustrate one in the next section on the elevator example.

3 Elevator Control System Example

For illustrating our approach, we will "develop" an elevator control system. The system controls multiple lift cabins that all service the same floors of a building. There are buttons to go up and down on each floor to request the lift (apart from the top-most and bottom-most floors). Inside an elevator cabin, there is a series of buttons, one for each floor. The arrival of a cabin at a floor is detected by a sensor. The system may ask the elevator to go up, go down or stop. In this example, we assume that the elevator's braking distance is negligible. The system may ask the elevator to open its door and it receives a notification when the door is closed—the door closes automatically after a predefined amount of time, which simulates the activity of letting people on and off at each floor. However, neither this function of the elevator nor the protection associated with the door closing (stopping it from squashing people) are part of the system to realize. Finally, for reasons of conciseness in this paper, we have removed the capability of canceling requests, therefore a request is definitive. The full worked example is available at [13].

The example illustrates a special situation where the actors have only very limited predefined usage protocols with the system. This is not always the case: for example, interaction with human actors is usually a lot more complex.

For this system, we could imagine a summary-level use case that describes the life cycle of the elevator. But for reasons of size, we concentrate instead on one user-goal level use case called Take Lift. Take Lift describes the activity of a user taking a lift from one floor to another. The use case description for Take Lift is shown in figure 1.

The Take Lift use case description, figure 1, follows, more or less, the template and style recommended by Cockburn [1]. It consists of seven different sections, in which the Main success scenario and the Extensions sections describe the different steps of the use case. The Main success scenario section describes the standard path through the use case. The Extensions section describes the alternatives to the standard path scenario. Sometimes an alternative supersedes the main step, e.g. step 2a, and sometimes it might happen in addition to the main step, e.g. step 7 || (interleaved or in parallel). An alternative might correspond to regular behavior, exceptional behavior that is recoverable, or unrecoverable erroneous behavior.

The use case takes the user's perspective and, for example, differentiates "the user takes the stairs" from "the user enters the lift but does not make a request", whereas the system's viewpoint would not do so.

Now taking a look at the interactions between the system and the actors which realize the Take Lift use case, we see in figure 2 the system interface necessary for the use case. In section 6, we will discuss how we derive these events and the corresponding operations that they invoke from the Take Lift use case, but for the moment we can just assume their existence. The System Context Model, figure 2, shows four different input events: externalRequest, internalRequest, doorIsClosed, and atFloor, and eight different types of output events: AckExtRequest, AckIntRequest, ServicedExtRequest, ServicedIntRequest, OpenDoor, GoUp, GoDown, and Stop.

The model also shows that there is some form of communication between the User actor type and the external request indicator (ExtRequestIndicator) and internal request indicator (IntRequestIndicator) to clarify that the requests originally come from the user. Although we admit this may not be valid UML, strictly speaking, we think showing external communication paths often clarifies the consistent overall working of a system.

Use Case: Take Lift
Scope: "System" means the Multi-Cabin Elevator Control System
Level: User goal
Goal: A User wants to go from one floor to another.
Context of Use: The Lift system has many lift cabins that service many users at any one time, taking them from one floor to another.
Primary Actor: User
Main Success Scenario:
1. The User requests a lift from a particular floor (source floor), also indicating the direction desired.
2. The System acknowledges the external request and commands the most suitable lift (which is currently idle) to go to the source floor [-> externalRequest].
3. The lift has reached the source floor, the System commands the lift to stop and open its Door, and the System dismisses the original external request of the User [-> atFloor].
4. The User enters the lift.
Steps 5 and 6 can happen in parallel (also implying any order)
5. The lift door closes.
6. The User requests a destination floor (inside the cabin).
7. The System acknowledges the internal request and commands the lift to go to the destination floor [-> internalRequest].
8. The lift has reached the destination floor, the System commands the lift to stop and open its Door, and the System dismisses the internal request of the User [-> atFloor].
9. The User exits the lift.
Extensions:
2a. A lift is already at the source floor with the door open.
  2a.1. The System acknowledges the external request and dismisses it [-> externalRequest]; and the use case continues at step 4.
2b. A lift is already at the source floor with the door closed and is currently idle (not servicing another request).
  2b.1. The System acknowledges the external request, commands the lift to open its Door, and dismisses the external request [-> externalRequest]; the use case continues at step 4.
2c. No lifts are currently available.
  2c.1. The System acknowledges and schedules the request [-> externalRequest].
  2c.2. A lift becomes available.
    2c.2.1 The System commands the lift to go to the destination floor [-> doorIsClosed]; continues step 3.
(2-3)||. The User leaves and takes the stairs: the use case ends after step 3.
3a. The lift never reaches the source floor or the Door does not open:
  3a.1.The User unhappily takes the stairs; the use case ends.
6a. The User does not make a request: the use case ends.
6b.The User(s) requests several different floors.
  6b.1. The System schedules all the internal requests, acknowledges them and commands the lift to go to the first floor that was requested [-> internalRequest].
  6b.2. The lift stops off at each floor requested, dismissing the requests on the way [-> atFloor] [-> doorIsClosed]; the user may exit the lift at any stop off; the use cases ends.
6c.The User requests a destination floor (inside the cabin), but the lift door is still open.
  6c.1. The System acknowledges and schedules the request [-> internalRequest].
  6c.2. The lift door closes: The System commands the lift to go to the destination floor [-> doorIsClosed]; the use case continues at step 8.
7||. The User requests another destination.
  7||.1. The System schedules the request, in addition to the current request [-> internalRequest].
  7||.2. same as 6.b.2
7a. The lift is already at the destination floor.
  7a.1. The System commands the lift to reopen its Door, and the System dismisses the internal request of the User [-> internalRequest]; the use case continues at step 9.
8a. The lift does not drop off the User at the destination floor, either because the Door doesn't open or the lift never reaches the destination floor.
  8a.1.The User, by mobile phone, sues the company who made the multi-cabin elevator system (not automated); the use case ends.

Fig. 1. Take Lift Use Case

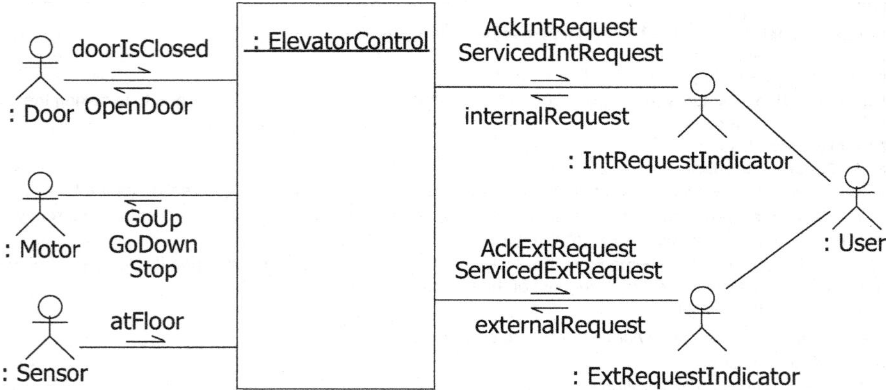

Fig. 2. Elevator Control System Context Model

The analysis-level class model for the elevator control system is shown in figure 3. It shows all the domain concepts and relationships between them. Inside the system there are five domain classes, Cabin, Floor, Request, IntRequest, and ExtRequest, and outside six actor classes, Motor, Door, IntRequestIndicator, ExtRequestIndicator, User, and Sensor. The system has five associations: IsFoundAt links a cabin to its current floor, HasIntRequest links a collection of internal requests to a particular cabin, HasCurrentRequest links a cabin to its current request, hasExtRequest models the collection of all external requests issued by users, and HasTargetFloor links requests to their target floor (source of call or destination). Finally, an <<id>> stereotyped association means that the system can identify an actor starting from an object belonging to the system, e.g., given a Cabin, cab, we can find its corresponding motor via the HasMotor association, denoted in OCL by cab.movedBy.

4 Supplementing Use Cases with Operation Schemas

Use cases are an excellent tool for capturing behavioral requirements because they describe the system from a user's point of view, which naturally allows one to describe not only normal behavior—successful scenarios—but also abnormal behavior—unsuccessful and exceptional scenarios. Another approach, or view on the system is where one looks purely at the interface and functionality offered by the system. This is the view provided by operation schemas.

The two views complement each other nicely: use cases provide the informal map of interactions between the system and actors, whereas operation schemas precisely describe a particular system action which executes atomically, called a system operation. A system operation corresponds to a transaction as defined by Jacobson (see section 2), a sequence of which forms a use case.

Operation schemas complement use cases in a number of ways. Firstly, use cases face the usual problems of descriptions written in natural language, i.e., they may be ambiguous and their level of description may vary, making it easy to fall into a design description. However, operation schemas are less likely to have such problems due to the use of OCL and are less likely to embody premature design decisions due to this single level of description. Secondly, operation schemas being precise and more formal than natural language offer a more rigorous basis on which we can reason about system properties, verify that invariants are obeyed, and provide a basis for specification-based testing. Potentially much of the verification and testing can be automated because of the formal nature of OCL. Thirdly, finding the right granularity for a use case is difficult, because there is a danger of decomposing use cases into pieces too small. On the contrary, operation schemas break the recursive decomposition at the level of operation schemas. Finally, operation schemas have a one-to-one mapping to collaboration diagrams, an important design artifact. One operation schema is realized by one collaboration diagram. A use case, on the other hand, does not map well to any single design artifact. As Cockburn [1] observed in the context of use cases:

"Design doesn't cluster by use case, and blindly following the use case structure leads to functional decomposition design".

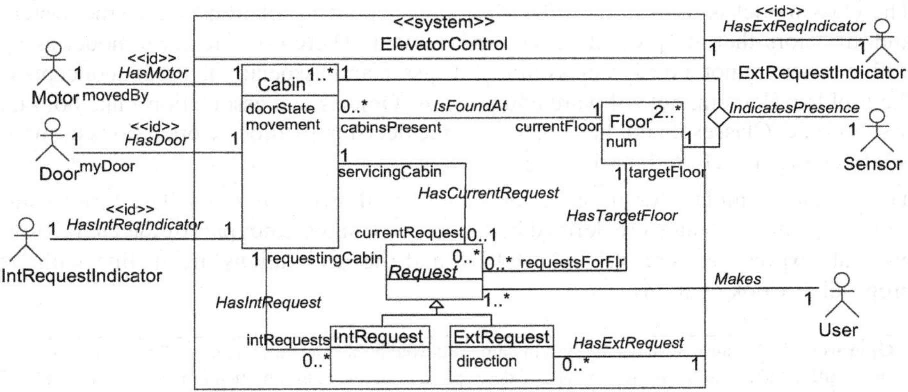

Fig. 3. Elevator Control System Class Model

It is worthwhile to note that operation schemas do not offer any advice on the allocation of behavior to objects: all the work is still to be done in terms of designing the objects of the system. The integration of collaboration diagrams into a coherent architecture is outside the scope of this paper, but interested readers are referred to [8].

We have found the approach of taking use cases to operation schemas enhances the development of reactive systems. However, we do acknowledge introducing operation schemas into a project requires an upfront cost for learning OCL and it forces one to spend longer in conceptual phases of development, which are often perceived by management as the "non-productive" phases.

5 Operation Schemas

An operation schema describes the effect of the operation on an abstract state representation of the system and any events sent to the outside world. It is written in a declarative form that abstracts from the object interactions inside the system which will eventually realize the operation. It describes the *assumed* initial state by a precondition, and the change in system state observed after the execution of the operation by a postcondition. Operation schemas use UML's OCL formalism, which was built with the purpose to be writable and readable by developers.

The system model is reactive in nature and all communication with the environment is achieved by asynchronous input/output events, termed signals in UML[1]. All system operations are triggered by input events, normally of the same name as the triggered operation.

The change of state resulting from an operation's execution is described in terms of objects, attributes and association links, which are themselves described in a class model. The postcondition of the system operation can assert that objects are created, attribute values are changed, association links are added or removed, and certain events are sent to outside actors. The association links between objects act like a network, guaranteeing that one can navigate to any state information that is required by an operation.

The class model is used to describe all the concepts and relationships in the system, and all actors that are present in the environment. Therefore, the class model as we define it here is not a design class model. Classes and associations model concepts of the problem domain, not software components. Objects and association links hold the system state. Classes do not have behavior; the decision to allocate operations or methods to classes is deferred until design.

The standard template for an operation schema is shown in figure 4. The various subsections of the schema were defined by the authors, and are not part of the OCL. However, all expressions are written in OCL, and the declarations are in line with the proposal of Cook et al. [4]

Operation: This clause displays the system name followed by the operation name and parameter list.
Description: This clause provides a concise description of the operation written in natural language.
Notes: This clause provides additonal comments.
Use Cases: This clause contains cross-references to superordinate use case(s).
Scope: This clause declares the classes, associations, and system-wide objects of the class model that are used in the schema.
Declares: This clause provides declarations of all constants and variables designating objects, datatypes, object collections, and datatype collections used in the **Pre** and **Post** clauses.
Sends: This clause specifies which kinds of events are sent to which actor types. Sending an event is modeled by placing the event into the local event queue of the destination actor. It is also possible to declare event instances and event collections, and to enforce event sequencing.
Pre: This clause is the operation's precondition written in OCL that evaluates to true or false. The precondition is made up of possibly many boolean OCL expressions separated by semi-colons (';'). A semi-colon replaces a "logical and" and is used as a boolean expression *terminator* (not separator).
Post: This clause is the operation's postcondition. Like the precondition, the postcondition is made up of possibly many boolean OCL expressions separated by semi-colons (';'). If the precondition is true, then the postcondition is true after the execution of the operation; if the precondition is false, the behavior of the operation is not defined by the schema. This is also the only clause that can refer to the pre-state, by the notation *@pre*.

Fig. 4. Operation Schema Format

---

1. According to UML, use cases use signals for the communication between the system and actors.

5.1 Presentation of OCL

UML [11] defines a navigation language called the Object Constraint Language (OCL) [15], a formal language whose principles are based on set theory. OCL can be used in various ways to add precision to UML models beyond the capabilities of the graphical diagrams. Two common uses of OCL are the definition of constraints on class models and the statement of system invariants. As we will see it can also be used to define pre- and postconditions for operations.

OCL is a declarative language. An OCL expression has no side effects, i.e. an OCL expression constrains the system by observation rather than simulation of the system. When describing operations, an OCL expression is evaluated on a consistent system state, i.e. no system changes are possible while the expression is evaluated. OCL is a typed language; it provides elementary types, like Boolean, Integer, etc., includes collections, like Set, Bag, and Sequence, and has an assortment of predefined operators on these basic types. It also allows user-defined types which can be any type defined in a UML model, in particular classes. OCL uses an object-oriented-like notation to access properties, attributes, and for applying operators.

We now highlight the atFloor operation schema, shown in figure 5. The atFloor operation schema describes the action of the system to stop at a particular floor or to continue on to the next one; the decision is based solely on whether there are any requests for the floor. The operation is triggered by a floor sensor when it detects the cabin at a particular floor. For the moment, we will ignore how we derived this operation schema from the Take Lift use case and just concentrate on the syntax and content of the schema itself.

The **Declares** clause defines a local boolean variable, makeStop, which results in true if there is an internal request or external request (that is requesting the same direction as the lift is currently going) for the supplied floor f. The **Sends** clause shows that the event types Stop, GoUp, GoDown, OpenDoor, ServicedExtRequest, ServicedIntRequest are in scope and that Stop and OpenDoor have named instances. Finally, it states that the two event instances are sent in the order stop followed by open. The **Pre** clause states that the cabin cab has a currentRequest, i.e., cab is servicing a request, and cab is moving.

The dot notation usually results in a set of objects or values, including the special cases of a single element or an empty set. For instance, self.cabin is the set of all cabins in the system, self denoting the system instance. When navigating on association links the dot notation is used together with the role name, e.g. cab.currentFloor. If there is no explicit role name, then the name of the target class is used as an implicit role name. For example, self.extRequest denotes the set of external requests that can be reached by navigating from self (the system instance) on the hasExtRequest association.

The arrow operator is used only on collections, in postfix style. The operator following the arrow is applied to the previous "term". For instance, dropOffRequest -> union (pickUpRequest) results in a set consisting of the union of the two sets dropOffRequest and pickUpRequest.

Operation: ElevatorControl::atFloor (cab: Cabin, f: Floor)
Description: The cabin has reached a particular floor, it may continue or stop depending on its destination and the requests for this floor.
Notes: The system can receive many atFloor events at any one time, each for a different cabin.
Use Case(s): TakeLift;
Scope: Cabin; Floor; Request; IntRequest; ExtRequest; HasIntRequest; HasExtRequest; HasCurrentRequest; HasTargetFloor; IsFoundAt;
Declares:
```
  directionHeading: Direction ::= if self.externalRequest->includes (cab.currentRequest) then
                    cab.currentRequest.direction; else cab.movement; endif;
  dropOffRequest: Set (IntRequest) ::= cab.intRequests->select (r | r.targetFloor = f);
  pickUpRequest: Set (ExtRequest) ::= self.extRequest->select (r | r.targetFloor = f and
                    r.direction = directionHeading);
  reqsForThisFloor: Set (Request) ::= dropOffRequest->union (pickUpRequest);
  makeStop: Boolean ::= reqsForThisFloor->notEmpty;
```
Sends:
```
  Motor::{Stop, GoUp, GoDown}, Door::{OpenDoor},
  ExtRequestIndicator::{ServicedExtRequest}, IntRequestIndicator::{ServicedIntRequest};
  stop: Stop, open: OpenDoor;
  Sequence {stop, open}; -- the output events are sent in the order stop followed by open
```
Pre:
```
  cab.currentRequest->notEmpty; -- cab was going somewhere
  cab.movement <> #stopped; -- cab was moving
```
Post:
```
  cab.currentFloor = f; -- new current floor for the cabin
  if makeStop then -- someone to drop off or pick up
    (cab.movedBy).events->includes (stop ()); -- stop sent to cab motor
    cab.movement = #stopped;
    (cab.myDoor).events->includes (open ()); -- open sent to door
    cab.doorState = #open;
    self.request->excludesAll (reqsForThisFloor); -- removed request(s) for this floor
    if pickUpRequest->notEmpty then
        (self.extReqIndicator).events->includes (ServicedExtRequest' (
            callingFlr => pickUpRequest.targetFloor, dir => pickRequest.direction));
    endif;
    if dropOffRequest->notEmpty then
        (self.intReqIndicator).events->includes (ServicedIntRequest' (
            destFlr => dropOffRequest.targetFloor));
    endif;
  endif;
```

Fig. 5. atFloor Operation Schema for Elevator Control System

The first line of the **Post** clause states that the cabin is now found at floor f. The next (compound) expression states that if a stop was made, then the cabin's motor was told to stop, the cabin's door was told to open, the state attributes of the cabin were updated, and the requests that were serviced by this stop were removed from the system. Note that the expression, self.request->excludesAll (reqsForThisFloor), not only removes the serviced request objects from the set of Request instances, but deletes also all the association links targeting one of these objects from the associations IntRequest, ExtRequest and CurrentRequest. For an explanation of the frame assumption for operation schemas which explains this sort of implicit removal, see [12].

In the **Post** clause, sending events is described by stating that an event instance was put into the event queue of the appropriate actor instance. For example, the third line of the postcondition states that the actor instance cab.movedBy, denoting a navigation from the cabin to its motor via the HasMotor association, has an event instance called stop in its local event queue. Looking closer at the OCL notation, an expression, such as cab.doorState = #open, means that the attribute, doorState, of the object cab has the value open (the '#' indicates an enumerated type value) after the execution of the operation.

In the description of postconditions we use the principle of minimum set [12] to clarify the semantics of the Post clause, to make postconditions more readable and to make it possible to state postconditions incrementally. For example, if request1 and request5 are linked to a cabin, cab, via the HasIntRequest association, then the following two conditions are equivalent:

```
cab.intRequests->includes (request1) and cab.intRequests-> includes (request5);     (1)
cab.intRequests = cab.intRequests@pre->union (Set {request1, request5})              (2)
```

The minimum set principle applied to the first condition guarantees that no extra elements are included in the cab.intRequests set after the execution of the operation (other than request1 and request5).

For a discussion on the semantic aspects of operation schemas see [12].

6 Mapping Use Cases to Operation Schemas

In this section, we describe the activity of deriving system operations from use cases. Generally, operation schemas are derived from user-goal level use cases, but sometimes sub-function level use cases can be useful too. The general rule is to decompose use cases until we get to use cases, where each step of the use case is a system operation, more or less.

This mapping activity is not necessarily straight-forward because the interaction with secondary actors can often be vague and may require further clarification of the use case in question. Before this mapping activity is started, a class model is made for the system which is a first approximation of the "system state", which will be needed to write the operation schemas. This class model (see figure 3 for an example) gets refined as the operation schemas are worked out. Moreover, the mapping activity exhibits iterations of refining the use case and writing/updating the corresponding operation schemas and the class model.

The general approach for mapping a use case to its corresponding operation schemas involves analyzing each step of the use case, looking for events sent by actors that trigger a system operation; once a trigger has been found, the system operation is described by an operation schema. The ultimate goal of the mapping activity is to partition the use case into a sequence of system operations. An important point to remember when deriving system operations from the use case is that for each system operation a triggering event must be found. Once we have decomposed the use case into system operations, we stop decomposition. Indeed, we have found that further decomposition often leads to structured design instead of object-oriented design.

We now show, stage-by-stage, the derivation of system operations from the Take Lift use case (figure 1). Step 1 of the Main success scenario describes the user making an external request for a lift—this is a trigger for a system action. The system action comes in step 2 where the system commands a lift to service the request. We, therefore, define a system operation called externalRequest which handles this action and specify it in an operation schema. To make the trace explicit, we add a hyperlink from the use case to the operation schema[1] (see the end of step 2 in figure 1).

Looking now at step 3, we see that the system performs an action, and we need, therefore, to trigger it. Looking closely at the text, we see that the situation was brought up by the lift reaching the source floor. We look back to the original problem description (section 3) and see that we receive an event whenever the lift reaches a certain floor, in our case the source floor. We, therefore, define a system operation called atFloor, triggered by the floor sensor, which handles the action of stopping the lift, opening the door and dismissing the request, and specify it in an operation schema.

Looking at the steps 4 and 5, we see that no obligation is placed on the system to do anything (although note that we will receive an event from the door informing us that the door is closed). Similarly to the steps 1 and 2, the steps 6 and 7 indicate a request and a corresponding system action, except this time the request is from inside the lift. We, therefore, define a system operation called internalRequest which handles this action and specify it in an operation schema. Similarly to step 3, step 8 is handled by the atFloor system operation. And looking at step 9, we see that no event or obligation is placed on the system.

Now let's look at the steps in the Extensions clause. The steps 2a and 2b, alternatives to step 2, detail other situations that need to be dealt with in the externalRequest system operation. Looking at step 2c, we have a condition that no lifts are available; this means that the externalRequest system operation is responsible for step 2.c.1, i.e., acknowledging and queuing the request. However, we see in step 2.c.2.1 that the system performs an action, and again we need a trigger. Examining closely the text, we see that a lift is in a position to go to another floor, in this case to do a pick up. We look back to the original problem description (section 3) and see that we receive an event whenever the lift closes it door. This event seems to be the best candidate for moving off the lift. We, therefore, define a system operation called doorIsClosed, triggered by the door, which is responsible for the action of calculating and handling where the lift is to go next, and specify it in an operation schema.

Step (2-3)|| means that the step can be done in parallel to the steps 2 or 3. This step along with steps 3a and 6a have no effect on the system functionality. The steps 6b and 7|| involve multiple stop offs by the lift, and therefore they queue the request with the internalRequest system operation and use a combination of atFloor and doorIsClosed system operations for stopping and moving off the lift, respectively. The step 7b details a situation that needs to be dealt with in the internalRequest system operation. Finally, the step 8a has no effect on the system functionality.

---

1. Our convention for referencing the operation schema is to put the system operation name (hyperlinked) inside square brackets with an arrow preceding the name, e.g. [-> sysOpX].

```
Operation: ElevatorControl::externalRequest (f: Floor, d: Direction)
Description: An external request to get a lift, indicating the direction desired, is made.
Notes: The system can receive many externalRequest input events at any one time.
Use Case(s): TakeLift;
Scope: Cabin; HasCurrentRequest; IsFoundAt; HasExtRequest; HasTargetFloor; ExtRequest;
Floor;
Declares:
  alreadyRequested: Boolean ::= self.extRequest->exists (r | r.direction = d and
     r.targetFloor = f);
  allAvailableCabins: Set (Cabin) ::= self.cabin->select (c | ((c.currentRequest->isEmpty and
     c.doorState = #closed) or (c.currentFloor = f and c.doorState = #open))) );
  -- the set of all cabins that are idle, or stopped with door open at the right floor
  cab: Cabin;
  req: ExtRequest;
Sends:
  Door::{OpenDoor}, Motor::{GoUp, GoDown},
  ExtRequestIndicator::{AckExtRequest, ServicedExtRequest};
Pre:
  true
Post:
  if not alreadyRequested then
     if allAvailableCabins->notEmpty then -- if cabins are available
        cab = bestSuitedCabin (allAvailableCabins, f); -- cab is best suited cabin
        if cab.currentFloor@pre = f then -- cab is currently at the requested floor
           cab.doorState = #open;
           (cab.myDoor).events->includes (OpenDoor' ()); -- note: door may have already been open
           (self.extReqIndicator).events->includes (ServicedExtRequest' (callingFlr => f,
              dir => d));
        else -- the lift was not on floor f
           req.oclIsNew (direction => d);
           req.targetFloor = f;
           self.extRequest->includes (req);
           cab.currentRequest = req;
           if (f.num > cab.currentFloor@pre.num) then -- if lift is to go up
              cab.movement = #up;
              (cab.movedBy).events->includes (GoUp' ());
           else -- if lift is to go down
              cab.movement = #down;
              (cab.movedBy).events->includes (GoDown' ());
           endif;
        endif;
     else -- else retain the request to deal with later when there is a lift that becomes free
        req.oclIsNew (direction => d);
        req.targetFloor = f;
        self.extRequest->includes (req);
     endif;
     (self.extReqIndicator).events->includes (AckExtRequest' ());
  endif;
```

Fig. 6. externalRequest Operation Schema for Elevator Control System

A summary of all the event exchanges between the system and the actors is shown by the System Context Model in figure 2. This model indicates that there are four kinds of input events: externalRequest, doorIsClosed, atFloor and internalRequest. These input events trigger the system operations of the same names. We have already discussed the operation schema for the atFloor system operation. We will now present the operation schema for the externalRequest system operation. For reason of size, the other system operation schemas are not shown. Interested readers, however, can find them on the web [13].

The parameterized predicate bestSuitedCabin (line 3) results in the lift cabin that is best suited for servicing the request; we do not provide the definition of this parameterized predicate in this paper; it would be defined by taking into account the cabins' scheduling policy.

The Post clause also shows a convention for sending unnamed event instances. The condition, (cab.movedBy).events->includes (GoUp□()), asserts that an unnamed event instance of the event type GoUp was put into the event queue of the actor instance cab.movedBy.

7 Related Work

The idea of operation schema descriptions comes from the work on the Fusion method by Coleman et al. [2]. They took many ideas for operation schemas from formal notations, in particular, Z and VDM. The operation schema notation that we present here has a similar goal to the original proposal, but we have made notable changes to the style and format of the schema. After the initial work on Fusion, Coleman introduced use cases into Fusion and briefly discussed the relationship between them and operation schemas [3]. Our work on relating operation schemas to use cases can be seen as an elaboration of this work.

Z [14] and VDM [7] are both rich formal notations but they suffer from the problem that they are very costly to introduce into software development environments, as is the case with most formal methods, because of their high requirements for mathematical maturity on the user. On the other hand, OCL, the language used in operation schemas, has the advantage of being a relatively small and mathematically less-demanding language that is targeted at developers. One of the secrets of OCL's simplicity is that it uses navigation and operators manipulating collections rather than relations. Also, OCL was created for the distinct and sole purpose of navigating UML models, making it ideal for describing constraints and expressing predicates when a system is modeled with the UML.

The Catalysis approach [5], developed by D'Souza and Wills, provides action specifications which, of all related work, is the closest to ours. Catalysis defines two types of actions: localized and joint actions. Localized actions are what we would term operations in our approach and joint actions are related to use cases. In the endeavor to support controlled refinement by decomposition through a single mechanism, Catalysis defines actions, which can be decomposed into subordinate actions, at a lower-level of abstraction, or composed to form a superordinate action, at a higher-level of abstraction. Furthermore, Catalysis defines joint actions to describe multi-party collaborations, and localized actions to describe strictly the services provided by a type. However, joint actions lack the ability of goal-based use cases to describe stakeholder concerns due to the focus of pre- and postconditions on state changes and not the goals and obligations of the participants/stakeholders. The activity of assuring stakeholder concerns, when writing use cases, is often a source for discovering new business rules, and it was for this reason that we chose to supplement use cases with operation schemas rather than replace them with operation schemas. In addition, effective use cases have the ability to describe complex sequencing in a understandable and intuitive way; more formal approaches, such as joint actions, in the presence of complex sequencing are less intuitive to understand and can be hard to produce due to inflexibility of formal languages. On the other hand, it could be argued against our approach that refining use cases to operation schemas is less direct and more heuristic-driven because of the gap between the two notations.

8 Conclusion

We described an approach that supplements use case descriptions with operation schemas. An operation schema is a declarative specification of a system operation written in OCL. We believe that we have shown that supplementing use cases with operation schemas provides the benefits of rigorous behavioral specification while still retaining the advantages of goal-based use cases. Moreover, we highlighted a possible mapping between a use case and its corresponding operation schemas on an elevator control system example.

Currently, we are focusing our work on the description of *concurrent* system operations and on the development of tool support for operation schemas.

References

[1] A. Cockburn. *Writing Effective Use Cases*. Addison-Wesley 2000.

[2] D. Coleman, P. Arnold, S. Bodoff, C. Dollin, H. Gilchrist, F. Hayes and P. Jeremaes. *Object-Oriented Development: The Fusion Method.* Prentice-Hall 1994.

[3] D. Coleman. *Fusion with Use Cases - Extending Fusion for Requirements Modelling*. OOPSLA Conference Tutorial Slides 1995.

[4] S. Cook, A. Kleppe, R. Mitchell, J. Warmer, A. Wills. *Defining the Context of OCL Expressions*. Second International Conference on the Unified Modeling Language: UML'99, Fort Collins, USA, 1999.

[5] D. D'Souza and A.Wills. *Objects, Components and Frameworks With UML: The Catalysis Approach*. Addison-Wesley 1998.

[6] I. Jacobson, M. Griss and P. Jonsson. *Software Reuse: Architecture Process and Organization for Business Success*. Addison-Wesley 1997.

[7] C.B. Jones. *Systematic Software Development Using VDM.* Prentice Hall, 1986.

[8] M. Kandé and A. Strohmeier. Towards a UML Profile for Software Architecture. Technical Report 2000, Swiss Federal Institute of Technology, Switzerland, 2000; submitted for publication.

[9] OMG Unified Modeling Language Specification, Version 1.3, June 1999; published by the OMG Unified Modeling Language Revision Task Force on its WEB site: http://uml.shl.com/artifacts.htm

[10] Presidents Information Technology Advisory Committee. *Report to the President "Information Technology Research: Investing in Our Future"*.National Coordination Office for Computing, Information, and Communications, February 1999 (http://www.ccic.gov/ac/report/pitac_report.pdf).

[11] J. Rumbaugh, I. Jacobson and G. Booch. *The Unified Modeling Language Reference Manual*. Addison-Wesley 1999.

[12] S. Sendall and A. Strohmeier. *Descriptive Object-Oriented Operation Specification for UML*. Technical Report 2000/326, Swiss Federal Institute of Technology, Switzerland, 2000.

[13] S. Sendall. *Specification Case Studies*. Electronic Resource: http://lglwww.epfl.ch/~sendall/case-studies

[14] J.M. Spivey. *The Z Notation: A Reference Manual.* Prentice Hall, 1989.

[15] J. Warmer and A. Kleppe. *The Object Constraint Language: Precise Modeling With UML*. Addison-Wesley 1998.

On the Extension of UML with Use Case Maps Concepts

Daniel Amyot[1,2] and Gunter Mussbacher[2]

[1] SITE, University of Ottawa, 150 Louis-Pasteur, Ottawa (ON), Canada, K1N 6N5
[2] Mitel Corporation, 350 Legget Dr., Kanata (ON), Canada, K2K 2W7
damyot@site.uottawa.ca | gunter_mussbacher@Mitel.com

Abstract. Descriptions of reactive systems focus heavily on behavioral aspects, often in terms of scenarios. To cope with the increasing complexity of services provided by these systems, behavioral aspects need to be handled early in the design process with flexible and concise notations as well as expressive concepts. UML offers different notations and concepts that can help describe such services. However, several necessary concepts appear to be absent from UML, but present in the Use Case Map (UCM) scenario notation. In particular, Use Case Maps allow scenarios to be mapped to different architectures composed of various component types. The notation supports structured and incremental development of complex scenarios at a high level of abstraction, as well as their integration. UCMs specify variations of run-time behavior and scenario structures through sub-maps "pluggable" into placeholders called stubs. This paper presents how UCM concepts could be used to extend the semantics and notations of UML for the modeling of complex reactive systems. Adding a "UCM view" to the existing UML views can help bridging the gap separating requirements and use cases from more detailed views (e.g. expressed with interaction diagrams and statechart diagrams). Examples from telecommunications systems are given and a corresponding design trajectory is also suggested.

1 Introduction

The modeling of reactive (event-driven) systems requires an early emphasis on behavioral aspects such as interactions between the system and the external world (including the users), on the cause-to-effect relationships among these interactions, and on intermediate activities performed by the system. Scenarios are particularly good at representing such aspects so that various stakeholders can understand them.

Owing to their distributed and critical nature, telecommunications systems are representative of complex reactive systems. Emerging telecommunications services require industries and standardization bodies (ANSI, ETSI, ISO, ITU, TIA, etc.) to describe and design increasingly complex functionalities, architectures, and protocols. This is especially true of wireless systems, where the mobility of users and of terminals brings an additional dimension of complexity. Recent and upcoming technologies based on agents and IP, which involve complex and sometimes unpredictable policy-driven negotiations between communicating entities, also raise new modeling issues as protocols and entities become more dynamic in nature and evolve at run time.

A. Evans, S. Kent and B. Selic (Eds.): «UML» 2000, LNCS 1939, pp. 16-31, 2000.

The design and standardization of telecommunication systems and services results from a design process frequently comprised of three major stages. At stage 1, services are first described from the user's point of view in prose form, with use cases, and with tables. The focus of the second stage is on control flows between the different entities involved, represented using sequence diagrams or *Message Sequence Charts* — MSC [13]. Finally, stage 3 aims to provide (informal) specifications of protocols and procedures. Formal specifications are sometimes provided (e.g. in SDL [11]), but they are still of marginal use [1]. ITU-T developed this three-stage methodology two decades ago to describe services and protocols for ISDN. Naturally, such descriptions emphasize the reactive and behavioral nature of telecommunications systems. In this methodology, scenarios are often used as a means to model system functionalities and interactions between the entities such that different stakeholders may understand their general intent as well as technical details.

1.1 Requirements for a Scenario Notation

Due to the inherent complexity and scale of emerging telecommunications systems, special attention has to be brought to the early stages of the design process. The focus should be on system and functional views rather than on details belonging to a lower level of abstraction, or to later stages in this process. Many ITU-T members recognize the need to improve this process in order to cope with the new realities cited above. In particular, Study Group 10, which is responsible for the evolution of standards such as MSC, SDL, and TTCN, recently approved a new research question that could lead to a new recommendation by 2003 [14].

This research question will focus on what notation may be developed to complement MSCs, SDL and UML in capturing user requirements in the early stages of design when very little design detail is available. Such notation should be able to describe user requirement scenarios without any reference to states, messages or system components. Reusability of scenarios across a wide range of architectures is needed with allocation of scenario responsibilities to architectural components. The notation should enable simpler modeling of dynamic systems, early performance analysis at the requirements level, and early detection of undesirable interactions among services or scenarios.

While UML activity diagrams provide some capability in this area [17], a notation with dynamic (run-time) refinement capability and better allocation of scenario responsibilities to architectural components is required.

1.2 Extending UML with Use Case Maps Concepts

Use Case Maps (UCMs) [7][8] visually represent causal scenarios combined with structures. UCMs show related use cases in a map-like diagram. They have a history of applications to the description of reactive systems of different natures (e.g. [1][2][3][9]), to the avoidance and detection of undesirable interactions between scenarios or services (e.g. [2][9][16]) and to early performance analysis (e.g. [21]). A more extensive bibliography can be found in the *UCM User Group* library [23].

The addition of several useful concepts found in the UCM notation to UML would make the latter a more appealing tool for designing reactive systems. UCMs have a number of properties that satisfy many of the requirements described in Section 1.1: scenarios can be mapped to different architectures, variations of run-time behavior and structures can be expressed, and scenarios can be structured and integrated incrementally in a way that facilitates the early detection of undesirable interactions. This paper presents how UCM concepts could be used to extend the semantics and notations of UML for the modeling of complex reactive systems. Adding a "UCM view" to the existing UML views can also help bridging the gap separating requirements and use cases (e.g. as found in stage 1 of the ITU-T methodology) from more detailed views expressed with interaction diagrams (stage 2) and statechart diagrams (stage 3).

Through examples from the telecommunications domain, this paper illustrates how UCM concepts can be used to extend UML semantics and notations in the modeling of reactive systems. Section 2 introduces Use Case Maps and defines its core concepts in terms of the UML semantic metamodel (version 1.3). Section 3 shows how UCMs combine behavioral scenarios and structures in a single view. The benefits of capturing dynamic run-time behavior are illustrated in Section 4. Section 5 goes beyond the core concepts and presents other potential benefits offered by UCMs, together with a UCM/UML design trajectory suitable for reactive systems.

2 Use Case Maps Core Concepts

The Use Case Maps notation is based on various core concepts. This section focuses on a subset of these concepts and links them to the existing UML semantic metamodel. Advanced concepts more specific to UCMs, which will lead to suggestions on how to improve the UML metamodel and notations, are discussed in Sections 3 and 4.

2.1 Overview of the UCM Notation

Use Case Maps are used as a visual notation for describing *causal relationships* between *responsibilities* bound to underlying organizational structures of abstract *components*. Responsibilities are generic and can represent actions, activities, operations, tasks to perform, and so on. Components are also generic and can represent software entities (objects, processes, databases, servers, etc.) as well as non-software entities (e.g. actors). The relationships are said to be causal because they involve concurrency and partial orderings of activities and because they link causes (e.g., preconditions and triggering events) to effects (e.g. postconditions and resulting events).

UCMs are useful for describing telecommunications services at an early stage in the design cycle, even when no component is involved. For example, Fig. 1(a) describes the basic call process of a simplified telecommunications system, the *Tiny Telephone System* (TTS), accompanied by the *Originating Call Screening* (OCS) feature in Fig. 1(b).

This map contains many of the elements that form the core of the UCM notation. Informally, a start point (filled circle) is where scenarios are caused, upon the arrival of a triggering event and/or the satisfaction of preconditions. The scenario effect is represented as an end point (bar), which describes some resulting event and/or post-conditions. Responsibilities are represented as crosses. UCM paths, which connect the different elements discussed so far and show the progression of a scenario along a use case, may fork and join in different ways. OR-forks represent alternative paths, which may be guarded by conditions. AND-forks (narrow bars) represent concurrent paths along which the scenario evolves. OR-joins are used to merge common paths whereas AND-joins (not shown here) are used to synchronize concurrent paths. The diamonds represent stubs and act as containers for sub-maps called plug-ins. For instance, the OCS map in Fig. 1(b) could be plugged in the `Originating` stub of the Basic Call

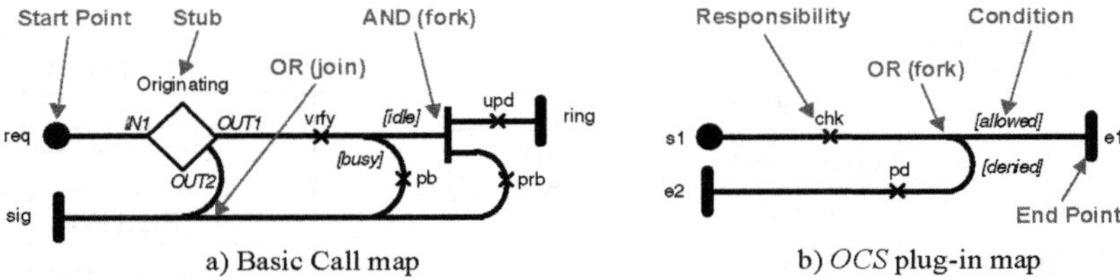

a) Basic Call map b) *OCS* plug-in map

map. This requires a *binding relationship* that would specify how the start and end points of the plug-in map would be connected to the path segments going into or coming out of the stub. In this example, the binding relationship is {`<IN1, s1>, <OUT1, e1>, <OUT2, e2>`}.

Fig. 1 Tiny Telephone System example, with one feature.

According to the UCM notation and semantics, the TTS scenarios are interpreted in the following way. Upon the arrival of a call request (`req`), the OCS feature checks whether the call should be allowed or denied (`chk`). If denied, then a call denied reply is prepared (`pd`) and signaled (`sig`). If allowed, then the system verifies whether the called party is busy or idle (`vrfy`). If busy, then a busy reply is prepared (`pb`) and signaled. If idle, then a ringback reply is prepared (`prb`) and signaled (`sig`) concurrently with the update of the system status (`upd`) and a resulting ringing event (`ring`).

This example illustrates how UCM descriptions abstract from messages, data and control, while focusing on general causal flows between causes, responsibilities, and effects. UCMs are neither dataflow diagrams nor control flow diagrams (where control is often associated to procedure calls or method invocations)

2.2 Current UCM Semantics

The UCM abstract syntax and static semantics are currently based on a graph structure (more specifically a hypergraph) and described in a XML document type definition [4]. The concrete syntax is visual and was introduced in the previous section. All of these are supported by a visual editing tool, the *UCM Navigator* [15], together with a set of valid transformations that ensure the satisfaction of well-formed rules. Dynamic semantics is yet informal, although one has been indirectly provided in terms of the formal language LOTOS [10], whose underlying semantics is based on labeled transition systems, on CCS and on CSP [2][3].

However, the main semantic concepts of Use Case Maps are hidden behind various details and implementation-related concerns. Fig. 2 captures, in general terms and independently of the current hypergraph-based semantics, the UCM core concepts in the form of a class diagram. This diagram abstracts from many class attributes, relationships, and constraints in order to focus on the essence of what concepts should be preserved in the context of an integration with UML.

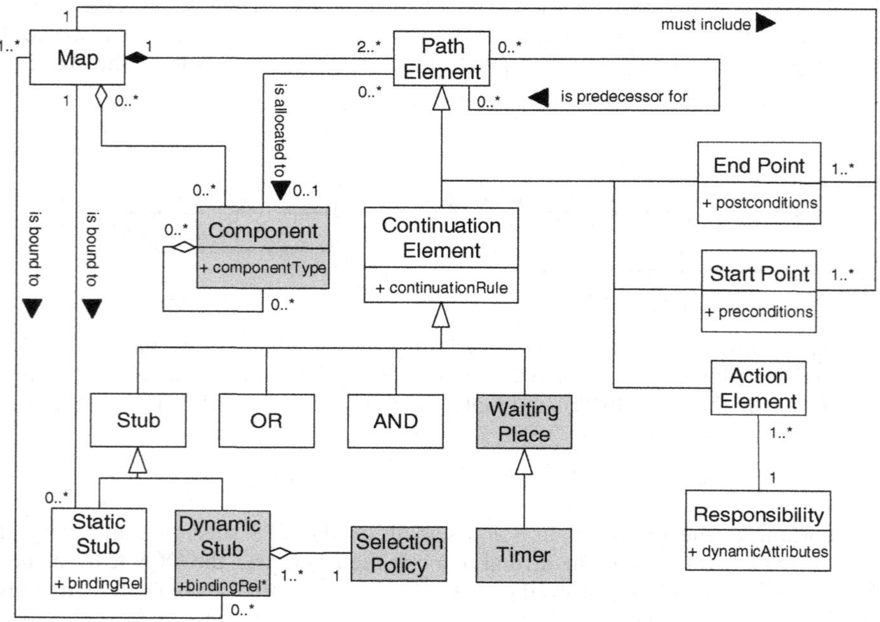

Fig. 2 Overview of UCM core concepts.

In this diagram, the white classes are the ones implicitly used by the TTS example in Fig. 1 and they are described in Table 1. The shaded classes will be discussed in other examples to be given in the remaining sections.

Table 1 Description of UCM concepts.

Class Name	Description
Map	Composition of path elements and components. Maps can be used as plug-ins for stubs. Maps must contain at least one start point and one end point.
Path Element	Superclass similar to a node in a connected graph.
Start Point	Beginning of a causal scenario (cause) possibly with preconditions.
End Point	End of a causal scenario (effect), possibly with postconditions.
Action Element	A path element on a causal path. References a responsibility.
Responsibility	Performs an action, activity, task, function, etc. Dynamic responsibilities (not discussed in this paper) possess additional attributes.
Continuation Element	Superclass representing a location where multiple path elements can connect together in a non-sequential way (i.e. with multiple predecessors and/or successors) as specified by a continuation rule. Each subclass de-

	fines its continuation rule (may be user-specified). In the case of a stub, the sub-map is the continuation rule.
OR	Composition (fork or join) of paths as alternatives. Conditions (guards) can be attached to paths that fork.
AND	Composition (fork or join) of concurrent paths.
Stub	Superclass representing a container for sub-maps (plug-ins).
Static Stub	Stub with a single sub-map (plug-in) and its binding relationship.

2.3 Linking UCM Concepts to UML

UCM concepts can be linked to UML in many ways. In this paper, we take advantage of similarities between UCMs and activity diagrams to facilitate this connection. Activity diagrams share many concepts with UCMs. They have common constructs and even the notations are alike, to some extent. The TTS example in Fig. 1 could effectively be described in terms of activity diagrams without any difficulty. The suggested uses of these notations are however slightly different. They both target the modeling of system-wide procedures and scenarios, but activity diagrams focus on internal processing, often found in business-oriented models (e.g. workflows), whereas UCMs are also concerned with external (asynchronous) events, which are essential to the modeling of systems that are reactive in nature.

Despite these usage differences, it seems appropriate to link the UCM concepts to the semantic model of activity diagrams: the *Activity Graphs* metamodel. Use Case Maps could be cast into this metamodel by using extension mechanisms that UML proposes, such as stereotypes, tagged values, additional OCL constraints and appropriate notation icons [17]. However in this paper, we suggest that several UCM concepts not supported by activity diagrams are important, simple, and useful enough to be included as part of the UML metamodel itself. In this way, the whole UML community would benefit from the suggested enhancements, whereas the use of extensions would lead to yet another notation based on UML which would not really be integrated to other notations that also extend UML (hence leading to interworking and compatibility issues).

Even in this context, the integration of UCMs to UML could be done in many ways. Fig. 3(a) presents an option where the UML *Behavioral Elements* package, found in the UML metamodel layer, is extended with a new sub-package for UCM concepts (shaded package). The latter depends on metaclasses found in Activity Graphs (for UCM paths) and on *Collaborations* (for UCM components, to be covered in Section 3,). However, this option would result in a new package with a lot of duplication in an already crowded set of packages and metaclasses.

Fig. 3(b) illustrates an alternative where the modifications are done directly to the Activity Graphs package. The latter would still depend on *State Machines* and, unlike the current UML standard, it would also depend on Collaborations.

Table 2 presents, through a simple mapping, how Activity Graphs metaclasses already support many UCM concepts discussed in Table 1.

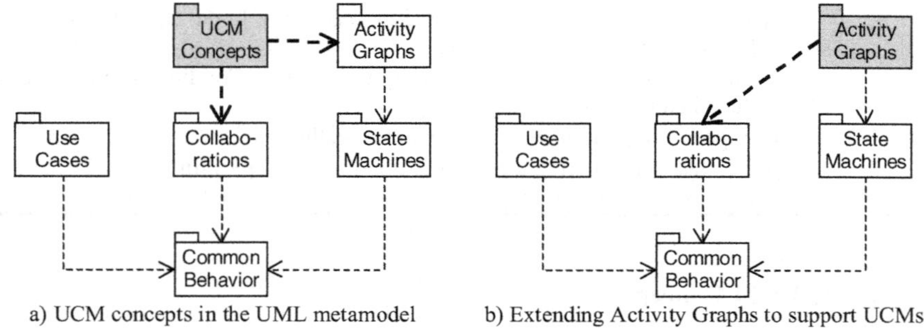

Fig. 3 Integrating UCM concepts to the UML metamodel layer.

Table 2 Mapping UCM concepts to Activity Graphs metaclasses.

UCM Concept	Corresponding Metaclasses
Map	ActivityGraph (from Activity Graphs), a child class of StateMachine.
Path Element	StateVertex (from State Machines), the parent class of State and PseudoState, which is also similar to a node in a graph.
Start Point	SimpleState (from State Machines), a State without nested states.
End Point	SimpleState (from State Machines), a State without nested states.
Action Element	ActionState (from Activity Graphs), an atomic action. In UML, an ActionState is a SimpleState with an entry action whose only exit transition is triggered by the implicit event of completing the execution of the entry action. This is similar to a UCM responsibility.
Responsibility	Associated with ActionState (from Activity Graphs), an atomic action referenced by an Action Element (in UCM terms).
Continuation Element	StateVertex (from State Machines), the parent class of PseudoState and (indirectly) of SubActivityState.
OR	PseudoState (from State Machines), of kind choice for an OR-fork and of kind junction for an OR-join.
AND	PseudoState (from State Machines), of kind fork for an AND-fork and of kind join for an AND-join.
Stub	CompositeState (from State Machines), which may contain submachines.
Static Stub	SubActivityState (from Activity Graphs), which may reference only one sub-ActivityGraph, just like a UCM static stub contains only one plug-in.

The Activity Graphs metamodel hence possess all the necessary elements to support the UCM concepts discussed so far. The different relationships in Fig. 2 are also covered by the underlying State Machines metamodel: "is predecessor for" is captured by the transitions linking the different states, "is bound to" is taken care of internally by the SubActivityState representing the UCM static stub, and "must include" could be refined as a new OCL constraint.

There are still minor differences between these UCM concepts and the semantics of Activity Graphs. In Activity Graphs, all of the paths leaving a fork must eventually merge in a subsequent join, and multiple layers of forks and joins must be well nested. There is currently no such restriction on UCMs. Also, UCM static stubs may have multiple incoming path segments, and plug-ins can have multiple start points, whereas a SubActivityState is limited to one initial state in the corresponding sub-ActivityGraph. However this can be overcome in a number of ways as SubActivity-

Graph is a child class of SubmachineState (see Fig. 7), which does not have such limitation. Enhancements to the binding relationship between SubActivityState and ActivityGraph could also solve this problem.

The next section will discuss the role of UCM components for linking scenarios to structures, as well as their potential impact on the UML metamodel.

3 Combining Scenarios and Structures

One of the main strengths of UCMs resides in their capacity to visually integrate scenarios and structural components in a single view. In the design of reactive systems, such view is most useful for understanding scenario paths in their context, and for enabling high-level architectural reasoning.

3.1 UCM Component Notation

UCM scenarios can be bound to structures by visually allocating path elements to underlying components. The UCM notation distinguishes, through different shapes, several types of components useful in a reactive system context (e.g. processes, objects, agents, interrupt service routines, etc.). However, such distinctions are beyond the scope of this paper, and simple rectangles will be used as a notation for generic UCM components representing software entities as well as non-software entities.

UCM paths can be bound to various component structures. Fig. 4 uses a simplified version of the TTS system in Fig. 1 to illustrate this concept. In Fig. 4(a), a UCM path is bound to an agent-based architecture where `Users` can communicate only through their respective `Agents`. Start points indicate where users initiate events (causes) whereas end points indicate where resulting events (effects) are observed. The various components are responsible for performing the responsibilities allocated to them.

As they can easily be decoupled from structures, UCM paths improve the reusability of scenarios and lead to behavioral patterns that can be utilized across a wide range of applications. For instance, Fig. 4(b) reuses the same scenario path in a very different context where components are based on the Intelligent Network (IN) reference model [1]. In this architecture, the `Switch` is the component responsible for establishing communication between users. However, the "intelligence" behind many IN features is located outside the switch, inside network elements called service nodes (`SN`). In this context, the `chk` responsibility, which is associated to the OCS feature, is performed by the `SN` component.

This UCM view, where scenarios and structures are combined, is most useful for architectural reasoning early in the design cycle. UCM paths are also more likely to survive evolutions and other modifications to the underlying architecture than scenarios described in terms of message exchanges or interactions between components. For instance, note how the two following message sequence charts differ in nature and complexity (UML sequence diagrams could have been used just as well). Fig. 4(c) is an MSC capturing the scenario from Fig. 4(a) in terms of message exchanges. This is a straightforward interpretation with artificial messages (in italic characters). Other such MSCs could possibly be derived from the same scenario path. Fig. 4(d) is a potential MSC of the same scenario path, but this time bound to the IN-based ar-

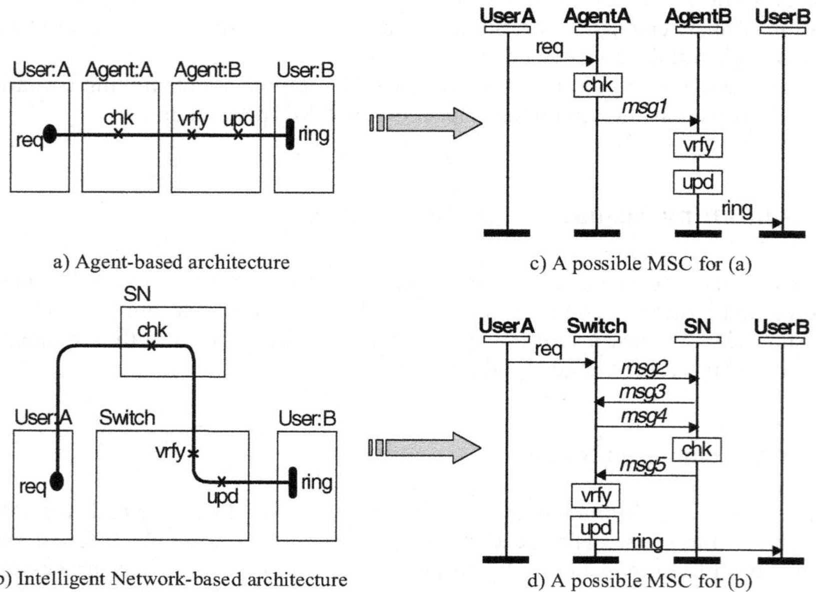

Fig. 4 UCM path bound to two different component structures, and potential MSCs.

chitecture. Complex protocols could be involved between the switch and the service node, hence resulting in multiple messages. Communication constraints also prevent users from communicating directly with service nodes; therefore the switch needs to be involved as a relay. By using a UCM view, all these issues related to messages, protocols, communication constraints, and structural evolutions (e.g. from one version of the structure to the next) can be abstracted from, and the focus can be put on reusable causal scenarios in their structural context. If a structure is modified, path elements need only to be rebound to appropriate components.

3.2 UML Semantics Support

The UCM core concepts (Fig. 2) contains a class representing the Component concept. Components may be of different types and may contain other sub-components. Path elements are allocated to such components, as discussed in the previous section.

In the UML metamodel, the *ClassifierRole* metaclass (from the Collaborations package) seems to fit best the concept of a UCM component. Like ClassifierRoles, UCM components are interpreted as roles rather than as particular instances; e.g. Fig. 4(a) uses two generic component types for users and agents, with roles `A` (originating party) and `B` (terminating party). Being UML *Classifiers* themselves, ClassifierRoles may declare other ClassifierRoles nested in their scope, just like UCM components may contain sub-components. A ClassifierRole specifies a restricted view of a more generic Classifier. Similarly, a UCM component shows only a partial view of the overall behavior of that component type. For all these reasons, we believe that the current ClassifierRole can support the UCM component concept as is. Note that the

UCM component concept is not equivalent to the UML *Component* metaclass (from the Core package), which represents a replaceable part of a system that packages implementation and provides the realization of a set of interfaces.

The need for ClassifierRole explains the additional dependency between Activity Graphs and Collaborations in Fig. 3(b). Still, the allocation of UCM path elements to their components cannot be easily captured by Activity Graphs. The latter possess the concept of *Partition*, which is a mechanism for dividing the states of an activity graph into groups. Partitions are visualized as *swimlanes* in UML activity diagrams. Unfortunately, Partitions have poor semantics because they simply regroup instances of the very abstract *ModelElement* metaclass (from the Core package) and they are quite removed from the rest of the UML metamodel. Hence, the metamodel needs to be enriched to support the useful "is allocated to" relationship found in Fig. 2. In that regard, Fig. 5 proposes two potential solutions:

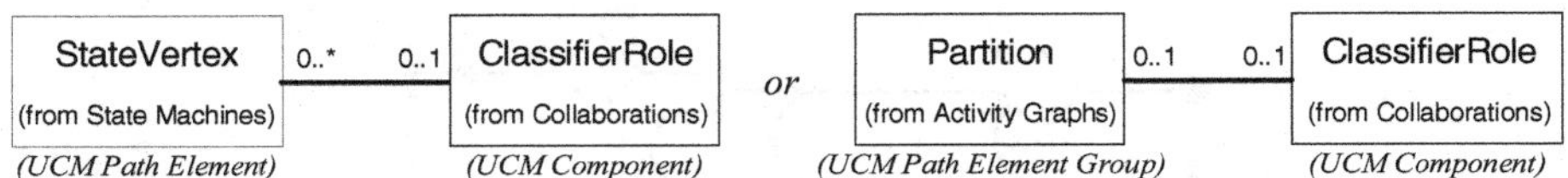

Fig. 5 Two possible solutions for the support of the UCM component concept.

Since StateVertex captures the essence of UCM path elements (see Table 2), they could be allocated directly to components, represented by ClassifierRole. Another solution would be to reuse the Partition concept of Activity Graphs and allocate a partition to a ClassifierRole (all relevant classes of Activity Graphs, and even StateVertex, are subclasses of ModelElement). Both solutions achieve our goal, but we prefer the second one because it is expressed in terms of Activity Graphs, not in terms of State Machines, and it has the capability of supporting non-StateVertex elements.

4 Modeling Dynamic Run-Time Behavior

Another important characteristic of the UCM notation is its capability of combining and integrating scenario paths in a way that enables the modeling of dynamic run-time behavior. This section presents how dynamic stubs can be used to localize and visualize, at design time, how alternative behavioral scenarios could evolve at run time.

4.1 UCM Notation for Dynamic Stub and Timers

UCMs can help structuring and integrating scenarios in various ways. The most interesting construct to do so is certainly the Dynamic Stub, shown as a dashed diamond. While static stubs contain only one plug-in map, dynamic stubs may contain multiple sub-maps, whose selection can be determined at run-time according to a *selection policy*. Such a policy can make use of preconditions, assertions, run-time information, composition operators, etc. in order to select the plug-in(s) to use. Selection policies are usually described with a (formal or informal) language suitable for the context where they are used.

Fig. 6(a) extends our original TTS Basic Call with two dynamic stubs. Whether the underlying architecture is based on agents, IN, or other types of components is not essential to the understanding of this example, hence components are not included.

This new system contains three features: the original *OCS* feature, Call Name Delivery (*CND* — displays the caller's phone number with `disp`), and *TEENLINE*. This last feature prevents several users (often teenagers) to use the phone for pre-set time intervals (e.g. from 7 PM to 10 PM), although users (e.g. parents) who provide a valid personal identification number (PIN) in a timely fashion can establish a call.

All these features are captured by plug-in maps (Fig. 6(b-e)). To simplify bindings, plug-in start/end points have been given the same names as the input/output stub segments to which they are bound. The `Originating` stub contains three plug-ins: *DEFAULT* (b), *TEENLINE* (d), and *OCS* (e). The `Display` stub contains only two: *CND* (c) and *DEFAULT* (b). The latter shows that a plug-in can be reused in multiple stubs. Together, these five UCMs integrate multiple end-to-end sequential scenarios in a structured and concise way.

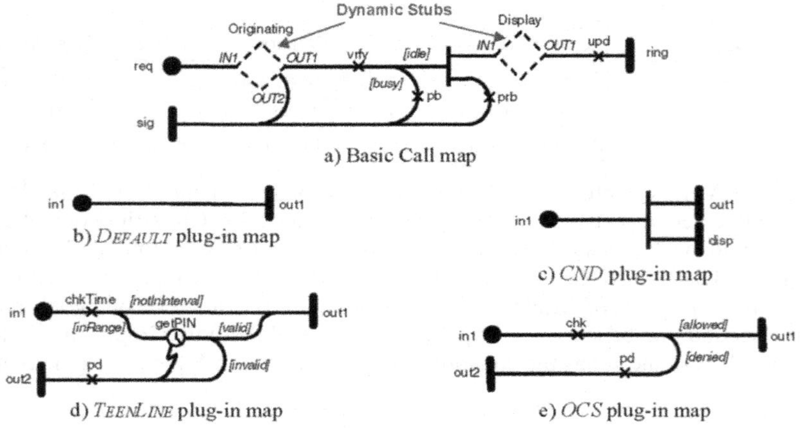

Fig. 6 Basic Call UCM with dynamic stubs and their plug-ins.

The *TEENLINE* plug-in contains a Timer named `getPIN` and shown with a clock symbol. Timers are special waiting places awaiting an event from their environment (which is the case here) or from other scenarios when visually connected to an end point (synchronous triggering) or to an empty path segment (asynchronous triggering). If the required event does not arrive in time, then the timeout path (shown with a zigzag symbol) is followed.

The selection policy for the `Display` stub could be as simple as: use *CND* if the called party has subscribed to the CND feature, else use *DEFAULT*. For the `Originating` stub however, the selection policy would need to be more complex because a user could have subscribed to both the *OCS* and *TEENLINE* features. There could potentially be an undesirable interaction between these two features, and the selection policy can be used to solve it, either in a fixed way (e.g. with priorities) or by stating a run-time resolution rule. Dynamic stubs make more local the potential conflicts that could arise between scenarios (hence leading to simpler analysis), and their selection policies can help avoiding or resolving these conflicts [2][9]. This particular way of looking at scenario combinations is at the basis of a feature interaction filtering method where undesirable interactions can be detected and dealt with early in the design cycle [16].

4.2 UML Semantics Support

As shown in Fig. 2, a Dynamic Stub is a Stub to which multiple Maps (plug-ins) are bound and to which a Selection Policy is associated. A selection policy instance should be defined as a potentially reusable object rather than as a mere attribute.

Stubs and Static Stubs were respectively mapped to CompositeState and SubactivityState in Table 2. Currently, the Activity Graphs and State Machines metamodels cannot represent, in a simple way, multiple bindings of sub-maps (i.e. ActivityGraph) to a stub. As a consequence, extensions appear necessary. Fig. 7 proposes a solution with *DynamicStub* as a new child class of CompositeState. Dynamic stubs may reference possibly many sub-maps, and they handle a binding relationship for each reference (instead of only one as in SubactivityState and SubmachineState). A *SelectionPolicy*, which is an abstract *Relationship*, is associated to each dynamic stub.

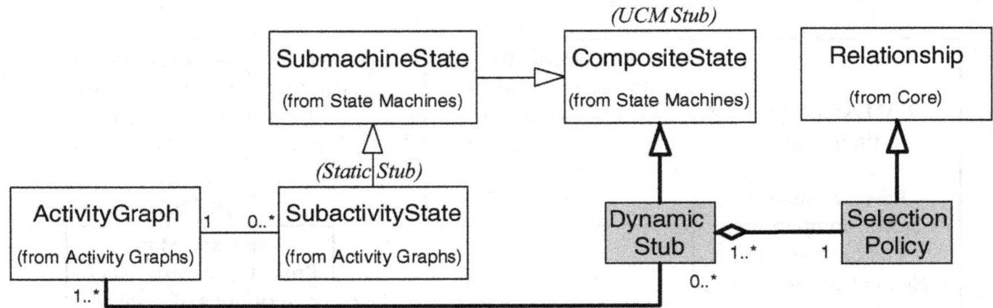

Fig. 7 Extending Activity Graphs with dynamic stubs.

The support of the Waiting Place and Timer concepts (as illustrated in the *TEENLINE* plug-in map, Fig. 6(d)) could be achieved with StateVertex. When such "wait states" are required, many UML methods suggest that statechart diagrams be used instead of activity diagrams [19]. However, we believe that wait states have their place in activity diagrams and UCMs for the modeling of reactive systems.

5 Beyond the Core Concepts

This section describes our vision on how Use Case Maps would fit in a UML-based design process. We go beyond the core concepts to address issues like connections between models and design trajectories suitable for telecommunications systems.

UML regroups various diagram techniques, which capture different views or partial representations of a same system. Some are more appropriate for the early stages of design (close to the requirements) while others are more appropriate for later stages (e.g. detailed design and implementation). These diagram techniques often focus on two orthogonal axes. *Structural diagrams* target software and conceptual entities and their relationships (e.g. class, object, component, and deployment diagrams), whereas *behavioral diagrams* emphasize behavior (e.g. sequence, collaboration, and statechart diagrams).

Structural diagrams can capture some aspects of system requirements such as the architecture and the application domain. They also share connections with behavioral diagrams, where the referenced entities often come from structural diagrams. Yet, there exists a conceptual gap between functional requirements (and use cases) and their realization in terms of behavioral diagrams, as illustrated in Fig. 8.

A UCM view represents a useful piece of the puzzle that helps bridge this gap. Requirements and use cases usually provide a black-box view where the system is described according to its external behavior. UML behavioral diagrams have a glass-box view describing the internal behavior in a detailed way. UCMs can provide a traceable progression from functional requirements to detailed views based on states, components and interactions, while at the same time combining behavior and structure in an explicit and visual way. Whereas sequence and collaboration diagrams usually show the behavior of several objects within a single use case and statechart diagrams show the behavior of a single object across many use cases, UCMs show the behavior of many objects for many use cases. In our experience, this view contributes greatly to the understanding of complex reactive systems.

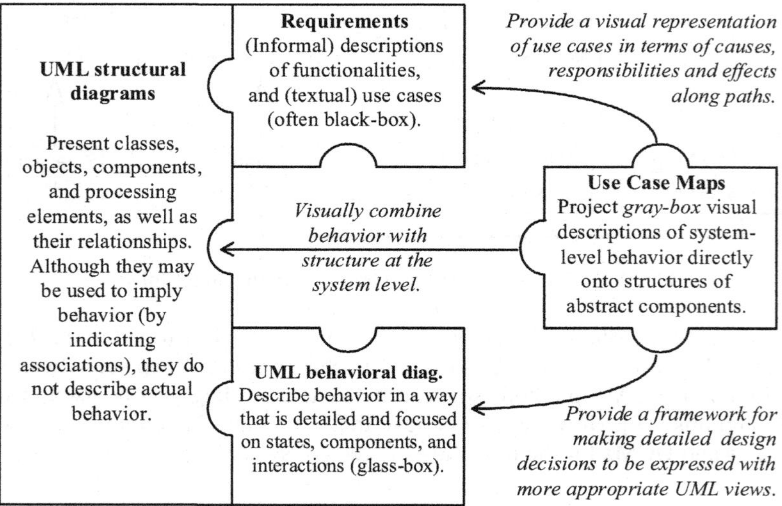

Fig. 8 UCMs as a missing piece of the UML puzzle.

Investment in UCMs can also be leveraged by connecting them to other UML views or to other modeling/specification languages. For instance:

- Buhr and Casselman use UCMs to generate class diagrams [7]. Similarly, Paech uses activity diagrams as a bridge between use cases and class diagrams [18].
- Once protocols and communication constraints are known (may be described by AssociationRoles connecting ClassifierRoles), UCMs can lead to various MSCs, sequence diagrams, and collaboration diagrams (e.g. Fig. 4). This generation is in the process of being formalized and automated in the UCM Navigator tool.
- Bordeleau presents a method for the generation of MSCs and hierarchical state machines (e.g. statechart diagrams and ROOMcharts) from UCMs [5][6]. Sales and Probert are doing similar work for the generation of SDL models [20].
- Amyot *et al.* use LOTOS as a formal means to validate UCMs and high-level designs and to detect undesirable interactions early in the design cycle [2][3].

Other research projects include the generation of performance models (e.g. in Layered Queuing Networks—LQNs) and of abstract test cases (e.g. in the Tree and Tabular Combined Notation—TTCN).

These connections enable the creation of many design trajectories relevant to telecommunications systems, as suggested in the introduction. In particular, we envision the following trajectory, inspired from [1][6]: requirements capture and architectural reasoning is done with UCMs (stage 1), which are first transformed into MSCs or interaction diagrams (stage 2), then into state machines in SDL/UML [12] or UML-RT [22] statechart diagrams (stage 3), and finally into concrete implementations (possibly through automated code generation). Validation, verification, performance analysis, interaction detection, and test generation could be performed at all stages.

6 Conclusions and Future Work

This paper illustrates how UCMs satisfy some of the requirements described in Section 1.1. Section 2 shows, at a semantic level, how the UML Activity Graphs metamodel already supports most of the core concepts behind the UCM notation. Advanced UCM concepts can be used to combine structure and behavior (through the allocation of path elements to components) and to model dynamic run-time behavior (with dynamic stubs and selection policies). These concepts can be integrated to the UML metamodel by extending Activity Graphs and connecting them to Collaborations (Sections 3 and 4). Other UCM concepts and notations not discussed in this paper include exceptions, failure points, (a)synchronous interactions between paths, and dynamic components and responsibilities [8], and they are left for future work.

In this paper, we attempted to minimize the number of modifications to the semantics of UML 1.3. However, in UML 2.0, Activity Graphs may be decoupled from State Machines. A reorganization of these packages could represent a good opportunity for including the UCM concepts discussed here.

Both the UCM notation and activity diagrams could be used to visualize these concepts. However, the latter would need to be extended to support bidimensional structures (swimlanes show partitions in one dimension only). As a consequence, straight lines used to represent causality between activities might need to become splines in order to adapt better to complex structures and to distinguish them from component boundaries. Also, the symbol used for activities might be too large to fit into these components. Hence, from a layout perspective, there are some advantages in using splines (as in UCM paths) and small crosses (as in UCM responsibilities). Note also that UCM may diminish the need for use case diagrams as many relationships between use cases (e.g. inclusion, extension, generalization) can be, to some extent, modeled by judicious use of stubs and plug-ins. Again, a good compromise between use case diagrams, activity diagrams, and UCMs requires further study.

The UCM notation enjoys an enthusiastic community of users and it has been used successfully in the domains of telecommunications and other reactive systems. However, users also complain about the lack of formal semantics and of a few concepts found in UML (such as actors distinguished from other components). We see in this an opportunity to add UCMs as a useful view of UML models, to integrate new expressive concepts to the UML metamodel, to precise the semantics of UCMs, to link UCMs to other languages and methodologies, and to move beyond reactive systems.

Acknowledgement. We are indebted towards Bran Selic and other members of the UCM User Group for their judicious comments, and to CITO for its financial support.

References

1. Amyot, D. and Andrade, R.: "Description of Wireless Intelligent Network Services with Use Case Maps". In: *SBRC'99, 17th Brazilian Symposium on Computer Networks*, Salvador, Brazil, May 1999. http://www.UseCaseMaps.org/pub/sbrc99.pdf
2. Amyot, D., Buhr, R.J.A., Gray, T., and Logrippo, L.: "Use Case Maps for the Capture and Validation of Distributed Systems Requirements". In: *RE'99, Fourth IEEE International Symposium on Requirements Engineering*, Limerick, Ireland, June 1999, pp. 44-53. http://www.UseCaseMaps.org/pub/re99.pdf
3. Amyot, D. and Logrippo, L.: "Use Case Maps and LOTOS for the Prototyping and Validation of a Mobile Group Call System". In: *Computer Communication*, 23(12), May 2000, pp. 1135-1157. http://www.UseCaseMaps.org/pub/cc99.pdf
4. Amyot, D. and Miga, A.: *Use Case Maps Document Type Definition 0.19*. Working document, June 2000. http://www.UseCaseMaps.org/xml/
5. Bordeleau, F. and Buhr, R.J.A.: "The UCM-ROOM Design Method: from Use Case Maps to Communicating State Machines". In: *Conference on the Engineering of Computer-Based Systems*, Monterey, USA, March 1997.http://www.UseCaseMaps.org/pub/UCM-ROOM.pdf
6. Bordeleau, F.: *A Systematic and Traceable Progression from Scenario Models to Communicating Hierarchical Finite State Machines*. Ph.D. thesis, SCS, Carleton University, Ottawa, Canada, August 1999. http://www.UseCaseMaps.org/pub/fb_phdthesis.pdf
7. Buhr, R.J.A. and Casselman, R.S.: *Use Case Maps for Object-Oriented Systems*, Prentice-Hall, USA, 1995. http://www.UseCaseMaps.org/pub/UCM_book95.pdf
8. Buhr, R.J.A.: "Use Case Maps as Architectural Entities for Complex Systems". In: *Transactions on Software Engineering*, IEEE, December 1998, pp. 1131-1155. http://www.UseCaseMaps.org/pub/tse98final.pdf
9. Buhr, R.J.A., Amyot, D., Elammari, M., Quesnel, D., Gray, T., and Mankovski, S.: "High Level, Multi-agent Prototypes from a Scenario-Path Notation: A Feature-Interaction Example". In: *PAAM'98, 3rd Conf. on Practical Application of Intelligent Agents and Multi-Agents*, London, UK, March 1998. http://www.UseCaseMaps.org/pub/4paam98.pdf.
10. ISO, Information Processing Systems, OSI: *LOTOS —A Formal Description Technique Based on the Temporal Ordering of Observational Behaviour*. IS 8807, Geneva, 1989.
11. ITU-T: *Recommendation Z.100, Specification and Description Language*. Geneva, 2000.
12. ITU-T: *Recommendation Z.109, SDL combined with UML*. Geneva, 2000.
13. ITU-T: *Recommendation Z. 120, Message Sequence Chart (MSC)*. Geneva, 2000.
14. ITU-T, SG10: *Proposal for a new question to define a notation for user requirements*. Canadian contribution, COM10-D56, November 1999.
15. Miga, A.: *Application of Use Case Maps to System Design with Tool Support*. M.Eng. thesis, Dept. of Systems and Computer Engineering, Carleton University, Ottawa, Canada, October 1998. http://www.UseCaseMaps.org/tools/ucmnav/
16. Nakamura, M., Kikuno, T., Hassine, J., and Logrippo, L.: "Feature Interaction Filtering with Use Case Maps at Requirements Stage". In: *Sixth International Workshop on Feature Interactions in Telecommunications and Software Systems (FIW'00)*, Glasgow, Scotland, UK, May 2000. http://www.UseCaseMaps.org/pub/fiw00_filter.pdf
17. Object Management Group: *Unified Modeling Language Specification, Version 1.3*. June 1999. http://www.omg.org
18. Paech, B. "On the Role of Activity Diagrams in UML". In: *Int. Workshop, UML'98*, pp. 267-277. http://www4.informatik.tu-muenchen.de/papers/Pae_UML98.html
19. Rumbaugh, J., Jacobson, I., and Booch, G.: *The Unified Modeling Language Reference Manual*. Addison Wesley, 1999.

20. Sales, I. and Probert, R.: "From High-Level Behaviour to High-Level Design: Use Case Maps to Specification and Description Language". Submitted to *SBRC'2000, 18th Brazilian Symposium on Computer Networks*, Belo Horizonte, Brazil, May 2000.
21. Scratchley, W.C. and Woodside, C.M.: "Evaluating Concurrency Options in Software Specifications". In: *MASCOTS'99, Seventh International Symposium on Modelling, Analysis and Simulation of Computer and Telecommunication Systems*, College Park, MD, USA, October 1999, pp. 330-338. http://www.UseCaseMaps.org/pub/mascots99.pdf
22. Selic, B.: *Turning Clockwise: Using UML in the Real-Time Domain*. In: Communications of the ACM, 42(10), October 1999, pp. 46-54.
23. *Use Case Maps Web Page* and *UCM User Group*, 1999. http://www.UseCaseMaps.org

HyperMSCs and Sequence Diagrams for Use Case Modelling and Testing

Peter Graubmann[1] and Ekkart Rudolph[2]

[1]Siemens AG, ZT SE, Otto-Hahn-Ring 6, D-81739 München, Germany
Peter.Graubmann@mchp.siemens.de

[2]Technische Universität München, Institut für Informatik, D-80290 München, Germany
rudolphe@informatik.tu-muenchen.de

Abstract. UML-Sequence Diagrams can be seen as an object oriented variant of the ITU-T standard language Message Sequence Chart (MSC) which is very popular mainly in the telecommunication area. Both notations would benefit from a unification together with a further elaboration. A comparison of Sequence Diagrams and MSCs demonstrates the big advantage of MSCs concerning composition mechanisms, particularly with respect to the branching construct in Sequence Diagrams. Therefore, MSC inline expressions and High Level MSCs (HMSCs) are of special interest for the inclusion into Sequence Diagrams. High Level MSCs may be employed for formalizing and structuring the construction of scenarios for Use Cases. In order to arrive at a most intuitive representation, HMSCs are re-interpreted in a way which has an analogy in hypertext-like specifications. Because of this analogy, the notation 'HyperMSC' is introduced. The scenarios derived from Use Cases in form of HyperMSCs can be employed also as a basis for the specification of test cases.

Keywords. UML, MSC, Sequence Diagrams, Use Cases, OO, software engineering, testing, distributed systems, real time systems, telecommunication

1 Introduction

Sequence Diagrams in UML resulted from two sources: Ivar Jacobson's interaction diagrams (Objectory) [7] and the 1992 version of the MSC language (MSC-92) [13]. From MSC-92 first an OO variant, called OMSC, was developed at Siemens which essentially combined a subset of MSC with constructs typical for OO design, in particular, the construct for method calls [2]. Sequence Diagrams are a further development and adjustment of OMSC [12]. They do not claim to have the same degree of formality yet as MSC. This refers to both syntax and semantics. The syntax is not equally fixed in UML as in the ITU-T Recommendation Z.120. Therefore, different authors referring to UML use slightly different variants and take over some more constructs from MSC. While Sequence Diagrams contain most of the basic MSC language constructs, the advanced MSC concepts concerning composition and refinement essentially are

A. Evans, S. Kent and B. Selic (Eds.): «UML» 2000, LNCS 1939, pp. 32-46, 2000.

missing. In particular, the inclusion of inline expressions and HMSCs into Sequence Diagrams may increase their power and applicability considerably.

MSC is an ITU-T standard trace language for the specification and description of the communication behaviour of system components and their environment by means of message exchange [5, 6, 10]. In general, MSCs are used in the area of reactive and distributed systems, and its main application area lies in the field of telecommunication systems. Traditionally, the MSC language is used primarily in connection with SDL. Indeed, it also arose from the same ITU-T study group as SDL. Contrary to Sequence Diagrams, MSC is a rather advanced language with a well defined syntax and semantics. Concepts to describe method calls and the flow of control have been introduced into MSC-2000 already [15], following our proposal for a harmonization of MSCs and Sequence Diagrams [9]. The MSC language can still benefit from taking over concepts of Use Case modelling from UML.

While Sequence Diagrams and Message Sequence Charts without any doubt are amongst the most popular and successful description techniques now, their real potential has not yet been exploited. Although MSC-2000 [15] contains very powerful composition mechanisms and other structural concepts, the language is still used essentially to define a set of sample behaviours. However, with the increasing popularity of the MSC language also a more comprehensive application is demanded by some user communities: MSCs have been proposed for the formalization of Use Cases already some years ago [1]. Recently, MSCs have been suggested for a graphical test format [11] which is more intuitive than the standard test notation TTCN [4]. Experiences with a comprehensive MSC based specification have shown, however, that the MSC language still needs certain extensions to make the MSC diagrams sufficiently readable and understandable and the MSC document manageable. These extensions are strongly related to a corresponding advanced tool support. In this paper, we use the analogy to hypertext documents and suggest a similar handling of large MSC documents. Because of this analogy we suggest the notation 'HyperMSC'. In particular, we claim that the full potential of High Level MSCs (HMSCs) and MSC references will show up only if they are treated in a hypertext-like manner.

Within section 2, the roles of Sequence Diagrams and MSCs are compared in the context of object oriented modelling. MSC language constructs which may be taken over to Sequence Diagrams are listed. In section 3, HyperMSCs are introduced in form of extended High Level MSCs for the derivation of scenarios from Use Cases. Section 4 summarises the new hypertext-like features of the HyperMSCs. Section 5 contains concluding remarks and an outlook.

2 Towards a Unification of MSCs and Sequence Diagrams

Sequence Diagrams and MSCs represent different views of system modelling and also refer to different application areas.

Sequence Diagrams offer a software oriented view where the target program in many cases is running on one processor and the flow of control is passing between various program modules. Within Sequence Diagrams the notion of flow of control plays an important role. A strict distinction is made between passive objects which do not have control and active objects which have control. 'Having control' means that an object which has control is able to execute its program code independently from other objects. An active object may calculate some data, may communicate with other objects and may call other methods.

Contrary to that, MSCs are typically applied to the description of logically and physically distributed systems with asynchronous communication mechanisms. The MSC language can be viewed as a special trace language which mainly concentrates on message exchange between communicating entities. The specification by means of MSCs normally refers to a fairly high level of abstraction focusing on the causal relations between the contained events. The introduction of control flow to these highly concurrent behaviour descriptions appears much less obvious than in the case of Sequence Diagrams. The harmonization of MSCs and Sequence Diagrams is intended to connect the software oriented view of Sequence Diagrams with the distributed conception of MSCs.

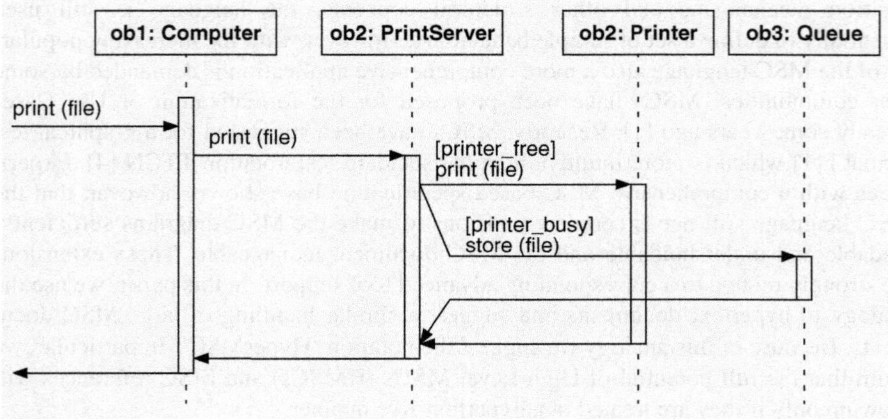

Fig. 1. UML Sequence Diagram containing guarded branching of messages

The possibility to explicitly indicate the flow of control in a way similar to Sequence Diagrams appeared to be important for the acceptance of the MSC language for OO modelling. It certainly offers a significant new visualization of the processes occurring in the system. Because of that, notations for method calls and replies have been introduced into MSC-2000 [15]. To a large extend, the constructs have been taken over from Sequence Diagrams (cf. fig. 2).

However, for a clear definition of flow of control in MSCs it turned out that the activation region alone is not sufficient. For the detailed specification of the flow of control, in addition a suspension region is employed [9].

The suspension region indicates the blocking state of a synchronizing call which is explicitly represented by a tall thin vertical white rectangle with dotted vertical border lines. The suspension region has no direct counterpart in Sequence Diagrams, it only may be distinguished in form of a non-shaded section if the actual computation part is shaded. However, we feel that the blocking state within a synchronizing call should be more clearly distinguished from the actual activation region. Within a detailed description, also for the activation region itself a substructure in form of shaded and non-shaded sections may be introduced.

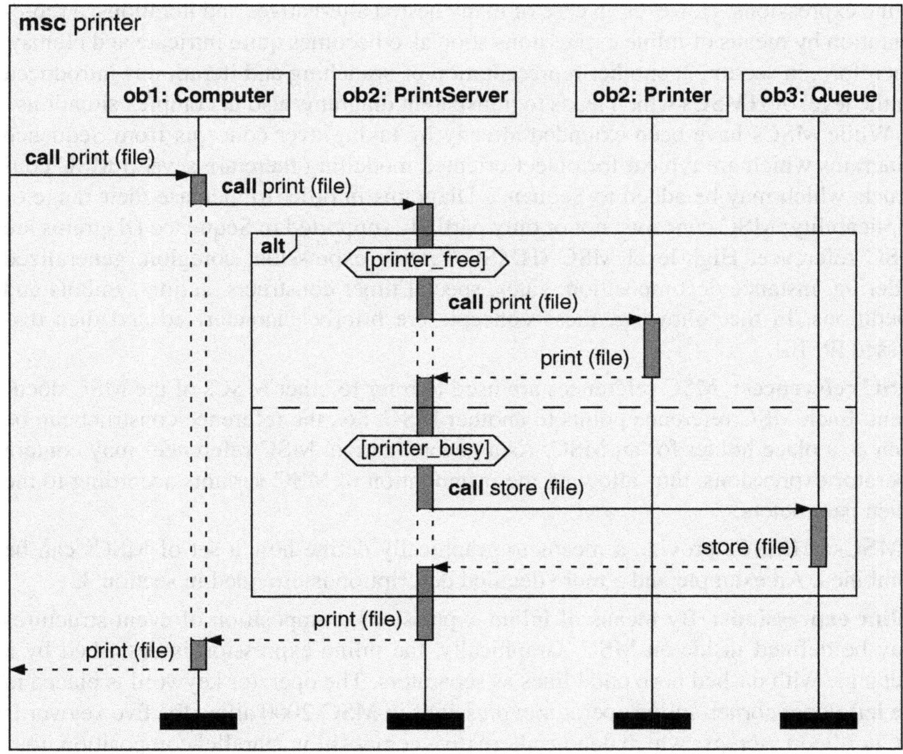

Fig. 2. Translation into an MSC containing an alternative inline expression

For modelling method calls in MSC, two kinds of calls are used: synchronizing calls with blocking mechanism for the calling instance and non-synchronizing calls without blocking mechanism. A synchronizing call is represented by a normal message with the keyword *call* and a message reply in form of a dashed arrow. The non-synchronizing call is represented only by a normal message with the keyword *call*. Due to the suspension region, synchronizing and non-synchronizing calls are sufficiently distinguished so that no special arrow head symbols are necessary as is the case in Sequence Diagrams. But keep in mind that specifying the flow of control remains optional.

Another significant difference between Sequence Diagrams and MSCs concerns the representation of branching [9]. In generic Sequence Diagrams, object life lines may branch and merge, thus showing alternatives. The branching of a method call is also allowed: it is represented by multiple arrows emanating from one common origin (cf. fig. 1). The guards for messages included in Sequence Diagrams can be interpreted as an if-statement, without else-part. Within MSCs, the branching and iteration constructs can be described by inline expressions (cf. fig. 2). Their clarity is an advantage of the MSC language which becomes obvious in more complicated situations. Guards are represented by means of guarding conditions containing a Boolean expression in brackets. Sequence Diagrams may benefit very much by taking over the concept of inline expressions. However, in case of many nested alternatives and iterations, a representation by means of inline expressions soon also becomes quite intricate and clumsy. Therefore, in section 3, another representation of branching and iteration is introduced on the level of HMSCs which leads to transparent diagrams also in complex situations.

While MSCs have been extended already by taking over concepts from Sequence Diagrams which are typical for object oriented modelling there are several MSC constructs which may be added to Sequence Diagrams in order to increase their range of applicability: MSC concepts, not or only partially supported in Sequence Diagrams are MSC reference, High-level MSC (HMSC), inline expression, coregion, generalized ordering, instance decomposition, gates, special timer constructs, action symbols and conditions. In the following, these concepts are briefly characterized and then discussed [9, 10].

MSC references: MSC references are used to refer to other MSCs of the MSC document. Each MSC reference points to another MSC, i.e., the reference construct can be seen as a place holder for an MSC. As a generalization, MSC references may contain operator expressions, thus allowing the instantiation of MSC variants according to the given parameters.

HMSCs: HMSCs provide a means to graphically define how a set of MSCs can be combined. An example and a more detailed description is provided in section 3.

Inline expressions: By means of inline expressions, composition of event structures may be defined inside an MSC. Graphically, the inline expression is described by a rectangle with dashed horizontal lines as separators. The operator keyword is placed in the left upper corner. Inline operator expressions in MSC-2000 allow the five keywords *alt*, *par*, *loop*, *opt*, *exc* which denote alternative composition, parallel composition, iteration, optional region and exception, respectively.

Coregions and generalized ordering: Along an MSC instance, normally a total ordering of message events is assumed. To cope with general time orderings, the coregion and generalized ordering are part of the MSC language. A coregion is graphically represented by a dashed section of an MSC instance. Within a coregion, the specified events are not ordered. The generalized ordering allows the specification of arbitrary event ordering.

Instance decompositions: By means of instance decomposition, a refining MSC may be attached to an instance which describes the events of the decomposed instance on a more detailed level.

Gates: Gates are used to define connection points for messages and order relations with respect to the interior and exterior of MSC references and inline expressions.

Special timer constructs: MSCs include language constructs expressing the setting, resetting and expiration of timers.

Actions: Actions are used to describe an internal activity of an instance. Graphically an action is represented by a rectangle containing arbitrary text. In Sequence Diagrams, an explicit action symbol is missing, however, an action being performed may be labelled in text next to the activation symbol or in the left margin.

Conditions: In MSC-2000, conditions may contain guards which we indicate in analogy to the UML- notation by enclosing the guarding expression in brackets (in MSC-2000, the keyword *when* is used instead). Otherwise, conditions are used to set the state of an instance.

3 The Role of HyperMSCs for Use Case Modelling and Testing

In case of many alternatives, the inline branching constructs, both for Sequence Diagrams and for Message Sequence Charts, described in section 2 (cf. fig. 1, 2) are not very transparent. In particular, they obscure the presentation of the complete message flow. Therefore, many users of UML are reluctant to employ these constructs at all. Instead, there is a tendency to indicate branching and iterations at the border line of the diagram either using special graphical constructs, e.g. for loops, or even using a program-like form. This way, the diagrams may be focusing on the representation of the pure message flow. In practice, however, such a notation again may soon become quite intricate and clumsy, particularly in case of nested alternatives or loops. In the following, we shall re-formulate High Level MSCs (HMSCs) which are part of the standard MSC language in such a way that they may serve for a similar purpose. At the same time, the obtained notation turns out to be very intuitive and simple also in more complicated situations.

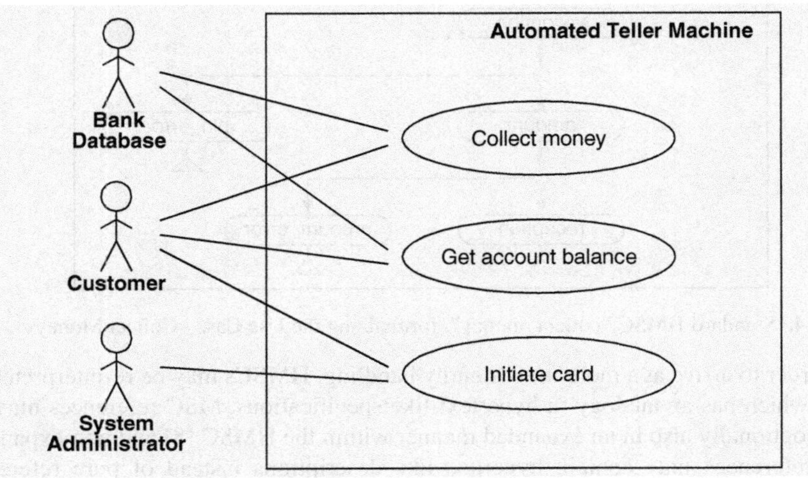

Fig. 3. Use Case diagram «Automated Teller Machine»

In the literature, High Level MSCs (HMSCs) have been suggested for the construction (derivation) of scenarios from Use Case Diagrams already several years ago [1]. HMSCs provide a means to define in form of a directed graph how a set of MSCs can be combined [8, 10]. A given Use Case is typically characterized by multiple scenarios on which a respective compositional structure may be imposed. This compositional structure suitably can be described in form of an HMSC. HMSCs allow the description of sequential, alternative and parallel composition. Repetitive behaviour may be represented by cyclic graphs. For the description of exceptional behaviour, additional operators may be defined, e.g., interruption and disruption, which are not yet included in the MSC standard. HMSCs are ideally suited to describe a main (normal) case with all accompanying side-cases.

HMSCs describe the composition of MSCs in form of a graph with MSC references and conditions as nodes. This way, they abstract from instances and messages which are not shown in the diagram. Each MSC reference points by means of the reference name to another MSC in the MSC document which defines the meaning of the reference. I.e., each reference symbol can be seen as a place holder for an MSC which has to be defined somewhere else in the MSC document. In case of many fairly small MSC reference definitions, such a representation soon becomes quite complex and in practice is difficult to handle. This may be demonstrated already by a rather small example, namely the HMSC representation of the Use Case «Collect money» (cf. fig. 4, 5) which is part of the Use Case diagram «Automated Teller Machine» (cf. fig. 3). Note, that in many cases much larger HMSCs have to be employed which may be even nested [10].

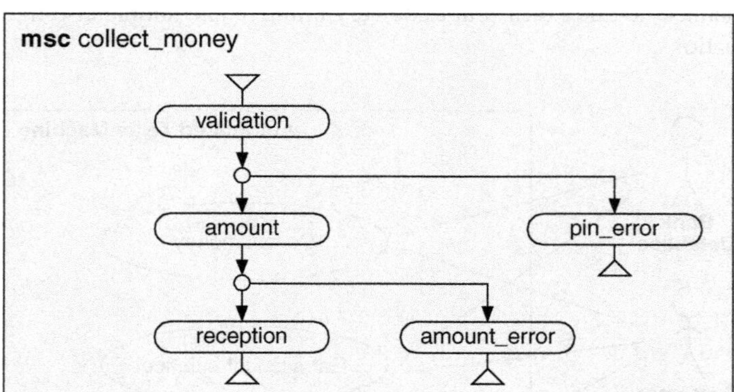

Fig. 4. Standard HMSC "collect_money", formalizing the Use Case «Collect Money»

In order to arrive at a more user-friendly handling, HMSCs may be re-interpreted in a way which has an analogy in hypertext-like specifications. MSC references may be shown optionally also in an expanded manner within the HMSC [8] and non-expanded MSC references may contain hypertext-like descriptions instead of pure reference names [11]. Note, that this implies a real extension of the MSC standard language. However, it essentially concerns the handling and the graphical layout only whereas it has no effect on the semantics. Thereby, we assume a corresponding tool support where the MSC references can be expanded within the HMSC in which they are contained or possibly in a separate window. The MSC references which can be expanded may be indicated similarly to hypertext by underlining the contained text or in a more compact form by variation of the symbol lines in line width or colour, or by adding additional symbols (like the asterisk, we choose in the examples). Such an approach is appropriate particularly in the usual case of many fairly small MSC reference definitions. Because of this analogy, we have introduced the notation 'HyperMSC' which shall indicate not only a special syntax form but also a corresponding tool support. The admittance of hypertext-like inscriptions within MSC reference symbols also provides a natural language interface to the user: On a higher level of design, the specification may be provided in form of purely textual descriptions which later on is specified in form of concrete MSCs. Within an advanced technology, the transition to concrete MSCs even may be automated.

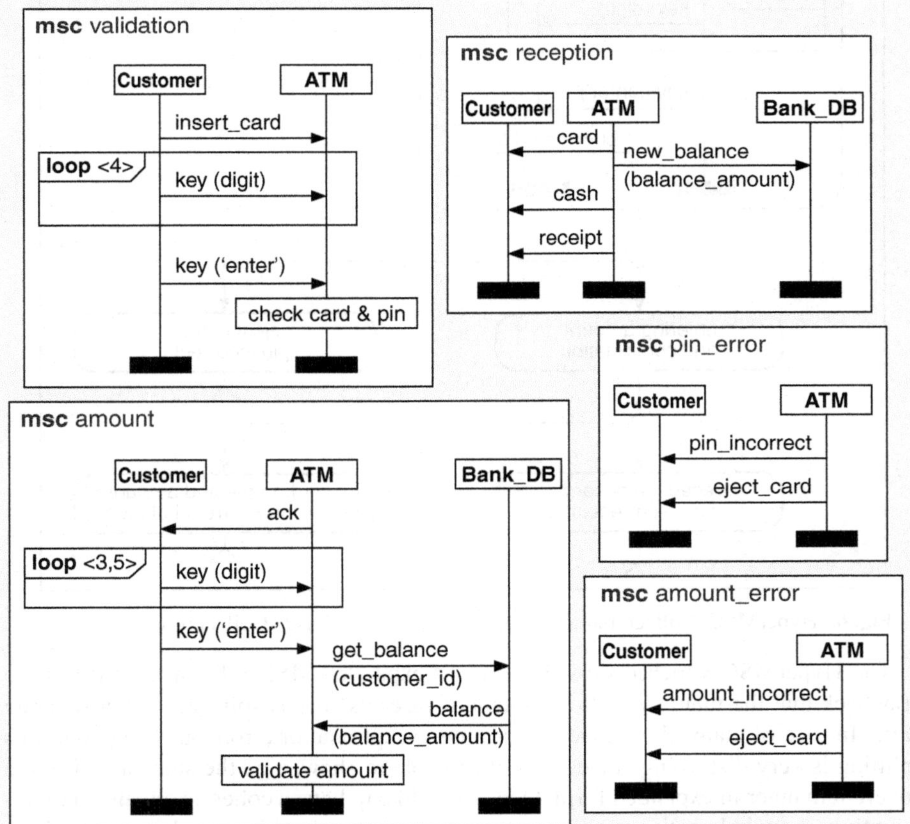

Fig. 5. The MSCs referenced in fig. 4: MSC "validation" (card and pin validation), MSC "amount" (entering amount and confirmation), MSC "reception" (reception of card, cash and receipt), MSC "pin_error" (eject card; pin incorrect), and MSC "amount_error" (discard; requested amount larger than current balance)

The transformation of the standard HMSC “collect_money” into a corresponding HyperMSC is shown in fig. 6. The MSC references may be expanded optionally within the diagram or in separate form, possibly even in a separate window. Within fig. 6, the MSC reference “validation” (card and pin validation) is shown in expanded form within the diagram.

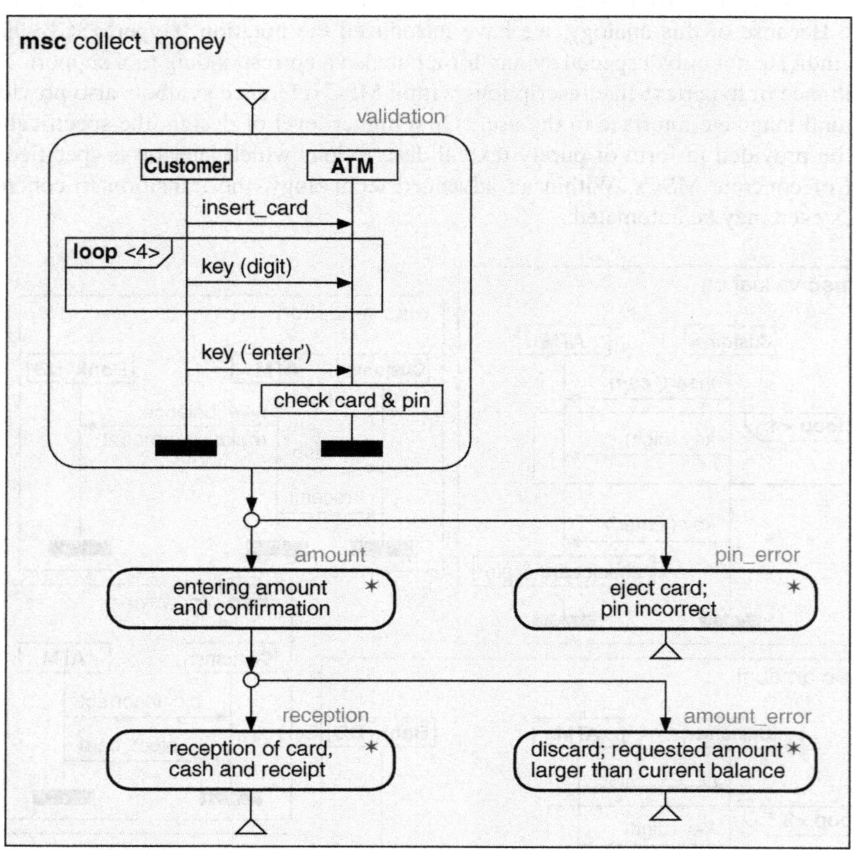

Fig. 6. HyperMSC “collect_money” representing the Use Case «Collect money»

The HyperMSC which results if we admit expanded MSC references still has the drawback that the main event flow (standard case) usually is split into many separate parts. In case of many alternatives describing exceptional or erroneous behaviour, this splitting is very disturbing since it is not possible to show, e.g., the standard case in a coherent manner in expanded form. One would like to have a coherent expanded representation of a whole path not only in a separate window but also in inline-form within the HyperMSC itself. We therefore suggest a further extension of HMSCs which somehow may be viewed also as a unification of High Level MSCs and plain MSCs. We allow the combination of several expanded MSC references which are interrupted by branching points to one coherent MSC reference. As a consequence, we have to shift the branching (or connection) point to the border line of the resulting MSC reference.

Thus, eventually, the complete main path of the Use Case «Collect money» may be represented in a coherent expanded form (cf. fig. 7).

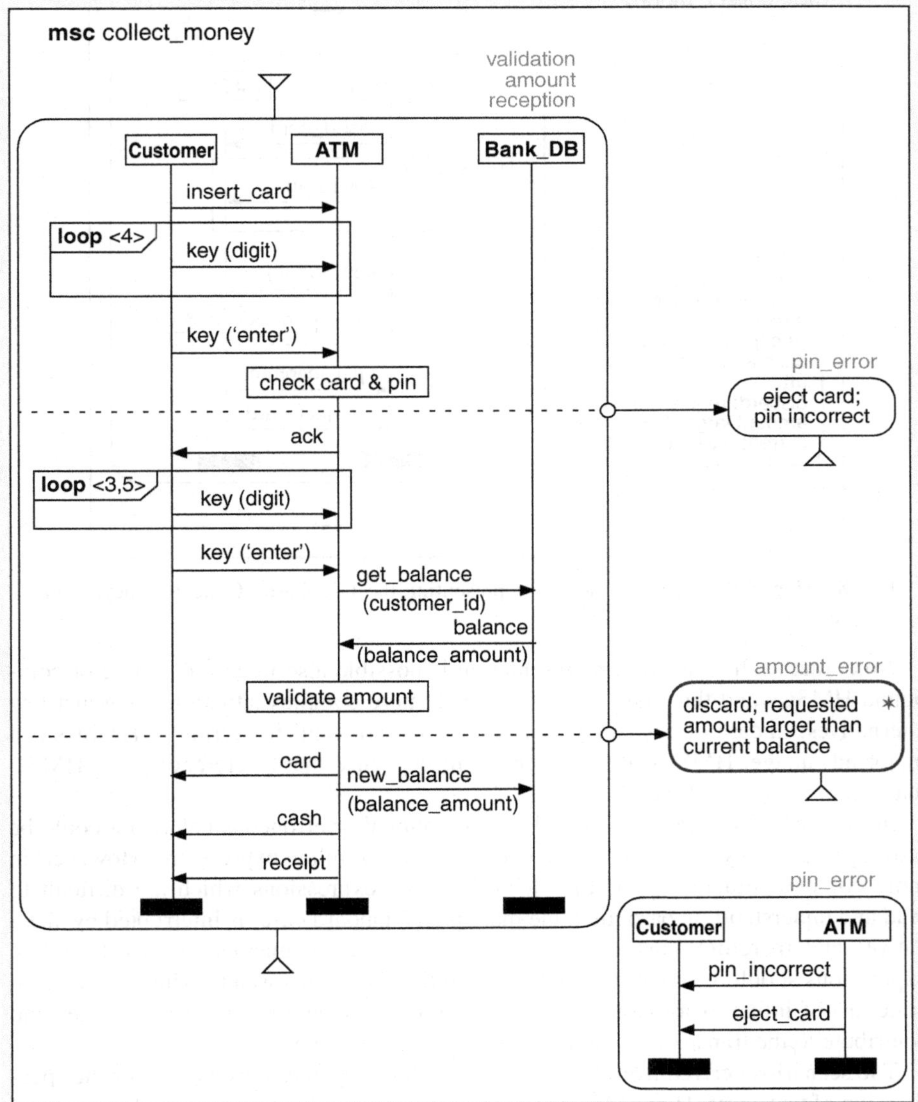

Fig. 7. HyperMSC "collect_money" with shifted branching point representing the Use Case «Collect money» in a coherent manner

The marked non-expanded references may be shown in expanded form separately as is demonstrated for the case where the PIN proofs itself to be incorrect. Another attractive solution is to change the roles of the main case and the side cases (cf. fig. 8).

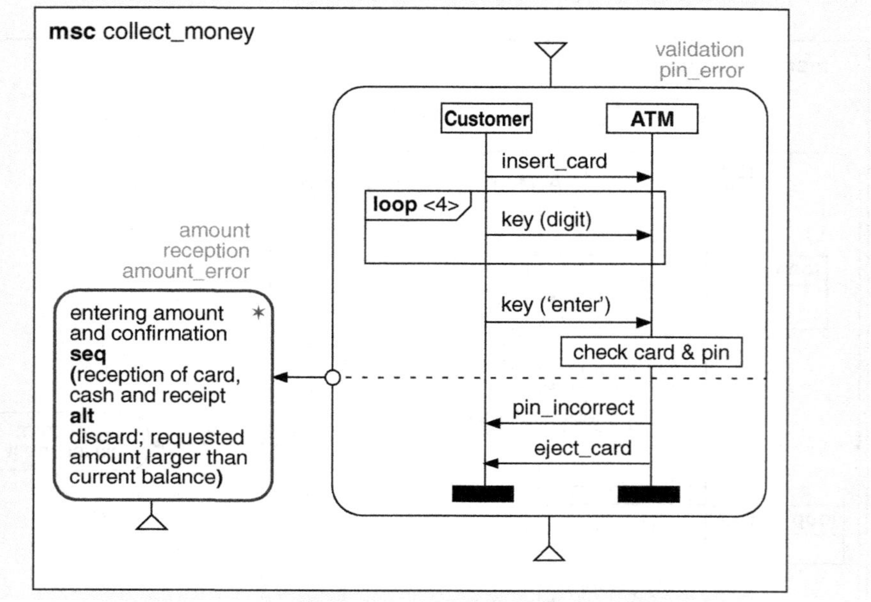

Fig. 8. HyperMSC "collect_money" representing the Use Case «Collect money» with changed roles

Note, that such a coherent representation is possible also in case of cyclic or compound HMSCs and thus may cope with much more complex situations than just few alternatives. In case of nested alternatives, the hierarchical structuring of HMSCs is a major advantage. HMSCs are hierarchical in the sense that a reference in an HMSC may again refer to an HMSC.

In principle, the side-cases describing exceptional or erroneous behaviour could be also represented by means of alternative or exception inline expressions. However, in more complex situations, this may lead to nested expressions which are difficult to read and understand. In particular, the main path (standard case) is interrupted by alternatives and therefore cannot be presented in a coherent manner. As a rule, inline expressions should be restricted to the description of small variants. This way, a moderate use of inline expressions instead of HMSC branches may have advantages and contribute to the transparency and readability of the diagrams.

The scenarios derived from Use Cases can be employed also as a basis for the specification of test cases. HyperMSCs appear to be particularly attractive for the graphical representation of such test cases. At present, the development of an MSC based graphical representation of the standard test notation TTCN (Tree and Tabular Combined Notation) is part of the ETSI project STF 156 on 'Specification of a Message Sequence Chart/UML format, including validation for TTCN-3' [11]. Because of the close relationship between MSCs and Sequence Diagrams, such a test format is also of great interest for UML particularly since there is no accepted test notation yet in UML. Practice has shown that the traditional tree and tabular representation of test cases in TTCN is not very intuitive even if tools are used. A representation in form of HyperMSCs may considerably increase the readability of test cases and make them more understandable, in particular, in case of many alternatives which may be even nested.

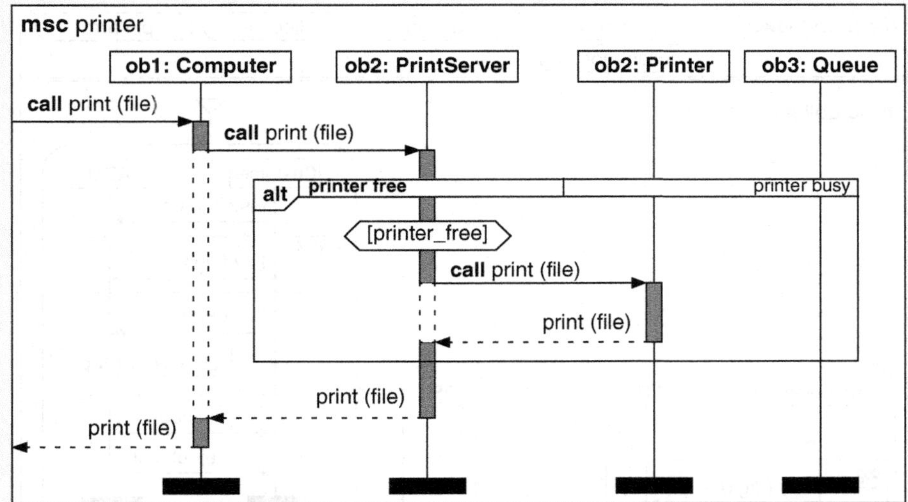

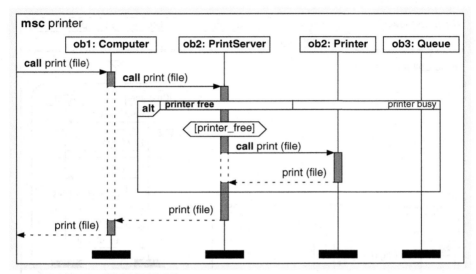

Fig. 9. Variant for inline expressions

4 Hypertext-like Features of the HyperMSCs

Let us here summarize the hypertext-like features of the HyperMSCs. The motivation to introduce those features was to provide flexible means for working with Sequence Diagrams. The basic assumption is

- that Use Cases start out as rather straight behaviour sequences, but further refinement introduces alternatives, identifies overlapping parts, adds exceptions, etc., and thus leads to diagrams consisting of rather small and fragmented portions.
- that the analysis, however, requires diagrams that express "logical units" where most of the alternatives are resolved; yet, the information about where behaviour alternatives commence is as well essential for the understanding of the system and should be indicated appropriately.
- that which parts of the diagram are focused on depends upon the aims of the analysis, i.e., they will change constantly during the work with the diagrams.

These considerations lead to a hypertext-like form of MSCs where a user can select the appropriate presentation by expanding or deflating MSC references. There are three ways to present an MSC reference: (a) by its proper name (cf. fig. 4), (b) by its textual description (cf. fig. 6), and (c) by its full blown MSC diagram (cf. fig. 6). All three forms may occur concurrently in one MSC representation. In addition, subsequent MSC diagrams are glued together, in order to show an uninterrupted behaviour flow (cf. fig. 7, where the three MSC references "validation", "amount", and "reception" are connected). Also textual descriptions can be combined in a simple way in order to produce clearly arranged diagrams (cf. fig. 8). To every diagram, an additional expansion of one of the MSC references can be added if necessary (see fig. 7).

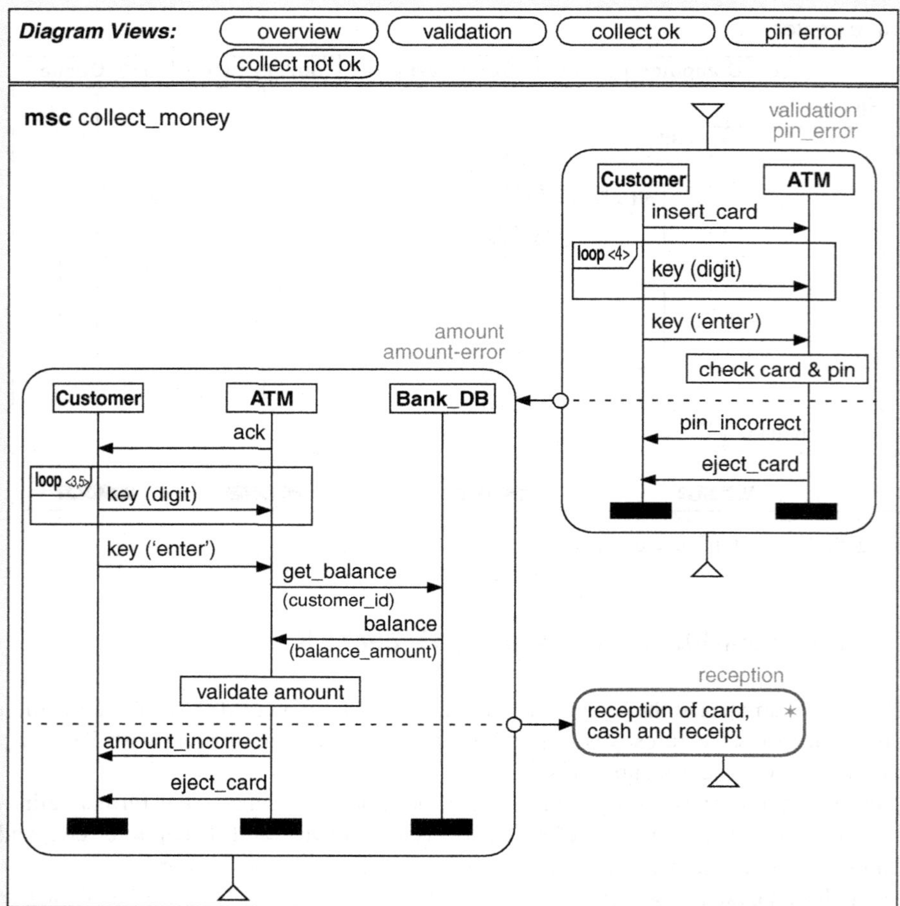

Fig. 10. HyperMSC "collect_money" in its view "collect not ok", together with the selection bar, where also the other views defined in this paper, i.e., "overview" (fig. 4), "validation" (fig. 6), "collect ok" (fig. 7), and "pin error" (fig. 8) can be selected for display

Inline expressions in MSCs can be also considered as candidates for a hypertext-like treatment. In particular, the *alt*-construct is well suited to express small alternatives. In order to simplify the presentation of the diagrams it is reasonable to provide a hypertext-like switching between the presented alternatives. In fig. 9, clicking into the "*printer busy*" field would change the presentation to the other alternative. Clicking into the "alt" field would change to the full presentation (all alternatives) as to be seen in fig. 2. Note, however, that the alternative could be realised with HMSCs and MSC references as well.

Hypertext-like mechanisms cannot be presented on paper very well. Thus, it needs to be mentioned explicitly that an appropriate tool support is expected for HyperMSCs where the user can freely change between the various representations. The tool has to rearrange the diagrams appropriately.

Each representation can be considered a specific view of the MSC. In our examples, fig. 6 describes the case where only the card and pin validation is of concern. The rest of the "collect_money" MSC is described in abbreviated form. In fig. 7, the focus is on the behaviour sequence which has to happen if both, the "check card & pin" and the "validate amount" actions give the ok and the money is dispensed. Another view is presented in fig. 10, where all behaviour sequences are displayed which lead to an abortion of the "collect_money" procedure.

Views are an essential means to analyse and explain the behaviour. Thus, it is necessary to preserve the selected view. In fig. 10, the selection bar above the diagram proposes the different views defined for the HyperMSC "collect_money". A click to the respective button would display the selected view. Obviously, starting with a given view, again new views can be created by expanding or deflating some MSC references.

5 Conclusion and Outlook

Both Sequence Diagrams and Message Sequence Charts, need extensions in order to be really applicable for Use Case modelling and testing. MSCs, however, contain already powerful language constructs for that purpose, in particular HMSCs, which only need to be slightly re-formulated in form of HyperMSCs. HyperMSCs offer the exciting possibility of a really comprehensive system modelling in form of diagrams which are easy to learn, use and interpret.

The general idea of HyperMSCs, i.e., to treat MSCs in a hypertext-like manner can be extended also to other MSC language constructs than HMSC and MSC references. The concept of decomposed instances [6] is quite close to MSC references and therefore can be viewed in a similar manner. Another application area concerns data descriptions in MSCs. According to the data concept of MSC-2000 [3, 15], data descriptions may occur at several places in an MSC, such as message parameters, action boxes and MSC reference parameters. The explicit inclusion of parameter lists within MSCs may soon lead to overloaded specifications. Thus, a hypertext-like reference may contribute to the transparency of the message flow description also in such cases. Such *constraint references* are already well established within TTCN test suites [4].

The usage of Sequence Diagrams and their role within the UML development process may greatly increase by taking over the concept of High Level MSCs and their extension to HyperMSCs, and other structural concepts, in particular, inline expressions from MSC. Most likely, Sequence Diagrams will then play a dominant role within the UML dynamic description techniques. As a future working program, it seems to us that more effort has to be put into a clear definition of the various communication mechanisms and their relationship. At the same time, additional constructs for a further differentiation of these communication mechanisms have to be provided. In particular, this applies to the MSC language which still only has one (asynchronous) message type. By means of a corresponding elaboration, Sequence Diagrams or MSCs may present a dynamic counterpart to the static class diagrams with a comparable usefulness and popularity.

References

1. M. Andersson, J. Bergstrand: Formalizing Use Cases with Message Sequence Charts. Master Thesis, Lund Institute of Technology, 1995
2. F. Buschmann, R. Meunier, H. Rohnert, P. Sommerlad, M. Stal: A System of Patterns, Pattern Oriented Software Architecture. John Wiley & Sons, 1996
3. A.G. Engels, L.M.G. Feijs, S. Mauw: MSC and Data: Dynamic Variables. In SDL'99, The Next Millennium, Proceedings of the 9th SDL Forum in Montreal, Canada, Yair Lahav and R. Dssouli (eds.), North Holland, June 1999
4. J. Grabowski, B. Koch, M. Schmitt, D. Hogrefe: SDL and MSC Based Test Generation for Distributed Architectures. In SDL'99, The Next Millennium, Proceedings of the 9th SDL Forum in Montreal, Canada, Yair Lahav and R. Dssouli (eds.), North Holland, June 1999
5. P. Graubmann, E. Rudolph, J. Grabowski: Towards a Petri Net Based Semantics Definition for Message Sequence Charts. In SDL'93 Using Objects, Proceedings of the 6th SDL Forum in Darmstadt, Germany, O. Faergemand and A. Sarma (eds.), North Holland, October 1993
6. O. Haugen: The MSC-96 Distillery. In SDL'97 Time for Testing-SDL, MSC and Trends, Proceedings of the 8th SDL Forum in Evry, France, A. Cavalli and A. Sarma (eds.), North Holland, September 1997
7. I. Jacobson et al.: Object Oriented Software Engineering, A Use Case Driven approach. Addison-Wesley, 1994
8. S. Mauw, M.A. Reniers: High Level Message Sequence Charts. In SDL'97 Time for Testing-SDL, MSC and Trends, Proceedings of the 8th SDL Forum in Evry, France, A. Cavalli and A. Sarma (eds.), North Holland, September 1997
9. E. Rudolph, J. Grabowski, P. Graubmann: Towards a Harmonization of UML Sequence Diagrams and MSC. In SDL'99, The Next Millennium, Proceedings of the 9th SDL Forum in Montreal, Canada, Yair Lahav and R. Dssouli (eds.), North Holland, June 1999
10. E. Rudolph, J. Grabowski, P. Graubmann: Tutorial on Message Sequence Charts (MSC-96). Forte/PSTV'96. Kaiserslautern, Germany, October 1996
11. E. Rudolph, I. Schieferdecker, J. Grabowski: Development of a Message Sequence Chart/UML Test Format. Proceedings of FBT-2000, Lübeck, Germany. Shaker-Verlag, 2000
12. J. Rumbaugh, I. Jacobson, G. Booch: The Unified Modelling Language, Reference Manual, Version 1.3, Rational, 1999
13. ITU-T Rec. Z.120 (MSC-92). Message Sequence Chart (MSC). E. Rudolph (ed.), Geneva, 1994
14. ITU-T Rec. Z.120 (MSC-96). Message Sequence Chart (MSC). E. Rudolph (ed.), Geneva, 1996
15. ITU-T Rec. Z.120 (MSC-2000). Message Sequence Chart (MSC). O. Haugen (ed.), Geneva, 1999

Business-Oriented Constraint Language

John Knapman

IBM, Hursley Park, Winchester, Hampshire, SO21 2JN, England
knapman@uk.ibm.com

Abstract. The Business-oriented Constraint Language (BCL) is proposed as a means of annotating diagrams in UML. BCL is grounded in the Object Constraint Language (OCL) but is designed particularly to address the needs of people who are concerned with enterprise application integration (EAI), although it may be more widely applicable. EAI often requires a loosely coupled event-based architecture in which timing and statistical measures are important; these are described in another paper (1). BCL provides these features together with a syntax that is flexible and extensible. It is intended to be accessible to most practitioners, including those who do not have a mathematical background.

1. Introduction

Business-process models, architectures and designs are all abstractions, in that they do not describe everything about an implementation but only aspects that the modeler considers salient. Models, including graphical models, are a form of constraint. However, despite their appeal, graphics are limited in what they can express. There is a need for architects to be able to state other constraints without having to go into implementation-level detail. It is highly desirable for these constraints to be readable to business people who do not have particular mathematical skills.

UML already provides a constraint language — OCL. It is somewhat mathematical in style and is based on the Syntropy method (2). An alternative syntax is presented that is intended to make the language more accessible to both IT professionals and business people — the Basic or COBOL of constraint languages. This includes approximate and statistical terms and phrases. Statistical extensions to OCL are described in another paper, "Statistical Constraints for EAI" (1).

It is proposed to name this extended language BCL. It subsumes OCL, for which it can substitute, and it includes OCL syntax as a special case. This document is a draft definition of BCL. Tools to implement it will require both a definition-time component (to check syntax and consistency with the graphical elements of models) and run-time components (to carry out monitoring and reporting).

A. Evans, S. Kent and B. Selic (Eds.): «UML» 2000, LNCS 1939, pp. 47-61, 2000.

2. Examples

The figure shows a UML class diagram in which associations between classes have been used to show links that carry messages. Here, modeling is being done at the level of application architecture. Some of the classes (Report Entry, Fault Management and Customer Care) represent parts (e.g., programs) of an application system. Some of the classes are stereotypes representing elements, such as transformation and subscription, that are commonly used in EAI. Stream and message class stereotypes (with streams containing messages) are shown with suitable attributes such as time stamp; streams have attributes that enable them to be implemented in queues (cf. JMS (3)) or service points (cf. OAMAS). In the application illustrated, fault reports are transformed and routed to Fault Management. Fault Management creates subscriptions so that the Publish and Subscribe (Pub/Sub) facility will selectively route follow-up reports to Customer Care. This is based on a business need to monitor the service that certain customers (a changing set of customers) receive. The annotations in brackets { } are in BCL, and they supplement the graphics. A tool that implements BCL will be able to read and validate these constraints, preferably using XMI (4). They have interpretations that apply at execution time; fault reports and other reports can be monitored, and a tool could report on the extent to which they conform.

Strictly, a class diagram does not show behavior. However, users commonly indicate behavior by adding notes. It is intended that BCL should be a usable alternative for such purposes.

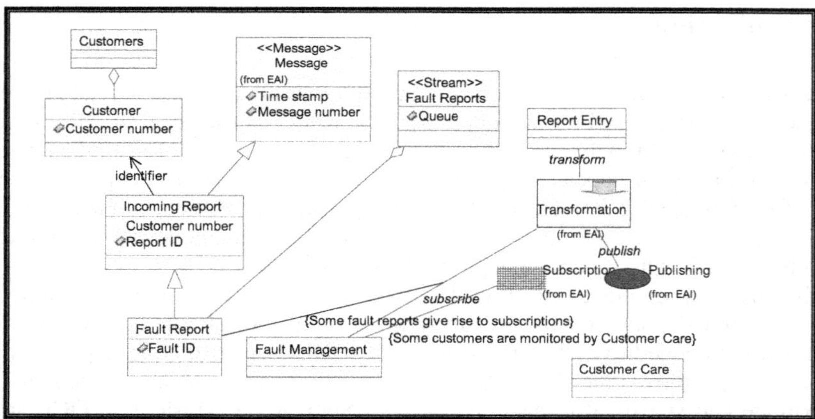

The first constraint asserts: "Some customers are monitored by Customer Care." Monitoring is a concept defined in terms of receiving identifiers. "Customers are monitored by X" can be rewritten as "X receives messages containing Customer IDs." The quantifier "some" implies that the assertion only applies to a subset of customers, the size of the subset being in a certain range (25% to 75% of superset size). This summarizes what is going on as a result of Pub/Sub. The definitions of these terms can be changed by users or administrators. If the implementation uses message queues, a monitoring tool can read messages and extract the statistics needed for reporting whether this constraint is satisfied.

The diagram itself comprises a set of constraints. It says that Customer Care receives fault reports directly and also publications that may include other message types. A monitoring tool could verify those constraints too. Another annotation asserts: "Some fault reports give rise to subscriptions." This can also be monitored to verify that subscriptions are indeed created in response to a subset (with size in a certain range) of fault reports received.

A UML interaction (sequence or collaboration) diagram could be used to give more detailed information about the order of operations, but many users rely on class diagrams with annotations in English or another natural language to add such information as they deem appropriate. BCL is intended to provide a human-readable language for some of these purposes. The style of these annotations may appear like natural language, but it conforms to the syntax of BCL, which allows terms to be defined as phrases that include blank spaces (e.g., "gives rise to"). Other styles are permissible, depending on preference, e.g.,

some (FaultReports) giveRiseTo Subscriptions
some (Customers) areMonitoredBy CustomerCare

In this style, the classes in the UML class diagram are labeled CustomerCare and FaultReports rather than Customer Care and Fault Reports. The following illustrates a style that is closer to Java:

(some (FaultReports)).giveRiseTo (Subscriptions)
(some (Customers)).areMonitoredBy (CustomerCare)

These examples illustrate the use of statistical quantification ("some") over a stream ("Fault Reports") and a set ("Customers"); they show an operation ("are monitored by") that is defined in terms of the model, and they indicate a syntactic flexibility that is intended to ease both reading and writing of constraints. If preferred, OCL syntax can be used with streams and statistical operations.

More detailed BCL annotations could be included that effectively refine the last one:

Fault reports, F, about some customers give rise to subscriptions, S.
Messages, M, about F **with** M following S are received by Customer Care.

The following variation on the second sentence may be preferable:

Messages about F **following** S are received by Customer Care.

The following sections summarize OCL collections, after which the syntax of BCL is defined and further operations are introduced.

3. Collections

UML is intended for modeling systems at a level of detail that is higher than an implementation (i.e., more abstract). As a graphical notation, there are some constraints that cannot readily be expressed in UML. For instance, we may require that the company's employees are all aged 18 or over. OCL users can express this constraint as follows:

```
Company
      self.employee->forAll( age >= 18 )
```

The header Company states the context of the constraint. Constraints may be written in the class diagram. For this one to be valid, 'Company' must appear as a class with the association 'employee' to another class that has attribute 'age'.

The arrow notation -> applies to a collection of employees. The forAll operation applies the predicate to all the employees of a company. A collection may be a set (repeated members forbidden), a bag (repeated members allowed) or a sequence (a bag with position numbering). For EAI, we define streams as a new collection type that can be sampled. Operations on a stream implicitly apply to a sample of messages, namely, those that have flowed since the last sample was taken. Such a sample is treated as an OCL sequence.

The BCL constraints given earlier can be rendered in OCL by defining 'some' as a collection operation returning another, smaller, collection:

```
FaultReports->some()
      ->forAll(f | f.giveRiseTo (Subscription))
Companies->some()
      ->forAll(c | c.areMonitoredBy (CustomerCare))
```

4. Syntax

Like OCL, BCL is intended to annotate UML models. The elements of OCL and BCL are names and operations. Names represent classes, types and objects that appear in the associated model or in the UML metamodel. OCL has a built-in but extensible set of operations, to which BCL adds more. Operations in OCL are typically of the form:

```
operation(parameter, parameter, ...)
```

or

```
object.operation(parameter, parameter, ...)
```

In BCL, operations are rendered with *keyphrases*. Smalltalk uses a similar form with each keyphrase ending in a colon (:), but it requires phrases to be run together (as do all programming languages). BCL does not require the use of colons, although a BCL user could choose to use them (as a stylistic choice) by defining keyphrases that end in a colon. BCL permits keyphrases to contain embedded blank spaces or special characters. For example, in OCL we might write:

```
person.income(date)
```

BCL offers other syntactic styles, so this could be "income of person as at date" or "person's income as at date". Here, person and date are names used as parameters; "income of", "'s income" and "as at" are keyphrases.

The basic form of an operation in BCL is:

$\text{expression}_1\ \text{keyphrase}_1 \ldots\ \text{keyphrase}_{n-1}\ \text{expression}_n$

In the basic form, n>=2 and the keyphrases are all infix operators. The case of two expressions (n=2) correponds to the familiar arithmetic operators (+, ,&/). Some operations have a prefix (keyphrase_0), a suffix (keyphrase_n) or both, giving three additional forms:

keyphrase$_0$ expression$_1$ keyphrase$_1$ .... keyphrase$_{n-1}$ expression$_n$ *(prefixed)*
expression$_1$ keyphrase$_1$ .... keyphrase$_{n-1}$ expression$_n$ keyphrase$_n$ *(suffixed)*
keyphrase$_0$ expression$_1$ keyphrase$_1$ .... keyphrase$_{n-1}$ expression$_n$ keyphrase$_n$ *(bracketed)*

With a prefix or suffix, n>=1. Unary operations (e.g., not A) are special cases in which n=1. A special case of a bracketed operation (i.e., having both a prefix and a suffix) is a bracketed identity operation such as "(...)", which can be used to determine nesting or operator precedence explicitly.

Because the language permits freedom in the use of overlapping names, the following conventions apply:

1. An expression may be a name (class, type or object), a literal or an operation.
2. A name or keyphrase may consist of an arbitrary string of characters, including blank spaces and special characters, but it must not be entirely blank. Generically, names and keyphrases are called *phrases.* Spaces between phrases are not significant. There is no case sensitivity.
3. Parsing is context sensitive. The first stage is *phrasing.* An expression is phrased (from left to right) by finding the longest phrase in the dictionary that matches the left-hand end of the expression and then phrasing the remainder of the expression.
4. Literals are marked conventionally with numerals or quotes as in OCL or other languages.
5. It is possible for phrases to overlap. Users can even choose names that include strings looking like literals or other phrases, although they can avoid such clashes through naming conventions or the use of extra spaces between phrases, and a parser may give warnings.
6. Prefixes can appear where names or literals are expected. If there is a clash so that a phrase equals both a name or a prefix, it is assumed to be a name. Similar considerations apply to a phrase that follows a suffix. The priority order is: name, prefix, literal. A bold font may be used to imply that a phrase is a keyphrase. A bold font may not be used for names or literals.
7. The language has an open-ended set of names and operations. Users can introduce new names or operations by using italics on their first appearance. Bold italics imply a new keyphrase and are necessary for new prefixes. The keyphrases are then added to the dictionary. Polymorphism is supported by allowing different operations to have overlapping keyphrases.
8. As in OCL, both the parameters and the results of BCL operations are typed. Hence, type-based polymorphism is supported, meaning that two operations may have an identical list of keyphrases if the types of one or more of the results differ.
9. Operator precedence is given to an operation on the right within the rules of type consistency. Hence, e.g., 2*3+5 is read as 2*(3+5). This convention is reversed if a bold font is used for the operators. So 2*3**+**5 and 2*3**+**5 are read as (2*3)+5).
10. Operator precedence is based on rules of type consistency. "A is a message if B is a sender" will parse as "(A is a message) if (B is a sender)" because the 'if' operation takes Boolean arguments. Otherwise, a non-typed rule of precedence on

the right would cause this to be parsed incorrectly as "A is a (message if (B is a sender))".

11. Ambiguities may arise when combining operations in an expression. If a keyphrase may be interpreted as a continuation of one operation or the start of another (nested), the continuation wins.

It is desirable for a parsing tool to warn users of clashes or overlapping names by checking all occurrences of name or keyphrase strings in an expression. A user can then introduce new names to avoid clashes or employ identity operations to server as punctuation. Users should be advised to use special characters sparingly in names and keyphrases, but the flexibility to use hyphens, apostrophes or other marks may sometimes be advantageous for readability. Optionally, a tool could show parsings explicitly as trees or using parentheses.

Identity operations, arithmetic operators (+, ,&/), functional forms and syntactic features like **if**...**then**...**else** ...**endif** are all special cases of operations. In multiplication, $keyphrase_1$ is "*" and the other keyphrases are blank. In a functional form f(..,..,...) $keyphrase_0$ is "f(" , $keyphrase_n$ is ")" and the others are ",". In a conditional, $keyphrase_0$ is "if", $keyphrase_1$ is "then", $keyphrase_2$ is "else" and $keyphrase_3$ is "endif". There are identity operations such as "(E)", "—E—" and "'E'" which are equivalent to "E", allowing users to add supplementary nesting to aid clarity or avoid ambiguity. Users can add their own operations.

A very basic operation has the form "A of B". This obtains the attribute A of B or applies the operation A to B. The OCL equivalent (also valid in BCL) is

```
B.A
```

or

<u>B</u>

```
self.A
```

BCL has the same typing scheme as OCL, which permits implicit type declarations in certain contexts, using the form

```
name : type
```

This carries over to BCL, where declaration is an operation having $keyphrase_1$ equal to ":". BCL also has the operations "is a" and "is an" as in "Ford is a company" or "X is an integer."

Newly introduced names or operations should be written in italics. If an operation is introduced in an expression, all its keyphrases should be in italics. Example:

If X *is monitored by* Y then Y receives messages about X.

This is not a complete definition of monitoring. Further assertions can be made about it in other constraints. Such open-endedness is inherent in constraint languages.

5. Summary of Grammar

sentence ::=	expression terminator
expression ::=	name
	literal

	unary-operation	
	operation-head operation-tail$_2$	
unary-operation ::=	keyphrase$_0$ expression	
	operation-head	
operation-head ::=	keyphrase$_0$ expression keyphrase$_1$	
	expression keyphrase$_1$	
operation-tail$_i$ ::=	expression keyphrase$_i$ operation-tail$_{i+1}$	(i=2,...,n-1)
operation-tail$_n$ ::=	expression	
	expression keyphrase$_n$	

Sentences are terminated by ". " (a dot followed by two spaces) or by a dot followed by a new line. A sentence appears as a unary operation with this terminator as a suffix, but implicitly it is treated as a bracketed unary operation (of form keyphrase$_0$ expression keyphrase$_1$), where keyphrase$_0$ is understood. It provides an outer bracket that can define the end of nested operations.

Parsing Strategy

As an operation is parsed, the keyphrases interpreted provide a context for interpreting those that follow. For any given list of parsed keyphrases, the parser carries the set of valid types and keywords that can follow immediately. This is called the *expected set* (ES) and consists of the expected type set (ETS) and the expected keyphrase set (EKS). Because operations can be nested, the parser stacks the sets. For a bracketed unary operation such as "(...)", for instance, the parser carries ")" in its ES. These lists and sets can be held efficiently in a repository, and new operations (indicated in italics) can be added to it.

Details of the parser are given in the appendix. The parsing strategy given is deterministic. More sophisticated parsing strategies are possible, such as constraint-based or probabilistic parsing, the method favored by many linguists for natural languages. Such strategies are able to resolve ambiguities with greater flexibility or to prompt users to resolve uncertain parsings, rather than following deterministic rules.

Syntactic Style

For the sake of readability and convenience, there are stylistic conventions in syntax that are not strictly part of the grammar. Users can choose (with appropriate definitions of class names and operations) and mix different styles. These are called cursive, bracketed, Javaesque and OCL, as illustrated, respectively:

Some fault reports give rise to subscriptions.
some (FaultReports) giveRiseTo Subscriptions
(some (FaultReports)).giveRiseTo (Subscriptions)
FaultReports->some(f | f.giveRiseTo (Subscription))

The cursive style is used in many of the examples in this paper. It carries certain conventions that should be implemented by a tool for greatest convenience. When properties are placed on the class diagram, they are implicitly associated with a pattern of operations. If class C has an attribute A, OCL will recognize ".A", "A of" and "'s A" as synonymous operations that can be applied to C as "C.A", "A of C" and "C's A", respectively. If class C has an operation B shown as Bx, where x stands for the parameters (as a sequence of keyphrases, "(..,..,..)" being a special case), then OCL will recognize ".Bx" and "'s Bx" as synonymous operations that can be applied to C as "C.Bx" and "C's Bx", respectively.

Decorations such as definite and indefinite articles can be defined as prefix unary operations equivalent to the identity function. Hence, "price of company", "the price of a company", "company's price" and "the company's price" are all equivalent provided the lexicon has the relevant plurals. The OCL rendering of these is:

```
Company
        self.price
```

Iterators

We use the notation

Collection, N,

and

Collection, N

to introduce iterators. The latter notation is suitable for the end of a sentence. An iterator is a variable that ranges over the members of a collection, as in the earlier examples:

Some fault reports, F, give rise to subscriptions, S.
Messages, M, following S...

In the first sentence, S is defined in a quantification context as follows:

```
someFaultReports->forAll(F|subscriptions
        ->forAll(S|F gives rise to S))
```

S is repeated in the second sentence. Implicitly, it applies to the same quantification context in a subsequent sentence as it appears in the first. Hence, the new sentence is nested in the same quantifiers, as follows:

```
someFaultReports->
        forAll(F|subscriptions->forAll(S|
        messages->select(M|M following S)... ))
```

Conventionally in BCL, collections have plural names. Hence, "messages" denotes a collection while "message" denotes a member of the collection. Concomitantly, plural verbs apply to collections: "messages are about F" whereas "a message is about F." A tool could implicitly define such plurals where singular nouns have been used for single instances in a UML diagram, but here we assume the plurals are defined in class diagrams using aggregations.

6. OCL Basis

BCL is based on OCL, rendering it in a form more suitable for users in business and commerce. The following headings align with the chapters in the OCL Specification.

Connection with the UML Metamodel
OCL includes class names and their operations as underscored headers to define a context. BCL relies on annotations in diagrams. OCL includes the labels 'invariant:', 'guard:', 'pre:' and 'post:'. BCL treats these as unary operations.

Basic Values and Types
Types may be implicitly determined by context, with a presumption of OclAny if there is no evidence for one of the other types, which are String, Integer, Real, Boolean, OclType, OclExpression, Enumeration, Collection, Set, Bag and Sequence. Explicit type statements are permitted in BCL through the 'is a' operation, e.g., X is a T. Here, T is equal to one of the types and X is a name.

Qualifying clauses and phrases of form 'E *such that* P' or 'E *with* Q' are permitted. Here, E is an expression and P is a predicate, that is, a Boolean operation; Q is a predicate on properties of E, e.g., "employees with age>50".

Expressions are permitted as in OCL, including ,+, ,&/,>,< 'and', 'or', 'implies' and if-then-else-endif. These are all BCL operations, albeit with different operator precedence rules.

In BCL an undeclared item is presumed to be of type OclAny. A supertype may be refined to one of its subtypes (e.g., OclType to Real, Real to Integer or Collection to Set — as with OCL retyping or casting) if an operation implies it, but contradictions are invalid. An advanced tool could hypothesize types on the basis of usage evidence and keep track of inconsistencies.

Enumerations include syntax for a collection of values. In OCL, the syntax is {v1, v2, v3}, where v1, etc., are literal values, either numeric or quoted strings. This syntax is a valid BCL operation with a recursive definition. Literals are conventional, with strings in surrounding quotes. There are also standard values true, false and empty. As in OCL, {} may be preceded by enum, Collection, Set, Bag or Sequence; enumeration values are preceded by #.

Objects and Properties
Properties may be attributes, operations and navigations (AssociationEnds) of a class or object and are generally written

```
Class
      self.attribute
```
or
```
      self.operation
```

in OCL, where `self` is an object of type `class`. For attributes and navigations (i.e., following associations between elements of the UML model), BCL treats the dot as the operation's keyphrase.

When OCL operations appear in BCL, they are declared so that the operation name is part of the initiator keyphrase. Consider the example:

```
aPerson.income(aDate)
```

This has ".income(" as its initiator keyphrase. UML class diagrams permit language-specific signatures to operations, so that we can write "*income as at* aDate". A BCL tool should interpret this as permitting operations “aPerson.income as at aDate” and “aPerson’s income as at aDate”. The use of keyphrases is intended to make for greater readability.

Navigation uses the same syntax as properties. So we may write “the employee’s manager” or “the employee’s company”. We may have “the company’s employees”, the plural indicating that this is a collection. We may want to refer to a set explicitly, as in “The size of the set of the company’s employees is 35” or “The set of the company’s employees is not empty.” The same applies to collections, sequences and bags. As in OCL, the properties of the members of a collection form another collection, as in ‘the birthdates of the company’s employees’.

Instance qualifiers, e.g., customer[8764423], are permitted as in OCL, treating [and] as the keyphrases.

In postconditions, the @pre postfix of OCL is permitted to refer to a previous value and is valid as a unary operation in BCL, as in:

```
post: age = age@pre + 1
```

In BCL, users or administrators could define operations to allow alternatives such as:

Final age is initial age plus 1.

Collection Operations
In BCL we may write ‘the set of’, ‘the collection of’, ‘the sequence of’ or ‘the bag of’ as operations on the following expression, normally followed by keywords ‘such that’ or ‘with’ and a predicate. These select from collections, normally properties of an object. They may form a collection from, for instance, the instances of a class (e.g., ‘the set of companies’, which is equal to `company.allInstances` in OCL). Collection operations (e.g., the size of) are permitted. As in OCL, collection operations are permitted on single elements too. Hence, we can write “The size of the set of an employee’s manager is 1” or “The size of the set of an employee’s managers is 1.”

7. Details of Examples

The examples introduced in section 2 are explained in more detail here. The first two sentences are:

Some fault reports give rise to subscriptions.
Some customers are monitored by Customer Care.

“Some” is a prefix operator and must be followed by a stream or other collection. The type-consistency rule of operator precedence dictates that the parsing is:
((Some (fault reports)) (give rise to) subscriptions).

This conforms to the rule that “some” is an operation on a stream that returns a substream which is then subject to the predicate that its messages give rise to subscriptions. The proposed definition of “some” constrains the size of the substream to be 25% to 75% of the messages. Without the type-consistency rule, the parsing would be:

(Some ((fault reports) (give rise to) subscriptions)).

This finds "some" applying to a Boolean, whereas it is defined over collections. Users could define the syntax of quantifiers in a functional form, e.g., "*some(...)*", as a way of being sure about the parsing, much as people often bracket arithmetic expressions because they can't remember the precedence rules. Thus the sentence can be written with parentheses, e.g.,

(Some fault reports) give rise to subscriptions.

The parsing of the second sentence is similar:

((Some (customers)) (are monitored by) (Customer Care))

Two more sentences introduced in the examples in section 2 are:

Fault reports, F, about some customers give rise to subscriptions, S.
Messages, M, about F **with** M following S are received by Customer Care.

These introduce iterator variables F, S and M using the comma syntax, as explained under "Syntactic style" in section 5. The variables are needed for the qualification of "messages" in the second sentence. Parsing needs a bold font or the introduction of parentheses to ensure that the "with" phrase in the second sentence applies to "messages, M," rather than to F. A more sophisticated parser could determine that the reference of this phrase must be to M because of its content. The interpretation of the first sentence (in a mixture of cursive and OCL style) is:

```
FaultReports->select(f|some(customers)->exists(c|f is about c))
        ->forAll(F|subscriptions ->forAll(S|F gives rise to S)))
```

The second sentence applies to the same context as the first. Hence, the full expression reads:

```
FaultReports->select(f|some(customers)->exists(c|f is about c))
        ->forAll(F|subscriptions->forAll(S|messages
        ->select(M|M about F)->select(m|m following S)
        ->forAll(m|m are received by Customer Care) )))
```

8. Future Directions

It is possible to continue extending the list of operations. A layering scheme would be appropriate, with a core set provided by a vendor, an industry set defined by a community of interest, a company set defined by an administrator and a set tailorable by each user.

A logical satisfiability (SAT) tool along the lines of Alcoa (5) could be introduced to check the validity of constraints. Alcoa uses a formal notation that does not map directly to UML (because UML still lacks formal semantics). A BCL tool could rewrite constraints to such a formal notation but, for completeness, a formal mapping of UML is needed too.

A non-deterministic or probabilistic parser could be introduced to permit greater flexibility in sentence forms. A more elegant, natural parser would be able to avoid iterator variables by allowing pronouns, coping with such pairs of sentences as:

Fault reports about some customers give rise to subscriptions.
Following messages about those faults are received by Customer Care.

This would require the ability to intepret anaphoric references ("those" or "them"), text matching to infer that faults are probably the subject of fault reports, and some temporal reasoning to assume that "following" refers to the events of the preceding sentence. Despite more than thirty years of effort, these are still regarded as research problems.

Appendix: State Machine for Parser

Because operations are allowed to overlap (a form of polymorphism), it is necessary to parse ahead to decide where an operation ends. Consider the parser in the middle of an expression, having identified keyphrases $K^a_0...K^a_i$ or $K^a_1...K^a_i$. There may be several operations with such a list of keyphrases, so that there are several possible keyphrases that might follow next. These are in the expected keyphrase set (EKS) $\{K^a_{i+1,j}\}$ of valid next keywords, where j>=1. If there is only one operation with keywords equal to the list to K^a_i and no overlapping operations, then there will be only one entry in the EKS. For example, in a functional form f(..,..,..), the EKS will contain only a comma or a right parenthesis. If K^a_i is the last keyphrase in an operation, the EKS will contain the token END or CLOSE. Here CLOSE indicates that K^a_i is a suffix (e.g., a right parenthesis, end of sentence, or **endif**), and END indicates that K^a_i is the last infix (e.g., an arithmetic operator or a logical **and** or **or**). These lists and sets should be maintained in the parser's repository. If ...K^a_i are in italics, indicating a new operation, the parser will place the token ITALIC in the EKS. Once the sentence has been parsed, the new operation is added to the repository.

In addition to the EKS, the parser maintains an expected type set (ETS). This lists, for the keyphrases $K^a_0...K^a_i$ or $K^a_1...K^a_i$, the permissible types of the following expression, i.e., the expression between K^a_i and $K^a_{i+1,j}$. This is used to help determine operator precedence in mixed expressions. The EKS and ETS together comprise the expected set (ES).

The parser scans phrases from left to right, maintaining a stack of ESs. At the top level, the ES contains only the sentence terminators. When one of these is recognized, its associated EKS contains only the token CLOSE, indicating that this is unambiguously a suffix and no continuation of the expression is possible. More generally, there may be operations with overlapping keyphrases so that a keyphrase is a suffix in one but not in another. Such an ambiguous keyphrase in a nested expression is called a candidate suffix; if it really is the end of the operation, it must be followed by another keyphrase belonging to the outer expression (in the next ES on the stack).

The state transition diagram for the parser shows that an expression may start with a prefix followed by a nested expression or may start with a name or literal. They are followed by a keyphrase. An expression then alternates between keyphrases and nested expressions, which are themselves dealt with by Expression Start. An expression may be terminated by a suffix, but this cannot always be determined until the next phrase is examined. A keyphrase is said to be a *candidate suffix* if it has CLOSE together with other values in its EKS. Some suffixes are unambiguous, such as a right parenthesis or a sentence terminator; they have EKS={CLOSE} (the only entry in the set).

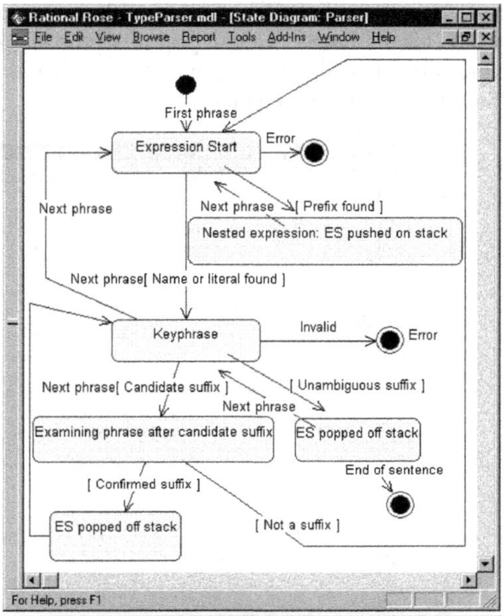

Pushing and popping the stack are shown for prefixes and suffixes; infix operators are dealt with in the Keyphrase diagram. A nested expression must be followed by another keyphrase (which must be in the next EKS on the stack), so the presence or absence of a following keyphrase belonging to the outer expression determines whether this candidate is really a suffix (confirmed) or not.

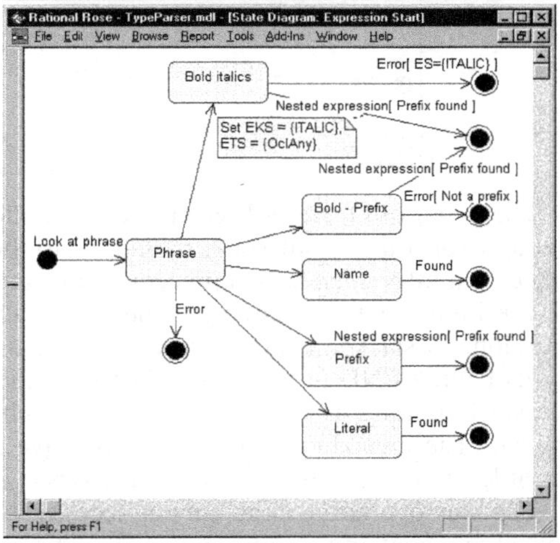

The Expression Start diagram shows detail of parsing an expression that starts with a prefix, including italics for a new operation. The order of the states follows the priority given first to bold italics denoting a prefix to a new operation, then to a bold font denoting an existing prefix. For ordinary font, the phrase is interpreted as a name, a prefix or a literal, in that order of preference.

The keyphrase diagram goes into detail of matching a keyphrase into the ES. Again, the highest priority state is at the top of the diagram and implements the principle of preferring the longest interpretation for an expression. If the keyphrase is not expected in the current expression, we look to see if it is an infix initiator. If so, the type information in the ETS is used to help determine operator precedence (see Operator Precedence diagram), ending preceding expressions when appropriate. A unary suffix is a special case (distinguished by setting EKS={CLOSE}). Otherwise, we consider whether the keyword is expected in an outer expression. If so, the nested expression must have terminated with the preceding phrase. If this is valid (indicated by END in its EKS), we can pop it off the stack. There could be more than one nested expression that has terminated with the same phrase, and they all need to have their ESs removed from the stack.

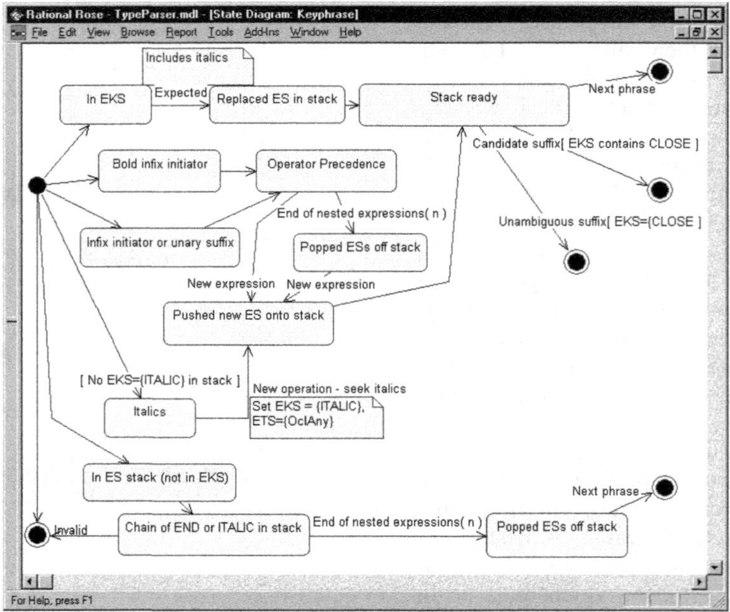

The detail of Operator Precedence shows how the decision is made, when an infix initiator (or a unary suffix) is parsed, as to the right level of nesting within the sentence. An infix must have a preceding operand, so the question is whether this should be the immediately preceding name or literal or whether it should be a stacked expression. A stacked expression can only be used if it can be terminated, as indicated by its having END in its EKS. Therefore, the state diagram shows a progression up the stack as long as there is an END in each EKS. We also require that the types match. The preceding expression must have a type, TP, that works with initiator, I, for at least one operation that has I as its infix initiator.

The new operation, although not necessarily nested at the lowest level, may still be nested in a containing expression. The type required by the containing expressions is recorded in the ETS for each ES in the stack. Although we don't know what type the result of the operation is until we have finished parsing, we can know the set of possible types that results of operations beginning with TP followed by I can yield. This information can be kept in the repository for all initiators; in the diagram, it is used to create the set VRTS of valid result types. In this way, many type conflicts can be avoided and best use can be made of the available information without going to the lengths of building a backtracking parser, which could be quite inefficient.

Bold font indicates an operation at an outer level of nesting compared with normal font. If there is no type information, bold font ensures that all preceding operations that can end (as indicated by END in their EKS) will be terminated and the highest one will be the initial operand of the new operation. Where there is type information, only those expressions that are type consistent will be considered.

If it is bold and the preceding expression can end (it has END in the EKS), the preceding expression is treated as the first operand of the new expression. If the key-

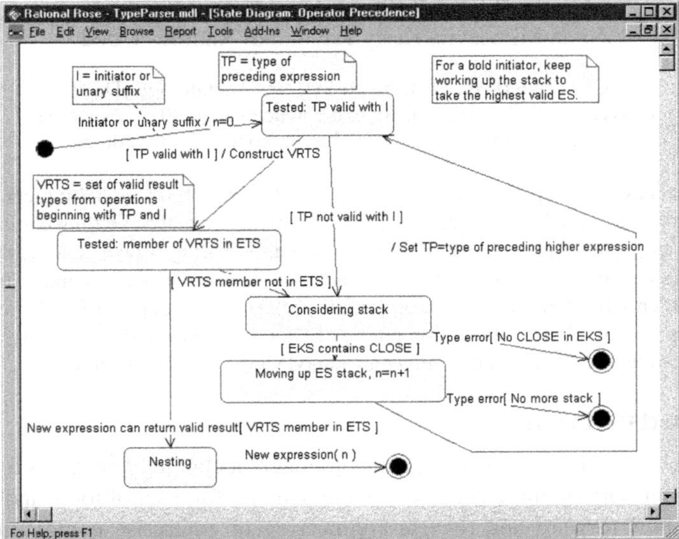

phrase is not bold, this indicates a nested expression (which continues the current expression). Because these checks are not exhaustive, a final check for type consistency is carried out after a sentence has been parsed.

References

1. "Statistical Constraints for EAI" by John Knapman, submitted to UML2000
2. Book "Designing Object Systems; Object-oriented modelling with Syntropy" by Steve Cook and John Daniels, Prentice Hall, 1994
3. The Java Message Service is documented at web site: java.sun.com/products/jms/docs.html
4. XML Metadata Interchange (XMI) at web site: www.omg.org/cgi-bin/doc?ad/99-10-02
5. "Alcoa: The Alloy Constraint Analyzer" by Daniel Jackson, Ian Schechter and Ilya Shlyakhter, Proc. International Conference on Software Engineering, Limerick, Ireland, 2000

Processes, Roles, and Events: UML Concepts for Enterprise Architecture

Alistair Barros, Keith Duddy, Michael Lawley,
Zoran Milosevic, Kerry Raymond, Andrew Wood

CRC for Enterprise Distributed Systems Technology (DSTC)
University of Queensland, Brisbane, Queensland 4072, Australia
{abarros, dud, lawley, zoran, kerry, woody}@dstc.edu.au

Abstract. This paper presents an integrated approach for modelling enterprise architectures using UML. To satisfy a need for a wide range of modelling choices, we provide a rich set of process-based and role-based modelling concepts, together with a flexible way of associating business events with business processes and roles. Our approach enriches Unified Modelling Language (UML) to support the requirements of enterprise distributed object computing (EDOC) systems and is currently being considered by the Object Management Group (OMG) for standardisation.

1 Introduction

As the maturing distributed object and component technology becomes more widely deployed in enterprises, there is an increasing demand for a set of tools and methodologies to support forward and reverse engineering of enterprise computing systems. These tools and methodologies are needed to: *i)* facilitate the building of enterprise computing systems that closely follow the structure, dynamics and policies of enterprises, and *ii)* allow for faster modifications of enterprise computing systems according to changing requirements of businesses. Such tools and methodologies need to support the use of object-oriented approaches across the analysis, design, implementation and deployment stages of enterprise distributed computing systems life cycle.

This paper focuses on providing a better support for the analysis phase in the life cycle of enterprise distributed computing systems. Our approach is based on the introduction of modelling concepts that represent dynamic, structural and policy aspects of enterprises. We provide support for enterprise concepts such as business process, business roles, business entities, and business events. We allow for flexible integration of these to closely model the operations of enterprises.

The goals for our work are to provide:

- a small but powerful set of enterprise modelling concepts
- an expressive graphical notation
- a basis for automatic generation of component-based enterprise systems (e.g. using CCM [1], EJB [2], COM [3]).

The application of modelling at the enterprise level is not new when one surveys the work done in requirements engineering [4], integrated CASE [5] and business process (workflow) automation [6]. However, there is a need for a more generic and integrated approach (e.g. process and policy versus procurement and service level agreement) with a broader technology target (inclusive of workflow management systems). Our immediate focus at present is on applying this approach to extend the modelling capability of

A. Evans, S. Kent and B. Selic (Eds.): «UML» 2000, LNCS 1939, pp. 62-77, 2000.

UML [7] and is in part influenced by the recent OMG Request for Proposal (RFP) for Enterprise Distributed Object Computing (EDOC) [8]. Therefore, in this paper we will demonstrate how our approach for modelling EDOC systems can be related to the existing version of Unified Modelling Language (UML).

The content of this paper is structured as follows. Section 2 motivates the paper by presenting key modelling concepts used in our EDOC modelling approach. Sections 3, 4, and 5 give an overview of our models for business processes, business entities, and business events. Section 6 concludes and outlines our future work plans.

Note that the full specification of our EDOC models is given in our EDOC submission to the OMG [9]. The full specification provides a UML model showing the relationship between all the concepts, and a detailed description of the rules and semantics applicable to each concept. It also provides a full description of the graphical notation, and presents a substantive example based on the work of a conference programme committee. Mappings of our EDOC models to various CORBA technologies are also presented to illustrate the generic nature of our proposal. We expect our EDOC models will continue to evolve as part of the OMG adoption process, including harmonisation with other parallel developments within the OMG's Analysis and Design Task Force, e.g. the forthcoming UML v2.0.

2 Key EDOC Concepts and Relation to UML

This section introduces key models we use to describe various aspects of Enterprise Distributed Object Computing (EDOC) systems. These models provide direct support for business processes, business roles, business entities, and business events and are well suited to extend UML to meet EDOC requirements, as specified in [8].

In fact, in deriving these models, our starting point was an analysis of how the EDOC requirements stated in this RFP can be met using the existing UML modelling concepts. Because UML is a general modelling language, there are many UML concepts that can be used to support the modelling of EDOC systems. However, we have also found that:

- many of the concepts are dispersed across different UML views and it is not easy to establish relationships between them
- there is a need for further extensions and refinement of the existing concepts to better meet *enterprise* requirements; this will further augment the richness of the UML in terms of its computational expressiveness. For example, we needed better support for capturing the coordination semantics of business processes (e.g. explicit support for business events and exceptional situations), semantics of business roles and business rules.

The above two points mean that it is not easy for an enterprise modeller to effectively and efficiently use UML 1.3. for modelling systems to support enterprise distributed object computing. Therefore, to provide a set of self-contained concepts suitable for practical enterprise modelling, we have integrated ideas from areas such as workflow systems, requirements engineering, and the ODP Enterprise Language standard [10].

2.1 Business Perspective to Process Modelling

Our approach to modelling *business processes* is based on our understanding of what are the critical *business* issues to be addressed when describing processes in the enterprise. A business process is represented as a dependency graph of business tasks linked in a specific way to achieve some particular objective. A business process can be control-driven or data-driven, or both, and our model provides a rich semantics for expressions of these task dependencies. Our model also supports the composition of business tasks in a way that is suitable for implementation as off-the-shelf components. In addition, we make provision for an association of business tasks with business roles to execute them.

Although our business process model uses concepts found in many workflow systems, nonetheless we view workflow as an IT solution to automating and managing business processes, mostly focusing on the execution semantics. Instead, in our approach, we have attempted to come up with a succinct business process model that encompasses different workflow execution semantics. In addition, we consider business processes in the context of other business determinants, such as business roles, business entities and business events resulting in an emphasis on business semantics over computational semantics. Our submission to the OMG [9] describes a number of alternate mappings from our business process concepts to various CORBA technologies, only one of which uses the OMG's Workflow Management Facility specification [11].

2.2 The Duality of Business Processes and Business Roles

We believe that business process modelling is only one (though frequent) approach to modelling a business. There are other possible ways of modelling and, in particular, we argue that *business role* modelling represents an alternative and/or complementary way of modelling the enterprise. This duality of role-based and process-based approaches is also reflected in our paper. In fact, we provide a separation of process-based and role-based modelling concepts as a way of offering different modelling choices. In addition, we separate the notion of business role and business entity, as this separation provides a powerful mechanism for distinguishing between required behaviour and business entities that can satisfy this behaviour.

2.3 Business Events

In both, process-based and role-based approaches, it is important to expose *business events* of significance to the enterprise. These events are associated with the modelling elements that can be their sources or sinks and our approach allows for flexible mapping of business event parameters onto the business process elements as well as business roles.

2.4 Business Processes and their Support in UML

It is our view that the modelling of *business processes* requires the ability to express:

- complex dependencies between the individual business tasks (i.e. logical units of work) constituting a business process. Both control dependencies and data dependencies, as well as rich concurrency semantics, must be supported.
- representation of several business tasks at one level of abstraction as being a single business task at a higher level of abstraction and precisely defining the relationships between such tasks. This must incorporate the activation and termination semantics for these tasks.
- representation of iteration in business tasks

- various time expressions, such as duration of a task and support for expressions of deadlines
- support for the detection of unexpected business events that need to be acted upon, i.e. exceptional situations
- initiation of specific tasks in response to business events arrival
- associations between the specifications of business tasks and business roles that perform these tasks and also those roles that are needed for tasks execution

While UML activity diagrams can provide support for most of the above requirements, we have identified a number of difficulties for their use in practical modelling:

- Swimlanes are not adequate to represent complex associations of responsibilities to activities (i.e. roles to tasks in our model), and in particular this mechanism does not scale (e.g. how we deal with tens or hundreds of activities) and how we deal with assigning several roles to one activity.
- External events cannot be used to start activities except by the intermixing of normal states from UML state machines and activity states from UML activity diagrams, as only the completion event of an activity state (and not an external event) can trigger the transition to another activity state.
- According to [12], "Normally, an activity graph assumes that computations proceed without external event-based interruptions (otherwise an ordinary state machine would be preferable)." Hence, most of the states in an activity diagrams are action states or sub-activity states. However, it is also legal to include ordinary states (from state machines) into activity diagrams. This presents the additional modelling problem of distinguishing between those transitions that are triggered by the completion of previous activity state and the external transitions.
- Activity graphs support only very simple forms of synchronization and impose a well nesting constraint such that every branch has a corresponding merge and every fork a corresponding join. It is common for a business process to not satisfy such a constraint, to require complex forms of synchronization and, in fact, to not be expressible using an explicit end-of-activity state but instead terminate when 'there is no work being done, and nothing more to be done'.

All of the above suggests that activity diagrams can be used for some business processes - those that include a well-defined sequence of business steps, each of which can be completed with certainty, and without external events involved. In general, business processes require support for more complex concurrency than supported by activity diagrams. For example, one needs a form of unrestricted concurrency that allows the dynamic creation of many parallel chains of execution without requiring that these independent chains need to be joined at a later stage.

Thus we believe that business process semantics requires a richer behaviour specification than that provided by UML state machines (the basis for UML activity diagrams). Therefore we derive our business processs model from more fundamental UML model elements: UML::NameSpace, UML::ModelElement, UML::Action and UML::Parameter as illustrated in Figure 1.

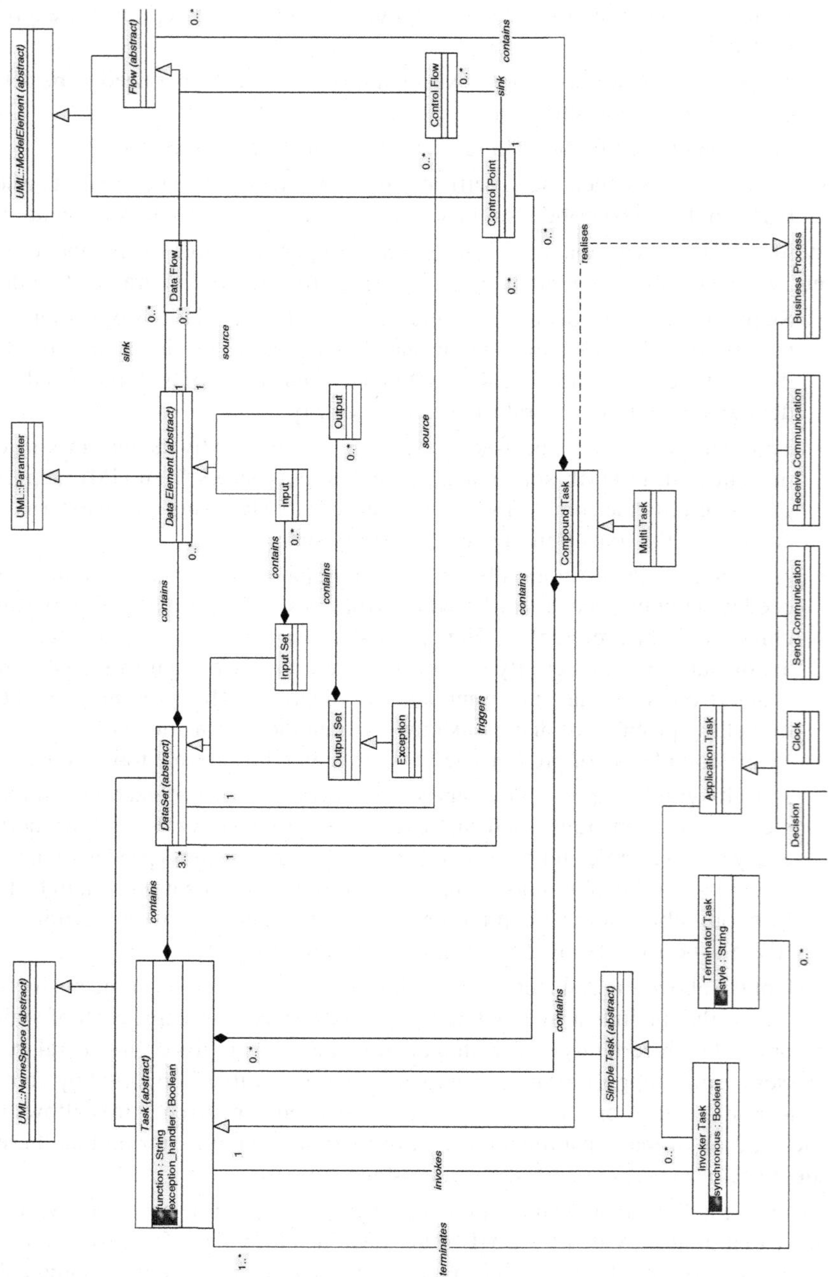

Figure 1 Business Process Model

2.5 Business Roles and their Support in UML

In terms of *business roles*, we believe that they should be described as fragments of behaviour of the enterprise - those that can then be fulfilled by specific *business entities*. The separation of the concepts of business entities and business roles enables the specification of the enterprise in terms of behaviour and not in terms of business entities. This modelling approach provides flexibility in assigning business entities to business roles; one business entity can fill more than one role and one role can be filled by different entities, as long as behaviour of such an entity is compatible with the behaviour of that business role. This allows flexibility in changing the assignments of business entities to business roles as new policy or resource requirements may demand. This is possible because of the way we partition the behaviour of business roles onto business entities.

Consequently, we believe that it gives more expressive power to describe business roles in terms of fundamental behaviour, as included in the UML common behaviour package (rather than as a concept within UML collaborations). In fact, we believe that the UML concepts of Action and Action Sequence can be used to define a business role and we derive our definition of a business role from these UML concepts.

Such treatment of business roles also provides a basis for flexible assignment of the performers of actions in a dependency graph of *business tasks* forming a *business process*. In fact, a business role can be regarded as a collection of actions that are involved in performing one or more business tasks and the grouping of these actions corresponds to the definition of business roles. This business task vs. business roles separation gives an additional power of expression to the already described business roles vs. business entities separation.

3 Business Process Model

The basic building block of business process model is the task. Tasks are then configured through the use of data flows and control flows into compound tasks, a larger building block. This is repeated until there is a compound task which describes the complete business process. Examples of business processes are issuing a Call for Papers for a conference and selecting from submitted papers. The business process model is shown in Figure 1.

3.1 Tasks in Isolation

A task defines a self-contained unit of work in terms of its inputs, its function, and its outputs. Tasks can be divided into two subtypes: simple tasks and compound tasks. A simple task refers to an activity that is carried out without further refinement at this level of abstraction, while compound task contains a set of statically-defined tasks that are co-ordinated to perform some larger scale activity (and will be discussed in Section 3.2).

Simple tasks can be divided into three subtypes: application task, invoker task, and terminator task. Application tasks (the most common variety) are just wrappers to enable applications (e.g. assign a paper ID to a paper) to be coordinated within a business process. Invoker task and terminator task subtypes are used to coordinate other tasks within a compound task; they enable tasks to be dynamically created and terminated (in a variety of ways) at run-time. For the purposes of the graphical notation, there are some common subtypes of application task: Decision, Clock, SendCommunication, and ReceiveCommunication; however, these are semantically indistinguishable from other application tasks.

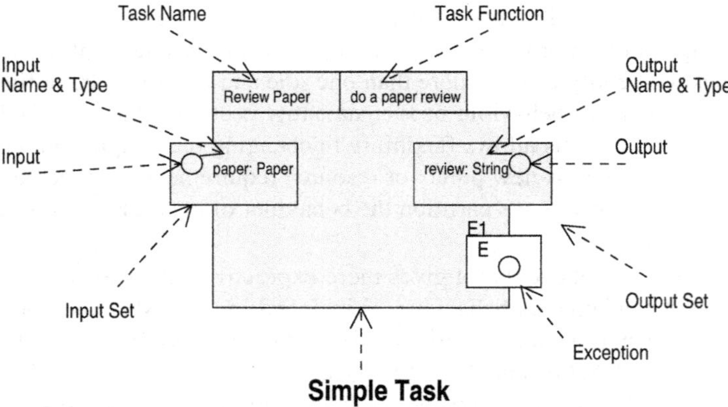

Figure 2 Example of a Simple Task

Tasks have input sets, output sets, and exceptions (which are subtypes of output set) as illustrated in Figure 2. An input set models the information required to commence execution of a task as a set of name-value pairs known as inputs. An output set represents a possible outcome of the execution of a task; it serves both as an indication that the task has terminated and provides a set of outputs (name-value pairs) associated with that outcome. An exception indicates that the task has terminated having failed to perform its function; it may have a set of outputs associated with that failure. There can be multiple input sets, output sets, and exceptions, modelling alternative circumstances in which the task may start, complete or fail. Note that a standard system exception is always available to signal a non-specific failure of a task (and is often omitted in the graphical representation). For example, the Review A Paper task takes a paper as input and provides a review as an output.

A task commences execution when one of its input sets is "enabled", which requires that values have been supplied for all the inputs in that input set. (A more complete definition of an enabled input set is given in Section 3.2.3). The execution of the task is parameterised by the nominated input set and the values of its input. Exactly one input set is associated with the execution of a task instance (*Exclusive OR semantics*).

When a task completes execution, one of its output sets will be enabled (see Section 3.2.3 for a definition of enabled output set). The completion of the task yields both the nomination of an enabled output set and values for the outputs defined by that output set. Exactly one output set (which may be an exception) is associated with the completion of a task instance (*Exclusive OR semantics*).

The lifecycle of a simple task is quite straightforward. Having been created, it waits until one of its input sets is enabled, executes its function and terminates, enabling one of its output sets by supplying data values for all of its outputs. The lifecycle of a compound task is discussed in Section 3.2.4.

3.2 Task Coordination

A compound task contains tasks, flows, and control point, as illustrated in Figure 3. Flows and control points are used to coordinate the execution of the tasks within a compound task.

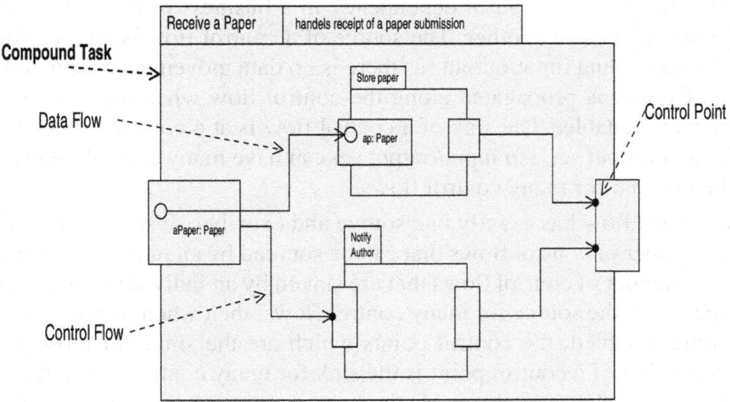

Figure 3 Example of a Compound Task

3.2.1 Flows

In abstract, a flow represents a causal relationship in a business process. Each flow has an associated source or sink (diagrammatically, the source is on the left and the sink on the right). The source of the flow must "happen" before the sink of the flow. For example, the conference proceedings cannot be printed until the best set of papers has been chosen.

Flows within a compound task must be acyclic; that is, things cannot happen in a circular order. This rule can be visualised as "all flows are drawn travelling from left to right, and do not cross task boundaries". A precise definition of legal flows based on relative positions in the containment hierarchy is given in [9].

We define two concrete subtypes of flow: data flow and control flow.

3.2.2 Data Flows

Data flows propagate data between causally-related inputs and outputs. For example, an input to a compound task is often the source of data flows leading to the inputs of some of its subordinate tasks. The outputs of subordinate tasks may supply values needed for the inputs to other subordinate tasks or as the outputs of the compound task. The data propagates along the data flow when the source of the data flow becomes *enabled*.

Although a data flow has exactly one source and exactly one sink, there is no restriction on the number of data flows that can be sourced or sinked by an individual input/output. If an input/output is a sink of more than one data flow, then the data value for that input/output can be supplied by any one of the enabled data flows (*Inclusive OR semantics*). If more than one of the data flows is enabled (to provide a data value), then the choice of data flow to supply the value is arbitrary. If there are many data flows with the same input/output as their source, then the data value will be transmitted along all data flows to their sinks (*AND semantics*).

3.2.3 Control Flows and Control Points

A control flow represents a causal dependency in a business process, by ensuring that one thing happens before another. The source of a control flow is an input/output set rather than an individual input/output (as there is no data movement associated with a control flow). Control is propagated along the control flow when the source of the control flow becomes enabled.The sink of a control flow is at a control point which is attached to an input/output set. An input/output set can have many control points, each of which can be the sink for many control flows.

Although a control flow has exactly one source and exactly one sink, there is no restriction on the number of control flows that can be sourced by an individual input/output set nor on the number of control flows that are sinked by an individual control point. If an input/output set is the source for many control flows, then when that source input/output set becomes enabled, the control points which are the sinks for those control flows becomes enabled. If a control point is the sink for many control flows, then only one control flow is needed to actually enable the control point (*Inclusive OR semantics*).

An input/output set is *satisfied* when all of its inputs/outputs have been assigned values and all of its attached control points have been enabled (*AND semantics*). An input/output set must be satisfied for it to be become *enabled*. Only one of a task's input sets can become enabled; the choice among the satisfied input sets is arbitrary. Similarly only one of a task's satisfied output sets can become enabled (when the task terminates); the choice again is arbitrary.

Unlike inputs/outputs, control points do not form part of an input/output sets, but are external to them. While inputs and outputs are part of the fundamental definition of a task, control points are not fundamental to a task's definition but rather to the configuration of this task into a larger piece of behaviour. As an analogy, tasks are bricks, while data flows, control flows, and control points are the mortar that binds them.

3.2.4 Lifecycle of a Compound Task

The lifecycle of a compound task is closely related to the lifecycle of its contained tasks. When a compound task commences execution (as a result of one of its input sets becoming enabled), it first creates instances of each of its contained tasks, each of which will then wait for one of its input sets to become enabled. Secondly, the compound task enables the flows from its enabled input set and its contained inputs (usually resulting in one or more of the contained tasks commencing execution). When a contained task terminates, its enabled output set (possibly an exception) becomes enabled, which (through flows) may enable further contained tasks to commence execution, and so on.

A compound task completes when all of its contained tasks have either completed their execution or are unable to execute (none of their input sets were ever enabled). It is quite normal for some contained tasks to never be executed; these will typically represented some alternative course of action, which was not taken in this instance. Normally, the completion of a compound task results in one of its output sets (possibly an exception) being suitable to be enabled (i.e. all outputs have received values, and all associated control points are enabled). This output set is then enabled, representing the outcome of the compound task. If there are more than one output set capable of being enabled, then one is arbitrarily chosen to be enabled. If a compound task completes and there is no output set that is capable of being enabled, then the compound task's system exception is enabled.

4 Business Entity Model

In this section, we describe our approach to business entity modelling by introducing our business entity concepts and showing their relationship to our other EDOC models. The business entity model is concerned with the descriptions of the behaviour of roles that will, as a collection, describe the behaviour of the enterprise system. Role-based specification represents a complementary specification of an enterprise to process-based specifications.

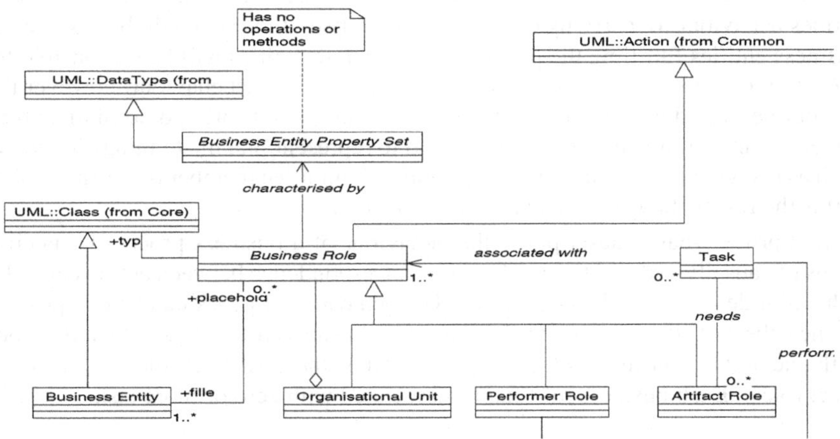

Figure 4 Business Entity Model

Central to our business entity model are the abstraction of business roles, as illustrated in Figure 4. A business role represents a characterisation of some part of the behaviour of the system being described. Performer and artifact roles are specialisations of business roles. Performer roles describe active behaviour while artifact roles characterise those things that are needed for the actions of performer roles (i.e. artifact roles do not initiate behaviour). A business entity can be said to fill a business role if it is capable of enacting the behaviour described by the role being filled. Organisational units are a composition of business roles, enabling the collective behaviour of a set of roles to be another (larger) role. This gives us the ability to describe behaviours at different levels of abstraction.

4.1 Business Role

A business role defines a placeholder for behaviour in a context. This context is an organisational unit (established with some objective in mind) and the behaviour of the role becomes part of the behaviour of the organisational unit as a whole. A business role is defined by its behaviour, its structure and a context in which it exists. For example, a Programme Committee Chair is a role in the context of a Programme Committee (an organisational unit).

Business role inherits from the UML concept of Action, which enables a generic description of behaviour. The behaviour can be expressed using different languages, varying from a program code to English statements (we do not assume any particular specification language). Each business role is associated with a UML Class to provide it with a structural description. Finally, each business role is defined within the context of an organisational unit, which is a specialisation of a business role that is composed of other business roles. Thus organisational units (as business roles) can be composed into larger organisational units, and so on, until the enterprise has been modelled.

Business role has two subtypes: performer role and artifact role. A performer role describes behaviour for carrying out tasks in enterprise - those that will be assigned to the business entities fulfilling the performer role. These entities will be responsible for the execution of some aspects of the tasks. Artifact roles have behaviour, however the behaviour described is in some sense passive in that artifact roles do not initiate the execution of any action. Artifact roles are used to represent inanimate things in the system such as resources. For example, a Programme Committee member (performer role) performs the review task using a paper (artifact role).

In a process-based description, the behaviour of a business process is specified in terms of causally-ordered tasks. There is a correspondence between actions of tasks and behaviour described by business roles. The behaviour of a task can be composed from (some subset of) the behaviour of one or more business roles. Thus a task is associated with one or more business roles (i.e. performed by the performer roles and using the artifact roles). Each business role can be associated with zero or more tasks.

4.2 Business Entity

A business entity describes an actual object that can carry out (some part of) a business role. A business role may be filled by one business entity or by a collection of them. Similarly, a business entity can fill more than one business role. For example, Prof. Smith (business entity) can fill the performer role of Programme Committee Chair and the paper "O-O for Fun and Profit" can fill the artifact role of Submitted Paper.

A business entity property set is used for specifying non-functional requirements of the behaviour of the business role. For a business entity to fill a business role, the object instantiating the business entity must match the properties specified in the business entity property set.

Instantiation of a business role is achieved by binding to a business entity that is able to fulfill the behaviour specified by business role. This binding is possible when the behaviour of the business entity is compatible with the behaviour of the business role in terms of structure and behaviour. However, binding of a business entity will commonly be based on more than just type compatibility. Some non-functional characteristics of a business role (e.g. QoS) may be specified as a business entity property set. Hence, business entities to be bound to a business role can also meet some additional criteria defined by the business entity property set. Bindings between roles and objects can be statically defined in the business entity model, or Yellow Pages services (e.g. the OMG Trader service [13]) can be used to automate the selection of the object instances to fill roles, allowing run-time binding.One approach for this is described in [18].

5 Business Event Model

The business event model provides for the attaching of sources and sinks of asynchronous broadcast events to various EDOC Model Elements to allow them to expose their actions or state changes to other parts of the enterprise. Restrictions can be placed on how widely the events are broadcast.

The notion of an "event" itself is not defined precisely in our model; it is sufficient to model only the business event type. A business event type explicitly exposes an action that has a significant business semantics with respect to the enterprise being modelled or its environment.

Business event sources emit events, while business event sinks receive events. For example, withdrawing a submitted paper from a conference is an event; the business event source for this event is the role Author while the business event sink is the Review A Paper task.

5.1 Business Event Type

A business event type is a declaration that provides the names and types of properties to be included in events that conform to this type. At runtime events are instantiated as lists of named data values that may be broadcast using some notification mechanism for consumption by subscribers to this event type.

Business event types have a name and a domain (within which the name is interpreted). Business event type inherits from UML::State Machine::Event, which enables the specification of the names and types of the properties (as UML::Parameters) that conforming events will contain. This approach to event types is compatible with a number of well-known event transmission systems [14] [15] [16] [17].

Business event types are used in the context of an event emission in order to check that the expected properties of a generated event are present and have correctly typed values. In the context of an event consumption they simply provide the author of a notification rule with a set of names and types to use as terms in a subscription expression. It is expected that these types will be used by the mapping of the model to perform type checking, and that they will be stored in a repository for reference from the application.

5.2 Business Event Sources and Sinks

A business event source represents the external exposure of some enterprise action, while a business event sink represents the need for awareness of some enterprise action.

A business event source defines the business event type to be emitted, the conditions under which a business event of that type is emitted (the event exposure rule), how the values in the event are obtained from the source's state (the event content mapping specification), and extent to which the event should be broadcast. Similarly, a business event sink defines the business event type to be received, the conditions under which such events should be received, how the event's values are assigned to the sink's state, and the extent from which events can be received.

Although events are primarily intended to support a decoupled communication paradigm, business event sources can be associated with specific business event sinks using the `transmit_to` association.

The extent to which the event is to be broadcast/received can be set to three built-in values:

- "global", indicating that the event can be broadcast/received outside the scope of the enterprise being modelled
- "application", indicating that this event can be broadcast/received by elements in this enterprise model
- "direct_only", indicating that the event can only be broadcast to, or received from, explicitly-defined transmission paths (as defined in the `transmit_to` association).

User-defined extents can also be supported (typically implemented using event filtering).

5.3 Actions of Interest

Business event source and sink are (deliberately) very general concepts to ensure many different model elements to be producers and consumers of events. However, it is necessary to nominate exactly what actions may be of interest for each kind of model element. All events are based on actions of interest, but not all actions of interest will be used as events. Note that it is theoretically possible to emit/receive all actions of interest as events, but the number of events becomes overwhelming in practice, hence our requirement that event sources and sinks are explicitly identified in the enterprise model.

The commencement of execution of a task is an "action of interest"; so is its termination. input sets and output sets have two actions of interest: becoming satisfied (once all its inputs and attached control points have been satisfied), and becoming enabled (when it is chosen by the task for its commencement and termination). The only action of interest for an input or output is to be assigned a value. The transmission of data or control along a flow is an action of interest.

For business roles and business entities, there are a number of actions of interest, including their creation and termination, the assignment or change of an attribute value, and the invocation or return of a method. The performing of a task by a performer role and the use of artifact role in a task are actions of interest. The assigning and de-assigning of business entities to fill business roles are also actions of interest.

5.4 Events as Data Flows

One of the by-products of the event content mapping is the ability to receive an event and assign the contents of the event to/from an input or output. Within an enterprise model, the values of inputs/outputs are normally transmitted via data flows (subject to the hierarchical structure of compound tasks). Events enable the values of inputs and outputs to be transmitted or received from beyond the scope of the containing compound task (or even the enterprise model itself). Such business event sources and sinks behave similarly to the sources and sinks of data flows for the purposes of propagation of data and determining whether an input/output set is satisfied.

6 Conclusion and Future Work

In this paper we have presented an object-based approach for modelling enterprise distributed object computing systems. We exploit the benefits of distributed object technology to enable an object-oriented description of enterprises, in terms of business processes, business entities, business roles and business events.

The benefits of using distributed object technology for modelling *business processes* stem from the fact that objects can represent key artifacts of business processes: tasks, data transferred between tasks, resources needed for task execution as well as performers that initiate these tasks. The purpose of a business process model is to describe how these different objects are related to each other, both in terms of their static (e.g. task-performer assignment) and dynamic (data flow and control flow) relationships. The use of objects allows for a more flexible approach in implementing and modifying business processes, as opposed to the monolithic structure of workflow products typical for an earlier generation of this technology. Further, the use of standard interfaces that specify behaviour of objects representing business process artifacts enables better interoperability of business processes specified by different organisations and/or supported by different underlying process engines.

The benefits of using objects for implementing *business entities* have been exploited since the very early days of object oriented technology. Distributed objects bring new capabilities in that the objects can be developed independently by different parties and they can interact by sending messages over the network. via their interfaces which expose their externally visible behaviour. The novelty of our approach is to further extend capabilities of object-oriented modelling by introducing the concept of *role*. Using roles it is possible to describe an enterprise in terms of fragments of behaviour that correspond to the positions in organisations. The benefit of this approach is that this allows many options for assigning objects to roles, even to the extent of run-time binding.

In addition, the use of latest distributed object platforms allows the exploitation of event-based interactions between objects. This mechanism is particularly suitable to be used as a way of communicating *business events* among parties involved in enterprise - be that as part of a streamlined business process, or as part of less prescriptive communication or collaboration between objects filling roles in an organisation.

In summary, this paper presents an integrated approach for modelling enterprise architectures to be implemented using distributed object technology. The approach presented deals mostly with *analysis* stage of system life cycle. To satisfy a need for wide range of modelling choices we provide a rich set of process-based and role-based modelling concepts and flexible ways of associating business events and business rules with business processes and roles. Our approach is well suited as a candidate for extending Unified Modelling Language (UML) to support the requirements of enterprise distributed object computing (EDOC) systems and is currently considered in the Object Management Group (OMG).

We note that in our approach we also support *design* and *implementation* phases of an object oriented life cycle. These aspects of our approach are beyond the scope of this approach and are presented elsewhere [18].

In the immediate future, we intend to pursue alignment with other proposed UML concepts, e.g. Capsule, Port, Connectors and Business Protocols [19]. We will also explore the use of UML collaboration diagrams and state diagrams for expressing the semantics of Application Tasks. There are interesting parallels between the role concept in our Business Entity model and the UML Classifier Role, which need to be thoroughly investigated.

In the longer term, we plan to more explicitly deal with various kinds of *business rules* and *policies*. Although some of these have been implicitly treated in the context of other EDOC modelling artifacts, we argue that there is a need for a more flexible ways of changing these business constraints than what is currently supported in our approach.

Finally, we also plan to investigate whether it is possible to identify certain business patterns, in particular those that could be useful for business process specification. The use of patterns would enable easier and more rapid specification of frequently occurring situations in the specification of business process and would enable shorter development time.

Acknowledgments

Our overall views on enterprise modelling have been substantially influenced by our involvement in the standardisation of the Open Distributed Processing Enterprise Language within ISO [10]. This standardisation work provided the basis for our business entity model. Our business process model has been substantially based on results from a workflow project [20] carried out at the Department of Computer Science, University of Newcastle upon Tyne, UK, and sponsored in part by Nortel Corporation. We especially thank Stuart Wheater at University of Newcastle upon Tyne for the many productive discussions we have had with him, and the feedback he has given us.

The work reported in this paper has been funded in part by the Co-operative Research Centre for Enterprise Distributed Systems Technology (DSTC) through the Australian Federal Government's CRC Programme (Department of Industry, Science & Resources).

References

[1] Object Management Group, "CORBA Components - Volume 1", OMG orbos/99-07-01, August 1999.

[2] Ed Roman, "Mastering Enterprise JavaBeans and the Java2 Platform, Enterprise Edition", John Wiley & Sons Inc, 1999.

[3] Dale Rogerson, "Inside COM", Redmond, WA: Microsoft Press, 1996. ISBN 1-572-31349-8.

[4] M. Jarke, J.A. Bubenko, C. Rolland, A. Sutcliffe, Y. Vassiliou, "Theories Underlying Requirements Engineering: An Overview of NATURE at Genesis", in Proceedings of the IEEE Symposium on Requirements Engineering, RE'93, San Diego, California, Jan. 1993, IEEE Computer Society Press.

[5] G.J. Ramackers, "Integrated Object Modelling, an Executable Specification Framework for Business Analysis and Information System Design", Ph.D. thesis, University of Leiden, The Netherlands, 1994.

[6] Y. Breibart, D. Georgakopoulos, H. Schek, "Merging Application-centric and Data-centric Approaches to Support Transaction-oriented Multi-system Workflows", SIGMOD Record, 22:3, Sept. 1993, pp 23-30.

[7] Object Management Group, "Unified Modelling Language v1.3", OMG ad/99-06-08, June 1999.

[8] Object Management Group, "Request for Proposal: UML Profile for Enterprise Distributed Object Computing", OMG ad/99-03-10, March 1999.

[9] DSTC, "UML Profile for Enterprise Distributed Object Computing", OMG ad/99-10-07, October 1999.

[10] ISO, "Open Distributed Processing - Enterprise Language", ISO/IEC JTC1/SC7/SC17 N0080, July 1999.

[11] Object Management Group, "Workflow Management Facility", OMG bom/98-06-07, July 1998.

[12] J. Rumbaugh, I. Jacobson, G. Booch, "The Unified Modeling Language Reference Manual", Addison Wesley, 1999.

[13] Object Management Group, "Trading Object Service", OMG formal/97-12-23, 1997.

[14] Object Management Group, "Event Management", OMG formal/97-12-11, 1997.

[15] Object Management Group, "Notification Service", OMG telecom/99-07-01, July 1999.

[16] B. Segall, D. Arnold, "Elvin has left the building: A publish/subscribe notification service with quenching", Proc. Australian Unix Users Group, Brisbane, Australia, September 1997.

[17] K. Riemer, "A Process-Driven Event-Based Business Object Model", Proc. 2nd International Enterprise Distributed Object Computing Workshop, November 1998, pp 68-74.

[18] A. Barros, K. Duddy, M. Lawley, Z. Milosevic, K. Raymond, A. Wood, "Mapping Enterprise Roles to CORBA Objects using Trader", 3rd IFIP/GI International Conference on Trends towards a Universal Service Market, Sept 2000.

[19] B. Selic, J. Rumbaugh, "Using UML for Modeling Complex Real-Time Systems", http://www.objectime.com/otl/technical/umlrt.pdf

[20] J.J. Halliday, S.K. Shrivastava, S.M. Wheater, "Implementing Support for Work Activity Coordination within a Distributed Workflow System", Proc. 3rd International Enterprise Distributed Object Computing Conference, Sept 1999, pp 116-123.

Statistical Constraints for EAI

John Knapman

IBM, Hursley Park, Winchester, Hampshire, SO21 2JN, England
knapman@uk.ibm.com

Abstract. Enterprise Application Integration (EAI) often requires a loosely coupled event-based architecture in which timing and statistical measures are important. Statistical constraints are proposed to address some of these requirements, although they may well have broader applicability. This idea is extended to the use of approximate terms such as "some" that can be given a statistical interpretation, as in "Some fault reports give rise to subscriptions." These can be a convenient way of expressing constraints that are important to the application architecture but are not absolute — abstraction through approximation. They may be used to annotate diagrams in UML and are based on the existing Object Constraint Language (OCL) (1). Some of the examples use a more flexible syntax that is the subject of another paper (2).

1. Introduction

At the OMG's special interest group on enterprise application integration (EAI SIG), work has started on an extension to UML — a Profile for Event-based Architectures in EAI (3). Its purpose is to help user companies to make connections between a business-process view and the implementations that generally exploit message-based loose coupling in an event-based architecture that includes message brokers, databases, application servers, groupware servers, ORBs and Internet servers. UML's interaction (collaboration and sequence) diagrams or activity diagrams will be augmented in the proposed profile with stereotypes and other features that better capture the needs of messaging and EAI users. This will be compatible with the textual rendering of UML that is defined in XML Metadata Interchange (XMI).

Business-process models, architectures and designs are all abstractions, in that they do not describe everything about an implementation but only aspects that the modeler considers salient. Models, including graphical models, are a form of constraint. However, despite their appeal, graphics are limited in what they can express. There is a need for architects to be able to state other constraints without having to go into implementation-level detail. In real-time business systems, many important constraints are statistical rather than absolute. Here are some examples:

1. It may be acceptable for a user to receive a few irrelevant messages so long as security is not violated and the needed ones get through.
2. It may be acceptable for occasional messages to arrive out of sequence provided that 99.9% of them are in sequence; this may be a design trade-off made for the sake of cost savings or time to market. It can be a business decision if it affects the company's agents or clients.

A. Evans, S. Kent and B. Selic (Eds.): «UML» 2000, LNCS 1939, pp. 78-92, 2000.

3. Timing, latency and response service levels are all naturally expressed statistically, usually as a percentile time (e.g., 95% in less than 0.8 seconds).

Constraints like these can be monitored at execution time by such techniques as checking logs, tracking with a message broker or using policy handlers. Policy handlers are defined in the Open Application Group's (OAG's) Middleware API Specification (OAMAS) (4). In the database and decision-support literature, the terms *approximate constraint* and *approximate dependency* have been used to refer to constraints that can be given a statistical interpretation (5). Statistical constraints are not rigidly enforced because systems may deviate by a certain amount rather than strictly violating them, but they are formally defined over OCL collections. Reports on conformance — and sometimes alerts to significant non-conformance — will be needed.

UML already provides a constraint language — the Object Constraint Language (OCL). It is somewhat mathematical in style and is based on the Syntropy method (6). The following extensions are proposed to OCL to adapt it to the needs of event-based architectures and EAI:

1. A specific type of collection — a stream — suitable for representing a succession of messages corresponding to real-time events
2. Predicates (Boolean operations) over streams that are statistical or temporal in nature

A separate paper (2) defines an alternative syntax, known as the Business-oriented Constraint Language (BCL). Some examples in this paper use it for illustrative purposes, but the statistical constraints are defined in OCL terms and can be written in OCL syntax (see section 5). Tools to implement them will require both a definition-time component (to check syntax and consistency with the graphical elements of models) and run-time components (to carry out monitoring and reporting).

2. Examples

The figure shows a UML class diagram in which associations between classes have been used to show links that carry messages. Some of the classes are stereotypes representing elements such as transformation and subscription that are commonly used in EAI. Stream and message class stereotypes (with streams containing messages) are shown with suitable attributes such as time stamp; streams have attributes that enable them to be implemented in queues (cf. JMS (7)) or service points (cf. OAMAS). In the application illustrated, incoming reports are augmented with information from a database and transformed and routed to some business systems, namely, Accounts, Repairs, Work Scheduling and Customer Care. Publish and Subscribe are used with Customer Care. The annotations in brackets {} are in BCL, and they supplement the graphics. A tool that implements BCL will be able to read and validate these constraints, preferably using XMI (8). They have interpretations that apply at execution time; fault reports and other reports can be monitored, and a tool could report on the extent to which they conform.

The first constraint asserts: "Some fault reports give rise to subscriptions." Fault Reports comprise a stream of messages (see class diagram). Streams have the property that they can be sampled (see section 4). The scope of the constraint is any one of these samples. "Some" is a quantifier implying that the constraint applies to a subset of each sample, the size of the subset being in a certain range. Subscriptions govern the publish/subscribe service, and "gives rise to" implies that the action of sending a subscription follows receipt of some fault reports. The definitions of these terms can be changed by users or administrators. If the implementation uses message queues, a monitoring tool can read messages and extract the statistics needed for reporting whether this constraint is satisfied.

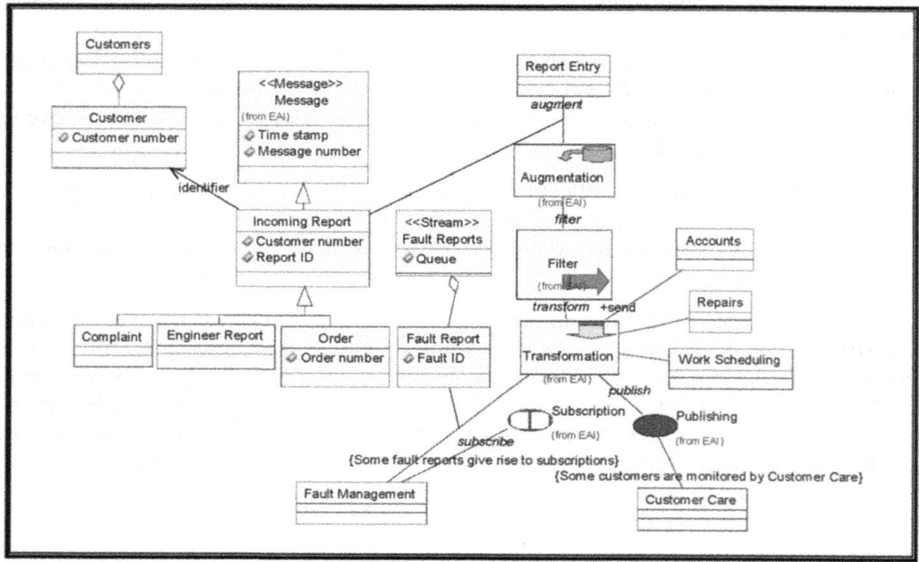

The diagram itself delineates a set of constraints. It says that Customer Care receives publications that may include several message types. A monitoring tool could verify such constraints too. Another annotation asserts: "Some customers are monitored by Customer Care." Customer and Customer Care are the names of classes in the diagram. Monitoring is a concept based on receiving identifiers. It can also be defined statistically in terms of commonality of data (see section 6). The assertion is true if there is an overlap between customer data and data in messages received by Customer Care; the overlap must fall within a defined range.

A UML interaction (sequence or collaboration) diagram could be used to give more precise information about the order of operations, but many users rely on class diagrams with annotations in English or another natural language to add such information as they deem appropriate. BCL is intended to provide a human-readable language for some of these purposes. The style of these annotations may appear like natural language, but it conforms to the syntax of BCL, which allows terms to be defined as phrases that include blank spaces (e.g., "gives rise to"). Other styles are permissible, depending on preference. The following examples illustrate four different styles, cursive, bracketed, Javaesque and OCL, respectively:

Some fault reports give rise to subscriptions.

some (FaultReports) giveRiseTo Subscriptions
(some (FaultReports)).giveRiseTo (Subscriptions)
FaultReports->some()->forAll(f | f.givesRiseTo (Subscription))

The cursive style is used in many of the examples in this paper. In some styles, embedded spaces are avoided, and so the classes in the UML class diagram are labeled CustomerCare and FaultReports rather than Customer Care and Fault Reports. The language is not case sensitive.

These examples illustrate the use of statistical quantification ("some") over a stream ("Fault Reports") and a set ("Customers"). They show a function ("are monitored by") that is defined in statistical terms (see section 6), and they indicate a syntactic flexibility that is intended to ease both reading and writing of constraints. If preferred, OCL syntax can be used with streams and statistical operations. The following sections review OCL and extend it to streams and statistical operations, after which further operations are introduced.

3. Review of OCL

UML is intended for modeling systems at a level of detail that is higher than an implementation (i.e., more abstract). As a graphical notation, there are some constraints that cannot readily be expressed in UML. For instance, we may require that the company's employees are all aged 18 or over. OCL users can express this constraint as follows:

```
Company
      self.employee->forAll( age >= 18 )
```

The header Company states the context of the constraint. Constraints may be written in the class diagram. For this one to be valid, 'Company' must appear as a class with the association 'employee' to another class that has attribute 'age'. In OCL terms, 'Company' is the type of the instance 'self', so that the following assertion is true:

```
Company
      self.oclType.name = 'Company'
```

The arrow notation `->` is required because there may be many employees; they form a collection. The forAll operation applies the predicate to all the employees of a company. A collection may be a set (repeated members forbidden), a bag (repeated members allowed) or a sequence (a bag with position numbering). For employees, a set would be normal because we would not want to record an employee twice. If an employee's job history formed a sequence, we could reference them by position number, as in:

```
Company
      self.employee.job->first.title = 'Trainee'
      if self.employee.job->size > 1 then
            self.employee.job->at(2).title = 'Associate'
      endif
```

The BCL constraints given earlier can be rendered in OCL by defining 'some' as a collection operation (see section 5):

```
FaultReports->some(f | f.givesRiseTo(Subscription))
Companies->some(c | c.isMonitoredBy(CustomerCare))
```

4. Operations and Semantics

One proposed version of the UML profile for Event-based Architectures and EAI is based on UML collaboration diagrams. In the formal syntax of the diagrams, a message M has a sender and a receiver object, an activator message and a set of predecessor messages. When an object receives an activator, it performs work that includes the sending of M after it has sent the predecessors of M. Because we are particularly interested in the flow of messages, the activator relationship is the most important to us. If work order is the activator of timed plan (see collaboration diagram), we say in BCL, "Work order *gives rise to* time plan." In OCL, this is:

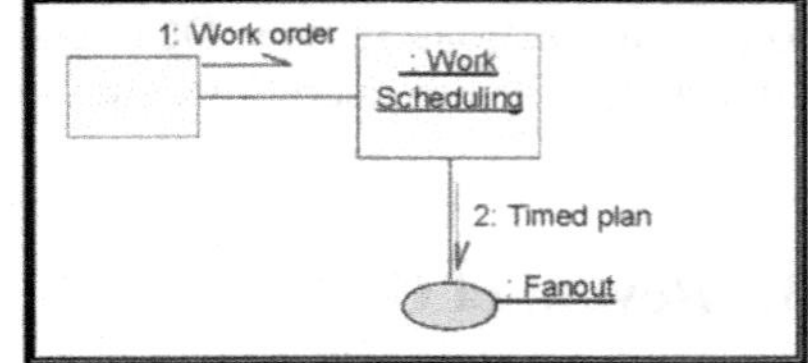


```
WorkOrder = TimedPlan.activator
```

In an OCL style, this can be written

```
WorkOrder.givesRiseTo(Timed Plan)
```

We can extend the definition to say

```
A.givesRiseTo(M)
```

if there are messages M_i (i=1,...,n-1) such that

$A.givesRiseTo(M_1)$ **and** $M_i.givesRiseTo(M_{i+1})$
and $M_n.givesRiseTo(B)$

Streams

OCL and BCL constraints naturally apply to classes and object instances because of the uniformity of object-oriented modeling and representations. UML collaboration diagrams represent the flows of messages between objects. We are interested in the collective properties and behavior of such messages, including matters of sequence and timing. It is useful to introduce streams as a particular type of collection in addition to sets, sequences and bags. It is characteristic of streams that they can be sampled. A sample from a stream is taken to be an OCL sequence. It contains those messages that have flowed since the last sample was taken (or since the stream was established). In the picture, each arrow represents the sequence of messages that have flowed between time t_{n-1} and t_n (n=1–5). In an OCL sequence the members are numbered sequentially from one up to the size of the sequence.

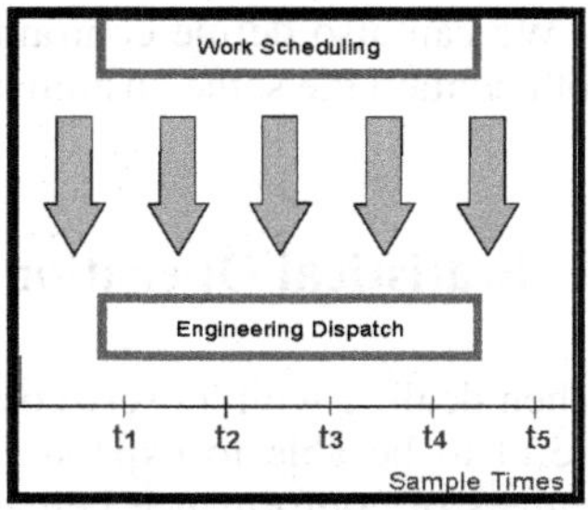

Streams contain messages, which have common attributes (e.g., time stamp, priority) in addition to the type-specific ones (e.g., customer number, company name) that are needed by the receiver. The proposed common attributes include the following:

time sent	local and universal date and time that message was sent
time received	on a copy in an audit trail or message warehouse, the local and universal date and time that the original message was received
message number	number (customarily sequential) that is unique within a given origin
priority	a value that allows selected queued messages to jump ahead
identifier	message type and origin (sender name)
message context	the business context (e.g., collaboration name, sender and receiver name)
reply context	the destination and identification of the reply, if any

To allow for various implementations, including parallel queues on multiple machines, there is only a partial ordering on messages. Message numbers are set by senders. In a stream of messages arriving from multiple senders, the message numbers do not define the order of arrival. Time stamps from different machines, as is well known, can only be compared approximately with degrees of uncertainty based on calibration and the magnitude of the difference. In implementations such as parallel queues, samples may overlap in time stamps and message numbers, although each sample is an OCL sequence and so has an internal sequence number that begins at one.

We define 'A *follows* B' as a Boolean expression for A and B in the same or different streams. Two time stamps may not be strictly comparable if their precision is insufficient, and this may include considerations of clock synchronization on different machines. However, this is a second-order consideration. We can compare the times of two messages, whether or not they have a pairwise ordering. When we state that message M gives rise to message N in a model (in a collaboration diagram, say), we are making a statement that applies to related instances, that is, for every message M_x in stream Ms there is a corresponding message N_x in stream Ns. A common special case is that N_x is a reply to M_x. We can compare the times of the two messages to see how long the intermediate (or server) process took. We may write:

N_x follows M_x in t seconds

OCL equivalents (briefer but less explanatory) would be:

```
A.follows(B)
Nx.follows(Mx,t)
```

We can also define contraints on fields in N based on values in M, e.g., that they both contain the same customer number but the reply also has the account balance.

5. Statistical Operations on Collections

When dealing with loosely coupled systems that communicate through messages, it is useful to be able to express requirements that are usually true, with exceptions or degrees of conformance being reported but not strictly imposed, since there may be good business reasons why a system should continue to operate with some exceptions. For example, an Internet server needs to be available continuously with high response times because of the low tolerance levels of general users (as opposed to employees who can be coerced into tolerating lower levels of service). If a component of a system suffers problems, occasional loss of sequence or delay in updating some records is probably better than holding up the entire service and hence annoying thousands or millions of users.

Loose coupling based on store-and-forward messaging provides the means of implementing such fail-safe architectures. Statistical constraints provide a means of expressing which kinds of conformance to rule are essential and which have a degree of latitude. Furthermore, the exact degree of latitude can be stated statistically so that, with appropriate tooling, it can be monitored and reported.

OCL has existential and universal quantification over collections with the Boolean operations `exists` and `forAll`, which are written:

```
collection->exists(v : Type |
      boolean-expression-with-v)
collection->exists(v | boolean-expression-with-v)
collection->exists(boolean-expression)
collection->forAll(v : Type |
      boolean-expression-with-v)
collection->forAll(v | boolean-expression-with-v)
collection->forAll(boolean-expression)
```

The following asserts that there is at least one employee called Jack and no two employees have the same forename:

```
Company
      self.employee->exists(forename = 'Jack')
      self.employee->forAll(e1 | self.employee
            ->forAll (e2 | e1 <> e2
            implies e1.forename <> e2.forename)))
```

When considering a stream of messages representing real-time events, an assertion about the existence of at least one of them that satisfies a certain condition is not much use, since we can not know whether some message may arrive eventually that satisfies it. It makes more sense to reason statistically about messages, since we must deal with those that have actually appeared at a point in time, as seen in a sample.

Statistical and Temporal Operations on Streams

UML collaboration, sequence and activity diagrams can describe the flow of messages through objects that represent application processes or infrastructure processes such as fanout or publishing. Streams are introduced to capture the particular semantics of messages flowing with time stamps, priorities and partial order. In addition to temporal and causal relations (following, giving rise to) it is important when dealing with large numbers to be able to associate timing and other requirements on such flows which are statistical in nature. For instance, based on the time lapse between two messages, we may write statistical expressions about time interval achievements in percentiles in a BCL style as follows:

x% of messages follow previous message in t seconds
Most complaints give rise to management reports in 10 seconds

Here, the quantifiers '% of' and 'most' have been introduced on streams or, more generally, collections. A quantifier with explicit bounds is the operation "x% *to* y% *of*" as in:

50% to 70% of messages have amount < 10,000

Whereas OCL quantifiers usually involve a single predicate, greater flexibility is achieved by separating them into two constraints. "Messages" denotes a stream, and "x% to y% of messages" or `messages->percent(x,y)` denote another stream satisfying the constraints:

```
X <= (100*((messages->percent(x,y))->size)
        / (messages->size)) <= y
 (messages->percent(50,70))->forAll(amount<10000)
```

Defining a quantified collection as a subcollection is more flexible than applying the predicate within the quantifier. It is better to write, for example,

```
FaultReports->some()
        ->forAll(f|f.givesRiseTo(Subscription))
```

rather than

```
FaultReports->some(f|f.givesRiseTo(Subscription))
```

As an example of flexibility, we can allow such phrases as "fault reports about some customers" referring to a substream of fault reports satisfying a condition (more details in "Monitoring and relatedness" in section 6) based on a subset of customers:

```
FaultReports->select(f|Customers->some()
        ->exists(c|f.isAbout(c)))
```

These operations are Boolean. However, future consideration can be given to the introduction of probabilistic or fuzzy logic, treating the upper and lower bounds as probability ranges or support pairs.

Quantifiers are constrained by size ratios, and it is useful to allow both closed bounds (<=) and open bounds (<). The following table gives a suggested initial list of them.

Quantifier	Lower bound %	Open lower		Upper bound %	Open upper	
some	25	true	<	75	true	<
most	75	true	<	100	true	<
few	0	false	<=	10	true	<
all	100	false	<=	100	false	<=
no	0	false	<=	0	false	<=
x% to y% of	x	false	<=	y	false	<=
x% of	x	false	<=	x	false	<=

A tool could allow an administrator to change these, or might even accumulate statistics on actual usage compared to operational results and revise the bounds accordingly.

6. Specific Operations

The operations described here are designed for application to streams of messages. They should be verifiable from the data available locally within a stream or within an object that sends or receives streams.

The datatype 'stream' refers to a stream of messages unless otherwise stated. A stream is an open-ended collection that can be sampled at a point in time. Each sample is a sequence (in the OCL sense) of messages that have flowed since the previous sample was taken (or since collecting began). A monitoring tool might extract samples from a log, an audit trail or a warehouse.

The operations are presented in the cursive style of BCL but are generally defined in OCL. A stream is conventionally represented by a plural noun, e.g., "messages", "fault reports", "orders". Hence we write "fault reports are followed by...". "Messages *are*..." or even "As are..." and "Bs are..." is written below for the sake of consistent style. Unless otherwise stated, "messages", "stream of messages" and "stream" all indicate the same datatype. Often, the stream in question will be a substream of another. For example, a quantifier such as "some" or "x% of" will indicate that an assertion applies to a substream of messages.

As described in the syntax, operations are introduced in italics. Many of them are defined using the equality constraint '=', so that A = B is equivalent to the OCL:

```
A
        post: result = B
```

There follows a proposed set of operations considered suitable for event-based architectures in EAI. These have a common pattern of participle (mapping to OCL select), plural verb (mapping to OCL forAll) and singular verb (mapping to OCL predicate, i.e., Boolean operation).

Giving Rise to

messages *giving rise to* stream : stream
messages *give rise to* stream : Boolean
message *gives rise to* message : Boolean

In a UML collaboration diagram, a message, A, *gives rise to* message, B, if A is the activator of B. B could be a reply to A, or there may be a chain of activation from A to B. The same concept is applicable to messages in streams that lead to activity in the receiving process, represented as a class. Taking givesRiseTo as the OCL style equivalent (see section 4), the definitions of the three operations are as follows:

A : message *gives rise to* B : message : Boolean ≡ A.givesRiseTo(B)
As : stream *give rise to* Bs : stream : Boolean
≡ As->forAll(a | Bs->exists (b | a.givesRiseTo(b)))
As : stream *giving rise to* Bs : stream : stream
≡ As->select(a | Bs->exists (b | a.givesRiseTo(b)))

This pattern is common to many of the operations and is not always shown in full.

Having
An attribute or combination of attributes can determine a selection of messages or other objects, indicated by 'having'. They can also be used to make assertions about messages (has/have). These operations use a predicate, which is a Boolean expression that involves attributes of the objects in the stream or other collection, as in OCL collection operations:

messages *having* P : predicate : stream
≡ messages->select{P : Boolean expression with attributes of messages}
message *has* P : predicate : Boolean
messages *have* P : predicate : Boolean

In each case the predicate P expresses conditions on the attributes of a message. Examples:

60% of orders have amount>100.
Requisitions having cost>1000 are received by Budget Checking.

Times
It is often important to measure the time that elapses between an activator and the sending or receiving of a message, since this can be critical to the successful use of an application system. The collaboration diagram (section 4) is taken to represent a stream of messages As (e.g., work orders) that give rise to a stream of messages Bs (e.g., timed plans). We are less interested in the timing of individual message pairs than in the statistics. A message has a time sent and a time received. We define the classes 'pair' and 'pairs' and operations '..from..to..' that line up messages in two streams so that each message is paired with the one it gives rise to. A pair has the attributes latency (or round trip time) and service time and may have others:

pair from A *to* B : pair
pair from A to B has A gives rise to B
and latency = B's time received - A's time sent
and service time = B's time sent - A's time received

pairs from As *to* Bs : stream
≡ Bs -> collect(b | pair from (As -> select(a | a.gives rise to b)) -> first() to b)

Here, the OCL first() operation on a sequence is used to get the message from the selection, which always yields just one message, since each pair consists of a single message. Here as in some other expressions styles have been mixed rather freely.

Where several messages come together to give rise to one (probably a reply), this is best treated as a correlation (fan-in). There may be interest in the arrival times and delays of the various messages. On the other hand, it may be that only a substream of As (possibly qualified noncommittally as "some As") give rise to Bs, in which case the latencies only apply to the substream.

Monitoring and Relatedness

Monitoring is defined in terms of the 'about' relationship, which is based on keys or similar identifiers, such as customer numbers or fault IDs. This concept is not represented in UML, although it is commonplace in database systems and is defined in OMG's recently adopted Common Warehouse Metamodel (9). We can use the metamodel that underlies UML, as that treats the fields in a message (attributes of a class) as a set:

messages *about* collection of objects : stream
S : messages *are about* C : collection of objects
≡ S->forAll(m | C->exists(j | m is about j))
message *is about* object ≡ message.attributes->exists(f | f=object.identifier)

collection of objects *monitored by* object : collection of objects,
P : object *is monitored by* Q : object : Boolean,
collection of objects *are monitored by* object : Boolean
≡ object receives messages about collection of objects

Any given stream sample will only be about a subset of objects. For example, a sample of 50 messages about customers will only be about at most 50 customers. In setting constraints, we may have two rather different interests: whether a stream of messages over time covers every object in a collection or whether messages about some objects are not received. The coverage question suffers from the same problem as existential and universal quantification over samples; we never know whether the next one will complete the picture. More useful is to consider the subset of objects actually referenced by a sample of messages from a stream. Since the 'about' relationship does not adequately address these requirements, we need a more explicit relationship 'referenced by':

C : collection of objects *referenced by* S : messages : collection
≡ C->select(j | S->exists(m | m is about j))
E : subset of collection of objects *are referenced by* S : messages : Boolean
≡ E->forAll(j | S->exists(m | m is about j))
object *referenced by* message ≡ message is about object

Constraints about monitoring can be made more specific by including a 'referenced by' clause (see Details of Examples in section 7). In this way, they can be written so that a monitoring tool is not expected to access databases but only to deal with the data in streams of messages. In fact, a tool implementer could choose to interpret constraints in this way, possibly subject to directives by an administrator. This would avoid excessive overhead for monitoring.

A more flexible definition of monitoring (but more expensive to record operationally) could be defined in terms of relatedness, which is itself defined statistically in terms of overlapping data (i.e., instance data from streams of messages, not metadata such as field names) using measures employed in data mining:

messages *related to* collection of objects : stream,
 message *is related to* object : Boolean,
 messages *are related to* collection of objects : Boolean
 ≡ some fields in messages are based on some fields in objects
A : stream of field in messages *is based on* B : collection of field in objects
 ≡ tokens of A are a subset of tokens of B
 ≡ union{tokens of A, tokens of B} = tokens of B

Tokens of a field are defined conventionally (as, e.g., by Java StringTokenizer), based on blank spaces and delimiters. Tokens of a collection of fields are unions of the sets of tokens from each field from each element (message or other object) in the collection. Other similarity measures between fields, messages and objects can also be defined.

As defined, monitoring implies that tools must be able to extract data from messages and check them against a database. Attributes need to be associated with the model to enable a tool to do this. Like other statistical tracking, the checking could be performed offline and reported with other statistics.

Receiving

messages *received by* object : stream
messages *is received by* object : Boolean
messages *are received by* object : Boolean

Following

messages *following* message : stream,
 A : message *follows* B : message : Boolean
 ≡ A's time stamp is after B's time stamp,
 messages *follow* message : Boolean

Position and sequences

Streams are based on OCL sequences, in which members (i.e., messages) have position numbers, n, by which they can be referenced using ->at(n):

messages *are in sequence*
 ≡ Sequence{2..stream->size}
 -> forAll (n | (messages->at(n)).messageNumber
 > (messages->at(n-1)).messageNumber)

Example: 99.9% of fault reports are in sequence.

We can define other related terms:

position of message *in* stream : Integer = n ≡ stream->at(n)=message
message *at* position *in* stream ≡ stream->at(position)
next message *in* stream : message
    ≡ if position of message in stream < size of stream
    then message at position+1 in stream else NIL endif
previous message *in* stream : message
    ≡ if position of message in stream > 1
    then message at position-1 in stream else NIL endif
message *is in sequence in* stream ≡ position of message in stream = 1
    or message number of message
    > message number of previous message in stream

Now we can write the definition more succinctly in mixed style:

S : messages *are in sequence*
    ≡ messages -> forall (m | m is in sequence in S)

Summary of Operations

Participle (select)	Singular verb (Boolean expression)	Plural verb (forAll)
(not) monitored by	is (not) monitored by	are (not) monitored by
(not) related to	is...	are...
(not) based on	is...	are...
(not) about	is...	are...
(not) received by	is...	are...
(not) in sequence	is...	are...
(not) such that	is...	are...
(not) giving rise to	gives rise to (does not give rise to)	give rise to (do not...)
(not) following	follows (does not follow)	follow (do not...)
(not) having	has (does not have)	have (do not have)
(not) monitoring	monitors (does not monitor)	monitor (do not...)
(not) receiving	receives (does not receive)	receive (do not...)
	latency is	latencies
	service time is	service times are

7. Details of Examples

The examples introduced in section 2 are explained in more detail here. The two annotations in the diagram are:

Some fault reports give rise to subscriptions.
Some customers are monitored by Customer Care.

"Some" is a prefix operator and must be followed by a stream or other collection. The parsing is:

((Some (fault reports)) (give rise to) subscriptions).

This conforms to the rule that "some" is an operation on a stream that returns a substream which is then subject to the predicate that its messages give rise to subscriptions. The definition of "some" constrains the size of the substream to be 25% to 75% of the messages. In the OCL style:

```
25<100*(FaultReports->some()->size()
      / FaultReports->size())<75
FaultReports->some()
      ->forAll(f|f.givesRiseTo(Subscription))
```

The parsing of the second sentence is similar:

((Some (customers)) (are monitored by) (Customer Care))

This may be paraphrased "Customer Care receives messages about some customers." In the class diagram, fault reports going to Customer Care inherit from Incoming Report and so contain Customer number, an identifier for Customer; this is the force of "about", as discussed in the paragraphs about monitoring in section 6. A version of this constraint can be written that avoids the implication that the customer database must be accessed. This is done by introducing a 'referenced by' clause. The sentence then becomes:

Some customers referenced by fault reports are monitored by Customer Care.

The parsing is:

((Some (customers (referenced by) (fault reports))
(are monitored by) (Customer Care))

This qualified constraint is more useful. As originally written, the constraint merely says that a subset of customers have reports about them sent to Customer Care. In any sample taken at a point in time, this is always true. Now it says that Customer Care receives a subset of messages about customers. A tool could be written to make the assumption that the domain of discourse of the original constraint is confined to data in the streams and not in the databases. This has a similar effect to the 'referenced by' qualification.

8. Future Directions

It is possible to continue extending the list of operations. These would eventually comprise an ontology (i.e., a set of terms and definitions that covers a subject) for EAI. Application-level terms could be developed for various industries and software packages.

A natural extension of the present statistical treatment is to deal with probabilities and probabilistic logic so that a constraint-based modeling tool could make plausible deductions and verify refinements of models.

9. References

1.The most recent updates, including OCL, are available at the web site: www.rational.com/uml
2."Business-oriented Constraint Language" by John Knapman, submitted to UML2000
3.The RFP is at web site: www.omg.org/cgi-bin/doc?ad/2000-03-07
4.See web site: www.openapplications.org/oamas/loadform.htm
5.Saharia, A.N., Barron, T.M., "Approximate dependencies in database systems", Decision Support Systems 13 (1995) 335-347, Elsevier Science
6.Book "Designing Object Systems; Object-oriented modelling with Syntropy" by Steve Cook and John Daniels, Prentice Hall, 1994
7.The Java Message Service is documented at web site: java.sun.com/products/jms/docs.html
8.XML Metadata Interchange (XMI) at web site: www.omg.org/cgi-bin/doc?ad/98-10-07
9.See web site: www.omg.org/cgi-bin/doc?ad/2000-01-01

Heaven or Hell? A "Real-Time" UML?
Panel

Moderator:
Bran Selic [1]

Panelists:
Prof. Alan Burns [2], Alan Moore [3], Prof. Theo Tempelmeier [4], Prof. Francois Terrier [5]

[1] Rational Software Inc., Canada
bselic@rational.com
[2] University of York, UK
burns@minster.cs.york.ac.uk
[3] Artisan Software, UK
AlanM@artisansw.com
[4] Fachhochschule Rosenheim, Germany
tt@extern.lrz-muenchen.de
[5] CEA-LETI, France
Francois.Terrier@cea.fr

1 Introduction

Of course everybody is special! But, among software developers, none more so than developers of real-time software. Theirs is a struggle not merely against the tyranny of literal-minded computer technology but also against an even mightier foe: the messy, unfriendly, unpredictable, driven-by-Murphy's-law physical world. Slowly and painfully, over decades, they first learned how to overcome software technologies that seemed to be designed for any domain but theirs, even reaching a point where they were able to turn these to advantage. Furthermore, almost uniquely among software practitioners, real-time developers started introducing elements of true engineering for these technologies, such as various forms of schedulability analysis and performance engineering.

And then, just as things seemed to be moving well, new technologies emerged sowing confusion and shattering this established order. First came the object paradigm. Like everyone else, real-time developers could not ignore the onrush of this technological wave that promised so much, but which, like all previous software technologies, never took into account their needs. How should this new paradigm be used for real-time applications? What should be done with all that good stuff that was developed around earlier generations of software technology? Even as these issues are being pondered, yet another technological wave has struck: UML. Once again, the payback potential is impossible to ignore: a common language providing higher-levels of abstraction, widely taught and used, supported by a large selection of tools.

A. Evans, S. Kent and B. Selic (Eds.): «UML» 2000, LNCS 1939, pp. 93-100, 2000.

At the same time, real-time developers are facing yet another onslaught from a different direction: With the advent of the Internet and the symbiotic relationship that our society has with computer technology, the demand for highly dependable real-time systems is increasing in leaps and bounds. This explosive growth is matched by an even greater growth in scope and complexity of applications. Systems of several millions of lines of "high-level" language code are no longer considered exceptional. Many are now in the tens of millions of lines of code. Yet, the vast majority of real-time developers use techniques and technologies that are twenty to thirty years old. It is clear that these are inadequate for dealing with the next order of magnitude of application complexity that is emerging and that more powerful techniques based on higher-level abstractions are required.

So, what should the real-time community do with UML? Does it help or hinder? Given the lack of widespread adoption of practically all real-time languages (e.g., Real-Time Euclid, PEARL, Flex) or even real-time dialects of standard programming languages (e.g., RTC++, Ada-95), is a "real-time" UML the right thing to do? If so, what should it look like? If not, what is the alternative?

The panelists were asked to provide their views on these and related issues. (Note that due to poor planning by the moderator, not all the panelists had the opportunity to submit their position papers in time to make the proceedings.)

2 Prof. Theodor Tempelmeier : Real-Time UML

Object-Orientation

Object-oriented design is currently the best way of building systems, and this also applies to real-time/embedded systems. Encapsulation, abstract data types, etc., and other concepts such as generics or templates, are a must when developing complex embedded systems[1]. The author is reluctant, though, to accept inheritance as a dominating design principle and prefers object composition instead, where possible.

As for analysis, the situation is less clear. In many cases the object-oriented paradigm may also be reasonable for analysis, but on the other hand there are situations in which the sheer algorithmic complexity suggests an "old-fashioned" functional decomposition approach. For instance, this may be the case in very complex control systems, e.g. in a flight control system ([8]).

In a still wider context, systems engineering (in its original meaning, i.e. not restricted to software systems, cf. [5]) poses again the problem of overwhelming complexity. For large and nontrivial systems from unfamiliar application domains, it is just difficult to understand, what the system does or has to do. Furthermore, in many real-time/embedded systems the hardware/firmware architecture is not fixed from the beginning. Even application-specific hardware, generated from some VHDL descriptions onto FPGAs, has become feasible [11] and is used in practice. From personal project experience, a functional decomposition into subsystems seems preferable in such cases[2].

[1] The over-cautious approach of embedded C++ [2] is hardly understandable to the author.

[2] Note that this holds only for analysis. The design should be object-oriented anyway.

Use cases are helpful in many cases. However, in projects with high algorithmic complexity or with a subsystem breakdown structure, which is difficult to find, the author was not able to manage all problems solely by use case analysis. So a non-dogmatic approach, i.e. allowing other forms of knowledge expression in requirements engineering when necessary seems appropriate.

UML

UML has its merits, no question. However, some aspects of UML need a special assessment with respect to application to real-time/embedded systems.

One of the biggest problems with UML is the question how its semantics are (or should be) defined. The many vague or undefined concepts and diagrams in UML are just a manifestation of this. Concerning design, there are obviously at least the following possibilities:

- UML is used as design language down to coding, i.e. UML is also used for "programming"
- UML is used for design, and a programming language is used for coding

The problem with the first approach is that UML (and similar modelling languages) do not have semantics as precise as it is necessary for programming. The problem with the second approach is that there may be a semantic discrepancy between the modelling language and the programming language (the programming language is in ultimate authority). From project experience, the author takes the following position.

- "Programming" in a "modelling language" is neither practicable nor reasonable nor desirable.
- A modelling language can be and should be used for a "visualisation" of the design. *From a practical point of view, this implies that the modelling language resembles the important design concepts within the programming language/target system on a one-to-one, or 'isomorphic" basis.* (Naturally, this is only valid if the programming language/target system include sound design concepts, e.g. programming languages such as assembler are ruled out.)

Obviously, the Unified Modeling Language fits the concepts of mainstream languages such as C++ or Java nicely. So the "isomorphic design representation principle" from above is mostly fulfilled in theses cases[3]. On the other hand, there are discrepancies between UML and Ada [13], probably because Ada is not a mainstream languages, notwithstanding its extremely valuable features for real-time, embedded, and safety-critical systems.

Real-Time/Embedded Systems

Real-time/embedded systems may be developed according to a number of paradigms, e.g. with StateCharts, along the ROOM method [9], or by Ada-related methods such as ADARTS [3]. StateCharts are a part of UML anyway. The concepts of ROOM have been implemented in UML using UML's extension mechanisms[4][10], and the

---

[3] However, what does, for instance, a UML package mean to the C++ programmer? A namespace?

same could be done in principle for the Ada-related methods. The "isomorphic design representation principle" is thus again fulfilled.

Despite all the merits of these methods, most real-time software in practical applications is probably implemented in C/C++ with calls to the underlying real-time operating system (RTOS) or by direct use of low-level hardware elements such as timers or interrupt systems. What are the essential design elements in this case?

For development in C/C++ with an RTOS, a number of UML elements can be used directly, e.g. class and object diagrams, sequence diagrams, and state charts.

But designers of real-time systems usually also require diagrams

for visualising concurrency and task interaction, and

for analysing timing properties (see e.g.[3][12]).

These requirements have been met by the UML community and by UML tool vendors, recently [1][6][7], in the form of timing diagrams, task diagrams, concurrency diagrams, concurrency and synchronisation object diagram, and the like. In the view of the author, this seems to be the right approach.

What is UML?

Given UML's extension mechanisms, all real-time modelling concepts existing so far can probably be incorporated into UML. In fact, (almost) any modelling concept can be integrated! This would mean that everything "is" UML, which clearly cannot be the case. As a consequence, it has to be distinguished, whether UML is only used as a meta-modelling tool (for method engineering) or whether core UML is used directly.

References

[1] Douglass, B.P.: Real-Time UML. Developing Efficient Objects for Embedded Systems. Addison-Wesley, Reading (Mass.) 1998.

[2] Embedded C++ Technical Committee: Rationale for the Embedded C++ specification Development. Version WP-RA-002, 6, Jan 1998. http://www.caravan.net/ec2plus.

[3] Gomaa, H.: Software Design Methods for Concurrent and Real-Time Systems. Addison-Wesley, Reading 1993.

[4] Rational: Rational Rose RealTime™. http:// www.rational.com/products/rosert.

[5] IEEE Standard for Application and Management of the Systems Engineering Process. IEEE Std 1220-1998. IEEE Computer Society, New York 1999.

[6] I-Logix Inc.: Rhapsody in C Code Generation Guide, Part No. 2065, Andover, Mass. 1999.

[7] McLaughlin, M.J., Moore, A.: Real-Time Extensions to UML. Timing, concurrency, and hardware interfaces. Dr. Dobb's Journal December 1998.

[8] Roßkopf, A., Tempelmeier, T.: Aspects of Flight Control Software - A Software Engineering Point of View. Control Engineering Practice 8 (2000), 675-680. Volume 8, Issue 6, June 2000.

[9] Selic, B., Gullekson, G., Ward, P.T.: Real-Time Object-Oriented Modelling. Wiley & Sons, New York, 1994.

[10] Selic, B., Rumbaugh, J.: Using UML for Modeling Complex Real-Time Systems. White paper. ObjecTime, http://www.objectime.com.

[11] Schrott, G., Tempelmeier, T.: Putting Hardware-Software Codesign into Practice. Control Engineering Practice, 6 (1998) 397-402. Volume 6, Issue 3, March 1998.

[12] Shumate, K., Keller, M.: Software Specification and Design: A Disciplined Approach for Real-Time Systems. Wiley & Sons, New York, 1992.

[13] Tempelmeier, T.: UML is great for Embedded Systems – Isn't it? In: P. Hofmann, A. Schürr (eds.): OMER ("Object-Oriented Modeling of Embedded Realtime systems") Workshop Proceedings. May 28-29, 1999, Herrsching (Ammersee), Germany. Bericht Nr. 1999-01, Mai 1999. Universität der Bundeswehr München, Fakultät für Informatik.

3 François Terrier (with Sébastien Gérard): For a Full Integration of Real-Time Concern into OO Models, or "*How to Popularize Real Time Programming ?*"

Several years ago, the market of real time and embedded systems was considered as a very specific and "confidential" sector (about 5% of the market of computer systems). Now several studies consider that they can represent near years 2003 more than 50% of the market (including PCs, client-server and information systems).

This explosion of the market and the increasing need of new embedded services urge engineers to face more and more to the hard problem of developing sophisticated real-time systems while competition through time to market and cost constraints increase day after day. Classical real-time development of software systems is reaching its limits in a world where in one hand hardware targets cannot be known in advance and where in the other hand version evolution becomes increasingly fast and time to market must be shorten drastically in order to meet economical requirements. In this context, reusability and evolvability become mandatory requirements for modelling methods and development techniques. In parallel, object oriented techniques have reached a sufficient level of maturity and efficiency in order to provide successfully the flexibility required by new applications. Up to now however, real-time community has long been reluctant to cross the Rubicon for mainly two reasons:

- OO offer was not mature enough to provide stability in their solutions;
- and real-time specificities were generally not well covered by existing methods.

Nowadays, *UML* becomes the lingua franca among system modellers all over the world and brings significant answers to both following needs:

- to have a fine level of modularity for component based development;
- and to improve reusability properties of subsystems.

Some commercially methods (and tools) are now available for *UML* real time development (e.g.: *ARTiSAN* [1], *UML/SDL & ObjectGeode* [2, 3], *ROOM/UML-RT & ObjecTime/Rose-RT* [4, 5] and *RT-UML & Rhapsody* [6]). Though a great effort has been done in order to provide a good compromise between task oriented modelling and object oriented one, these proposals reflect a great diversity in the possible methodological choices offered to handle real-time and object orientation together [7]. These proposals generally maintain two separate conceptual models: the object one and the task one. Designers are also required to have a high level of expertise to maintain consistent these two different views, all along the development process. It is clear that the solutions and concepts proposed address more specialist of real time system development than common users whose primary interest is not on computing technologies but a given application domain (e.g.: automotive industry). In particular, three examples of divergence between approaches for real-time specialists and the common object oriented programming paradigms can be pointed out:

The interface role of active objects (or "capsules" or "reactive objects") becomes unclear. While in traditional OO development, it defines the behaviour of the object (i.e.: the only way to communicate with it and the processing triggered by the messages it receives), in current proposals, either active objects have no such interface, either they have one. But in this last case, the most important part of their behaviour is defined outside, in the object state machine.

The communication schemes are also considered with different points of view. Indeed, real-time approaches have based the communication schemes essentially on signals that can not be mapped to usual operation calls. So, execution models of signal processing and of operation calls can be completely different (asynchronous communications triggering processing in independent thread of the target versus synchronous communications processed in the caller).

The state machines used to specify active object behaviour mix both following concerns: control and actions. In one hand, they specify which messages the object can process and under which conditions. On the other hand, they specify too which actions are performed to implement the object reaction to the messages it receives. This breaks the usual structure of OO approaches where the program is first described in terms of objects. So, at a finest detail level, each object is described in terms of operations and attributes. And finally, at the lowest detail level, each operation is described in terms of a set of elementary actions.

In addition, timing specifications are always introduced either through informal information (e.g.: time points identified in sequence diagrams) or by timer definitions in state diagrams. This implies that developers always need to translate real-time constraints defined in requirement documents into specific implementation mechanisms. Moreover, setting of priorities on task and definition of scheduling policies (either for the application task management or for the messages management in the queues) are not really integrated in the models. This requires again to the developers to have a deep knowledge of these real-time mechanisms.

These points can be tackle by enriching and clarifying semantics of current *UML* concepts connected to real-time modelling. But this leads also to the necessity of proposing new modelling concepts at higher level, hiding completely underlying implementation techniques [8, 9, 10, 11, 12, 13]. This requires consequently to provide more elaborated procedures (and also tools) to automatically generate application implementations.

Moreover, validation of embedded systems remains a main issue that requires, at this time, long and costly procedures. One of the great challenges is then to provide some supports to help the validation and automatically provide model simulation, property verification and test generation [14]. This leads to the necessity of defining formal *UML* models able to support these essential functionalities.

In conclusions, all these needs underline the importance of having open developing environments supporting facilities for meta-modeling (for notation and method extension, model analysis and translation), model exchange among various tools and definition of implantation optimization profiles.

References

[14] A. Moore and N. Cooling, "Real-time Perspective - Overview (Version 1.0)", ARTISAN Software, 1998.

[15] P. Leblanc, V. Encontre, "ObjectGeode : Method Guidelines", VERILOG SA, 96

[16] S. J. Mellor, S. R. Tockey, R. Arthaud, P LeBlanc, "An Action Language for UML", in proc. <<UML'98>> Beyond the Notation, Mulhouse, France, June 98.

[17] B. Selic, G. Gullekson, and P. T. Ward, "Real time Object-oriented Modeling", John Wiley & Sons, Inc., 1994.

[18] B. Selic and J. Rumbaugh, "Using UML for Modeling Complex Real-Time Systems", ObjecTime Limited 1998.

[19] B. P. Douglass, "Doing Hard Time : Developing Real-Time Systems with UML, Objects, Frameworks, and Patterns", Addison-Wesley Pub., 1999.

[20] F. Terrier, S. Gérard, "Real time system modeling with UML: current status and some prospects", in proc. SAM'2000, Grenoble, France, June 2000.

[21] Y. Ishikawa et al., "Object-oriented real-time language design: Constructs for timing constraints", ECOOP'90 & OOPSLA'90, Ottawa, 1990.

[22] K. Takashio and M. Tokoro, "DROL: An object-oriented programming language for distributed real-time systems", OOPSLA'92, 1992.

[23] L. Nigro and F. Tisato, "RTO++: A framework for building hard real-time systems", Journal of object-oriented programming (JOOP), pp. 35-47, 1993.

[24] F. Terrier, G. Fouquier, D. Bras, L. Rioux, P. Vanuxeem, and A. Lanusse, "A Real Time Object Model", TOOLS Europe'96, Paris, France, February, 1996.

[25] A. Lanusse, S. Gérard, and F. Terrier, "Real-Time Modeling with UML : The ACCORD Approach", UML'98, Mulhouse, France, June, 1998.

[26] S. Gérard, "Modélisation UML exécutable pour les systèmes embarqués de l'automobile", Ph.D. Report, to be published, Evry, France, September 2000.

[27] J.-P. Gallois, "Analyse de spécifications industrielles et génération automatique de tests", in proc. ICSEA'99, Paris, France, November, 1999.

4 Bran Selic: Using UML for Real-Time Systems Analysis and Design—An Engineering Approach

The purpose of most real-time systems is to interact with the physical world and to control its state in some way. In contrast to the logical world of "pure" forms, the physical world, as Plato reminds us, is imperfect. This imperfection is reflected by a variety of limitations, all of them with physical underpinnings. Thus, no matter how fast our processors, computing still takes finite time, there are always limits on the amount of memory that we can assume, and components sometimes fail to behave according to their specifications.

This imposes a need to take into account the *quantitative* aspects when designing real-time software. In most software models, this dimension is captured somewhat loosely through the generic notion of a *resource*. A resource typically represents something finite, something that can run out. The concept covers both physical devices, such as processors, memory, and other hardware facilities, as well as logical resources, such as buffers, queues, and process control blocks. If we choose to ignore the finite nature of resources, our designs will not deal effectively with situations where resources run out. In real-time systems in particular, this may mean missing deadlines with potentially catastrophic consequences.

Therefore, the ability to accurately model resources, including their physical characteristics, is key to successful real-time design. It is also the key to an *engineering-oriented approach* to real-time software development. Such an approach relies on quantitative analysis methods (such as schedulability analysis), which can determine the salient real-time properties of a proposed design before it is fully elaborated and implemented. The economic and other benefits of that hardly need to be justified when we consider the high failure rate of software projects.

It is particularly useful to develop such an approach in the context of UML, since UML is an industry standard that is rapidly becoming prevalent among software practitioners and is supported by a large number of different tools from different vendors.

One such engineering-oriented approach to real-time software development based on UML has been proposed for adoption as an OMG standard [28][28]. A fundamental feature of this proposal is the notion of *quality of service* (or *QoS* for short).

In this proposal, a resource is modeled as a server whose services are characterized not only by their functional effect, but also by their non-functional aspects, such as response time, capacity, availability, etc. A QoS characteristic specifies (usually quantitatively) some aspect of how well a resource *can* perform a service (or *offered QoS*) or, how well a service *needs* to be performed (*required QoS*). (Usually the offered QoS specification is conditional on the resource having its own QoS requirements met, since a resource typically uses other resources to perform its services.)

Once the required QoS and offered QoS are explicitly specified in a UML model, it may be possibly to numerically verify the adequacy of the corresponding real-time design. This verification is typically not a simple thing and often requires some very sophisticated analysis techniques. However, provided that there is a standard way of specifying QoS information in a UML model, the analysis can be done by specialized tools. This also removes a significant and frequent impediment to the use of analysis methods: the dearth of qualified experts who know how to apply them.

QoS characteristics can be associated with UML models in a variety of ways, but the most effective and simplest is to define standard stereotypes of common UML concepts such as Class, Instance, or Link. The key challenge is to do this in a way that is flexible enough not to restrict the modeler in any significant way. For example, different analysis methods will require different perspectives on a given UML model. In that case, it is much better to have a single model that is decorated with multiple different types of QoS annotations instead of a different UML model for every analysis that might be performed on that model. Maintaining multiple models of a single system is not only time-consuming it also introduces potential consistency problems.

The intent of such a standard is to pave the way towards a discipline of real-time software design that is based on the principle of predictive modeling that is fundamental in classical engineering disciplines.

References

[28] Object Management Group, RFP for Scheduling, Performance, and Time, OMG document number ad/99-03-13 (March 1999).

[29] B. Selic, "A generic framework for modeling resources with UML", IEEE Computer, June 2000.

Towards a UML Profile for Interaction Design: The Wisdom Approach

Nuno Jardim Nunes[1], João Falcão e Cunha[2]

[1] Universidade da Madeira, Unidade de Ciências da Computação, Dep. de Matemática, 9000-390 Funchal, Portugal
njn@math.uma.pt
[2] Universidade do Porto, GEIN, Faculdade de Engenharia, 4099 Porto CODEX, Portugal
jfcunha@fe.up.pt

Abstract. The UML is recognized to be the dominant diagrammatic modeling language in the software industry. However, it's support for building interactive systems is still acknowledged to be insufficient. There is a common misconception that the same models developed to support the design of the application internals are also adequate to support interaction design, leveraging the usability aspects of the applications. In this paper we identify and discuss the major problems using the UML to document, specify and design interactive systems. Here we propose a UML profile for interactive systems development that leverages on human-computer interaction domain knowledge under the common notation and semantics of the UML. Our proposal integrates with existing object-oriented software engineering best practice, fostering co-evolutionary development of interactive systems and enabling artifact change between software engineering and human-computer interaction.

1 Introduction

Building interactive systems that are efficient and reliable in use, easy to learn and remember, and that provide user satisfaction is one of the greatest challenges of the software industry. Such requirements are increasing with the widespread use of the Internet, the advent of the information appliances and agent-based systems. In fact the Internet changed the importance of usability because the user interface is increasingly becoming the customer-interface, hence, a business critical factor.

The Unified Modeling Language (UML) has found widespread use in many different application domains and is increasingly becoming the *de facto* standard language for object-oriented analysis and design. However, UML support for interactive system development is recognized to be insufficient.

Although it is acknowledged that in interactive applications about 50% of the code is devoted to the user interface the UML and related methods and tools still focus more the application internals and less the usability aspects [1]. Moreover there

A. Evans, S. Kent and B. Selic (Eds.): «UML» 2000, LNCS 1939, pp. 101-116, 2000.

is a common misconception that the same models developed to support the design of the application internals are adequate to support user interface development.

In order to adequately support interactive system development we need to leverage on human-computer interaction (HCI) domain knowledge. Model based notations and formalism proliferate in the HCI field; however, they lack a common language that enables co-evolutionary development and artifact change with the software-engineering field. The same argument that led to the adoption of the UML, by the software engineering (SE) community, applies in bridging the gap between HCI and SE. The UML provides a common language for specifying, visualizing and documenting software intensive systems and enables tool interoperability at the semantic level, all of these issues are of ultimate importance for interactive system development [1].

HCI methods and techniques usually require modeling constructs to:

- describe users and their relevant characteristics;
- describe user behavior while performing the envisioned or supported tasks;
- specify abstract (conceptual) and concrete (physical) user interfaces.

The adoption of use-cases in the UML acknowledges the importance of identifying the different roles users play when interacting with an application to support their tasks. However they are still mainly used to structure the application internals and don't provide an efficient way to support the usability aspects of the interactive system. Essential use-cases [2] identified some of the requirements for user interface development enabling the connection between the structure of use and the structure of the user interface. An essential use-case is "*a simplified, abstract, generalized use-case defined in terms of user intentions and system responsibilities*" [3], it contrasts Jacobson's original definition of a concrete use-case "*a class describing the common pattern of interaction of a set of scenarios*" [4]. Essential use-cases define user role maps, a set of relationships between actors (affinity, classification and composition) that reveal how the different roles in a system fit together defining who will use the system and how [3]. Other approaches, used in goal-driven interaction design, rely on archetypal descriptions of users. In one of those proposals [5] the author defines a *persona*, a hypothetical archetype of a user defined with precision and detail. The author claims that instead of designing for a broad audience of users, interaction designers should design for a small set of archetypal users – the cast of characters [5]. The requirements in such proposals are substantially different from the common interpretation of use-cases in OO analysis and design – they recognize the peculiarities of interaction design and they focus on users' goals and the structure of use. A proposal for structuring use-cases with goals [6] already recognizes some of the above problems distinguishing goals as a key element of use-cases.

The descriptions of user behavior are intimately associated with the technique (and underlying concepts) used to abstract the end-users. In the UML, and related methods, descriptions of user behavior are usually captured detailing use-cases with scenarios, activity diagrams or interaction diagrams. From an HCI perspective the descriptions of user behavior usually encompass a task model, which, at least to some degree, can be achieved with the mentioned UML diagrams – in [1] and [7] two UML extensions are proposed to accommodate task analysis. However the major problem with descriptions of user behavior are related to the system-centric nature of use-cases. In [3] the authors argue that "*conventional use-cases typically contain too many built-in assumptions, often hidden and implicit, about the form of the user interface that is yet to be designed.*" Such argument led the authors to propose the essential use-case narrative, a technology-free, implementation independent, structured scenario expressed in the language of the application domain and end-users. The essential quality (technology free and implementation independent) of descriptions of user behavior can also be applied to diagrammatic representations, in [8] we propose to detail use-cases with activity diagrams following the same principle. Goal-driven interaction design also relies on descriptions of user behavior structured in terms of users' goals, for instance in [5], the author proposes to drive design in terms of personal, corporate and practical goals.

The above discussion concerns early models of interest to interactive system development, in particular models of user roles and models describing user behavior. The ideas described here are of ultimate importance to support interaction design and interactive system development. They should, in our opinion, be considered in further UML revisions and extension profiles. Although use-cases have proved to be an effective tool to structure application internals, alternate interpretations should be clearly defined and put into context to avoid misused in interactive system design. Experience reports on the mentioned approaches show benefit gains in terms of reduced complexity and cost of producing and maintaining the systems; enhanced user satisfaction and productivity; and even improvements in project management and resource allocation.

In this paper we focus on the analysis and design models of interactive systems, the models required to specify conceptual and concrete models of user interfaces. While the requirement model concerns an external view of the system described in the language of the users/customer, the analysis model concerns an internal view of the system described in the language of the developers [9]. In analysis the focus is to build a sound architecture that outlines how to realize the functionality captured in the different use-cases. In section 2 we discuss the analysis framework of the UML profile for software development processes and present a new proposal specifically adapted to develop interactive systems. Also in section 2 we present the design level models of our approach and how they complement the standard UML profile design model in order to foster the physical realization of the use-cases in interactive applications. Section 3 outlines the semantics of the UML extensions. In section 4 we present a worked example of our approach and, finally, in section 5 the conclusions and further developments.

2 Analysis and Design Level Models in Interactive System Development

The third type of descriptions of interest to HCI mentioned in the previous section are conceptual and physical models of the user interface. A conceptual model of the user interface is a model used by interaction designers to anticipate the user's mental model of the envisioned system. Conceptual models are important since they enable designers to ensure that the system under development will ultimately meet the expectations of the end-users, i.e., the usability requirements that define the quality of the user interface. Usually, conceptual models encompass the *things* (entities) the users manipulate to perform the tasks, hence, they can be conceived as refinements of domain models. However, the intents that drive such refinement are distinct for the purpose of the application internals and interaction. A good user interface, amongst other factors, should match as much as possible the user's conceptual model and not the internal application implementation model.

Conversely, a physical or concrete model of a user interface is a specific representation of the user interface designed to accommodate the tasks the users must perform. A physical model of the user interface is sometimes called a designer's model and should also match the user's conceptual model of the system. However, physical models include additional information required to design and implement the user interface, not present in conceptual models. For instance, an abstract physical model considers the task decomposition and the interaction spaces required,, while a concrete physical model also takes into consideration the interaction styles and the user interface technology available. In the following sections we discuss the relationship between the analysis and design models in the UML standard profile for software development processes and the corresponding descriptions necessary to support conceptual and physical models of the user interface.

2.1 The Analysis Framework of the UML Profile for Development Processes and Interactive Systems

The UML profile for software development processes [10] defines an analysis framework that divides the analysis classes in three stereotypes. This partitioning, originally from the OOSE method [4], encompasses three dimensions:

- The information dimension (<<entity>> stereotype) specifies the information held in the system in both short and long term – the state of the system;
- The behavior dimension (<<control>> stereotype) specifies the behavior the system will adopt – when and how the system changes state;
- The interface dimension (<<boundary>> stereotype) specifies the details for presenting the system to the outside world.

The reason behind this partitioning of analysis classes into information, behavior and interface is to promote a structure more adaptable to changes. Assuming that all systems change, stability will occur in the sense that changes affect (preferably) only one object in the system, i.e., they are local [4]. Therefore, the UML analysis framework aims at concentrating changes to the interface and related functionality in boundary objects; changes to (passive) information and related functionality in entity objects; and changes to complex functionality (e.g., involving multiple objects) in control objects.

This approach is conceptually similar, although at a different granularity level, to conceptual architectural models for interactive system's, for instance, PAC [11] and MVC [12]. In fact, the PAC distinction between presentation, abstraction (application) and control relate, conceptually, to the boundary, entity and control class stereotypes. However, such similarities are misleading in the sense that they do not comply with some of the requirements defined in interactive system architectures.

The major issue in conceptual and implementation architectures for interactive systems is the separation of concerns between the semantics of the application functional core and the user interface provided to the user. Such separation of concerns fosters portability, reusability, multiple interfaces and customization. The logical components of an interactive system architecture were originally identified in the Seeheim workshop [13] and later revised in the Arch workshop [14]. The initial three component proposal of the Seehim model encompassed the presentation, dialogue control and application interface components – a division that also closely maps the MVC and PAC models. The Arch model expanded this proposal on a five component model balanced around the dialogue component. The components of this model are:

- The interaction toolkit component - implements the physical interaction with the end-user;
- The presentation component - provides a set of toolkit independent objects;
- The dialogue component – responsible for task-level sequencing, providing multiple interaction space consistency, and mapping the between domain specific and user interface specific formalisms;
- The domain adapter component - implements domain related tasks required but not available in the domain specific component;
- The domain specific component - controls, manipulates and retrieves domain data and performs other domain-related functions.

The Arch model provides developers with guidance to tackle the difficult engineering compromises that affect the development process of interactive systems and the quality of the end product. On the one hand, the user and the functional core play a symmetric role driving the dialogue component, hence, at high levels of abstraction there is no a priori imposition on the control of the interaction. On the other hand, both the domain adapter and interaction toolkit components serve as buffers for the functional core and the user, therefore, isolating and absorbing the effects of change in its direct neighbors [15].

2.2 The Analysis Framework for Interactive Systems

In [16] we present a proposal for an UML based analysis architecture for interactive systems (depict in Fig. 1). This new proposal builds on UML's analysis framework but introduces two additional dimensions: the presentation and dialogue dimensions. The new dimensions accomplish two goals, on the one hand, the presentation dimension detaches the human-interface from the existing interface dimension, on the other hand, the dialogue dimension regulates task-level sequencing while providing multiple interaction space consistency and mapping between domain specific and user interface specific formalisms. In addition, the information dimension is shared among both the user interface specific dimensions and the internal application dimensions, postponing domain adaptation to other models at lower levels of abstraction.

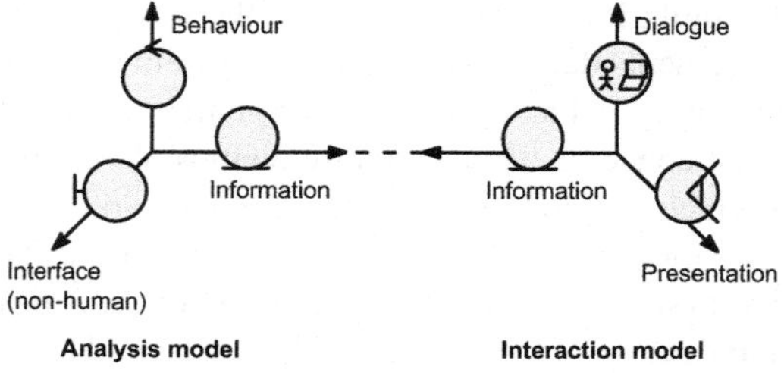

Fig. 1. The revised analysis framework for interactive systems

The proposal for the UML analysis framework for interactive systems includes a new UML interaction model to accommodate the two new dimensions, plus the shared information dimension. Therefore, the interaction model encompasses the information, dialogue and presentation dimensions, clearly mapping the conceptual architectural models for interactive systems, while maintaining the desired separation of concerns. Accordingly, the analysis model accommodates the UML profile architecture dimensions, also including the shared information dimension. Note that the presentation dimension in the UML analysis framework is reduced to capture the interface (not the presentation) to external systems.

The new interaction model defines the user interface architecture, like the analysis model defines the internal system architecture. Here we consider that an architecture for interactive systems involves the description of the elements from which those systems are built, the overall structure and organizations of the user interface, patterns that guide their composition and how they are connected in order to support the interactions with the users in their tasks [16]. In the following sections we describe the design models necessary to realize the user-interface architecture. For further details regarding the proposal for this architectural model refer to [8].

2.3 The Dialogue Design Level Model

The interaction model suffers further refinement on two design level models: the dialogue model refines the dialogue dimension and the presentation model refines the presentation dimension.

The dialogue model specifies the dialogue structure of the application using an UML based adaptation of the *ConcurTaskTrees* visual task formalism [17]. According to the author, the main purpose of *ConcurTaskTrees* is to support the specification of flexible and expressive task models that can be easily interpreted even by people without formal background. *ConcurTaskTree* is an expressive, compact, understandable and flexible notation representing concurrent and interactive activities by task decomposition and supporting cooperation between multiple users. *ConcurTaskTrees* defines three types of task allocations:

- user tasks (tasks performed by the user);
- application tasks (tasks completely executed by the application);
- interaction tasks (tasks performed by the user interacting with the system);
- abstract tasks (tasks which require complex activities whose performance cannot be univocally allocated).

An important feature of the *ConcurTaskTrees* notation, essential to bring detail in the dialogue model, is the ability to express temporal relationships between tasks. In our adaptation of the formalism we use the UML constraint extension mechanism to express such temporal relationships between tasks. A constraint is a semantic relationship among model elements that specifies conditions and propositions that must be maintained as true [10]. The temporal relationships in *ConcurTaskTrees* adapted in our approach are depict in Fig. 2 and described bellow (including the original notation from [17] in parenthesis next to their name):

- Independent concurrency (T1|||T2) – denotes that actions belonging to two tasks (T1 and T2) can be performed in any order without any specific constraint;
- Choice (T1[]T2) – denotes that it is possible to choose form a set of tasks and once the choice has been made the chosen task can be performed, while other tasks are not available;
- Concurrency with Information Exchange (T1|[]|T2) – same has independent concurrency but the tasks have to synchronize in order to exchange information;
- Deactivation (T1[>T2) – denotes that the first task (T1) is definitely deactivated once the second task (T2) terminates;
- Enabling (T1>>T2) – denotes that the second task (T2) is activated once the first task (T1) terminates;
- Iteration (T*) – denotes the task (T) is performed repeatedly until the task is deactivated by another task;
- Finite Iteration(s) (T1(n)) – same as iteration but the task (T) is performed n times;
- Optional Tasks ([T]) – denotes that the performance of a task is optional.

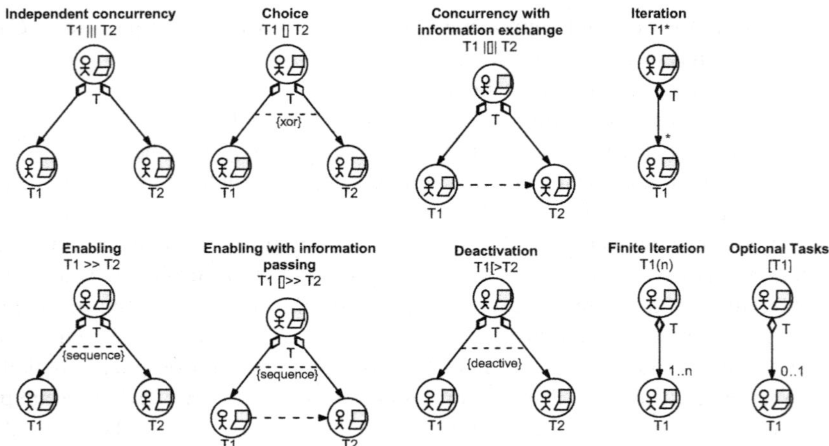

Fig. 2 – UML adaptation of *ConcurTasktrees*. Note that the icon circle with a sticky man and a stylized computer inside denote a UML stereotype <<task>>. Also, all the associations between <<task>> classes are stereotyped <<refine task>> associations. Finally {xor}, {sequence} and {deactivate} are UML constraints (refer to section 3 for definitions). For a complete reference of ConcurTaskTree involving all the possible uses of such formalism, specifically for evaluation and pattern expression, refer to [17].

2.4 The Presentation Design Level Model

The other design level model defined in our approach is the presentation model. Recently several authors proposed the idea of using object models to specify presentational aspects of interactive applications. In the Ovid method Roberts and colleagues proposed the concept of an (object) view – the modeling concept responsible for presenting to the users and allowing them to use information to accomplish tasks [18]. However the initial proposal of Ovid relies on UML annotations to express relevant information of views and, hence, have little semantic significance. Ovid organizes views in designers and implementation models through class, sequence and statechart diagrams. This model organization maps the well-known HCI distinction between the different conceptual models of users, designers and implementation – the aim is to bring the implementation model as close to the user's model as possible, hence, preventing the user interface from reflecting the internal system architecture.

A similar concept is also proposed in usage-centered design (UCD), the authors of essential use-cases propose interaction contexts as the main building block of the presentation aspects of the user interface. An interaction context represents the places within the user interface of a system where the user interacts with all the functions, containers and information needed for carrying out some particular tasks or set of interrelated tasks [3]. However the authors don't provide any information regarding the definition of interaction contexts in the UML framework. Contrasting

Ovid, UCD emphasizes the navigational structure of the user interface architecture. Interaction contexts are organized in navigation maps and relationships between interaction contexts are defined (context changes). This characteristic enhances the capability of reasoning about the navigational structure of the interactive application, supporting one of the important compromises in interaction design – the balance between the number of interaction contexts and the number of context transitions.

Both Ovid and UCD classify the presentation objects in terms of generic graphical interaction elements, e.g., contents, composed, properties and user assistance in Ovid; and window, screen, display, message and panel in UCD. This classification scheme imposes a dependency on the user interface technology - the WIMP graphical user interface – which restricts the ability of the modeling concepts to serve multiple interaction styles and interface technologies.

In our approach the presentation model defines the physical realization of the perceivable part of the interactive system (the presentation), focusing on how the different presentation entities are structured to realize the physical interaction with the user. The presentation model provides a set of implementation independent modeling constructs (the <<interaction space>> class stereotype[1]) for use by the dialogue model, hence, leveraging independence of the interaction techniques provided by the user interface technology (e.g. UI toolkit). Interaction spaces are responsible for receiving and presenting information to the users supporting their task. Interaction spaces are typically organized in hierarchies and containment relationships can occur between interaction spaces. In the next section we present the UML's extensions to support the presentation model.

3 The UML Profile for Interactive System Development

In the previous sections we presented and discussed different approaches and contributions to define adequate interactive system architectures. We also discussed the analysis framework of the standard UML profile for software development, argued about its system-centric nature and proposed some modeling concepts to overcome this nature while staying within the UML and related SE methods. In this section we present a minimal set of extensions to the UML to support the concepts introduced in the previous section. We call this extension set the Wisdom UML profile because it was originally developed to support the Wisdom software development method [19]. Wisdom is a UML based method specifically adapted to develop interactive system by small software developing companies. In this paper we intentionally detached the extension profile from its methodological background because it is our belief that the Wisdom extensions are broadly applicable in different process contexts.

---

[1] In previous versions of the Wisdom method the concept described here as an interaction space was named view. The change is related with: (i) the belief that interaction space reflected more the notion of a human user interacting with a computer system (as opposed with a more passive notion in view); and (ii) the existence of an equally named stereotype (<<view>>) in the data modeling profile very common in industry modeling tools.

3.1 Revised Stereotypes for the Analysis Model

As we mentioned in the previous section the new analysis framework for interactive system development expands the UML standard profile framework, while introducing some subtle but important changes in the conceptual definitions of the class stereotypes. For that purpose we present the modified definitions of the Wisdom profile (where required partial definitions are retrieved from [10] and [9]):

- <<Boundary>> class stereotype – the boundary class is used, in the analysis framework for interactive systems, to model the interaction between the system and external systems (non-human). The interaction involves receiving (not presenting) information to and from external systems. Boundary classes clarify and isolate requirements in the system's boundaries, thus isolating change in the communication interface (not human-interface). Boundary classes often represent external systems, for example, communication interfaces, sensors, actuators, printer interfaces, APIs, etc.
- <<Control>> class stereotype – the control class represents coordination, sequencing, transactions and control of other objects. Control classes often encapsulate complex derivations and calculations (such as business logic) that cannot be related to specific entity classes. Thereby, control classes isolate changes to control, sequencing, transactions and business logic that involves several other objects.
- <<Entity>> class stereotype – the entity class is used to model perdurable information (often persistent). Entity classes structure domain (or business) classes and associate behavior, often, representing a logical data structure. As a result, entity classes reflect the information in a way that benefits developers when designing and implementing the system (including support for persistence). Entity objects isolate changes to the information they represent.

3.2 Stereotypes for the Interaction Model

The elements of the interaction model are interaction classes, defined as stereotypes of UML class constructs. The three stereotypes proposed in the analysis framework for interactive systems are:

- <<Task>> class stereotype – task classes are used to model the structure of the dialogue between the user and the system. Task classes are responsible for task level sequencing, multiple interaction space consistency and mapping back and forth between entities and interaction space classes. Task classes often encapsulate complex behavior that cannot be related to specific entity classes. Thereby, task classes isolate changes in the dialogue structure of the user interface
- <<Interaction space>> class stereotype – the interaction space class is used to model interaction between the system and the human actors. An interaction space class represents the space within the user interface of a system where the user interacts with all the functions, containers, and information needed for carrying out some particular task or set of interrelated tasks [3]. Interaction space classes are

responsible for the physical interaction with the user, including a set of interaction techniques that define the image of the system (output) and the handling of events produced by the user (input). Interaction space classes isolate change in the user interface of the system, they are technology independent although they often represent abstraction of windows, forms, panes, etc.

The UML profile for software development processes also defines association stereotypes. Although, the UML profile for interactive systems doesn't change the semantics of those association stereotypes, they can be applied to the new class stereotypes introduced before:

- <<Communicate>> is an association between actors and use cases denoting that the actor sends messages to the use case or the use case sends messages to the actor. It can also be used between boundary, control and entity. In addition it can be used between actor and boundary, with the new specific constraint that actor is an external system. Communicate can also be used between entity, task and interaction space. In addition it can be used between actor and interaction space, with the specific constraint that actor is human. The direction of communication can be one way or two ways;
- <<Subscribe>> is an association between two class states that objects of the source class (subscriber) will be notified when a particular event occurs in objects of the target class (publisher). Subscribe can be used from boundary, entity and control to entity. In addition, subscribe can also be used between task and entity. The direction of subscribe is one way.

3.3 Additional Stereotypes for the Dialogue Model

- <<Refine task>> is an association between two tasks denoting that the target class (subtask) specifies the source task (parent task) at a different (lower) level of detail. The refine task association is unidirectional can only be used between task classes.

Constraints for the Refine task association (assuming all objects or classes maintain their own thread of control, i.e., they are active and run concurrently with other active objects):

- {xor} – is the UML standard constraint and applies to a set of associations, specifying that over that set, exactly one is manifest for each associated instance;
- {sequence} - is applied to a set of <<refine task>> associations, specifying that over that set, associated instances become active in sequential order, i.e., one associated instance activates the other when it becomes inactive;
- {deactivate} - is applied to two <<refine task>> associations, specifying that one associated instance explicitly deactivates the other when it becomes active.

For the purpose of task allocation the following tagged values apply to the task classes:

- {abstract task} – tasks which require complex activities and whose performance cannot be univocally allocated;

- {user task} - tasks performed by the user with no interaction with the system. For instance, thinking about which option to choose;
- {application task} - tasks completely executed by the application;
- {interaction task} - tasks performed by the user interacting with the system;

3.4 Additional Stereotypes for the Presentation Model

- <<Navigate>> is an association stereotype between two interaction space classes denoting a user moving from one interaction space to another. The navigate association can be unidirectional or bi-directional, the later usually meaning there is an implied return in the navigation. Users navigate in interaction spaces while performing complex tasks and a change between interaction spaces usually requires a switch of thinking from the user;
- <<Contains>> is an association stereotype between two interaction space classes denoting that the source class (container) contains the target class (content). The contains association can only be used between interaction space classes and is unidirectional.
- <<input element>> – is an attribute stereotype denoting information received from the user, i.e., information the user can manipulate;
- <<output element>> – is an attribute stereotype denoting information presented to the user, i.e., information the user can perceive but not manipulate;
- <<action>> – is an operation stereotype denoting something a user can do in the physical user interface that causes a significant change in the internal state of the system, i.e., changes in the long term information of the system (entities), request for signification functionality, changes in context of the user interface, etc.

3.5 Valid Association Stereotypes Combinations

To: From:	Actor	Boundary	Control	Entity	Task	Interaction space
Actor		communicate				communicate
Boundary	communicate	communicate	communicate	communicate subscribe		
Control		communicate	communicate	communicate subscribe	communicate	
Entity				communicate subscribe		
Task			communicate	communicate subscribe	communicate refine	
Interaction space					communicate	navigate contain

Fig.3 – Valid association stereotypes combinations

4 The Wisdom Approach in Practice: A Worked Example

We've applied our approach in different development contexts and projects, of variable size and complexity. For the purpose of illustrating the notation presented in this paper, we present, throughout this section, several artifacts from a well-known example of a simple hotel reservation system (refer to [18] for other worked examples of the same problem). The "toy examples" bellow are not intended to demonstrated the applicability of the approach in a real-world scenario, that is the aim of a case-study and is out of the scope of this paper.

To the left-hand side of Fig. 4 we show a possible use-case structure for the above problem statement. The use-case model is depict to illustrate how different interaction and analysis classes collaborate in their realization. For example, the *customer browser* class, the *identify customer* task and the *customer* entity all collaborate in the realization of the three use-cases depict in Fig. 4. In the middle left-hand side of the illustration are interaction model classes (interaction space and task classes). The task classes accommodate the dialogue of the interactive system, hence, for example, *check availability* and *identify customer* are high-level tasks belonging to the dialogue structure of this particular architecture. Task objects also guarantee consistency between interaction spaces, one example of such responsibility is visible between the *confirm reservation* task class, the *customer browser* and *customer reservations*. To the middle right-hand side of Fig. 4 is the internal analysis model. In this example there are no boundary objects to interface external systems. Finally rightmost in the figure we present a hypothetical traditional solution (i.e., following the boundary/control/entity division). This "traditional" solution was adapted from other examples in the literature (e.g., [4], [9] or [20]). It is not our remit here to build a thorough discussion of both alternatives, but we can easily observe that in traditional approaches typically:

- boundary classes tend to follow the same functional decomposition of use-cases, i.e., there is usually a 1-to-1 mapping between use-cases and boundary classes. Such decomposition is less adaptable to change, compromises the reuse potential of the UI compromising the consistency and coherency of the UI (a major usability factor);
- boundary classes presuppose a user-interface technology or style (window, screen, etc.). Although we can argue that this is not explicitly a notational problem, we believe it is closely related to the lack of lower level extensions supporting the reification of the presentation aspects of the UI;
- logic related to the UI usually goes into control or boundary classes. Again this is a problem of ineffective support for the required separation of concerns for interactive applications. The result is a structure less adaptable to changes, reuse, and even existing n-tier physical architectures. For instance, we have successfully exploited mappings of our approach to n-tier architectures promoted in the UML profiles for web applications [20];

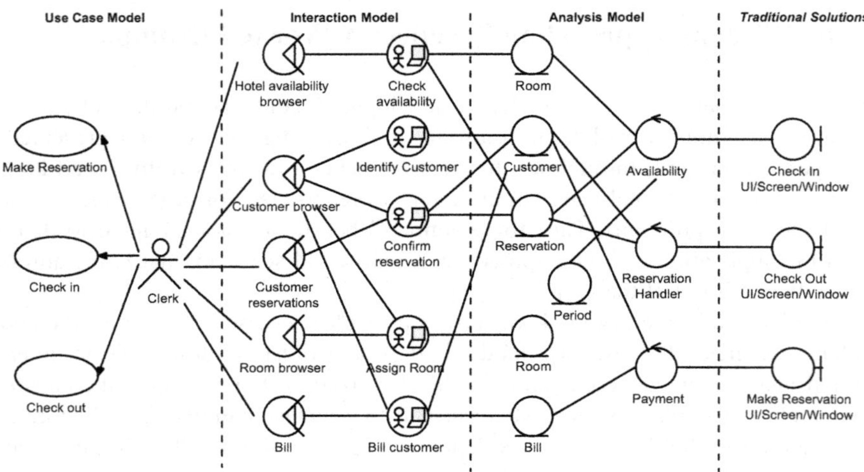

Fig. 4. Example of a use-case model, an user interface architecture, an internal architecture and a "traditional" solution for a simple Hotel Reservation System.

The following two artifacts (Fig. 5 and 6) depict the reification of parts of the architecture in Fig. 4. The artifacts, shown bellow, typically belong to design level models, in this particular case part of the task model (Fig. 5) and part of the presentation model (Fig. 6).

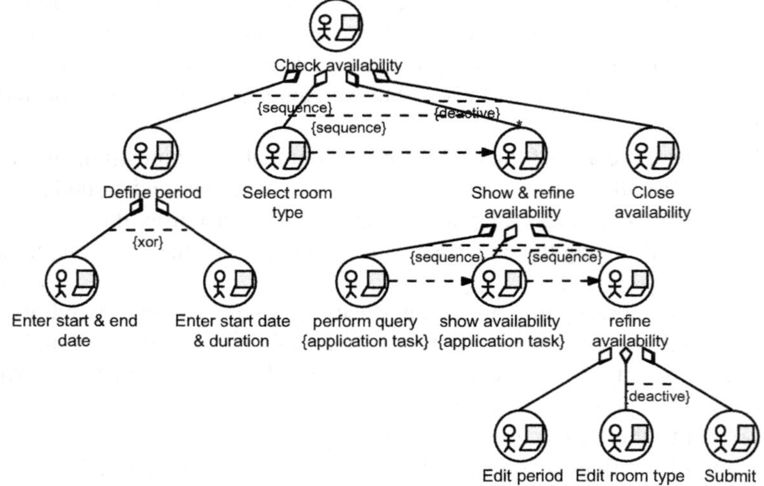

Fig. 5. Example of a task model for the check availability top-level task. Note that in this diagram the <<task>> stereotype uses a special icon as an alternate representation. This icon enables further usage for task allocation, i.e., removing alternately the sticky man and the stylized computer we can define stereotypes for task allocation to user tasks and application tasks. Also the associations in this example omit the stereotype reference for clarity, obviously all associations are <<refine task>> stereotypes.

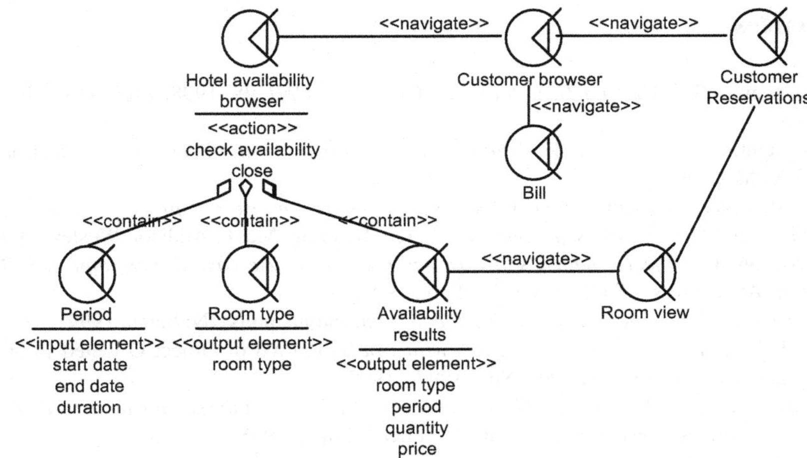

Fig. 6. Example of a presentation model for the hotel availability browser. Note that in this diagram the <<interaction space>> stereotype uses a special icon as an alternate representation.

5 Conclusions

In this paper we discussed the major problems using the UML for interactive system development and present several contributions that enable adequate development of user interfaces. Our proposal leverages on HCI domain knowledge, while staying within the UML framework, fostering co-evolutionary development of interactive systems, enabling artifact change between HCI and SE and providing the basis for tool support and interoperability. The proposed interactive system analysis framework supports both the internal system architecture and the interactive architecture required to build good user interfaces that foster reuse, portability, multiple user interfaces and customization. The dialogue and presentation design level models support model based development of user interfaces using a set of UML notational extensions based on a experimented software engineering method – the Wisdom method. The extensions described here are also effective for expressing task and interaction patterns. Our experience using and evolving these notational extensions shows that they can be actually applied in a practical development environment, taking full advantage of the increasing tool support for the UML.

References

[1]. Kovacevic, S. *UML and User Interface Design.* in *UML'98.* 1998. Mulhouse - France, Year.

[2]. Constantine, L., *Essential Modeling: Use cases for user interfaces.* Communications of the ACM, , 1992.

[3]. Constantine, L.L. and L.A.D. Lockwood, *Software for use : a practical guide to the models and methods of usage-centered design*, Reading, Mass.: Addison Wesley, 1999.

[4]. Jacobson, I., *Object-oriented software engineering: a use case driven approach*, New York: ACM Press - Addison-Wesley Pub., 1992.

[5]. Cooper, A., *The inmates are running the asylum*, Indianapolis, IN: Sams, 1999.

[6]. Cockburn, A., *Structuring Use Cases with Goals.* Journal of Object-Oriented Programming, (Set.-Out. 1997 and Out.-Nov. 1997), 1997.

[7]. Artim, J., *et al.*, *Incorporating work, process and task analysis into industrial object-oriented systems development.* SIGCHI Bulletin, **30**(4), 1998.

[8]. Nunes, N. and J.F.e. Cunha. *Detailing use-case with activity diagrams and object-views.* in *Workshop on Integrating Human Factors into Use Cases and OO Methods.* 1999. Lisbon - Portugal: http://www.crim.ca/~aseffah/ecoop/, Year.

[9]. Jacobson, I., G. Booch, and J. Rumbaugh, *The unified software development process.* The Addison-Wesley object technology series, Reading, Mass: Addison-Wesley, 1999.

[10]. OMG, *Unified Modeling Language 1.3*, , Object Management Group, 1999.

[11]. Coutaz, J. *PAC: An object-oriented model for dialogue design.* in *INTERACT'87.* 1987: Elsevier Science Publisher, Year.

[12]. Beck, K. and W. Cunningham. *A laboratory for teaching object oriented thinking.* in *OOPSLA'89.* 1989, Year.

[13]. Pfaff, G. and P.J.W.t. Haguen, eds. *User Interface Management Systems.* , Springer-Verlag: Berlin, 1985.

[14]. Bass, L., *A metamodel for the runtime architecture of an interactive system: The UIMS developers workshop.* SIGCHI Bulletin, **24**(1): p. 32-37, 1992.

[15]. Coutaz, J., *Software Architecture Modeling for User Interfaces*, in *Encyclopedia of Software Engineering*, Wiley, 1993.

[16]. Nunes, N.J. and J.F.e. Cunha. *Wisdom – A UML based architecture for interactive systems.* in *DSV_IS'2000.* 2000. Limerick - Ireland: (submitted), Year.

[17]. Paternò, F., *Model Based Design and Evaluation of Interactive Applications.* Applied Computing, London: Springer-Verlag, 1999.

[18]. Roberts, D., *et al.*, *Designing for the user with OVID : bridging user interface design and software engineering.* lst ed, Indianapolis, IN: Macmillan Technical Pub., 1998.

[19]. Nunes, N.J. and J.F.e. Cunha, *Whitewater Interactive System Development with Object Models*, in *Object-Oriented User Interface Design*, M.v. Harmelen, Editor, Addison-Wesley, 2000.

[20]. Conallen, J., *Building Web Applications with UML.* Object Technology Series: Addison-Wesley, 1999.

UML*i*: The Unified Modeling Language for Interactive Applications

Paulo Pinheiro da Silva and Norman W. Paton

Department of Computer Science, University of Manchester
Oxford Road, Manchester M13 9PL, England, UK.
e-mail: {pinheirp,norm}@cs.man.ac.uk

Abstract. User interfaces (UIs) are essential components of most software systems, and significantly affect the effectiveness of installed applications. In addition, UIs often represent a significant proportion of the code delivered by a development activity. However, despite this, there are no modelling languages and tools that support contract elaboration between UI developers and application developers. The Unified Modeling Language (UML) has been widely accepted by application developers, but not so much by UI designers. For this reason, this paper introduces the notation of the Unified Modelling Language for Interactive Applications (UML*i*), that extends UML, to provide greater support for UI design. UI elements elicited in use cases and their scenarios can be used during the design of activities and UI presentations. A diagram notation for modelling user interface presentations is introduced. Activity diagram notation is extended to describe collaboration between interaction and domain objects. Further, a case study using UML*i* notation and method is presented.

1 Introduction

UML [9] is the industry standard language for object-oriented software design. There are many examples of industrial and academic projects demonstrating the effectiveness of UML for software design. However, most of these successful projects are silent in terms of UI design. Although the projects may even describe some architectural aspects of UI design, they tend to omit important aspects of interface design that are better supported in specialist interface design environments [8]. Despite the difficulty of modelling UIs using UML, it is becoming apparent that domain (application) modelling and UI modelling may occur simultaneously. For instance, tasks and domain objects are interdependent and may be modelled simultaneously since they need to support each other [10]. However, task modelling is one of the aspects that should be considered during UI design [6]. Further, tasks and interaction objects (widgets) are

A. Evans, S. Kent and B. Selic (Eds.): ≪UML≫ 2000, LNCS 1939, pp. 117–132, 2000.

interdependent as well. Therefore, considering the difficulty of designing user interfaces and domain objects simultaneously, we believe that UML should be improved in order to provide greater support for UI design [3,7].

This paper introduces the UML*i* notation which aims to be a minimal extension of the UML notation used for the integrated design of applications an their user interfaces. Further, UML*i* aims to preserve the semantics of existing UML constructors since its notation is built using new constructors and UML extension mechanisms. This non-intrusive approach of UML*i* can be verified in [2], which describes how the UML*i* notation introduced in this paper is designed in the UML meta-model.

UML*i* notation has been influenced by model-based user interface development environment (MB-UIDE) technology [11]. In fact, MB-UIDEs provide a context within which declarative models can be constructed and related, as part of the user interface design process. Thus, we believe that the MB-UIDE technology offers many insights into the abstract description of user interfaces that can be adapted for use with the UML technology. For instance, MB-UIDE technology provides techniques for specifying static and dynamic aspects of user interfaces using declarative models. Moreover, as these declarative models can be partially mapped into UML models [3], it is possible to identify which UI aspects are not covered by UML models.

The scope of UML*i* is restricted to form-based user interfaces. However, form-based UIs are widely used for data-intensive applications such as database system applications and Web applications and UML*i* can be considered as a baseline for non-form-based UI modelling. In this case, modifications might be required in UML*i* for specifying a wider range of UI presentations and tasks.

To introduce the UML*i* notation, this paper is structured as follows. MB-UIDE's declarative user interface models are presented in terms of UML*i* diagrams in Section 2. Presentation modelling is introduced in Section 3. Activity modelling that integrates use case, presentation and domain models is presented in Section 4. The UML*i* method is introduced in Section 5 when a case study exemplifying the use of the UML*i* notation is presented along with the description of the method. Conclusions are presented in Section 6.

2 Declarative User Interface Models

A modelling notation that supports collaboration between UI developers and application developers should be able to describe the UI and the application at the same time. From the UI developer's point of view, a modelling notation should be able to accommodate the description of users requirements at appropriate levels of abstraction. Thus, such a notation should be able to describe abstract task specifications that users can perform in the application in order to achieve some goals. Therefore, a *user requirement model* is required to describe these abstract tasks. Further, UI sketches drawn by users and UI developers can help in the elicitation of additional user requirements. Therefore, an *abstract presentation model* that can present early design ideas is required to describe these UI sketches. Later in the design process, UI developers could also refine abstract presentation models into *concrete presentation models*, where widgets are selected and customised, and their placement (layout) is decided.

From the application developer's point of view, a modelling notation that integrates UI and application design should support the modelling of application objects and actions in an integrated way. In fact, the identification of how user and application actions relate to a well-structured set of tasks, and how this set of tasks can support and be supported by the application objects is a challenging activity for application designers. Therefore, a *task model* is required to describe this well-structured set of tasks. The task model is not entirely distinct from the user requirement model. Indeed, the task model can be considered as a more structured and detailed view of the user requirement model.

The application objects, or at least their interfaces, are relevant for UI design. In fact, these interfaces are the connection points between the UI and the underlying application. Therefore, the application object interfaces compose an *application model*. In an integrated UI and application development environment, an application model is naturally produced as a result of the application design.

UML*i* aims to show that using a specific set of UML constructors and diagrams, as presented in Figure 1, it is possible to build declarative UI models. Moreover, results of previous MB-UIDE projects can provide experience as to how the declarative UI models should be inter-related and how these models can be used to provide a declarative description of user interfaces. For instance, the links (a) and (c) in Figure 1 can be explained in terms of state objects, as presented in Teallach [5]. The link (d) can be supported by techniques from TRIDENT [1] to generate concrete presentations. In terms of MB-UIDE technology there is not a common sense of the models that might be used for describing a UI. UML*i* does not aim to present a new user interface modelling proposal, but to reuse some of the models and techniques proposed for use in MB-UIDEs in the context of UML.

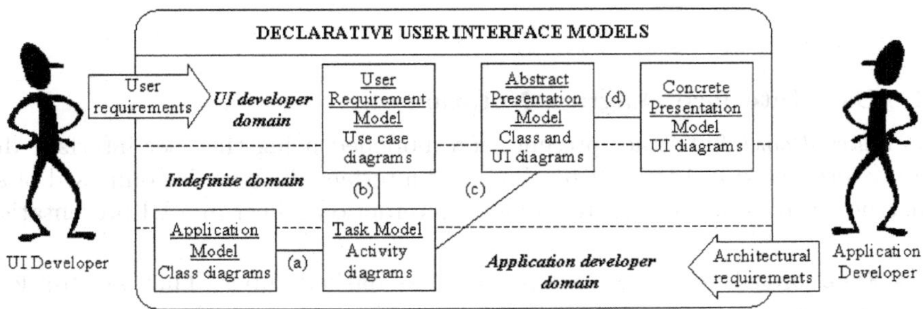

Fig. 1. UML*i* declarative user interface models.

3 User Interface Diagram

User interface *presentations*, the visual part of user interfaces, can be modelled using object diagrams composed of *interaction objects*, as shown in Figure 2(a). These interaction objects are also called *widgets* or *visual components*. The selection and grouping of interaction objects are essential tasks for modelling UI presentations. However, it is usually difficult to perform these tasks due to the large number of interaction objects with different functionalities provided by graphical environments. In a UML-based environment, the selection and grouping of interaction objects tends to be even more complex than in UI design environments because UML does not provide graphical distinction between domain and interaction objects. Further, UML treats interaction objects in the same way as any other objects [3]. For instance, in Figure 2(a) it is not easy to see that the *Results* Displayer is contained by the *SearchBookUI* FreeContainer. Considering these presentation modelling difficulties, this section introduces the UML*i* *user interface diagram*, a specialised object diagram used for the conceptual modelling of user interface presentation.

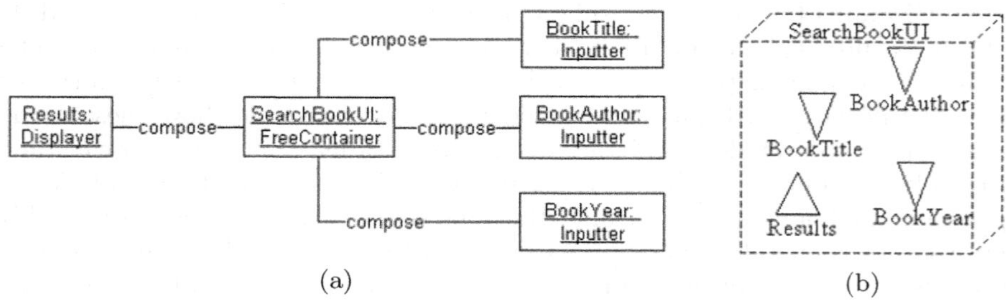

Fig. 2. An abstract presentation model for the SearchBookUI can be modelled as an object diagram of UML, as presented in (a). The same presentation can alternatively be modelled using the UML*i* user interface diagram, as presented in (b).

3.1 User Interface Diagram Notation

The *SearchBookUI* abstract presentation modelled using the user interface diagram is presented in Figure 2(b). The user interface diagram is composed of six constructors that specify the role of each interaction object in a UI presentation.

- `FreeContainers`, ⬚, are rendered as dashed cubes. They are top-level interaction objects that cannot be contained by any other interaction object, e.g. top-level windows. They are also called *presentation units* since the interaction objects in a FreeContainer are always presented at the same time. An interaction object can be visible and disabled, which means that the user can see the object but cannot interact with it.

- `Containers`, ⌸, are rendered as dashed cylinders. They can group interaction objects that are not FreeContainers. Containers provide a grouping mechanism for the designing of UI presentations.
- `Inputters`, ∇, are rendered as downward triangles. They are responsible for receiving information from users.
- `Displayers`, $\triangle$, are rendered as upward triangles. They are responsible for sending visual information to users.
- `Editors`, $\diamond$, are rendered as diamonds. They are interaction objects that are simultaneously Inputters and Displayers.
- `ActionInvokers`, ⊳, are rendered as a pair of semi-overlapped triangles pointing to the right. They are responsible for receiving information from users in the form of events.

Graphically, Containers, Inputters, Displayers, Editors and ActionInvokers must be placed into a FreeContainer. Additionally, the overlapping of the borders of interaction objects is not allowed. In this case, the "internal" lines of Containers and FreeContainers, in terms of their two-dimensional representations, are ignored.

3.2 From an Abstract to a Concrete Presentation

The complexity of user interface presentation modelling can be reduced by working with a restricted set of abstract interaction objects, as specified by the user interface diagram notation. However, a presentation modelling approach as proposed by the UML*i* user interface diagram is possible since form-based presentations respect the *Abstract Presentation Pattern*[1] (APP) in Figure 3. Thus, a user interface presentation can be described as an interaction object acting as a FreeContainer. The APP also shows the relationships between the abstract interaction objects.

As we can see, the APP is environment-independent. In fact, a UI presentation described using the user interface diagram can be implemented by any object-oriented programming language, using several toolkits. Widgets should be bound to the APP in order to generate a concrete presentation model. In this way, each widget should be classified as a `FreeContainer`, `Container`, `Inputter`, `Displayer`, `Editor` or `ActionInvoker`. The binding of widgets to the APP can be described using UML [3].

Widget binding is not efficient to yield a final user interface implementation. In fact, UML*i* is used for UI modelling and not for implementation. However, we believe that by integrating UI builders with UML*i*-based CASE tools we can

[1] The specialised constructors under the Inputter, Displayer, Editor and ActionInvoker classes in Figure 3 indicate that many concrete interaction objects (widgets) can be bound to each one of these classes. This constructor is an adaptation of a similar one used in Gamma *et al.* [4] (see page 233).

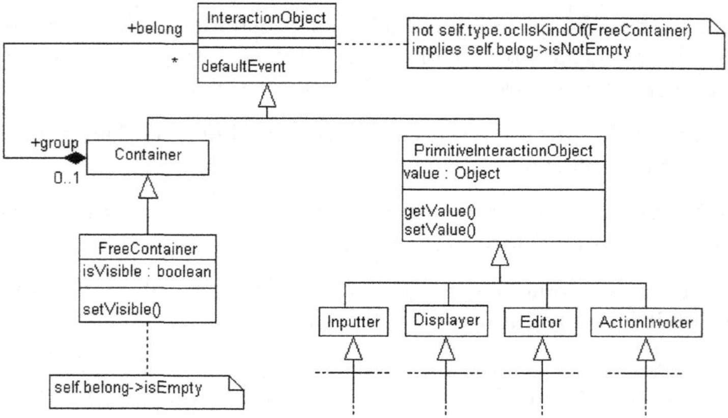

Fig. 3. The Abstract Presentation Pattern

produce environments where UIs can be modelled and developed in a systematic way. For instance, UI builder facilities may be required for adjusting UI presentation layout and interaction object's colour, size and font.

4 Activity Diagram Modelling

UML interaction diagrams (sequence and collaboration diagrams) are used for modelling how objects collaborate. Interaction diagrams, however, are limited in terms of workflow modelling since they are inherently sequential. Therefore, concurrent and repeatable workflows, and especially those workflows affected by users decisions, are difficult to model and interpret from interaction diagrams.

Workflows are easily modelled and interpreted using activity diagrams. In fact, Statechart constructors provide a graphical representation for concurrent and branching workflows. However, it is not so natural to model object collaboration in activity diagrams. Improving the ability to describe object collaboration and common interaction behaviour, UML*i* activity diagrams provide greater support for UI design than UML activity diagrams.

This section explains how activities can be modelled from use cases, how activity diagrams can be simplified in order to describe common interactive behaviours, and how interaction objects can be related to activity diagrams.

4.1 Use Cases and Use Case Scenarios

Use case diagrams are normally used to identify application functionalities. However, use case diagrams may also be used to identify interaction activities. For instance, a ≪*communicates*≫ association between a use case and an actor indicates that the actor is interacting with the use case. Therefore, for example, in Figure 4 the `CollectBook` use case cannot identify an interaction activity since its association with `Borrower` is not a ≪*communicates*≫ association. Indeed, the `CollectBook` use case identifies a functionality not supported by the application.

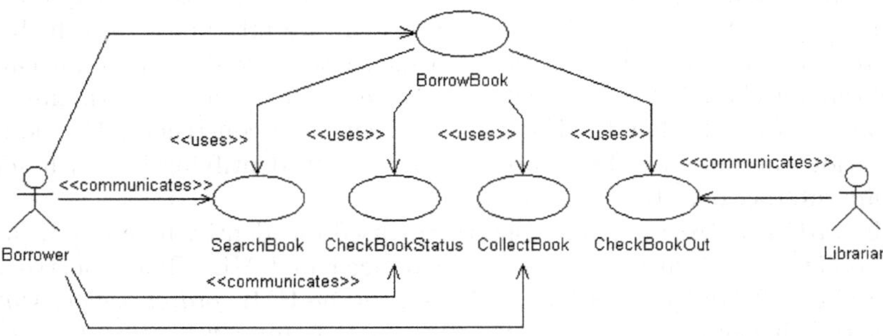

Fig. 4. A use case diagram for the `BorrowBook` use case with its component use cases.

Use case scenarios can be used for the elicitation of actions [12]. Indeed, actions are identified by scanning scenario descriptions looking for verbs. However, actions may be classified as Inputters, Displayers, Editors or ActionInvokers. For example, Figure 5 shows a scenario for the `SearchBook` use case in Figure 4. Three interaction objects can be identified in the scenario: $\underline{\nabla \textit{providing}}$ that receives book's title, author and year information; $\underline{\nabla \textit{specify}}$ that specifies some query details; and $\underline{\triangle \textit{displays}}$ that presents the results of the query. Therefore, UMLi can start the elicitation of interaction objects, using this transformation of actions into interaction objects, during requirements analysis. These action transformations are often possible since the interaction objects of UMLi are abstract ones. The elicitation of these interaction objects early, as describe here, is important since it provides an initial description for abstract presentations. Indeed, user interface diagrams can initially be composed of interaction objects elicited from scenarios.

John is looking for a book. He can check if such book is in the library catalogue $\underline{\nabla \textit{providing}}$ *its title, authors, year, or a combination of this information. Additionally, John can* $\underline{\nabla \textit{specify}}$ *if he wants an exact or an approximate match, and if the search should be over the entire catalogue or the result of the previous query. Once the query has been submitted, the system* $\underline{\triangle \textit{displays}}$ *the details of the matching books, if any.*

Fig. 5. A scenario for the `SearchBook` use case.

4.2 From Use Cases to Activities

UML*i* assumes that a set of activity diagrams can describe possible user interactions since this set can describe possible application workflows from application entry points. Indeed, transitions in activity diagrams are inter-object transitions, such as those transitions between interaction and domain objects that can describe interaction behaviours. Based on this assumption, those activity diagrams that belong to this set of activity diagrams can be informally classified as *interaction activity diagrams*. Activities of interaction activity diagrams can also be informally classified as *interaction activities*. The difficulty with this classification, however, is that UML does not specify any constructor for modelling application entry points. Therefore, the process of identifying in which activity diagram interactions start is unclear.

The *initial interaction state* constructor used for identifying an application's entry points in activity diagrams is introduced in UML*i*. This constructor is rendered as a solid square, ■, and it is used as the UML *initial pseudo-state* [9], except that it cannot be used within any state. A *top level interaction activity diagram* must contain at least one `initial interaction state`. Figure 6 shows a top level interaction activity diagram for a library application.

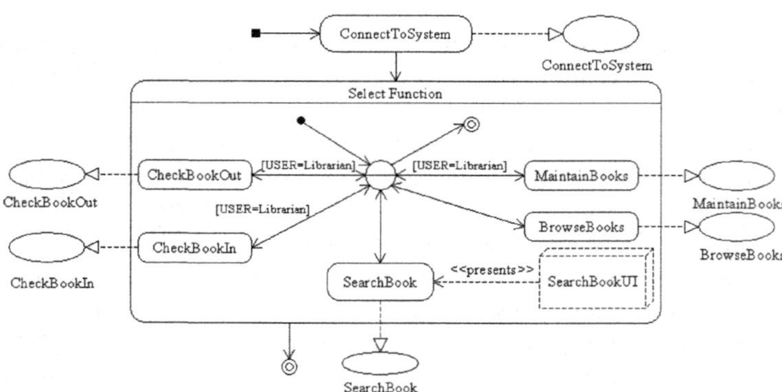

Fig. 6. Modelling an activity diagram from use cases using UML*i*.

Use cases that communicate directly with actors are considered *candidate interaction activities* in UML*i*. Thus, we can define a *top level interaction activity* as an activity which is related to a candidate interaction activity. This relationship between a top level interaction activity and a candidate interaction activity is described by a realisation relationship, since activity diagrams can describe details about the behaviour of candidate interaction activities. The diagram in Figure 6 is using the UML*i* activity diagram notation explained in the next section. However, we can clearly see in the diagram which top level interaction activity realises which candidate interaction activity. For instance, the `SearchBook` activity realises the `SearchBook` candidate interaction activity modelled in the use case diagram in Figure 4.

In terms of UI design, interaction objects elicited in scenarios are primitive interaction objects that must be contained by FreeContainers (see the APP in Figure 3). Further, these interaction objects should be contained by FreeContainers associated with top-level interaction activities, such as the `SearchBookUI` FreeContainer in Figure 6, for example. Therefore, interaction objects elicited from scenarios are initially contained by FreeContainers that are related to top-level interaction through the use of a ≪*presents*≫ object flow, as described in Section 4.4. In that way, UI elements can be imported from use case diagrams to activity diagrams. For example, the interaction objects elicited in Figure 5 are initially contained by the `SearchBookUI` presented in Figure 6.

4.3 Selection States

Statechart constructors for modelling transitions are very powerful since they can be combined in several ways, producing many different compound transitions. In fact, simple `transitions` are suitable for relating activities that can be executed sequentially. A combination of `transitions`, `forks` and `joins` is suitable for relating activities that can be executed in parallel. A combination of `transitions` and `branches` is suitable for modelling the situation when only one among many activities is executed (choice behaviour). However, for the designing of interactive applications there are situations where these constructors can be held to be rather low-level, leading to complex models. The following behaviours are common interactive application behaviours, but usually result in complex models.

- The `order independent` behaviour is presented in Figure 7(a). There, activities `A` and `B` are called *selectable activities* since they can be activated in either order on demand by users who are interacting with the application. Thus, every selectable activity should be executed once during the performance of an order independent behaviour. Further, users are responsible for selecting the execution order of selectable activities. An order independent behaviour should be composed of one or more selectable activities. An object with the execution history of each selectable activity (*SelectHist* in Figure 7(a)) is required for achieving such behaviour.
- The `optional` behaviour is presented in Figure 7(b). There, users can execute any selectable activity any number of times, including none. In this case, users should explicitly specify when they are finishing the `Select` activity. Like the order independent behaviour, the optional behaviour should be composed of one or more selectable activities.
- The `repeatable` behaviour is presented in Figure 7(c). Unlike the order independent and optional behaviours, a repeatable behaviour should have only one associated activity. `A` is the associated activity of the repeatable behaviour in Figure 7. Further, a specific number of times that the associated activity can be executed should be specified. In the case of the diagram in Figure 7(c), this number is identified by the value of `X`.

An optional behaviour with one selectable activity can be used when a selectable activity can be executed an unspecified number of times.

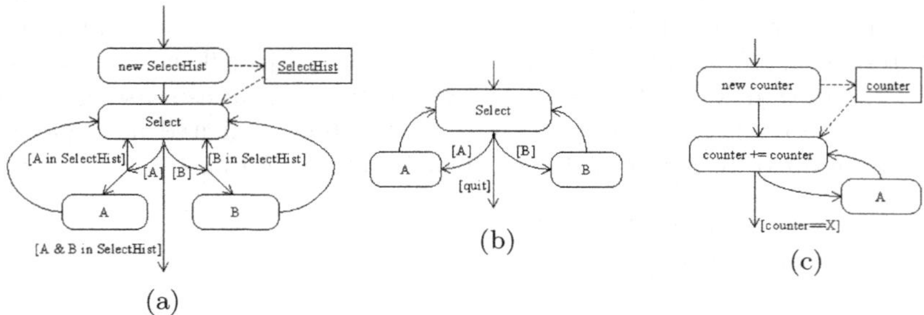

Fig. 7. The UML modelling of three common interaction application behaviours. An **`order independent`** behaviour is modelled in (a). An **`optional`** behaviour is modelled in (b). A **`repeatable`** behaviour is modelled in (c).

As optional, order independent and repeatable behaviours are common in interactive systems [5], UML*i* proposes a simplified notation for them. The notation used for modelling an order independent behaviour is presented in Figure 8(a). There we can see an *order independent selector*, rendered as a circle overlying a plus signal, $\oplus$, connected to the activities `A` and `B` by *return transitions*, rendered as solid lines with a single arrow at the selection state end and a double arrow at the selectable activity end. The order independent selector identifies an *order independent selection state.* The double arrow end of return transitions identify the selectable activities of the selection state. The distinction between the selection state and its selectable activities is required when selection states are also selectable activities. Furthermore, a return transition is equivalent of a pair of Statechart transitions, one single transition connecting the selection state to the selectable activity, and one non-guarded transition connecting the selectable activity to the selection state, as previously modelled in Figure 7(a). In fact, the order independent selection state notation can be considered as a macro-notation for the behaviour described in Figure 7(a).

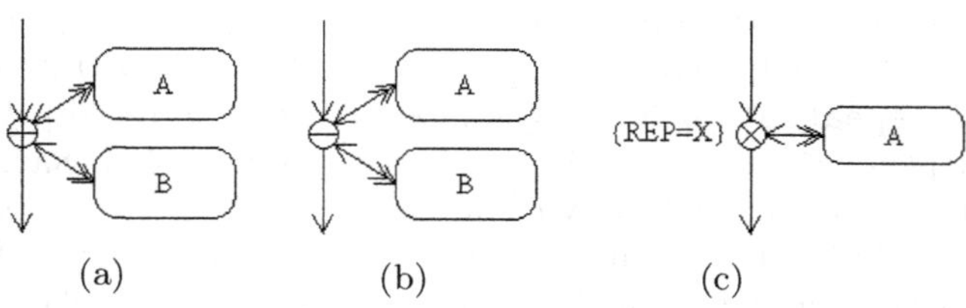

Fig. 8. The UML*i* modelling of an **`order independent`** selection state in (a), an **`optional`** selection state in (b), and a **`repeatable`** selection state in (c).

The notations for modelling optional and repeatable behaviours are similar, in terms of structure, to the order independent selection state. The main difference between the notation of selection states is the symbols used for their selectors. The *optional selector* which identifies an *optional selection state* is rendered as a circle overlaying a minus signal, $\ominus$. The *repeatable selector* which identifies a *repeatable selection state*[2] is rendered as a circle overlaying a times signal, $\otimes$. The repeatable selector additionally requires a `REP` constraint, as shown in Figure 8(c), used for specifying the number of times that the associated activity should be repeated. The value `X` in this `REP` constraint is the `X` parameter in Figure 7(c). The notations presented in Figures 8(b) and 8(c) can be considered as macro-notations for the notation modelling the behaviours presented in Figures 7(b) and 7(c).

4.4 Interaction Object Behaviour

Objects are related to activities using *object flows*. Object flows are basically used for indicating which objects are related to each activity, and if the objects are generated or used by the related activities. Object flows, however, do not describe the behaviour of related objects within their associated activities. Activities that are action states and that have object flows connected to them can describe the behaviour of related objects since they can describe how methods may be invoked on these objects. Thus, a complete decomposition of activities into action states may be required to achieve such object behaviour description. However, in the context of interaction objects, there are common functions that do not need to be modelled in detail to be understood. In fact, UML*i* provides five specialised object flows for interaction objects that can describe these common functions that an interaction object can have within a related activity. These object flows are modelled as stereotyped object flows and explained as follows.

- An ≪*interacts*≫ object flow relates a primitive interaction object to an action state, which is a primitive activity. Further, the object flow indicates that the action state involved in the object flow is responsible for an interaction between a user and the application. This can be an interaction where the user is invoking an object operation or visualising the result of an object operation. The action states in the `SpecifyBookDetails` activity, Figure 9, are examples of Inputters assigning values to some attributes of the `SearchQuery` domain object. The △ `Results` in Figure 9 is an example of a Displayer for visualising the result of `SearchQuery.SearchBook()`. As can be observed, there are two abstract operations specified in the APP (Figure 3) that have been used in conjunction with these interaction objects. The `setValue()` operation is used by Displayers for setting the values that are going to be presented to the users. The `getValue()` op-

[2] UML*i* considers a *repeatable selection state* as a "selection" state since users might have the possibility of cancelling the repeatable state iteration.

eration is used by Inputters for passing the value obtained from the users to domain objects.

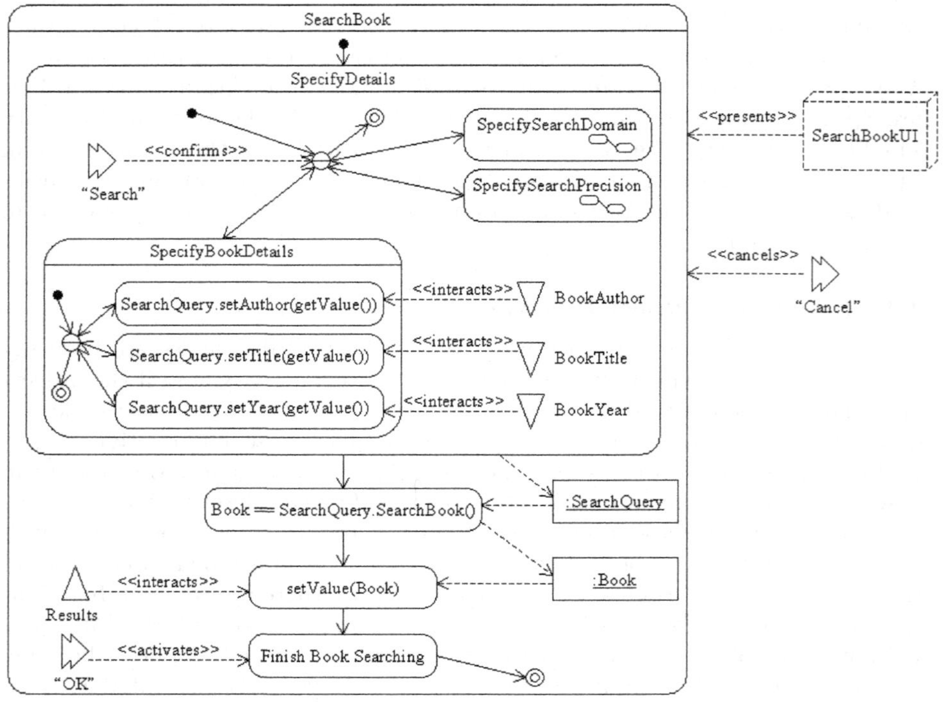

Fig. 9. The `SearchBook` activity.

- A ≪*presents*≫ object flow relates a FreeContainer to an activity. It specifies that the FreeContainer should be visible while the activity is active. Therefore, the invocation of the abstract `setVisible()` operation of the FreeContainer is entirely transparent for the developers. In Figure 9 the `SearchBookUI` FreeContainer and its contents are visible while the `SearchBook` activity is active.
- A ≪*confirms*≫ object flow relates an ActionInvoker to a selection state. It specifies that the selection state has finished normally. In Figure 9 the event associated with the ▷"Search" is responsible for finishing the execution of its related selection state normally. An optional selection state must have one ≪*confirms*≫ object flow directly or indirectly related to it. The optional selection state in the `SpecifyDetails` activity in Figure 9 has the ▷"Search" directly related to it. The optional selection state in the `SpecifyBookDetails` relies on the ▷"Search" that is indirectly related to it. In fact, confirming the optional selection state in

SpecifyDetails a user is also confirming the optional selection state in SpecifyBookDetails.

- A ≪*cancels*≫ object flow relates an ActionInvoker to any composite activity or selection state. It specifies that the activity or selection state has not finished normally. The flow of control should be re-routed to a previous state. The ⇨"Cancel" object in Figure 9 is responsible for identifying the user cancelling of the SearchBook activity.
- An ≪*activate*≫ object flow relates an ActionInvoker to an activity. In that way, the associated activity becomes a triggered activity, that waits for an event to effectively start, after being activated. This event that triggers the activity is the defaultEvent presented in the APP (Figure 3).

5 Using UMLi: Method and Case Study

The UMLi method is composed of eight steps. These steps are not intended to describe a comprehensive method for the modelling of a UI in an integrated way with the underlying application. For example, these steps could be adapted to be incorporated by traditional UML modelling methods such as Objectory and Catalysis.

A case study describing a Library Application [3] is used for exemplifying the use of the UMLi method. Many results of this case study are used as examples of the UMLi notation in previous sections.

Step 1 *User requirement modelling. Use cases can identify application functionalities. Use cases may be decomposed into other use cases. Scenarios provide a description of the functionalities provided by use cases.*

The use cases in Figure 4 identified some application functionalities. Scenarios can be used as a textual description of the use case goals. For instance, the scenario presented in Figure 5 is a textual description of the SearchBook use case in Figure 4. Further, scenarios can be used for the elicitation of sub-goals that can be modelled as use cases. Use cases that are sub-goals of another use case can be related using the ≪*uses*≫ dependency. Thus, the use of ≪*uses*≫ dependencies creates a hierarchy of use cases. For instance, SearchBook is a sub-goal of BorrowBook in Figure 4.

Step 2 *Interaction object elicitation. Scenarios of less abstract use cases may be used for interaction object elicitation.*

Scenarios can be used for the elicitation of interaction objects, as described in Section 4.1. In this case, elicited interaction objects are related to the associated use case. Relating interaction objects directly to use cases can prevent the elicitation of the same interaction object in two or more scenarios related to the same use case. Considering that there are different levels of abstraction for use cases, as described in Step 1, it was identified by the case study that interaction objects of abstract use cases are also very abstract, and may not be useful for exporting to activity diagrams. Therefore, the UML*i* method suggests that interaction objects can be elicited from less abstract use cases.

Step 3 *Candidate interaction activity identification.*

Candidate interaction activities are use cases that communicate directly with actors, as described in Section 4.1.

Step 4 *Interaction activity modelling. A top level interaction activity diagram can be designed from identified candidate interaction activities. A top level interaction activity diagram must contain at least one initial interaction state.*

Figure 6 shows a top level interactive activity diagram for the Library case study. Top level interaction activities may occasionally be grouped into more abstract interaction activities. In Figure 6, many top level interaction activities are grouped by the `SelectFunction` activity. In fact, `SelectFunction` was created to gather these top level interaction activities within a top level interaction activity diagram. However, the top level interaction activities, and not the `SelectFunction` activity, remain responsible for modelling some of the major functionalities of the application. The process of moving from candidate interaction activities to top level interaction activities is described in Section 4.2.

Step 5 *Interaction activity refining. Activity diagrams can be refined, decomposing activities into action states and specifying object flows.*

Activities can be decomposed into sub-activities. The activity decomposition can continue until the action states (leaf activities) are reached. For instance, Figure 9 presents a decomposition of the `SearchBook` activity introduced in Figure 6. The use of ≪*interacts*≫ object flows relating interaction objects to action states indicates the end of this step.

Step 6 *User interface modelling. User interface diagrams can be refined to support the activity diagrams.*

User interface modelling should happen simultaneously with Step 5 in order to provide the activity diagrams with the interaction objects required for describing action states. There are two mechanisms that allow UI designers to refine a conceptual UI presentation model.

- The inclusion of complementary interaction objects allows designers to improve the user's interaction with the application.
- The *grouping* mechanism allows UI designers to create groups of interaction objects using Containers.

At the end of this step it is expected that we have a conceptual model of the user interface. The interaction objects required for modelling the user interface were identified and grouped into Containers and FreeContainers. Moreover, the interaction objects identified were related to domain objects using action states and UML*i* flow objects.

Step 7 *Concrete presentation modelling. Concrete interaction objects can be bound to abstract interaction objects.*

The concrete presentation modelling begins with the binding of concrete interaction objects (widgets) to the abstract interaction objects that are specified by the APP. Indeed, the APP is flexible enough to map many widgets to each abstract interaction object.

Step 8 *Concrete presentation refinement. User interface builders can be used for refining user interface presentations.*

The widget binding alone is not enough for modelling a concrete user interface presentation. Ergonomic rules presented as UI design guidelines can be used to automate the generation of the user interface presentation. Otherwise, the concrete presentation model can be customised manually, for example, by using direct manipulation.

6 Conclusions

UML*i* is a UML extension for modelling interactive applications. UML*i* makes extensive use of activity diagrams during the design of interactive applications. Well-established links between use case diagrams and activity diagrams explain how user requirements identified during requirements analysis are described in the application design. The UML*i* user interface diagram introduced for modelling abstract user interface presentations simplifies the modelling of the use of visual components (widgets). Additionally, the UML*i* activity diagram notation provides a way for modelling the relationship between visual components of the user interface and domain objects. Finally, the use of selection states in activity diagrams provides a simplification for modelling interactive systems.

The reasoning behind the creation of each new UML*i* constructor and constraint has been presented throughout this paper. The UML*i* notation was entirely modelled in accordance to the UML*i* meta-model specifications [2]. This demonstrates that UML*i* is respecting its principle of being a non-intrusive extension of UML, since the UML*i* meta-model does not replace the functionalities of any UML constructor [2]. Moreover, the presented case study indicates that UML*i* may be an appropriate approach in order to improve UML's support for UI design. In fact, the UIs of the presented case study were modelled using fewer and simpler diagrams than using standard UML diagrams only, as described in [3].

As the UML*i* meta-model does not modify the semantics of the UML meta-model, UML*i* is going to be implemented as a plug-in feature of the ARGO/UML case tool. This implementation of UML*i* will allow further UML*i* evaluations using more complex case studies.

Acknowledgements. The first author is sponsored by Conselho Nacional de Desenvolvimento Científico e Tecnológico - CNPq (Brazil) – Grant 200153/98-6.

References

1. F. Bodart, A. Hennebert, J. Leheureux, I. Provot, B. Sacre, and J. Vanderdonckt. Towards a Systematic Building of Software Architectures: the TRIDENT Methodological Guide. In *Design, Specification and Verification of Interactive Systems*, pages 262–278, Vienna, 1995. Springer. 119
2. P. Pinheiro da Silva. On the Semantics of the Unified Modeling Language for Interactive Applications. In preparation. 118, 131, 131
3. P. Pinheiro da Silva and N. Paton. User Interface Modelling with UML. In *Proceedings of the 10th European-Japanese Conference on Information Modelling and Knowledge Representation*, Saariselkä, Finland, May 2000. IOS Press. (To appear). 118, 118, 120, 121, 129, 131
4. E. Gamma, R. Helm, R. Johnson, and J. Vlissides. *Design Patterns: Elements of Reusable Object-Oriented Software*. Addison-Wesley, Reading, MA, 1995. 121
5. T. Griffiths, P. Barclay, J. McKirdy, N. Paton, P. Gray, J. Kennedy, R. Cooper, C. Goble, A. West, and M. Smyth. Teallach: A Model-Based User Interface Development Environment for Object Databases. In *Proceedings of UIDIS'99*, pages 86–96, Edinburgh, UK, September 1999. IEEE Press. 119, 126
6. P. Johnson. *Human Computer Interaction: Psychology, Task Analysis and Software Engineering*. McGraw-Hill, Maidenhead, UK, 1992. 117
7. S. Kovacevic. UML and User Interface Modeling. In *Proceedings of UML'98*, pages 235–244, Mulhouse, France, June 1998. ESSAIM. 118
8. B. Myers. User Interface Software Tools. *ACM Transactions on Computer-Human Interaction*, 2(1):64–103, March 1995. 117
9. Object Management Group. *OMG Unified Modeling Language Specification*, June 1999. Version 1.3. 117, 124
10. M. B. Rosson. Integrating Development of Task and Object Models. *Communications of the ACM*, 42(1):49–56, January 1999. 117
11. P. Szekely. Retrospective and Challenges for Model-Bases Interface Development. In *Computer-Aided Design of User Interfaces*, pages xxi–xliv, Namur, Belgium, 1996. Namur University Press. 118
12. R. Tam, D. Maulsby, and A. Puerta. U-TEL: A Tool for Eliciting User Task Models from Domain Experts. In *Proceedings of Intelligent User Interfaces'98*, pages 77–80, San Francisco, CA, January 1998. ACM Press. 123

A Diagrammatic Tool for Representing User Interaction in UML

Patrícia Vilain[1,2], Daniel Schwabe[1], Clarisse Sieckenius de Souza[1]

[1] Depto. de Informática, PUC-Rio, Rua Marques de São Vicente 225
Rio de Janeiro, RJ 22453-900 Brazil
{vilain, schwabe, clarisse}@inf.puc-rio.br
[2] Depto. de Informática e Estatística, UFSC, Campus Universitário
Florianópolis, SC 88040-900 Brazil
vilain@inf.ufsc.br

Abstract. The UML suggests the employment of use cases for capturing the requirements and for specifying the interaction between the users and the system being modeled. Use cases are easily understood by users since they are essentially textual descriptions, but lack the precision and the conciseness accomplished by the other diagrammatic tools of UML. Besides, there is no systematic method that helps the designer to obtain such UML diagrams from a set of use cases. In this paper we present a diagrammatic tool to represent the users/system interaction called User Interaction Diagram (UID). UIDs have proven to be a valuable tool to gather requirements since they describe the exchange of information between the system and the user in a high level of abstraction, without considering specific user interface aspects and design details as in other UML diagrams. We show how UIDs can be incorporated into the requirements and analysis workflows of the Unified Process for software development.

1 Introduction

Interaction is the communication activity that takes place between the user and the system [8]. From the user-system interaction, it is possible to identify the information manipulated by the system and the functionality that the system must offer. Thus, the specification of the user-system interaction is fundamental to the development of the system, mainly for requirements gathering.

In the Unified Modeling Language (UML), interaction is seen as the exchange of messages between system objects [1], which differs from the concept we use here in that the exchange occurs between the user and the system. Thus, the UML diagrams representing the interaction, such as the sequence diagrams, collaboration diagrams, statechart diagrams, and activity diagrams, are more appropriately used during system design. For the requirements gathering, the UML suggests the employment of use cases to model user interaction instead of using those diagrammatic tools.

A. Evans, S. Kent and B. Selic (Eds.): «UML» 2000, LNCS 1939, pp. 133-147, 2000.

Use cases are defined as different ways of using the system [5] [6]. They deal only with the interaction between the user and the system or with the information perceptible by the user, and they do not deal with the internal aspects of the system. Use cases have gained wide acceptance, and are used to specify the software requirements as well as the basis for the development cycle, including the analysis, design, implementation and testing activities [5] [7].

Although other approaches for requirements gathering employ use cases [2] [10], this may not be the best tool for this purpose. Use cases employ textual descriptions, which are unwieldy when used in a validation process with users, mainly because of the lack of precision and conciseness. Graphical notations, on the other hand, do not suffer from these shortcomings, and are well suited for requirements gathering. However, we are not aware of any graphical technique that represents the user/system interaction sequence specified in use cases independently of design aspects.

We propose a diagrammatic modeling tool, User Interaction Diagrams (UID), to represent the interaction between the user and the system. UIDs are a tool used mainly to support the communication between the designer and users in requirements gathering. In addition, during system analysis, UIDs also serve as input for obtaining the class diagram. UIDs can also be used as a basis for the design of Web-based applications, as described in [4]. Also, we propose an extension of The Unified Process [5], where UIDs and the guidelines to obtain the class diagram from these UIDs are incorporated in the requirements and analysis workflows. In this proposal, requirements are expressed as a powerful combination of use cases and UIDs, and are also employed as a validation tool during requirements gathering. Thus, we can have increased confidence that the information represented in the class diagram will be correct and complete.

The UIDs presented in this work are taken from a case study about an online CD shop. This case study involved 6 participant users and resulted in 14 use cases and 14 UIDs. Other projects in which UIDs have been applied resulted in much large numbers of use cases and UIDs.

The remainder of paper is organized as follows. Section 2 presents the user interaction diagram. Section 3 shows how to define UIDs from use cases. Section 4 presents rules to obtain the class diagram using as basis the UIDs. In section 5, an extension of the Unified Process is proposed and section 6 highlights our conclusions.

2 User Interaction Diagrams

A user interaction diagram (UID) represents the interaction between the user and the system. This diagram describes only the exchange of information between the system and the user, without considering specific user interface aspects. It depicts the interaction information that is textually described in a use case.

Next, we present some examples of UIDs; the complete notation of the UID is shown in the appendix. Fig. 1 shows the UID that has been defined to represent the interaction in the task *Selection of a CD based on a given title.*

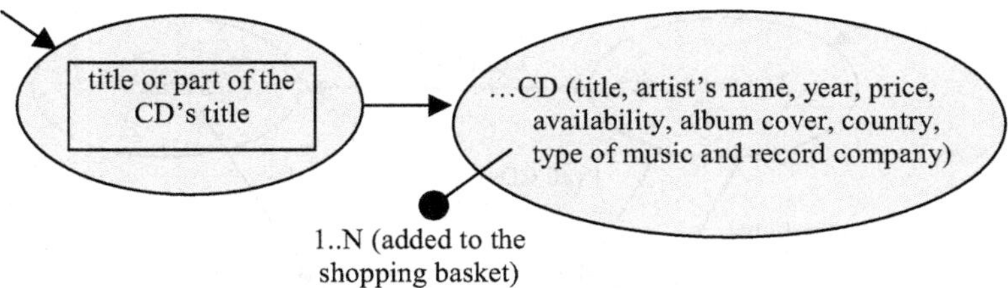

Fig. 1. Selection of a CD based on a given title: UID

The ellipses represent the interaction between the user and the system. The interaction begins with the ellipse that has the arrow without a source. In this example, the user must enter the title of the CD, denoted by a rectangle with a continuous border. After the user enters the title of the CD, the system presents the set of CDs that match the user's input. The results of each interaction that causes processing in the system should be represented as a separate ellipse, connected to the preceding interaction by an arrow.

In the example, since the presentation of the set of CDs implies processing in the system, the resulting set is represented in another interaction that is connected to the previous by an arrow. A *set* of CDs is represented by ellipsis in front of the set name (*...CD* in the example). For each CD shown by the system, the following data items are given: *title, artist's name, year, price, availability, album cover, country, and record company*, shown within parenthesis next to the item's name. From this last interaction, it is possible to select 1 to N CDs and execute the operation of adding them to the shopping basket, which is represented by the line connected to the text *1..N (add to the shopping basket)* with a black bullet in one end.

Fig. 2 shows the UID that has been defined to represent the interactions in the task *Selection of a CD based on the type of music*. In this example, at the first interaction, the system presents a set of types of music, represented by the label *.Type of mus ic*. After this interaction, the user must select one type of music followed by the choice of one of the following options: *artists, all CDs, suggestions*. The selection of a single type of music is represented by the number 1 attached to the outgoing arrow.

If the user selects the option *artists*, then the interaction that shows the set of artists (for the chosen type of music) occurs. Following this interaction, the user must select one artist and the system shows the CDs related to this artist.

If the user selects the option *suggestions*, then the system shows the CDs that are recommended for the chosen type of music. If the user selects the option *all CDs*, then the system shows all CDs under the chosen type of music.

For each of the CDs shown by the system, the following data items are given: *title, artist's name, year, price, availability, image cover, country, and record company*.

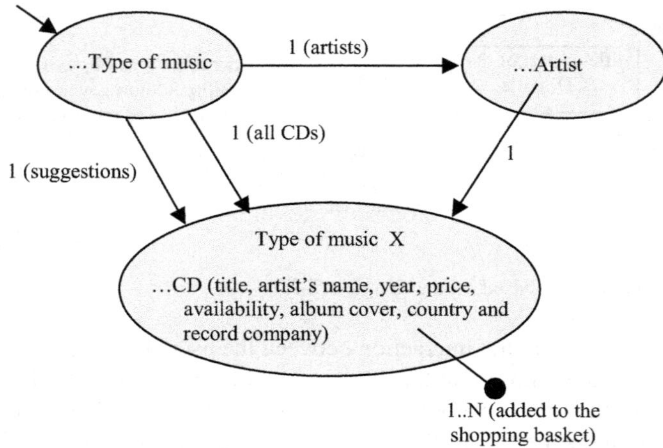

Fig. 2. Selection of a CD based on the type of music: UID

Fig. 3 shows the UID that has been defined to represent the interaction in the task *Buying the selected CDs*.

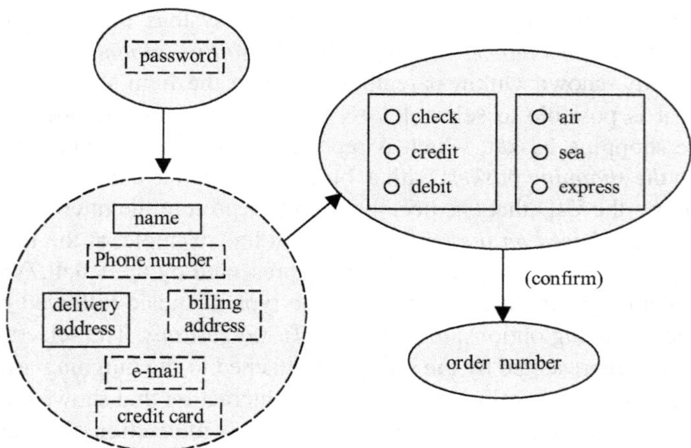

Fig. 3. Buying the selected CDs: UID

In the first interaction the user may enter his password. This data item is optional and is represented by a rectangle with a dashed border. If the user enters a valid password the second interaction does not occur. Thus, this interaction is represented by a dashed border as well.

If the second interaction occurs, the user must enter the mandatory data items, namely *name* and *delivery address*, and the optional data items, *phone number, bill-*

ing address, e-mail, credit card. Provided the user enters at least the mandatory data items, the third interaction occurs.

In the third interaction, the user must select the payment option by *check, credit,* or *debit,* and the shipping method, namely *air, sea* or *express.* After the user enters these data items, the user can execute the operation confirming the purchase, followed by the system returning the order number, which is represented as another interaction.

3 From Use Cases to User Interaction Diagrams

According to the UML, sequence diagrams, collaboration diagrams, and statechart diagrams can specify the realizations of use cases [1]. However, the specification of use cases using these techniques is a workaround for not having an appropriate tool and may unexpectedly anticipate some design decisions. Thus, we propose to use UIDs to represent the interaction described by use cases.

In order to obtain a UID from a given use case, the sequence of information exchanged between the user and the system must be identified and organized into interactions. Identifying this information exchange is crucial since it is the basis for the definition of the UID.

In this section, we present a method to map a use case to a UID. To exemplify the application of this method, we show the mapping of the use case *Selecting a CD based on a given artist's name* into a UID.

Use Case Selecting a CD based on a given artist's name: *The user enters the name of the artist or part of it. He can inform the year or period of the CD being sough if he wants to. The system returns a set with the names of the artists matching the value entered. The user selects the artist of interest. The system returns a set with the CDs by the artist. For every CD found, the title, name of the artist, year, price, availability, image of the album cover, country, and record company are shown. If the user wishes to buy one or more CDs, he selects the CDs and adds to the shopping basket to perform the purchase later (use case Purchase).*

Step 1. We start by analyzing the use case to identify what information is exchanged between the user and the system. Generally these data items are represented by nouns. It is also important to identify which data items are given by the user and which are returned by the system.

In the example, we can identify the following information exchanged between the user and the system: *name of the artist or part of the name* (user), *the year or period of the CD being sought* (user); *a set with the names of the artists matching the value entered* (system), *the artist of interest* (user); *a set with the CDs by the artist, for every CD found, the title, name of the artist, year, price, availability, image of the album cover, country and record company* (system).

Step 2. After identifying the information exchanged, we have to split the data items into interactions. Data items are placed in the same interaction, unless they require processing by the system before being presented; in such cases they are placed in another interaction. Next, we try to place the remaining data items in this interaction, and so on. To keep track of the sequence among the interactions, each new interaction yielded by this process is temporarily given an order number.

In the example, we begin with the *name of the artist or part of it* data item, which is placed in the first interaction of the UID. The next data item exchanged, *the year or period of the CD sought*, given by the user, does not require processing by the system, so it can be placed in the same interaction as the previous data item. Since the next data item exchanged, *set with the names of the artists*, is returned by the system after processing a query over the artists database, it is placed in a second interaction. The next data item exchanged, *the artist of interest*, requires the system to verify the selection of an artist given by the user. Thus, it will be shown in the third interaction. The last data items (*the title, name of the artist, year, price, availability, image of the album cover, country and record company*) are returned by the system as a result of the same processing as selection of the artist. Consequently, they are also placed in the third interaction.

Step 3. The data items given by the user and returned by the system must be distinguished. Mandatory data items given by the user are placed into rectangles with a continuous border and the optional data items are placed into rectangles with a dashed border. The data items returned by the system are placed directly in the interaction, without rectangles around them. The data items that are associated with an element are placed inside parenthesis and the set of elements is represented by ellipsis before the set's name.

In the example, in the first interaction, since the *name of the artist or part of it* data item is mandatory data entered by the user, it is placed inside a rectangle with a continuous border. The *year or period of the CD sought* data item is optional, so it is represented inside a rectangle with a dashed border. In the second interaction, since the *set with the names of the artists* data item is returned by the system it is placed directly in the interaction preceded by an ellipsis. In the third interaction, despite the fact that *artist of interest* data item depends on the user selection, it is presented by the system, and therefore it is represented directly in the interaction. The set of CDs is also represented in the interaction preceded by an ellipsis. The other data items are related to each CD, so, they are placed within parenthesis next to the CD.

Fig. 4 presents the first, second and third interactions with their data items.

Phase 4. The interactions are connected by arrows. When interactions are connected, the target interaction must have a sequence number greater than that of the source interaction. It is possible to connect one interaction to two or more interactions, thus representing several alternative succeeding interactions. In this case, the information entered by the user determines which of the alternative interactions occurs next. If the change of interaction is the result of an element selection, the number of selected elements is attached to the arrow, and the source of this arrow is the set from which the selected elements are taken. The initial interaction always has an arrow without source.

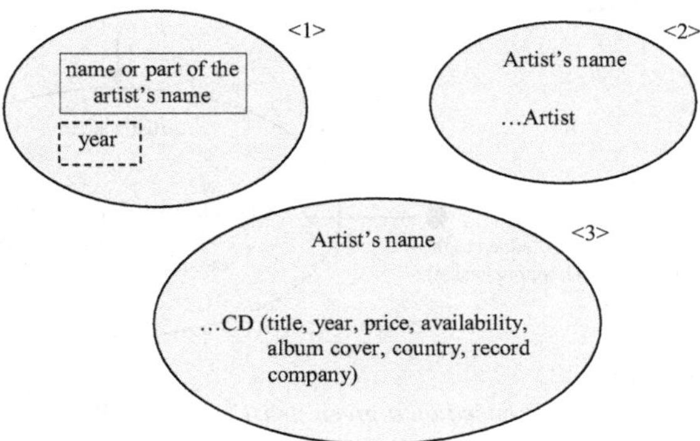

Fig. 4. Use case *Selecting a CD based on a given artist's name*: interactions and data items

In the example, since the second interaction occurs after all the data items in the first interaction have been entered, the source of the arrow connecting the first interaction to the second interaction is attached to the whole interaction. The third interaction occurs after the user has selected exactly one artist, so the arrow connecting the second and third interactions has the number 1 attached to it, and its source is the set of artists (and not the entire interaction).

Phase 5. The operations performed over the data items must also be identified. They are generally represented in the use cases by verbs. An operation is represented in the diagram by a line with a bullet. If after the execution of the operation another interaction occurs, then the operation is represented attached to the arrow instead of the line.

In the example, the last information presented in the use case is an operation that allows the user to include the selected CDs in the shopping basket. Note that the line representing this operation is connected to the set of CDs indicating that set serves as input for the operation. The number of CDs selected and the operation are placed next to the line. The name of the operation is placed inside parenthesis.

Phase 6. Non-functional requirements are not specified in UIDs. Although use cases do not specify these requirements, sometimes a non-functional requirement can appear. In this case, it should appear attached to the UID as text.

Fig. 5 represents the complete UID.

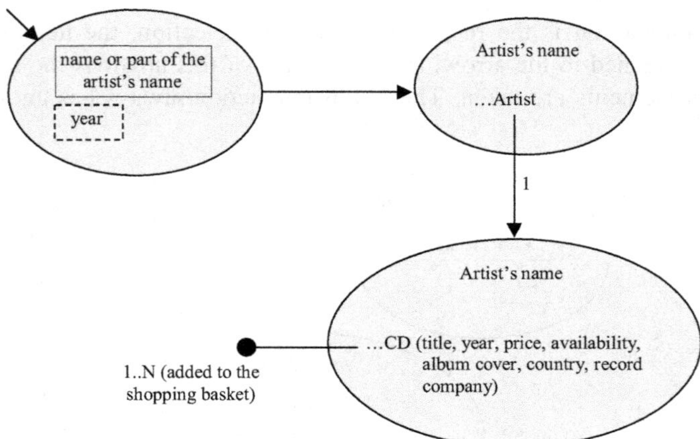

Fig. 5. Use case *Selecting a CD based on a given artist's name*: UID

4 Specifying the Class Diagram

The class diagram is defined according to some guidelines that are applied to the UIDs. Some of these guidelines are resultant from adapting schema normalization techniques [3] to UID elements. The rules to obtain a class diagram from UIDs are the following:

1. For each UID, define a class for each element, set element and specific element. For each defined class, assume the existence of an identifier attribute OID.
2. For each data item of the set elements that appears in each UID, define an attribute according to the following:
   Verify if the data item is functionally dependent[1] on the OID in each class, i.e., if OID data item. Verify if the data item is not transitively dependent[2] on the OID. If these conditions are satisfied, then the data item must become an attribute of the class. The verification should preferably begin with the class that represents the set, because there is a higher probability that this data item be an attribute of this class.

---

1 Defined in [3] as "A functional dependency, denoted by X Y, between two sets of attributes X and Y that are subsets of R specifies a constraint on the possible tuples that can form a relation instance r of R. The constraint states that, for any two tuples t_1 and t_2 in r such that $t_1[X] = t_2[X]$, we must also have $t_1[Y] = t_2[Y]$. This means that the values of the Y component of a tuple in r depend on, or are determined by, the values of the X component; or alternatively, the values of the X component of a tuple uniquely (or functionally) determine the values of the Y component. We also say that there is a functional dependency from X to Y or that Y is functionally dependent on X."

2 Defined in [3] as "A functional dependency X Y in a relation schema R is a transitive dependency if there is a set of attributes Z that is not a subset of any key of R, and both X Z and Z Y hold."

Verify if the data item is functionally dependent on the OID of two or more different classes and if the data item is not transitively dependent on these OIDs. If these conditions are satisfied, then the data item must become an attribute of an association between the classes.
If the data item is not functionally dependent on the OID of any existent class, or if it is only transitively dependent of existent OIDs, a new class needs to be defined with its own OID. The data item must be added as an attribute of the newly created class.

3. For each data item entered by the user, represented by an single rectangle, define an attribute according to the following:
Verify if the data item is functionally dependent on the OID in each class, i.e., if OID data item. Verify if the data item is not transitively dependent on the OID. If these conditions are satisfied, then the data item must become an attribute of the class. The verification should begin preferably with the class that represents the set, because there is a higher probability that this data item be an attribute of this class.
Verify if the data item is functionally dependent on the OID of two or more different classes and if the data item is not transitively dependent on these OIDs. If these conditions are satisfied, then the data item must become an attribute of an association between the classes.
If the data item is not functionally dependent on the OID of any existent class, or if it is only transitively dependent of existent OIDs, a new class needs to be defined with its own OID. The data item must be added as an attribute of the newly created class.
4. For each attribute *a* that appears in a set different from its class, proceed as the following:
If the OID of the class of *a* functionally depends on the OID of the class corresponding to the set and the OID of the class of *a* does not depend transitively on that OID, create an association between the class that contains *a* and the class representing the set. The maximum cardinality of the class that contains *a* in the association is 1. Verify if the resulting association is semantically correct (i.e. if it makes sense in the domain being modeled).
If the OID of the class of *a* functionally depends on the OID of the class of another attribute *b* in the same set, but the OID of the class of *a* does not depend transitively on that OID, create an association between the class that contains *a* and the class that contains *b*. The maximum cardinality of the class that contains *a* in the association is 1. Verify if the resulting association is semantically correct (i.e. if it makes sense in the domain being modeled).
5. For each interaction flow (represented by an arrow), if there are different classes in the source interaction and the target interaction, define an association between these classes. It is also necessary to verify if this association is semantically correct (i.e. if it makes sense in the domain being modeled).
If N elements can be selected in the source interaction, then the maximum cardinality of the source interaction class is N.

If a set of elements can be returned in the target interaction, then the maximum cardinality of the target interaction class is N.
If the element or set of elements returned in the target interaction is optional (i.e the element or set in the target interaction can be empty), then the minimal cardinality of the target interaction class is 0.

6. For each operation that appears connected to an element or set, if it is an operation of the corresponding class, add it to that class.
7. At the end of the process, do the necessary adjustments in the resulting class diagram, for instance, identify generalizations and missing association cardinalities.

We next show some steps of the definition of the class diagram synthesized from the UIDs in the case study. Due to space constraints, the use cases were not included in this paper.

Step 1: Definition of the classes. In each UID, a class was defined for each element, set element and specific element. The following classes were identified for each UID:

CD: UIDs 1, 3, 4, 5, 6, 7, 8, 9, 10, 11, 12, 13, 14	Composer: UID 10
Song: UIDs 1, 5, 6	Music: UID 10
Artist: UIDs 4, 7	Purchase: UID 2
Type of music: UID 7	

Step 2: Definition of the attributes. The following attributes were identified from the information of the set elements of the UIDs:

CD: title, year, price, availability, album cover, country, price-offer, record company	Composer : name
Song: time	Music: title, lyrics
Artist: name	Purchase: number
Type of music: name	CD – Purchase: quantity

Step 3: Definition of the attributes. The following attributes were identified from the information entered by the users:

CD: title, year	Composer: name
Song: -	Music: title, sample
Artist: name	Purchase: payment-option, shipping method, delivery-address
Type of music: name	Person: name, e-mail, password, phone number, billing address, credit-card

The class Person had to be created in this step in order to hold the attributes corresponding to the data items entered by the users.

Step 4: Definition of the associations. The following associations were identified from the attributes belonging to distinct classes but appearing as data items of the same set:

Composer 1 - Music	Artist 1 - CD
Music 1 - Song	CD - 1 Type of music
Song - 1 Artist	

Step 5: Definition of the associations. The following associations were identified from the different classes presented in the source and target interactions:

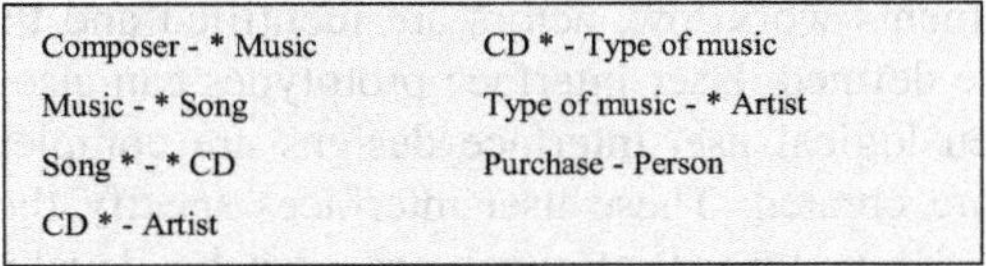

Composer - * Music
CD * - Type of music
Music - * Song
Type of music - * Artist
Song * - * CD
Purchase - Person
CD * - Artist

Step 6: Definition of the operations. The following operations were identified from the UIDs:

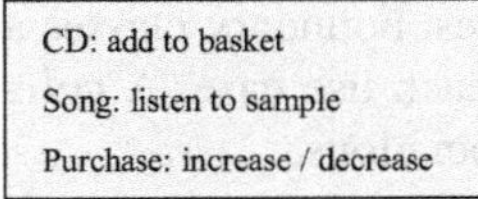

CD: add to basket
Song: listen to sample
Purchase: increase / decrease

Fig. 6 shows the class diagram that results from the six steps:

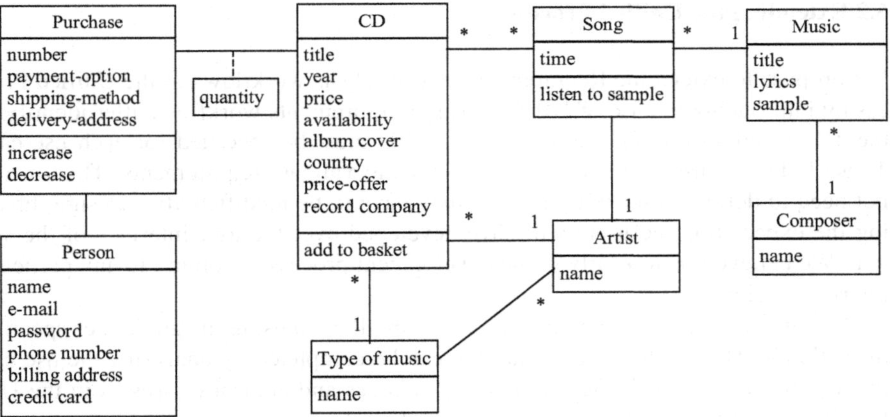

Fig. 6. Final resulting class diagram

5 UIDs within the Unified Process

In this section, we propose extending the Unified Process to include UIDs and the definition of the class diagram from UIDs. This extension is applied specifically to the Requirements and Analysis workflows.

5.1 Unified Process

Application development according to the Unified Process [5] is divided into several cycles. Each cycle results in a product and is composed by four phases: inception, elaboration, construction and transition. Over these phases, five workflows take place: Requirements, Analysis, Design, Implementation, and Test.

During Requirements workflow, actors are identified and the use cases in which each actor plays are defined. User-interface prototypes can also be used to gather the requirements. When logical user-interface designs are complete, the physical user-interface designs are created. These user-interfaces specify the interaction between human actors and the system. Prototypes can also be developed for some of the physical user-interfaces.

During Analysis workflow, classes and associations needed to realize the use case are suggested. The entity classes, boundary classes and control classes are defined by examining the description of each use case. A collaboration diagram is also defined based on these classes and associations.

5.2 Extending the Unified Process

We propose to extend the Requirements and Analysis workflows of the Unified Process by introducing the use of UIDs. During Requirements workflow, after identifying the actors and specifying the use cases, a UID must be specified for each use case. These UIDs are used together with use cases to validate requirements. Thus, we do not need to define a user-interface that may have to be modified after Design, breaking the expectation the users will have developed over the user-interface of the system. We believe it is too early in the development process to commit to any particular interface design.

During Analysis workflow, entity classes are defined using the guidelines specified in section 4. The resulting class diagram can be completed by analyzing the use case descriptions and by defining the boundary classes and control classes as in the Unified Process. Thus, for each human actor, entity class, and external system actor, one boundary class is defined. For each use case, it is necessary to verify if one or more control classes are required. The attributes of boundary and control classes can be gathered as in the Unified Process, looking at the entity classes and their attributes. To complete the Analysis, the collaboration diagram is defined as in the Unified Process.

The succeeding workflows proceed in the same way as the Unified Process workflows.

6 Conclusion

We have presented UIDs, a graphical notation that represent the interaction between the user and the system. UIDs have been proposed as a higher abstraction level tool that can be used without concern over user interface and design details. Further, UIDs can also be used to validate use cases and constitute the basis for the definition of the class diagram.

We have also proposed guidelines to define the class diagram from UIDs. Some of these guidelines are based on the well-known concept of functional dependency. Even though the resulting class diagram may need some adjustments, it can be defined based on accurate steps. We have been working on improvements for the notation and the set of rules presented here. We intend to incorporate guidelines for dealing with more complex representations, such as multivalued data items and nested sets.

UIDs can be used to gather the requirements in any software methodology. Here, we have presented how to use UIDs in the Unified Process. We have shown the proposed extensions in the Requirements and Analysis workflows to support UIDs and the definition of the class diagram. UIDs could also be mapped to logical user-interface definitions during the Design workflow.

UIDs and the specification of the class diagrams presented in this work are being used as the basis of a method for gathering requirements and achieving the conceptual design of web applications [12]. This method emphasizes the importance of modeling user interaction and involving users in this process. It starts by capturing the requirements expressed in use cases and UIDs. These UIDs serve as a requirement validation tool and as input for obtaining the class diagram. UIDs have been tested within a joint project with a large oil company in Brazil, to design the website for the intranet of their training division. It consists of 52 use cases, which were used to obtain a class diagram with 51 classes and 54 associations.

UIDs are also being used for navigation design within the Object Oriented Hypermedia Design Method [9] [11]. In that method, UIDs are re-examined after the conceptual class diagram has been synthesized, in order to define navigational views that will constitute the navigation class diagram. In addition, the interactions in the UIDs are examined, and some are mapped onto navigation steps that will determine the navigational topology of the final web application.

References

1. Booch, G., Rumbaugh, J., Jacobson, I.: The Unified Modeling Language User Guide. Addison-Wesley, Reading (1999)
2. Imaz, M., and Benyon, D.: How Stories Capture Interactions. In: Proceedings of Human-Computer Interaction - INTERACT'99. IOS Press (1999) 321-328
3. Elmasri, R., and Navathe, S.B.: Fundamentals of Database Systems, Second Edition. Benjamin/Cummings (1994)
4. Güell, N., Schwabe, D., Vilain, P.: Modeling Interactions and Navigation in Web Applications. In: Proceedings of the Second Workshop on Conceptual Modeling and the WWW - ER'2000. Lecture Notes in Computer Science (2000) - forthcoming
5. Jacobson, I., Booch, G., and Rumbaugh, J.: The Unified Software Development Process. Addison-Wesley, Reading (1999)
6. Jacobson, I.: The Use-Case Construct in Object-Oriented Software Engineering. In: Scenario-Based Design: Envisioning Work and Technology in System Development. John Wiley & Sons (1995) 309-336

7. Jacobson, I., Christerson, M., Jonsson, P., and Övergaard, G: Object-Oriented Software Engineering - A Use Case Driven Approach. Addison-Wesley, Wokingham (1992)
8. Preece, J., Rogers, Y., Sharp, H., Benyon, D., Holland, S., and Carey, T.: Human-Computer Interaction. Addison-Wesley, Wokingham (1994)
9. Schwabe, D., Rossi, G.: An Object Oriented Approach to Web-Based Application Design. Theory and Practice of Object Systems 4, 4 (1998) 207-225
10. Sutcliffe, A.G., Maiden, N.A.M., Minocha, S., and Manuel, D.: Supporting Scenario-Based Requirements Engineering. IEEE Transactions on Software Engineering 24, 12 (1998) 1072-1088
11. Rossi, G., Schwabe, D., Lyardet, F.: Web application models are more than conceptual models. In: Proceedings of the World Wild Web and Conceptual Modeling'99 Workshop, ER'99 Conference. Lecture Notes in Computer Science. Springer (1999) 239-252
12. Vilain, P., Schwabe, D., de Souza, C. S.: Use Cases and Scenarios in the Conceptual Design of Web Applications. Technical Report MCC 12/00, Departamento de Informática, PUC-Rio (2000)

Appendix: User Interaction Diagram Notation

To represent the user-system interaction UIDs use the following notation for the different types of information:

Initial Interaction: represents the beginning of the interaction between the user and the system.

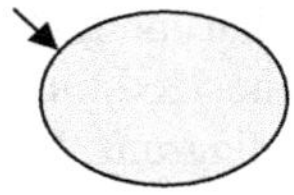

Interaction: represents one interaction between the user and the system. The information given by the user and returned by the system is shown inside the ellipse.

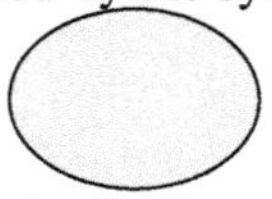

Optional Interaction: represents an interaction that depends on the previous interaction. Depending on the previous result this interaction may occur or not. If it does not occur then the output of the previous interaction will be the input of the next interaction.

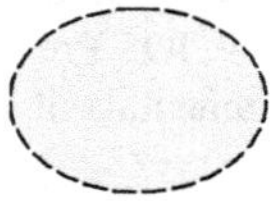

Interaction Alternatives: this representation is used when there are two alternative outputs from an interaction. The subsequent interaction depends on the elements or operation chosen by the user.

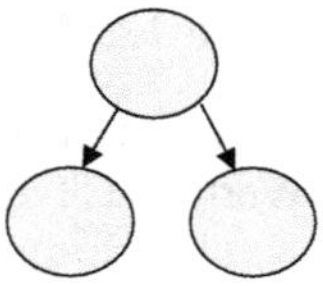

Data Entry: represents mandatory data entered by the user.

Optional Data Entry: Represents optional data entered by the user.

Element and its data items: represents an element and its data items. The data items are optional.

Element (data items)

Element Set: represents an element set. The data items associated to the element are also presented.

... Element (data items)

Specific Element: represents the specific element selected or entered by the user in the previous interaction.

Element X

Text: represents some additional data that participates of the interaction.

XXXX

Optional Text: represents some optional data that participates in the interaction.

XXXX *

New Interaction: represents a new interaction that occurs after the user has entered the required data and the system has returned other information in the previous interaction.

Selection of N Elements and New Interaction: represents that N elements must be selected prior to the new interaction.

N

Call of Operation Z and New Interaction: represents that the operation Z must be called prior to the new interaction.

(Z)

Selection of N Elements and Call of Operation Z and New Interaction: represents that N elements must be selected and the operation Z must be called prior to the new interaction.

N (Z)

Selection of N Elements and Call of Operation: represents that N elements may be selected and the operation Z called.

N (Z)

Call of operation Z: represents that the operation Z may be called. The calling is optional.

(Z)

UML Extension for ASAM-GDI Device Capability Description

Eugen Brenner[1] and Ivo Derado[2]

[1] Institute for Technical Informatics, Technical University Graz,
Inffeldgasse 16, 8010 Graz, Austria
brenner@iti.tu-graz.ac.at

[2] AVL List GmbH, Hans-List-Platz 1, 8020 Graz, Austria
ivo.derado@avl.com

Abstract. The ASAM standard has identified subsystems within automation and measuring systems as well as standard interfaces between these subsystems. One of these interfaces, called GDI (Generic Device Interface), defines the connection to measurement devices and intelligent subsystems. ASAM-GDI ensures the interoperability of real-time subsystems by separating the implementation code of device drivers and their interface descriptions, called DCD (Device Capability Description). DCD describes an object-like interface of procedural real-time components (device drivers) using the DCD language. In this paper it is shown how the DCD language and its constructs can be mapped to UML notation using the standard UML extension mechanisms. Advantages of modeling DCD using UML are numerous: uniform and standard graphical representation of device capabilities, improvement in DCD development, straightforward extension of DCD using UML notation, standard exchange text format of DCD documents using XMI (XML Metadata Interchange), etc. The definition of UML extensions for DCD contributes to the acceptance of the ASAM-GDI standard and simplifies the development of ASAM-GDI tools in the future. It is also an example how similar constructs, i.e. blocks with inputs and outputs, can be specified using UML.

1 Introduction

Test and measurement tasks in different industries (automotive, aerospace, railway, etc.) use complex computer based tools and applications running on different platforms. The situation in these areas is characterized by a large number of individual and incompatible solutions, which make it often very difficult to exchange data, operate subsystems together or compare results. Furthermore, considerable effort and expense is needed for maintenance and adaptation of these individual systems. When combining components of different vendors, cost and effort often increase significantly. The solution to these problems can be achieved using one of the technologies that provide interoperability between components in a heterogeneous distributed environment, such as CORBA or DCOM, and by defining standard interfaces between them. The use of standard interfaces

A. Evans, S. Kent and B. Selic (Eds.): ≪UML≫ 2000, LNCS 1939, pp. 148–161, 2000.

reduces costs, effort and implementation time, but also ensures compatibility, reusability, easy maintenance and portability of applications to different platforms. In 1991, five German automobile manufacturers, namely Audi, BMW, Daimler, Porsche and VW established the Activity Group for the Standardization of Automation and Measuring Systems (ASAM) in order to encourage and support these standardization efforts. Today more than 60 companies out of different industrial areas are working together (see [1]). ASAM has identified subsystems within test- and measurement systems as well as standard interfaces between them (see fig. 1).

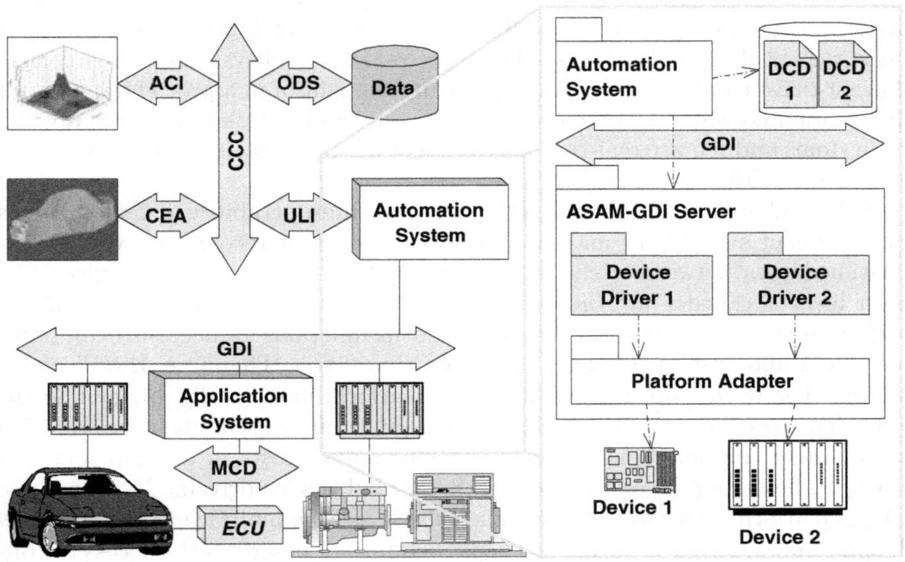

Fig. 1. ASAM Interfaces

The following interfaces are defined by ASAM:

- ASAM-MCD (Measurement Calibration and Diagnosis): interfaces for the description and integration of microcontroller-based open-loop and closed-loop control systems (ECU[1])
- ASAM-GDI (Generic Device Interface): interfaces to measurement devices and intelligent subsystems
- ASAM-ULI (Upper Level Interfaces): common standards for interfaces to applications
- ASAM-ACI (Automatic Calibration Interface): the interface between optimization and ECUs

[1] Engine Control Unit

- ASAM-ODS (Open Data Service): interfaces for storage, interpretation and exchange of data
- ASAM-CEA (Components for Evaluation and Analysis): a component interface and the necessary basic functionality for the creation of project-specific overall applications from modular measured data evaluation and analysis tools
- ASAM-CCC (Component Communication and Coordination): methods facilitating comprehensive communication between software components

The communication between subsystems is based on CORBA technology with communication services defined in ASAM-CCC. Exceptions are subsystems, which communicate via ASAM-GDI and ASAM-MCD interfaces, such as ECUs, application systems and different drivers for intelligent subsystems and measurement devices (see fig. 1). These are real-time subsystems, which consist of event-driven and cyclic programs typically thought of in a procedural and not object-oriented way. Furthermore, they run on variety of platforms and operating systems and require real-time services that are not supported by technologies such as CORBA and DCOM.

ASAM-GDI specifies interfaces that support interoperability of device drivers for intelligent subsystems and measurement devices. It recognizes two communication layers between a client (e.g. automation system) and a device. The lower layer is called *Platform Adapter* and has features similar to those of virtual machines. It exports platform independent functions for accessing computer peripheral and system resources (memory, time, etc.). Therefore, the Platform Adapter has to be implemented for every platform individually, but not so the code that uses these functions. This technique is often used when dealing with two or more computer platforms in order to reduce costs in development and testing. The second layer consists of ASAM-GDI device drivers. To keep these drivers platform independent, they exclusively use the interface to the *Platform Adapter* and to ANSI-C libraries. The GDI-Interface describes the access to constructs that are common to all device drivers and is therefore generic[2]. Using these common constructs, a manufacturer can describe specific device driver functionalities in a separate ASCII document called *Device Capability Description* (DCD). This description is given in a specific language, which is a slight modification to the well known Interface Definition Language (IDL). The syntax for this language with all possible constructs is defined using BNF notation in [2]. For each ASAM-GDI device driver exists one DCD. Thus, the integration of an ASAM-GDI device driver involves two components: device driver code and corresponding DCD document. The client, i.e. an automation system, analyzes the DCD document and obtains the information about device driver functions that can be accessed via the GDI interface. In companion standards, ASAM-GDI defines common device driver functions that make it possible for an automation system to coordinate its work with different device drivers.

The most important advantage of this approach is the separation of the code (device driver) and the interface description (DCD document). Hence, the

[2] These constructs are defined in the ASAM-GDI specification [2]

client's code has to be changed only if the DCD has been changed. This is also a characteristic of CORBA and COM technologies. ASAM-GDI device drivers have to be written in ANSI-C and export the GDI interface. During the integration process the device driver has to be compiled and linked with Platform Adapter and the corresponding DCD has to be parsed. These restrictions and routine jobs can be somewhat eased off with new ASAM-GDI tools in the future.

In this paper the abstract syntax of the DCD language is examined using UML[3] notation. It is shown that DCD constructs can be mapped to UML constructs using UML extensibility mechanisms. Also, since there are XML DTD[4] definitions for UML (see [13] and [15]), it is possible without any additional effort to represent the context of a DCD document with XML, i.e. using a standard text exchange format. With future XSL[5] definitions it will be possible to present DCD in different graphical forms.

2 DCD Abstract Syntax

Since the complete description of the DCD abstract syntax is outside the scope of this document, we concentrate on the major elements. Every DCD contains one DCD header structure, which includes information about the device manufacturer, the device and the device driver. It also has a reference to the DIT document[6] that includes all text descriptions, such as error descriptions. Apart from *DCD Header* structure, DCD document consists of *User Types*, *Constants*, *Operations*, *Device Functions* and *Modules* (see fig. 2). *User Types* are based on standard C-types. *Constants* are values, which cannot be changed and can represent e.g. certain device setting. A *Device Function* describes certain device functionality which can be parameterized, used and influenced via *Attributes*[7] and *Operations* (see fig. 3). *Operations* are typically defined within *Device Functions.* However, as DCD syntax supports forward declaration operations can be defined globally. *Operations* can be referenced from any *Device Functions.* A *Module* is a DCD construct used to encapsulate a group of *Device Functions.* The reason for grouping is typically device complexity or modularity. A *Module* can represent a type of I/O card in a system, but also a group of software functions in a device driver. *Modules* can again contain *User Types*, *Constants*, *Operations* and *Device Functions.* It can also include other *Modules* (sub-modules). In this way a complex functionality of a device driver can be built by using basic functions. However, no module inheritance is supported. The *Module* description is included in the information function block (*IFnBlock*), which has references to text descriptions in the DIT document.

[3] Unified Modeling Language (see [12])

[4] XML (Extensible Markup Language) and DTD (Document Type Definition) are defined in [16]

[5] XSL (Extensible Style Language) is defined in [17]

[6] Device Information Text document; it includes information, error messages and questions (see [2] for details)

[7] It is important in the further text to differ between *Attributes* and one of the *Comm-Types* also called *Attribute* (see table 1)

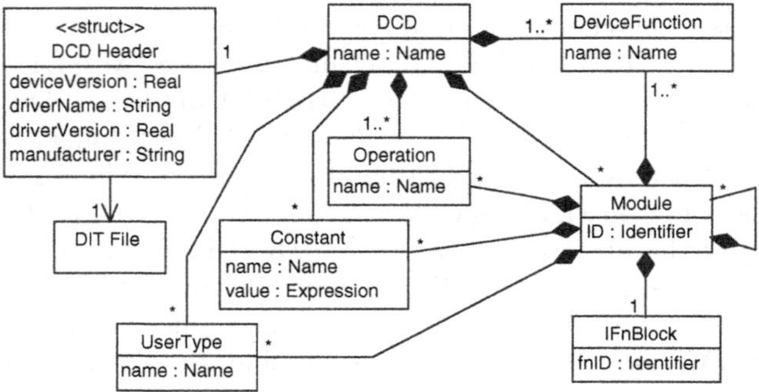

Fig. 2. Main DCD Constructs

Device Functions consist of *Operations* and *Attributes. Operations* are uniquely defined by an *IFnBlock* and a list of parameters (*OperParameter*). *Operations* return no value (void). Every parameter is defined by its *name*, default value, data type and operation type (*OperParamType*) that defines whether a parameter is an input value (*In*), an output value (*Out*) or both (*InOut*). An *Attribute* is defined by its communication type (*CommType*), which specifies its role in communication (described later), and its data type (*Type*). An *Attribute* can be *Global* (static for all instances of *Device Function*) or *Local*[8]. It has an initial value, an information block (*IBlock*) and an identifier (*name*), which makes the *Attribute* unique within the *Device Function*.

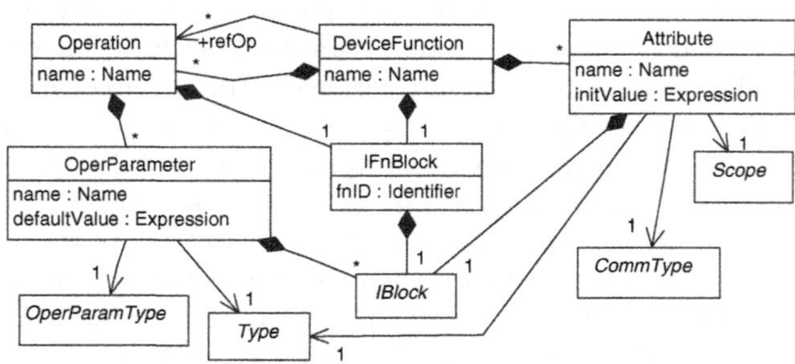

Fig. 3. *Device Function*

ASAM-GDI recognizes five different communication types:

- *Attribute* – defines an input of a *Device Function*
- *readonly Attribute* – defines an output of a *Device Function*

[8] defined within *Scope*

- *Param* – defines a parameter of a *Device Function.* The user can set its value, but not in the 'Working'[9] state of the device driver's communication.
- *readonly Param* - defines a parameter of a *Device Function* which cannot be altered and therefore is 'read only'
- *CreateParam* - defines parameters, that have to be set before the *Device Function* is instantiated; they are treated as constants after initialization.

3 Device Functional Configuration

In order to build more complex, application-specific functions, the *Attributes* of *Device Functions* can be connected using GDI interface. In this document the generated scheme with connected instances of *Device Functions* is called Device Functional Configuration (DFC). A DFC is application-specific and therefore not a part of the ASAM-GDI standard. Nevertheless, the process of connecting *Device Functions* is not application-specific, but a standard ASAM-GDI service. DFC uses instances of DCD constructs, i.e. *Device Functions*, *Attributes*, etc. In order to represent an instance of a connection between two *Attributes* an additional construct must be introduced. We call this new construct *Data Link.* A *Data Link* represents a connection between two *Attributes* having the same

Table 1. Possible connections between *Device Functions*

DATA LINK End / Start	*Attribute*	*readonly Attribute*	*Param*	*readonly Param*	*Create Param*
Attribute	Yes	No	No	No	No
readonly Attribute	Yes	No	No	No	No
Param	No	No	Yes	No	No
readonly Param	No	No	Yes	No	No
CreateParam	No	No	No	No	No

data type (*Type*, see fig. 3). Rules[10] for connecting two *Attributes* concerning their *CommTypes* are as follows:

- Input *CommTypes* (*Attribute* and *Param*) cannot be connected to output *CommTypes* (*readonly Param* and readonly *Attribute*)
- *CreateParam* cannot be connected to any other *Attribute*, since it must be possible to instantiate *Device Functions* independently.
- On-line data flow i.e. *CommTypes Attribute* and *readonly Attribute* are separated from parameter data flow i.e. *CommTypes Param* and *readonly Param*
- An output *CommType* cannot be connected to another output *CommType*

[9] ASAM-GDI defines the state machine for every device driver, see sect. 4.2

[10] These rules are not directly specified in ASAM-GDI specifications ([2] and [3])

In table 1 are shown possible connections. The meta-model of *Data Link* is described in figure 4 with a UML class diagram. Rules for connecting two *Attributes* are specified using an OCL[11] expression.

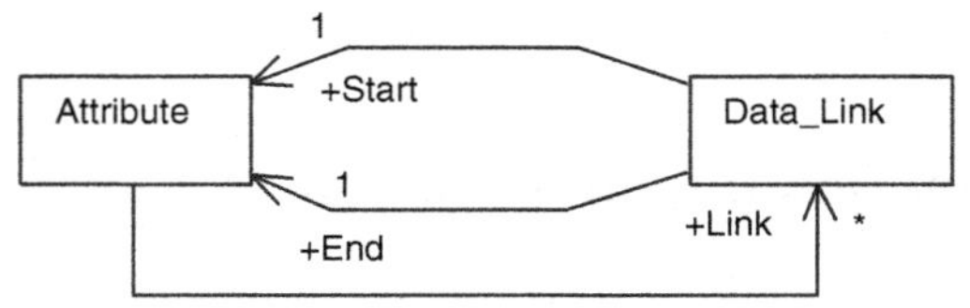


```
context Data Link
inv (self.Start.Type.oclType=self.End.Type.oclType)
     and
    (self.End.CommType.oclIsTypeOf(Attribute) or
     self.End.CommType.oclIsTypeOf(Param))
     and
    (if self.End.CommType.oclIsTypeOf(Attribute)
     then (self.Start.CommType.oclIsTypeOf(Attribute) or
          (self.Start.CommType.oclIsTypeOf(readonly Attribute))
     else if self.End.CommType.oclIsTypeOf(Param)
          then (self.Start.CommType.oclIsTypeOf(Param) or
          (self.Start.CommType.oclIsTypeOf(readonly Param)))
```

Fig. 4. Meta-model of *Data Link* described with UML class diagram and OCL constraint

4 Modeling DCD with UML

The extensibility mechanisms of UML offer a way to embed specific model elements without defining new ones. There are a series of examples for UML extensions in different areas of applications, like UML extension for complex real-time systems [9], UML Extension for Objectory Process for Software Engineering [10], or UML extension for hypermedia design [8].

The first step towards an UML extension for DCD is to define new UML model elements, which would represent DCD elements[12]. Three basic constructs are recognized:

- *Module*
- *Device Function*

[11] OCL stands for Object Constraint Language and it is a standard semi-formal language

[12] This does not have to be a one-to-one relation

– *Communication Object*

For DFC documents an additional construct called *Data Link* is necessary.

4.1 Structure

Module A Module is a DCD construct, which can contain one or more *Device Functions*, but also different *User Types* and *Constants* (see fig. 2). A Module represents a namespace, therefore the same names can be used in different modules. Modules are modeled with UML packages and sub-modules with sub-packages. No extensions for the UML package are needed.

Device Function A *Device Function* is the central modeling construct. It describes certain device or device driver functionality from a client point of view. It is neither a procedure nor a function and cannot be executed by calling it. It has more similarity to a class because it can be instantiated, its *Attributes* can be read and written (similar to class attributes) and its *Operations* can be executed (similar to class operations). Like UML ≪Interface≫ classes, a *Device Function* represents only an interface specification to the real implementation i.e. the device driver's code. The underlying mechanism for accessing the correct *Device Function*, *Attribute* and *Operation* including other ASAM-GDI services is based on the GDI interface. Hence, a *Device Function* is represented by an UML class element having a stereotype name ≪Device Function≫. A DCD specification, which describes a series of *Device Functions*, is represented with the same number of ≪Device Function≫ classes in an UML class diagram. The concept of communication objects (see sect. 3 and [2]) adds an additional characteristic to ≪Device Function≫'s attributes that UML class attributes do not have. To avoid the discrepancy, *Device Function Attributes* are modeled as special UML elements, called *Communication Objects* (see sect. 4.1). Thus a ≪Device Function≫ class does not contain any attributes. The exception is the *CreateParam Attribute* that has the same characteristic as template parameter of UML template class i.e. its value can not be changed after the instantiation of a *Device Function*. Consequently, the ≪Device Function≫ class can also be modelled using an UML template class (see fig. 5), where *CreateParam Attributes* are represented as parameters.

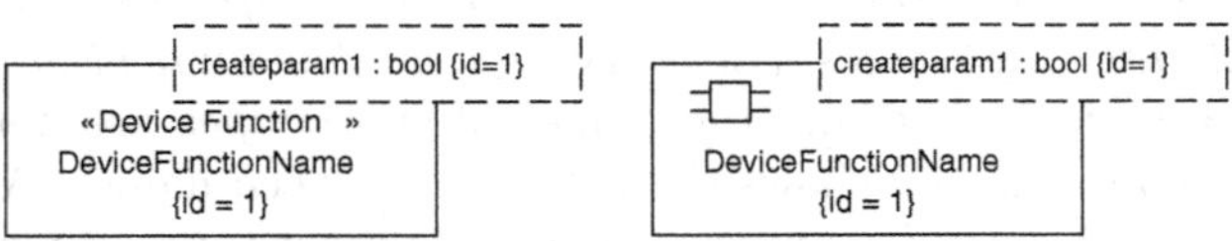

Fig. 5. *Device Function* stereotype

Device Functions can contain *Operations*, which are mapped to UML class operations. An *Operation* within a *Device Function* does not return a value (*void*) and its visibility is always public. An *Operation* parameter has a data type and *OperParamType* (see fig. 3). There is no special compartment for *Operations* in a ≪Device Function≫ class. It is assumed that all *Operations* listed in the operation compartment of a ≪Device Function≫ class are ASAM-GDI *Operations*. The only type of association that a ≪Device Function≫ can have is the 1-to-1 composition association to its *Communication Objects*. However, in the future it would be possible to add additional associations and dependencies to ≪Device Function≫ classes, such as generalization. A nice example for using generalization is the support of ASAM-GDI companion standards. Each companion standard defines a set of standard *Device Functions*, which can be used as base ≪Device Function≫ classes for other non-standard ≪Device Function≫ classes. Generalization offers an easier and more flexible way of using ASAM-GDI device drivers, but at the same time it is more difficult to support it.

For defining the identification number of a *Device Function* a special tagged value *id* can be used (see fig. 5). The ≪Device Function≫ stereotype also has its own icon ( ), which can be used to graphically denote a *Device Function*.

Communication Objects A *Communication Object* represents an arbitrary *Device Function Attribute* with the exception of *CreateParam*. It has the following features:

- It acts as a boundary object of a *Device Function* i.e. it is a part of a *Device Function* and exists as long as *Device Function* instance exists.
- It represents four types of ASAM-GDI *Attributes* i.e. *Attribute*, *readonly Attribute*, *Param* and *readonly Param* (see table 2)
- It has exactly one attribute, which represents its data type and value, which can be either only read or read and written depending on type of the *Communication Object* and the state of the *Device Function*[13].
- It can be "connected" to other *Communication Objects* following the rules defined in table 1.

A *Communication Object* is specified as an UML class with the composition association to a *Device Function* having one attribute, which represents its value and data type (see fig. 6). A composition association ensures that the *Communication Object* will live only as long as the associated *Device Function* exists. Values of *Communication Objects* with types *readonly Attribute* and *readonly Param* can be only read (*Get* method), values of type *Attribute* and *Param* can be read and set (*Set* method). The *Communication Object* describes four types of *Device Function*'s *Attributes*. For every type of *Communication Object* a special stereotype is defined, where the names of stereotypes are not identical to ASAM-GDI names. Table 2 shows the mapping between names. An example of a class diagram with a *Device Function* having different types of *Communication Objects* is shown in figure 7.

[13] The state machine of *Device Function* is described in 4.2

Table 2. Stereotypes for *Communication Objects*

ASAM-GDI	STEREOTYPE	
Name	Name	Icon
Attribute	≪Input≫	●——▶
readonly Attribute	≪Output≫	——▶●
Param	≪InParam≫	■——▶
readonly Param	≪OutParam≫	——▶■

It is obvious, that the representation of a *Device Function* having more *Communication Objects* can get very complex. Defining stereotype icons for each stereotype name can loosen this problem. Furthermore, the association between a *Communication Object* and a *Device Function* is always a composition association with the multiplicity one on both ends, and therefore a stereotype icon represents not only a UML class, but also the corresponding association. It is convenient to show *Communication Object* stereotypes with their role names and data types. Additionally, for every *Communication Object* a tagged value *id* with an identification number can be defined.

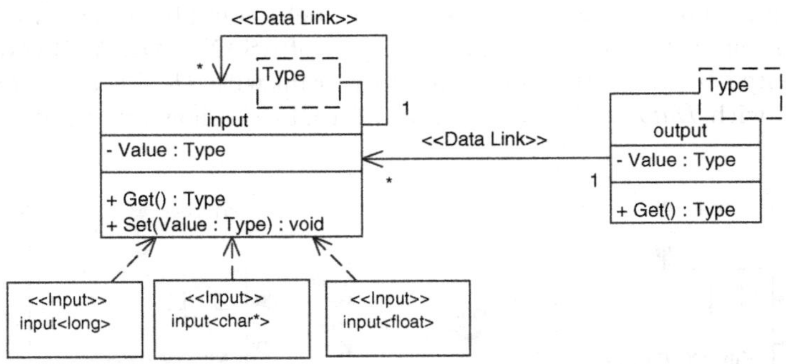

Fig. 6. This figure shows the definition of three *Attribute* (≪Input≫) *Communication Objects*. They are all instances of the template class *input* that provides common features for all *Attribute* (≪Input≫) *Communication objects.*

Data Links A *Data Link* is a communication channel that enables data exchange between two *Communication Objects*. It is modeled using an UML binary association, which is represented with a solid line, and it is declared in a collaboration diagram. *Data Links* exist only between *Communication Objects*. A *Data Link* has a special stereotype (≪Data Link≫), which is optionally denoted, since it is the only association that can exist between instances of *Communication Objects*.

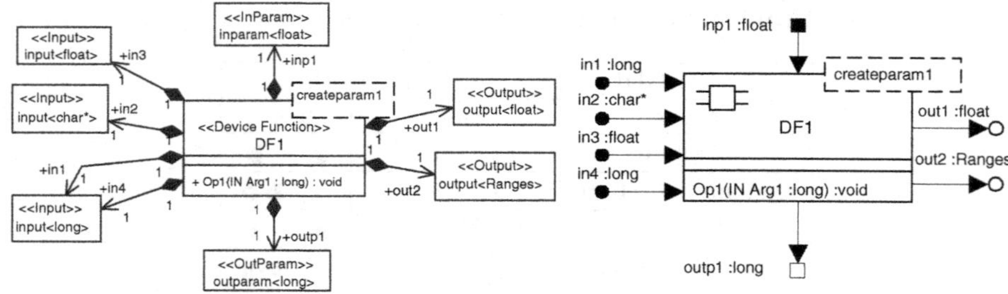

Fig. 7. *Device Function* graphical representation

Via a *Data Link* two *Communication Objects* can exchange their values. Two constraints has to be fulfilled in order to link two *Communication Objects* (see fig. 4):

- only certain types of *Communication Objects* can be linked (table 1)
- only *Communication Objects* with identical data types can be linked.

When two *Communication Objects* are linked, the value of data source (*Start*) overwrites the value of data sink (*End*). The ability to trigger this activity either at a particular time (polling) or when a certain time interval has expired from a given point in time is part of a time service, which should be generally assessable. The definition of this time service is not a part of ASAM-GDI. A DFC document is represented by an UML collaboration diagram with *Device Function* objects connected with *Data Links*. An example of a DFC is shown in figure 8.

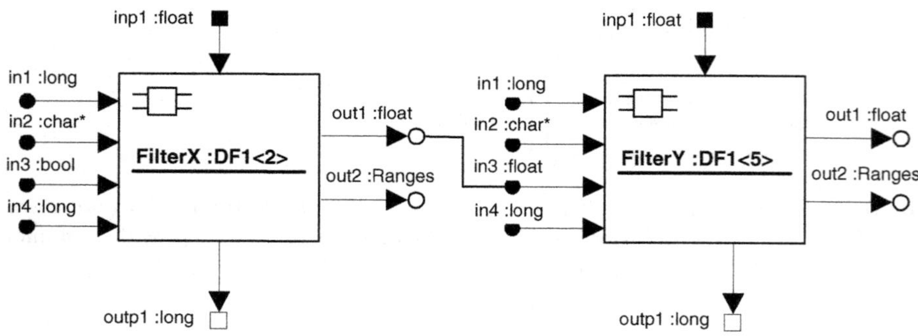

Fig. 8. DFC example

4.2 Behavior

ASAM-GDI defines a standard state machine for device drivers. This is an abstract state machine that can be refined with states specific for certain device driver. It has impacts on the behavior of *Device Functions.* An abstract state machine for *Device Function* is not explicitly defined within DCD. Using UML notation we can define it as a state machine of a *DeviceFunctionBase* class (see fig. 9).

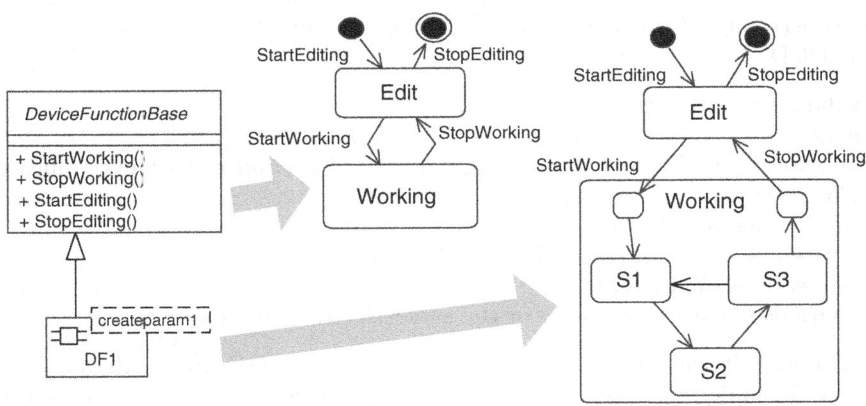

Fig. 9. Abstract state machine (*DeviceFunctionBase*) and possible refinement

Transitions in this state machine are equivalent to those in device driver's state machine [2]. *CreateParam Attributes* have to be defined before a ≪Device Function≫ object is being instantiated. In the states 'Edit' and 'Working', parameter- and on-line data-flows are separated i.e. reading and writing to *≪InParams≫* and *≪OutParams≫* is allowed in the state 'Edit' and reading and writing to *≪Inputs≫* and *≪Outputs≫* in the state 'Working'. *Operations* can be executed in both states. As already mentioned, this is an abstract state machine for a *DeviceFunctionBase* that can be refined with additional states specific for a certain ≪Device Function≫ class (see fig. 9). This refinement mechanism was first used in [6] in ROOMcharts, and was later captured in [9] as a usage pattern called the abstract behavior pattern. UML supports state machine refinement by defining chain states (small circles in fig. 9) and chained transitions. This feature is not supported by standard DCD language and it would mean a significant improvement toward better control of *Device Functions.*

4.3 Constraints

In order for DCD to be a contract document it is necessary to extend it with constraints, which describe obligations and benefits for both client and supplier ([4]). Constraints are commonly written as annotations (assertions) of a source text and are checked at run-time [7]. However, in a world of components, where the interface description of one component is separated from its source code, constraints become a part of each component interface description i.e. DCD.

Apart from stereotypes and tagged values, UML extension mechanisms include constraints. UML constraints are restrictions defined on UML elements, which can add new semantics or change existing rules. Constraints can be specified using free-form text or formal language. UML specifies the Object Constraint Language (OCL, [5]) as a standard UML formal language. An OCL expression is purely a declaration of what must be true, not of what should be done (declarative constraints). Constraints can be used to describe the following conditions in the DCD:

- valid areas for *User Types*
- maximum number of instances of a *Device Function*
- maximum number of instances of a *Device Function* concerning values of *CreateParams*
- valid areas for *Attributes*
- invariants, pre- and post-conditions for *Operations*
- connections of *Attributes*
- relations between *Attributes* of the same *Device Function*

Constraints help the client to integrate and test ASAM-GDI device driver. They improve the understanding and usage of *Device Functions* and increase formality level of DCD documents[14].

4.4 Well-Formedness Rules

In order to model DCD with UML constructs, well-formedness rules for the static semantic have to be defined for every UML stereotype. Because DCD is an interface language, no general dynamic semantic is needed. The dynamic semantic i.e. the implementation of a DCD is specific to a certain device driver implementation. The definition of the static semantic of the individual modeling constructs is outside the scope of this document.

5 Conclusion and Future Work

ASAM-GDI defines standard interfaces to real-time subsystems. It supports interoperability for various real-time operating systems by separating the implementation code (device driver) and the interface description (DCD). A DCD document describes an object-like interface of a device driver, which can be written in ANSI-C. Thus, ASAM-GDI bridges the gap between procedural thinking, which is efficient at the low engineering levels, to powerful object-oriented thinking at higher system design levels. Integration and test of ASAM-GDI device drivers will be simplified and speeded up in the future with new ASAM-GDI tools. The definition of the UML extension for DCD is a contribution to this process. It provides not only a standard graphical notation (UML) for DCD, but

[14] It is important to notice the difference between constraints and formal languages, such as VDM or Z, that are used to define the formal specification of interfaces and also their implementation

also a standard exchange text format (XMI, see [15]). Furthermore, the existing features of DCD language can be extended with additional UML features, such as inheritance, state machine refinement and constraints. Using standard UML tools it is possible to generate and understand DCD documents much faster than before.

Finally, using UML for the definition of DCD not only provides a better way to specify *Device Functions*, but also a possibility to define application-specific procedures, such as test scenarios by using UML scenario diagrams. This is one of the important steps towards a ASAM-GDI test development environment.

References

1. ASAM WebServer: http://www.asam.de 149
2. ASAM-GDI Teil A: Spezifikation der Device Capability Description eines ASAM-GDI-Treibers, Der technische Beirat des ASAM-GDI und ASAM-GDI-Plenum, Rev.4.1, 1999 150, 150, 151, 153, 155, 159
3. ASAM-GDI Teil B: Spezifikation der Schnittstellen eines ASAM-GDI-Treibers, Der technische Beirat des ASAM-GDI und das ASAM-GDI-Plenum, Rev.4.1, 1999 153
4. Applying "Design by Contract", B.Meyer, Interactive Software Engineering, IEEE Transactions on Computer, 1992 159
5. The Object Constraint Language, Precise Modeling with UML, Jos Warmer, Anneke, Kleppe, Addison-Wesley, November 1998, ISBN 0-201-37940-6 160
6. Real-time Object-Oriented Modeling, B.Selic, G.Gullekson, P.T.Ward, Joh Wiley & Sons, Inc., 1994, ISBN 0-471-59917-4 159
7. A Practical Approach to Programming With Assertions, D.S.Rosenblum, AT&T Bell Laboratories, IEEE Transactions on Software Engineering, Vol.21, No.1, January 1995 159
8. Towards a UML Extension for Hypermedia Design, H.Baumeister, N.Koch, L.Mandel, UML'99 Second International Conference, Fort Collins, CO, USA, October 28-30. 1999, Proceedings 154
9. Using UML for Modeling Complex Real-Time Systems, Bran Selic, ObjecTime Limited and Jim Rumbaugh, Rational Software Corporation, March, 1998 154, 159
10. UML Extension for Objectory Process for Software Engineering, version 1.1, OMG Document ad/97-08-06, www.omg.org, 1997 154
11. OMG Unified Modeling Language Specification, 1.3, June 1998
12. The Unified Modeling Language, User Guide, G.Booch, J.Rumbaugh,I.Jacobson, Addison-Wesley, 1999, ISBN 0-201-57168 151
13. Making UML models interoperable with UXF, J.Suzuki, Y.Yamamoto, 1999 151
14. A Defensive Approach to Certifying COTS Software, Jeffrey Voas, Reliable Software Technologies Corporation, RSTR-002-97-002.01, August 1997
15. XML Metadata Interchange (XMI), OMG Document ad/98-10-05, www.omg.org, October 20, 1998 151, 161
16. Extensible Markup Language (XML), Version 1.0 Recommendation, W3C, 1998, http://www.w3.org/TR/1998/REC-xml-19980210 151
17. Extensible Stylesheet Language (XSL), Version 1.0, W3C Working Draft, 2000, http://www.w3.org/TR/2000/WD-xsl-20000301 151

Swinging UML
How to Make Class Diagrams and State Machines Amenable to Constraint Solving and Proving

Peter Padawitz

University of Dortmund
padawitz@cs.uni-dortmund.de
http://ls5.cs.uni-dortmund.de/~peter

Abstract. *Swinging types* (STs) provide a specification and verification formalism for designing software in terms of many-sorted logic. Current formalisms, be they set- or order-theoretic, algebraic or coalgebraic, rule- or net-based, handle either static system components (in terms of functions or relations) or dynamic ones (in terms of transition systems) and either structural or behavioral aspects, while STs combine equational, Horn and modal logic for the purpose of applying computation and proof rules from all three logics.
UML provides a collection of object-oriented pictorial specification techniques, equipped with an informal semantics, but hardly cares about consistency, i.e. the guarantee that a specification has models and thus can be implemented. To achieve this goal and to make verification possible a formal semantics is indispensable. Swinging types have term models that are directly derived from the specifications. The paper takes first steps towards a translation of class diagrams, OCL constraints and state machines into STs. Partly, we proceed along examples, partly we describe generally how, e.g., classes can be turned into signatures.
Swinging types are particularly suitable for interpreting UML models because they integrate static and dynamic components. UML treats them separately, STs handle them within the same formalism. Hence, one may check, for instance, whether static operations are correctly refined to local message passing primitives.
A crucial point of a formal semantics of UML models is a reasonable notion of *state*. If constraints involve static data as well as states and state transitions, the modal-logic view on states as (implicit) predicates is less adequate than the ST representation as terms denoting tuples of attribute values, "histories" of object manipulations or compositions of substates (*composite states*).

1 Introduction

Given a system to be analyzed or synthesized, there are two conceptionally and technically rather different views on the relationship between its static structure on the one hand and its dynamic behavior on the other. We call them the **two-tiered view** and the **one-tiered view**, respectively. The former is the prevailing one. It is based on temporal and modal logic where each state is associated with its own interpretation of all syntactic entities building up assertions about

A. Evans, S. Kent and B. Selic (Eds.): ≪UML≫ 2000, LNCS 1939, pp. 162–177, 2000.

the system. The formal semantics is a *Kripke structure*, i.e. a collection (e.g. a sequence) of models each of which describes a single state. The state structure does not interfere with the transition relation that captures the dynamics and only the dynamics of the system. In contrast to this, formal approaches adopting the one-tiered view regard states not as different models ("worlds"), but as different elements of a single model. This allows one to keep to predicate logic, but in its *many-sorted* version: state domains must be distinguished from *visible* domains such as numbers or finite lists. The approaches that favor a one-tiered view are: process algebra [3], dynamic data types [2], hidden algebras [12,13] and swinging types. Hidden algebras are closely related to models of behavioral specifications [5] and subsumed by models of coalgebra specifications [29,32,21]. Hidden algebras handle behavioral equivalence, dynamic data types specify transition relations, only swinging types do both.

A swinging type (ST) separates from each other *visible sorts* that denote domains of data identified by their structure; *hidden* ("state") *sorts* that denote domains of data identified by their behavior in response to *observers*; *μ-predicates* (least relations) that represent inductive(ly provable) properties; and *ν-predicates* (greatest relations) that represent complementary "coinductive" properties.

Swinging types combine features of model-oriented approaches with those of axiomatic, deduction-oriented formalisms because their standard models are *Herbrand structures* and thus consist of terms. This is natural, opens up the use of powerful proof rules like unfolding, induction and coinduction [25,28] and generalizes the syntax and semantics of functional, logic or constraint languages. The models that are usually associated with such languages are the "godfathers" of ST models.

The ST approach evolved from 25 years of research and development in the area of formal methods for software construction. It aims at keeping the balance between a wide range of applications and a simple mathematical foundation. To this end boundaries between many research communities had to be crossed. STs employ concepts, results and methods from many-sorted and modal logic, algebraic specification, term rewriting, automated theorem proving, structural operational semantics, functional and logic programming, fixpoint and category theory, universal algebra and coalgebra. Whatever was adopted from these areas, could be reformulated in terms of many-sorted logic with equality.

Section 2 illustrates the ST specification of UML classes at an example presented in [18]. Section 3 deals with refinements or (abstract) implementations of STs. A refinement of an ST is another ST that meets certain correctness conditions on the Herbrand models of both types and on a given *signature morphism* from the "abstract" type to the "concrete" one. Section 4 proposes a rule-based transformation of class diagrams into STs with product and sum sorts that reflect the inheritance relationships in a class diagram. Section 5 confronts OCL with logic-based constraint languages. Section 6 deals with the integration of state machines into STs representing class diagrams. Here we present two examples involving guards, *generic* states and action-event communication.

2 UML and Algebraic Specification

[18] asserts a conceptual difference between the algebraic specification methodology and the object-oriented modelling approach: the former favors if not demands a high degree of data encapsulation and constraint locality, while the latter admits, at least on higher design levels, the "free use of information from almost anywhere in the current system state." On lower levels, the object-oriented approach achieves locality "by enriching the operation lists of the classes and by switching to a message-passing semantics. Sending a message to a locally known object and reading the result may be the equivalent to a complex navigation over the object community—however, the global actions, which are caused by sending a message, are invisible to the invoking object."

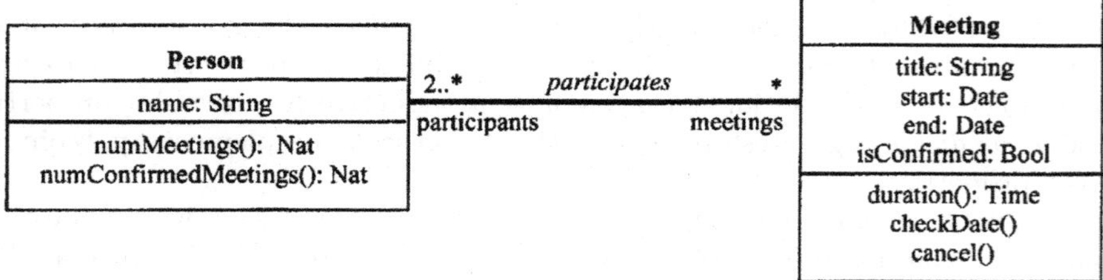

Figure 1. *Two associated classes (Figure 3 of [18])*

It might be a widespread practice in algebraic specification to enforce a high degree of locality and encapsulation, but this is not inherent to the approach. [18] claims a general one-to-one correspondence between a class and a specification unit. However, a simple look at the graph structure of a class diagram reveals that this cannot work as soon as the graph involves cycles such as those created by bidirectional associations (cf. Fig. 1). A class does not correspond to a whole specification, but just to a single *sort*. Due to the "static" semantics, an algebraic specification is structured hierarchically: the use relationships form a collapsed *tree*.

Even the finest specification structure reflecting a class diagram has to encapsulate all data and operations involved in a use cycle into a single specification unit. But this does not mean that the other extreme, recommended by [18], must be adopted, i.e., translating the entire class diagram into a single specification with a global state sort. The "coalgebraic features" of STs allow us to avoid the introduction of state sorts that are not sums or products of sorts representing classes.

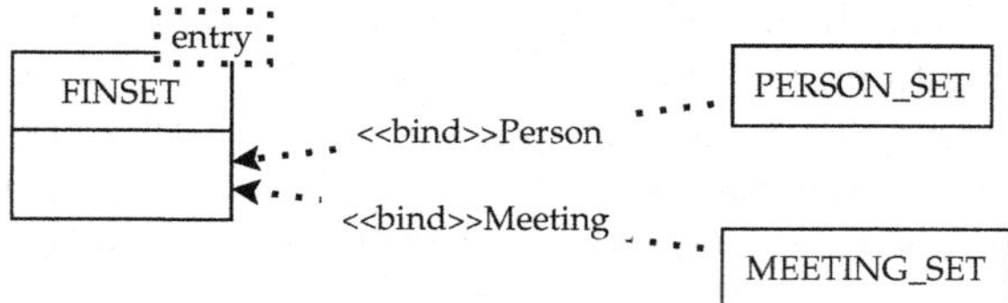

Figure 2. *FINSET as a template (parameterized class)*

A swinging type starts out from constructors (`constructs`) for visible sorts (`vissorts`) or hidden sorts. Each sort is equipped with a structural and a behavioral equality. For visible sorts, both equalities coincide. Constructors build up data, but only visible constructors do this uniquely w.r.t. structural equality. Object constructors (`oconstructs`) are hidden constructors that build up data uniquely w.r.t. behavioral equality. On the basis of constructors, an ST defines functions (`defuncts`) and *μ-predicates* (μ-`preds`) in terms of *finitary implications* (Horn clauses with or without universal quantifiers in the premise) whose purpose ranges from stating pre/postconditions of functions to specifying transition systems in an SOS style. Complementary *ν-predicates* (ν-`preds`) are specified in terms of *co-Horn clauses* that mostly describe aspects of behavior "in the infinity", such as reachability or invariance conditions on state sequences. μ-predicates are interpreted as least, ν-predicates as greatest solutions of their Horn resp. co-Horn axioms. Structural equalities are μ-predicates induced by usual congruence axioms. Behavioral equalities are ν-predicates induced by axioms expressing the compatibility with all defined functions that are declared as *destructors* (`destructs`), all predicates that are declared as *separators* (`separators`) and all *dynamic predicates* (cf. Section 6) that are declared as *transition predicates*. Destructors, separators and transition predicates build up the set of *observers*. ν-predicates and further μ-precicates, which are specified in terms of *generalized Horn clauses*, are sufficient for specifying most operators of any modal or temporal logic. While co-Horn clauses may involve existentially quantified conjunctions in the conclusion, generalized Horn clauses may involve universal quantified implications in the premise. A μ-predicate is *static* or *dynamic*. Structural equalities are dynamic. Other dynamic predicates represent "non-deterministic functions". In general, behavioral equalities are only *zigzag* compatible with dynamic predicates.

The set of hidden sorts of an ST splits into *reachable* or *finitely generated sorts* (`gensorts`), *destructor sorts* (`dessorts`) and *constructor sorts* (`consorts`). A reachable sort is interpreted as a set of behavioral-equivalence classes of constructor terms and thus represents a domain of finitely generated data. A destructor sort s represents a class and is interpreted as a set of—usually infinite—tuples of *context* functions that represent *behaviors* of s-objects. The contexts are composed of destructors (see above). A constructor sort is interpreted as a set of constructor terms, which are built upon constructor terms of a reachable sort and constants of a destructor sort. In UML, constructor sorts denote sets of composite states. *Data constraints* (`constraints`) for a sort s are formulas that restrict the set of s-term classes resp. s-object behaviors to a certain subdomain. In the latter case, data constraints for s correspond to invariants for the class represented by s. In contrast to defined functions (see above), *auxiliary functions* (`auxfuncts`) need *not* preserve the data constraints. They are specified in a special section with *defining axioms* (`defaxioms`). For precise definitions, consult [25,28].

Example 2.1 The bidirectional association between the classes *Person* and *Meeting* in Fig. 1 suggests a single ST, but two sorts for person states and meeting states, respectively. The following ST covers Fig. 1 and the OCL constraint of [18], Fig. 4 (see Section 5). For specification operators and symbol mappings, we adopt the syntax of CASL [6]. The ST extends a *parameterized* specification FINSET of finite subsets of the set of instances of a class (sort) *entry* that is part of the *parameter* specification ENTRY (cf. [25,26]). ENTRY is supposed to include a total ordering $<: entry \times entry$. BOOL and NAT are further imports of FINSET providing Boolean resp. natural number arithmetic. FINSET constructs all finite sets of entries from the sum (disjoint union) $\amalg_{n\in\mathbb{N}} entry^n$ of n-tuples of entries over all $n \in \mathbb{N}$. The constraint of FINSET restricts the tuples to ordered ones and thus ensures that each set has a unique term representation. Sums and products are also crucial for translating inheritance relationships into STs (cf. Section 4). FINSET might look more as an implementation than as a specification. The reason is that the alternative specification of sets with hidden elements use set membership as a destructor and thus violate the—reasonable—condition that destructors have only one hidden argument.

FINSET = ENTRY **and** BOOL **and** NAT **then**

`dessorts`	$set = set(entry) = \amalg_{n\in\mathbb{N}} entry^n$	
`oconstructs`	$\kappa_n : entry^n \to set$	for all $n \in \mathbb{N}$
`auxfuncts`	$add : entry \times set \to set$	
`defuncts`	$\emptyset : \to set$	
	$insert, remove : entry \times set \to set$	
	$filter : (entry \to bool) \times set \to set$	
	$map : (entry \to entry) \times set \to set$	
	$forall : (entry \to bool) \times set \to bool$	
	$\lvert\_\rvert : set \to nat$	
μ-`preds`	$\_ \in \_ : entry \times set \to bool$	
`vars`	$x, y, x_1, \ldots, x_n : entry \quad f : entry \to entry \quad g : entry \to bool$	
`defaxioms`	$add(x, \kappa_n(x_1, \ldots, x_n)) \equiv \kappa_{n+1}(x, x_1, \ldots, x_n)$	
`constraints`	$is_{set}(\kappa_n(x_1, \ldots, x_n)) \Rightarrow x_1 < \cdots < x_n$	
`Horn axioms`	$\emptyset \equiv \kappa_0()$	
	$insert(x, \kappa_0()) \equiv \kappa_1(x)$	
	$insert(x, \kappa_{n+1}(x, x_1, \ldots, x_n)) \equiv \kappa_{n+1}(x, x_1, \ldots, x_n)$	
	$insert(x, \kappa_{n+1}(y, x_1, \ldots, x_n)) \equiv \kappa_{n+2}(x, y, x_1, \ldots, x_n) \Leftarrow x < y$	
	$insert(x, \kappa_{n+1}(y, x_1, \ldots, x_n)) \equiv add(y, insert(x, \kappa_n(x_1, \ldots, x_n))) \Leftarrow x > y$	
	$remove(x, \kappa_0()) \equiv \emptyset$	
	$remove(x, \kappa_{n+1}(x, x_1, \ldots, x_n)) \equiv \kappa_n(x_1, \ldots, x_n)$	
	$remove(x, \kappa_{n+1}(y, x_1, \ldots, x_n)) \equiv add(y, remove(x, \kappa_n(x_1, \ldots, x_n))) \Leftarrow x \not\equiv y$	
	$filter(g, \kappa_0()) \equiv \emptyset$	
	$filter(g, \kappa_{n+1}(x, x_1, \ldots, x_n)) \equiv filter(g, \kappa_n(x_1, \ldots, x_n)) \Leftarrow g(x) \equiv false$	

$$
\begin{aligned}
& filter(g, \kappa_{n+1}(x, x_1, \ldots, x_n)) \\
& \quad \equiv \; add(x, filter(g, \kappa_n(x_1, \ldots, x_n))) \\
& \qquad \Leftarrow \; g(x) \equiv true \\
& map(f, \kappa_0()) \; \equiv \; \emptyset \\
& map(f, \kappa_{n+1}(x, x_1, \ldots, x_n)) \\
& \quad \equiv \; insert(f(x), map(f, \kappa_n(x_1, \ldots, x_n))) \\
& forall(g, (x_1, \ldots, x_n)) \; \equiv \; g(x_1) \wedge \cdots \wedge g(x_n) \\
& |\kappa_n(x_1, \ldots, x_n)| \; \equiv \; n \\
& x \in \kappa_{n+1}(x, x_1, \ldots, x_n) \\
& x \in \kappa_{n+1}(y, x_1, \ldots, x_n) \; \Leftarrow \; x \in \kappa_n(x_1, \ldots, x_n)
\end{aligned}
$$

PERSON_SET = FINSET[$entry \mapsto Person,\ < \mapsto <_{lex}$] **and** STRING **then**

`destructs`	$name : Person \rightarrow String$
`vars`	$p, p' : Person$
`Horn axioms`	$p < p' \Leftarrow name(p) <_{lex} name(p')$

MEETING_SET = FINSET[$entry \mapsto Meeting,\ < \mapsto <_{lex}$] **and** STRING **then**

`destructs`	$title : Meeting \rightarrow String$
`vars`	$m, m' : Meeting$
`Horn axioms`	$m < m' \Leftarrow title(p) <_{lex} title(p')$

PERSON&MEETING = PERSON_SET **and** MEETING_SET **and**
DATE&TIME **then**

`dessorts`	$Person \;\; Meeting$
`constructs`	$checkDate : Meeting \rightarrow Meeting$
	$cancel : Meeting \rightarrow Meeting$
`destructs`	$meetings : Person \rightarrow set(Meeting)$
	$participants : Meeting \rightarrow set(Person)$
	$start, end : Meeting \rightarrow Date$
	$isConfirmed : Meeting \rightarrow bool$
`defuncts`	$numMeetings : Person \rightarrow Nat$
	$numConfirmedMeetings : Person \rightarrow Nat$
	$duration : Meeting \rightarrow Time$
	$consistent : Meeting \times Meeting \rightarrow bool$
`vars`	$p : Person \;\; m, m' : Meeting \;\; ms : set(Meeting)$
	$ps : set(Person)$
`constraints`	$is_{Meeting}(m) \Rightarrow |participants(m)| \geq 2$
`Horn axioms`	$numMeetings(p) \equiv |meetings(p)|$
	$numConfirmedMeetings(p)$
	$\quad \equiv |filter(isConfirmed, meetings(p))|$
	$duration(m) \equiv end(m) - start(m)$
	$consistent(m, m') \equiv not(isConfirmed(m'))\ or$
	$\quad end(m) < start(m')\ or$
	$\quad end(m') < start(m)$
	$isConfirmed(checkDate(m))$

$$\begin{array}{rcl} & \equiv & forall(\lambda m'.consistent(m,m'),remove(m,ms)) \\ & \Leftarrow & participants(m) \equiv ps \wedge map(meetings,ps) \equiv ms \\ isConfirmed(cancel(m)) & \equiv & false \end{array}$$

A UML template of FINSET and its two instances (see below) is given by Fig. 2. Non-composite methods (here: *checkDate* and *cancel*) come as constructors. Unspecified function symbols have the expected meaning. The standard model that we associate with the above ST is the Herbrand model of the ST's **coalgebraic completion** [28]. The domain of this model is the set of all ground terms built up of constructors of ST and of constants that denote states of *Person*-, *Meeting*-, *set*(*Person*)- or *set*(*Meeting*)-objects. ❑

[25] presents the theoretical foundations of STs, in particular standard models, criteria for their existence and basic proof rules. [26] explores various application areas and integrates traditional special-purpose approaches. Sections 3 and 6 of [26] provide more UML-related examples than the lack of space allows us to work out here. [27,28] deal with extensions, such as the coalgebraic completions, and refinements of STs.

3 Refinements

Notions of refinement or abstract implementation notions have a long tradition in data type theory (cf., e.g., [1]). They define more or less implicit *abstraction* operators transforming models of the implementing—*concrete*—specification, say *SP*, into models of the implemented—*abstract*—specification, say *SP'*. While the original approaches focused on particular models of *SP* and *SP'* like initial or final ones (cf. [16,15,14,9]), later approaches consider model *classes* (cf. [34,33,23,4]). The correctness requirement that abstraction operators generate *SP'*-models from *SP*-models is sometimes strengthened by the condition that a refinement does not identify data that are distinct with respect to *SP'* [9,23].

Which are—intuitively—the operators, which transform an *SP*-model A into an *SP'*-model B? A refines B if B can be constructed from A by **translating** the symbols of *SP'* to symbols of *SP* along a signature morphism *rep* (*representation function*), by **restricting** the set of data of A to the *rep*-image of B, and, finally, by **identifying** concrete data with respect to the kernel of an *abstraction homomorphism* from A to B, which, intuitively, hides the implementation details. STs cope with visible and hidden sorts and thus allow us to design behavioral refinements as well as "structural" implementations along the lines of [9] within a common framework.

[34,23,4,20] pay particular attention to the identification step and consider congruences induced by behavioral equivalences. In other words, visible "abstract" sorts are mapped to hidden "concrete" sorts. Accordingly, *rep* may map structural by behavioral equalities. Another practically important class of refinements involves mappings from global operations to local message passing primitives. [18] claims that such steps require the change of the underlying logics, namely from algebraic to object-oriented formalisms. If the ST approach is adopted, the formalism need not be changed because STs integrate functional and state-based logics. For instance, a refinement of global operations by local message passing primitives could be formalized by a signature morphism that maps static to dynamic predicates.

The formal definition of a refinement of *SP* by *SP'* is based on the notion of a signature morphism $rep : \Sigma \to \Sigma'$ where $\Sigma = (S, F, P)$ and $\Sigma' = (S', F', P')$ are the signatures of *SP* resp. *SP'*. *rep* consists of functions $rep_S : S \to S'$, $rep_F : F \to F'$ and $rep_P : P \to P'$ such that for all $f : s_1 \dots s_n \to s \in F$ and $r : s_1 \dots s_n \in P$, $rep_F(f) : rep_S(s_1) \dots rep_S(s_n) \to rep_S(s)$ and $rep_P(r) : rep_S(s_1) \dots rep_S(s_n)$.

A **Σ-structure** A consists an interpretation of S, F, P by an S-sorted set $\{A_s\}_{s \in S}$, a set $\{f^A : A_w \to A_s\}_{f:w \to s \in F}$ and a set $\{r^A \subseteq A_w\}_{r:w \in P}$, respectively. Given a Σ'-structure A', the *rep*-**reduct** $A'|_{rep}$ is the Σ-structure that is defined by $(A|_{rep})_s = A_{rep(s)}$ and $f^{A|_{rep}} = rep(f)^A$ for all $s \in S$ and $f \in F \cup P$. The least Σ-substructure of $A'|_{rep}$ is denoted by A'_{rep}. Given the Herbrand models A of *SP* and A' of *SP'*, *SP'* **refines** *SP* **along** *rep* if A'_{rep} satisfies the axioms of *SP* and *SP'* is *consistent w.r.t. SP*, i.e., negation-free formulas valid in A'_{rep} are also valid in A. If *SP* has complements and *rep* preserves them, then the second follows already from the first condition [25,27].

Hence even when designing refinements and proving them correct we need not reason about other than Herbrand models. When several models are under consideration, they should first be related to each other syntactically, i.e., in terms of signature morphisms. It often turns out that what seems to be two structures A and B of a single signature is better handled if A and B are represented as Herbrand structures of different signatures related by signature morphisms.

4 From Classes to Signatures

STs combine results obtained in thirty years of research on applying equational, Horn or modal logic to program specification and verification. Readers who are familiar with at least one of these logics or those the common language CASL [6] is based upon should be able to follow the outlined proposals to equip UML with some algebra and logic, although the lack of space enforces a rather sketchy presentation.

As was already stated, a class *cl* corresponds to a hidden sort s_0. An **attribute** of *cl* with values in a domain denoted by the sort s' yields a destructor $att : s_0 \to s'$. An **operation** $op(x_1 : s_1, \dots, x_n : s_n)\{: s\}$ of *cl* provides a function symbol $f_{op} : s_0 \times s_1 \times \dots \times s_n \to s_{i_1} \times \dots \times s_{i_k}$ where $\{i_1, \dots, i_k\}$ is the set of $0 \le i \le n$ such that some "call" $op(a, a_1, \dots, a_n)$ causes a change of (the state of) a_i.

An n-ary **association** that connects n classes $cl_1, \dots, cl_n$ is a relational object of a (hidden) set sort *rel* with the membership function $\in: (cl_1 \times \dots \times cl_n) \times rel \to bool$ as the destructor. **Rolenames** attached to the **ends** of *rel* correspond to attributes in a relational database [7,8]. If the association is binary and **anonymous**, we need not introduce a sort for the asscociation. Instead, each rolename becomes a destructor of one of the two connected classes as in Ex. 2.1. The range sort of the destructor depends on the **multiplicity** at the target end of the association. If the multiplicity is 1, 0..1 or something else, the range sort is s, $1 + s$ or $set(s)$, respectively. Further multiplicity constraints are modelled as data constraints on $set(s)$ (cf. Ex. 2.1).

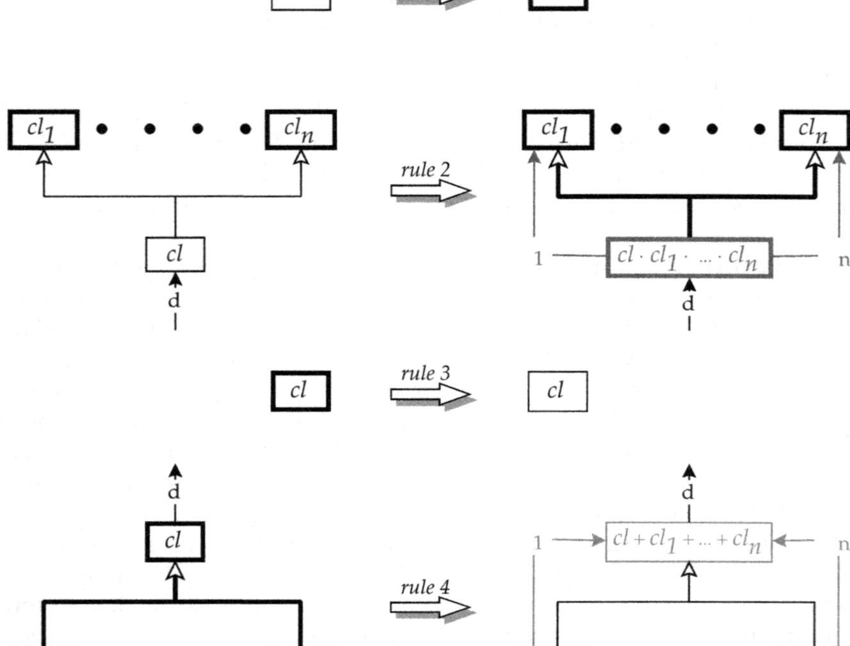

Figure 3. *Sorts induced by generalizations*

Generalizations in a class diagram yield additional product or sum sorts. They are obtained if the graph replacement rules of Fig. 3 are applied to the diagram in the following order. At first, rule 1 is applied to all maximal classes (w.r.t. the inheritance relationships). Then sequential applications of rule 2 traverse the diagram **top-down** and turn each local subclass to the product of itself and all its parent classes. In addition, rule 2 introduces projections $\pi_1, \ldots, \pi_n$ as unidirectional associations that allow *cl*-objects returned by a function d to access attributes and operations of $cl_1, \ldots, cl_n$. Subsequently, rule 3 is applied to all minimal classes. Then applications of rule 4 traverse the diagram **bottom-up** and turn each local superclass to the sum of itself and all its children. Finally, rule 4 introduces injections $\kappa_1, \ldots, \kappa_n$ as unidirectional associations that allow a function d defined on *cl* to access cl_i-objects. The boldface-framed nodes denote intermediate class states that disappear at the end of the described transformation of the diagram.

In accordance with [31], classes with **qualifiers** establish further product sorts. [11] compiles generalizations and qualifiers into more basic UML concepts. But since the target language is again UML (and OCL), the translation does not take us closer to a verifiable model.

5 On Constraints

UML class diagrams are equipped with invariants, associations with multiplicity or Boolean constraints, operations with pre/postconditions, often in terms of state transitions. All these conditions are expressed in OCL, the "object constraint language" UML is associated with (cf. [35]). In the ST approach, pre/postconditions are presented as Horn axioms for defined functions, while invariants and multiplicity constraints become data constraints (cf. Ex. 2.1). Some of the latter, however, are better regarded as requirements, which are not satisfied automatically by models constructed from the class specification (like the Herbrand model of a corresponding ST), but are passed to a model checker or program verifier to prove them against the models. But this can be done only when the class specification contains all operations that shall generate or modify class instances.

Ex. 2.1 includes an ST version of an OCL constraint that describes the effect of *checkDate* and originally reads as follows:

```
context Meeting :: checkDate()
        post : isConfirmed =
               self.participants ->
               collect(meetings) ->
               forAll(m | m <> self and m.isConfirmed implies
                          (after(self.end,m.start) or (after(m.end,self.start)))
```

(cf. [18], Fig. 4). The syntax of OCL is horrible! Striving for a language far from mathematical notation the authors of the language created a cryptic, error-prone formalism that only disguises mathematical notions with which one *must* be familiar for using that language correctly. For instance, the **collection operations** of OCL re-invent basic second-order functions on sets, bags or lists and are folklore for any functional programmer. As Ex. 2.1 shows, the above constraint can be expressed easily in terms of classical equational logic.

"In order to write unambiguous constraints, so-called formal languages have been developed. The disadvantage of formal languages is that they are useable only to persons with a strong mathematical background, but difficult for the average business or system modeler to use. OCL has been developed to fill this gap." [24] "Although it seems a good candidate for a precise unambiguous notation, a mathematical notation cannot be used as a standard constraint language. The aim of a standard is that it be widely used and not that it be exact but rarely used. We need the rigor and precision of mathematics, but the ease of use of natural language. These are conflicting requirements, so we need to find the right balance." [35]

In fact, OCL is not a bit closer to natural language than any other specification formalism—which is not surprising because any formalism relies on mathematical concepts and notations, no matter whether this is acknowledged or denied. Still, it is annoying if one wants to sell us for an inherent drawback of formal methods ("conflicting requirements") what only follows from the bad training of software engineers in basic logic and algebra. Admittedly, the above citations also put a shame on formal-methods communities, which—after 30 (!) years of intense research—have not achieved a little more acknowledgement among their clients.

I doubt that OCL is easier to use than a specification language based on well-established functional-logic concepts. Moreover, OCL's lack of a formal semantics favors inconsistent, i.e. non-implementable specifications. "Rigor and precision" is not the main purpose of a formal semantics. Natural-language specifications can also be rigorous and precise. However, only a formal semantics *ensures* the existence of models and thus of implementations of what has been specified. Only a formal semantics can establish evaluation, solution and proof rules that are indispensible for analyzing the specified systems.

A bare class diagram usually contains only a small subset of all desired use relationships between attributes, operations and rolenames. As [18] points out, it is the additional constraints like invariants or pre/postconditions that define "strongly connected" subdiagrams. Each of them covers all attributes and rolenames that occur in some constraint because all of these must be navigated for checking the constraint. For accomplishing an adequate class hierarchy, [18] proposes the refinement of a class diagram in a way that turns the strongly connected subdiagrams into new superclasses (generalizations). This strategy raises the question whether a reasonable grouping of operations into classes can be achieved at all *before* most of the constraints have been fixed. One may plead for hierarchical, parameterized specifications rather than class diagrams in those early design phases where many constraints are not yet known. But this is debatable because class diagrams allow people, as a referee puts it, "to look at parts of the map" without being bothered by a "counter-productive" hierarchy "when the design is still rather vague and prone to changes".

6 Adding State Machines

State machines are labelled transition systems that adopt (part of) the *statechart* approach [19].[1] A transition from state st_1 to state st_2 may have many components:

$$st_1 \xrightarrow{e(x)[g(x)]/act(x)} st_2.$$

The transition is triggered by a parameterized **event** $e(t)$ if the **guard** (= Boolean expression) $g(x)$ applied to t evaluates to true. During the state transition, the **action** $act(t)$ is executed. UML distinguishes between several kinds of events and actions.

The crucial point in a formal semantics of state machines is the notion of a *state* and what it is to represent. [35] regards states as values of a particular attribute. What distinguishes state attributes from other attributes? That they can take only finitely many values so that state machines are representable as graphs? Are all state attributes determined by class attributes? If so, it would be reasonable to define states as tuples of values over all attributes of a class. Consequently, state sets will usually be infinite.

[17] associates states with predicates whose validity may change when transitions take place. Then there should be some guidelines telling us which predicates

[1] For differences between statecharts and state machines concerning the semantics of synchronization, see [22], Section 2.4.

form states and which ones form guards. At some stage of a refinement of the state model, the predicate denoting a state s should imply the guards that label transitions starting out from s. States-as-predicates realize the *two-tiered view* of modal logic and Kripke models: a state is a world, state transitions change worlds, the structure of states and the structure of transition systems are expressed on different levels in different languages. Alternatively, process algebra [3], dynamic data types [2], hidden algebra [12,13] and swinging types proclaim the *one-tiered view* where states and state transitions pertain to the same world.

UML uses state machines only as a *description* tool. If they shall provide the models against which system properties are to be *verified*, the choice between the one- and the two-tiered view becomes crucial. We consider the former to be more adequate especially when—as in UML state machines—events and actions are calls of functions that belong to the static part of a system.

STs represent states as hidden-sorted *normal forms*, i.e., terms built up of constructors. In the beginning of a system development, constructors may just be constants (cf., e.g., $s = resource$ in Ex. 6.2). In later stages, a state may obtain many, though *behaviorally equivalent*, normal form representations. Normal forms consisting of *object* constructors (cf. Sect. 2) are behaviorally equivalent *only if* they are equal. However, *objects* cannot be identified by the normal forms representing their possible states. Their identity is determined by **object identifiers** or **key attributes** (address, name, number, etc.) in the sense of relational data bases (cf., e.g., [8]). Object identifiers are particular attributes (cf. Ex. 2.1).

State transitions should preserve behavioral equivalence, which makes this relation into a *bisimulation*: it is not fully, but only *zigzag* compatible with transitions. This means that the ability of a transition to be executed and the result of the execution do not depend on the source state's term representation. Full versus zigzag compatibility motivates the distinction between static predicates (`static preds`) and dynamic ones (`dynamic preds`) of STs.

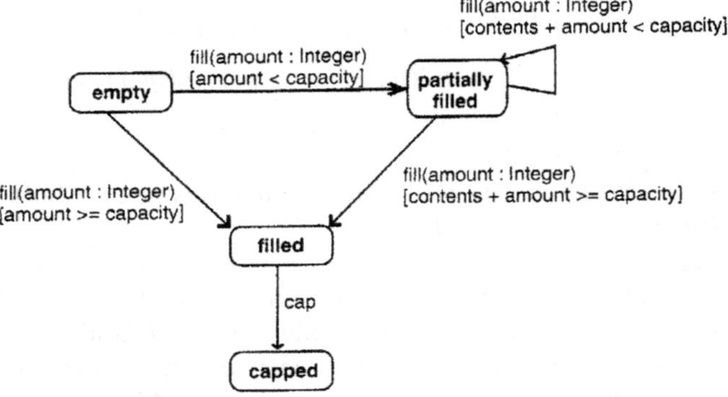

Figure 4. *A state machine with events and guards, but no actions (Figure 4-4 of [35])*

Example 6.1

BOTTLESTATE = NAT `then`
`gensorts` *Bottle*

`constructs`	$makeBottle : nat \to Bottle$
	$fill : Bottle \times nat \to Bottle$
	$cap : Bottle \to Bottle$
`destructs`	$capacity, contents : Bottle \to nat$
`separators`	$capped : Bottle$
`static` μ`-preds`	$empty, filled, partially\_filled : Bottle$
`vars`	$n : nat \quad b : Bottle$
`Horn axioms`	$capacity(makeBottle(n)) \equiv n$
	$contents(makeBottle(n)) \equiv 0$
	$capacity(fill(b,n)) \equiv capacity(b)$
	$contents(fill(b,n)) \equiv min(contents(b) + n, capacity(b))$
	$capacity(cap(b)) \equiv capacity(b)$
	$contents(cap(b)) \equiv contents(b)$
	$capped(cap(b))$
	$empty(b) \Leftarrow contents(b) \equiv 0$
	$filled(b) \Leftarrow contents(b) \equiv capacity(b)$
	$partially\_filled(b) \Leftarrow 0 < contents(b) < capacity(b)$

The specification reveals that each state in Fig. 4 represents a set of attribute (destructor or separator) values. Hence there is no need for an additional state attribute (cf. [35], Section 4.1.5). The example also shows that state predicates and transition guards encompass similar semantical information. Both provide preconditions for executing a transition.

BOTTLETRANS = BOTTLESTATE `then`

`vissorts`	$event$
`constructs`	$Fill : nat \to event$
	$Cap : \to event$
`dynamic preds`	$\_ \xrightarrow{\_} \_ : Bottle \times event \times Bottle$
`Horn axioms`	$b \xrightarrow{Fill(n)} fill(b,n) \Leftarrow empty(b)$
	$b \xrightarrow{Fill(n)} fill(b,n) \Leftarrow partially\_filled(b)$
	$b \xrightarrow{Cap} cap(b) \Leftarrow filled(b)$

$Fill(n)$ and Cap are the events that cause transitions from a bottle state b to the state $fill(b,n)$ resp. $cap(b)$. ❑

An advantage of representing states as terms is the possibility to identify a state with its **entry action**. There are two kinds of state constructors: object generators like *makeBottle* and object modifiers like *fill* and *cap*. Object generators have a hidden-sorted range, while object modifiers have a distinguished hidden-sorted argument and a range of the same sort. **Composite states** are built up of *non-recursive* object generators, i.e. the sort of a composite state differs from the sorts of its substates.

Example 6.2 The following ST specifies the mutually-exclusive access of several users to a single resource. It presents a state machine with action-event communication and thus involves multiple-object transitions. Functions on collections of objects of a class cl represent **class-scope operations**. They induce the events that trigger multiple-object transitions.

MUTEX = NAT **and** BOOL **and** FINSET[$entry \mapsto user$] **then**

`vissorts`	$event \;\; label$
`dessorts`	$user \;\; resource \;\; environment = set(user) \times resource$
`oconstructs`	$free, used :\rightarrow resource$
`constructs`	$new : int \rightarrow user$
	$access, release : user \rightarrow user$
	$New : nat \rightarrow event$
	$Request, Access, Release :\rightarrow event$
	$\_.\_ : int \times event \rightarrow event$
	$\_/ : event \rightarrow label$
	$/\_ : event \rightarrow label$
	$\_/\_ : event \times event \rightarrow label$
`destructs`	$id : user \rightarrow nat$
	$uses : user \rightarrow bool$
`dynamic preds`	$\_ \stackrel{-}{\longrightarrow} \_ : user \times label \times user$
	$\_ \stackrel{-}{\longrightarrow} \_ : resource \times label \times resource$
	$\_ \stackrel{-}{\Longrightarrow} \_ : set(user) \times label \times set(user)$
	$\_ \stackrel{-}{\Longrightarrow} \_ : environment \times label \times environment$
`ν-preds`	$mutex, \Box mutex : environment$
`vars`	$i : nat \;\; u, u' : user \;\; r, r' : resource \;\; s : set(user)$
	$e, a : event \;\; l : label \;\; env, env' : environment$
`Horn axioms`	$id(new(i)) \equiv i$
	$uses(new(i)) \equiv false$
	$id(access(u)) \equiv id(u)$
	$uses(access(u)) \equiv true$
	$id(release(u)) \equiv id(u)$
	$uses(release(u)) \equiv false$
	$u \stackrel{/Request}{\longrightarrow} u \;\Leftarrow\; uses(u) \equiv false$
	$u \stackrel{Access/}{\longrightarrow} access(u) \;\Leftarrow\; uses(u) \equiv false$
	$u \stackrel{/Release}{\longrightarrow} release(u) \;\Leftarrow\; uses(u) \equiv true$
	$free \stackrel{i.Request/i.Access}{\longrightarrow} used$
	$used \stackrel{i.Release/}{\longrightarrow} free$
	$s \stackrel{New(i)/}{\Longrightarrow} insert(new(i), s)$
	$s \stackrel{/i.a}{\Longrightarrow} insert(u', remove(u, s)) \;\Leftarrow\; u \stackrel{/a}{\longrightarrow} u' \wedge id(u) \equiv i$
	$s \stackrel{i.e/}{\Longrightarrow} insert(u', remove(u, s)) \;\Leftarrow\; u \stackrel{e/}{\longrightarrow} u' \wedge id(u) \equiv i$
	$(s, r) \stackrel{e/}{\Longrightarrow} (s', r') \;\Leftarrow\; s \stackrel{/e}{\Longrightarrow} s' \wedge r \stackrel{e/a}{\longrightarrow} r'$
	$(s, r) \stackrel{/a}{\Longrightarrow} (s', r') \;\Leftarrow\; r \stackrel{e/a}{\longrightarrow} r' \wedge s \stackrel{a/}{\Longrightarrow} s'$
	$(s, r) \stackrel{e/}{\Longrightarrow} (s', r') \;\Leftarrow\; s \stackrel{/e}{\Longrightarrow} s' \wedge r \stackrel{e/}{\longrightarrow} r'$
	$mutex(s, r) \;\Rightarrow\; ((u \in s \wedge u' \in s \wedge uses(u) \wedge uses(u'))$

$$\begin{array}{rcl} & \Rightarrow & id(u) \equiv id(u')) \\ \Box mutex(env) & \Rightarrow & mutex(env) \\ \Box mutex(env) & \Rightarrow & (env \stackrel{l}{\Longrightarrow} env' \Rightarrow \Box mutex(env')) \end{array}$$

The main requirement to MUTEX is an invariant: $\Box mutex(\emptyset, free)$. It can be show by classical means. ❑

7 Conclusion

We have presented first steps towards a translation of UML class diagrams, constraints and state machines into swinging types. Since STs have term models, they admit constraint solving and proving with the help of powerful and efficient rule systems [25,26,28]. STs represent both the statics of class diagrams and the dynamics of state machines within many-sorted logic. They also allow us to reason about the interaction between static and dynamic features. This could include the refinement of class operations by transition relations that break down a function call to action/event communication. Which other UML concepts should and could be integrated? May the ST interpretation suggest a redesign of certain UML constructs for the purpose of avoiding inconsistencies that remain unnoticed as long as UML has no logical foundation? Would it not be better to equip UML with a little more well-known logic instead of inventing new notations for old concepts even if the old notations have proved useful and adequate? The aim of this paper is to provoke debates on such questions rather than to give final answers.

References

1. E. Astesiano, H.-J. Kreowski, B. Krieg-Brückner, eds., *Algebraic Foundations of Systems Specification*, IFIP State-of-the-Art Report, Springer 1999 168
2. E. Astesiano, G. Reggio, *Algebraic Specification of Concurrency*, Proc. WADT'91, Springer LNCS 655 (1993) 1-39 163, 173
3. J.C.M. Baeten, W.P. Weijland, *Process Algebra*, Cambridge University Press 1990 163, 173
4. M. Bidoit, R. Hennicker, *Proving the Correctness of Behavioural Implementations*, Proc. AMAST '95, Springer LNCS 936 (1995) 152-168 168, 168
5. M. Bidoit, R. Hennicker, M. Wirsing, *Behavioural and Abstractor Specifications*, Science of Computer Programming 25 (1995) 149-186 163
6. The CoFI Task Group on Language Design, *CASL: The Common Algebraic Specification Language*, 1998, www.brics.dk/Projects/CoFI/Documents/CASL 166, 169
7. E.F. Codd, *A Relational Model for Large Shared Data Banks*, Communications of the ACM 13 (1970) 377-387 169
8. B. Demuth, H. Hußmann, *Using UML/OCL Constraints for Relational Database Design*, Proc. UML '99, 1999 169, 173
9. H. Ehrig, H.-J. Kreowski, B. Mahr, P. Padawitz, *Algebraic Implementation of Abstract Data Types*, Theoretical Computer Science 20 (1982) 209-263 168, 168, 168
10. H. Ehrig, B. Mahr, *Fundamentals of Algebraic Specification 1*, Springer 1985
11. M. Gogolla, M. Richters, *Transformation Rules for UML Class Diagrams*, Proc. UML '98, Springer LNCS 1618 (1998) 92-106 170
12. J.A. Goguen, R. Diaconescu, *An Oxford Survey of Order Sorted Algebra*, Mathematical Structures in Computer Science 4 (1994) 363-392 163, 173

13. J.A. Goguen, G. Malcolm, *A Hidden Agenda*, UCSD Technical Report CS97-538, San Diego 1997, www-cse.ucsd.edu/users/goguen/ps/ha.ps.gz 163, 173
14. J.A. Goguen, J.W. Thatcher, E.G. Wagner, *An Initial Algebra Approach to the Specification, Correctness and Implementation of Abstract Data Types*, in: R. Yeh, ed., Current Trends in Programming Methodology 4, Prentice-Hall (1978) 80-149 168
15. J. Guttag, E. Horowitz, D.R. Musser *Abstract Data Types and Software Validation*, Report ISI/RR-76-48, University of Southern California 1976 168
16. C.A.R. Hoare, *Proof of Correctness of Data Representations*, Acta Informatica 1 (1972) 271-281 168
17. A. Hamie, F. Civello, J. Howe, S. Kent, R. Mitchell, *Reflections on the Object Constraint Language*, Proc. UML '98, 1998 172
18. H. Hußmann, M. Cerioli, G. Reggio, F. Tort, *Abstract Data Types and UML Models*, Report DISI-TR-99-15, University of Genova 1999 163, 164, 164, 164, 164, 166, 168, 171, 172, 172
19. D. Harel, M. Politi, *Modeling Reactive Systems With Statecharts: The STATEMATE Approach*, McGraw-Hill 1998 172
20. B. Jacobs, *Behaviour-Refinement of Coalgebraic Specifications with Coinductive Correctness Proofs*, Proc. TAPSOFT '97, Springer LNCS 1214 (1997) 787-802 168
21. B. Jacobs, J. Rutten, *A Tutorial on (Co)Algebras and (Co)Induction*, EATCS Bulletin 62 (June 1997) 222-259 163
22. J. Lilius, I.P. Paltor, *The Semantics of UML State Machines*, TUCS Technical Report 273, Turku Centre for Computer Science 1999 172
23. G. Malcolm, J.A. Goguen, *Proving Correctness of Refinement and Implementation*, Technical Monograph PRG-114, Oxford University Computing Lab 1994 168, 168, 168
24. OCL Specification, Version 1.1 171
25. P. Padawitz, *Swinging Types = Functions + Relations + Transition Systems*, Report, University of Dortmund 1998, ls5.cs.uni-dortmund.de/~peter/Rome.ps.gz, to appear in Theoretical Computer Science 163, 165, 166, 168, 169, 176
26. P. Padawitz, *Sample Swinging Types*, Report, University of Dortmund 1998, ls5.cs.uni-dortmund.de/~peter/BehExa.ps.gz 166, 168, 168, 176
27. P. Padawitz, *Modular Swinging Types*, Report, University of Dortmund 1999, ls5.cs.uni-dortmund.de/~peter/MST.ps.gz 168, 169
28. P. Padawitz, *Swinging Types and Coalgebras*, Report, University of Dortmund 2000, ls5.cs.uni-dortmund.de/~peter/BehCoalg.ps.gz 163, 165, 168, 168, 176
29. H. Reichel, *An Approach to Object Semantics based on Terminal Coalgebras*, Math. Structures in Comp. Sci. 5 (1995) 129-152 163
30. M. Richters, M. Gogolla, *On Formalizing the UML Object Constraint Language OCL*, in: Proc. Conceptual Modeling- ER '98, Springer LNCS 1507 (1998) 449-464
31. J. Rumbaugh, I. Jacobson, G. Booch, *The Unified Modeling Language Reference Manual*, Addison-Wesley 1999 170
32. J.J.M.M. Rutten, *Universal Coalgebra: A Theory of Systems*, Report CS-R9652, CWI, SMC Amsterdam 1996 163
33. D. Sannella, A. Tarlecki, *Toward Formal Development of Programs from Algebraic Specifications: Implementations Revisited*, Acta Informatica 25 (1988) 233-281 168
34. M. Wand, *Specifications, Models, and Implementations of Data Abstractions*, Theoretical Computer Science 20 (1982) 3-32 168, 168
35. J.B. Warmer, A.G. Kleppe, *The Object Constraint Language*, Addison-Wesley 1999 171, 171, 172, 173, 174
36. M. Wirsing, *Algebraic Specification*, in: J. van Leeuwen, ed., Handbook of Theoretical Computer Science, Elsevier (1990) 675-788

UML Based Performance Modeling of Distributed Systems

Raffaela Mirandola Vittorio Cortellessa

Dipartimento di Informatica Sistemi e Produzione
Università di Roma "Torvergata"
Via di Tor Vergata, 00133 Roma, Italy

Abstract. The development of distributed software systems satisfying performance requirements is achievable only spending careful attention to performance goals throughout the lifecycle, and especially from its very beginning. The aim of our approach is to encompass the performance validation task as an integrated activity within the development process of distributed systems. To this end we consider object oriented distributed systems based on UML, the Unified Modeling Language. We show how a system modeled by UML diagrams can be translated into a queueing network based performance model. The main contribution of this work consists of an extensive application to a case study of our methodological approach for the automatic generation of performance models. The considered case study falls in the domain of distributed software systems, where the proposed methodology suitably exploits and combines information derived from different UML diagrams to generate a quite accurate performance model.

1 Introduction

In the last few years UML [9,11,37,38,39] is becoming a standard notation for software/hardware system modeling, mostly because the same conceptual framework and the same notation can be used from specification through design to implementation. Besides, the UML syntax allows to embed into the model both static and dynamic aspects of the system through the usage of different diagrams, each of them representing different aspects of the system itself. Both these considerations make UML suitable to a systematic performance evaluation throughout the development process.

Goal of this paper is showing how a UML based methodology that encompasses the performance validation task as an integrated activity within a development process can be extensively applied to a distributed case study. Indeed, if unacceptable performances are discovered late in the project, it is necessary to either abandon the system entirely or go through redefinition, redesign and redevelopment phases until the system becomes acceptable. Both of these options are much more expensive than validating performance goals from the beginning of the project.

A. Evans, S. Kent and B. Selic (Eds.): ≪UML≫ 2000, LNCS 1939, pp. 178–193, 2000.

The performance validation task consists of two main steps: the model generation and the model evaluation. Our target performance model, basing on the Software Performance Engineering (SPE) methodology [30], consists of two parts: the Software Model (SM), based on Execution Graphs (EG) and the Machinery Model (MM) (i.e., the hardware platform model), based on Extended Queueing Network Models (EQNM). The combination of SM and MM yields a complete (parameterized) EQNM based performance model. Once the model generation step is completed, classical solution techniques based on well-known methodologies [17,19,22] are applied to perform the model solution step. The performance indices of interest are thus obtained and, if they result unsatisfactory, modifications to the software and/or hardware design can be made.

We have proposed a methodological approach that extracts from different UML diagrams the main factors affecting the system performance and combines these data to generate a performance model [7]. In this paper we briefly go through the methodology and we rather focus on the performance model solution. We show how the model produced is exploited for a non trivial early performance evaluation. The results of this evaluation give insights on the crucial (eventually distributed) aspects of the system and allow to refine the UML diagrams basing on the feedback gained from the performance evaluation.

The proposed methodology makes use of: the UML Use Case Diagram to derive the user profile and the software scenarios (i.e., the use cases themselves), the Sequence Diagrams to derive an Execution Graph, and the Deployment Diagram to derive an EQNM and to identify the hardware/software relationships that improve the accuracy of the performance model. The level of modeling detail does not directly depend on the set of diagrams adopted to describe the hardware/software system, it rather depends on the depth of knowledge acquired in the requirement analysis phase. Besides, extracting information from other UML diagrams would be helpful to keep into the performance model other characteristics of the system that are not explicitly captured from the diagrams we have considered. An extended approach considering, for example, State Transition Diagrams would give rise to a more detailed performance model. The latter is indeed a work in progress, and therefore is out of this paper scope.

With regard to the class of hardware/software systems we cope with our approach, the set of diagrams we consider allows to suitably model distributed applications. Software systems with different features (e.g., real-time systems, mobile code based systems) could gain advantage (in terms of appropriateness of the performance model produced) from using different/additional UML diagrams.

The paper is organized as follows. Section 2 contains a short introduction to SPE and a survey of related work on software performance. Section 3 describes our methodological approach for the derivation of a queueing network based performance model. In section 4 an exhaustive description of the methodology application to a case study is presented. Finally, in Section 5 the conclusions are sketched.

2 Background

In this section we present both a short introduction to SPE and a survey of the related work on performance modeling mostly focused on UML based systems.

2.1 Software Performance Engineering

The systematic assessment of performance issues throughout the lifecycle is a methodology known as Software Performance Engineering (SPE). SPE concepts, tools and methods have been firstly presented in [30]. The SPE basic concept is the separation of the software model from its execution environment model (i.e., machinery model). This distinction, on the one hand helps to define software and machinery models and to solve their combination, on the other hand improves the portability of the models (i.e., the performance of a specific software system can be evaluated on different platforms, and the performance of a specific platform can be validated under different software systems).

As already stated a performance model based on SPE consists of two parts: the Software Model (SM) and the Machinery Model (MM).

The SM captures essential aspects of software behaviour and is based on Execution Graphs (EG) [30]. An EG is a graph whose nodes represent software workload components and edges represent transfer of control. A software workload component is a set of instructions or procedures performing a specific task. EGs include several types of nodes, such as basic, cycle, conditional, fork and join nodes. Each node is weighted by use of a *demand vector* that represents the resource usage of the node (i.e., the demand for each resource).

The MM is the model of the hardware platform and is based on Extended Queueing Network Models (EQNM) [22]. EQNM are extensively applied in the literature for the modeling of resource contention. In order to specify an EQNM it is necessary to define: components (i.e., service centers), topology (i.e., connections among centers) and parameters (such as job classes, job routing among centers, scheduling discipline at service centers, service demand at service centers). Component and topology specification is performed according to the system description, while the specification of parameters is obtained from information derived by SM and knowledge of resource capabilities. The so obtained parameterized EQNM has to be solved to obtain the values of the performance indices of interest.

The steps of the model solution are: assigning environment-based parameters to the EQNM; processing EG (with reduction analysis techniques) to obtain software-based parameters and assigning them to the EQNM; solving parameterized EQNM with classical techniques based on simulation and/or analysis [23,30].

If the obtained results indicate that the performance objective are met then the development process can go on, otherwise some hardware and/or software alternatives should be considered and the performance validation task repeated for the new hardware/software system.

2.2 Related Work

In literature there exist several papers presenting SPE application to distributed object oriented systems [8,16,23,31,32,34]. Different approaches to performance model generation and/or evaluation have been presented in [3,5,12,13,14,15,28,36]. Recently, the growing interest in software architectures [2] leads to extending performance model generation to also encompass the software architecture concept [1,35].

With regard to UML based systems, preliminary ideas on using UML diagrams for performance modeling have been first presented in [25].

In [24] Sequence Diagrams are considered and a prototype simulation tool (built around them) is presented. The obtained result consists of an animated Sequence Diagram as a trace of events. The main drawback of this approach is the lack of effectiveness on complex systems.

In [20,21] has been proposed the use of a Collaboration Diagram with State Diagrams of all possible objects embedded within them. All possible behaviors of the system are captured. Starting from this new combined diagram a Generalized Stochastic Petri Net model is generated. The translation of the State Diagram representing each object into a Stochastic Petri Net is obtained by associating to each state in the State Diagram a place in the Petri Net and to each transition in the State Diagram a transition in the Petri Net. A complete Petri Net representing the global system can be obtained by merging the different models with support of the Collaboration Diagram. In [21] it is highlighted that the major drawback of the mapping of State Diagrams to Petri Nets is the identification of transitions to be shared with other components when the individual Petri Nets are combined. The direct generation of a continuous time Markov chain starting from Collaboration and State Diagrams is also investigated in [21] through a simple example.

A formal approach is considered in [26] where the translation of UML diagrams into Process Algebras models is dealt with.

A framework that allows UML diagrams to be used for building performance models is presented in [18]. Performance modeling is carried out basing on a precise textual notation, called Performance Modeling Language to represent the UML characteristics relevant to performance models. These UML based performance models are then transformed into stochastic queueing networks with simultaneous resource possession. Resource (queues) are derived from Class Diagram, workload from Collaboration Diagram and service demands are partially derived from triggering properties of Class Diagram. The framework provides an algorithm for performance model solution based on classical analytical techniques, such as MVA, and therefore inherits all the limitation due to this kind of model solution [17,19,22].

Our methodology, starting from a set of UML diagrams, leads to the generation of a performance model, whereas in [13,25,24,28,34,35,36] several steps along the path from analysis/design output to performance models are not explicitly given. The definition of algorithms within the methodology allows automatic generation of the software performance model whereas several works [13,28,25,24,26] are not very concerned with automatic aspects.

In the rest of the paper we show on a case study how the combined use of different diagrams (in a distributed domain) leads to the generation of a quite accurate and complete performance model, early in the lifecycle, so allowing early identification of factors that yield performance degradation.

3 The Methodology

Our methodology only considers a restricted set of UML diagrams, that are: Use Case Diagrams, Sequence Diagrams and Deployment Diagrams. Therefore a performance model can only be obtained for those systems that are modeled by means of *at least* these diagrams. Even if this appears as a limitation of the approach (i.e., the UML modeling approach is not aimed at requiring some diagrams rather than other ones), we show how this set of diagrams contain the basic hardware/software features to build a suitable queueing network based performance model.

The basic steps to be performed in order to build such a performance are the following:

1) Deduce from Use Case Diagram the user profile. The UML original UCD diagram is enriched with further data that are helpful to build the performance model. In practice, a probability is assigned to every edge that links a type of user to an use case. More formally, let us suppose to have a Use Case Diagram with m types of users and n use cases. Let p_i $(i = 1, ..., m)$ be the i-th user type frequency of usage of the software system (i.e., $\sum_{i=1}^{m} p_i = 1$) and let P_{ij} be the probability that the i-th user makes use of the software system by performing the functionality corresponding to the use case j $(j = 1, ..., n)$ (i.e., $\sum_{j=1}^{n} P_{ij} = 1$). The probability for whatever Sequence Diagram corresponding to the use case x to be executed is given by:

$$P(x) = \sum_{i=1}^{m} p_i \cdot P_{ix} \tag{1}$$

2) For each use case in the UCD, process the corresponding set of Sequence Diagrams (SDs) to obtain the meta-EG.

The UML original SD diagrams are also enriched with further data ([1]). Each interaction in the SDs is identified by the tuple $(l, A1, A2)$, where l is the shortened label of the SD interaction arrow, A1 is the name of the SD axis where the arrow starts, and A2 is the name of the SD axis where the arrow ends. In Appendix the algorithm that translates the SDs into a *meta*-EG is given. The application of the algorithm to the distributed case study is given in Section 4. The algorithm deals with SDs that does have neither *no-reply* nor *asynchronous* interactions. The Execution Graph obtained in this step includes only five types

[1] We remark that enriching the UML diagrams with further data is similar to introducing *annotated* specifications [18].

of nodes: basic nodes, branching nodes, cycle nodes, fork and join nodes [30]. Every basic node is labeled with the tuple $(l, A1, A2)$ identifying an interaction, and it corresponds to the set of operations that are carried out by the component A1 before interacting with A2 through $(l, A1, A2)$. We basically translates this set of operations with an EG node and a pending arrow exiting the node. The end of the arrow has to be properly connected, in the subsequent steps, to another node of the EG.

3) Use the Deployment Diagram to obtain the extended queueing network model (EQNM) of the hardware platform and to appropriately tailor the meta-EG to the latter, so obtaining an EG-instance.

The usage of information contained in the Deployment Diagram is twofold. On the one hand, an Extended Queueing Network Model (EQNM) can be obtained representing the hardware platform hosting the software system, on the other hand the tailoring of the EG to the specific platform can be performed, so obtaining an EG-*instance*.

In order to build a suitable EQNM does not suffice the topology of the platform and the type of the sites; several basic features of devices placed on each site have also to be known, in order to assign numeric values to service center parameters of the EQNM. Besides, basing on the names of the interacting component within the *meta*-EG block labels, the overhead delays due to communications among software components can be captured into the performance model. We consider this as a very important aspect of our methodology and in Section 4 we show how to combine this information with the description of the hardware platform.

4) Assign numerical parameters to the EG-instance. In this step we assign probabilities to the edges outgoing branching nodes and *net weights* to the basic blocks of the EG-*instance*, that means giving probabilities to interactions of the SDs. Probabilities have been associated to use cases, i.e. to sets of SDs. But, given a set of SDs, not all the SDs have the same probability to be executed.

Recall that we denote with $P(j)$ the probability of executing the use case j, for $j = 1, ..., n$ (see 1). Let $s(j)$ be the number of SDs that refer to the use case j. Let the designer, basing on his/her experience, be able to determine, for $k = 1, ..., s(j)$ the frequency $f_j(k)$ of execution of the k-th SD with respect to the other ones referring to the same use case (i.e., $\sum_{k=1}^{s(j)} f_j(k) = 1$). The *actual* probability to execute a transition belonging the k-th SD that, in turn, refers to the j-th use case, is given by $P(j) \cdot f_j(k)$. In order to apply the SPE approach we need to assign to the set of edges outgoing every branching node in an EG-*instance* a probability distribution (i.e., such probabilities must sum to 1). So, after assigned a probability to each interaction corresponding to an outgoing edge, a normalization operation has to be performed.

Assigning a *net weight* to a basic block means evaluating the expected *resource demand vector* of this block [8,23,30]. This vector is the combination of the expected block requests for each device of the site where it is executed before the interaction identified by the block label takes place.

Net weights of EG basic blocks are available only if both the consistency of the operations performed into each block and the size of the data exchanged are known in advance (at least their orders of magnitude). This is true for the probabilities as well (e.g., user profile). In some of cases where this information is not sufficient to give numerical values to the model parameters a symbolic performance evaluation can be carried on. In these cases upper and lower bounds of performance metrics are obtained.

Finally, the combination of EG-instance and EQNM to solve the obtained performance model is achieved through the approach of Section 2.1.

4 Case Study

In this section we show the application of the methodology in Section 3 to a distributed application that is an Information Retrieval System (IRS).

In IRS an user, through a main interface, accesses to a software system that, basically, can performs two types of operations, that are local and remote research of data. If the user requires a local research of an item then the system, after identified such user, accesses to a local database system, searching for the item requested. If a remote research is instead required then no identification is performed as no "local private" data can be accessed, and three different browsers are asked to find the item on the Net.

4.1 Execution of the Methodological Steps

In Figure 1 the Use Case Diagram for the IRS example is drawn. Only one type of user and two use cases are considered that correspond to the functionalities provided by this software system. Labels p and $1-p$ represent the probabilities that User executes, respectively, the local or the remote research functionality of the IRS system.

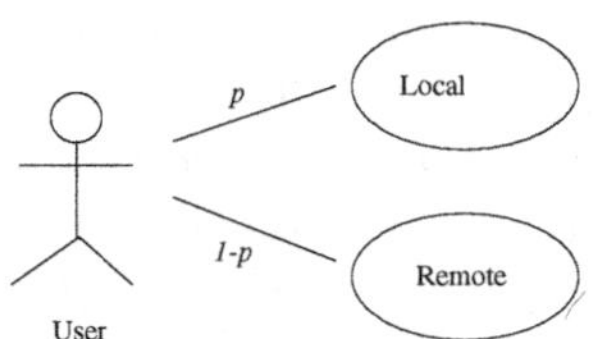

Fig. 1. Use Case Diagram of IRS.

In Figures 2 and 3 the set of Sequence Diagrams corresponding, respectively, to the *Local* and to the *Remote* use case of Figure 1 are shown. We refer to each SD axis as an object, but for sake of generality we call it component in the rest of the paper. The *Local* use case gives rise to three diagrams, that describe, respectively, situations of: non failure, user authentication failure, non existing item in local DB. The *Remote* use case gives rise to one only diagram, because we do not consider any possible failure.

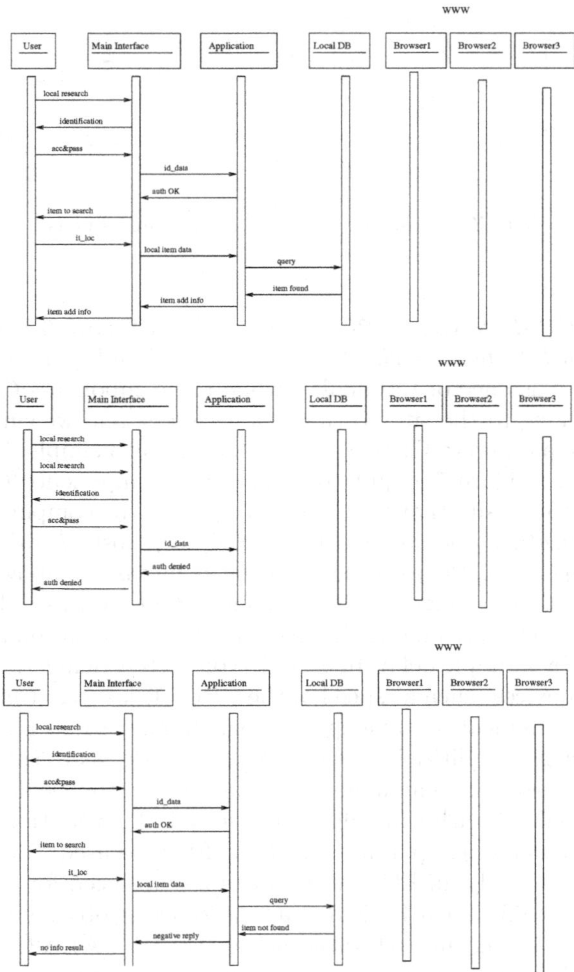

Fig. 2. Sequence Diagrams of *Local* use case.

Figure 4 shows the meta-EG obtained applying our algorithm to the SDs in Figure 2 and 3.

In Figure 5 two candidate Deployment Diagrams for our IRS example are drawn, and the corresponding EQNMs are shown in Figures 6 and 7. The internal structure of the two sites of the *Centralized platform* is very simple. The

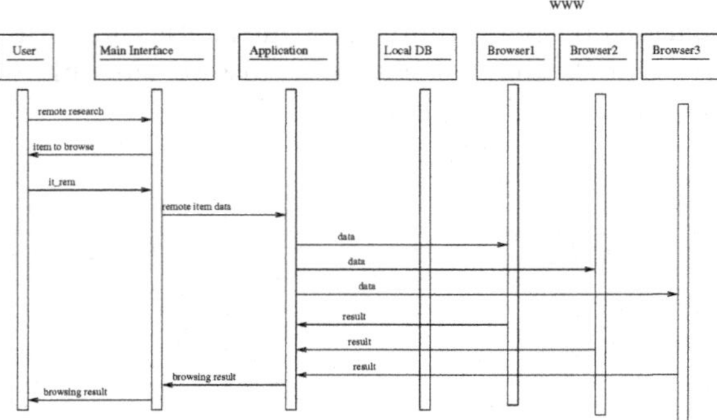

Fig. 3. Sequence Diagram of *Remote* use case.

components $TERMINALS$, CPU_A and $DISK$ in Figure 6 belong to the site that hosts *Main Interface*, *Application* and *Local DB* in Figure 5 (plus *User* that determines the existence of terminals), while the components CPU_{B1}, CPU_{B2} and CPU_{B3} belong to the site hosting the browsers, and we suppose that each browser runs on a different CPU. WAN is modeled by a simple delay. The structure of EQNM in Figure 7 is quite different. The components $TERMINALS$, CPU_M belong to the site that hosts *Main Interface*, the component CPU_A here only runs *Application*, the component $DISK$ only hosts *Local DB* and finally CPU_{B1}, CPU_{B2} and CPU_{B3} accomplish the same task as above. This alternative platform requires changes in the communication layer as well. A LAN is introduced to connect three among the sites in the deployment diagram. The LAN is also modeled by a simple delay. In order to completely define the EQNMs, basic features of the devices (such as speed of the CPU, disk access time) and size and delay of the communications among components have to be given. In a similar way as we do for probabilities in Use Case Diagram, we ask to the designer to put the characteristics of the communication means within the Deployment Diagram (as shown in Figure 5 with symbolic values u and v). In Section 4.2 we provide details of all the numerical parameters of the EQNMs used. A specific instance of the *meta*-EG (namely an EG-*instance*) can be produced for each deployment diagram and hence for each EQNM. Each instance is obtained by visiting the *meta*-EG and replacing, in each basic node, the pair (A1,A2) with a numeric value representing the overhead delay due to the communication between A1 and A2. This delay depends on the mapping of components to hardware sites (given by the Deployment Diagrams), on the size of data exchanged, but it also depends on the type of communication mean used to interact (represented by the additional data in the deployment diagram).

In Section 4.2 will be given several examples of numerical values assigned to the net weights and the branching point probabilities of the EG-*instances*.

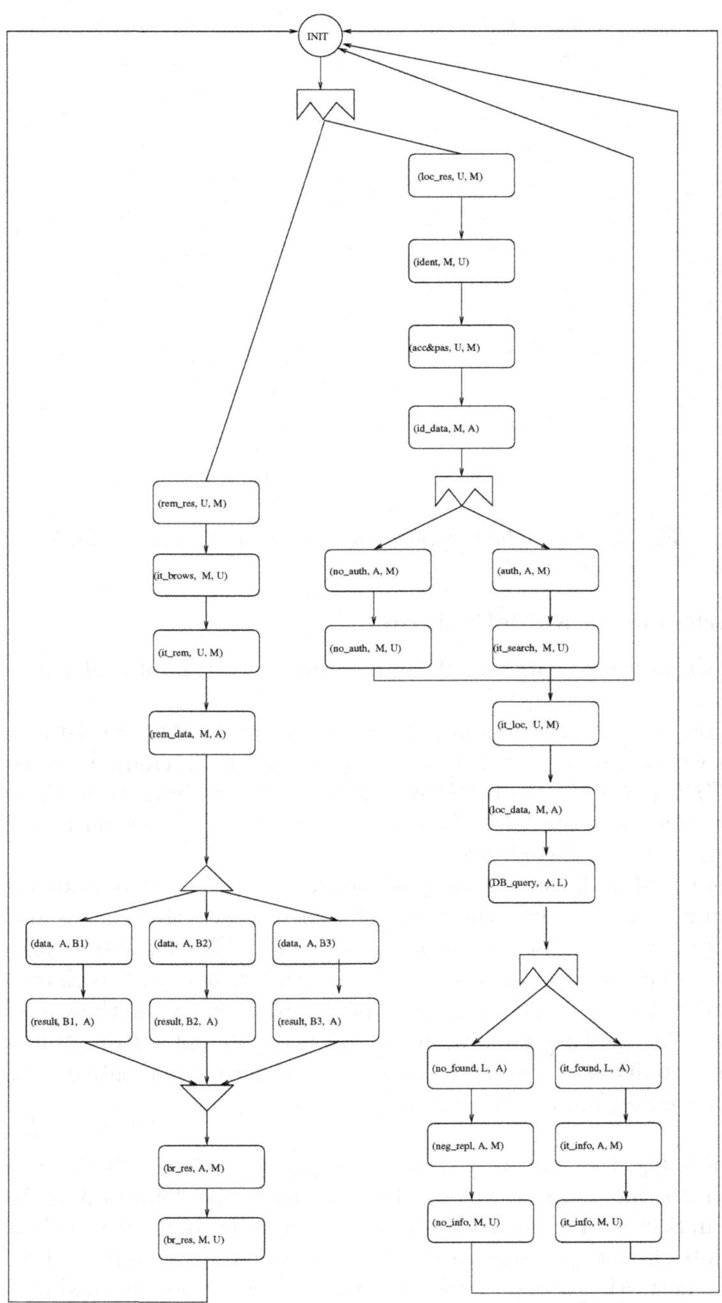

Fig. 4. *Meta*-EG of IRS example.

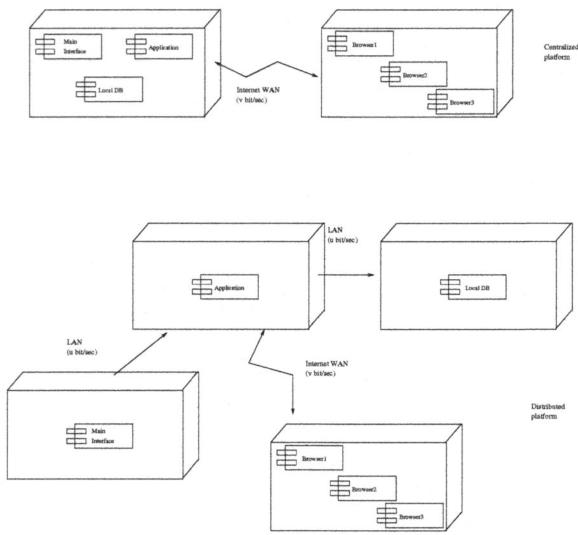

Fig. 5. Candidate Deployment Diagrams for IRS example.

4.2 Performance Model Solution

In this Section we describe how to obtain the prediction of performance indices of interest.

We have considered different sets of service center characteristics and in the following we identify each set as a *Characterization*. In characterization C_1 the devices CPU_A, CPU_M and $DISK$ are quite slow. Characterization C_2 introduces a higher speed for CPU_A and CPU_M. In addition the characterization C_3 has a higher performing $DISK$.

Standard values have been assigned to the service center parameters in terms of minimum time spent into the center (for the center x this time is given by T_x). For example, in the characterization C_1 the value of T_{CPU_A} and T_{CPU_M} are both 0.1 msec, while the value of T_{DISK} is 0.5 msec. Instead in the characterization C_3 the value of T_{CPU_A} and T_{CPU_M} are both 0.01 msec, while the value of T_{DISK} is 0.1 msec. At the same time we have assigned different set of numerical values to the probability p of Figure 1, to consider different percentage of *Local* and *Remote* use cases, namely $p = 0.2, 0.5, 0.8$.

For each C_i $(i = 1, 2, 3)$ a completely parameterized EQNM, as described in Section 2.1, has been obtained. More precisely, the definition of the EQNMs obtained in Section 4.1 has to be completed with environment based parameters, such as job classes, job service demands at different centers and job routing among the network centers. To this end, the EG-*instances* obtained in Section 4.1 have been reduced following the technique described in [30], so obtaining reduced EG-*instances*. The EG-*instances* differ in structure and values of the basic block demand vectors. For example, the demand vector of the block obtained reducing

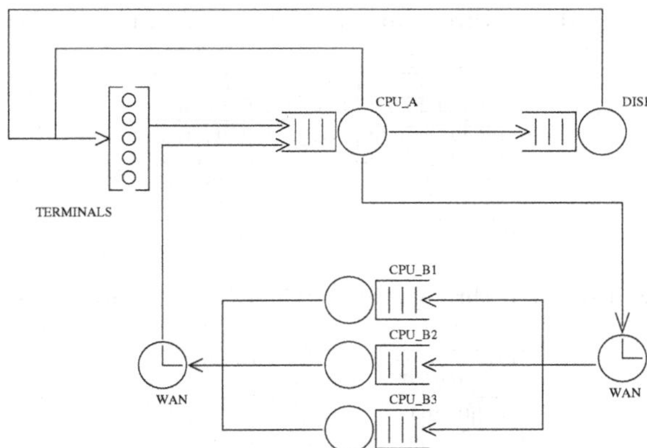

Fig. 6. Extended Queueing Network Model for *Centralized platform* of IRS example.

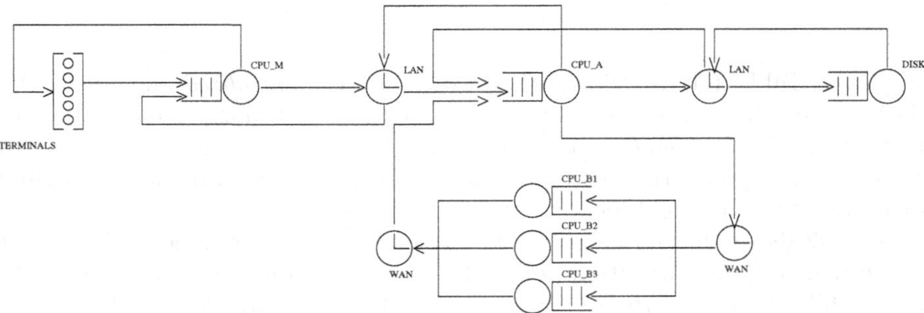

Fig. 7. Extended Queueing Network Model for *Distributed platform* of IRS example.

all the operations successfully performed by the local users in the Distributed platform is given by (1, 3, 3, 3, 2, 1), where each value represent the multiplier of the minimum time spent in the corresponding resource (e.g., the third value of the vector makes the block spending $3 \cdot 0.1$ msec as global time in CPU_A). These values have been used as service demands at EQNM centers. The job routing among the EQNM centers is defined according to the branching probabilities and the non-null values of the demand vector in the reduced EG-*instances*.

The final step to obtain prediction of performance indices of interest is the parameterized model solution and it has been carried out by use of the IBM/RESQ tool [10]. The EQNMs have been solved (by simulation) for the three C_i by varying the total number of users in the IRS and the values of p.

Tables 1 and 2 show the predicted throughput for local users for both *Centralized* and *Distributed* platforms for characterization C_1 and characterization C_3, respectively, vs both the global number of users and the percentage of local users.

Table 1. Predicted throughput for Characterization C_1 (local users)

C_1	Centralized			Distributed		
	0.2	0.5	0.8	0.2	0.5	0.8
10	0.22	0.58	1.02	0.36	0.92	1.43
20	0.24	0.60	1.04	0.49	1.12	1.74
40	0.23	0.63	1.06	0.59	1.18	1.73
60	-	-	-	0.60	1.17	1.74

Table 2. Predicted throughput for Characterization C_3 (local users)

C_3	Centralized			Distributed		
	0.2	0.5	0.8	0.2	0.5	0.8
10	0.69	1.70	2.67	0.66	1.71	2.67
20	1.33	3.37	5.15	1.35	3.36	5.30
40	2.49	5.96	9.18	2.60	6.42	9.95
60	3.40	6.55	10.34	3.95	9.16	11.97
80	3.81	6.30	10.37	5.20	11.12	12.80
100	-	-	-	6.50	11.94	13.09

¿From Table 1 it is evident that for C_1 both *Centralized* and *Distributed* platforms reach a saturation point quite early: the *Centralized* one for 10 global users, while the *Distributed* one for 60 global users. Anyway we remark that, at the saturation point, the *Distributed* platform guarantees a higher throughput for all the percentages of local users.

Table 2 shows that for C_3 the system tolerates an higher value of global users before reaching the saturation point: the *Centralized* one holds up to 80 global users, while the *Distributed* one more than 100 global users. Also in this case, at the saturation point, the *Distributed* platform guarantees a higher throughput for all the percentages of local users.

Basing on these results the designer can primarily perform a choice between *Centralized* and *Distributed* platform, looking at the configuration that better achieve the performance requirements. Thereafter a fine tuning of the number of users to be introduced into the system can be achieved by keeping into account the growth towards the saturation and, eventually, additional performance index values (such as the device utilizations).

5 Conclusions

In this paper we have shown how to apply to a complete case study a methodology for the automatic generation of a performance model from a UML based software/hardware distributed system description. We have outlined how the characteristics of some UML diagrams (i.e., Use Case, Sequence and Deployment Diagrams) can be exploited to build a non-trivial performance model early in the software development process. Two different design alternatives have been considered for the case study in order to show that our approach can be helpful as a support to early design decisions. Evident differences on the numerical results of the performance model solution for the considered alternatives prove that this kind of decisions could actually affect the quality of the final product. We also show that once such a decision has been taken, the iterative solution of the performance models allows to finely tune several model parameters, hence to produce enhanced systems specifications.

Future work follows two parallel directions: extending the methodology to cope with a wider range of Sequence Diagrams (including, for example, dynamic creation of objects), and to work with different UML diagrams (for example, Activity Diagrams could be used for workload derivation); different types of performance models (i.e., not SPE based) should be also considered.

Acknowledgements

The authors thank the anonymous referees for their helpful comments which have improved the content and the presentation of the paper. This work has been supported by MURST project "SALADIN: Software architectures and languages to coordinate distributed mobile components".

References

1. Balsamo, S., Inverardi, P. and Mangano, C. "An Approach to Performance Evaluation of Software Architectures", *Proc. of WOSP98*, 1998. 181
2. Bass L., Clements P., Kazman R. "Software Architecture in Practice" *Addison-Wesley*, 1998. 181
3. Bernardo M., Donatiello L., Gorrieri C. "A Formal Approach to the Integration of Performance Aspects in the Modeling and Analysis of Concurrent Systems" *Information and Computation 144, 83-154*, 1998. 181
4. Booch, G. "Object oriented analysis and design with applications", *Redwood City, CA, Benjamin/Cummings*, 1991.
5. Buhr, R.J.A. and Casselman, R.S. "Use case maps for Object oriented systems", *Prentice Hall*, 1996. 181
6. Coad, P. and Yourdon, E. "Object-Oriented analysis", *Yourdon Press/Prentice-Hall, Englewood Cliffs, NJ*, 1990.
7. Cortellessa, V. and Mirandola R. "Deriving a queueing network based performance model from UML diagrams", to appears in Proceedings of WOSP2000 179
8. Cortellessa, V., Iazeolla, G. and Mirandola R. "Early Performance Verification for Object-Oriented Software Systems" Technical Report, University of Rome "Torvergata", 1999. 181, 183
9. Fowler, M. and Scott, K. "UML Distilled: Applying the Standard Object Modeling Language", *Addison Wesley Object Technology Series*, 1997. 178
10. Gordon, R.F. Loewner, P.G. and MacNair, E.A. "The Research Queueing Package Version 3" IBM T.J. Watson Research Center, March 1992. 189
11. Harmon, P. and Watson, M. "Understanding UML: the Developer's Guide", *Morgan Kaufmann*, 1997. 178
12. Herzog, U. "Stochastic Process Algebras" *Proc. of 2nd Workshop on Process Algebras and Performance Modeling, Regensberg, Germany*, 1994. 181
13. Hills, G., Rolia, J.A. and Serazzi, G. "Performance Engineering of Distributed Software Process Architectures", *LNCS, Springer Verlag, vol.977, pp.357-371*, 1995. 181, 181, 182

14. Hrischuk, C., Rolia, J. and Woodside, C.M. "Automatic generation of a software performance model using an object oriented prototype", *Proc. of Third International Workshop on Modeling, Analysis and Simulation of Computer and Telecommunication Systems, Durham, NC*, 1995. 181
15. Hrischuk, C., Woodside, C.M., Rolia, J. and Iversen, R. "Trace-Based Load Characterization for Generating Performance Software Models", *IEEE Trans. on Software Engineering, vol.25, no.1, pp.122-135*,January/February 1999. 181
16. Iazeolla, G., D'Ambrogio, A. and Mirandola, R. "Software Performance Validation Strategies", *Proc. of Performance'99, Special Sessions*, Istanbul, Turkey, October 1999. 181
17. Jain, R. "Art of Computer Systems Performance Analysis", *New York Wiley*, 1990. 179, 181
18. Kahkipuro P. " UML based Performance Modeling Framework for Object-Oriented Distributed Systems", *Proc. of Second International Conference on the Unified Modeling Language, October 28-30, 1999, USA, LNCS, Springer Verlag, vol.1723*, 1999. 181, 182
19. Kant, K. "Introduction to Computer System Performance Evaluation", *McGraw Hill, Int. Editions*, 1992. 179, 181
20. King, P. and Pooley, R. "Estimating the Performance of UML Models using Petri Nets", private communication, 1999. 181
21. King, P. and Pooley, R. "Using UML to Derive Stochastic Petri Net Models", *Proceedings of the Fifteenth UK Performance Engineering Workshop, Department of Computer Science, The University of Bristol, N. Davies and J. Bradley, editors, UKPEW '99* July 1999. 181, 181, 181
22. Lavenberg, S.S. "Computer Performance Modeling Handbook", *Academic Press, New York*, 1983. 179, 180, 181
23. Mirandola, R. and Hollinger, D. "A new approach to performance modeling of Client/Server distributed data bases architectures", Performance Evaluation, 29, 1997. 180, 181, 183
24. Pooley, R. and C. Kabajunga, "Simulation of UML Sequence Diagrams" *Proc. of 14th UK Performance Engineering Workshop, Edinburgh,R. Pooley and N. Thomas Eds., UK PEW '98* July 1998. 181, 181, 182
25. Pooley, R. and King, P. "The Unified Modeling Language and Performance Engineering", *IEE Proceedings - Software, vol.146, no.1, pp.2-10*, February 1999. 181, 181, 182
26. Pooley, R. "Using UML to Derive Stochastic Process Algebras Models", private communication, 1999. *Proceedings of the Fifteenth UK Performance Engineering Workshop, Department of Computer Science, The University of Bristol, N. Davies and J. Bradley, editors, UKPEW '99* July 1999. 181, 182
27. Raymond, K.A. "Reference Model for Open Distributed Processing: a Tutorial", *Open Distributed Processing, II (C-20)*, 1995.
28. Rolia, J.A. and Sevcik, K.C. "The Method of Layers", *IEEE Trans. on Software Engineering, vol.21, no.8, pp.689-699*, August 1995. 181, 181, 182
29. Shlaer, S. and Mellor, S.J. "Object lifecycles: modeling the world in states", *Prentice-Hall Building, Englewood Cliffs, NJ, Yourdon Press*, 1992.
30. Smith, C.U. "Performance Engineering of Software Systems", *Addison-Wesley, Reading, MA*, 1990. 179, 180, 180, 180, 183, 183, 188
31. Smith, C.U. and Williams, L.G. "Software Performance Engineering: a Case Study including Performance comparison with Design alternatives", *IEEE Transactions on Software Engineering, 19 (7)*, 1993. 181

32. Smith, C.U. and Williams, L.G. "Performance Engineering Evaluation of Object-Oriented Systems with SPE-ED", *LNCS , Springer Verlag, vol.1245, pp.135-153*, 1997. 181
33. Smith, C.U. and Williams, L.G. "Software Performance Engineering for Object-Oriented Systems: A Use Case Approach", *Technical Report, Performance Engineering Services*, 1998.
34. Williams, L.G. and Smith, C.U. "Information Requirements for Software Performance Engineering", *LNCS, Springer Verlag, vol.977, pp.86-101*, 1995. 181, 181
35. Williams, L.G. and Smith, C.U. "Performance Evaluation of Software Architecture", *Proc. WOSP 98, pp. 164-177*, 1998 181, 181
36. Woodside, C.M. "A Three-View Model for Performance Engineering of Concurrent Software", *IEEE Transactions on Software Engineering, 21 (9)*, 1995. 181, 181
37. "UML 1.3 Documentation", *Rational Rose Resource Center*, 1999. 178
38. http://www.omg.org. 178
39. http://www.rational.com/uml/documentation.html. 178

Appendix

Here below the algorithm that derives the *meta*-EG from the SDs is given. The rationale behind this algorithm is that each SD contributes by a certain number of different nodes to the EG. The complete EG is thereon incrementally obtained.

```
Sequence Diagrams to Execution Graph:
place into EG the INIT node
place a pending arrow after INIT
for all SD's do
    do
        consider next interaction (l, A1, A2)
        Translation Operations
    while there is another interaction
    if (pending arrow) then link it to INIT
```

```
Translation Operations:
Case 1: Interaction (l, A1, A2) already translated
    if (pending arrow) then
        link it to (l, A1, A2)
        if (a cycle not including INIT has been generated) then
            place into EG a cycle node
    else skip
Case 2: Interaction (l, A1, A2) never translated
    subcase 2.1: (l, A1, A2) is a single interaction
        if (pending arrow) then
            place a new (l, A1, A2) node into EG after the pending arrow
        else
            place a branching node into EG after the last visited node, if any, or after INIT
            place the already existing path on one branch
            place a new (l, A1, A2) node on the other branch
        place a pending arrow after (l, A1, A2)
    subcase 2.2: (l, A1, A2) is a multiple interaction (*, A1, *) with cardinality c
        if (pending arrow) then
            place a fork node with multiplicity c into EG after the pending arrow
        else
            place a branching node into EG after the last visited node, if any, or after INIT
            place the already existing path on one branch
            place a fork node with multiplicity c on the other branch
        – follow and translate, one at a time, all the c threads starting from (*, A1, *) –
        place a join node into EG after all the c threads translated
        place a pending arrow after the join node
        resume translation from the first interaction after the multiple interaction
```

A Radical Revision of UML's Role Concept

Friedrich Steimann

Institut für Technische Informatik
Rechnergestützte Wissensverarbeitung
Universität Hannover, Appelstraße 4, D-30167 Hannover
steimann@acm.org

Abstract. UML's current definition of the role concept comes with many problems, not the least being that it is difficult to understand and communicate. This paper proposes a revised UML metamodel building on a much simpler role definition. Moreover, it replaces the rather unusual notions of association role and association end role as well as the rarely used association generalization with the more popular concept of overloading, thereby leading to a considerable reduction in the number of modelling concepts. Despite the rather radical nature of the proposed alterations, no changes in UML notation become necessary. However, a notable change in modelling style including in particular a clearer separation of structure and interaction diagrams are among the likely effects of the proposed revision.

1 Introduction

UML's current version [OMG 1999] has three different definitions of the role concept:

- roles as names of association ends,
- roles as slots in collaborations, and
- roles as dynamic classes.

The first two are heritage from the entity-relationship diagram and object-oriented methods such as OORAM [Reenskaug et al. 1996], respectively, and, as will be seen, are mostly independent of each other. The third is only mentioned in passing [§ 3.27.1, p. 3-46] and is presumably a tribute to a view of roles commonly found in the literature [Steimann 1999].

Of course there are various other uses of the term spread over the UML specification, for instance the roles of an actor in different use case diagrams or the roles in a state chart, but these uses are either instances of one of the three definitions listed above or merely a way of speaking. After all, role is one of the most elementary terms not only in modelling (cf. sect. 5), and it is difficult, if not impossible, to get along without it.

The rationale of the first definition of the role concept is simple: to uniquely identify it, every end of an association (like every place of a relationship in the entity-relationship diagram) can be assigned a rolename, and this end is then referred to as a role [§ 3.42.2]. The second definition, the definition of roles as slots of a collaboration, involves more:

A. Evans, S. Kent and B. Selic (Eds.): «UML» 2000, LNCS 1939, pp. 194-209, 2000.

"... *while a classifier is a complete description of instances, a classifier role is a description of the features required in a particular collaboration, i.e. a classifier role is a projection of, or a view of, a classifier. The classifier so represented is referred to as the base classifier of that particular classifier role.*" [§ 2.10.4, p. 2-112]

and

"*Each association role represents the usage of an association in the collaboration, and it is defined between the classifier roles that represent the associated classifiers. The represented association is called the base association of the association role. As the association roles specify a particular usage of an association in a specific collaboration, all constraints expressed by the association ends are not necessarily required to be fulfilled in the specified usage. The multiplicity of the association end may be reduced in the collaboration, i.e. the upper and the lower bounds of the association end roles may be lower than those of the corresponding base association end, as it might be that only a subset of the associated instances participate in the collaboration instance.*" [ibid.]

These definitions become more transparent when looking at the corresponding excerpt of UML's metamodel, as compiled from figures 2-5, 2-6, and 2-17 of the original specification (shown in figure 1). For the sake of conciseness, classifiers other than *Class* and *Interface* have been omitted; the complete list can be found in [Rumbaugh et al. 1999]. It must be noted, however, that much of UML's complexity is due to this generalization and the resultant genericity, and that the correctness of the following and all other argumentation critically depends on what is comprised under the classifier term. Also notice that *AssociationClass*, a common subclass of *Association* and *Class*, has been omitted; although a handy modelling concept, it entails certain consistency problems that are not dealt with here.

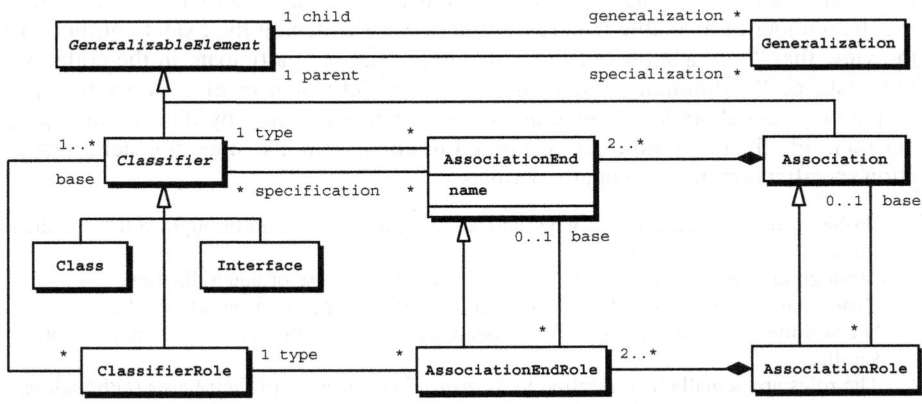

Figure 1: An excerpt of the abstract syntax that forms the structural part of the UML metamodel. More than one base for one classifier role may only be specified if classification is multiple.

Closer inspection of the original specification reveals that there are many problems in association with roles. Some of them are obvious and easily avoided. For instance, a classifier role must not specify a classifier role as its base, and association ends and association end roles must not be mixed in one association.[1] Other things are subtler and become apparent only when working through the textual specification. Some of these will be discussed next.

2 Problems

2.1 Base vs. Projection

The use of the term base in connection with collaboration roles (as reflected in the metamodel of figure 1) suggests that the roles of a collaboration are derived from their bases. And indeed, one well-formedness rule for association end roles states that the base classifier of the classifier role connected to the association end role must be the same as or a specialization[2] of the classifier connected to the association end role's base [§ 2.10.3, p. 2-108]:

```
self.type.base = self.base.type
or
self.type.base.allParents->includes (self.base.type)
```

But this observation is superficial. The rule only requires that the base itself, if not the same classifier, is a specialization, not that the classifier role is a specialization of its base. Quite the contrary: a role repeats only parts of the features of its base (the *availableFeatures* [§2.10.2, p. 2-106]) and in case of the classifier role, lets instances of any classifier engage in the association as long as it conforms to whatever is required by this role. Therefore, the extent of the role is bigger than that of its base,[3] and use of the term base (reminiscent of base type/derived type) is misleading.[4]

But if the classifier role is more general than its base, why is this base allowed to be a specialization of the original type? Why should one first restrict the extent of a classifier role (by selecting a specialization as its base) and then widen it (by reducing the number of available features)? And doesn't widening the extent conflict with the view that "only a subset of the associated instances participate in the collaboration instance"? Admittedly, it does make sense to let instances of arbitrary type participate in a collaboration as long as they do what is required by the role they play, but then this liberty should not be limited to collaborations, since a general association specification may be equally permissive.[5]

---

1 Problems of this kind can easily be (and some actually are) fixed through well-formedness rules.

2 Throughout this text, specialization is defined as the inverse of generalization.

3 Note that the semantics of the base relation differs depending on what is being related, because the same does not hold for association and association end roles: their extents are samller.

4 The roles are actually also referred to as *projections* or *views* of their bases (although *partial specifications* would seem more adequate).

5 In fact, several extensions of the entity-relationship model allow ad hoc disjunctions (which are not generalizations!) of entity types to occur in the places of relationship types [Steimann 1999]. Interfaces may serve as such ad hoc disjunctions [Steimann 2001], but this is not discussed in the UML specification.

2.2 Interface Specifiers vs. Classifier Roles

In UML, each association end can specify one or more classifiers as *interface specifiers* (mapped to the *specification* pseudo-attribute, see figure 1) which are to restrict the access to the instances of the classifier across the association. In a way, these interface specifiers parallel the specification of base classifiers with a classifier role, but despite the symmetric structure of the metamodel this parallelism is unapparent. Instead, the UML specification offers various nebulous explanations, for instance

> "*A role may be static (e.g., an association end) or dynamic (e.g., a collaboration role)*"

in the glossary or

> "*The use of a rolename and interface specifier are equivalent to creating a small collaboration that includes just an association and two roles, whose structure is defined by the rolename and attached classifier on the original association. Therefore, the original association and classifiers are a use of the collaboration. The original classifier must be compatible with the interface specifier (which can be an interface or a type, among other kinds of classifiers)*"

in the notation guide [§ 3.42.2, S. 3-66]. Undoubtedly, both interface specifiers of an association end and base classifiers of a collaboration role serve to specify what is required from the instances engaging in an association (or collaboration). However, *AssociationEnd* generalizes *AssociationEndRole*, not *ClassifierRole*, and it lets the former inherit the rolename attribute. But what happened to the *specification* pseudo-attribute that should also be inherited from *AssociationEnd*? Has it been dropped? If an association end role in a collaboration specifies an association end as its base and this base lists interface specifiers, must the classifier role of such an association end role conform to these interface specifiers? And while the interface specifiers only serve to restrict access, not to constrain the type of the instances (this is the task of the connected type classifier), the classifier role does both: it provides a partial specification of the classifiers whose instances can play the role, and it restricts access to the features of this partial specification. Last but not least, while the base classifier of a classifier role must connect to the base association of its association role, no such constraint is imposed on the interface specifiers. Thus, the alleged symmetry is really an asymmetry (and a very confusing one at that).

2.3 Static Structure Diagrams vs. Collaboration Diagrams

The duality of concepts just criticized is paralleled by a second one: that of static structure and collaborations. For an example of this, look at the diagram of figure 2a. According to the UML specification it is a perfect collaboration diagram, albeit one without interaction information. But where is the collaboration? Is the structural information given in figure 2a less generally relevant than that of figure 2b, which is a class diagram? Or is the existence of (classifier) roles the true (and only) reason to declare one as a collaboration diagram and not the other? Indeed, one might prefer to model *Teacher* and *Student* as subclasses (rather than roles) of *Person*[6] — would this

---

[6] admittedly a poor preference: roles are no subtypes [Firesmith & Henderson-Sellers 1998; Steimann 1999]

simple modification turn the collaboration diagram into an ordinary class diagram? Hardly.

Note well, the problem here is not that collaboration diagrams express structure, but that roles (other than the rolenames of association ends) are excluded from class diagrams. Many kinds of constraints on associations (including multiplicities, exclusive ors etc.) have been devised, but it is impossible to express in a class diagram that of all persons only teachers can be members of a staff and give courses, even though this may very well be a fundamental structural property of a modelling problem. In such cases, the introduction of an extra collaboration diagram to express structure (but lacking an actual interaction) must appear artificial, as is the case for figure 2.

(a)

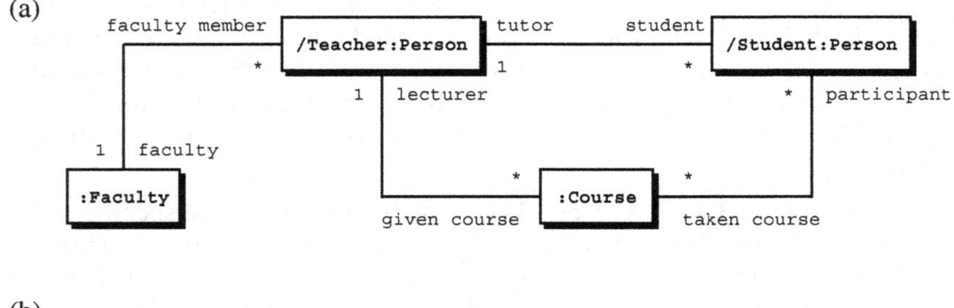

(b)

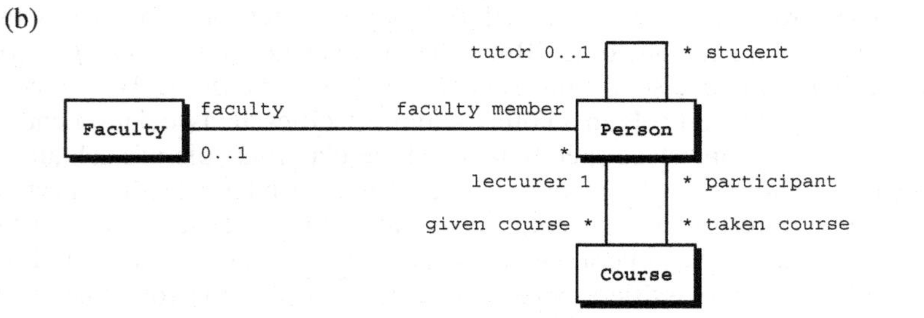

Figure 2: (a) Collaboration diagram without interaction information (from [OMG 1999]) (b) corresponding class diagram (adapted from [Övergaard 1999])

2.4 Specification vs. Instance Level

In UML, interaction diagrams are offered at two levels: the specification (or classifier) and the instance level [§ 2.10.4, p. 2-112]. However, interactions (and collaborations) always take place between actual objects, not their roles or classes, and it seems that the specification level is needed only insofar as interactions require or impose additional structure, structure that, because of its generality, should indeed be expressed on the classifier level. The specification of interaction itself however must be able to distinguish different objects even if they play the same role and, more importantly, must be able to express that the same object plays different roles in one interaction. Such is not possible on the classifier level, and it would appear that the instance level is the natural domain for interaction specification. The definition of collaborations with generic interaction patterns on the classifier level tends to blur this distinction, and is rather difficult to communicate.

2.5 Association Roles vs. Association Generalization

As quoted above, association roles "specify a particular usage of an association in a specific collaboration" in which the "constraints expressed by the association ends are not necessarily required to be fulfilled in the specified usage" [OMG 1999, § 2.10.4, 2-112]. For instance:

> *"The multiplicity of the association end may be reduced in the collaboration, i.e. the upper and the lower bounds of the association end roles may be lower than those of the corresponding base association end, as it might be that only a subset of the associated instances participate in the collaboration instance."*

In other words: the extent of an association role is a subset of the extent of its base association. And the UML specification continues:

> *"Similarly, an association may be traversed in some, but perhaps not all, of the allowed directions in the specific collaboration, i.e. the isNavigable property of an association end role may be false even if that property of the base association end is true.* [...] *The changeability and ordering of an association end may be strengthened in an association-end role, i.e. in a particular usage the end is used in a more restricted way than is defined by the association."* [§ 2.10.4, 2-112]

But association roles are not the only way to restrict the use of an association in a UML model: as indicated by the metamodel in figure 1, associations can also be generalized. Whereas the current OMG specification is very brief about association generalization ("Generalization may be applied to associations as well as classes, although the notation may be messy because of the multiple lines. An association can be shown as an association class for the purpose of attaching generalization arrows." [OMG 1999, § 3.49.2, S. 3-80] is the only textual mention I found), other sources go into more detail:

> *"As with any generalization relationship, the child element* [of an association generalization] *must add to the intent (defining rules) of the parent and must subset the extent (set of instances) of the parent. Adding to the intent means adding additional constraints. A child association is more constrained than its parent."* [Rumbaugh et al. 1999, p. 163].

But isn't disallowing navigation more constrained than leaving navigability open (that is, allowing it), and isn't being sorted more constrained than not being sorted (it is implied by an additional condition, that of the elements being ordered)? All in all, it seems that the semantics of association roles is largely covered by the specialization of their base associations, but his duality of concepts (yet another one!) is never mentioned.

2.6 Interfaces vs. Classes

For some unapparent reason, UML doesn't make much use of interfaces. In fact, even though there appears to be a basic awareness of the general importance of interfaces, the metamodel has no dedicated use for it (as it has, e.g., for collaboration roles). Instead, the more general *Classifier* (comprising classes and interfaces) is consistently (ab)used to specify interfaces where the use of the *Interface* concept were in place. For instance, the interface specifiers of an association end may be classes, and classifier roles are general classifiers although their purpose is clearly that of a partial specification and hence that of an interface[7].

3 Revision

It should be clear from the above that UML's current role concept is problematic. The alleged symmetry of association end and collaboration role is only seeming, and particularly the introduction of association roles and association end roles which share only superficial properties with classifier roles (such as having bases and being slots in a collaboration) appears to be a peculiarity of UML that is difficult to transport. As a matter of fact, the description of the connection between associations and association roles remains rather sketchy, and it may be speculated that any attempt to pin it down precisely would lead to more problems.

Fortunately, there is a simple solution to all this. Roles are no specialty of collaborations and the interactions they enable, they are a core structural element (although not necessarily a static one). Roles are bridges between instantiable classifiers and their associations, be it in the scope of a collaboration or outside the context of any interaction. But roles are no association ends (or the names thereof) — a role (more precisely, a *role type*) is a classifier like a class, only that it does not have instances of its own. Instead, a role recruits its instances from those classifiers that are declared compatible with the role, that is, that comply with the partial specification that makes the role.

As for the remaining UML roles, namely the association roles and association end roles: they too are not limited to the scope of collaborations. But unlike classifier roles, they are rivaled by an equally suitable (an much better understood) concept: *association overloading*. Overloading, expressing that the same association (operation, relation, or function) has different properties depending on the classifiers (types) being associated, is ubiquitous in object-oriented programming as well as in the theory of type structures [Bläsius et al. 1989], and it gracefully accounts for the fact that an association in a collaboration (with only a subset of the instances involved) may have different properties than the same association outside the scope of the collaboration. At the same time, overloading accounts for most of the semantics of association specialization as a purely structural modelling element — the only obvious difference is that a specialized association can have a different name than its generalization.

Note well, the suggested revision is not a plea against collaborations. Collaborations remain as an important means of zooming into particular structural aspects of a model and as a basis for expressing the interactions that build upon them. The point here is that the structural aspects of a collaboration can be expressed with the same modelling concepts as any classifier structure, be it in or outside the scope of collaboration.

7 perhaps not an interface in the definition of UML, but that is another issue

More specifically, the revision of UML's role concept is comprised by the following four commitments.

1. The metaclasses *Interface* and *ClassifierRole* are merged into a new metaclass *Role*. The restrictions regarding interfaces in UML (that they cannot have attributes or occur in other places than the target ends of directed associations) are dropped. *Class* and *Role* are strictly separated: while classes can be instantiated (unless of course they are abstract), roles cannot.
2. The association between classifier roles and their base classifiers is replaced by a new relationship, named *populates*[8], which relates classes with the roles their instances can play. (It is convenient to speak of a class as *populating* a role and of an instance as *playing* a role. It is important that these are distinguished: populating roughly corresponds to the subclass relationship among classes, and playing to the instance-of relationship of an instance to its class. The diction in this regard is often ambiguous in the literature.)
3. Association ends are required to connect to roles exclusively. Because roles are interfaces and subroles can combine several interfaces, both pseudo-attributes *type* and *specification* are replaced by one new relationship *specifies* associating each association end with one role. The classes whose instances actually participate in an association are specified only indirectly via the *populates* relationship between classes and roles. Association ends need not be given a rolename; if they are, this name must equal the connected role's. Every role must be unique within an association, i.e., no two association ends of one association must specify the same role.
4. The metaclasses *AssociationEndRole*, *AssociationRole*, and the generalization of associations are replaced by *association overloading*. For this purpose, a new metaclass, *Signature*, is introduced whose instances stand between an association and its (overloaded) association ends. Thus, rather than giving rise to an association role, an association restricted in the context of a collaboration specifies a new instance of *Signature*, comprising new association ends, each connected to a role defined by the collaboration.

The metamodel the suggested changes result in is presented in figure 3. First and foremost, it does not distinguish between core and collaboration modelling elements: association ends are always connected to roles, which are always populated by classes (representative of all other classifiers), although a particular diagram may choose not to show this. Second, UML's indifference with regard to a classifier's being a class or an interface is lifted: interfaces, now termed roles, exclusively occur at associations' ends, and classes exclusively as populating them. Last but not least, it accounts for the fact that the same association can occur multiply in one model, each occurrence disambiguated by a different signature, always involving different association ends and usually also connecting to a different set of roles.

---

[8] Alternative terms for *populates* would be *implements* or *realizes*, but these are rather technical.

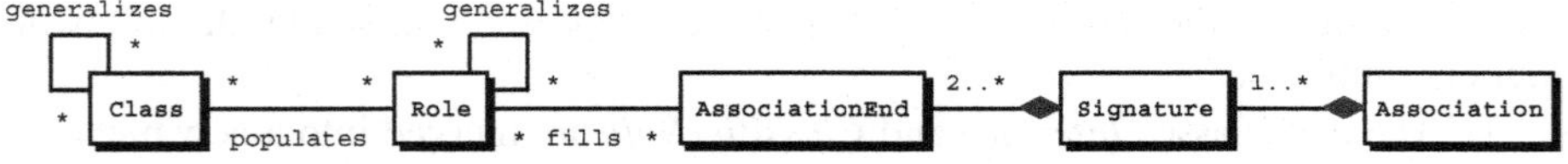

Figure 3: The revised metamodel for UML

A final note on the representation of generalization in figure 3. UML introduces *Generalization* as an instantiable metaclass (see figure 1). In order to avoid inconsistencies, it must be declared for all generalizable elements what is inherited down each generalization relationship (instance of the *Generalization* metaclass). The changed metamodel takes a simpler approach: it represents generalization as an overloaded relationship of the metamodel. Note that *generalizes* is of the same order as *populates*[9], while all instances of *Association* are of a lower order. This way, no precautions avoiding inconsistencies and paradoxes need to be taken.

4 Changes for the Modeller

The good news first: there are no changes of notation necessary. The definition of the new role concept as a merger of collaboration roles and interfaces and the emphasis on the interface aspect suggests that roles are drawn like interfaces, i.e., as stereotyped classifiers or, preferably, as circles. The overloading of associations covering both association generalization and association roles is implicitly expressed by different associations with the same name (and, under certain conditions, may be explicated by generalization arrows). All other changes have no impact on the *notation* itself, only on the *style* diagrams are composed.

4.1 A New Style for Structure Diagrams

The most obvious consequence of the new metamodel on diagram style is that all associations must end at roles. Thus, roles (formerly interfaces) should be seen more frequently in class diagrams, where they function as interface specifiers restricting access to instances across the association, but also as partial specifications of the classes whose instances link. In fact, placing roles, not classes, at association ends means lifting the ‘program to an interface’ maxim (that is considered good practice in object-oriented programming [Gamma et al. 1995; D’Souza & Wills 1998; Steimann 2001]) to the modelling level; it entails that instances of various classes can interchangeably engage in the same association as long as their classes populate the role specified.

In a collaboration diagram at specification level, all associations already end at roles (formerly, classifier roles). However, the classes that (by default) populate the roles, the former base classes (if provided), are no longer implicit parts of the role symbols, but have to be shown explicitly. Note that roles in a collaboration diagram serve no

---

9 UML specifies a similar relationship of types and implementation classes: “[...] types may only specialize other types and implementation classes may only specialize other implementation classes. Types and implementation classes can be related only be realization” [3.27.1, p. 3-46]. But the distinction of types and implementation classes is not that of roles and classes.

different purpose than roles in a (new style) class diagram: they specify the interface (including attributes!) that are required from the collaborators, but they do not commit the collaboration to the classes whose instances can play the role. Figure 4 shows a collaboration diagram and a class diagram in the new style, showing structure, but no behaviour.

Because with the new style class diagrams and the structural aspects of collaboration diagrams rely on the same modelling concepts, there is no syntactical difference between the two diagram types: both show associations connecting roles and classes populating them. Consequently, the difference between the two can be based only on intention: drawing a separate collaboration diagram is useful if and only if (a) interaction information is to be provided or (b) associations that are relevant only within the scope of an actual collaboration (formerly: association roles) are to be shown.

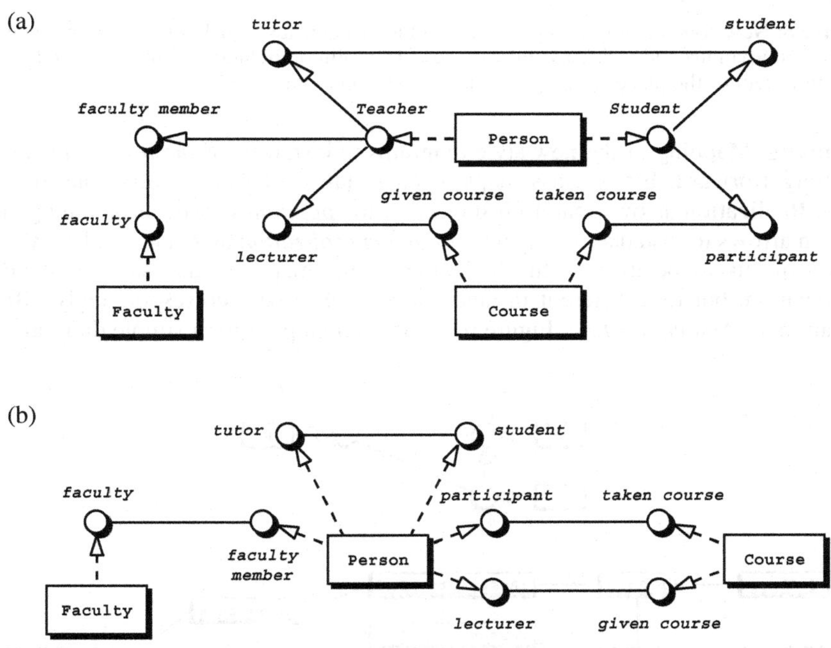

Figure 4: New style collaboration diagram (a) and class diagram (b) corresponding to the diagrams of figure 2. Note that collaboration diagram differs from the class diagram only by the introduction of the subroles *Teacher* and *Student*.

Finally, a collaboration diagram at instance level specifies behaviour by showing prototypical objects as they interact. Although not reserved for the instance level, it is here that UML's lollipop notation unfolds its intuitive expressiveness: in an interaction, objects should be accessed exclusively via the roles they play, and these roles (which are themselves no instances) are connected to their players by unlabeled lines to express that they are the plugpoints between (substitutable) objects and the specified interaction. Figure 5 gives an example of this.

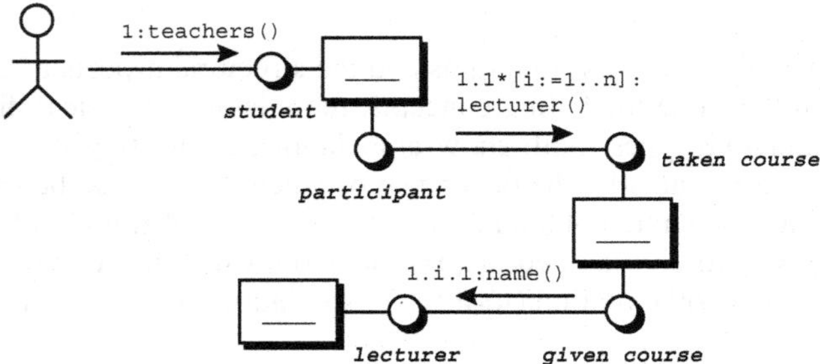

Figure 5: New style collaboration diagram on the instance level. All objects can, but need not, remain anonymous and lack class information. The lollipop notation of an object and its roles is reminiscent of the pieces of a jigsaw puzzle, which is intentional.

Mapping. Mapping of the new style diagrams to instances of the revised metamodel is straightforward. Every class maps to an instance of *Class*, every role to one of *Role*. Realization arrows map to instances of the *populates* association, and generalization arrows to instances of the respective *generalization* associations. Every occurrence of an association with the same name maps to the same instance of Association, but to a different instance of *Signature* with correspondingly different instances of *AssociationEnd*. Figure 6 shows the mapping for a simple diagram.

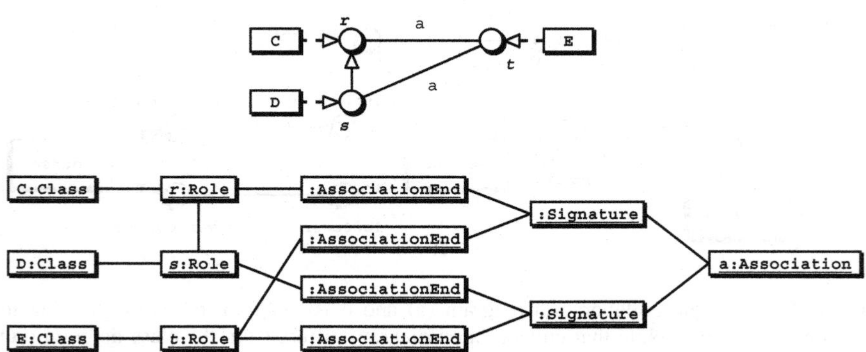

Figure 6: Mapping of a new style structure diagram to an instance of the revised metamodel. Association labels of the object diagram are omitted, but can easily be reconstructed from the class diagram of figure 3.

4.2 Retaining Old Style Diagrams

Every diagram of the new style is valid UML diagram, mapping to the old as well as the revised metamodel. But there are even better news: all diagrams of the old style that map to instances of the old metamodel also map to the revised one. However, as one may imagine, the mapping is not straightforward, and it is more instructive to look at a systematic transformation of conventional diagrams into diagrams of the new style, for which mapping is one-to-one.

The outline of the mapping procedure is as follows: First, it is ensured that every association end connects to a suitable role. Then, the classifier formerly occupying the association end is related to that role, either as populating, as specializing, or as being identical to it. Finally, in case the association is a specialization or an association role, the necessary overloading is declared. During this procedure it may become necessary to introduce a (default) role for a class that is defined as the class's complete interface. In these cases, the role is given the same name as the class (only that the name is set in italics), and it is understood that the two are different types even though they carry the same names.[10]

Mapping. In class diagrams of the old style classifiers (mostly classes) directly connect to association ends. However, these association ends usually come with rolenames. Even though these rolenames are no roles, but mere labels, they could be, and the first step in mapping is to introduce a role for every association end with the rolename as its name, and to let the classifier formerly connected to the association end populate that role. If no rolename is provided, the role is given the class's name (the default role), and if the classifier is an interface, it is considered a direct subrole of the role introduced by the rolename (if provided), or everything is left as is (if no extra rolename is provided). Figure 7 a shows the mapping for all four cases.

Next come the interface specifiers. The interface specifiers at association ends always come with rolenames, but the association ends may connect to classes or interfaces. The mapping to the new drawing style in either case is as above, only that each interface specifier is made an immediate superrole of the role connected to the association end. If an interface specifier is a class, its default role is assumed. Figure 7 b shows the details. Note that the interface specifiers are independent of the association end, since it is not required that they participate in the same association.

Finally the collaboration roles. Here, we restrict ourselves to single classification, which is still predominating in the object-oriented world. Thus, only one base classifier is listed with each classifier role. If this base classifier is a class the classifier role is mapped to an interface with the base classifier populating that interface (figure 7 c). Whether or not the role is the default role of the class depends on whether the classifier role is a partial specification of the base class, i.e., whether it restricts the available features. By default, we must assume that this is the case so that a new role is introduced carrying the classifier role name if specified or a new name otherwise; if not, the default role can be used. Finally, if the base classifier is an interface, it replaces the new role and the class populating it (figure 7 d). Note in particular that the mapping of interface specifiers and classifier roles have not much in common.

---

[10] The names may be thought of as being qualified by a Class or a Role suffix, respectively, but this suffix is left implicit for the sake of readability.

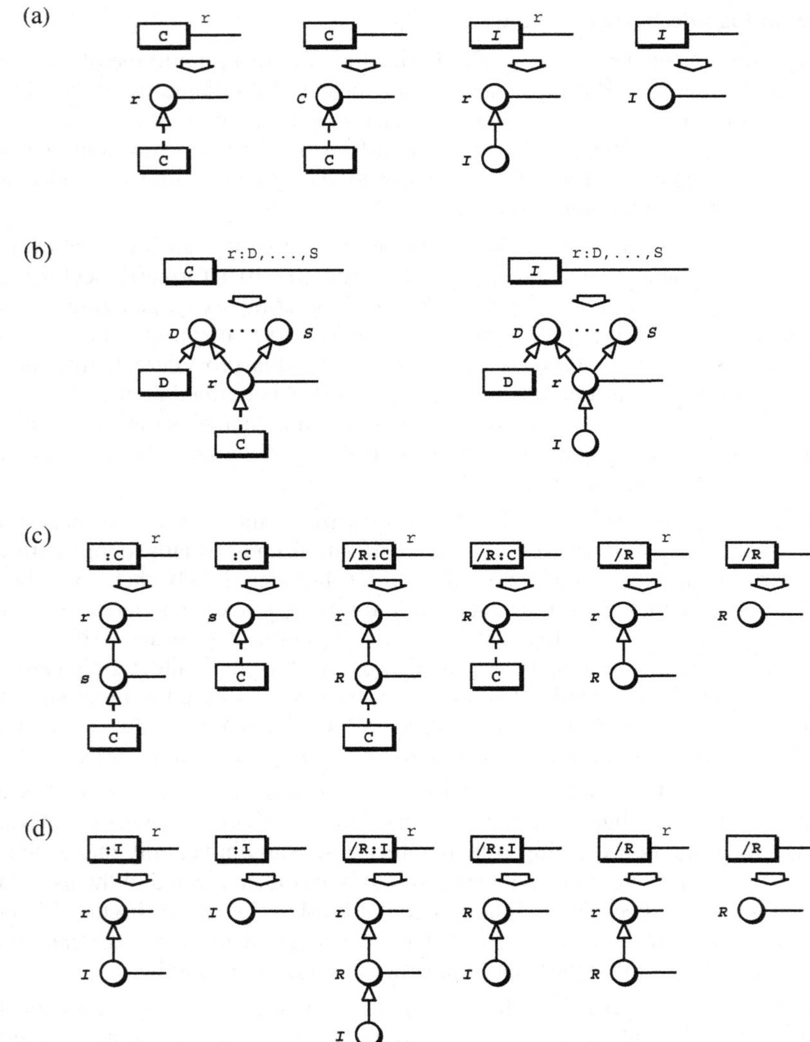

Figure 5: Mapping of old style notation to the new style
(a) for association ends,
(b) for association ends with interface specifiers,
(c) for collaboration roles with classes as bases, and
(d) for collaboration roles with interfaces as bases.

A collaboration diagram does not only introduce classifier roles, but also association roles and association end roles. These roles are implicitly given if (a) the association is unique to collaboration diagrams or (b) the use of the association is restricted in the context of the collaboration (so that the association has a base association). The latter may result from a restriction in multiplicity, navigability, etc. and results in an overloading of associations (and their ends). Thus, to provide complete mapping rules it would be necessary to consider all other uses of the association. In figure 5, overloading is shown only in the context of classifier roles connecting to association ends with rolenames, because it is assumed that the rolename is heritage from a class diagram with the same association[11] and that this association is being restricted within the scope of the collaboration.

Given these mapping rules the diagrams of figure 2 are easily transformed to the new style diagrams of figure 4 (with multiplicities and overloaded associations omitted). However, a couple of things deserve mention. First, if an association end (of a class diagram) is to be filled with instances of the specified classifier only, the corresponding role must not be populated by other classes. Second, if the same rolename occurs in different associations, it must be checked whether the corresponding roles are actually the same or different. Chances are good that they are the same if they comprise the same set of instances (the role players) and if they come with the same set of features. In case they are different, rolenames can be qualified by their association names.

5 The Big Picture

The definition of roles as presented here is not just another formalization of the same old concept — the relation of roles and classes or *natural types* (as opposed to role types) of individuals as reflected by the metamodel in figure 3 is easily formalized using order sorted predicate logic (including a theory of overloading), and is at the same time deeply founded in disciplines as diverse as sociology, linguistics, and ontology [Steimann 2000]. Particularly the latter two have an obvious influence on modelling, and both leave no doubt that roles and relations are mutually dependent concepts. In this dependency, classes merely serve as the providers of instances (which roles don't have) and as takers of the responsibility for the realization of whatever the roles of a model promise.

The biggest advantage of this separation is that structure and interaction are specified largely independently of the classes that deliver instances and implementation. As a result, classes are kept exchangeable even on the model level. In fact, it seems that modelling with roles delivers on the long requested decoupling of classes in a natural and intuitive way. This has been recognized not only by several object-oriented modelling methods such as OORAM [Reenskaug et al. 1996], OPEN [Firesmith & Henderson-Sellers 1998] and CATALYSIS [D'Souza & Wills 1998], but also in different application areas of object-oriented modelling, for instance by the pattern community [Buschmann 1998] and in framework design [Riehle 2000]. With roles defined as above at hand, instantiating the Composite pattern in a model simply amounts to the involved classes populating (or realizing) the *Component*, *Composite*, and *Leaf* roles.

A major advantage of the introduction of roles as *partial specifications of classes* is that polymorphism and substitutability in modelling are no longer bound to the generalization hierarchy of classes (which mainly serves as an abstraction mechanism

---

[11] *introducing* rolenames for association ends in collaboration diagrams is redundant, since classifier roles can have rolenames

and, not only in UML, to specify the paths of inheritance), but apply equally to roles and their implementors. The advantage here is that substitutability, if bound to roles, is less demanding than requiring the full substitutability of (the instances of) one class for another[12], because a role promises only limited functionality and behaviour. In fact, the literal meaning of the term polymorphism is that objects (not functions) have different forms, and an object playing different roles may indeed be considered polymorphic in this literal sense [Steimann 1999].

Last but not least, roles give interfaces a prominent conceptual abstraction that would otherwise be missing in object-oriented modelling. Perhaps this lack explains why UML treats interfaces so negligently, but be that as it may, with roles as a natural and intuitive modelling concept (comprising the purposes of interfaces and classifier roles), interfaces should finally get their rightful place in object-oriented modelling.

6 Conclusion

The distinction between class diagrams as static structure diagrams (with classifiers as types and as interface specifiers of association ends) on one side and collaboration diagrams as behaviour diagrams (with classifier roles and their base classifiers) on the other is notoriously difficult to understand (and even more difficult to write about). This unfortunate situation is worsened by the fact that UML's offered diversity of modelling concepts opens the door wide up for introducing inconsistencies into models that are not easily caught unless an automated tool with full mastery of the UML specification is used. In fact, it may be conjectured that the building of such a tool (mapping all diagrams into a single instance of the metamodel) would unveil many more flaws in the UML specification. Keeping this specification is likely to result in practitioners ignoring large parts of it, if only to be on the safe side.

What is equally disappointing is that the UML specification does not promote the use of the interface concept, which is today a proven design and implementation construct. Instead, the metamodel allows it that interfaces and other classifiers are interchangeably used where either one or the other is required. For instance, in UML neither the interface specifiers of association ends nor the base classifiers of classifier roles need be interfaces, although their purpose is clearly that of specifying an interface. Instead, it seems that UML has adopted JAVA's notion of interfaces and follows it rather slavishly to the point that interfaces can only occur at the target ends of directed associations — an undue limitation that is unacceptable for the role concept. CORBA and IDL, other OMG standards, are much more flexible in this regard.

References

[Bläsius et al. 1989]
KH Bläsius, U Hedtstück, CR Rollinger (eds) *Sorts and Types in Artificial Intelligence* Lecture Notes in Artificial Intelligence 418 (Springer 1989).

[12] which is never really given because otherwise there would be no need to have different classes

[Buschmann 1998]
F Buschmann "Falsche Annahmen (Teil 2)" *OBJEKTspektrum* 4 (1998) 84–85.

[D'Souza & Wills 1998]
DF D'Souza, AC Wills *Objects, Components and Frameworks with UML: The Catalysis Approach* (Addison-Wesley, Reading 1998).

[Firesmith & Henderson-Sellers 1998]
DG Firesmith , B Henderson-Sellers "Upgrading OML to version 1.1 part 2: additional concepts and notations" *Journal of Object-Oriented Programming* 11:5 (1998) 61–67.

[Gamma et al. 1995]
E Gamma, R Helm, R Johnson, J Vlissides *Design Patterns: Elements of Reusable Object-Oriented Software* (Addison-Wesley 1995).

[OMG 1999]
OMG *Unified Modeling Language Specification* Version 1.3 (www.omg.org, June 1999).

[Övergaard 1999]
G Övergaard "A formal approach to collaborations in the Unified Modeling Language" in: *UML '99* LNCS 1723 (Springer, 1999).

[Reenskaug et al. 1996]
T Reenskaug, P Wold, OA Lehne *Working with Objects — The OOram Software Engineering Method* (Manning, Greenwich 1996).

[Riehle 2000]
D Riehle *Framework Design: a Role Modeling Approach* doctoral dissertation (ETH Zürich, 2000).

[Rumbaugh et al. 1999]
J Rumbaugh, I Jacobsen, G Booch *The Unified Modeling Language Reference Manual* (Addison-Wesley, Reading 1999).

[Steimann 1999]
F Steimann "On the representation of roles in object-oriented and conceptual modelling" *Data & Knowledge Engineering* to appear.
http://www.kbs.uni-hannover.de/~steimann

[Steimann 2000]
F Steimann *Formale Modellierung mit Rollen* thesis (Universität Hannover, 2000).

[Steimann 2001]
F Steimann "Role = Interface: a merger of concepts" *Journal of Object-Oriented Programming* (2001) to appear.
http://www.kbs.uni-hannover.de/~steimann

The Role of "Roles" in Use Case Diagrams

Alain Wegmann[1], Guy Genilloud[1]

[1] Institute for computer Communication and Application (ICA)
Swiss Federal Institute of Technology (EPFL)
CH-1015 Lausanne, Switzerland
icawww.epfl.ch
{alain.wegmann, guy.genilloud}@epfl.ch

Abstract: Use cases are the modeling technique of UML for formalizing the functional requirements placed on systems. This technique has limitations in modeling the context of a system, in relating systems involved in a same business process, in reusing use cases, and in specifying various constraints such as execution constraints between use case occurrences. These limitations can be overcome to some extent by the realization of multiple diagrams of various types, but with unclear relationships between them. Thus, the specification activity becomes complex and error prone. In this paper, we show how to overcome the limitations of use cases by making the roles of actors explicit. Interestingly, our contributions not only make UML a more expressive specification language, they also make it simpler to use and more consistent.

1 Introduction

The Unified Modeling Language (UML), standardized by the Object Management Group (OMG) in 1996, aims at integrating the concepts and notations used in the most important software engineering methods. UML is today widely used by the software development community at large. While the bulk of the integration of the concepts is completed, there are still improvements to be made in their consistency. Such improvements could increase the expressive power of UML while reducing its complexity.

System design frequently starts with business modeling, i.e. modeling the context of the system to be developed. The aim is to understand the processes in which the system participates and the system's functionality. UML proposes the *use case model* to describe the system's functionality.

Ivar Jacobson initially defined use case models in [p. 127, 7]: "*The use case model uses actors and use cases. These concepts are simply an aid to defining what exists outside the system (actors) and what should be performed by the system (use cases)*". According to this description, a use case represents a part of the system's functionality. UML defines use cases in a similar manner in [p. B-19, 12]: "*the specification of*

A. Evans, S. Kent and B. Selic (Eds.): «UML» 2000, LNCS 1939, pp. 210-224, 2000.

a sequence of actions, including variants, that a system (or other entity) can perform, interacting with actors of the system..."

Use case models are similar to role models because their intent is to capture the roles of each participant in an action. Role models are defined by Trygve Reenskaug in the OOram method [14]. The method aims at achieving a design by an understanding of how roles collaborate to achieve a goal (i.e. defining a "role model"). Roles are then implemented by programming language objects. For our discussion, the OOram important elements are: (1) roles help with the separation of concerns; even if an object can fulfill more than one role, the designer can still analyze each role individually; (2) roles focus on the notion of responsibilities (i.e. messages accepted and those sent by a role), as opposed to classes that focus on capabilities (i.e. putting more emphasis on the message accepted as opposed to those sent by a class). This method influenced significantly UML and, in particular, the interaction diagrams (i.e. collaboration and sequence diagrams). A good overview of the importance of role models can be found in [11].

Use case models can be used to model functionality of entities at different levels of abstraction: for example business entities (e.g. companies) [8], sub-systems (e.g. existing IT systems to be integrated), components or even programming language classes. In this paper we are particularly concerned with the refinement from business models to system specification models. In the business model, the system of interest is the enterprise and the actors are the people, companies or IT systems interacting with the enterprise. In the system specification model, the system of interest is usually an IT system, which needs either to be developed or modified and the actors are the entities in direct contact with the system of interest. From our experience in consulting, we raised several modeling questions about the utilization of use case diagrams that document system specification models.

The modeling questions we identified are related to the representation of the systems in UML diagrams, to the impossibility of specifying some important requirements of use cases, and to the reuse of use cases. Ian Graham mentions already some of these problems in [4].

Desmond D'Souza and Allan Wills provide a partial answer with their Catalysis method [1]. In their method, they first analyze the role of an IT application in its business environment, and define the system specification independently from the implementation details. They then implement the system by defining a collaboration of "pluggable-parts" such as programming language classes or components. They define collaboration as a "*set of related actions between typed objects playing defined roles in collaboration*" [p. 716, 1]. In Catalysis, the use case is a means to specify a collective behavior of entities without specifying the individual behavior of each entity. This idea came originally from DisCo [9].

Our paper proposes to extend the Catalysis definition of use cases by leveraging on the concept of role. Our propositions allow for the improvement of the use case expressiveness and should lead to a simplification of UML.

The plan of this paper is: Section 2: identification of modeling questions related to use cases, Section 3: discussions of the questions and proposition of extensions to the use case modeling technique, Section 4: propositions of modifications to UML, Section 5: case study revisited using the extended use case modeling technique, Section 6: future work.

2 Modeling Questions

In this section, we present five modeling issues related to use cases. We illustrate these issues with an example of Company, a chain store. The Company has one Corporate HQ (headquarter) and several Stores (see Fig. 1).

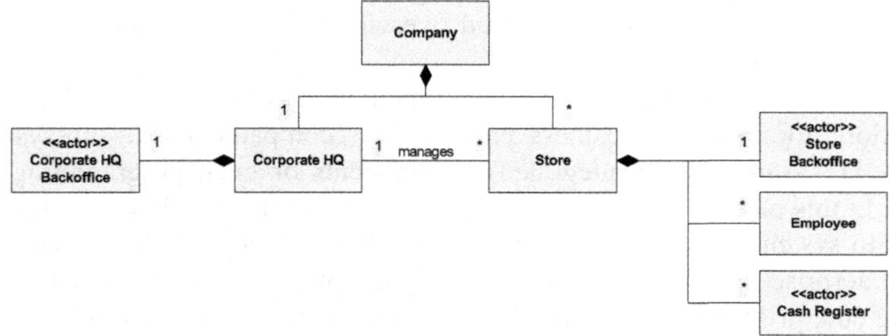

Fig. 1: Class diagram describing Company structure

The Company began an IT project to automate the Cash Registers of its Stores. The functionality to be provided is (see Fig. 2): "sell Goods" (i.e. the Cashier computes price to be paid by the Customer and then proceed with the payment), "till Balance" (i.e. the Cashier and the Manager check the content of the cash drawer) and "transfer Price" (i.e. new price lists are transferred from the Corporate HQ to all Cash Registers with the collaboration of the Store Backoffice).

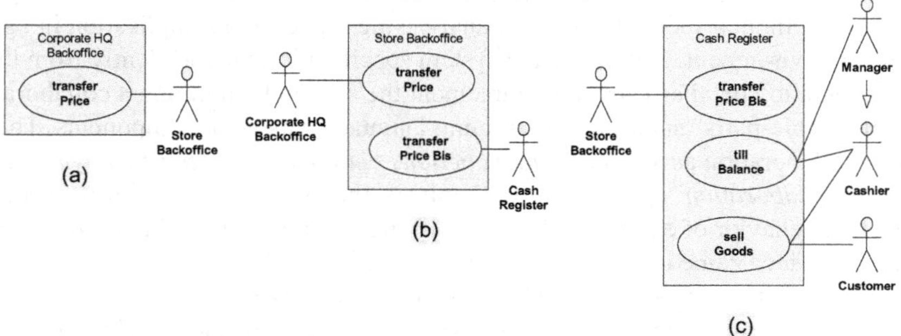

Fig. 2: (a) Corporate HQ Backoffice use case diagram, (b) Store Backoffice use case diagram, (c) Cash Register use case diagram

This example raises the following points:

1. As the "transfer Price" business process specification involves three types of IT systems (Corporate HQ, Store Backoffice and Cash Register), we must have three separate use case diagrams (one per system type). We would much rather have one diagram representing all system types to better understand the role of each system type relative to the other system types. We could use an interaction diagram. We would not necessarily reject this solution if in UML, as in Catalysis, interaction diagrams could represent use case occurrences (in a similar manner as stimuli are represented). Without the ability to represent use case occurrences, we would have to refine the interactions between the systems down to the level of stimuli exchanges. That is, we would be forced to provide too many details for what is needed. This raises Question 1: "How can we model, in one use case diagram, a business process specification between multiple system types and actor types?"
2. As represented in Fig. 2b, the Store Backoffice system will perform occurrences of two use cases: "transfer Price" and "transfer Price bis". These two use case specifications are identical, except for, in each occurrence, the actors are different and the system plays a different role (sender in one case and receiver in the other case). This forces the designer to have two independent use case specifications ("transfer Price" and "transfer Price bis"). Of course, we want to have just one use case specification "transfer Price". This raises Question 2: "How can a system play different roles in different occurrences of a same use case specification?"
3. Traditionally use case diagrams do not express multiplicities. In our example, this prevents the modeler from specifying if the "transfer Price" use case involves only one recipient (unicast) or many (multicast). This raises Question 3: "How can we capture constraints on the number of actor instances in a use case occurrence?"
4. When the prices are transferred, "transfer Price" should occur first, followed by "transfer Price bis". UML use case diagrams alone do not provide a way to specify such relationships between use cases. As a result the semantics of use case diagrams are often unclear. This raises Question 4: "How could we represent constraints on when use cases may occur?"
5. The concept Store Backoffice is shown as an actor (Fig. 2c) or as a system (Fig. 2b) in the use case diagrams and as a class, possibly stereotyped with <<actor>>, in the class diagram (Fig. 1). The same concept is shown with a different diagram element, so what is specific to actors? This raises Question 5: " What is an actor?"

3 Extension to Use Case Modeling Technique

In this section, we will analyze the questions of Section 2 and propose possible solutions.

To be precise, this paper will use the RM-ODP definition [Section 9, 6] of the terms *type*, *class*, *specification*[1], *instance* (used for concepts such as objects, components, etc.) or *occurrence* (used for concepts such as messages, actions, etc). The use of these terms is illustrated in the following example: an actor specification defines the features of an actor, an actor instance defines an actual actor entity, an actor class defines a set of actors that share common characteristics, and an actor type defines the common characteristics of the actors belonging to the class.

3.1 Representation of the System

In this section, we answer Question 1: "How can we model, in one use case diagram, a business process specification between multiple system types and actor types?"

To model a business process that involves multiple system types and actor types, we need to be able (1) to indicate which system type realizes which use case, and (2) to model the use cases that do not directly involve systems (i.e. those use cases that are only between actors). Currently UML use case diagrams force the designer to have only one system of interest in a use case diagram by either representing only one system (drawn as a box around the use cases) or none at all. This excludes from the diagram, the use cases not involving directly the system of interest.

A possible answer can be found in Catalysis [1], a method that defines use cases as not system-centric. Their definition of use case is "*a joint action with multiple participant objects that represent a meaningful business task, usually written in a structured narrative style. Like any joint action, a use case can be refined into a finer-grained sequence of actions*" [p. 722, 1]. A joint action is defined as: "*a change in the state of some number of participant objects without stating how it happens and without yet attributing the responsibility for any of it to any one of the participants*" [p. 158, 1]. A use case may be described on two levels. First level is a declarative description, defined as the change of state of all use case participants resulting from its execution. The declarative description is composed of pre- and post-conditions. It puts an emphasis on the collective behavior of all participants. Second level is an operational description defined as a refinement of the declarative description in which the joint action is decomposed into smaller grain actions. These actions are either joint actions or localized actions. A localized action is defined as "*a one-sided speci-*

[1] To have a terminology closer to UML, we define *specification* as a synonym for the RM-ODP term *template.* We also consider *occurrence* as a synonym for the RM-ODP term *instance.*

fication of an action focused entirely on a single object and how it responds to a request, without regard to the initiator of that request" [p. 715, 1]. The operational description puts an emphasis on the individual behavior of each participant.

Fig. 3: Use case diagram representing systems with actors (UML requires that actors are used as participants to use cases)

The Catalysis definition of the use case does not make any reference to "the system". Use cases are therefore no longer system centric[2]. The implication is that three use case diagrams shown in Fig. 2 may now be represented in one diagram, as shown in Fig. 3.

3.2 Reuse of Use Case Specifications

We answer Question 2: "How can a system play different roles in different occurrences of a same use case specification?"

The Catalysis use case definition does not answer this question. Catalysis, as well as UML, forces the designer to have one use case specification for each group of actors involved (see "transfer Price bis" use case in Fig. 3). A possible answer with Catalysis is to use a collaboration framework [p. 346, 1] to show that two use cases with different names are of the same type. However this does not solve the problem, as a same use case specification cannot be used by two different groups of actors.

Use case specifications explicitly refer to actors and this is the source of the reuse problem. Introducing roles instead of actors solves it. This is consistent with the UML definition of actors as a set of roles.

UML defines role as: "*the named specific behavior of an entity participating in a particular context. A role may be static (e.g., an association end) or dynamic (e.g., a collaboration role).*" We focus on the first part of the definition, the second part is not important for the present discussion. By using this definition and replacing entity by actor and context by use case we can show that an actor may be identified by its role in the use case context (rather than by its name). Thus, roles provide the mechanism needed for making use case specifications independent of actors. Use case specifications may then be reused between different groups of actors and can also refer to a same actor instance playing different roles in different occurrences. Of course, we must have a mechanism to bind roles to actors. This can be done in use case diagrams by writing the role as the associationEndRole on the association between the use case and the actor (see Fig. 4).

---

[2] We will propose a use case definition for UML in Section 4.0

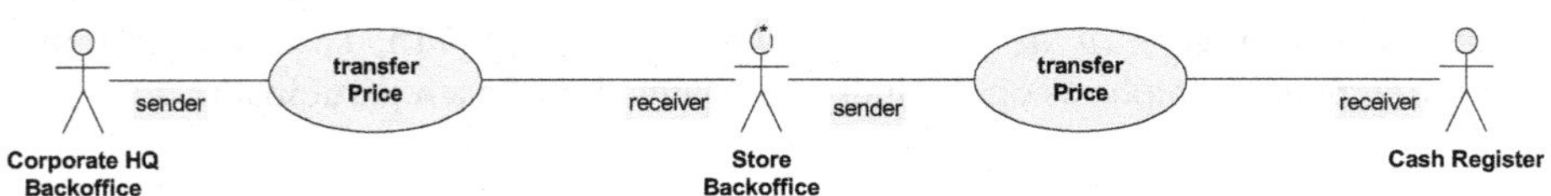

Fig. 4: Example of use case specification reuse in one use case diagram

Some readers may be puzzled to see two use cases with the same name involving two different groups of actors. This is not uncommon as it is analogous to having two associations with the same name but between different classes in a class diagram. We still need to understand what is meant by two "transfer Price" use cases in a same diagram. For example, in Fig. 4, the use case on the left corresponds to the class of use cases that are instantiations of the "transfer Price" use case specification with its role sender referring to Corporate HQ Backoffice and the role receiver referring to the Store Backoffice.

Our approach to explicitly represent roles enables reusing a same use case specification between different groups of actors in a same use case diagram or in different diagrams. In addition, it is consistent with UML and in particular with: (1) the definition of role, (2) the meta-model (use cases and actors are classifiers with an association between them), (3) the notation of roles in class diagrams (in which the roles are represented at the association end).

3.3 Constraints about Number of Instances Participating in a Use Case

We address Question 3: "How can we capture issues related to number of actor instances in a use case occurrence?".

It is not clear whether the use case modeling technique has provisions for representing the number of actor instances (of the same actor type) participating in a use case occurrence. The UML notation guide shows a few examples of multiplicities [p. 3-93, 12]. However, the meta-model does not acknowledge the existence of an actor instance and it is not clear if role is a type or an instance.

The difference between type and instance is often unclear as illustrated in the following two examples "*roles (in collaborations) are somewhat between types and instances*" [p. 3-15, 12] and "*if there can be more than one instance corresponding to a given ClassifierRole, one of these instances is selected to represent them all*" [13]. We believe that the difficulty in deciding if something is a type or an instance is based on the fact that people tend to think in terms of prototypes (i.e. an instance of a type). This is thoroughly discussed by George Lakeoff in [10]. The prototype defines a type by using a specific instance especially representative of the type. But, at the same time, the prototype denotes one or more actual instances. For example an instance of a policeman in uniform is considered as defining a type (i.e. the predicate that allows to decide whether a man is a policeman) but is an instance at the same time (i.e. the man currently in the middle of the crossing). This mechanism of prototype explains why, sometimes, concepts are difficult to categorize as type or instance. Unfortunately, the prototype mechanism is not applicable in UML. Types have to be defined explicitly. For this reason, *type models* (e.g. class diagrams) and *instance models* (e.g. object diagrams) have to be developed. Based on this, we state:

1. All concepts exist as instances (at a specific location in time and space).
2. All concepts may be categorized into classes by means of types (i.e. predicates).
3. Instances are useful for considering interactions between concepts
4. Classes are useful for working with instances in the sense that we do not need to look at each instance separately.

We propose that UML defines all concepts as both a concept type and a concept instance. For most concepts, this duality type / instance already exists. The terms chosen to denote the types and the instances are usually quite different from each other, for example: message and stimulus, object and class, use case [class] and use case [instance].... Our proposition is to add definitions for actor [instance] and role [instance] to the UML meta-model. Acknowledging the existence of actor instances in UML is consistent with the possibility to express multiplicities in use case diagrams (as multiplicities express constraints on the number of instances). This is illustrated in Fig. 5.

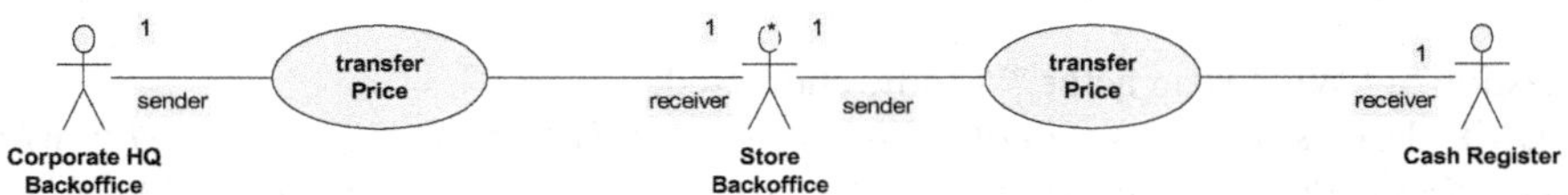

Fig. 5: Example of multiplicity in use case diagram

Fig. 5 illustrates the use of multiplicities in use case diagrams. Considering the "transfer Price" use case, writing a multiplicity of 1 on the receiver role indicates that a use case corresponds to a unicast. On the other hand, writing a multiplicity of 1..* would indicate a multicast of price information.

The multiplicity notation is analog to the one used in class diagrams. The multiplicity is on the actor side of the association and expresses constraints on the number of instances involved in one use case occurrence. We purposely omit multiplicity on the use case's side of the association, as an actor may almost always participate in an unlimited number of occurrences of use case.

Our approach is to systematically define all concepts as types and instances. This allows multiplicities to be represented in type models (e.g. class diagram or use case diagram) as multiplicities represent constraints on the number of instances.

3.4 Constraints on Use Case Occurrences

We analyze Question 4: "How could we represent constraints on when use cases may occur?"

Actor instance and use case occurrence concepts enables the drawing of use case instance diagrams as shown in Fig. 6. By numbering the occurrences of use cases, it is then possible to illustrate the sequence in which use cases will be executed. The sequence-numbering notation is the same as the one defined in collaboration diagrams. Its limitations are also the same. Further work needs to be done on specifying execution constraints beyond what is already defined in interaction diagrams (e.g. "*constraints may include for example sequentiality, non-determinism, concurrency or real-time constraints*" [Section 8, 6]).

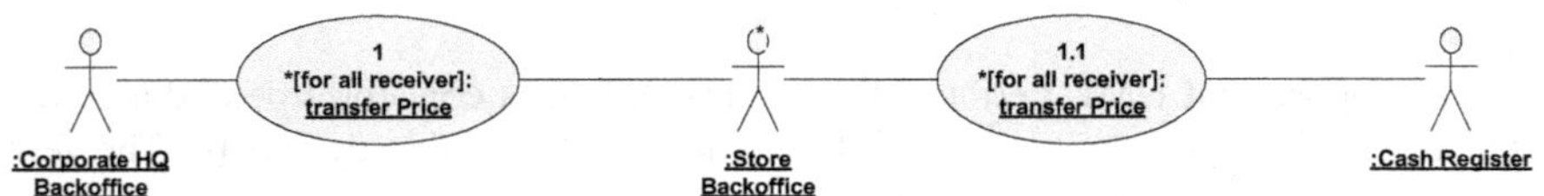

Fig. 6: Example of use case instance diagram

Note that Pavel Hruby proposes to use state diagrams to specify execution constraint between use cases [5]. His approach is complementary to our proposal.

3.5 The Role of Actors

Question 5: "What is an actor?" is now addressed.

UML defines actors as "*a coherent set of roles that users of use cases play when interacting with these use cases. An actor has one role for each use case with which it communicates*". As all entities realize a set of roles, it is not clear what is so unique about actors?

Catalysis defines actors as "*external roles participating in an action*" [p. 592, 1]. In general, they represent the use case participants with diagram elements corresponding to the actual entity (e.g. actor, system, component, programming language class, etc.). Unfortunately UML specifies that participants in use cases are actors (and not any other possible entities such as sub-system, components, programming language classes). Should this restriction be lifted?

To understand the specificity of actors and whether entities other than actors can be represented in use case diagrams, we need to consider how actors are used:

1. Traditionally actors represent entities exterior to the system of interest. For example, in Fig. 2c, the Customer actor represents a person coming in the Store to purchase goods.
2. An actor links use cases together by performing a number of roles. For example, in Fig. 5, the Store Backoffice actor receives the prices by participating in a class of "transfer Price" use cases and then sends these prices by participating in a second class of "transfer Price" use cases.
3. An actor represents, in a use case diagram, an entity coming from another diagram (or vice-versa). Using the same name for an actor and an entity in another

diagram establishes this relation. For example, in Fig. 5, the Store Backoffice actor represents the Store Backoffice shown in the class diagram in Fig. 1.

4. An actor is sometimes used as a means to indicate explicitly which entity realizes a set of roles. This is done either by using a <<realize>> relationship between an actor (representing the roles) and an entity (realizing the roles) diagram elements, or by adding "/name" to an entity identifier to represent its role (where "name" is the name of an actor).
5. An actor may have a generalization relationship with another actor [p. 3-92, 12]. For example, in Fig. 2c, Manager is a generalization of Cashier. That is, all Managers are also Cashiers. Or, in other words, the Manager actor type is a subtype of Cashier in the sense that a Manager can perform all the roles of a Cashier.

The first use illustrates the specificity of the actor concept compared to the other entity concepts. An actor is used when the designer needs to model only a part of the behavior of an entity (which is typically the case for entities external to the systems of interest as the designer does not have to consider or to specify their full behavior).

The second use does not require a specific actor concept. All entities may realize multiple roles; so all entities may be used in use case diagram for linking two use cases together. Only the definition of the use case diagram forces the systematic use of actors.

The third use is quite artificial and is a direct consequence of the use case diagram definition that allows for the representation of actors only, use cases and possibly one system. If the actual entities could be represented in the use case diagram (with their original diagram element as done in Catalysis), the use case diagram would gain in clarity as the designer could decide to represent the actual entity fulfilling roles rather than using an indirection via an actor.

The fourth use becomes marginal if use case diagram elements can represent any entities as participants in the use cases. Actors can still be used when the designer does not want to specify which entity will realize the role (e.g. definition of a collaboration framework involving multiple use cases). In such cases, an actor represents a composite role (called "actor role") played in a specific context (called "actor context"). The actor context is the set of use cases in which the actor participates. The role played by one actor in one specific use case is called "use case role". The actor role is the composition of all the use case roles. Based on this, we recommend defining actor as a composition of roles (as opposed to a set of roles, which is not a role). Note: when needed, the designer explicitly states which entity realizes the actor role. In such cases, an entity plays a composite role (called "entity role") in a specific context (called "entity context"). The entity role is the composition of all actor roles the entity realizes. The entity context is the composition of the corresponding actor contexts.

The fifth use of actors is to show generalization relationships between participants in use cases. In our example, the generalization relationship between Manager and Cashier shows that a Manager can perform the roles of a Cashier. It is not intended to signify that the role of the Cashier in "sell Goods" is a Manager's role (only that it is a role that a manager can realize). It would be preferable to express that a same Employee could realize the Manager's roles and the Cashier's roles (by making explicit who realizes the two sets of roles) rather than to merge these two sets of roles into one (by using the generalization relationship). This allows the designer to keep both set of roles separate. The generalization between actors should be carefully used. In general, the <<realize>> relationship is more appropriate for assigning a set of roles to an entity.

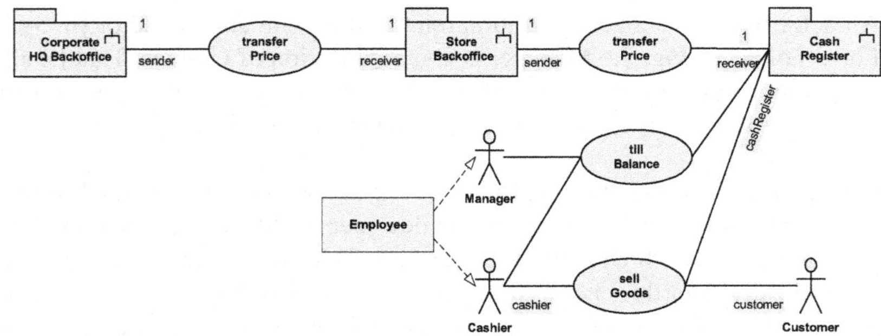

Fig. 7: Example of use case diagram in which participants are subsystems and actors.

Fig. 7 illustrates our recommendation for the representation of any entity diagram elements in a use case diagram and to redefine Actor (see Section 4.0). CorporationHQ Backoffice, Store Backoffice, and Cash Register are represented using the diagram element corresponding to the actual entity (a subsystem to represent an IT system). Customer remains an actor, as it is an entity that will remain partially specified (as an external participant, only its role in the context of "Sell Goods" is interesting to us). Manager and Cashier remain actors, as they represent roles, which will have to be mapped to an actual entity. This mapping is made explicit by using the two <<realize>> relationships. Even if the resulting diagram appears more complex than a diagram using only actors (more type of entities are represented), it is actually simpler to use (as it removes unnecessary indirection between diagram elements).

4 Modifications to UML

In this section we discuss the impact of our proposal on UML. We propose the following definitions:

Use case [class[3]] - the specification of the change of state of a group of entities willing to achieve some purpose. This change of state can be described either as the result of the occurrence of one abstract action involving all the entities or as the result of the occurrences of sequences of individual actions involving individual entities.

Use case [instance] – an occurrence of a use case [class].

[3] Class is used here with its UML meaning, i.e. specification (or ODP template).

Actor [class] –the specification of a role defined as the composition of the roles that a participant of use cases play when interacting with these use cases..
Actor [instance]- an instance of an actor [class].

By introducing the above definitions in UML and further by relaxing the constraints on the diagram elements allowed in use case diagrams, we address most of the raised modeling questions. This implies that current UML case tools need only minimal changes to apply our extended modeling technique.

To express execution constraints on use cases, the meta-model needs to be extended to incorporate the missing concepts of: Actor Instance, Subsystem Instance, and Instance Role[4].

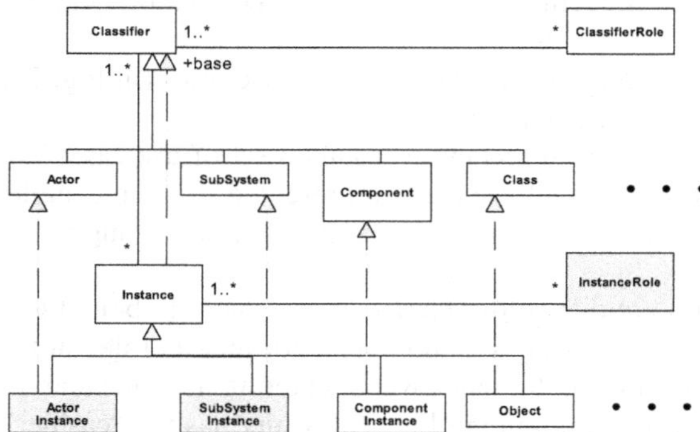

Fig. 8: Elements of meta-model related to the classifier – instance relationship

The proposed modifications to the meta-model are illustrated in Fig. 8. They make it more consistent as they remove some exceptions (Classifier concepts without corresponding Instance concepts).

5 Application of our Suggestions

In Section 2, we presented "classic" use case models (Fig. 1 and Fig. 2). Fig. 7 and Fig. 9 present analog models that reflect the use of our new definitions of use case and actor. Note the consistency between the class diagram (Fig. 9) and the corresponding use case diagram (Fig. 7), which is not the case in the classic models (Fig. 1 and Fig. 2).

[4] We name the meta-class InstanceRole rather than RoleInstance to be consistent with ClassifierRole.

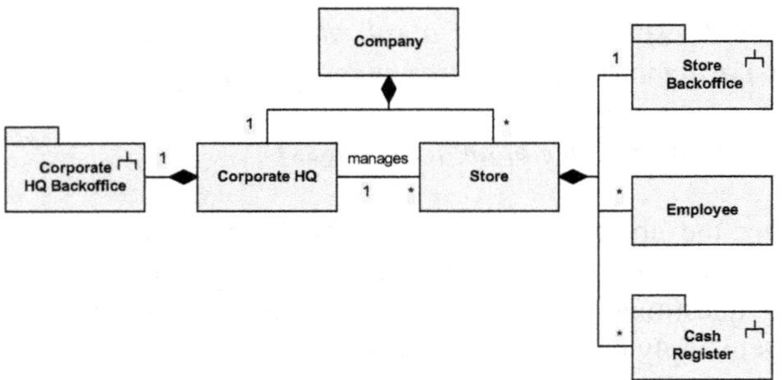

Fig. 9: Class diagram describing Company organization

Our new use case modeling technique can be compatible with the standard UML technique by:

1. Allowing optional representation of use case roles (in Fig. 7 the use case roles in "till Balance" are not specified).
2. Allowing the use of a rectangle around a set of use cases to represent that an actor participates in all use cases represented in the rectangle. Note that a use case diagram might have more than one of these rectangles.

Sometimes, roles are difficult to name. As the roles are bound to the use case, it is possible to use the same name to denote an actor and its roles in the use cases. This name might start with a capital letter when denoting an actor and a lower case when denoting the role. In our example in Fig. 7, Cashier has the "cashier" role in the "sell Goods" use case. This convention is consistent with the one used in class diagrams to denote AssociationEndRole.

6 Future Work

In this paper, we proposed new definitions for actor and use case, as well as the addition of new classes to the UML meta-model. An advantage with these changes is that all entities may be represented in all UML diagrams. The notational techniques, that we propose for use case and use case instance diagrams, are similar from those of class diagrams and interaction diagrams. We believe that this is more than a mere coincidence: the essence of these diagrams is the same, however they differ by their notational techniques. We believe that they can be integrated or unified. Further work needs to be done towards this integration. The results would simplify UML further and would lead to the following benefits: (1) simpler utilization, (2) better specification capabilities, and (3) simplification of case tools.

Conclusion

Use cases are the modeling technique of UML for formalizing the functional requirements placed on systems. In this paper, we have shown several quite important limitations of this technique. It is not possible to model the context of a system beyond its immediate environment (e.g., if two actors exchange information related to their use of a system, this communication cannot be shown in a use case diagram). Likewise, it is impossible to show how several systems are related, even though those systems support a same business process. Reuse opportunities for use case specifications are denied, because use case specifications are directly tied to their associated actors. And execution constraints between use case occurrences cannot be shown or specified in any way.

These limitations can be overcome to some extent by the realization of multiple models and multiple diagrams of various types. But the more diagrams and models there are, the larger the amount of work to be done, and there is the problem of specifying and maintaining the relationships between all these models and diagrams. In this paper, we showed that another approach was possible and quite effective.

This approach relies on three principles: making the roles of use case participants explicit, representing use case participants with their actual diagram elements, and treating the system as any other use case participants. These three principles would require very limited changes to UML: the definitions of actor and use case must be revised.

A complementary idea is to enable modeling at the level of use case occurrences and actor instances (the diagrammatic techniques are borrowed from those of interaction diagrams). We think that modeling at this level is invaluable for relating use cases together and for expressing execution constraints between them. The necessary changes to UML are again quite modest. The meta-model needs to be extended to incorporate the missing concepts of: Actor Instance, Subsystem Instance, and Instance Role.

Quite importantly, all the modifications we propose for UML increases its consistency. As a result, they not only contribute to make UML a more expressive specification language, they also make it a simpler language to understand and use.

Acknowledgments

John Donaldson (Compaq Professional Services, Geneva, Switzerland) and Frederic Bouchet (Nortel Professional Networks, Bussigny, Switzerland) helped to identify the problems of modeling the reengineering of a business process at the abstraction level of IT systems. Special thanks to an anonymous reviewer for providing us with numerous useful suggestions.

References

1. D'Souza Desmond F., Wills Alan Cameron: Objects, Components, and Frameworks with UML – The Catalysis Approach. Addison-Wesley (1999) (ISBN 0-201-31012-0).
2. Genilloud Guy, Wegmann Alain: On Types, Instances, and Classes in UML. European Conference - Object-oriented Programming (ECOOP), Sophia-Antipolis, France (2000) (http://icawww.epfl.ch).
3. Genilloud Guy, Wegmann Alain: A Foundation for the Concept of Role in Object Modelling. Enterprise Distributed Object Computing Conference (EDOC), Makuhari, Japan. (2000) (http://icawww.epfl.ch).
4. Graham Ian: Requirements Engineering and Rapid Development: an Object-oriented approach. Addison-Wesley (1998) (ISBN 0-201-36047-0).
5. Hruby Pavel: Structuring Specification of Business Systems with UML (with an Emphasis on Workflow Management Systems). OOPSLA Workshop: Business Object Design and Implementation IV: From Business Objects to Complex Adaptive Systems, Vancouver B.C. (1998).
6. ISO/IEC ITU-T: Open Distributed Processing – Basic Reference Model – Part 2: Foundations. Standard 10746-2, Recommendation X.902 (1995) (http://isotc.iso.ch /livelink/livelink/fetch/2000/2489/Ittf_Home/PubliclyAvailableStandards.htm).
7. Jacobson Ivar, Christerson Magnus, Jonsson Patrick, Övergaard Gunnar: Object-Oriented Software Engineering. Addison-Wesley (1992) (ISBN 0-201-54435-0).
8. Jacobson Ivar, Ericsson Maria, Jacobson Agneta: The Object Advantage – Business Process Reengineering with Object Technology. Addison-Addison Wesley (1995) (ISBN 0-201-42289-1).
9. Kellomäki Pertti, Mikkonen Tommi: Design Templates for Collective Behavior. European Conference – Object-oriented Programming (ECOOP), Sophia-Antipolis, France (2000) 277 – 295.
10. Lakoff George: Women, Fire and Dangerous Things – What Categories Reveal about the Mind. Chicago Press (1987) (ISBN 0-226-46804-6).
11. Li Qing, Wong Raymond: Multifaceted object modeling with roles: A comprehensive approach. In: Information Sciences 117, Springer-Verlag, (1999) 243-266.
12. OMG: Unified Modeling Language Specification, Version 1.3 (1999) (www.omg.org).
13. Reenskaug Trygve: UML Collaboration and OOram semantics – New version of green paper. 2nd ed, Nov. 8, 1999 (http://www.ifi.uio.no/~trygver/documents).
14. Reenskaug Trygve, Wold Per, Lehne Odd Arild, Working With Objects: The OOram Software Engineering Method. Manning Publications (1996) (ISBN 0-13-452930-8).

Ensuring Quality of Geographic Data with UML and OCL*

Miro Casanova, Thomas Wallet, and Maja D'Hondt

System and Software Engineering Laboratory
Vrije Universiteit Brussel, Pleinlaan 2, 1050 Brussels Belgium
mcasanov | twallet | mjdhondt@vub.ac.be

Abstract. Geographic data is the backbone of sophisticated applications such as car navigation systems and Geographic Information Systems (GIS). Complexity quickly arises in the production of geographic data when trying to ensure quality. We define quality as the integrity and well-formedness of the contents of the geographic data, usually enforced by external applications where constraints ensuring quality (referred to as *quality constraints*) are implicit, low-level and scattered throughout the application code. This has significant consequences with respect to manageability, adaptability and reuse of these constraints.
This paper explains our use of UML class diagrams as conceptual model for geographic data, and how we exploited the Object Constraint Language (OCL) for describing the quality constraints in an explicit, declarative and high-level way. As our use of OCL is slightly different than it was originally intended, we present our adaptations and explain the main issues of evaluating the resulting OCL.
We are confident that our specific application of OCL can be put to use in other domains where complex constraints need to be expressed in a knowledge-oriented domain.

1 Introduction

This paper recounts how we use class diagrams from the *Unified Modeling Language* to represent geographic data in a conceptual model, and how the *Object Constraint Language* can be exploited to describe quality criteria on this domain in the form of complex constraints.

Section 2 gives a general overview of the domain of geographic data, describes the challenges in its production process, and reports on the current practices and their problems. It becomes clear that most difficulties are encountered ensuring the quality of the produced geographic data. Such quality is indeed defined by means of implicit domain constraints which are generally expressed in a low-level and implementation-dependent way, thus hard to localise, understand and modify. We explain how to overcome these drawbacks: a high-level representation of

* This research, in collaboration with *Tele Atlas Data Gent NV*, is part of the project *GeoObjects (IWT 990025)*, funded by the *Flemish Institute for the Improvement of the Scientific-Technological Research in the Industry* (IWT).

A. Evans, S. Kent and B. Selic (Eds.): ≪UML≫ 2000, LNCS 1939, pp. 225–239, 2000.

the domain knowledge is required, accompanied by a high-level, unambiguous, explicit and modular representation of the quality ensuring constraints (hereafter referred to as *quality constraints*). In this research, we use the class diagrams from UML together with a subset of OCL to achieve this. Considering the subtle differences between our application of OCL and the way OCL is usually employed, we had to make some adaptations in order to express elegantly the quality constraints. These adaptations are described in Sect. 3, where they are also extensively illustrated with real-world examples taken from the domain of geographic data.

This research is the by-product of a project we are involved in with TeleAtlas – an important supplier of geographic data in Europe – as the other partner. Since our partner manipulates a vast amount of geographic data, the checking of the quality constraints in OCL should be performed automatically. Although the development of an OCL evaluator is still ongoing work, we discuss some pertinent issues in evaluating OCL in Sect. 4.

In Sect. 5 we touch upon a few more advanced adaptations to OCL. We conclude in Sect. 6 that although this research originated in the domain of geographic data, we strongly believe that the results can be reused in other domains where complex constraints need to be expressed on a conceptual, knowledge-oriented model. In addition to this we provide some issues about our ongoing work, and hint at related work performed by other research groups or companies.

2 Quality of Geographic Data

2.1 Geographic Data

Digital geographic data, and especially data concerned with the road network, is used in sophisticated applications such as Geographic Information Systems (environmental planning and control, alarm call and dispatch), Fleet Management Systems, car navigation and geo-marketing. Suppliers of geographic data are responsible for the production process, which consists of capturing the real-world geographic data and storing it in a persistency layer. The source material typically comes from satellite images, scanned maps, Global Positioning System data, and so on. Since this may lead to mistakes creeping into the geographic data, an important and ever continuing concern in the production process is quality assurance.

The most widely accepted format for geographic data is the Geographic Data Files (GDF) standard [GDF], which has been created in order to improve the efficiency of capturing and producing road related geographic information. GDF achieves this efficiency by providing a common reference model on which clients can base their requirements and suppliers can base their product definition. The foundation of the GDF standard consists of a general, non-application specific planar-graph representation of the real world. On top of this model, a road network specific application model has been built. The last model describes real-world concepts in the domain of geographic road network data, as well as attributes of these concepts and relations between these.

2.2 Challenges in Producing Geographic Data

The geographic data market is highly competitive. Factors that determine success are among others adaptability, flexibility and time to market. Moreover, enormous effort goes into eliminating errors and inaccuracies in the contents of the geographic data in order to guarantee high quality and reduce maintenance. *Quality* of geographic data is defined here as the integrity and well-formedness of the data, and is specified at the hand of specific domain constraints. The importance of delivering high-quality geographic data is easily understood when thinking of the consequences of using data of poor quality in applications such as car navigation and alarm call and dispatch.

2.3 Current Practices and Their Drawbacks

Although most suppliers of geographic data use the high-level and implementation independent GDF standard for interchange and as a common reference model, we observe that in practice no actual model is actively and explicitly employed in the production process. In other words, an implicit mental picture is used instead of a tangible high-level representation of the geographic data and the corresponding quality constraints. The only tangible model of geographic data in current practices is its specific implementation in a file system, a commercially available database or any other medium. Since there is the inevitable impedance mismatch between the high level and the implementation level, the concepts, attributes, relations and quality constraints residing in the high level are irretrievably lost in the actual production process.

More specifically, in today's production processes, high quality of the geographic data is usually ensured by a pool of software applications that check the quality constraints. Since these applications can only operate on a low-level description of geographic data, the quality constraints are consequently described on an equally low level, i.e. in terms of the actual implementation of the geographic data. This approach results in a tangling of the implicit quality constraints in the application code, hence causing them to be non-modular and hard to localise. This has significant consequences with respect to manageability, adaptability and reuse of the constraints, making the production process prone to mistakes and resulting in increased time to market.

2.4 Setting an Approach to Satisfy the Requirements

From the previously described drawbacks of the current approaches we observe that we need a high-level, conceptual description of the knowledge in the domain of geographic data. Preferably this model should be based on a standard, such as GDF, to facilitate exchange. But more importantly, the conceptual nature of the model will ensure implementation independence and a close match with reality to minimise loss of information.

Current descriptions of geographic data, with GDF as representative example, are compatible with the philosophy of object-orientation: geographic features or concepts can be mapped to classes, whereas relations between concepts correspond to associations between classes. Because of this, but also because it is a standard in modelling, UML was selected in this project for representing a conceptual model of the geographic data.

The quality constraints that reason about the geographic data should also be expressed explicitly on a conceptual level for the same reasons. But there are other requirements involved: they need to be described in a modular manner, allowing for easy localisation and flexible manipulation of a particular constraint. Additionally, we should be able to change a quality constraint without this having to affect other constraints. Moreover, the medium for expressing these constraints should embody a level of intuitiveness and declarative power comparable to that of natural language, yet be formal and unambiguous.

These requirements and the fact that the quality constraints reason about domain knowledge that is described in UML class diagrams, point to the use of UML's accompanying OCL [KW99] [UML1.3]. OCL is used to express constraints on UML models by attaching constraints to classes (class invariants), operations on classes (pre- and postconditions), and more. This means that OCL has built-in constructs for navigating UML models, more specifically class diagrams. OCL fulfils our desires for a formal and unambiguous language, while still being relatively simple and intuitive.

3 Using OCL for Quality Constraints

We present in Sect. 3.1 parts of the conceptual model, both to illustrate the result of modelling geographic data in UML class diagrams, and to provide a context for the examples we use later on, which are realistic examples directly taken from the domain of geographic data.

In Sect. 3.2 to 3.5 we present a set of adaptations to OCL as well as their motivating reasons.[1]

We will elaborate on the consequences of these adaptations for the semantics of OCL in Sect. 4.

3.1 The Conceptual Model in UML

We will discuss one theme of geographic data here in order to use this throughout the rest of the paper as the entirely realistic context in which the example quality constraints are defined. It concerns `Relationships`, where a relationship refers to a real-world entity that needs to be represented as a mutual link between concepts and may indicate the sequence of those concepts. We will discuss two kinds of relationships: the first is `Manoeuvre`, where we can distinguish `PriorityManoeuvre`, `RestrictedManoeuvre` and `ProhibitedManoeuvre`,

[1] Note that as a starting point only a subset of OCL is selected since not all of its language constructs are required. For example, constructs related to pre- and postconditions are discarded.

and the second is ServiceBelongingToServices. Figure 1 shows the relevant part of the Relationship hierarchy.[2]

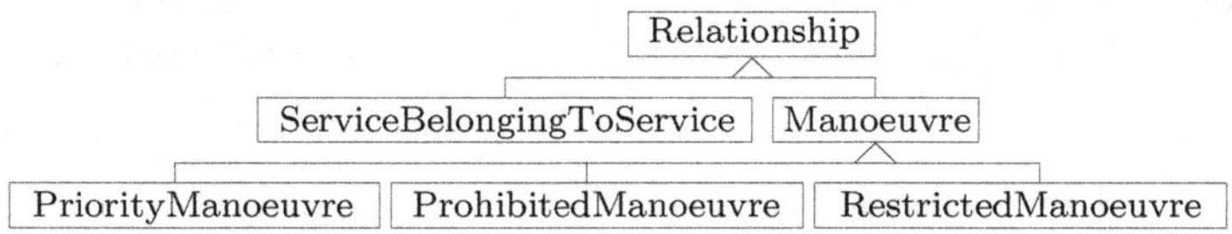

Fig. 1. The Relationship hierarchy.

Manoeuvre. A Relationship such as Manoeuvre forms a link between a number of RoadElements and a Junction, where the order of these concepts is important. A Manoeuvre indicates a certain path that can be followed by a vehicle. Figure 2 depicts the exact associations between the concepts that are involved. Moreover, it also shows the relations between RoadElement and Junction.

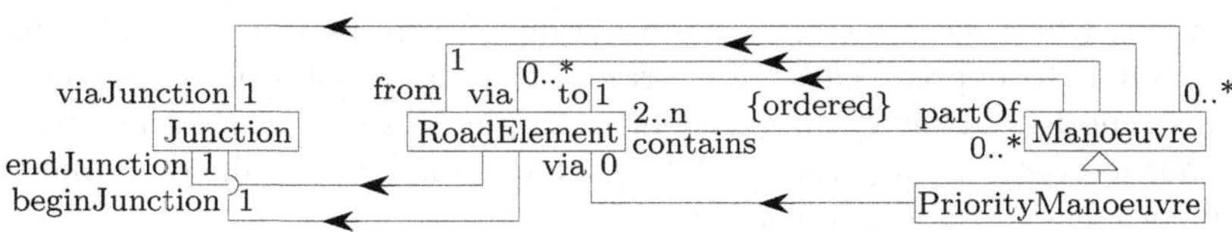

Fig. 2. The relationship Manoeuvre and its relation to RoadElement and Junction.

A PriorityManoeuvre represents a manoeuvre that has priority over other manoeuvres at an intersection. A ProhibitedManoeuvre indicates a manoeuvre that is prohibited, whereas a RestrictedManoeuvre is obligatory. Note in Fig. 2 that a PriorityManoeuvre has exactly two RoadElements which it refers to, thereby overriding Manoeuvre's behaviour.

ServiceBelongingToService. Another kind of relationship is ServiceBelongingToService, which represents the fact that two Services functionally belong to each other. Examples of services are Restaurant, RestArea, PetrolStation, AirlineAccess, Airport, etc. When a Restaurant belongs to a RestArea, they are linked together by a

[2] Since the applied modelling method in itself is outside the scope of this paper, we only show the resulting conceptual model of the examples of geographic data that are described.

ServiceBelongingToService relationship. Likewise, a PetrolStation can belong to a RestArea. Figure 3 shows the conceptual class diagram. A special kind of Service is EntryPoint, which denotes a location from which one has to leave the publicly accessible road network in order to a enter a Service. Most services are connected to the EntryPoint via a ServiceBelongingToService.

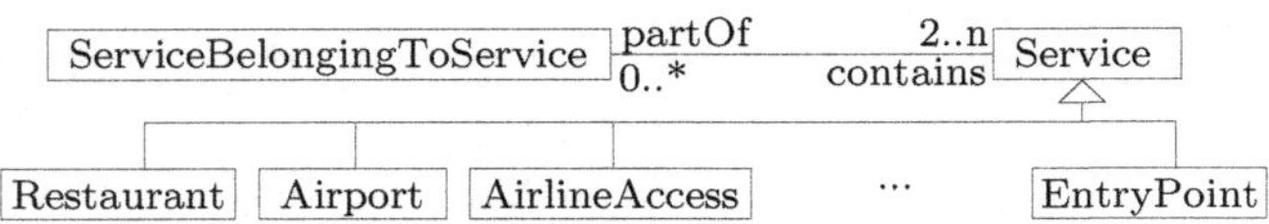

Fig. 3. The relationship ServiceBelongingToService and its relation to Service.

3.2 Constraints on Multiple Classes

The original purpose of OCL is to write *local* constraints on parts of the UML model, such as class invariants, pre- and postconditions on operations, etc. In our context, where we use UML class diagrams to represent a knowledge model, we need OCL to express *global* constraints that may potentially reason about the entire model. Below is an excellent example of a constraint that expresses some characteristic of geographic data that cannot be restrained to one single concept or class of the conceptual model.

Constraint. *A road-element shall not be the first road-element of a restricted-manoeuvre and a prohibited-manoeuvre in case both these manoeuvres refer to the same via-junction.*

It is clear that this constraint reasons about the concepts RestrictedManoeuvre and ProhibitedManoeuvre, and that neither one can be preferred over the other to serve as main context. Nevertheless, if we would choose for example the first concept as context, the constraint in current OCL would be:

```
context RestrictedManoeuvre inv:
ProhibitedManoeuvre.allInstances->forall(p : ProhibitedManoeuvre |
self.viaJunction = p.viaJunction implies self.from <> p.from)
```

This constraint shows signs of imbalance: there is an implicit looping over all instances of RestrictedManoeuvre, whereas for ProhibitedManoeuvre the loop is expressed explicitly, using the undesirable allInstances construct.[3] We would like to use this built-in language construct for all classes that occur in a

[3] In OCL specifications [UML1.3], it is explicitly said that the use of allInstances is problematic and is discouraged in most cases.

constraint. This issue was introduced in [GKR99], where they propose to allow multiple type names after the keyword `context`. We adopted a different notation, illustrated in the new version below of the example constraint:

```
RestrictedManoeuvre.viaJunction = ProhibitedManoeuvre.viaJunction
implies RestrictedManoeuvre.from <> ProhibitedManoeuvre.from
```

We use the name of the class of the conceptual model to denote the context and at the same time as the contextual instance. Note that as a result of this notation the reserved word `self` becomes obsolete.

3.3 Constraints on Multiple Instances

Class invariants in the original OCL specifications are meant principally to allow manipulation of one instance of a class at a time,[4] whereas our quality constraints require access to more than one instance of the same class at the same time in order to express some characteristic about them. The following constraint exemplifies this (see class diagram on Fig. 3):

Constraint. *Every airport which is in relation with an airline-access, shall also be related to an entry-point of this airline-access. Consequently, this airline-access itself relates to at least one entry-point.*

The services `Airport`, `AirlineAccess` and `EntryPoint` are related through some `ServiceBelongingToService` relationships. More specifically, a first one connects `Airport` and `AirlineAccess`. The constraint expresses that this should imply the connection by means of a second `ServiceBelongingToService` between `Airport` and `EntryPoint` of the `AirlineAccess`. The last two services are in turn connected by a third relationship. The main context of this constraint is the class `ServiceBelongingToService`. However, this constraint involves three different instances of this class, which cannot be expressed gracefully, as is shown below:

```
ServiceBelongingToService.allInstances->exists(s1 |
     ServiceBelongingToService.allInstances->exists(s2 |
          ServiceBelongingToService.allInstances->exists(s3 |
        <expression with s1 s2 s3>) ) )
```

Again, the undesirable explicit iteration over all instances with `allInstances` is required because different instances need to be referred to in the same constraint. Therefore we propose the introduction of *identifiers* in the context of a constraint. The syntax we adopt is:[5]

```
constraint :: ('id' idDecl 'in')? exp
idDecl :: <name> (',' <name>)* (':' <type>)? '=' exp (';' idDecl)*
```

[4] It is however possible to refer to multiple instances of a same class, but this can only be achieved in a complex way using the undesirable construct `allInstances`.

[5] Syntax definitions are given in extended BNF.

An identifier consists of a name, an initial value, and an optional type. The identifier can be referred to several times within a constraint by means of its name, thus accessing its value. This value cannot be altered since constraints are side-effect free due to their declarative nature. The initial value of an identifier can be any valid OCL expression, including navigation paths such as `Manoeuvre.contains->first` and `Manoeuvre.contains->select(m | m.oclIsTypeOf(RoadElement))`.

Consequently, the previous constraint can be expressed as follows:

```
id s1, s2, s3 : ServiceBelongingToService in
    <expression with s1 s2 s3>
```

Note that our notion of identifiers closely resembles that of the *let* expression presented in [CHH+98] and adopted in the specification of OCL 1.3 [UML1.3]. It is not clear though if this construct can only be used as an abstraction and reference mechanism for expressions that are used more than once in a constraint, or if the semantics also allows it to express constraints about different instances of the same class, as does our approach.

In any case, our syntax adaptation is equally suited to name a repeated expression in a particular constraint and refer to it in this constraint. This avoids repeatedly writing long and complicated navigation paths, an advantage when trying to reduce the complexity and length of constraints, and thus the chance of making mistakes.

3.4 Dot and Arrow Notations

In [KW99] and [UML1.3] navigation through elements of a model is achieved through navigation paths using dot and arrow notations. Associations or attributes on a class in the user-defined model are accessed through the dot notation as in the following expressions: `Manoeuvre.contains`, `RoadElement.endJunction`, etc. OCL contains a set of predefined classes and corresponding operations. Examples of these operations are `attributes` and `supertypes` defined on `OclType`, whose instances are all the types (user-defined or predefined) existing in the UML model, and `oclIsTypeOf` defined on `OclAny` which is the superclass of all types. Another category of predefined OCL classes is the `Collection` hierarchy. This class and its subclasses `Set`, `Sequence` and `Bag`, have predefined operations such as `size` and `isEmpty`, but also for instance `select` and `forall` which iterate on all elements of a `Collection`. Inconsistency results from the fact that the notation for applying operations from the `Collection` hierarchy is the arrow operator, whereas for the other predefined operations it is also the dot operator.

Therefore it is complicated to distinguish when an OCL predefined operation or a user-defined property is used. The fact that many OCL predefined classes or operations have a prefix *Ocl* highlights this.

We adopted a more consistent notation, which is easier to understand for users of OCL, and easier to evaluate. Our notation stresses the difference between user-defined and predefined properties by using the dot notation to express navigations from the former and the arrow notation from the latter, even if it does not concern an instance of the `Collection` hierarchy.

3.5 Accumulators

The *accumulator* concept, used in the predefined `iterate` operation for iterations over a `Collection`, lacks a clear definition in [KW99] and [UML1.3]. For this reason we adopted the following syntax for the single parameter `oclExpression` of this `iterate` operation:

```
oclExpression :: <name> (',' <name>)* accumulator '|' expression
accumulator :: '[' <name> (':' <type>)? '=' expression ']'
```

`accumulator` is assigned an initial value before the iteration mechanism. Then for each iteration step, the result of the evaluation of the expression following the horizontal bar is assigned to the accumulator. At the end of all the iterations, the current value of the accumulator is returned as the result of the evaluation of the iterate operation.

Our experience highlighted the fact that accumulators are necessary for context propagation in iterations. However accumulators must be expressed with a procedural-like syntax which definitely contrasts with the relatively intuitive and declarative way to write constraints with OCL. The following example presents a constraint where the use of an accumulator is needed. In the same time it shows that such a constraint requires a procedural-like syntax, thus loosing part of the intuitiveness and declarativity of OCL.

Constraint. *The set of road-elements which a manoeuvre refers to is continuous, meaning that it is an ordered set of road-elements and that each road-element, except for the last, has exactly one junction in common with the following road-element.*

```
id res = Manoeuvre.contains in
res->subSequence(2,res->size)->iterate( item
    [path = Sequence{res->at(1).endJunction}] |

    if path->isEmpty
    then Sequence{}
    else
        if item.beginJunction = path->last
        then path->append(item.endJunction)
        else
            if item.endJunction = path->last
            then path->append(item.beginJunction)
            else Sequence{}
            endif
        endif
    endif)->notEmpty
```

As presented in Fig. 2, a Manoeuvre refers to a sequence of RoadElements through the association contains, and each RoadElement has two extremities (startJunction and endJunction). We iterate over this sequence (except its first RoadElement, which is the starting point), to check if each of its elements (represented by the identifier item) have a shared extremity with the previous one. The accumulator path is used to store the continuous sequence of shared extremities already encountered. Particularly, path->last is the extremity of the previous RoadElement that should be shared with the current element. Consequently, either the beginJunction, either the endJunction of the current element must be equal to this extremity, otherwise the continuity is broken. When the continuity is broken, a null sequence (Sequence{}) is assigned to the accumulator path. For simplification we suppose here that we know that the first RoadElement of the sequence is linked to the second by its end junction.

4 Evaluating Constraints

In this section we explore the main issues of evaluating constraints which are expressed using our modified version of OCL (as proposed in Sect. 3). For a further description of OCL evaluation issues, we refer to [HHK98].

4.1 Checking Navigations Paths

OCL constraints make extensive use of navigation path expressions, referring to associations, attributes or methods described in the UML class diagrams of the conceptual model. For this reason an important issue in constraint evaluation is the checking of navigation path validity against the conceptual model. Such checking must actually be done statically, in order to avoid run-time interruptions of costly quality routines due to type errors.

Whereas classical OO-language type checking is typically performed through the checking of property names, return types and parameter types, the type checking on OCL constraints is based on checking navigation paths against associations described in the conceptual model (according to role names, association cardinalities, etc.). Note however that dot and arrow notations, in the way we adopted them (see Sect. 3.4), involve a simple mechanism of navigation path checking. When type checking a constraint, a property of an expression accessed using the dot notation is checked in the user-defined conceptual model in UML (for searching the specified property, its return type, etc.). In a similar way, an operation of an expression accessed using the arrow notation is checked in the UML class diagram of the predefined OCL types.

4.2 Evaluating Constraints on Multiple Classes

As explained in Sect. 3.2, our OCL can be used for expressing constraints on several classes. The mechanism of evaluating an OCL constraint depends on the number of classes it involves. Based on the checking of navigation paths, classes involved can be identified. The constraint evaluation is achieved in as many evaluation loops as the number of classes involved. Evaluation loops are nested loops which aim to evaluate the given OCL constraint for each permutation of the instances of the classes involved, as shown in the following example:

```
RestrictedManoeuvre.viaJunction = ProhibitedManoeuvre.viaJunction
implies RestrictedManoeuvre.from <> ProhibitedManoeuvre.from
```

In such case, the constraint will be evaluated through two evaluation loops, the first one over the `RestrictedManoeuvre` instances, and the second one, nested within the first one, over the `ProhibitedManoeuvre` instances. For each loop iteration the constraint will be evaluated with the current pair of instances.

4.3 Evaluating Constraints with Identifiers

Constraints with identifiers (as presented in Sect. 3.3) are evaluated through the same evaluation loop mechanism. Evaluation of a constraint with identifiers is equivalent to the evaluation of that same constraint with the references to the identifiers within the constraint textually replaced by their value. For instance, the constraint below will be evaluated in exactly the same way as the constraint given in Sect. 4.2.

```
id rm = RestrictedManoeuvre ; pm = ProhibitedManoeuvre in
  rm.viaJunction = pm.viaJunction implies rm.from <> pm.from
```

However, when having two or more global identifiers with the same initial value, as in the following example, the evaluation mechanism is slightly different.

```
id re1, re2 = RoadElement in
  <some_constraint_using_re1_and_re2>
```

Evaluation of such a constraint will be achieved through two nested evaluation loops, each over all instances of the class `RoadElement`. The reason for having two identifiers (`re1` and `re2`) with the same value (`RoadElement`) is to be able to refer to two instances of the same class which are guaranteed to be distinct.

5 Advanced Adaptations to OCL

We already proposed some syntactic modifications to OCL and defined informally their procedural semantics. However we plan some further modifications that will simplify the process of writing and reusing quality constraints on geographic data, by introducing constraint referencing and composition as well as parametric constraints.

5.1 Referencing Constraints

In OCL specifications [UML1.3], a constraint name can optionally be written after the `inv` keyword. Because we chose to not link explicitly a context to each constraint, we had to replace this way of naming a constraint. That is the reason why we propose a mechanism for naming each constraint within its OCL definition. Sections 5.2 and 5.3 will highlight the interest of referencing such names in other OCL constraints.

The naming mechanism is compulsory for each constraint definition and is done through the following syntax:[6]

```
constraint  :: <name> ':' constraintBody
```

The following constraint illustrates the naming mechanism:

> *A restaurant-service shall always be referred to by a service-belonging-to-service relationship in which the other object is an entry-point*

```
entryPointBelongsToRestaurant :
id s = ServiceBelongingToService.services in
s->select(s1 | s1->oclIsTypeOf(Restaurant))->notEmpty implies
s->select(s2 | s2->oclIsTypeOf(EntryPoint))->notEmpty
```

5.2 Parametric Constraints

Let's consider the three following constraints (see class diagram on Fig. 3):

> *1- A* ***restaurant****-service shall always be referred to by a service-belonging-to-service relationship in which the other object is an entry-point*
>
> *2- An* ***airline-access****-service shall always be referred to by a service-belonging-to-service relationship in which the other object is an entry-point*
>
> *3- An* ***airport****-service shall always be referred to by a service-belonging-to-service relationship in which the other object is an entry-point*

Since only the class name changes, it is useful to factor it out of the OCL constraint definition, enabling us to write the OCL rule only once and reuse it with different classes. To achieve this we propose to have *parametric OCL constraints*. As with C++ templates, such constraints take one or more parametric types as arguments that can be used in the OCL expressions composing the parametric constraint.

It is important however to provide a way to bound the parametric types of a parametric constraint to avoid a defined parametric constraint from being used

[6] This is a simplified syntax. The complete syntax, allowing parametric constraints, will be presented in Sect. 5.2

with any parametric type. Inspired by *Pizza*[7] [OW97] we specified a bounding mechanism for parametric types through a `where` clause. For instance, parametric types can be bounded in the `where` clause using some predefined OCL operations such as `supertypes` (to get the direct superclasses of a class), `name` (to get the name of a class) or `allSupertypes` (to get all the ancestor classes of a class). Note that a `where` clause can only hold meta-constraints on the parametric types.

The syntax for parametric constraints is given below:

```
constraint    :: <name> parametrics? ':' constraintBody
parametrics   :: '<' <parametric> (',' <parametric>)* '>' whereExp?
whereExp      :: 'where' expression
parametric    :: "@" "a"-"z" ( "a"-"z" | "A"-"Z" | "0"-"9" | "_" )*
```

The following example shows the OCL definition of a parametric constraint that can be used for the three constraints given at the beginning of this subsection:

```
entryPointBelongsToService<@param>
where @param->supertypes->includes(Service) :
id s = ServiceBelongingToService.services in
s->select(s1 | s1->oclIsTypeOf(@param))->notEmpty implies
s->select(s2 | s2->oclIsTypeOf(EntryPoint))->notEmpty
```

The `where` clause of this example specifies that the parametric type of the constraint (`@param`) must be a direct subclass of the class `Service`.

To obtain a concrete constraint out of a parametric constraint, its parametric type(s) must be filled in. This can be done within a new OCL constraint by referencing the parametric constraint with the % symbol. For instance, the first of the three previous constraints is obtained as follows:

```
entryPointBelongsToRestaurant :
%entryPointBelongsToService<Restaurant>
```

Checking the validity of such an expression will be achieved by evaluating the `where` clause of the parametric constraint with the `Restaurant` type.

We can construct an OCL constraint that can be evaluated by textually assigning the parametric type of the constraint to a given type. This means that the above constraint is equivalent to:

```
entryPointBelongsToRestaurant :
id s = ServiceBelongingToService.services in
s->select(s1 | s1->oclIsTypeOf(Restaurant))->notEmpty implies
s->select(s2 | s2->oclIsTypeOf(EntryPoint))->notEmpty
```

[7] *Pizza* is an extension to Java, which offers parametric and bounded parametric types.

5.3 Constraints Composition

In geographic data quality, quality constraints are often reused or grouped together. Composing existing quality constraints reduces copy-pasting, or rewriting of parts or entire OCL constraints. With the referencing mechanism introduced in the previous subsection, it becomes relatively straightforward to realise constraint composition. As explained before, existing constraints can indeed be reused within any OCL expression by referencing them with the % symbol.

For instance we can compose the three constraints of the previous subsection into a more general one as follows:

```
entryPointBelongsToAllServices :
%entryPointBelongsToService<Restaurant>
and
%entryPointBelongsToService<AirlineAccess>
and
%entryPointBelongsToService<Airport>
```

This is a basic example of an `and` composition, but more complicated compositions can be created, using the full expressive power of OCL.

It is important to note that composite constraints are always independently evaluated, i.e. only their final result is used to compose the final constraint. This mechanism enables powerful features for reusing or grouping constraints.

6 Conclusion

6.1 Ongoing Work

We are currently applying the results presented in this paper to the development of an OCL evaluator. Our objective is to provide an efficient way for checking OCL constraints on the extensive geographic data of our industrial partner TeleAtlas. The resulting OCL evaluator will be integrated into a distributed quality assurance system for the geographic data production process of TeleAtlas.

6.2 Related Work

UML is well suited for modelling on a conceptual level, as is described in [BFS99]. Therefore, UML class diagrams, conforming to the principles of entity-relationship modelling, are frequently used for modelling domains that consist of large amounts of static knowledge.

A body of work exists concerning OCL and its syntax and semantics performed by the *Software and Systems Engineering Research Group* at the University of Kent, Canterbury [HHK98] [CHH+98] [GKR99]. A few other research groups and companies are working on OCL improvements. The *Klasse Objecten* [KO] holds pointers to most of these projects.

6.3 Conclusion

This paper reports on the exploitation of OCL to describe quality ensuring constraints on a domain which is essentially knowledge-oriented. This domain is represented at a conceptual level by means of UML class diagrams. The source of inspiration for this work is the domain of geographic data where constraints embody criteria for the integrity and well-formedness, in other words quality of the vast amount of knowledge.

Although this use of OCL results in an explicit, high-level and unambiguous description of the quality constraints, some adaptations to the syntax and semantics, and some additional language constructs were necessary. Once more, these adaptations originated and were established in the domain of geographic data. Nevertheless they are of a general kind and therefore applicable in other domains that require conceptual modelling of extensive amounts of domain knowledge, enriched with quality ensuring constraints. Examples of such domains are broadcast management for television and radio stations, and resource schedulers, for instance for the management of passengers, cargo, transport and so on at airports and railways.

7 Acknowledgments

Viviane Jonckers and Tom Toutenel reviewed earlier drafts of this paper. We thank them for their corrections and valuable comments.

References

BFS99. G. Booch, M. Fowler, K. Scott. "UML Distilled: A Brief Guide to the Standard Object Modeling Language". Addison-Wesley. 1999. 238

CHH+98. F. Civello, A. Hamie, J. Howse, S. Kent, M. Mitchell. "Reflections on the Object Constraint Language". In Post Workshop Proceedings of UML98. Springer Verlag, June 1998. 232, 238

GDF. "The Geographic Data Files Standard". Committee for Road Transport and Traffic Telematics of the Comité Européen de Normalisation. 226

GKR99. S. Gaito, S. Kent, N. Ross. "A Meta-model Semantics for Structural Constraints in UML". In H. Kilov, B. Rumpe, and I. Simmonds editors, Behavioural specifications for businesses and systems, chapter 9, pages 123-141. Kluwer Academic Publishers, Norwell, MA, September 1999. 231, 238

HHK98. A. Hamie, J. Howse, S. Kent. "Interpreting the Object Constraint Language". In Proceedings of Asia Pacific Conference in Software Engineering. IEEE Press, July 1998. 234, 238

KO. Klasse Objecten group. `http://www.klasse.nl` 238

KW99. A. Kleppe, J. Warmer. "The Object Constraint Language: Precise Modeling with UML". Addison-Wesley, 1999. 228, 232, 233

OW97. M. Odersky, P. Wadler. "Pizza into Java: Translating theory into practice". In Conference Record of POPL 97': The 24th ACM SIGPLAN-SIGACT Symposium on Principles of Programming Languages, pages 146-159, Paris, France, 15-17 January 1997. 237

UML1.3. "UML 1.3 Specifications" (including OCL). `http://www.omg.org/uml` 228, 230, 232, 232, 233, 236

Contextual Diagrams as Structuring Mechanisms for Designing Configuration Knowledge Bases in UML

Alexander Felfernig, Dietmar Jannach, and Markus Zanker

Institut für Wirtschaftsinformatik und Anwendungssysteme, Produktionsinformatik, Universitätsstrasse 65-67, A-9020 Klagenfurt, Austria, email: felfernig@ifi.uni-klu.ac.at.

Abstract. Lower prices, shorter product cycles, and the customer individual production of highly variant products are the main reasons for the success of product configuration systems in various application domains (telecommunication industry, automotive industry, computer industry). In this paper we show how to employ UML in order to design complex configuration knowledge bases. We introduce the notion of contextual diagrams in order to cope with the intrinsic complexity of configuration knowledge. Since domain experts mostly think in terms of contexts, this approach leads to a more intuitive way of modeling configuration knowledge.

1 Introduction

The mass customization paradigm [18] created big challenges for the development of software supporting the product development process. A successful approach to master these challenges is to employ knowledge-based systems with domain specific, high level, formal description languages which allow a clear separation between domain knowledge and inference knowledge. Especially product configuration systems are increasingly applied for supporting product development processes. However, these systems are not integrated in the industrial software development process and their representation formalisms are not understandable for domain experts. In order to meet these challenges we propose the employment of the Unified Modeling Language (UML [20]) as domain specific notation for a conceptual design of configuration knowledge bases which can automatically be translated into the representation formalism of the corresponding configurator. The application of UML is motivated by the wide spread use of the language, the high degree of understandability, the extendability for domain specific purposes, and the availability of a build-in constraint language which allows the definition of complex constraints.

A configuration task can be characterized through a set of components, a description of their properties (attributes and their domains), available connection points (ports), and constraints on legal configurations. Given some customer requirements, the result of computing a configuration is a set of components,

A. Evans, S. Kent and B. Selic (Eds.): ≪UML≫ 2000, LNCS 1939, pp. 240–254, 2000.

corresponding attribute valuations, and connections satisfying all constraints and the customer requirements. In order to enable the construction of product models in UML we have defined a profile which contains domain-specific modeling concepts including the corresponding well-formedness rules. Furthermore, we have defined a set of translation rules which allow the automatic translation of the conceptual representation into an executable logic representation [8], [9] based on the component port model [16], [11].

The proposed development process for configuration knowledge bases is shown in Figure 1. First, a conceptual model of the configurable product is designed in UML (1). After syntactic checks on the correct usage of the concepts, the resulting model is non-ambiguously translated into logical sentences (2) which can be exploited by a general configuration engine for computing product configurations. The resulting knowledge base is validated by the domain expert using test runs on examples (3). A valid configuration knowledge base is employed in productive use (4).

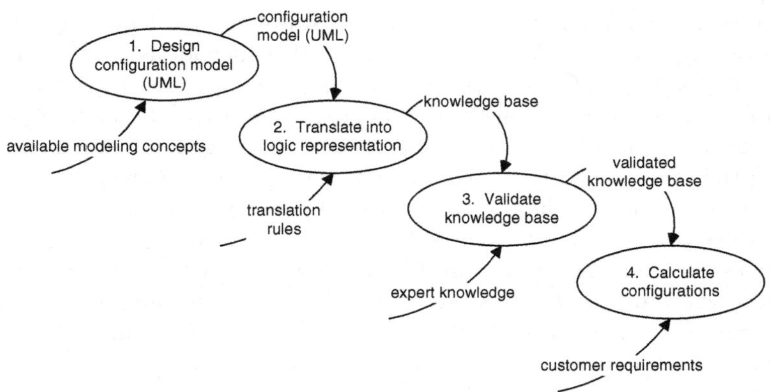

Fig. 1. Configuration system development process

Designing configuration knowledge bases using a conceptual modeling language combined with the automatic translation into an executable logic representation results in significant reductions of development efforts. However, when applying our approach for representing complex configuration knowledge bases, we have made the experience that the structuring mechanisms provided by UML do not suffice. In order to improve the understandability and maintainability of configuration models we introduce the notion of contextual diagrams[1], which provide a means for structuring the domain knowledge in a more intuitive way.

The paper is organized as follows. After giving a simple example for modeling configuration knowledge bases using UML (Section 2) we briefly discuss the properties of a configuration task and give a formal definition which is further used as basis for translating UML models (Section 3). In the following we motivate the usage of contextual diagrams by showing the limits of conventional

[1] This notion of context must not be confused with an OCL context.

structuring mechanisms provided by UML. Furthermore, we give an example for the construction of contextual diagrams (Section 4). In Section 5 we show how to translate contextual diagrams into a logic representation discussed in Section 3. Finally, Sections 6 and 7 contain related work and conclusions.

2 Building Configuration Models Using UML

Figure 2 shows how a configurable product can be modeled using an UML class diagram. Such a diagram describes the generic product structure, i.e. all possible variants of the product. The set of possible products is restricted through a set of constraints which relate to customer requirements, technical restrictions, economic factors, and restrictions according to the production process. Figure 2 shows how UML can be employed for modeling configurable products using the built-in extension mechanisms (stereotypes). A configuration model created with the defined concepts can automatically be translated into an executable logic representation[2].

For presentation purposes we introduce a simplified model of a configurable car as working example. We use standard UML concepts as well as newly introduced domain-specific stereotypes, whereby their usage is restricted through OCL constraints (Object Constraint Language) in the UML metamodel. The basic structure of the product is modeled using classes, generalization and aggregation of the well-defined parts (component-types) the final product can consist of. The applicability of these object-oriented concepts for configuration problems has been shown in [17]. The following modeling concepts (represented as stereotypes) are typical for the product configuration domain [22]*: component types*, *resources*, and *ports* are stereotyped classes, *connections* and *compatibility constraints* are stereotyped relations, *requires*, *produces*, and *consumes* are stereotyped dependencies.

- **Component types** Component types represent parts the final product can be built of. They are characterized by attributes (e.g. the component type *lights* is characterized by the attribute *color*).
- **Generalization** Component types with a similar structure are arranged in a generalization hierarchy[3].
- **Aggregation** Aggregations between components represented by part-of structures state a range of how many subparts an aggregate can consist of. Within the configuration domain the part of concept has the following semantics. A component is either a compositional part of another component, i.e. it must not be part of another component, or it is a non-composite (shared) part, i.e. the component can be shared between different components.
- **Resources, produces, and consumes** Parts of a configuration problem can be seen as a resource balancing task, where some of the component types *produce* some resource and others *consume* a *resource* (e.g. a *radio* represents a consumer of the resource *battery*).

[2] A detailed discussion on the translation rules is given in [8], [9].

- **Ports and connections** In addition to the amount and types of the different components also the product topology may be of interest in a final configuration, i.e. how the components are interconnected to each other. Ports represent connection points between connected components. E.g. a *radio power supply* must be connected to the *battery*.
- **Compatibility and requirements relations** Some types of components cannot be used in the same final configuration - they are *incompatible* (e.g. a *4-wheel gearing* is incompatible with a *diesel engine*). In other cases, the existence of one component type *requires* the existence of another special type in the configuration (e.g. an *automatic gearing* requires an *otto engine*).
- **Additional modeling concepts and constraints** Constraints on the product model, which can not be expressed graphically, are formulated using the language OCL (Object Constraint Language), which is an integral part of UML. As it is done for the graphical modeling concepts, OCL expressions are translated into a logical representation executable by the configuration engine[4]. The discussed modeling concepts have shown to cover a wide range of application areas for configuration [17]. Despite this, some application areas may have a need for special modeling concepts not covered so far. To introduce a new modeling concept a new stereotype has to be defined. Its semantics for the configuration domain must be defined by stating the facts and constraints induced to the logic theory when using the concept.

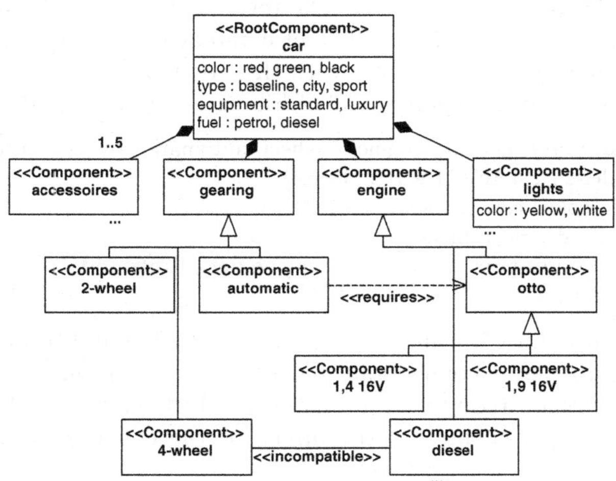

Fig. 2. Simple configuration model of a car

[3] Note that the car type in Figure 2 could also be represented in a generalization hierarchy.

[4] A detailed discussion on the translation of OCL expressions can be found in [9].

After having defined the configurable product, the actual configuration can take place. The user (the customer) specifies the requirements for the actual variant of the product. Let {*color:red, type:city, equipment: standard, engine:diesel*} be the customer requirements. The configuration system selects a *2-wheel* gearing since a *diesel* engine is incompatible with a *4-wheel* gearing as well as with an *automatic gearing* (*automatic* gearing requires an *otto engine*). Furthermore, a set of *yellow lights* and one *accessoire* (not further refined in this example) are added to the configuration.

3 Configuration Task

The following definition of a configuration task is based on a consistency-based approach. A configuration problem can be seen as a logic theory that describes a component library, a set of constraints, and customer requirements. Components are described by attributes and ports. Ports are used as connection points between components. The result of a configuration task is a set of components, their attribute values, and connections that satisfy the logic theory. This model has proven to be simple and powerful to describe general configuration problems and serves as a basis for configuration systems as well as for representing technical systems in general [16], [24], [14].

The formulation of a configuration problem can be based on two sets of logic sentences, namely *DD* (domain description) and *SRS* (System Requirements Specification). We restrict the form of the logical sentences to a subset of range restricted first-order-logic with a set extension and interpreted function symbols. In order to assure decidability, we restrict the term-depth to a fixed number.

DD includes the description of the different component types (*types*), named ports (*ports*), and attributes (*attributes*) with their domains (*dom*).

The *DD* of the car configuration model of Figure 2 is represented as follows:

types = {car, accessoires, gearing, engine, 4-wheel, automatic, 2-wheel, otto, diesel, 1,4 16V, 1,9 16V, lights}.
attributes(car) = {color, type, equipment, fuel}. ...
dom(car, color)= {red, green, black}. ...
ports(car) = {accessoires-port, gearing-port, engine-port, lights-port}[5].
ports(engine) = {car-port}. ...

Additionally, constraints are included, reducing the possibilities of allowed combinations of components, connections and value instantiations.

SRS includes the user requirements on the product which should be configured. These user requirements are the input for the concrete configuration task.

The configuration result is described through sets of logical sentences (*COMPS*, *ATTRS*, and *CONNS*). In these sets, the employed components, the attribute values (parameters), and the established connections are represented.

[5] The *part of* relationship between components is translated into connections between component ports in the logical representation.

- *COMPS* is a set of literals of the form *type(c,t)*. *t* is included in the set of types defined in *DD*. The constant *c* represents the identification for a component.
- *CONNS* is a set of literals of the form *conn(c1,p1,c2,p2)*. *c1* and c2 are component identifications from *COMPS*, *p1* (*p2*) is a port of the component *c1* (*c2*).
- *ATTRS* is a set of literals of the form *val(c,a,v)*, where c is a component-identification, a is an attribute of that component, and v is the actual value of the attribute (selected out of the domain of the attribute).

Example for a configuration result:

```
type(c1, car).
type (a1, accessoires).
type(g1, 2-wheel).
type(e1, diesel).
type(l1, lights).
conn(c1, accessoires-port, a1, car-port).
conn(c1, gearing-port, g1, car-port).
conn(c1, engine-port, e1, car-port).
conn(c1, lights-port, l1, car-port).
```

Based on these definitions, we are able to specify precisely the concept of a consistent configuration:

Definition (Consistent Configuration) If (*DD*, *SRS*) is a configuration problem and *COMPS*, *CONNS*, and *ATTRS* represent a configuration result, then the configuration is consistent exactly iff *DD* ∪ *SRS* ∪ *COMPS* ∪ *CONNS* ∪ *ATTRS* can be satisfied.

Additionally we have to specify that *COMPS* includes all required components, *CONNS* describes all required connections, and *ATTRS* includes a complete value assignment to all variables in order to achieve a *complete configuration.*

This is accomplished by additional logical sentences which can be generated using *DD*, *COMPS*, *CONNS*, and *ATTRS*. A configuration, which is consistent and complete w.r.t. the domain description and the customer requirements, is called a *valid configuration.* A detailed formal exposition is given in [11].

Using this component port formalism the following sentence can be derived expressing the *requires* relation between *automatic* gearing and *otto engine*[6]:

$$\text{type(ID1, automatic)} \wedge \text{type(ID2, car)} \wedge \text{conn(ID1, car-port, ID2, gearing-port)} \Rightarrow \\ \exists\ \text{ID3 type(ID3, otto)} \wedge \text{conn(ID3, car-port, ID2, engine-port)}.$$

The *incompatible* relation between a *4-wheel* gearing and a *diesel engine* can be translated as follows:

$$\text{type(ID1, 4-wheel)} \wedge \text{type(ID2, diesel)} \wedge \text{conn(ID1, car-port, ID3, gearing-port)} \wedge \\ \text{type(ID3, car)} \wedge \text{conn(ID2, car-port, ID3, engine-port)} \Rightarrow \text{false}.$$

---

[6] A detailed discussion on the translation rules can be found in [8].

The reason for applying the component port model as formal representation of UML configuration models lies in the direct executability of this representation in various configuration systems (e.g. [14], [24]).

In addition to the constraints derived from the UML model of Figure 2 further constraints are derived, e.g. *if component X is connected to component Y then component Y is connected to component X too,* or *one port can be connected to exactly one other port*, or *components have a unique type.* These constraints are called application independent constraints, which can automatically be generated from the domain description *(DD).*

In order to express constraints not representable graphically (using the concepts presented in Section 2), OCL constraints can be employed. These constraints often concern different model classes sometimes stored in different packages. The maintenance of these constraints becomes difficult, even if only a small set of constraints is formulated in the model (see Figure 3). The definition and maintenance of textually represented constraints is a real challenge for the knowledge engineer as well as the technical expert, whereas graphical representations significantly enhance the flexibility regarding human computer interaction and consequently reduce development and maintenance costs. In order to improve knowledge acquisition of such constraints we introduce the notion of contextual diagrams which will be presented in the next section. The idea is to divide the configuration model into different contexts in which different constraints must hold, e.g. *if the customer selects a car of type baseline, the gearing must be of type automatic* (see constraint C1 in Figure 3). The expression *gearing must be of type automatic* must hold, if a car of type *baseline* is selected, i.e. it must only hold in the context *car is of type baseline.* These kinds of constraints can be expressed graphically by their specification in a separate diagram denoted as contextual diagram, which is itself an UML class diagram. The argument for the application of contextual diagrams lies in the user centered knowledge acquisition support and in the reduction of textual constraints in the model. In order to represent the dependency between different contextual diagrams a diagram hierarchy must be introduced.

In the following sections we show how to employ contextual diagrams as structuring mechanism for modeling complex (configuration) knowledge bases.

4 Building Contextual Diagrams

UML packages and views primarily support the grouping of model elements not regarding the structure of complex constraints as shown in Figure 3. In order to tackle this challenge we propose the notion of contextual diagrams (representing contexts[7]), which allow the organization of (configuration) knowledge in a more intuitive way. The notion of context has been discussed in different research areas [4], [15], [21], [3], [25] using quite different interpretations. An overview of different interpretations of the notion of context can be found in [3].

[7] We assume that contextual diagrams and the corresponding contexts are denoted by the same name.

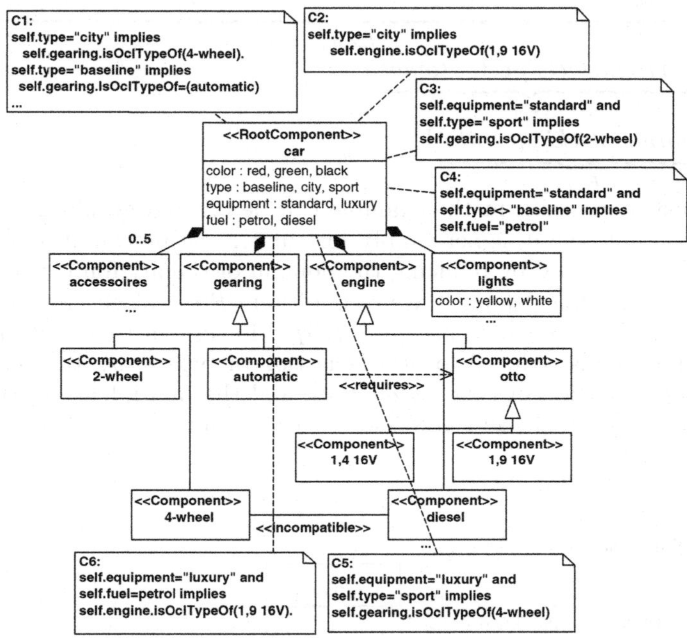

Fig. 3. Car model with additional sales constraints (defined in OCL)

Our interpretation of context is similar the the notion of context defined by McCarthy [15], who proposes a formalism *ist(c,p)* in order to define a context *c*, in which the proposition *p* must hold, i.e. *p is true* in *c*.

Definition (context) A context *c* is a tuple *(Prec, Expr)*, which is to be taken as assertion that *Expr* is *true* if *Prec* holds, i.e. *Prec⇒Expr*. *Prec* denotes a conjunction of logical expressions $Prec_i$, *Expr* either denotes a set of logical expressions $Expr_i$, or denotes a further context c' represented by the tuple *(Prec', Expr')*.

Following this definition we are able to construct a hierarchy of contextual diagrams (UML class diagrams), in which each contextual diagram c_i either represents the root of the hierarchy, or is derived from a contextual diagram c_j ($c_i \neq c_j$); Figure 4 shows a simple context hierarchy consisting of the root context c_{root} and the derived contexts $c_{baseline}$, c_{sport}, and c_{city}. *Prec* and *Expr* of the context $c_{baseline}$ can be expressed as OCL constraints as follows[8].

$$c_{baseline} = \{ \underbrace{(car.type =' baseline',}_{Prec_1}$$

[8] Note, that in many cases (also in this example) the designer of the configuration model does not have to formulate the constraints textually.

$$\underbrace{(car.accessoires \rightarrow size \succeq 0 \; and \; car.accessoires \rightarrow size \leq 2))}_{Expr_1},$$
$$\underbrace{gearing.isOclType(automatic)}_{Expr_2},$$
$$\underbrace{engine.isOclType(otto)\}}_{Expr_3}$$

The constraints given in the example can be entered graphically as shown in Figure 5. First, the designer simply formulates the precondition of the new context c_i - in this case by reducing the domain of the attribute *type*, i.e. *type: baseline*. After having defined the precondition *(Prec)* of the new context c_i, the designer enters a set of constraints *(Expr)* for c_i - in this case the domain of the engine type is reduced to *otto* (selection of type *otto*), the gearing type to *automatic* (selection of type *automatic*), and the multiplicity of the part of relationship between *car* and *accessoires* to *0..2* (upper bound of multiplicity reduced to 2).

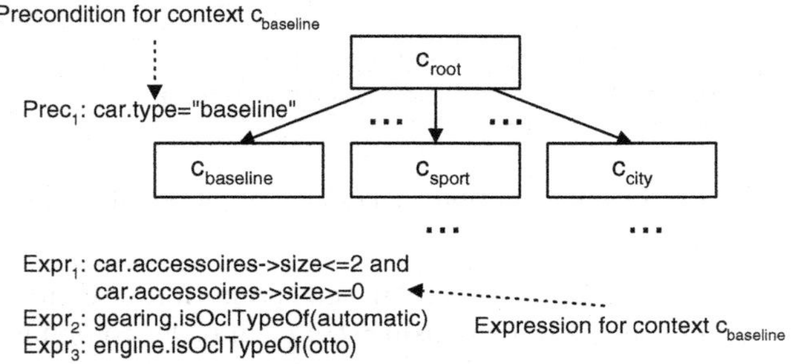

Fig. 4. A simple context hierarchy

Assuming that the contextual diagram c_{root} exists, a contextual diagram c_i ($c_i \neq c_{root}$) is constructed as follows (see Figure 6).

1. Select an existing contextual diagram c_j.
2. Define a precondition $Prec_i$ for c_i. Preconditions can either be defined graphically by specialization of classes of c_j, by restriction of the multiplicity of classes of c_j, or restriction of attribute domains of c_j. Furthermore, a precondition can be formulated as OCL expression.
3. Add the additional expressions $Expr_i$ valid in c_i by specialization of classes of c_j, by restriction of the multiplicity of classes of c_j, by restriction of attribute domains of c_j, or by using the following concepts presented in Section 2 *(requires, incompatible, produces, consumes, connected)*. Furthermore, $Expr_i$ can be formulated as OCL expression.
4. Derive the new contextual diagram c_i, i.e. represent only the selected (specialized) classes, relevant multiplicities, attribute domains, and constraints (also including additionally added constraints).

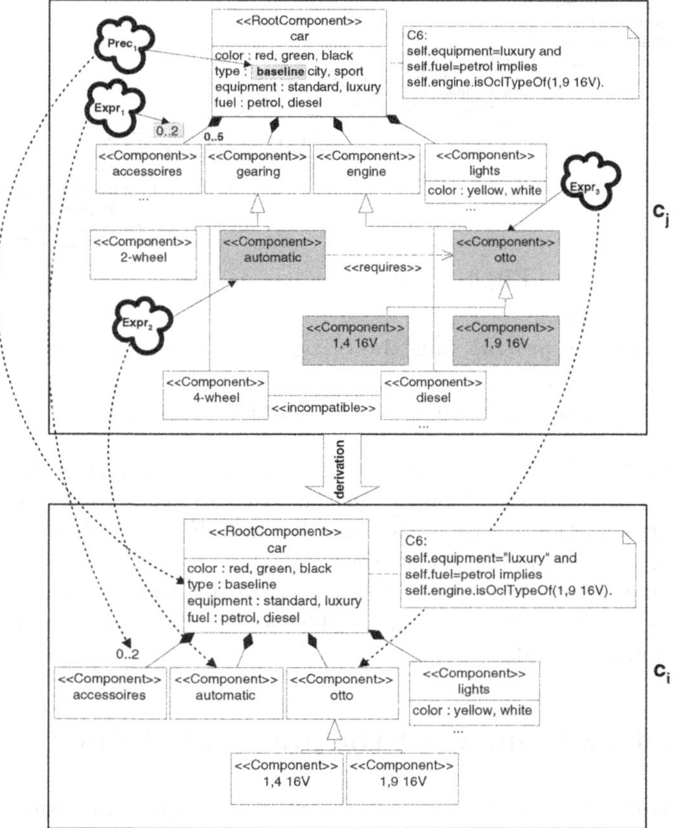

Fig. 5. Building the context $c_{baseline}$

Note, that a contextual diagram can contain only classes, attributes, generalization hierarchies, part of relations, and multiplicities, which were already defined in the diagram of the root context, i.e. no additional elements can be added in the context c_i ($c_i \neq c_{root}$). We impose this restriction since our goal is the structuring of constraints belonging to a given component hierarchy, which is defined in the *root* context.

Following the above rules we are able to construct a contextual diagram for the context $c_{baseline}$ as follows.

1. The existing contextual diagram c_{root} is selected.
2. A precondition *(Prec)* for the new context $c_{baseline}$ is formulated. In this example this is done by reducing the domain of the attribute *type* to *baseline* (see Figure 5).
3. The designer defines a set of restrictions *(Expr)* for $c_{baseline}$, namely at most two *accessoires* (not further refined in this example) can be part of the

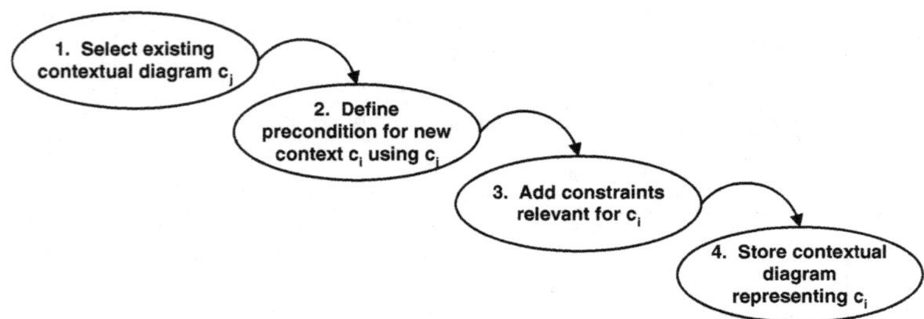

Fig. 6. Context building process

configuration, the *gearing* must be of type *automatic*, and the *engine* unit must be of type *otto*.

4. The new contextual diagram c_i can be derived (see Figure 5).

We assume that graphically entered expressions of *(Prec, Expr)* are internally stored as OCL constraints, which are further used in order to derive a component port representation of the contextual diagram. Figure 4 shows the entered selections represented as OCL constraints.

After having defined *Prec* and *Expr*, a corresponding contextual diagram $c_{baseline}$ can be derived. This diagram can be used for the construction of further contextual diagrams inside $c_{baseline}$.

5 Translating Contextual Diagrams into Logic

In order to translate contextual diagrams into our logic representation (component port representation discussed in Section 3), the following rules must be considered:

1. Let c_{root} be the root contextual diagram representing our configuration model. Then *DD* of c_{root} is derived conforming the translation rules given in [8], [9], i.e. c_{root} is translated into the component port represention.
2. All additional expressions added in a contextual diagram c_i ($c_i \neq c_{root}$) are translated as follows. Let *Prec* be a conjunction of preconditions defined for c_i, and *Expr* a set of expressions defined for c_i. Then c_i is translated as follows: *Prec* $\Rightarrow$ *Expr*, i.e. $\forall$ $Expr_i \in Expr$ $(Prec \Rightarrow Expr_i)$ is added to *DD*. Furthermore, if c_i is a subcontext of a context c_j with preconditions *Prec'*, then c_i is translated as follows: $Prec' \Rightarrow (Prec \Rightarrow Expr)$.

Example: translation of the context $c_{baseline}$

$Prec_1$: *car.type="baseline"*
$Expr_1$: car.accessoires→size≤2 and car.accessoires→size≥0
$Expr_2$: gearing.isOclTypeOf(automatic)
$Expr_3$: engine.isOclTypeOf(otto)

Conform to $c_{baseline}$, i.e. $\text{Prec}_1 \Rightarrow (\text{Expr}_1 \wedge \text{Expr}_2 \wedge \text{Expr}_3)$ must be translated into the component port representation. An alternative representation of the implication is the following: $(\neg\text{Prec}_1 \vee \text{Expr}_1) \wedge (\neg\text{Prec}_1 \vee \text{Expr}_2) \wedge (\neg\text{Prec}_1 \vee \text{Expr}_3)$, i.e. $(\text{Prec}_1 \Rightarrow \text{Expr}_1) \wedge (\text{Prec}_1 \Rightarrow \text{Expr}_2) \wedge (\text{Prec}_1 \Rightarrow \text{Expr}_3)$. The component port representation for these constraints valid in $c_{baseline}$ is the following:

type(X, car) $\wedge$ val(X, type, baseline) $\Rightarrow$
parts(X, accessoires, Count) $\wedge$ (Count $\leq$ 2) $\wedge$ (Count $\geq$ 0).

type(X, car) $\wedge$ val(X, type, baseline) $\wedge$ type(Y, gearing) $\wedge$
conn(X, gearing-port, Y, car-port) $\Rightarrow$ type(Y,automatic).

type(X, car) $\wedge$ val(X, type, baseline) $\wedge$ type(Y, engine) $\wedge$
conn(X, engine-port, Y, car-port) $\Rightarrow$ type(Y, otto).

Note, that the generated sentences belong to one single *DD*. The automatic generation of the knowledge base is done by traversing the derived context hierarchy, translating the contextual diagrams into the component port representation, and adding the result to *DD*.

In order to support the debbugging of knowledge bases we propose a consistency-based formalism (model-based diagnosis) discussed in [10], where the constraints in the generated configuration knowledge base are interpreted as components which are diagnosed in order to find contradicting components. The resulting diagnoses are presented to the user indicating the corresponding classes in the conceptual configuration model.

6 Related Work

The formalization of the semantics of conceptual modeling languages like OMT [19], UML [20] and OCL is an actual research area [2], [5], [6]. These formalizations are mostly based on mathematical models and specification languages. The work is focused on getting precise definitions of the employed concepts for general models. In order to support the graphical representation of complex constraints [12] propose the notion of constraint diagrams, which are basically extensions of Venn Diagrams. We view our work as complementary, since our goal is to generate formal descriptions which can be interpreted by logic-based problem solvers restricted to a special domain (solvers based on the logic representation discussed in Section 3). However, the consideration of the concepts presented in [12] could be useful for our work in order to provide additional modeling concepts for configuration domains.

There is a long history in developing configuration tools in knowledge-based systems (see [23]). However, the automated generation of logic-based knowledge bases by exploiting a formal definition of standard design descriptions like UML has not been discussed so far. Comparable research has been done in the fields of automated and knowledge-based Software Engineering, e.g. the derivation of programs in the Amphion [13] project.

Research dealing with knowledge representation in the configuration domain regards declarative constraint representation as the basic representation formalism, since the development and maintenance of rule-based systems like R1/XCON [1] have shown to be error-prone. Using declarative constraint representation is not enough since knowledge bases become increasingly complex so that conventional structuring mechanisms do not suffice. Conventional mechanisms for structuring knowledge bases in the configuration domain are described in [7]. The notion of context has been discussed in several research areas using different interpretations depending on the application area. In [25] a context is denoted as a higher order conceptual entity, which describes a group of conceptual entities from a particular point of view. Rules and operations are provided to organize the manipulation of contexts. Furthermore, an example for the application of contexts in a cooperative document design environment is given, where documents represent collections of objects. In [4] the notion of context is employed for supporting cooperative work in hypermedia design providing a set of context operations on hypermedial objects (e.g. editing, inquiry, attribute operations). Compared to these approaches we view our approach as complementary, since our goal is to effectively support the knowledge acquisition for complex (configuration) knowledge bases not regarding any operations for combining different contexts (all contexts are translated into the same DD). In AI research the notion of context is interpreted in a different sense. [15] denotes a context as an abstract object representing a particular meaning not true outside the context. Our approach applies these concepts in order to support knowledge acquisition for complex knowledge bases on a conceptual (UML) level, especially improving the representation of complex constraints in order to be understandable for domain experts. Furthermore, an overview of different interpretations of context in the design area is given in [3].

7 Conclusions

Extensible standard design languages like UML are able to provide a basis for introducing and applying rigorous formal descriptions of application domains. This approach helps us to combine the advantages of various areas. First, high level formal description languages reduce the development time and effort significantly, because these descriptions are directly executable. Second, standard design languages like UML are far more comprehensible and are widely adopted in the established industrial software development process. We defined a logic-based formal semantics for UML constructs, which allows us to generate logical sentences and to process them by a problem solver. The intrinsic complexity of configuration knowledge requires the provision of concepts which effictively support the representation of complex constraints, i.e. support a graphical representation. We have shown how to represent and organize complex (configuration) knowledge bases using the concept of contextual diagrams which especially support an understandable representation of complex constraints.

Applying these concepts enables us to automate the generation of specialized software applications and allows for rapid generation of prototypes. An improvement in the requirements engineering phase through short feedback cycles is achieved. The design model is comprehensible for domain experts and can be adapted and validated without the need of specialists. Consequently, time and costs for the development and maintenance of product configuration systems can be reduced significantly. We chose product configuration systems because of the economic and technical relevance and the challenges to be tackled by software engineering of these systems.

References

1. V.E. Barker, D.E. O'Connor, J.D. Bachant, and E. Soloway. Expert systems for configuration at Digital: XCON and beyond. *Communications of the ACM*, 32, 3:298–318, 1989. 252
2. R.H. Bourdeau and B.H.C. Cheng. A formal Semantics for Object Model Diagrams. *IEEE Transactions on Software Engineering*, 21,10:799–821, 1995. 251
3. Charles Charlton and Ken Wallace. Reminding and context in design. In *Proceedings 6th International Conference on Artificial Intelligence in Design (AID'00)*, pages 569–588, Boston/Worcester, MA, USA, 2000. Kluwer Academic Publishers. 246, 246, 252
4. N.M. Delisle and M.D. Schwartz. Contexts – a partitioning concept for hypertext. *ACM Transactions on Information Systems*, 5,2:168–186, 1987. 246, 252
5. A. Evans. Reasoning with UML class diagrams. In *Proceedings Workshop on Industrial Strength Formal Methods(WIFT'98)*, Florida, USA, 1998. IEEE Press. 251
6. A. Evans and S. Kent. Core Meta-Modeling Semantics of UML: the pUML aproach. In *Proceedings ¡¡UML¿¿'99*, pages 140–155, Fort Collings, Colorado, USA, 1999. 251
7. F. Feldkamp, M. Heinrich, and K.D. Meyer Gramann. SyDeR System Development For Reusability. *AIEDAM, Special Issue: Configuration Design*, 12,4:373–382, 1998. 252
8. A. Felfernig, G. Friedrich, and D. Jannach. UML as domain specific language for the construction of knowledge-based configuration systems. In *11th International Conference on Software Engineering and Knowledge Engineering*, pages 337–345, Kaiserslautern, Germany, 1999. 241, 242, 245, 250
9. A. Felfernig, G. Friedrich, and D. Jannach. Generating product configuration knowledge bases from precise domain extended UML models. In *Proc. 12th International Conference on Software Engineering and Knowledge Engineering*, pages 284–293, Chicago, USA, 2000. 241, 242, 243, 250
10. A. Felfernig, G. Friedrich, D. Jannach, and M. Stumptner. An Integrated Development Environment for the Design and Maintenance of Large Configuration Knowledge Bases. *Artificial Intelligence in Design (AID'00) (to appear), Kluwer Academic Publisher*, 2000. 251
11. G. Friedrich and M. Stumptner. Consistency-Based Configuration. In *AAAI Workshop on Configuration, Technical Report WS-99-05*, pages 35–40, Orlando, Florida, 1999. 241, 245
12. J. Gil, J. Howse, and S. Kent. Constraint Diagrams: A Step Beyond UML. In *Proceedings TOOLS USA'99*. IEEE Press, 1999. 251, 251
13. M. Lowry, A. Philpot, T. Pressburger, and I. Underwood. A formal approach to domain-oriented software design environments. In *Proc. 9th Knowledge-Based Software Engineering Conference*, pages 48–57, Montery, CA, USA, 1994. IEEE Computer Society. 251
14. D. Mailharro. A classification and constraint-based framework for configuration. *AIEDAM, Special Issue: Configuration Design*, 12,4:383–397, 1998. 244, 246

15. J. McCarthy. Notes on formalizing context. In *Proc. of the 13th IJCAI*, pages 555–560, Chambery, France, 1993. 246, 247, 252
16. S. Mittal and F. Frayman. Towards a Generic Model of Configuration Tasks. In *Proc. of the 11th IJCAI*, pages 1395–1401, Detroit, MI, 1989. 241, 244
17. H. Peltonen, T. Mnnist, T. Soininen, J. Tiihonen, A. Martio, and R. Sulonen. Concepts for Modeling Configurable Products. In *Proceedings of European Conference Product Data Technology Days*, pages 189–196, Sandhurst, UK, 1998. 242, 243
18. B.J. PineII, B. Victor, and A.C. Boynton. Making Mass Customization Work. *Harvard Business Review*, Sep./Oct. 1993:109–119, 1993. 240
19. J. Rumbaugh, M. Blaha, W. Premerlani, F. Eddy, and W.Lorensen. Object-Oriented Modeling and Design. In *Prentice Hall International Editions*, New Jersey, USA, 1991. 251
20. J. Rumbaugh, I. Jacobson, and G. Booch. *The Unified Modeling Language Reference Manual.* Addison-Wesley, 1998. 240, 251
21. M. Siegel, E. Sciore, and S. Salveter. A method for automatic rule derivation to support semantic query optimization. *ACM Transactions on Database Systems*, 17:563–600, 1992. 246
22. T. Soininen, J. Tiihonen, T. Mnnist, and R. Sulonen. Towards a General Ontology of Configuration. *AIEDAM, Special Issue: Configuration Design*, 12,4:357–372, 1998. 242
23. M. Stumptner. An overview of knowledge-based configuration. *AI Communications*, 10(2), June, 1997. 251
24. M. Stumptner, G. Friedrich, and A. Haselbck. Generative constraint-based configuration of large technical systems. *AIEDAM, Special Issue: Configuration Design*, 12, 4:307–320, Sep. 1998. 244, 246
25. Manos Theodorakis, Anastasia Analyti, Panos Constantopoulos, and Nikos Spyratos. Context in information bases. In *Proceedings of the 3rd International Conference on Cooperative Information Systems (CoopIS'98)*, pages 260–270, New York City, NY, USA, August 1998. IEEE Computer Society. 246, 252

The UML Family: Profiles, Prefaces and Packages

Steve Cook

IBM UK Ltd, 79 Staines Road West, Sunbury-on-Thames, Middlesex TW16 7AN
sj_cook@uk.ibm.com

Abstract. This paper overviews the status of UML (Unified Modeling Language) considered as a *family* of languages, and reviews critically various approaches to defining variants of UML within this family.

1 The UML Family

UML is very successful. We may reflect back to the time before UML, when there were several competing notations for object-oriented modelling and design, such as Object Modeling Technique (OMT) [1], Booch [2], OORAM [3], Syntropy [4] and many others. Although each of these approaches had its particular strengths and weaknesses, the sheer number of competing approaches was a major inhibitor to the ability of practitioners to understand each others' models, to get effective training in constructing models, and to exchange models. UML, introduced in 1997, has been rapidly and widely adopted and has almost completely superseded all of these earlier approaches. This demonstrates that the industry is more interested in a common modelling approach than in the particular philosophies that distinguished the earlier approaches from each other.

Nonetheless, as the use of UML mounts we are recognising that UML is in fact a family of languages, rather than a single language. As UML develops and matures we may expect its variety of uses to continue to expand. Today UML is used for numerous purposes, including but not limited to:

diagrammatic depiction of program code: the UML models can be directly transformed into program code (typically in Java or C++) and (sometimes) vice-versa. This is the typical interpretation given to UML by popular CASE (Computer-Aided Software Engineering) tools.

precise declarative modelling of system behaviour (see e.g. Catalysis [5]).

diagrammatic depiction of directly-executable models, where an interpreter exists to execute the UML models directly (see e.g. the activities of the Action Semantics Consortium [6]).

hypermedia and website design (see e.g. Conallen's book [7] and the paper by Baumeister et al [8]).

It is very clear that the semantics of UML cannot be exactly the same for all of these uses. This can be demonstrated, for example, by observing that the semantics of

A. Evans, S. Kent and B. Selic (Eds.): «UML» 2000, LNCS 1939, pp. 255-264, 2000.

inheritance for Java and C++ are different. Java makes a formal distinction between classes and interfaces and enforces different inheritance schemes on each (single inheritance for classes, multiple for interfaces), while C++ makes no such distinctions. If UML is to represent both Java and C++, the set of legal UML-C++ models and the set of legal UML-Java models must be different. The position of this paper is that there should be some way of representing these differences within the structure of UML itself, i.e. that UML-C++ and UML-Java are different (although similar) members of the UML language family.

The difference between C++ and Java inheritance is just one of a huge number of differences between the possible applications of UML. In this paper we will call a specific application of UML a "UML variant". The remainder of this paper discusses and proposes various approaches to dealing systematically with UML variants.

2 The Definition of UML

To improve our understanding of how to represent UML variants we must first understand how UML is itself defined. Formally, UML is defined by a document controlled by the Object Management Group [9] containing the following sections:

UML Summary. Overview, history, acknowledgements, etc.

UML Semantics. This section defines the UML "abstract syntax" in the form of a set of UML packages. Thus UML is defined using a subset of itself: this definition is called the UML "meta-model". Each class in the meta-model is explained by English paragraphs. Well-formedness rules for UML models are expressed in Object Constraint Language (OCL) [10]. Each package within the meta-model is further described by additional English text that describes the intended interpretation of the elements in the package. This section is itself called "Semantics".

UML Notation Guide. This section describes the pictorial elements that make up the UML diagrams, and how they fit together. Examples are used together with English text. Each diagrammatic element has a "Mapping" that describes in English how it corresponds to elements in the meta-model. The notation document also contains paragraphs entitled "Semantics".

UML Standard Profiles. This section briefly introduces two standard Profiles, which are variants of UML: UML Profile for Software Development Processes, and UML Profile for Business Modeling. We return to the subject of UML Profiles later.

UML CORBAfacility Interface Definition. This section gives the CORBA IDL[11] (Interface Definition Language) interface to a repository for creating, storing and retrieving UML models. The UML meta-model is subjected to transformations that map it into the facilities supported by the OMG's Meta-Object Facility (MOF) standard, and then systematically mapped into IDL interface definitions.

UML XMI DTD Specification. This section gives an alternative physical specification of UML, represented using XML (eXtensible Markup Language), specifically intended for interchanging UML models between tools and/or repositories. As with the IDL definition, the UML meta-model is subjected to transformations that create a "physical meta-model", which is then systematically mapped into XML Data Type Definitions – schemas that govern the structure of legal XML representations of UML models.

Object Constraint Language Specification. This section introduces and defines the Object Constraint Language that is used to formulate well-formedness rules in the UML specification, and is also intended to be an adjunct to UML for modellers who wish to add more precision to their models.

UML Standard Elements. This appendix lists standard values for UML Stereotypes, Constraints and Tags.

OMG Modeling Glossary. This appendix lists definitions of terminology.

The UML definition is positioned within a hierarchy of levels called the four-layer architecture. The four layers are:

M0: domain-specific information
M1: model of the domain-specific information, e.g. in UML
M2: meta-model, e.g. definition of UML
M3: meta-meta-model, e.g. definition of the way that UML is defined.

M3 is defined using itself, obviating any need for M4, M5 etc.

In this document we will call all classes in an M2 level model M2-classes.

We observe that the current definition of UML possesses a number of inhibitors to developing a systematic approach to UML variation.

1. The UML semantics is informally specified, and this specification is scattered in a number of places. There is no definitive statement of what is meant by the phrase "UML semantics"; in general, the definition of semantics contains English prose that adds additional information about the intended meaning of UML constructs. This additional prose covers various kinds of subject matter, including:
   Statements about the dynamic behaviour of the systems described by models under various circumstances
   Statements about the well-formedness of models
   Statements about different approaches to modelling a particular concept.

   We observe that the UML semantics have no operational method of checking or enforcement; whether a UML model conforms to the semantics or not is purely a matter of human interpretation based on a reading of the prose. This means in practice that the proposed semantics may be ignored if desired. Furthermore, it remains a subject of pure conjecture whether a given variant of UML, for example a particular vendor's mapping of UML into Java, actually conforms to the UML semantics.

2. The UML definition is uneven in the level of abstraction at which it defines semantics. Some parts of the specification are defined with considerable operational precision, for example the behaviour of Statecharts is defined in terms of an event queue, an event dispatcher, and an event processor. This (unless the semantics are ignored) precludes the use of UML's state machine modelling techniques for modelling purely declarative, observational state machines as might,

for example, be associated with interfaces. On the other hand, parts of the specification, such as the meaning of a Flow (a relationship between two versions of an object) have very loose semantics, and are intended to be specialised in particular circumstances.

3. The meta-model contains significant redundancy. Some M2-classes that represent very similar concepts, such as Package and Model, are identical from the perspective of well-formedness and differ only in the English description of their semantics, and a minor difference in their notation.

4. UML defines a set of diagram types, but there is no meta-model representation of a diagram itself. According to the UML notation definition, "individual class diagrams do not represent divisions in the underlying model". In consequence, interoperability of models is severely restricted, because without extending UML in some way it is not possible to interchange the information about which elements appear in which diagrams. In fact, diagram interoperability is not supported in general because there is not a functional mapping between meta-model elements and diagrammatic elements.

3 Current Approaches to UML Variation

The current definition of UML does allow the possibility of variation. There are two main techniques used within the portfolio of OMG technologies for dealing with UML variation: Profiles and Meta-model Extensions.

3.1 Profiles

The concept of a Profile was first introduced in the UML definition itself, and defined to be "a predefined set of Stereotypes, TaggedValues, Constraints, and notation icons that collectively specialize and tailor the UML for a specific domain or process. ... A profile does not extend UML by adding any new basic concepts." We have to explain these terms.

A UML Stereotype is 'a way of classifying (marking) UML elements so that they behave in some respects as if they were instances of new "virtual" meta-model concepts. Instances have the same structure (attributes, associations, operations) as a similar non-stereotyped instance of the same kind. The stereotype may specify additional constraints and required tagged values that apply to instances. In addition, a stereotype may be used to indicate a difference in meaning or usage between two elements with identical structure' [9]. The definition of Stereotype also includes a notation icon.

A *UML TaggedValue* is 'a (Tag, Value) pair that permits arbitrary information to be attached to any model element'[9].

A *UML Constraint* 'allows new semantics to be specified linguistically for a model element. The specification is written as an expression in a designated constraint language' [9].

Together these three concepts offer a lightweight means for extending UML with new kinds of modelling element. It is lightweight because it is easily supported by tools without requiring "meta-CASE" facilities, and because it does not impact the interchange formats.

The definition of profile has evolved significantly since the original quoted above. An enhanced definition appeared in the OMG Requests for Proposals for UML Profiles for CORBA, for Enterprise Distributed Object Computing, and for Scheduling, Performance and Time. Within each Request for Proposal (RFP) there is a working definition of a UML profile, which states:

'For the purposes of this RFP, a UML profile is a specification that does one or more of the following:

- Identifies a subset of the UML meta-model (which may be the entire UML meta-model)
- Specifies "well-formedness rules" beyond those specified by the identified subset of the UML meta-model. "Well-formedness rule" is a term used in the normative UML meta-model specification to describe a set of constraints written in UML's Object Constraint Language (OCL) that contributes to the definition of a meta-model element.
- Specifies "standard elements" beyond those specified by the identified subset of the UML meta-model. "Standard element" is a term used in the UML meta-model specification to describe a standard instance of a UML stereotype, tagged value or constraint.
- Specifies semantics, expressed in natural language, beyond those specified by the identified subset of the UML meta-model.
- Specifies common model elements, expressed in terms of the profile.'

Further work within the OMG Analysis and Design Task Force, not yet published publicly, has refined this definition further in preparation for the next version (1.4) of UML.

As already observed, Profiles offer a lightweight mechanism for creating extensions of UML. However, Profiles are not satisfactory as a *general* mechanism for UML variation, because every concept must be represented either directly by an existing UML M2-class, or by a stereotype that directly extends such an M2-class. There is no way to add associations to the meta-model when defining a profile, and if an existing M2-class cannot be found to provide an effective basis for a new concept, the extension cannot be accomplished. Furthermore, the extension ought to be consistent with the existing UML semantics, insofar as they can be established.

3.2 Meta-model Extensions

More "heavyweight" extensions to UML can be accomplished by using the OMG's Meta-Object Facility (MOF) standard [12] directly to create additional M2-classes, as extensions to the UML meta-model. This approach has been taken within the OMG itself to define the Common Warehouse Meta-model [13], a meta-model designed to support interchange data warehouse metadata.

This approach is significantly more flexible than the profiles approach, because new M2-classes can be created either as subclasses of M2-classes in the UML definition, or as separate M2-classes with associations to UML M2-classes.

However there are a number of drawbacks with this approach.

The UML meta-model is not directly expressed using the MOF standard, and must be subjected to simplifying transformations.

No rules exist about what happens to notational mappings when the UML meta-model is extended.

No rules exist about what happens to semantics when the UML meta-model is extended.

Apart from subclassing, no way exists to add new associations or attributes to an existing M2-class within a new meta-model. As showed by D'Souza et al [14], this capability would provide a simple and powerful technique for defining UML extensions using packages at the M2 level.

3.3 UML Prefaces

More encompassing proposals for UML extensibility were made in the paper by Cook et al [15], which introduced the concept of a UML *Preface*. A preface would be a document that would define a UML extension by specialising, tailoring and extending:

the meta-model
the abstract syntax
the semantics
the concrete syntax
the context conditions on all of the above
the allowed transformations and generations.

A preface, then, would be a much more substantial and wide-ranging document than a profile or a meta-model extension. The range of subject-matters that a preface could cover are suggested in the paper [15] as follows:

'extensions of the UML by new elements through
- stereotype definitions
- allowable tags
- pragmas (expressed as tagged values)

class diagrams
- meaning of aggregation: strong or weak?
- special symbols for better visual perception
- treatment of n-ary associations (n>2)
- implicit adding of methods for persistence, Jini-Interfaces, etc.

statechart diagrams
- meaning of guards

- what to attach statecharts to (methods or classes?)
- what happens if a message cannot be processed? Throw an error? Ignore?
- relationship of guards and control states to preconditions
- inheritance of statecharts between superclasses and subclasses

inheritance

- allowed forms (multiple, public and private, repeated)
- meaning of repeated inheritance (C++ rules? Eiffel rules?)
- redefinition rules for overriding (extending types of parameters, how to deal with pre- and postconditions)

framing rules to specify which actions do or don't affect which parts of a system, on the

- specification level
- operational level

underlying model of time

- what is an object? what is a system state?
- causes of transitions: events, operations, conditions that become valid, timeouts, etc
- concurrency issues: deadlock, transaction privacy, etc.

connecting OCL constraints to diagrams

- how UML-diagram elements become available to OCL expressions

programming language specific support

- C++ (with multiple inheritance)
- Java (without multiple inheritance, but a useful exception mechanism)
- Smalltalk (with possibility to dynamically change a class during runtime)
- Eiffel (with support for runtime checking of assertions)

communication paradigms

- buffered (asynchronous) communication vs. synchronous vs. procedure call
- synchronous with deadlocks, or loss of messages not processed in time
- event notification mechanisms, priority, transmission privacy (encryption) through protocols

persistence mechanisms

- automatic persistence for all or some objects
- predefined mapping to a given data-base
- logging of object-changes; undo policy
- predefined transaction-mechanism
- error recovery'

4 Towards a Language for Defining Language Families

If we reflect upon the design of UML and its various extension mechanisms we conclude that it has not been well designed as a family of languages. Its original designers considered that purely syntactic elements, stereotypes and tags, were sufficient for defining extensions of the language. Experience is increasingly telling us that this is insufficient, and that the industry wants a more robustly extensible construct for UML.

We can think of such a construct as a *language for designing language families.* According to a feasibility study being carried out by Clark et al [16], such a language should have the following properties:

- It should be general. There should be as few special cases and unmotivated restrictions as possible.
- It should be coherent and consistent.
- There should be as few key concepts as possible. The core concepts should be orthogonal. One concept should not totally subsume another.
- It should be appropriate for language design. In particular, it should be able to describe syntax (both textual and visual), concepts and semantics, including well-formedness rules.
- It should provide explicit support for the definition and evolution of language families.
- It should be precise and unambiguous.
- It should itself be a language. Thus its definition should distinguish between syntax, concepts and semantics, and these should be defined in a clear and unambiguous way.
- It should be declarative.
- It should support reflection, i.e. should support the treatment of a definition as data.

Clark et al point out that the MOF does not satisfy all of these criteria; notably it provides no support for defining concrete syntax or semantics and it mixes up language definition properties with issues to do with storage models in a repository. These aspects should be kept separate.

Clark et al propose an architecture for a *language for defining language families.* This architecture explicitly distinguishes at its core between concepts (i.e. abstract syntax), syntax (i.e. concrete syntax), semantics, and the mappings between them. A key construct of the approach is the use of *packages* to encapsulate chunks of definition. The paper specifies a semantics for packages and package instances that allows the definition of language concepts to be built up progressively in several packages, in a similar way to that proposed by D'Souza et al in [14].

One of the important contributions of [16] is a more precise definition of *semantics* in the context of diagrammatic language definition. We saw earlier that the UML definition document itself uses the word *semantics* to mean a variety of things, including abstract syntax and various discussions about the restrictions of that syntax. A clarification of the meaning of *semantics* is urgently needed.

In general, the formal study of semantics is a huge and challenging enterprise. Within computer science, large amounts of effort have gone into studying the meaning of textual programming languages, giving rise to branches of study called (amongst others) *denotational* semantics, *operational* semantics, *axiomatic* semantics and *algebraic* semantics. We can expect a similar challenge and diversity of approach in giving meaning formally to diagrammatic languages such as UML.

The approach adopted in [16] is a denotational approach, i.e. one that maps each concept of the language to a corresponding denotation in a semantics domain. To make things simpler, the language used to express the semantics domain is UML itself. OCL is used to specify constraints between language concepts and their counterparts in the semantic domain. The resulting framework would allow a great deal more checking of the overall validity of UML models than is possible given the current definition.

5 The Future

At the time of writing, an intensive activity is progressing within the OMG to define a Request for Proposals for version 2 of UML. This follows on from the results of a Request for Information on this topic that produced some 32 responses from a large number of companies and academic institutions. This Request for Proposals (which may be split into two or more requests) will ask for revisions to UML in two major areas: content and architecture. The revisions in the area of content will both refine and extend the existing content; we may hope that these improvements will retain all of the existing strengths of the language and notation while making it more extensible and better abstracted. The revisions in the area of language architecture will hopefully be driven by the kinds of considerations reviewed in this paper and transform UML into a well-defined family of languages that can be fully interchanged between tools, and with much more capability for model checking than now.

References

1. Rumbaugh, J., Blaha, M., Premerlani, W., Eddy, F., & Lorensen, W.: Object-Oriented Modeling and Design. Prentice-Hall, Englewood Cliffs (1991).
2. Booch, G.: Object-Oriented Analysis and Design with Applications (2nd ed.). Benjamin/Cummings, Redwood City (1994).
3. Reenskaug, T.: Working with Objects. Manning, Greenwich (1996).
4. Cook, S. & Daniels, J.: Designing Object Systems: Object-oriented modelling with Syntropy. Prentice-Hall, Hemel Hempstead (1994).
5. D'Souza, D. & Wills, A.C.: Objects, Components and Frameworks with UML: The Catalysis Approach. Addison-Wesley, Reading, Massachusetts (1999).
6. The Action Semantics Consortium - http://www.kc.com/as_site/home.html
7. Conallen, J.: Building Web Applications with UML. Addison-Wesley, Reading, Massachusetts (2000).
8. Baumeister, H., Koch, N. & Mandel, L.: Towards a UML Extension for Hypermedia Design. In: France, R. & Rumpe, B. (eds): UML'99 – The Unified Modeling Language: Beyond the Standard. Lecture Notes in Computer Science, Vol. 1723. Springer-Verlag, Berlin Heidelberg New York (1999) 614-629
9. OMG Unified Modeling Language Specification, Version 1.3: ftp://ftp.omg.org/pub/docs/formal/00-03-01.pdf
10. Warmer, J.B. & Kleppe, A.G.: The Object Constraint Language : Precise Modeling with UML, Addison-Wesley, Reading, Massachusetts (1999).
11. CORBA IDL definition http://cgi.omg.org/cgi-bin/doc?formal/99-10-07.pdf

12. OMG Meta-Object Facility (MOF) Specification, Version 1.3: ftp://ftp.omg.org/pub/docs/formal/00-03-01.pdf
13. OMG Common Warehouse Metamodel (CWM) definition http://cgi.omg.org/cgi-bin/doc?ad/00-01-01.pdf
14. D'Souza, D., Sane, A., Birchenough, A.: First Class Extensibility for UML – Packaging of Profiles, Stereotypes, Patterns. In: France, R. & Rumpe, B. (eds): UML'99 – The Unified Modeling Language: Beyond the Standard. Lecture Notes in Computer Science, Vol. 1723. Springer-Verlag, Berlin Heidelberg New York (1999) 265-277
15. Cook, S., Kleppe, A., Mitchell, R., Rumpe, B., Warmer, J., Wills, A.C.: Defining UML Family Members using Prefaces. In: Mingins. C., & Meyer, B. (eds): Proceedings of TOOLS 32, IEEE (1999).
16. Clark, T., Evans, A., Kent, S.: Feasibility Study in Rearchitecting MOF, UML and XMI. To be published.

Validating UML Models and OCL Constraints

Mark Richters and Martin Gogolla

University of Bremen, FB 3, Computer Science Department
Postfach 330440, D-28334 Bremen, Germany
{mr|gogolla}@informatik.uni-bremen.de,
WWW home page: http://www.db.informatik.uni-bremen.de

Abstract. The UML has been widely accepted as a standard for modeling software systems and is supported by a great number of CASE tools. However, UML tools often provide only little support for validating models early during the design stage. Also, there is generally no substantial support for constraints written in the Object Constraint Language (OCL). We present an approach for the validation of UML models and OCL constraints that is based on animation. The USE tool (UML-based Specification Environment) supports developers in this process. It has an animator for simulating UML models and an OCL interpreter for constraint checking. Snapshots of a running system can be created, inspected, and checked for conformance with the model. As a special case study, we have applied the tool to parts of the UML 1.3 metamodel and its well-formedness rules. The tool enabled a thorough and systematic check of the OCL well-formedness rules in the UML standard.

1 Introduction

The Unified Modeling Language (UML) [9] has been widely accepted as a standard for modeling software systems. A great number of CASE tools exists which facilitate drawing and documentation of UML diagrams. Many of the tools also offer automatic code generation and reverse engineering of existing software systems. However, often there is only little support for validating models during the design stage. Also, there is generally no substantial support for constraints written in the Object Constraint Language (OCL) [8,13]. While it seems feasible to translate constraints into program code as part of the code generation process, we argue that a model and its constraints should be validated before coding starts. Mistakes in the design can thus be detected very early, and they can easily be corrected in time.

In this paper, we present an approach for the validation of UML models and OCL constraints that is based on animation. We have built a tool called USE (UML-based Specification Environment) for supporting developers in this process. The main components of this tool are an animator for simulating UML models and an OCL interpreter for constraint checking. A UML model is taken as a description of a system. System states are snapshots of a running system. They can be manipulated, inspected, and checked for conformance with the

A. Evans, S. Kent and B. Selic (Eds.): ≪UML≫ 2000, LNCS 1939, pp. 265–277, 2000.

model. The tool implements and continues ideas and results from our previous work on formalizing the OCL and introducing a metamodel for OCL [11,12].

Our validation tool can be generally applied to models from any domain. As a special case, we have applied it to parts of the UML 1.3 metamodel and its well-formedness rules. This is the first time (at least to our knowledge) that a tool enabled a thorough and systematic check of the OCL well-formedness rules in the UML standard. This also opens up a number of other useful applications. For example, the well-formedness of arbitrary models with respect to the UML standard can be automatically checked by validating them as instances of the UML metamodel.

There are currently only a few tools available which are specifically designed for analyzing UML models and OCL constraints. Probably, this is mostly due to the lack of a precise semantics of UML and OCL. A well-defined semantics is a prerequisite for building tools offering sophisticated analysis features. Work on precise semantics has been carried out in, e.g., [3,11]. The following summarizes some work related to tools for checking UML designs. Alcoa is a tool for analyzing object models [5]. It does not use OCL but has its own input language, Alloy, which is based on Z. RTUML [7] focuses on real-time modeling aspects and offers a methodology for mechanized verification of design properties with PVS. An OCL compiler and code generator combined with an OCL runtime library implemented in Java has recently been developed at the Dresden University [4]. A beta release of a commercial tool offering animation of UML models and OCL support is ModelRun by BoldSoft [1].

The rest of this paper is structured as follows. In Sect. 2 we describe our approach to validating UML and OCL. Section 3 gives an overview of the USE architecture. A case study is used in Sect. 4 to demonstrate the key features of our tool with respect to the validation process. In Sect. 5, we report on applying the USE tool to the Core package of the UML metamodel. We close with a summary and draw some conclusions for future work.

2 The USE Approach to Validation

The goal of model validation is to achieve a good design before implementation starts. There are many different approaches to validation: simulation, rapid prototyping, etc. In this context, we consider validation by generating snapshots as prototypical instances of a model and comparing them against the specified model. This approach requires very little effort from developers since models can be directly used as input for validation. Moreover, snapshots provide immediate feedback and can be visualized using the standard notation of UML object diagrams – a notation most developers are familiar with.

The result of validating a model can lead to several consequences with respect to the design. First, if there are reasonable snapshots that do not fulfill the constraints, this may indicate that the constraints are too strong or the model is not adequate in general. Therefore, the design must be revisited, e.g., by relaxing the constraints to include these cases. On the other hand, constraints may be too weak, therefore allowing undesirable system states. In this case, the constraints must be changed to be more restrictive. Still, one has to be careful about the fact that a situation in which undesirable snapshots are detected during validation and desired snapshots pass all constraints does not allow a general statement about the correctness of a specification in a formal sense. It only says that the model is correct with respect to the analyzed system states. However, some advantages of validation in contrast to a formal verification are the possibility to validate non-formal requirements, and that it can easily be applied by average modelers without training in formal methods.

The diagram in Fig. 1 illustrates the basic use cases for validating a model with USE. First, a model specification can be checked by the validation system. The *check specification* use case includes a syntax, type and semantic check. The syntax check verifies a specification against the grammar of the specification language which is basically a superset of the OCL grammar defined in [8,13] extended with language constructs for defining the structure of a model. The type check makes sure that every OCL expression can be correctly typed. Finally, a semantic check verifies a number of context-sensitive conditions. Among these conditions are the well-formedness rules defined as part of the UML Semantics [10]. An example for such a well-formedness rule is the requirement that a generalization hierarchy must not contain cycles.

When a specification has passed all checks, a developer may start producing and *changing system states*. A system state can be changed by issuing commands for creating and destroying objects, inserting and removing links between objects, and setting attribute values of objects. The developer can *check a system state* at any time. A system state check includes two phases. First, all model-inherent constraints must be verified. A model-inherent constraint is a constraint which is inherent to the semantics of all UML models. For example, the set of links between objects is verified against the multiplicity specifications of the association ends. The number of objects participating in an association must conform to the multiplicities defined at the association ends. Second, if the developer has defined explicit OCL constraints, all the constraint expressions are evaluated. If any of the constraints is false or has an undefined result, the system state is considered illegal.

The *inspect system state* use case describes facilities for getting information about a system state. This is very important for helping a user to understand the effects of commands resulting in system state changes. Furthermore, when a constraint fails and a system state is found to be invalid, the developer has to find the reason for the failure. Inspecting a system state involves the inspection of individual objects, their attribute values and links. Another powerful way for inspection is the use of OCL as a query language. For example, consider a model where each object of class A must have at least one link to an object of class B, i.e., the association end at class B has multiplicity `1..*`. If this multiplicity constraint is violated in some system state, the objects of class A which do *not* have a link to a B object can easily be found by the expression `A.allInstances->select(a | a.b->size = 0)`.

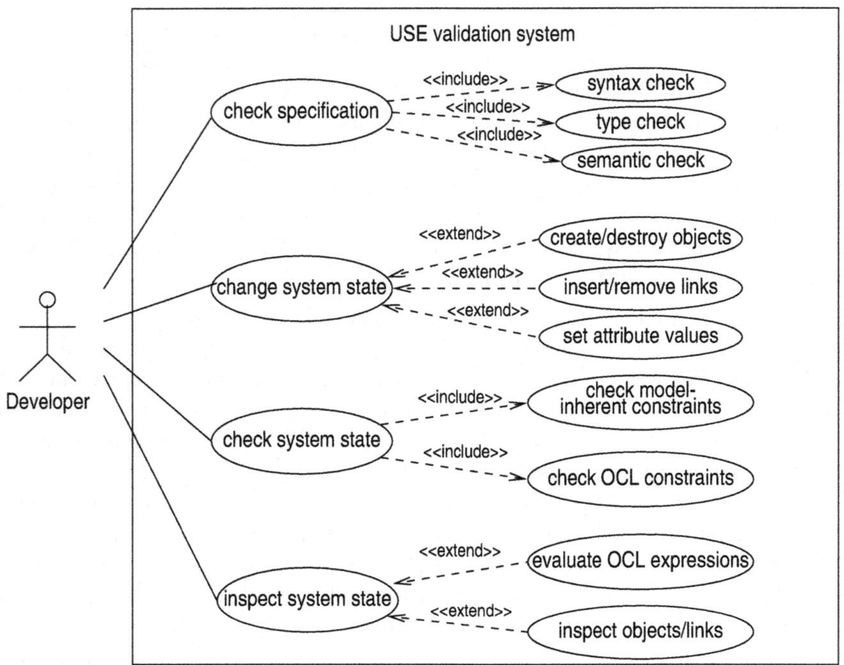

Fig. 1. Use case diagram showing basic functionality of USE

3 Architecture of USE

A high-level overview of the USE architecture is given in Fig. 2. We distinguish between a *Description Layer* at the top, and an *Interaction Layer* below. The description layer is responsible for processing a model specification. The main component is a *Parser* for reading *Specifications* in USE syntax and generating an abstract syntax representation of a model. A USE specification defines the structural building blocks of a model like classes and associations. Furthermore, OCL expressions may be used to define constraints and operations without side-effects.

The output of the parser is an abstract representation of a specification containing a *Model* and *OCL* expressions. The representation of the model is done with a subset of the Core package of the UML metamodel [10, p. 2-13]. The subset excludes all model elements which are not required during the analysis and early design phase of the software development process. For example, model elements like Permission, Component, and Node seem to be more adequately applied in extended design and implementation models. The abstract representation of OCL expressions closely follows the OCL metamodel we have presented in [12].

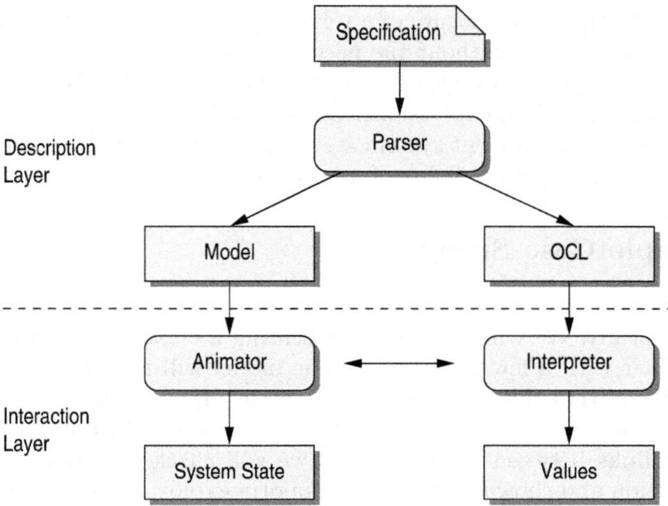

Fig. 2. Overview of the USE architecture

The *Interaction Layer* provides access to the dynamic behavior and static properties of a model. The main task of the *Animator* component is the instantiation and manipulation of *System States*. A system state is a snapshot of the specified system at a particular point in time. The system state contains a set of objects and a set of association links connecting objects. As a system evolves, a sequence of system states is produced. Each system state must be well-formed, i.e., it must conform to the model's structural description, and it must fulfill all OCL constraints. Furthermore, a transition from one system state to the next must conform to the dynamic behavior specification. Specifying and checking state transitions is not yet available in USE.

The *Interpreter* component is responsible for evaluating OCL expressions. An expression may be part of a constraint restricting the set of possible system states. In order to validate a system state, the animator component delegates the task of evaluating all constraints to the interpreter. The interpreter is also used for querying a system state. A user may query a system state by issuing expressions that help inspecting the set of currently existing objects and their properties.

The Model and OCL branches in Fig. 2 are tightly related to each other. For example, a model depends on OCL since operations of classes defined in a model may use OCL expressions in their bodies. A dependency in the other direction exists because the context of OCL constraints is given by model elements. However, it is in general possible to define models which do not use OCL at all, or there may be OCL expressions which do not require a user model. For example, the realization of various general purpose algorithms with OCL (like sorting, determining the transitive closure of a relation [6], etc.) is an interesting task on its own and can be done without the need for any particular model.

Animator and interpreter closely work together. The animator asks the interpreter for evaluating OCL expressions. On the other hand, the Interpreter needs information about the current system state, e.g., when evaluating an expression which refers to the attribute value of an object.

4 Example Case Study

In this section, we will demonstrate the validation of a UML model by means of a small case study. We will start with presenting a class diagram of a company model together with a few constraints. The model will then be specified in the textual USE notation. This specification serves as input to the validation tool. In an interactive session, a sequence of system states will be produced by creating objects and links between them. Finally, we will check a system state against the specification and show how the tool supports exploring the system state and helps in finding the reason for a constraint violation.

Figure 3 shows a UML class diagram of our example model. Employees have name and salary attributes and work in departments. A department controls projects on which any number of employees can work. Both department and projects have attributes specifying the available budget.

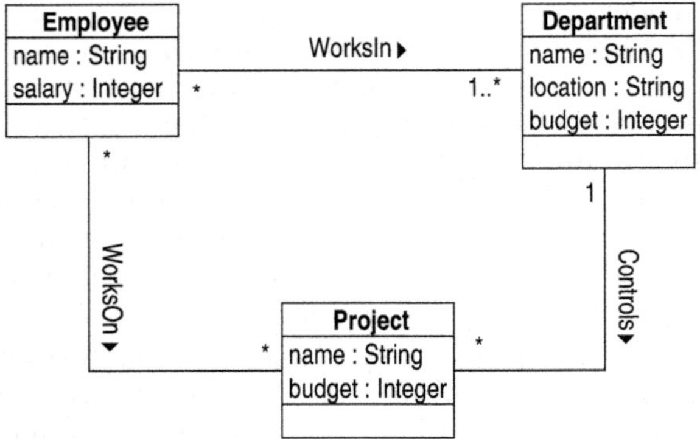

Fig. 3. Class diagram of example model

The result of translating the class diagram into the textual USE notation is shown in Fig. 4. The specification contains definitions for each of the classes and associations. The definition of a class includes its attributes, an association defines references to the participating classes for each association end. Multiplicity ranges are specified in brackets. Not used in this example but also supported by the USE language are UML features like generalization, operations, different association types, role names, etc.

```
model Company

class Employee
attributes
  name : String;
  salary : Integer;
end

class Department
attributes
  name : String;
  location : String;
  budget : Integer;
end

class Project
attributes
  name : String;
  budget : Integer;
end

association WorksIn between
  Employee[*];
  Department[1..*];
end

association WorksOn between
  Employee[*];
  Project[*];
end

association Controls between
  Department[1];
  Project[*];
end
```

Fig. 4. USE specification of the example model

In order to make the example more interesting, we add some constraints which cannot be expressed graphically with the class diagram. The following five conditions have to be satisfied by a system implementing the given model.

[1] The salary and budget attributes are always positive.
[2] A department has at least as many employees as projects.
[3] An employee working on more projects than another employee gets a higher salary.
[4] The budget of a project must not exceed the budget of the controlling department.
[5] Employees working on a project must work in the controlling department.

For each of these constraints we have specified OCL expressions that are used as invariants on the classes. We continue the specification begun in Fig. 4 with a section defining the set of constraints shown in Fig. 5. Each invariant is named for allowing an easy reference to the list above. Note that constraint [1] actually maps to three OCL invariants (i1a, i1b, i1c) since it states a condition on each of the three classes.

We can run the USE tool with the specification and start with an empty system state where no objects and no association links exist. As a next step, we are going to populate the system with objects and link them together. There are three kinds of commands which allow us to modify a system state: (1) creating and destroying objects, (2) changing attribute values, and (3) inserting and

constraints

context Department
  inv i1a: self.budget >= 0
  inv i2: self.employee→size >= self.project→size

context Employee
  inv i1b: self.salary >= 0
  inv i3: Employee.allInstances→forAll(e1, e2 |
      e1.project→size > e2.project→size **implies** e1.salary > e2.salary)

context Project
  inv i1c: self.budget >= 0
  inv i4: self.budget <= self.department.budget
  inv i5: self.department.employee→includesAll(self.employee)

Fig. 5. USE specification of OCL constraints

deleting association links. Figure 6 shows a screenshot of USE visualizing a system state after several objects and links have been created.

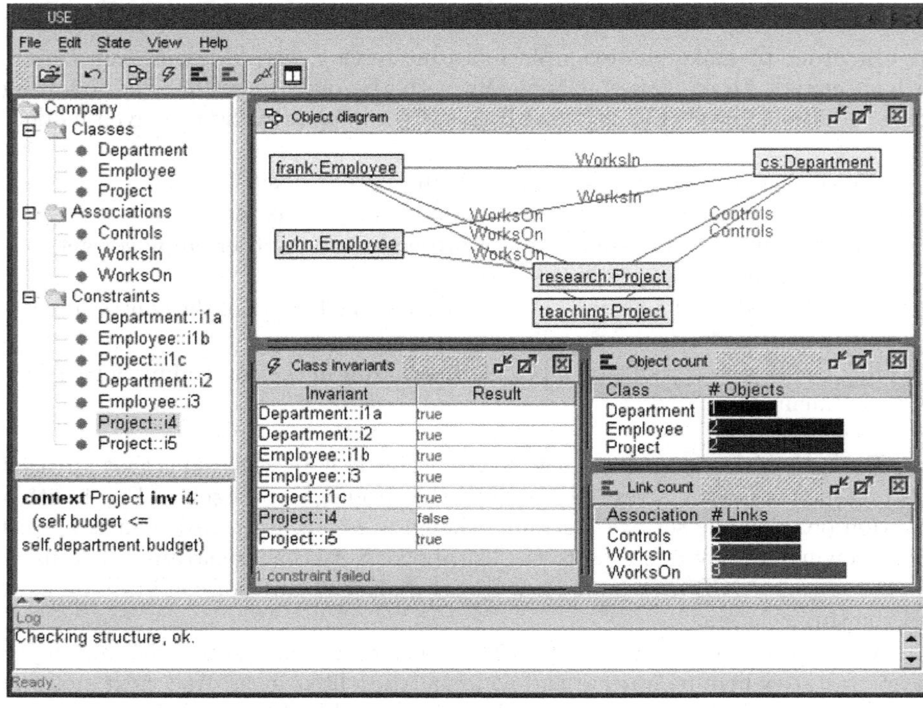

Fig. 6. USE screenshot

On the left side, the user interface provides a tree view of the classes, associations, and constraints in the model. The pane below shows the definition of the currently selected component (the invariant `Project::i4`). The pane on the right contains several different views of the current system state. These views are automatically updated as the system changes. A user can choose from a number of different available views each focusing on a special aspect of a system state. In this example, there are views showing an object diagram, a list of class invariants with their results, and two views displaying the number of objects and links.

The highlighted constraint `Project::i4` in the class invariant view has the result false indicating that the system state does not conform to the specification. The plain information that an invariant has been violated is usually not very helpful in finding the reason for the problem. The invariant from the example is quite short (see Fig. 5), and we can infer from the specification that there must be at least one project with a budget exceeding the budget of its controlling department. We could proceed by inspecting all projects until we find one violating the constraint. For larger systems, this quickly becomes a laborious task. Our tool therefore offers special support for analyzing OCL expressions.

The details of evaluating an OCL expression can be examined by means of an evaluation browser which provides a tree view of the evaluation process. Figure 7 displays such a browser for the failing invariant. The root node shows the complete OCL expression defined as the body of the invariant (actually, the original expression is first expanded into a self-contained expression which does not require a context). Child nodes represent sub-expressions which are part of their parent node's expression. Evaluating the `forAll` expression requires the evaluation of the source collection (`Project.allInstances`) and the argument expression (`self.budget <= self.department.budget`). By looking at the current binding of `self`, we can conclude that it is the budget of the "research" project which invalidates the whole invariant.

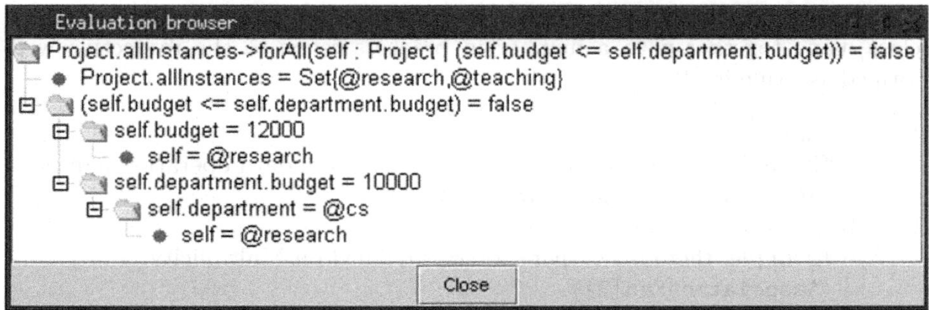

Fig. 7. OCL evaluation browser

5 Validating the UML Metamodel

The USE validation tool can be generally applied to models from any domain. As a special case, we have applied it to the Core package of the UML 1.3 metamodel and its well-formedness rules. The tool enabled a systematic check of the OCL well-formedness rules in the UML standard. This section describes the procedure for checking the metamodel and some results.

In the first step, we had to translate the class diagrams defining the UML Core ([10, Sect. 2.5.2]) into the textual USE notation. Next, all well-formedness rules as well as additional operations in Sect. 2.5.3 of [10] were added. Some minor syntactical changes required by the USE syntax were necessary following these rules:

1. If an association does not have a name, add one.
2. Append an underscore to identifiers which are reserved keywords in USE (e.g., `association`).
3. Append a pair of parentheses '()' to calls of additional (user-defined) operations when they have no arguments.
4. Replace all implicit occurrences of collect by an explicit invocation.
5. Replace all implicit occurrences of collection flattening by using a predefined operation `flatten`.
6. Replace occurrences of Boolean enumeration types with the OCL type Boolean.

The final specification[1] has 31 classes and 24 associations. There are 43 well-formedness rules and 28 additional operations resulting in a total of 71 OCL expressions. The expressions in the UML document had a number of errors which could quickly be located by analyzing the error messages signaled by the USE parser. Some errors could easily be corrected, others indicated more serious problems with the constraints. We classified the problems into the following categories (with increasing severity) and give an example for each category. A class name together with a number in brackets refers to the respective well-formedness rule in [10].

E1: *Syntax errors*
  - Example: wrong spelling of keywords and standard operation names (`Association[3]`, `AssociationEnd[1]`)

E2: *Minor inconsistencies*
  - Example: there is no operation `max` defined on Multiplicity (`AssociationEnd[2]`)

E3: *Type checking errors*
  - Example: union of sets with incompatible element types (`Classifier[4]`, `Classifier[5]`)
  - Example: implicit collect expression returns a bag not a set (`ModelElement::supplier()`)

[1] Available at `http://www.db.informatik.uni-bremen.de/~mr`

E4: *General problems*

- Example: the operation `contents()` in class Namespace has syntax errors and an identical description as `allContents()`. It remains unclear how these operations should look like.

The results from analyzing the OCL expressions are summarized in Table 1. We found that there were errors in 39 out of 71 expressions. Some expressions contained two or more errors belonging to different categories. Approximately, every second erroneous expression had errors of category E1 which could be fixed without much effort. The other errors generally required more work and detailed knowledge of the metamodel.

Table 1. Results from analyzing OCL expressions in the UML Core

	Classes	Associations	Invariants	Operations	Errors	E1	E2	E3	E4
Count	31	24	43	28	39	20	7	13	5

It is not very surprising that a tool-based mechanical check of OCL expressions greatly helps in finding frequently occurring errors such as spelling mistakes. The fact that OCL provides strong typing also helps in getting complex expressions right. Another general observation that we have made is related to the style of the OCL syntax. In some cases, a single notation is used for many different things. This makes it sometimes quite difficult to understand an expression and requires a lot of context knowledge. From a human's point of view this complicated the task of reading, understanding and checking OCL expressions. Consider, for example, the definition of the operation allParents in class GeneralizableElement:

```
allParents : Set(GeneralizableElement);
allParents = self.parent->union(self.parent.allParents)
```

The syntax of the expression `self.parent` is the same for referring to an attribute, an operation, or a role name of an associated class. Furthermore, `parent.allParents` may again be an attribute reference, an operation call, or a navigation by role name. Additionally, it may be an implicit collect expression written in shorthand notation. To find out which case is actually present, one has to look at the attributes, the operations and associations of all the referenced classes. However, this is still not enough since all these features might be defined in superclasses so that the generalization hierarchy also has to be taken into account. We therefore "re-engineered" most expressions to an explicit form making the intended meaning much clearer. The example from above was augmented with an explicit collect, a flattening operation, and a conversion of the result to a set which is required by the declaration.

```
allParents = self.parent()->union(
  self.parent()->collect(g | g.allParents())->flatten)->asSet
```

We found the USE tool to be very beneficial for understanding and analyzing the well-formedness rules of the UML metamodel. A number of errors in the OCL expressions could be quickly located and corrected. For future work, we plan to extend the analysis to the complete UML metamodel including all of its well-formedness rules and making it available in USE. This might not only be useful for improving the state of the standard but also implies another very nice application: in principle, any UML model can then be checked for conformance to the UML standard. A model conforms to the UML standard if it can be represented as an instance of the UML metamodel. The general idea is to (1) import a UML model (preferably in XMI representation), (2) traverse the model and execute a sequence of USE commands for instantiating the model elements as objects of the UML metamodel, and (3) check all constraints on the resulting snapshot. All these steps can be done mechanically. If the last step fails, the model is not conform to the UML standard.

6 Conclusion

In this paper, we have presented a tool-based approach to validating UML models and OCL constraints. The ideas presented here have been implemented in the USE tool. The functionality of USE has been shown by means of use cases and a small example case study. We have also applied the tool for checking a part of the UML metamodel which makes extensive use of OCL constraints. As a result we could identify a number of errors in the standard document. Using the metamodel as a specification of arbitrary UML models, the tool enables a mechanical check for conformance of these models with the standard.

The OCL parser and interpreter that is part of USE implements most of the core features of OCL like expression syntax, strong type checking, and evaluation of expressions. We have implemented almost all of the more than 100 standard operations on predefined OCL types. Features we are currently working on include the syntax of path expressions and qualifiers, type checking of empty collection literals, and syntax and semantics of pre- and postconditions. For validating postconditions it might also be desirable to have some kind of an action language to specify side effects of operations.

There are several possible future extensions which would fit within the USE framework. First, it would be nice if the animation could be automated to some extent by deriving test cases from the model. Another extension could apply the validation techniques of USE to implementations of a model. Program code could be generated which mirrors the state of a system at runtime. The state traces can be observed and analyzed in parallel with USE. With this approach there is no need for transforming OCL expressions into program code since the interpretation of expressions is already part of USE. Also very useful would be an analysis of OCL constraints with respect to properties like consistency. However, there is currently no clear definition of what it means for a set of OCL constraints to be consistent. A discussion of this can be found in the OCL Semantics FAQ [2].

Acknowledgments

We thank Frank Finger, Heinrich Hussmann, and Jos Warmer for fruitful discussions.

References

1. BoldSoft. Modelrun, 2000. Internet: `http://www.boldsoft.com/products/modelrun/index.html`. 266
2. Tony Clark, Stuart Kent, Jos Warmer, et al. OCL Semantics FAQ, Workshop on the Object Constraint Language (OCL) Computing Laboratory, University of Kent, Canterbury, UK. Internet: `http://www.cs.ukc.ac.uk/research/sse/oclws2k/index.html`, March 2000. 276
3. Andy Evans and Stuart Kent. Core meta-modelling semantics of UML: The pUML approach. In Robert France and Bernhard Rumpe, editors, *UML'99 - The Unified Modeling Language. Beyond the Standard. Second International Conference, Fort Collins, CO, USA, October 28-30. 1999, Proceedings*, volume 1723 of *LNCS*, pages 140–155. Springer, 1999. 266
4. Frank Finger. Design and implementation of a modular OCL compiler. Diplomarbeit, Dresden University of Technology, Department of Computer Science, Software Engineering Group, Germany, March 2000. 266
5. Daniel Jackson, Ian Schechter, and Ilya Shlyakhter. Alcoa: the Alloy constraint analyzer. In *Proc. International Conference on Software Engineering, Limerick, Ireland, June 2000*, 2000. (to appear). 266
6. Luis Mandel and María Victoria Cengarle. On the expressive power of OCL. In *FM'99 - Formal Methods. World Congress on Formal Methods in the Development of Computing Systems, Toulouse, France, September 1999. Proceedings, Volume I*, volume 1708 of *LNCS*, pages 854–874. Springer, 1999. 270
7. Darmalingum Muthiayen. *Real-Time Reactive System Development - A Formal Approach Based on UML and PVS.* PhD thesis, Department of Computer Science at Concordia University, Montreal, Canada, January 2000. 266
8. OMG. Object Constraint Language Specification. In *OMG Unified Modeling Language Specification, Version 1.3, June 1999* [9], chapter 7. 265, 267
9. OMG, editor. *OMG Unified Modeling Language Specification, Version 1.3, June 1999.* Object Management Group, Inc., Framingham, Mass., Internet: `http://www.omg.org`, 1999. 265, 277, 277
10. OMG. UML Semantics. In *OMG Unified Modeling Language Specification, Version 1.3, June 1999* [9], chapter 2. 267, 268, 274, 274, 274
11. Mark Richters and Martin Gogolla. On formalizing the UML Object Constraint Language OCL. In Tok Wang Ling, Sudha Ram, and Mong Li Lee, editors, *Proc. 17th Int. Conf. Conceptual Modeling (ER'98)*, volume 1507 of *LNCS*, pages 449–464. Springer, 1998. 266, 266
12. Mark Richters and Martin Gogolla. A metamodel for OCL. In Robert France and Bernhard Rumpe, editors, *UML'99 - The Unified Modeling Language. Beyond the Standard. Second International Conference, Fort Collins, CO, USA, October 28-30. 1999, Proceedings*, volume 1723 of *LNCS*, pages 156–171. Springer, 1999. 266, 268
13. Jos Warmer and Anneke Kleppe. *The Object Constraint Language: Precise Modeling with UML.* Addison-Wesley, 1998. 265, 267

Modular Architecture for a Toolset Supporting OCL

Heinrich Hussmann, Birgit Demuth, and Frank Finger

Dresden University of Technology, Department of Computer Science

Abstract. The practical application of the Object Constraint Language, which is part of the UML specification since version 1.1, depends crucially on the existence of adequate tool support. This paper discusses general design issues for OCL tools. It is argued that the nature of OCL will lead to a large variety of tools, applied in combination with a variety of different UML tools. Therefore, a flexible modular architecture for a UML/OCL toolset is proposed. The paper reports on the first results of an ongoing project which aims at the provision of such an OCL toolset for the public domain.

1 Introduction

Since version 1.1, the UML standard comprises a formal annotation language for UML models, the Object Constraint Language (OCL) [19]. This language is used in the UML standard for precisely defining the well-formedness rules of UML models on the metamodel level. Moreover, OCL is currently gaining popularity in the definition of other OMG standards. Besides this usage on a meta-level there is also high potential in using OCL in the actual development process of software to improve software quality.

- In the analysis phase, business rules can be expressed precisely. Usually, OCL invariants are attached to class diagrams and enable the specification of constraints which go far beyond the possibilities of "plain" UML (i.e. UML without OCL). Some of the most useful constructs of plain UML for the analysis phase can be seen just as abbreviations for simple OCL invariants (e.g. the construct of association multiplicities), and as soon as more complex constraints appear, OCL is the language of choice.
- In the design phase (mainly), constraints can be used to precisely specify pre- and postconditions for operations, and therefore provide a precise contract [13] for the implementor and user of the operations.
- In development tools, OCL can be used as a simple query and navigation language.
- At various other places in UML models, object constraints can be used for preciseness, e.g. in guards of statechart diagrams.

An example for a full UML-based development method which incorporates OCL usage is Catalysis [10].

A. Evans, S. Kent and B. Selic (Eds.): ≪UML≫ 2000, LNCS 1939, pp. 278–293, 2000.

Recently, at several places experiments have been started to introduce OCL into the practical object-oriented software development process (e.g. [2]). However, all such attempts are facing the problem that there is a definite lack of tool support for OCL. With a few exceptions [5], the tool industry seems to ignore OCL. There are at least two good reasons for this lack of commercial support: First, it has still to be proven that the theoretical potential of OCL leads to practical improvements in real software projects. Second, the needed functionality of OCL support tools is still rather unclear. So there is a need for significant further research before OCL can achieve a status of broad market acceptance and commercial tool support.

In this paper, we report on an attempt to enable serious practical experiments with OCL. We describe a software platform for OCL tool support which is designed for openness and modularity, and which is provided as OpenSource. The goal of this platform is to enable practical experiments with various variants of OCL tool support. In this paper, we analyze the requirements for this tool platform and describe the key design decisions.

This paper is structured as follows: In section 2, an overview of the full range of possibilities for OCL tool support is given, setting the scene for the analysis of the requirements for the tool platform. Section 3 describes the actual architecture chosen, based on key requirements derived from section 2. Several examples for possible configurations of the tool platform are given, and the current status of the implementation is described. Section 4, finally, summarizes our results and gives ideas for further investigations and projects.

2 Potential for OCL Tool Support

The specification of OCL constraints enhancing a UML model causes a significant amount of additional effort, so the crucial question is an economic one: How can we ensure that the additional development effort spent on adding all this detailed information really pays back? From this perspective, several kinds of tools are required:

- Tools that use the high precision present in OCL-based specifications for a thorough analysis of the UML/OCL model.
- Tools that help the modeler to ensure that the actual constraints together with other UML diagrams make up a sensible model of the problem domain.
- Tools that reduce the development, testing and maintenance effort by making use of the information given in OCL.
- Tools that enable a higher level of trust in the implementation of an OCL specification, and therefore are suitable e.g. for development of safety-critical applications.

When discussing tool support for OCL, an important difference between OCL and many other formal specification languages has to be pointed out: OCL constraints are *executable* in the sense that they can be evaluated mechanically for a given snapshot of a universe of objects. Nevertheless, OCL contains all language constructs of classical first-order logic, like the classical quantifiers "forAll" and "exists", and these quantifiers can be applied in arbitrary nesting. In contrast to general predicate logic, however, OCL always ensures that these constructs are applied only to a finite set, so they can be checked mechanically by enumeration of the set. This property of OCL was less clear in early versions of the UML specification (due to constructs like `Integer.allInstances`). However, for UML 1.3 several changes have been applied which prohibit the usage of infinite sets, and which even ensure that the evaluation of a constraint on a snapshot always terminates. The executability of OCL is a key feature for effective and simple tool support.

Let us briefly discuss the most important kinds of tools supporting OCL.

Syntactical analysis The simplest form of support is of course parsing OCL expressions. This form of tool support, however, is able to find only very basic OCL errors.

Typechecking After some amendments to the standard, there is now a relatively stable type system for OCL which enables mechanical static typechecking of OCL constraints, much in the same way as typechecking of a typed programming language. However, OCL constraints always make reference to an underlying class model. So an OCL typechecker has to have access to the underlying UML model information. Practical experience shows that this relatively simple tool feature already significantly improves the quality of OCL specifications.

Logical consistency checking Since OCL is a logic language, it is possible to write down sets of constraints which are contradictory in themselves. Although it would be very helpful to have a tool checking statically for such inconsistencies, there are many open questions still to be solved before such tools can be built. In general, it is even likely that consistency is undecidable, so one may want to develop appropriate criteria for decidable subcases. Moreover, links to recent research prototypes for symbolic constraint solving (e.g. [9]) may lead to interesting results.

Dynamic invariant validation From the point of view of the tool builder, an invariant is a Boolean-valued function which can be evaluated on a given snapshot of the system. So it makes sense to provide tools which actually do this evaluation during the evolution of a system. There are several approaches to such a dynamic verification: To integrate assertion tests into standard generation of code (fragments); to generate specific code doing automatic invariant checking, as it is possible for database integrity constraints [6]; or to provide a simulation tool for construction of sample system states [5], [17].

Dynamic pre/postcondition validation In a very similar way to the treatment of invariants, pre- and postconditions can be evaluated at runtime of a system constructed from the specification. In this case, the most appropriate approach seems to be to integrate assertion statements into the generation of code (fragments).

Test automation An automated test tool may make use of the OCL pre- and postconditions to achieve an automatic check of test results against the specification. Moreover, it may be possible to derive test cases from an analysis of the functional specification written in OCL. This class of tools may be the most interesting one from an economic point of view, since it helps to save some of the usually high costs for quality assurance. Also maintenance costs can be reduced by such tools since automatic regression testing against the formal specification is enabled, and the semantic consistency of specification and code is enforced.

Code verification and synthesis In the long run, OCL may also form a basis for code verification and synthesis. First projects in this direction have been started (e.g. the Karlsruhe KeY project [8]), but this is clearly the most ambitious kind of tool which may be appropriate only for special, safety-critical development projects.

From the list above, it becomes obvious that there is a large variety of different tools, all of which rely on a rather small common functionality. This observation is reflected in the toolset architecture described below.

3 Toolset Architecture

3.1 Requirements

From an analysis of potential OCL tools, as summarized above, a number of requirements can be derived:

Requirement 1: The architecture shall enable interworking with various CASE tools and repositories, regarding the access to model information for type-checking. A simple and flexible interface is required which supports the construction of stand-alone experimental tools (working e.g. on a file representation of the model) as well as a tight integration into CASE tools, for more user-friendly versions of tools.

Requirement 2: Syntax analysis and type checking of OCL constraints is the functionality which is common to all tool variants. So a simple interface to this functionality is needed in order to enable integration into various OCL tools.

Requirement 3: The tool platform has to provide a simple and easily reusable interface for accessing the actual constraint information (the abstract syntax of the constraints) from different kinds of tools. Ultimately, the solution should be compliant with an OCL metamodel [16], which is still under discussion.

Requirement 4: Different tools want different levels of abstraction in accessing the representation of OCL constraints. For example, a tool generating programming language code may want to expand automatically all `select` operations into the generic `iterate` mechanism. In contrast, a tool generating SQL integrity conditions may want to keep the `select` operations since they can be mapped easily and directly to SQL [6].

3.2 Key Design Decisions

In the following, a modular architecture for an OCL toolset satisfying the above listed requirements is presented. The architecture is designed based on our experience with a prototype implementation [14]. We decided to develop the OCL toolset in Java because of the high popularity of Java as implementation language in the Open Source Community and therewith the availability of useful tools like parser generators and the possibility to integrate the OCL toolset with free CASE tools such as Argo/UML.

A further decision was that an OCL toolset should be fully compliant to the UML/OCL specification version 1.3 [15]. Unfortunately, this specification contains some ambiguities and contradictions. These have to be solved in a sensible way, and aspects where the implementation deviates from the specification have to be documented in detail.

The first requirement from above means that a toolset should be adaptable to different environments. This adaptability can be achieved if all external interfaces are designed and documented carefully. Dependencies between the OCL toolset and the environment have to be minimized.

With the adaptibility comes the extensibility of the design. As discussed in section 2, a large variety of OCL tools is imaginable that the toolset architecture should support. While it is very hard or even impossible to achieve this fully for very sophisticated tools like consistency checkers, the architecture should at least offer the possibility to use the toolset as the first stage of such a tool. As a result, the new tool can benefit from the adaptability of the toolset to different environments, and reuses existing functionality.

The reuse of functionality can be achieved by the design of small, configurable modules with clearly defined responsibilities. Information can be passed between modules using a *blackboard strategy* [3] with each module being implemented as a separate traversal of the abstract syntax tree of the OCL expression. Additional dependencies, such as type information offered by the type checker module, are restricted to Java interfaces to allow different implementations (*strategy pattern* [7]).

3.3 Modules and the Abstract Syntax Tree

According to the above listed requirements and design decisions as well as common compiler implementation principles, the toolset architecture consists of the modules presented below. Figure 1 gives an overview of the basic modules of the OCL toolset. Following classical techniques from compiler design, the essential internal interface of the OCL toolset is the abstract syntax tree.

Abstract Syntax Tree Abstract syntax tree classes are created out of a grammar description using the the parser generator SableCC [18]. The parser generator creates abstract classes for productions and a concrete subclass for each of the alternatives of the production. These classes, generated for a straightforward translation of the OCL grammar in [15] into the specification format of SableCC,

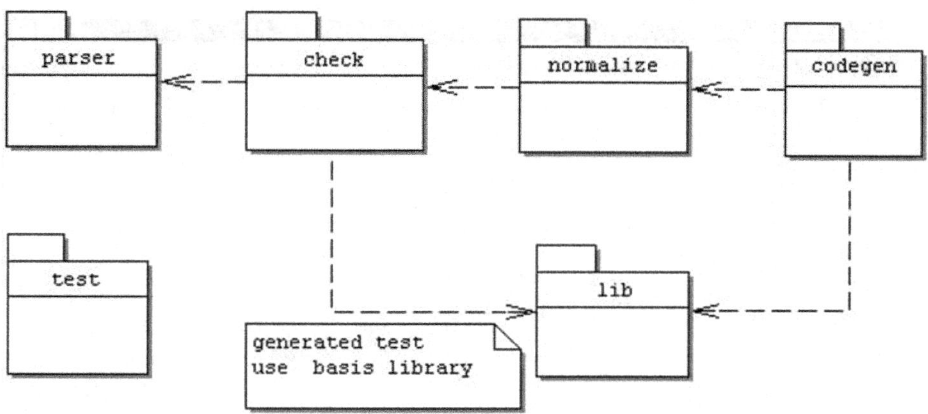

Fig. 1. Modules of the OCL toolset

are used as the primary information exchange data structure between modules. Figure 2 shows a screenshot displaying the abstract syntax tree of the prototype implementation. The current user interface is more targeted towards test and demonstration of the core functionality of the toolset. It is easy to replace this user interface by other interfaces, which are for instance more integrated with other UML tools.

The decision to use an abstract syntax tree as internal storage form of the OCL toolset was taken for very pragmatic reasons. The SableCC system provides quite a number of helpful mechanisms to deal with abstract syntax trees effectively, which could be reused. Moreover, in the current situation, the evolving OCL metamodel [16] is not yet an alternative since it is not fully stabilized (and will probably not become stable before UML 2.0). The current decision allows a very loose coupling between the OCL toolset and its environment and is based on current standards. As soon as the metamodel is stable, it will be easily possible to introduce an additional layer of abstraction on top of the syntax tree, which will be based on an OCL metamodel. In fact, a metamodel view was already used in some of the typechecking algorithms (see below).

Parser The parser transforms the input OCL expression into an abstract syntax tree. Of course it is straightforward to use a SableCC-generated parser for this task, but it can be fulfilled by an arbitrary parser that creates the appropriate instances of the SableCC-generated abstract syntax tree classes.

Semantical Analysis The abstract syntax tree classes can be seen as a representation of a static UML metamodel[1]. By formulating invariants that constrain this model, consistency rules (well-formedness rules) on the abstract syntax tree

[1] This metamodel is not the one proposed in [16], but the UML model corresponding to the classes generated by SableCC.

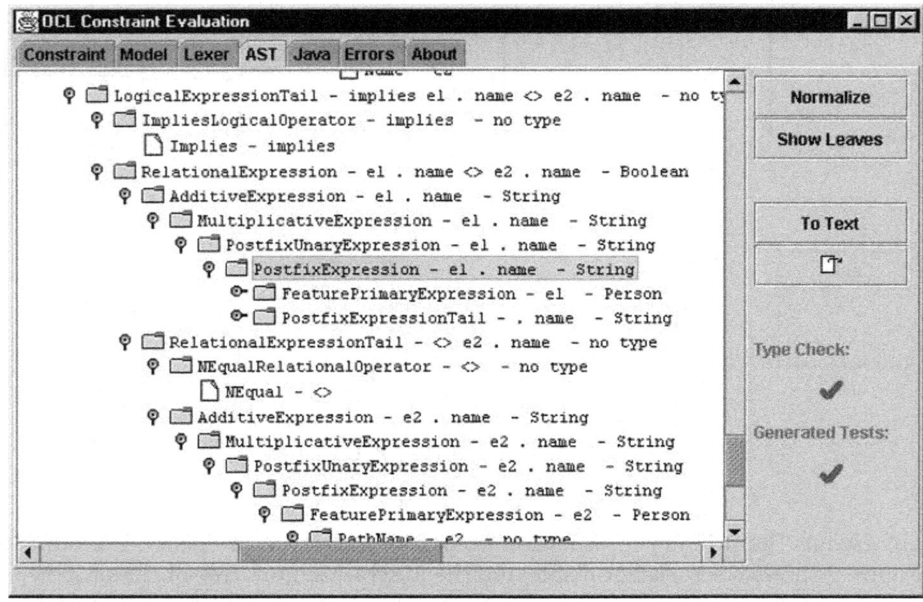

Fig. 2. User interface of the OCL toolset prototype

can be defined. The Java code generator of the OCL toolset can be used to automatically transform these constraints into Java code which can then be used as a part of semantical analysis. In fact, part of the typechecking in the prototype was "bootstrapped" already this way.

Type checking is implemented as a module that, in addition to checking semantical correctness with reference to the OCL type system, offers type information about syntax tree nodes and variables towards other modules. To minimize inter-module dependencies, this information is made available through a clean Java interface. It is important to note that OCL type checking is not possible without information about the UML model the OCL constraint is part of. Such information is not available within the OCL toolset, but has to be extracted from the toolset's environment. An external interface for this purpose is described in subsection 3.4.

Normalisation In order to be able to support a variety of tools, it is desirable to avoid that every tool has to implement the execution of any OCL expression completely. This can be achieved by defining a *normal form* of OCL terms, such that all terms can be mapped into a simpler subset of the OCL language. Such a normal form could for example disallow multiple iterators for the collection property `forAll`, since they can be replaced by nested iteration.

As it was mentioned in requirement 4 above, different normal forms are preferable for different purposes: For consistency checking it might be helpful to normalise collection properties like `forAll` and `exists` to `iterate`, but a

Java code generator might produce less efficient code after this modification. Customized normalisation is made possible in our tool architecture by defining and implementing small normalisation steps, like "remove multiple iterators" or "expand shorthand for `collect`". The implementors of OCL tools based on our platform are free to combine these steps as desired, or even to add further normalisation steps.

While the normalisation module does not define an additional internal interface, other modules depend on properties of the abstract syntax tree achieved by normalisation. These dependencies can be made explicit by managing a list of asserted invariants for the syntax tree. Normalisation steps can add invariants to this list, and modules dependent on certain invariants can assure that these have been asserted before.

Code Generation Code generator modules transform the normalised syntax tree into a target language. How this is done is to a large extent dependent on the target language. For the implementation of a Java code generator, a combination of a class library and a comparatively simple syntax-directed translation has proven to be sufficient. The class library offers Java-representations for the predefined OCL types, and the code generator can make straightforward translations of OCL property accesses into Java method calls for most cases.

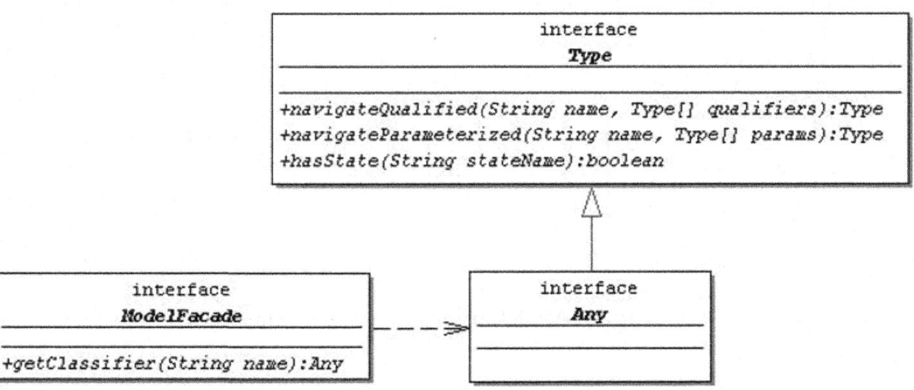

Fig. 3. Model information source interfaces

3.4 Interfaces of Tool Modules to the Environment

An OCL toolset needs at least two interfaces for communication with its environment, as stated above in requirements 1 and 2.

The first interface allows the environment to pass OCL expressions into the toolset. Constraints are here represented as simple String objects.

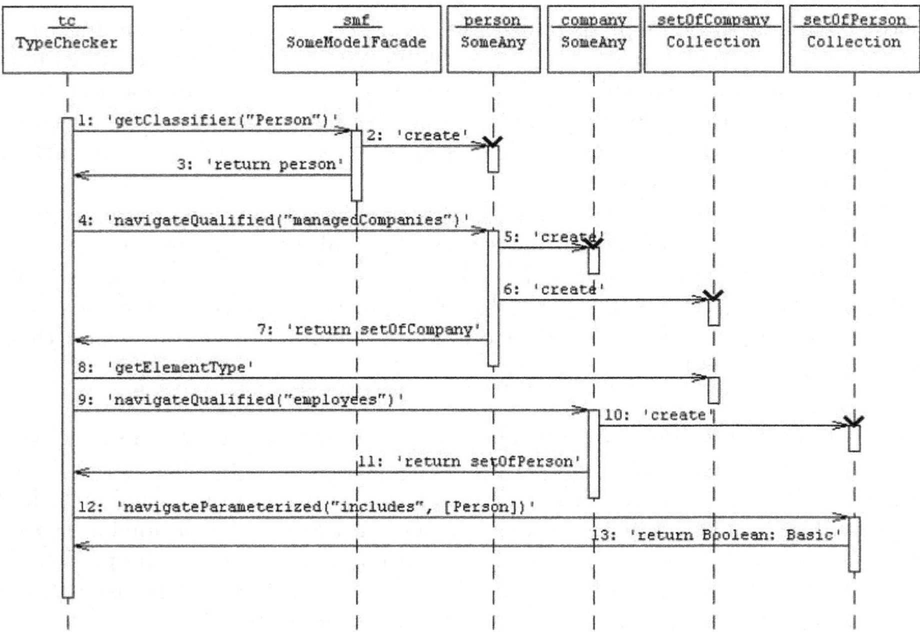

Fig. 4. Communication between type checker and model information source

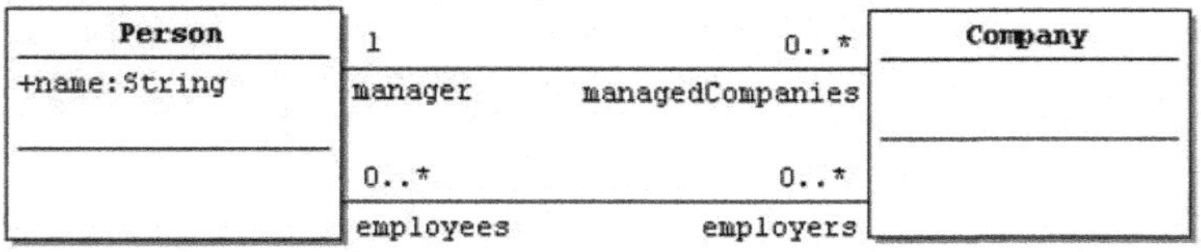

Fig. 5. Model for example constraints

The second external interface is used by the type checker of the toolset to access model information. Since OCL expressions are dependent only on a small part of the UML meta model (classifiers, behavioural and static features, associations, and states), the necessary queries can be restricted to the small and elegant interfaces `ModelFacade` and `Any` shown in figure 3. These have to be implemented for a toolset environment. Figure 4 shows how the type checker and implementations of these interfaces cooperate to examine the following constraint:

```
context Person inv:
managedCompanies->forAll(employees->includes(self))
```

All example constraints refer to the model in figure 5.

Several experimental implementations of the `ModelFacade` interface have been realised already. For instance, there is an implementation which reads the model information out of a file in the XML-based UML exchange format XMI (compatible with the XMI export facility of Rational Rose), and an implementation which takes the model information directly from the repository of the OpenSource CASE tool Argo/UML. Another implementation extracts model information from Java classes that are enriched with Javadoc comments which show the element type of collections.

Additional external interfaces may be added by other modules. For example, for a code generator it makes sense to offer an interface where produced code can be queried. Such an interface should not only make the generated code itself available, but also offer information such as the constrained class and operation or, for procedural target languages, the variable that holds the result of the evaluation.

3.5 Java Assertion Generation

As a first complete configuration of the modules of the described toolset, a compiler has been realised which translates OCL constraints into Java assertion code [14]. According to the classification given in section 2, this OCL tool has the functionalities of dynamic invariant validation and dynamic pre/postcondition validation. It can also be used for test automatisation. The approach to generate code which is executed at runtime as part of an actual implementation of the UML model is less straightforward that e.g. an OCL interpreter and model animator [5]. However, we believe that for the application of OCL in larger projects, the compilation into assertions is much more important, whereas the interpretative approach is more suited to education in OCL.

The prototype compiler uses the XMI-based implementation of the `ModelFacade` interface. Therefore it can be used to generate Java assertion code out of two files: a text file containing OCL constraints and a UML/XMI file (containing the class diagram), which is created by export from standard UML CASE tools. Internally to the compiler, the normalisation module is used to transform the input constraint into a sublanguage of OCL that avoids the use of multiple iterators, iterating properties without declarator, multiple use of the same variable name, and use of the default navigation context[2]. Figure 6 shows a normalisation example.

The Java code generator module then follows syntax-driven rules to produce Java code, a sample of which is shown in figure 7. The classes used in this code, like `OclAnyImpl` or `OclSet`, are defined in a class library, which defines among other things implementations for the standard collection data types of OCL. As usual with compilers, the generated code is not meant for human readers but for execution by machine. It uses a number of auxiliary variables to break down the code in relatively small pieces (a standard compiler construction technique).

[2] Not using the default navigation context means that every navigation expression has to begin with a bound name, like `self` or an iterator name, or a literal.

input expression

```
context Company inv:
employees->forAll(e1, e2 | e1 <> e2 implies e1.name <> e2.name)
```

normalised expression

```
context Company inv tudOclInv0:
let tudOclLet0 : Set(Person) = self.employees in
tudOclLet0 -> forAll (
  e1 : Person | tudOclLet0 -> forAll (
    e2 : Person | e1 <> e2 implies e1.name <> e2.name
  )
)
```

Fig. 6. Example for normalisation

```
final OclAnyImpl tudOclNode0=Ocl.toOclAnyImpl( Ocl.getFor(this) );
final OclSet tudOclNode1=
  Ocl.toOclSet(tudOclNode0.getFeature("employees"));
final OclIterator tudOclIter0=tudOclNode1.getIterator();
final OclBooleanEvaluatable tudOclEval0=new OclBooleanEvaluatable() {
  public OclBoolean evaluate() {
    final OclIterator tudOclIter1=tudOclNode1.getIterator();
    final OclBooleanEvaluatable tudOclEval1=new OclBooleanEvaluatable(){
      public OclBoolean evaluate() {
        final OclBoolean tudOclNode2=
          Ocl.toOclAnyImpl(tudOclIter0.getValue()).
          isNotEqualTo(Ocl.toOclAnyImpl(tudOclIter1.getValue()));
        final OclString tudOclNode3=
          Ocl.toOclString(Ocl.toOclAnyImpl(tudOclIter0.getValue()).
          getFeature("name"));
        final OclString tudOclNode4=
          Ocl.toOclString(Ocl.toOclAnyImpl(tudOclIter1.getValue()).
          getFeature("name"));
        final OclBoolean tudOclNode5=
          tudOclNode3.isNotEqualTo(tudOclNode4);
        final OclBoolean tudOclNode6=tudOclNode2.implies(tudOclNode5);
        return tudOclNode6;
      }
    };
    final OclBoolean tudOclNode7=
      tudOclNode1.forAll(tudOclIter1, tudOclEval1);
    return tudOclNode7;
  }
};
final OclBoolean tudOclNode8=tudOclNode1.forAll(tudOclIter0,tudOclEval0);
```

Fig. 7. Generated Java code for the example of figure 6

After executing this code, the result variable (tudOclNode8) contains a value which indicates whether the examined object fulfills the constraint. In order to access the actual snapshot of the model at runtime, again a simple and elegant Java interface has been defined (using the *Factory Method* design pattern) that makes it easy to adapt the assertion code to any chosen representation of UML constructs in Java. This feature is particularly important for the representation of associations, where many significantly different design choices exist.

In order to make practical use of our prototype OCL compiler, a separate tool is required which takes this code and inserts it as the body of a new method assertOcl() into a Java source code file. Figure 8 shows the effect of this tool for the file Company.java from the running example. Using such generated tests, component testing can be greatly simplified. For instance, in the *JUnit* testing framework [11], assertions are made that usually compare the result of a method call with the desired result. Using the automatic generation of assertions, it is sufficient to just make calls to the methods that are being tested. The validation of the result is automatised based on an OCL post-condition for the method which was formulated during modelling.

Figure 9 gives an overview of the interaction of client and compiler modules for Java assertion generation.

```
import tudresden.ocl.lib.*;
import java.util.*;

public class Company {

  public int numberOfEmployees;

  protected Person manager;
  protected Vector employees;

  public void assertOcl() {
      tudOclAssert0();
  }

  private void tudOclAssert0() {
    // generated Java code is inserted here

    if ( ! tudOclNode8.isTrue() ) {
      throw new RuntimeException("constraint violated");
    }
  }
}
```

Fig. 8. Java class with assert method (generated code is omitted)

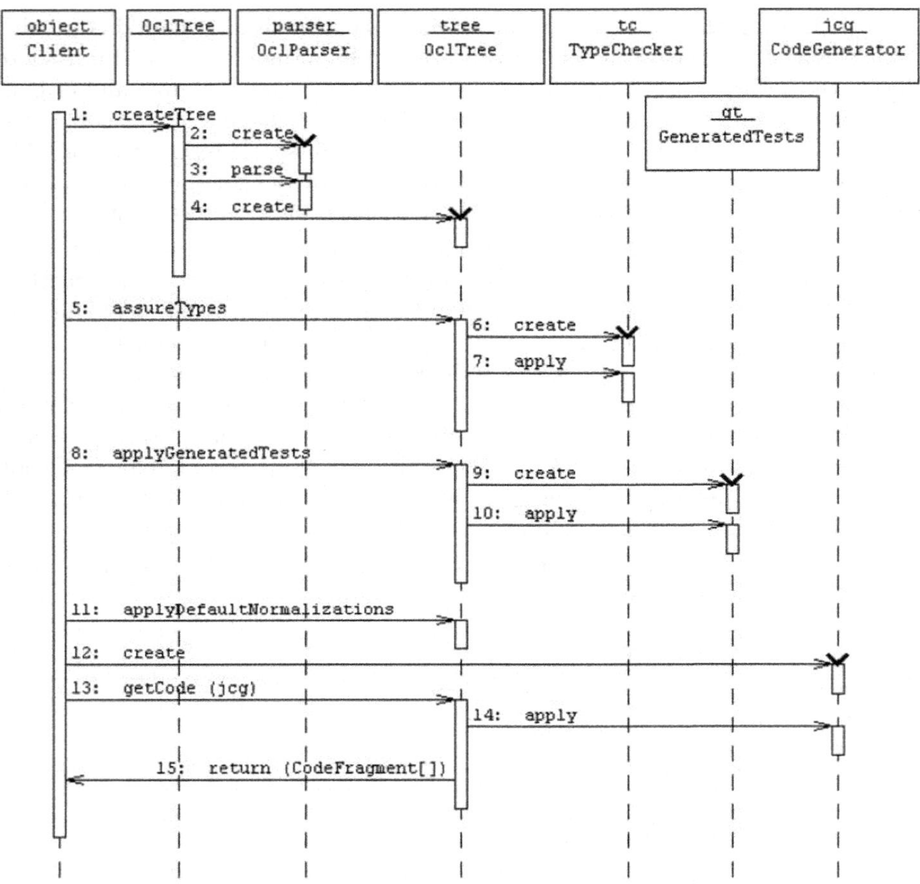

Fig. 9. Inter-module communication for Java code generation

3.6 SQL Integrity Constraint Generation

Another configuration of the modules of the presented OCL toolset architecture is currently under development, which aims towards an integration with database schema generation tools. The intention is to automatically generate SQL integrity constraints [12] as part of a relational database schema. The integrity constraints are derived from OCL expressions that are specified in form of business rules on UML models. Basic mappings from OCL invariants to SQL constraints (`create assertion` et al.) are given in [6]. For this purpose, the parser and type checker can be reused without change. However, SQL as declarative language requires in contrast to Java other properties of the abstract syntax tree. For example, it makes no sense to normalise the above given example (see figure 6) in the same way as presented above. In this case, it would be better to normalise the OCL expression into an abstract syntax tree representing the equivalent OCL constraint:

```
context Company inv: employees->isUnique(name)
```

This expression can be easily transformed into a SQL unique key constraint. Therefore, specific normalisation steps have to be developed and added to the normalisation module. A further development step is then the implementation of the code generation interface for the generation of SQL statements. Because of the large number of relational database system vendors that offer different implementations of the SQL standard, a flexible approach for code generation is needed. One way to achieve this is the separation of the SQL code generator from the mapping rules by their description in XML. The structure of such a document is predefined by a document type definition (DTD) and can be seen as a catalog that contains SQL code templates related to the grammar rules of the OCL specification. Using this approach, the generated SQL code is to a large extent independent of the compiled code and can easily be adapted to different SQL dialects using XML-Editors. The current OCL prototype toolset supports both SQL-92 [12] and Oracle/SQL code generation. Although this development is not yet completed, the design of it already gives some proof for the adequateness of the chosen modular structure of our OCL toolset.

4 Summary and Outlook

The purpose of this paper was not just to describe a particular implementation of an OCL tool. Instead, a rather general discussion of the potential tool support for OCL has been given, and the described design contains a number of ideas which may be transferable also to other tool environments. Moreover, the described tool platform may be interesting for a wide audience, since the full source code is freely available under GNU Library General Public License [14].

The current status of realisation comprises a complete and stable implementation of all the modules which were mentioned in figure 1. The compiler from OCL constraints to Java assertions is available and thoroughly tested. The compiler from OCL to SQL integrity constraints is currently under development. There are already several other (academic) projects which have decided to take the tool platform described here as the basis for their development of OCL tools.

The design of the toolset is oriented towards an easy integration into all kinds of other (Java-based) environments. It was an encouraging experience regarding the toolset design that a first prototype of the integration into the OpenSource UML tool Argo/UML was produced within just a few hours of development time (as could be observed "live" by the participants of an OCL workshop taking place in Canterbury/UK in March 2000). The core parts of our OCL toolset will be fully integrated into future releases of Argo/UML. Moreover, experiments for integration with other Java-based CASE tools, e.g. Together, are going on in cooperation with other research institutions.

Further work from our side will concentrate on additional modules for the toolset which enable practical experimentation with fully automatic tool support for OCL. Among the future plans is to develop an OCL interpreter based on our toolset and to connect it with a CASE tool in order to automatically check meta-level OCL constraints on UML models. Such a tool may provide significant help in stabilizing the formal OCL parts of the current OMG standard for UML. Another goal for the near future is to provide adequate tool support for automatic testing based on OCL, and to carry out pilot studies for the use of such tools in small but realistic development projects.

From the viewpoint of tool developers, we can summarize that effective support for the OCL part of UML is possible, and that the language is in principle well designed to achieve a high level of automatisation within such tools.

Acknowledgment: The authors would like to thank Ralf Wiebicke and Sten Loecher for their contributions to the prototype implementation.

References

1. Argo/UML Page, http://www.ArgoUML.com
2. Baar, Th.: Experiences with the UML/OCL-Approach to Precise Software Modeling: A Report from Practice, Unpublished report 2000, see http://i12www.ira.uka.de/˜projekt/publicat.htm 279
3. Buschmann, F. et al.: Pattern-Oriented Software Architecture - A System of Patterns. John Wiley and Sons Ltd, Chichester, UK, 1996 282
4. Booch, G., Rumbaugh, J., Jacobson, I.: The Unified Modeling Language User Guide. Addison-Wesley, 1999
5. BoldSoft, Object Constraint Language Support Information, http://www.boldsoft.com/products/bold/ocl.htm 279, 280, 287
6. Demuth, B., Hussmann, H.: Using OCL Constraints for Relational Database Design. in: UML'99 The Unified Modeling Language, Second Int. Conference Fort Collins, CO, USA, October 1999, Springer, 1999 280, 281, 290
7. Gamma, E., Helm, R., Johnson, R., Vlissides, J.: Design Patterns. Addison-Wesley, 1995 282
8. Haehnle, R., Menzel, W., Schmitt, P.H. KeY - Integrated Deductive Software Design, see http://i12www.ira.uka.de/˜key 281
9. Jackson, D. et al. (MIT Software Design Group): Alcoa. http://sdg.lcs.mit.edu/alcoa/ 280
10. D'Souza, D.F., Wills, A.C.: Objects, Components, and Frameworks with UML - The Catalysis Approach, Addison-Wesley 1999. 278
11. JUnit, http://www.xprogramming.com/software.htm 289
12. Melton, J., Simon, A.: Understanding the New SQL: A Complete Guide. Morgan Kaufmann, 1993 290, 291
13. Meyer, N.: Applying "Design by Contract", IEEE Computer, 25(10), Oktober 1992, pp. 40-51. 278
14. OCL Page, Dresden University of Technology, http://dresden-ocl.sourceforge.net/ 282, 287, 291
15. OMG UML v. 1.3 specification, http://www.omg.org/cgi-bin/doc?ad/99-06-08 282, 282
16. Richters, M., Gogolla, M.: A Metamodel for the UML Object Constraint Language OCL. in: UML'99 The Unified Modeling Language, Second Int. Conference Fort Collins, CO, USA, October 1999, Springer, 1999 281, 283, 283

17. Richters, M., Gogolla, M.: Validating UML Models and OCL Constraints. in: UML2000 The Unified Modeling Language, contained in this proceedings, Springer, 2000 280
18. SableCC Homepage, http://www.sable.mcgill.ca/sablecc/ 282
19. Warmer, J., Kleppe, A.: The Object Constraint Language. Precise Modeling with UML. Addison-Wesley, 1999 278

Strict Profiles: Why and How

Colin Atkinson and Thomas Kühne

AG Component Engineering,
University of Kaiserslautern,
67653 Kaiserslautern, Germany
{atkinson,kuehne}@informatik.uni-kl.de

Abstract. The definition of a clean profile mechanism will play a crucial role in the UML's future in terms of how useful it will be to modellers and how well tool vendors may implement the new facilities. Unfortunately, in an attempt to restrict profile definitions to a single meta level, predefined modeling elements are currently specified exclusively at the meta-model level, and therefore can be applied solely through the mechanism of meta-instantiation. We identify the problems associated with such a restriction and explain why model level inheritance also has a role to play in the definition of predefined modeling elements. We point out the fundamental differences and relationships between the two mechanisms in the context of defining UML profiles and provide guidelines as to which mechanism should be used under which circumstance. We conclude by describing the necessity for the use of both mechanisms in the definition of UML profiles within a strict metamodeling framework.

Introduction

The uptake of the UML in a remarkably wide range of application domains has raised the imperative to view the standard more as a *family* of languages, sharing a common core, rather than as a *single* language having a few minor context-specific extensions. Current plans for the UML's evolution therefore envisage a significant shrinkage of the UML core, coupled with the definition of an enhanced extension mechanism to support the addition of domain and user specific modeling concepts [1]. Several different extension mechanisms have been proposed to date [2, 3], with the most prominent being the "profile mechanism" defined in a white paper for the OMG Analysis and Design Platform Task Force [4].

Although the proposed tailoring mechanisms differ significantly in their details, they all take the view that the definition of the standard UML core, and the extension of the core with user-specific modeling concepts, is achieved at the M2 (commonly known as "meta") level in the OMG's standard four layer modeling architecture. In this paper we argue that this assumption is fundamentally flawed, and that inheritance at the M1 level should also be utilized where appropriate. After demonstrating how, for specific purposes, inheritance enables the predefinition of modeling elements and/or their properties in a much more natural way than meta-instantiation (e.g. stereotyping), we apply the two mechanisms to an example to compare their different effects. We then explain why both mechanisms have their appropriate contexts of use and warrant a unifying notation.

A. Evans, S. Kent and B. Selic (Eds.): «UML» 2000, LNCS 1939, pp. 309-322, 2000.

Profiles and the Standard Model Architecture

All UML modeling takes place within the context of the standard four-level OMG model architecture depicted in Fig. 1.

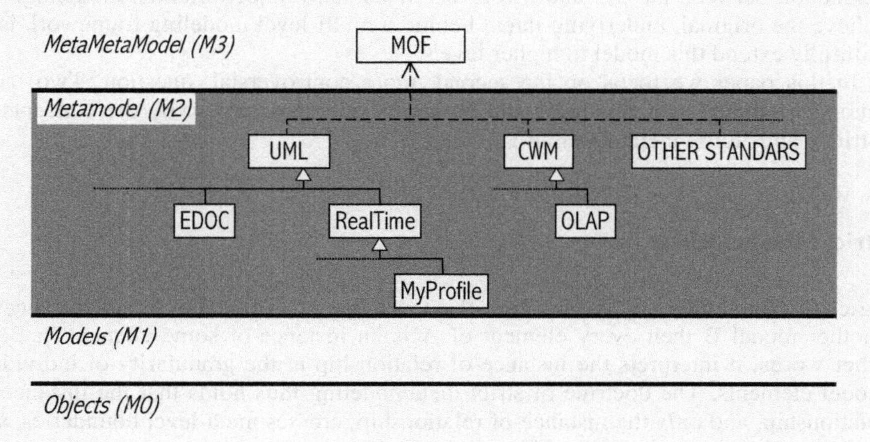

Fig. 1. The OMG view of profiles

The top (M3) level in this model is the so called meta-metamodel, or meta-object facility (or MOF), which defines the basic concepts from which specific metamodels are created at the meta (M2) level. This includes the UML metamodel, which as illustrated in Fig. 1 is regarded as being an instance-of the MOF residing at the M2 level. Other data representation standards, such as the CWM are also viewed as being "instances of" the MOF residing at the M2 level. Normal user models, created using the concepts of the UML or CWM, are regarded as residing at the M1 level, and the ultimate run-time data is regarded as residing at the M0 level.

The fundamental relationship between these layers is intended to be the instance-of relationship. This view is clearly expressed in the UML specification [5], which, in defining the four level model architecture states that "...a model is an instance of a metamodel...". Although this definition has a superficial simplicity and appeal, it is actually the source of significant confusion. In particular, it leaves two main questions unanswered.

1. What is the definition of the instance-of relationship in general?
2. What does the instance-of relationship between models mean in terms of the relationships between the model elements within the models?

In a document the size of the UML specification, one might expect a precise definition of instance-of, e.g., in terms of set theory. Critical issues that need to be clarified in such a definition are the difference between the direct instance-of relationship between an object and the immediate template from which it is created, and the indirect instance-of (or is-member-of) relationship which describes sets of objects with related properties. This relates to the idea of polymorphism in object-oriented systems whereby a direct-instance of a class can be viewed as an (indirect) instance-of all of the class's superclasses. For the purposes of this paper, however, we simply appeal to the long established semantics of the instance-of relationship that forms the foundation of class-based programming and modeling. The idea that an object is an instance-of a class, and that subclasses convey to their objects properties (and thus set memberships) inherited from their superclasses, is one of the most fundamental tenets of object-oriented development, and also the basis for the distinction between the M1 and M0 levels in standard object-oriented modeling. We believe the original, underlying intent behind a multi-level modeling framework is to faithfully extend this model to higher levels.

In this paper we focus on the second, more controversial, question. Two basic schools of thought on this issue can be identified characterized by the concepts of "strict-" and "loose metamodeling".

Strict Metamodeling

Strict metamodeling [6] is based on the tenet that if a model A is an instance of another model B then every element of A is an instance-of some element in B. In other words, it interprets the instance-of relationship at the granularity of individual model elements. The doctrine of strict metamodeling thus holds that the instance-of relationship, and *only* the instance-of relationship, crosses meta-level boundaries, and that every instance-of relationship must cross exactly one meta-level boundary to an immediately adjacent level. This can be captured concisely by the following rule -

> Strict Metamodeling: *In an n-level modeling architecture, M_0, M_1 ..M_{n-1}, every element of an M_m level model must be an instance-of exactly one element of an M_{m+1} level model, for all $m < n-1$.*

This definition deliberately rules out the top level in a hierarchy of levels, since some way has to be employed to terminate the hierarchy of meta-levels. A common approach is to model the top level so that its elements can be viewed as instance-of other elements in the same level[1].

In essence, the strict metamodeling approach simply seeks to faithfully extend the time-honored class/object duality from classic object-oriented development to all levels in a multi-level modeling architecture.

Loose Metamodeling

Loose metamodeling essentially encompasses all approaches which claim that one model is an "instance of" another model, but where the instance-of relationship between individual model elements does not hold as defined above. In practice, this means that the location of model elements is not determined by their place in the instance-of hierarchy, but instead by other criteria. In other words, in a loose metamodeling hierarchy one simple places model elements in the model where one

[1] In terms of the model-level "instance-of" relationship, this is described as a model being an instance of itself.

finds a need to mention them. Although this makes the initial definition of metamodels much easier, it also gives rise to some subtle, but significant problems.

The first problem is the blurring of the level-boundaries that arises when the contents of models are chosen from a utilitarian perspective. An immediate consequence of this blurring is that all kinds of relationships have to cross the boundary between meta-levels, including inheritance relationships, associations and links. This in turn impacts upon the integrity of the model levels, which effectively end up playing the role of packages that only serve to group elements into subgroups of like purpose. This is not a bad thing in itself, since the value of grouping related model elements within packages has long been established. However, wrapping up what essentially amounts to an application of packages in all the baggage and paraphernalia of "meta" modeling not only becomes confusing, but is also directly misleading. Why characterize the relationship between model levels as the instance-of relationship, when, if loose metamodeling is employed, the instance-of is not even the most common form of relationship between the levels?

A second, and more significant problem, is the need to deviate from the well-established mechanism of instantiation in object-oriented approaches to make loose metamodeling work. An example which exemplifies this problem is the problem of defining a prototypical instance of a concept (such as the prototypical class instance, Object) which serves to convey upon entities the basic property of being an object. We call this the "Prototypical Object Problem". The approach used in the specification of the UML (based on loose metamodeling) is to define the prototypical instance at the same level of the class from which it is instantiated. The model elements Class and Object both appear within the (M2) metamodel, and are related by an unnamed association. But this requires that -

1. a modeling element at the M0 level must be an instance of an M2 element.
2. a modeling element at the M0 level must be the direct instance of two classes.

This is clear in the work of Alhir [7], who has to resort to double, direct instance-of relationships when attempting to fully characterize the relationships between modeling elements within the context of loose metamodeling.

Predefining Model Elements

Although the instance-of relationship, as elaborated above, is claimed to be the criterion separating model levels in the UML standard, in fact a different unstated principle is actually used. This principle is essentially that everything "predefined" by the UML standard should be at the meta-model level (M2), and everything that is user-defined should be at the model level (M1). Thus, something is chosen to be at the meta-level because it is predefined, not because of its location in the instance-of hierarchy.

This unstated premise lies behind many of the distortions that exist in the current version of the UML standard. The premise that "meta predefined" also appears to underpin the various profile (i.e. tailoring) mechanisms that have been proposed to date. As an example, consider Fig. 1, an adaptation of an OMG diagram [4] that illustrates the profile concept. This clearly indicates that all tailoring of the UML for specific applications is expected to take place at the M2 level.

The UML's preoccupation with meta-level modeling as the only way to provide a predefined set of concepts upon which users can base their work is actually somewhat surprising, since object technology has a well established and successful mechanism for providing predefined building blocks – the inheritance mechanism. Object-oriented programming languages, such as Smalltalk, Eiffel, and Java feature a whole hierarchy of predefined classes, rooted in a class called Object from which all other classes either explicitly or implicitly inherit. Note that this predefined "object" class is *not* a meta concept residing at the M2 level, but is purposely provided at the M1 level.

We believe that many of the current problems with the UML standard and the proposed profiling mechanisms stem from a failure to recognize the importance of M1 level inheritance as a mechanism for providing predefined modeling elements. Before discussing how proper utilization of this mechanism can aid in a clean definition of the profile mechanism, we first investigate, in the following section, the difference between inheritance and instantiation.

Inheritance versus Meta-Instantiation

In order to compare meta-instantiation to inheritance as a mechanism for applying predefined modeling elements we will use the well-known Observer pattern [8]. Since the UML has no generally accepted notation to depict the meta-class of an M1 level class (i.e. the meta class from which a class is instantiated), we use the stereotype notation, with the understanding that this form is normally intended only for indicating instantiation from user-defined modeling elements.

Predefining a Subject Role

The Observer pattern identifies a subject role, whose task it is to notify a set of attached observers whenever the subject's state changes. The observers then in turn query the subject about its state in order to synchronize their own state (e.g., a rendered view of the subject's contents). Fig. 2 shows that a subject role may attach and detach multiple observers. Whenever the subject's state changes it will call its own notify method, causing an update message to be sent to each attached observer instance. Fig. 2 also shows that the subject and observer roles are actually performed by concrete subclasses. Only concrete observers have an association to a concrete subject so that they can exploit a particular interface to inquire about the subject's state (e.g., `getState()`).

This pattern is common enough to be supported at both the implementation and the modeling level. The Java package, `java.util`, for instance defines two interfaces `Observer` and `Observable` with methods similar to the corresponding classes in Fig. 2. The question we wish to address is how can one best support the above mentioned roles within the UML? Assuming that we want to apply the Observer pattern to the visualization of a data table object (e.g., for displaying multiple diagram types of the same data), we have two options: meta-instantiation and inheritance.

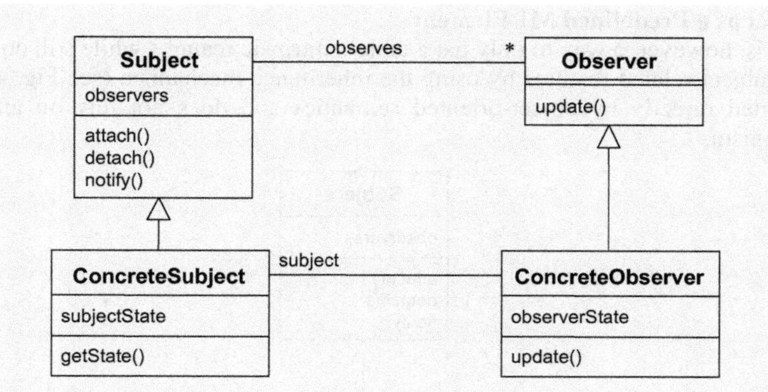

Fig. 2. The structure of the Observer pattern

Note that we do not strive to present the best implementation of the Observer pattern or attempt to find its optimal representation using the UML. The focus here, is on comparing the mechanisms of meta-instantiation and inheritance with respect to their properties when used to apply predefine modeling elements.

Subject as a Predefined M2 Element

When we try to capture the properties of an observer's subject at the M2 level, we have to introduce a stereotype named "Subject" which is used to mark classes which ought to play the role of a subject (see Fig. 3). In order to use the "predefined" subject properties, we then have to use the meta-instantiation mechanism, i.e., apply the stereotype. However, since a stereotype can not equip the class it is applied to with attributes, class `Table` has to feature a list of its observers and a `notify()` method in addition to its internal state (`cells`) and inquiry methods (`getState()`).

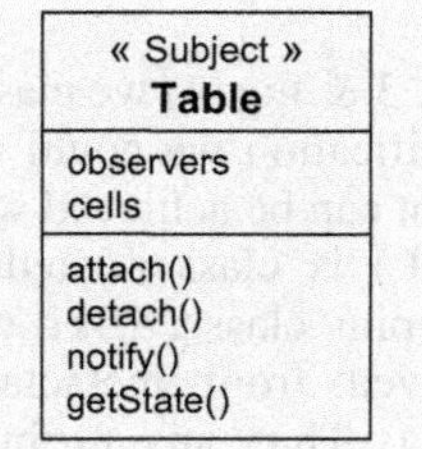

Fig. 3. Subject modeled with a stereotype

If we want to omit any subject related features from class `Table` then we have to rely on a code generator to automatically fill in that boilerplate code for all classes being stereotyped with "Subject". This is the approach most likely to be taken when stereotyping is used because a table's role as a subject is to be communicated through the stereotype tag, rather than through a set of subject related features, added to a table's intrinsic features.

Subject as a Predefined M1 Element

There is, however, a way to only list a table's intrinsic features while still equipping it with subject related features by using the inheritance mechanism (see Fig. 4). This is supported directly by object-oriented semantics and does not rely on an external mechanism.

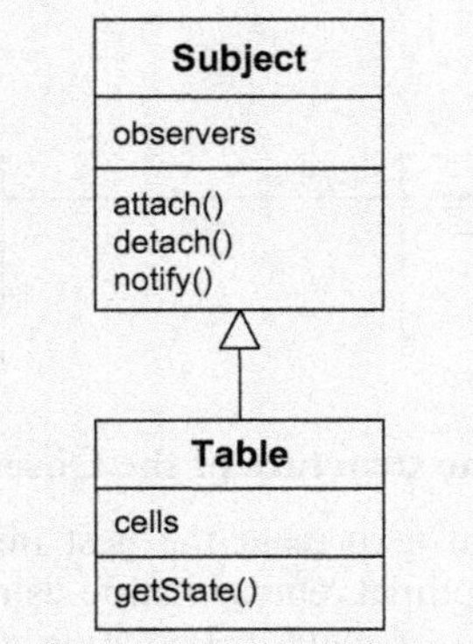

Fig. 4. Subject modeled with inheritance

If the subject role is modeled as a class at the M1 level then a `Table` class may inherit from it, receiving all its features. Note that if the subject class only defines abstract features then class `Table` only receives constraints (i.e., the obligation to implement the abstract features). If, however, class `Subject` defines concrete attributes and methods then class `Table` is able to fulfill a subject role by only providing a specific `getState()` method. The rest is predefined by class `Subject`.

Comparing the Mechanisms

In both variants above (see Fig. 3 & Fig. 4) we classified a table to be a subject. When we used stereotyping for classification we could not influence the structure of table instances directly. The most that can be achieved without resorting to the specification of constraints (e.g., with OCL) is class related information such as "author" or "version" information. Stereotyping class `Table` with "Subject" actually means that a metaclass `Subject` is derived from metaclass `Class` and then `Table` is instantiated from it (see Fig. 5 a). Thus, any attributes specified in `Subject` become class-level attributes of `Table`.

When inheritance is used, however, (i.e., class `Subject` resides at the M1 level, see Fig. 5 b) one can straightforwardly predefine features, associations, invariants, etc. in class `Subject` to be received by class `Table`. As the "jump" across the metalevel border has already been performed by class `Subject`, class `Subject` may predefine properties for `Table` at the same meta level. Interestingly, the two mechanisms both use instantiation and derivation but in reversed order:

meta-instantiation first *derives* `Subject` and then *instantiates* it to `Table`, whereas

inheritance first *instantiates* `Subject` and then *derives* `Table` from it.

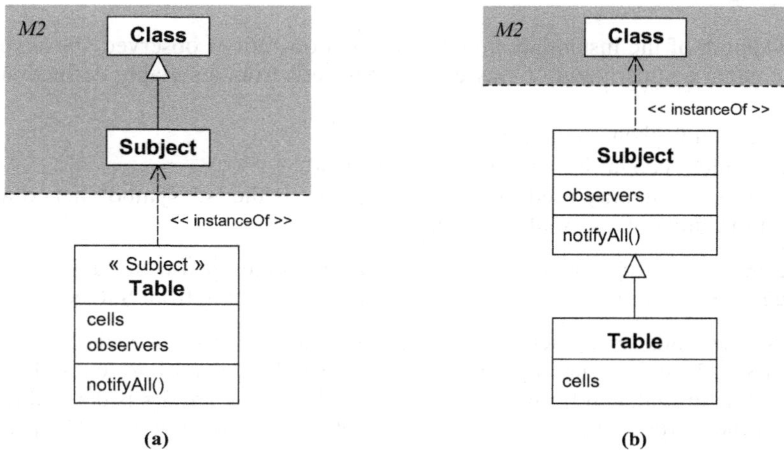

Fig. 5. Meta-Instantiation versus Inheritance

The only difference, in effect, is that in the latter case a link between the classes `Table` and `Subject` is established to denote inheritance. The fact that `Table` is then free not to provide subject related features again is just a consequence of this link. This observation makes it clear that predefining elements through stereotyping is not fundamentally different to predefining element through M1-level inheritance. However, some of the practical effects of the two mechanisms are different:

meta-instantiation does not affect the structure of the new M1 elements. It is, therefore, optimally used to express non-code related information (e.g., project relevant information) or to capture implementation details which have no effect on the stereotyped classes but on other classes (e.g., marker interfaces, such as "`Serializable`" which are only used to signal this property to other classes which actually implement serialization).

inheritance may shape a new M1 element through predefined constraints, interfaces, features, etc. It obviates the need for writing constraints within stereotypes which check that instantiated M1 level elements obey a certain structure (e.g., provide a certain attribute). With inheritance this attribute (or an association to another class, or corresponding methods) can directly be specified.

As a general observation, inheriting from M1 level elements seems to considerably reduce the need for constraints. In the above example, the stereotype "Subject" is likely to contain a constraint checking that the stereotyped element actually features an `observers` attribute. This property, in contrast, is guaranteed by construction when inheritance is used for the classification of subjects. As a further example, one can provide a many-to-many association and let new association types inherit from it saving the trouble of using a constraint language, such as OCL, to specify the meaning of a many-to-many property for associations at the M1 level.

A Unifying Notation

The swapping of the instantiation and derivation operations observed above suggests that the name compartment of classes would benefit from a suitably defined notation that -

highlights this phenomenon, and

allows quick recognition of the situation at hand.

A notation commonly used to express subtyping is the "<" symbol, hence with ":" denoting instantiation as usual, one obtains:

Table : (Subject < Class) (Table stereotyped with Subject)
Table < (Subject : Class) (Table inheriting from Subject)

The first line reads "First metaclass Subject is derived from metaclass Class and then class Table is instantiated from it", whereas the second line reads "First class Subject is instantiated from class Class and then class Table is derived from it".

When the stereotype syntax is used to denote instantiation and stereotypes prefix their elements the two lines become:

«Subject < Class» **Table** abbreviates to: «Subject» **Table**
Table < «Class» Subject abbreviates to: **Table** < Subject

In this version, the guillemets nicely enclose all elements at the M2 level (i.e., the gray parts in Fig. 5).

In a further evolution one may write Subject > Table (instead of Table < Subject) and for the sake of conformance with the existing stereotype notation even write <Subject> Table. Note that the ">" operator between Subject and Table still points in the right direction. Now denoting meta-instantiation and inheritance reads:

«<Class> Subject» **Table** abbreviates to: «Subject» **Table**
<«Class» Subject> **Table** abbreviates to: <Subject> **Table**

Here, guillemets (« ») and the new subtype notation (< >) visually depict the "distance" of the new M1 element in terms of meta levels. In particular, in the abbreviated forms on the right (which could be used as usual within a class icon) it can readily be seen that Table is an instance of a metaclass in the first line above, and that it is derived from a class in the second line above.

Clearly, there is already a graphical means to express that one element is derived from another one (namely the generalization arrow). However, such redundancy already has a precedent in the UML. For example, there are three ways to express instantiation in the UML:

1. Two names separated by a colon.
2. A dependency arrow stereotyped with instance-of.
3. The stereotype notation.

Although these are strictly speaking redundant notations, each variant has an intended application context where it communicates a particular variation of instantiation. Likewise, we believe that the above proposed notation for deriving elements could specifically communicate that inheritance is used to obtain predefined modeling properties, whereas the graphical notation is typically employed to express a generalization relationship between elements within a domain.

Strict Profiles

Having discussed the subtle differences between introducing new modeling concepts at the M2 level (for instantiation) or at the M1 level (for specialization), we are now in a position to describe how we believe UML profiles should be defined in the context of a strict metamodeling framework. Fig. 6 gives a more faithful rendering (in comparison to Fig. 1) of how profiles are located in the four-layer meta architecture. As a mechanism for predefining a modeling environment, we believe that a profile should contain elements at both the M2 and M1 levels. Hence, profiles conceptually span metalevels. Although Fig. 6 does not give the organized impression of Fig. 1, it is simply the result of taking the doctrine of strict metamodeling seriously, given that M1 elements constitute an important part in a profile's definition. Fig. 7 gives a more detailed view of how the contents of profiles (depicted as the gray rectangle labeled L_3) are distributed over metalevels. Note that the boxes now depict individual classes while in Fig. 6 they depict profiles. Another view, that more clearly emphasizes the levels in the four-layer meta architecture, is contained in Fig. 8. In this figure, corresponding shades of gray belong to the same profile.

Predefined □ Meta

The basic goal of a profile is to define a set of modeling elements which users in a specific domain can build upon for their own modeling work. Thus, from the perspective of an individual user of the UML, a profile defines the set of predefined modeling elements that he/she can use as the basis of his/her own modeling work. This includes the so called "root profile" (labeled L_2 in Fig. 7) which defines the standard set of predefined elements which are part of the UML's specification.

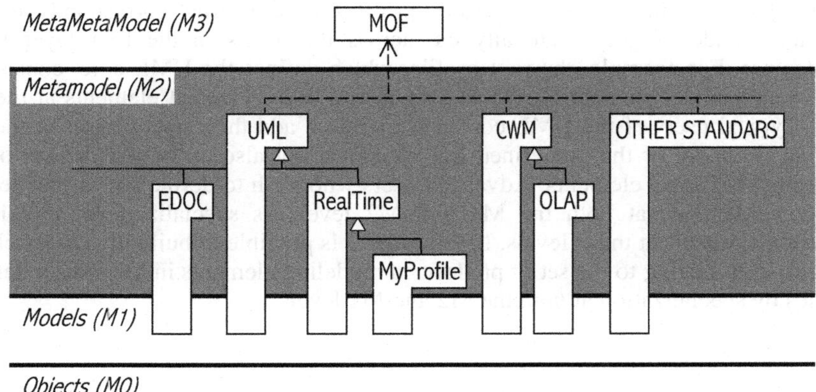

Fig. 6. Profiles containing M2 and M2 elements

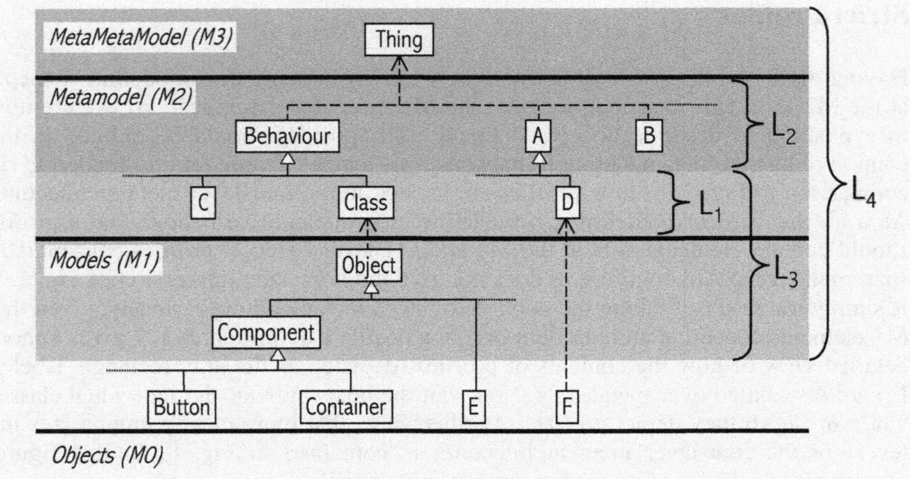

Fig. 7. Naming the modeling layers

The key difference between the new way of defining profiles proposed in this paper, and the approach described in the existing literature, is that a profile is no longer restricted to just one level in the meta hierarchy. On the contrary, profiles (including the root profile) will typically consist of elements at both the M2 and M1[2] levels. Rather than blindly allocate model elements to levels based on whether or not they are "predefined" or "user defined", the model elements in a profile are allocated to meta-levels according to their logical place in the "instance-of " hierarchy. This reflects the fundamental observation that definition time (i.e. being predefined) and level occupancy (i.e. being at a particular metalevel) are two completely different concerns. In a nutshell: "predefined meta".

As illustrated in Fig. 8, therefore, profiles (one profile corresponds to one particular shade of gray) generally cut across the levels in the four layer meta-architecture. For example, the root profile, which defines the UML core, consists of regular metamodel elements at the M2 level, and several model elements at the M1 level. Typical users of the UML core will therefore add their own classes at the M1 level as *instances* of the predefined M2 elements, but also as *specializations* of the predefined M1 level elements. Advanced users who wish to define a new profile, can add new elements at both the M1 and M2 levels as specializations of existing modeling elements at those levels. In this way, it is possible to build up a hierarchy of profiles, each adding to the set of predefined modeling elements in previously defined profiles by specialization at *both* the M2 and M1 levels.

---

[2] In principle it is also possible for a profile to contain predefined elements at the M0 level. For example, the "constant" objects in Smalltalk (e.g. integers, characters, Boolean values), could be viewed as special predefined objects at the M0 level. However, we do not expect this to be common in practical UML modeling scenarios.

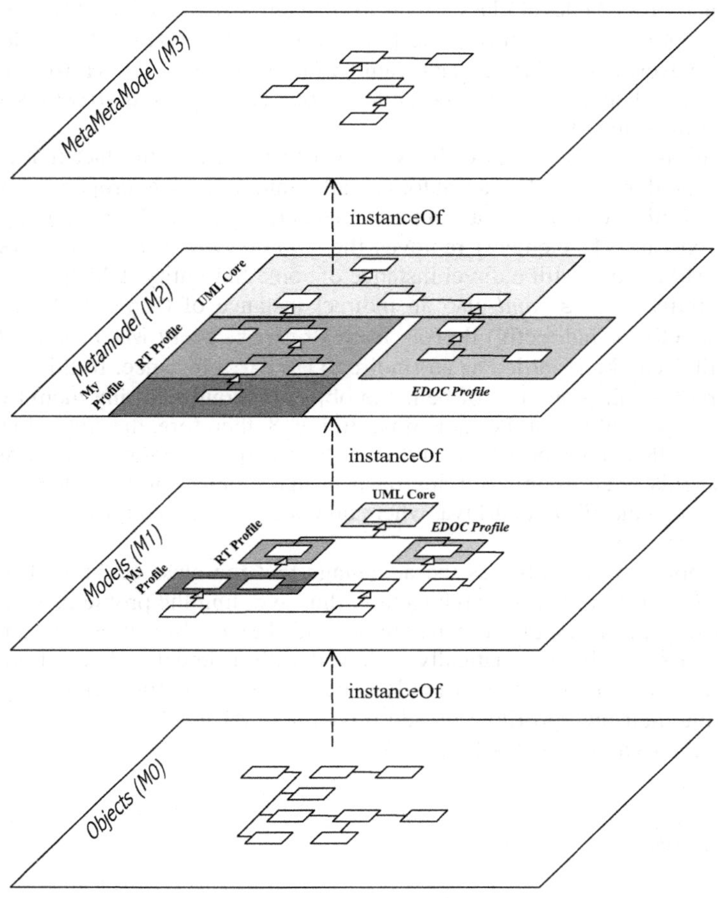

Fig. 8. Predefined entities at the M2 and M1 levels

The Prototypical Instance Problem

The model of profiles depicted in Fig. 7 illustrates how the "predefined meta" principle helps solve the prototypical instance problem outlined at the beginning of the paper in a way that is consistent with the principles of strict metamodeling. Instead of forcing prototypical instances[3], such as the class `Object` and the class `Link` to reside at the M2 level, these classes are instead allowed to reside at the M1 level, which represents their natural location as far as the instance-of hierarchy is concerned. It is true that is conceptually possible to regard an M0 entity as having all object properties (i.e., being an instance of an M2 entity `Object`), as well as being

[3] Meaning that their properties and type are prototypical for all elements derived from them.

an instance of a M1 level class which itself is an instance of the M2 entity `Class`. This conceptual view would enable both `Object` and `Class` to reside at the M2 level. However, in standard object-oriented modeling, e.g., known from modeling in the M0 and M1 levels, it is not possible for one entity to be a *direct* instance of two entities at the same time.

Therefore, moving `Object` to the M1 level and defining the fact that all M1 level classes would be regarded as automatically inheriting the properties of the class `Object`, (either directly, in an implicit manner, or indirectly by inheriting from an already existing M1 element) removes the "*double direct instance*" anomaly. Note that any M0 entity is still a direct instance of some M1 entity (which is an instance of the M2 entity `Class`) *and* also an indirect instance of `Object`. Since every M1 entity (directly or indirectly) derives from `Object`, every M1 instance (i.e. an M0 level entity) can be regarded as an (indirect) `Object` instance. In this way M0 level entities receive all properties of being an object without requiring them to be a *direct* instance of two entities at the same time. In Fig. 8, therefore, the single M1 level class within the UML core profile would correspond to the prototypical class `Object`. Note that this is an established approach in many object-oriented language models, such as Smalltalk, Eiffel and Java, where all classes have a common `Object` class as their root ancestor.

This approach not only has the advantage that the class `Object` has its natural place in the multi-level meta-architecture, thus avoiding the problems that arise when contravening the rules of strict metamodeling, but it also allows instances of user defined classes to be automatically endowed with a predefined set of attributes and methods. Although this is not currently done with the predefined class `Object`, users who define their own profiles can add predefined M1 level classes with a predefined set of attributes and/or methods.

Conclusion

With the envisaged shrinkage of the UML core, and the growing emphasis on user tailorability, the quality and flexibility of the profile (i.e. extension) mechanism will play an increasingly critical role in the language's future success. This is reflected in the level of interest in the subject of UML extensibility, and the growing set of proposals for the next version of the UML extension mechanism. However, as pointed out in this paper, the current set of proposals are based on an implicit, but fundamentally flawed, assumption that tailoring of the UML must necessarily be achieved at the metamodel (M2) level. This assumption is not only invalid, but as explained in the paper, is fundamentally at odds with fundamental principles of object modeling. Strict metamodeling offers the best opportunity to place future versions of the language specification on a sound footing and, hence, is envisaged in current plans for the UML's evolution [1].

The definition of a profiling mechanism that is consistent with the rules of strict metamodeling (a so called *strict profile*) requires model elements to be allocated to meta-levels according to their natural location in the instance-of hierarchy rather than whether or not they are predefined form the perspective of a user. The result is an approach to UML extension which uses regular M1 level inheritance as well as meta-instantiation to enable users to build upon a predefined set of building blocks. The predefined building blocks, therefore, are distributed across multiple levels in the meta-architecture, rather than being concentrated at one specific (M2) level in the meta hierarchy. Distributing predefining elements among multiple levels in this way not only avoids the numerous semantic distortions that are necessary to support the unstated "meta predefined" principle, but also facilitates a more flexible allocation of properties to user classes and objects according to the mechanisms discussed in this paper. By directly shaping the structure of M1 elements through the use of M1 level inheritance, the need to use a constraint language in order to check on a desired structure is avoided in many places.

The strict profiling principles outlined in this paper are essentially independent of the notation used to define, instantiate, or specialize individual modeling elements. For example the approaches described by D'Souza et al. [2] and Cook et al. [3] are both compatible with, and could be use to embody, the notion of strict profiles. Nevertheless, the practical application of the approach would greatly benefit from appropriate notational support that applies the concepts of instantiation and specialization in a level independent way. The UML currently supports two main notations for instantiation, one between the M1 and M0 levels (regular class instantiation) and one between the M2 and M1 levels (stereotyping), but this paper provides suggestions for unifying the two approaches together with a shorthand notation for inheritance. When supported by an appropriate notation, we believe that the notion of a strict profile outlined in this paper will help the UML make the transition towards a truly universal and sound modeling language.

References

1. Kobryn, C.: UML 2001: A Standardization Odyssey. Communications of the ACM (42):10 (1999) 29–37
2. D'Souza, D., Sane, A., Birchenough, A: First Class Extensibility for UML – Packaging of Profiles, Stereotypes, Patterns. In: UML'99 (1999) 265–277
3. Cook, S., Kleppe, A., Mitchel, R., Rumpe, B., Warmer, J. and Wills, A., C.: Defining UML Family Members Using Prefaces. In: Proceedings of TOOLS 32, IEEE (1999)
4. OMG: "White Paper on the profile mechanism", OMG Document ad/99-04-07 (1999)
5. OMG: OMG Unified Modeling Language Specification, Version 1.3. OMG document ad/99-06-08 (1999)
6. Atkinson, C.: Supporting and Applying the UML Conceptual Framework. In: UML'98 (1998)
7. Alhir, S., S.: Extending the Unified Modeling Language. At: home.earthlink.net/~salhir (1999)
8. Gamma, E., Helm, R., Johnson, R., E., Vlissides, J.: Design Patterns: Elements of Reusable Object-Oriented Software. Addison-Wesley (1994)

Dynamic Meta Modeling: A Graphical Approach to the Operational Semantics of Behavioral Diagrams in UML

Gregor Engels, Jan Hendrik Hausmann, Reiko Heckel, Stefan Sauer

University of Paderborn, Dept. of Mathematics and Computer Science
D-33098 Paderborn, Germany
engels|corvette|reiko|sauer@uni-paderborn.de

Abstract. In this paper, dynamic meta modeling is proposed as a new approach to the operational semantics of behavioral UML diagrams. The dynamic meta model extends the well-known static meta model by a specification of the system's dynamics by means of collaboration diagrams. In this way, it is possible to define the behavior of UML diagrams within UML.

The conceptual idea is inherited from Plotkin's structured operational semantics (SOS) paradigm, a style of semantics specification for concurrent programming languages and process calculi: Collaboration diagrams are used as deduction rules to specify a goal-oriented interpreter for the language. The approach is exemplified using a fragment of UML statechart and object diagrams.

Formally, collaboration diagrams are interpreted as graph transformation rules. In this way, dynamic UML semantics can be both mathematically rigorous so as to enable formal specifications and proofs and, due to the use of UML notation, understandable without prior knowledge of heavy mathematic machinery. Thus, it can be used as a reference by tool developers, teachers, and advanced users.

Keywords: UML meta model, statechart diagrams, precise behavioral semantics, graph transformation

1 Introduction

The UML specification [20] defines the abstract syntax and static semantics of UML diagrams by means of (meta) class diagrams and OCL formulas. The dynamic (operational) semantics of behavioral diagrams is only described informally in natural language. However, when using UML models for communication between development teams, for project documentation, or as a contract between developers and customers, it is important that all partners agree on a common interpretation of the language. This requires a semantics specification which captures, in a precise way, both the structural and the dynamic features of the language.

A. Evans, S. Kent and B. Selic (Eds.): ≪UML≫ 2000, LNCS 1939, pp. 323–337, 2000.

Another fundamental requirement for the specification of a modeling language is that it should be readable (at least) by tool developers, teachers, and advanced users. Only in this way, a common understanding of the semantics of the language can be developed among its users.

Presently, most approaches to dynamic UML semantics focus on the implementation and simulation of models, or on automatic verification and reasoning. Reggio et al. [23], for example, use algebraic specification techniques to define the operational semantics of UML state machines. Lillius and Paltor [17] formalize UML state machines in PROMELA, the language of the SPIN model checker. Knapp uses temporal logic [15] for formalizing UML interactions. Övergaard [21] presents a formal meta modeling approach which extends static meta modeling with a specification of dynamics by means of a simple object-oriented programming language that is semantically based on the π-calculus. The formalisms used in the cited approaches provide established technologies for abstract reasoning, automatic verification, execution, or simulation of models, but they are not especially suited for explaining the semantics to non-experts.

In contrast, the technique of meta modeling has been successful, because it does not require familiarity with formal notations to read the semantics specification. Our approach to UML semantics extends the static meta model based on class diagrams [20] by a dynamic model which is specified using a simple form of UML collaboration diagrams. The basic intuition is that collaboration diagrams specify the operations of a goal-driven interpreter. For instance, in order to fire a transition in a statechart diagram, the interpreter has to make sure to be in the source state of the transition, and it might have to ask for the occurrence of a certain trigger event. This trigger event may in turn depend on the existence of a link mediating a method call, invoked by the firing of a transition in another statechart diagram, etc. Conceptually, this may be compared to the behavior of a Prolog interpreter trying to find a proof for a given goal.

Despite the graphical notation, the specification is mathematically rigorous since collaboration diagrams are given a formal interpretation based on graph transformation rules (see, e.g., [24,6,7] for a recent collection of surveys and [1] for an introductory text) within our approach. In particular, they can be considered as a special form of graphical operational semantics (GOS) rules [4], a generalization of Plotkin's structured operational semantics (SOS) paradigm for the definition of (textual) programming languages [22] towards graphs.

The paper is organized as follows: The approach to dynamic meta modeling is exemplified using an important fragment of UML statechart and object diagrams which is introduced along with a sample model in Sect. 2. In Sect. 3, we introduce the structural part of our meta model, a fragment of the standard meta model with meta classes extended by meta operations. The semantics specification in terms of collaboration diagrams is presented in Sect. 4, and in Sect. 5 it is shown how this specification can be used to compute the behavior of the sample model introduced in Sect. 2. Finally, in Sect. 6 we summarize and outline some future perspectives.

2 Statechart and Object Diagrams

Our approach to dynamic meta modeling shall be exemplified by the operational semantics of UML statechart and object diagrams. Statechart diagrams are used to specify the local behavior of objects (of a certain class) during their lifetime. Similarly to an event-condition-action rule, a transition consists of a triggering event, an activation condition, and a list of actions. Additionally, we regard the invocation of operations on an object as well as the calls to operations of other objects by the object under consideration as particularly relevant for this purpose. Therefore, we restrict our specification to transitions with call events and/or call actions. Conditions, other kinds of events and actions, composite and pseudo states, as well as more advanced structural concepts like inheritance and composition of classes are not considered.

The considered model extract refers to a problem of general importance, since the life cycle description of objects in a statechart diagram has to be related to the messaging mechanisms between interacting objects and the invocation of methods on such objects. A recent solution [3] suggests to model dynamic behavior by state machines and to view methods as private virtual objects to allow for concurrent execution by delegation. In contrast, we propose dynamic meta modeling as a basis for an integration of events, messages, and method invocation. In the following, we present an example that will allow us to demonstrate the application of our approach.

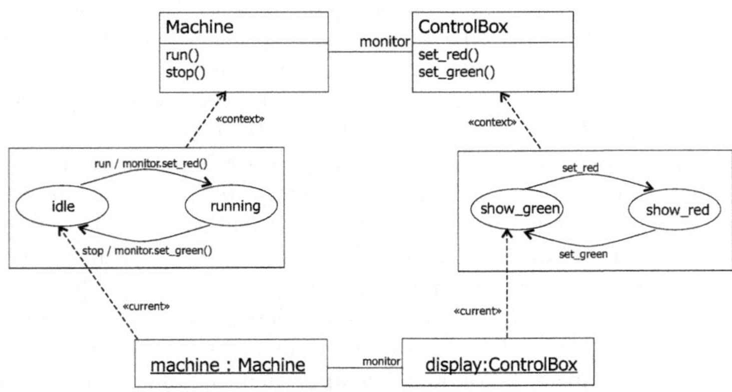

Fig. 1. A sample model (initial configuration)

Figure 1 shows a model consisting of two classes Machine and ControlBox related by an association stating that objects of class Machine may be monitored by objects of class ControlBox. In the Machine statechart diagram, transitions are labeled with combined event/action expressions like run/monitor.set_red(). That means, in order for the transition to fire, a call event for the operation run()

has to occur, and by firing the transition the method set_red() shall be called on the ControlBox object at the opposite end of the monitor link. As a result, the ControlBox object should change its state from show_green to show_red. No further actions are issued by the ControlBox statechart diagram. Notice that we do not model the implementation of operations. Therefore, the relevant interaction between objects (like switching the display by the machine) is described using call actions on the statechart level (rather than implementing it in the method run()).

The initial configuration of the system is given by an object diagram together with a specification of the control state of each object. In our example, machine is in state idle and display is in state show_green as shown in Fig. 1 by the stereotyped ≪current≫ relationships.

After presenting the static meta model and the firing rules of UML statechart diagrams in the next sections, we shall examine part of the life cycle of the objects introduced above.

3 Meta Classes and Meta Operations

In the UML semantics specification [20], the abstract syntax of statechart diagrams is specified by a meta class diagram. In order to define the structural model of an interpreter for this languages, this model has to be extended by state information, for example to represent the current control state of an object.

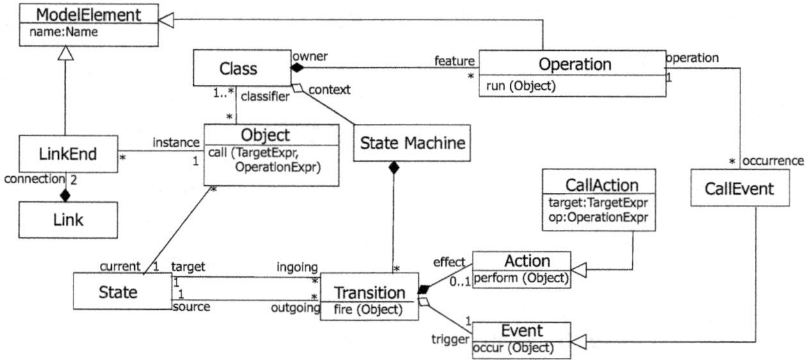

Fig. 2. Meta class diagram

Figure 2 shows the classes from the UML meta model that are relevant for the subclass of statechart diagrams we are considering (partly simplified by flattening the meta class hierarchy). A statechart diagram, represented by an instance of meta class StateMachine, controls the behavior of the objects of the class it is associated with. For this purpose, we extend the meta model by an association current which designates the current control state of an object within the state diagram. States and transitions are represented by instances of the corresponding meta classes, and transitions are equipped with a trigger CallEvent (like run in our scenario) and an effect CallAction (like control.set_red()). A CallEvent carries a link to the local operation which is called. Unlike in the standard meta model, a CallAction is not directly associated with an operation, as this would result in static binding. Instead, an attribute OperationExpr is provided.

The state space of the diagrammatic language consists of all instance graphs conforming to the meta class diagram. Each instance graph represents the state of an interpreter given by the "programs" (e.g., statechart diagrams) to be executed, the problem domain objects with their respective data states (given, e.g., by the values of attributes and links), and their control states.

The relation between class and instance diagrams can be formally captured by the concept of *type* and *instance graphs* [5].[1] Given a type graph TG, representing a class diagram, a *TG-typed instance graph* consists of a graph G together with a typing homomorphism $g : G \to TG$ associating to each vertex and edge x of G its type $g(x) = t$ in TG. For example, the instance graph of the meta class diagram in Fig. 2 that represents the abstract syntax of the model in Fig. 1 is shown in Fig. 3.

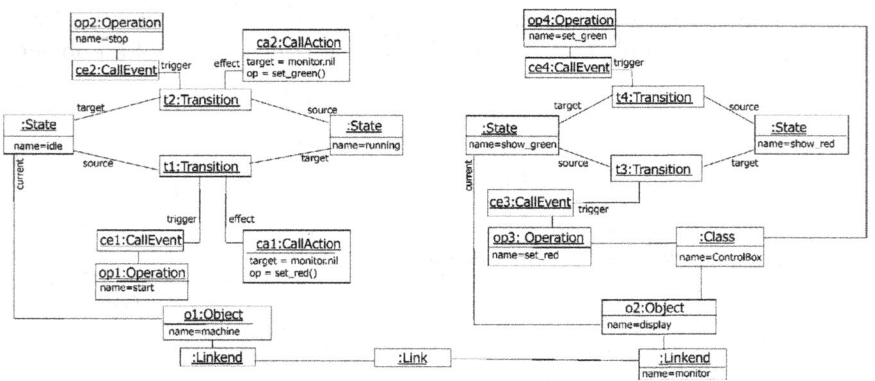

Fig. 3. Abstract syntax of sample model

The class diagram in Fig. 2 does not only contain meta classes and associations, but also *meta operations* like perform(Object) of class Action. They are the operations of our interpreter for statechart diagrams. Given the type graph

[1] By *graphs* we mean directed unlabeled graphs $G = \langle G_V, G_E, src^G, tar^G \rangle$ with set of vertices G_V, set of edges G_E, and functions $src^G : G_E \to G_V$ and $tar^G : G_E \to G_V$ associating to each edge its source and target vertex. A graph homomorphism $f : G \to H$ is a pair of functions $\langle f_V : G_V \to H_V, f_E : G_E \to H_E \rangle$ compatible with source and target.

TG representing the structural part of the class diagram, the meta operations form a family of sets $M = (MOP_w)_{w \in TG_V^+}$ indexed by non-empty sequences $w = v_1 \ldots v_n$ of parameter class names $v_i \in TG_V$. By convention, the first parameter v_1 of each meta operation represents the class to which the operation belongs (thus there has to be at least one argument type). For example, the meta operation perform(Object) of class Action is formally represented as perform $\in MOP_{\mathsf{Action,Object}}$.

After having described the abstract syntax of our model in terms of meta classes and meta operations, the implementation of the meta operations shall be specified using collaboration diagrams in the next section.

4 Meta Modeling with Collaboration Diagrams

The static meta model of the UML defines the abstract syntax of the language by means of meta class diagrams. Seen as a system specification, these class diagrams represent the structural model of an UML editor or interpreter. In this section, we shall extend this analogy to the dynamic part of a model, i.e., we are going to specify the dynamics of an interpreter for statechart and object diagrams. Interaction diagrams and, in particular, collaboration diagrams are designed to specify object interaction, creation, and deletion in a system model. Dynamic meta modeling applies the same language concepts to the meta model level to specify the interaction and dynamics of model elements of the UML.

The specification is based on the intuition of an interpreter which has to demonstrate the existence of a certain behavior in the model. Guided by a recursive set of rules stating the conditions for the execution of a certain meta operation, the interpreter works its way from a goal (e.g., the firing of a transition) towards its assumptions (e.g., the occurrence of a trigger event). The behavioral rules are specified by collaboration diagrams consisting of two compartments. The head of the diagram contains the meta operation which is specified by the diagram. The body specifies the assumptions for the execution of the meta operation, its effect on the object configuration, and other meta operations required.

For example, the conditions for a transition to fire and its effect on the configuration are specified in the collaboration diagram of Fig. 4: An object o may fire a transition if that object is in the corresponding source state, the (call) event triggering the transition occurs, and the operation associated with this call event is invoked by the meta operation run(o). In this case, the object o changes to the target state of the transition, which is modeled by the deletion and re-creation of the current link.

Thus, in order to be able to continue, the interpreter looks for a call event triggering the transition. This call event can be raised if the associated operation is called on the object o as specified in Fig. 5 using the meta operation call. The signature of this meta operation of meta class Object contains two parameters: The first one holds a path expression to direct the call to its target object (it equals nil when the target object is reached), and the second one specifies the

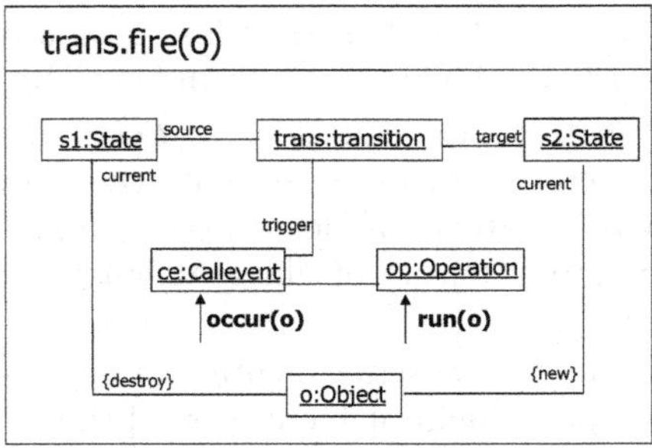

Fig. 4. The firing of a transition by an object

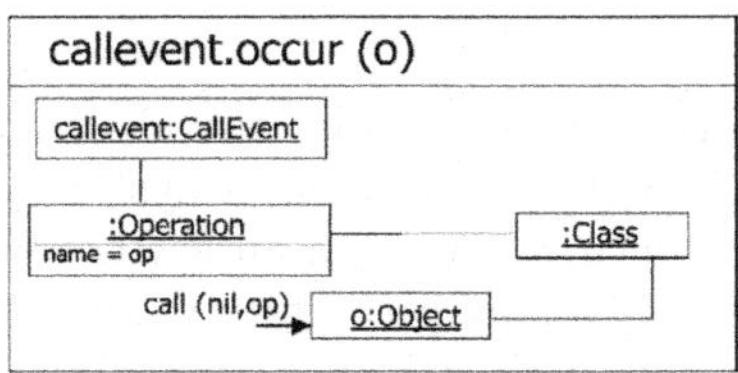

Fig. 5. Issuing a CallEvent

name of the operation to be called (and possibly further parameters). The name of the operation op has to match the operation expression transmitted by call.

Note that this does not guarantee the execution of the body of the called operation. In fact, no rule for meta operation run of meta class Operation is provided. The specification of the structure and dynamics of method implementations is the objective of *action semantics* as described by the corresponding request for proposals [18] by the Object Management Group. So far, UML provides only "uninterpreted strings" to capture the implementation of methods. We believe that our approach is extensible towards a dynamic semantics of actions once this is precisely defined.

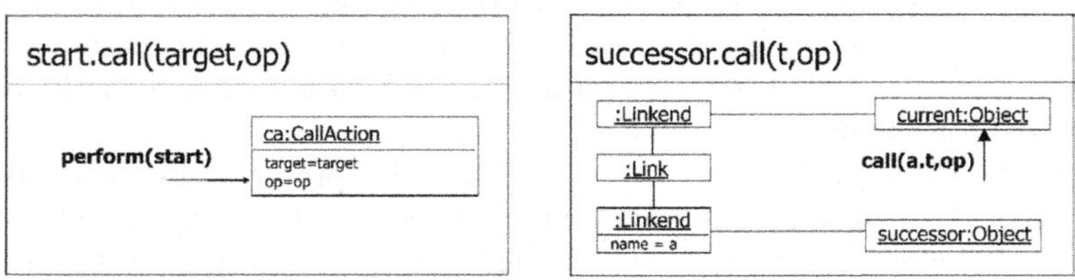

Fig. 6. Evaluating the target expression

An operation call like o.call(nil, op) in Fig. 5 originates from a call action which specifies by means of a path expression the target of the call. Thus, in order to find out whether a call is pending for a given object o, our interpreter has to check two alternatives: Either a call action is performed on o directly with target = nil, or there is a call at a nearby object with a target expression pointing towards o. These two cases are specified by the two collaboration diagrams for meta operation call in Fig. 7. The left diagram specifies the invocation of the meta operation by a CallAction on an object start. (The object is not depicted since it is given by the parameter of the premise.) Notice that the values of the meta attributes target and op have to match the parameters of meta operation call.

If the meta operation is not directly invoked by a call action, an iterative search is triggered as specified by the right diagram: To invoke the meta operation call(t,op) on an object successor which is connected to object current via a link, whose link end named a is attached to the successor object, the meta operation call(a.t,op) has to be invoked on current with the identical operation parameter op and the extended path expression a.t. (We assume target to be in a Java-like path syntax where the names of the links to be followed form a dot-separated list.)

Notice, that the right rule in Fig. 7 is potentially non-deterministic: In a state where the successor object has more than one incoming a link, different instantiations for the current object are possible. In this case, the link to be followed would be chosen non-deterministically.

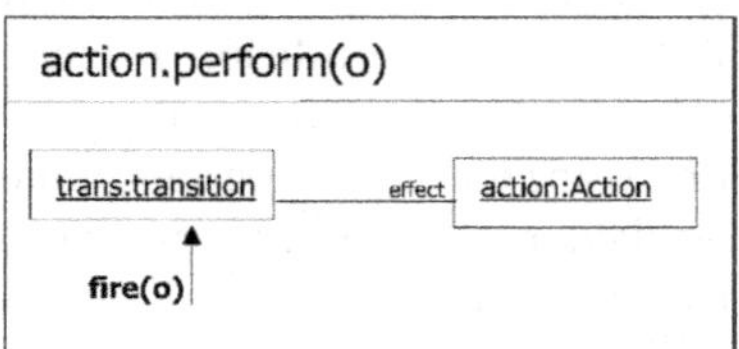

Fig. 7. The performing of an action by an object

Figure 7 presents the rule for performing an action. In our scenario this should be a CallAction initiating a call to another object, but the rule is also applicable to other kinds of actions. An action is the (optional) effect of firing a transition, i.e., the invocation of meta operation perform of meta class Action depends on the firing of the associated transition. Thus, the rule in Fig. 4 has to be applied again in order to derive the firing of the transition at the calling object.

As already mentioned in the introduction, this goal-oriented style of semantics specification is conceptually related to the proof search of a Prolog interpreter. This intuition is made precise by the paradigm of graphical operational semantics (GOS) [4], a graph-based generalization of the structured operational semantics (SOS) paradigm [22], for the specification of diagram languages. In the GOS approach, deduction rules on graph transformations are introduced in order to to formalize the derivation of the behavior of models from a set of meta-level diagrams, which is implicitly present in this section. In the next section, we describe a simplified form of this approach especially tailored for collaboration diagrams.

5 Computing with Collaboration Diagrams

In the previous section, collaboration diagrams have been used to specify the firing rules of statechart transitions and the transmission of calls between objects. Now, concrete computations shall be modeled as collaboration diagrams on the instance level. This allows us to represent changes to the object structure together with the operations causing these changes. Moreover, even incomplete computations can be modeled, where some of the method calls are still unresolved. This is important if we want to give semantics to incomplete models like the one in Sect. 2 which requires external activation in order to produce any activity.

The transition from semantic rules to computations is based on a formal interpretation of collaboration diagrams as graph transformation rules. A rule representing the collaboration diagram for operation trans.fire(o) in Fig. 4 is shown in Fig. 8. It consists of two graphs L and R representing, respectively, the pre- and the post-condition of the operation. In general, both L and R are instances of the type graph TG representing the class diagram, and both are subgraphs of a common graph C that we may think of as the object graph of the collaboration diagram. Then, the pre-condition L contains all objects and links which have to be present before the operation, i.e., all elements of C except for those marked as {new} or {transient}. Analogously, the post-condition contains all elements of C not marked as {transient} or {destroy}. In the example of Fig. 8, graph C is just the union $L \cup R$ since there are no transient objects in the diagram of Fig. 4.

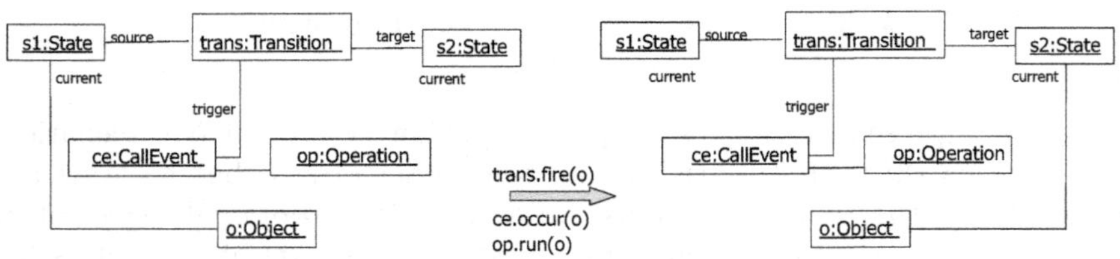

Fig. 8. Collaboration diagram as a labeled graph transformation rule

Besides structural modifications, the collaboration diagram describes calls to meta operations ce.occur(o) and op.run(o), and it is labeled by the operation trans.fire(o), the implementation of which it specifies. This information is recorded in the rule-based presentation in Fig. 8 by means of additional labels above and below the arrow. Abstractly, a collaboration diagram is denoted as

$$C : L \xrightarrow[b]{a} R$$

where C is the object graph of the diagram, L and R are the pre- and post-conditions, a is the label representing the operation specified by the diagram, and b represents the sequential and/or concurrent composition of operations referred to (that is, called) within in the diagram. The expression ce.occur(o) × op.run(o) in Fig. 8, for example, represents the concurrent invocation of two operations.

We shall use the rule-based interpretation of collaboration diagrams in order to derive the behavior of the sample model introduced in Sect. 2. The idea is to combine the specification-level diagrams by means of two operators of *sequential composition* and *method invocation*. The sequential composition of two diagrams

$$C_1 : L_1 \xrightarrow[b_1]{a_1} R_1 \text{ and } C_2 : L_2 \xrightarrow[b_2]{a_2} R_2$$

is defined if the post-condition R_1 of the first equals the pre-condition L_2 of the second. The composed diagram is given by

$$C_1 \cup_{L_2=R_1} C_2 : L_1 \xrightarrow[b_1;\,b_2]{a_1;\,a_2} R_2$$

where $C_1 \cup_{L_2=R_1} C_2$ denotes the disjoint union of the graphs C_1 and C_2, sharing only $L_2 = R_1$. The second operator on diagrams models the invocation of a method from within the implementation of another method. This is realized by substituting the method call by the implementation of the called method, thus diminishing the hierarchy of method calls. Assume two rules

$$C : L \xrightarrow[b[c]]{a} R \text{ and } C' : L' \xrightarrow[d]{c} R'$$

where the call expression $b[c]$ of the first rule contains a reference to the operation c specified by the second rule. (In the rule of Fig. 8, $b[c]$ corresponds to ce.occur(o) × op.run(o), and c could be instantiated with either ce.occur(o) or op.run(o).) Then, the composed rule is given by

$$C \cup_c C' : L \cup_c L' \xrightarrow[b[d]]{a} R \cup_c R'.$$

The call to c is substituted by the expression d specifying the methods called within c. By $C \cup_c C'$ we denote the union of graphs C and C' sharing the *self* and parameter objects of the operation c.[2] In the same way, the pre- and post-conditions of the called operation are imported inside the calling operation.

[2] Notice that, in order to ensure that the resulting diagram is consistent with the cardinality constraints of the meta class diagram, it might be necessary to identify further elements of C and C' with each other (besides the ones identified by c). For instance, when identifying two transitions, we also have to identify the corresponding source and target states. Formally, this effect is achieved by defining the union as a pushout construction in a restricted category of graphs (see, e.g., [16]).

In Fig. 9 it is outlined how these two composition operators are used to build a collaboration diagram representing a possible run of our sample model. The given diagrams are depicted in iconized form with sequential composition and invocation as horizontal and vertical juxtaposition, respectively. This presentation is inspired by the *tile model* [12], a generalization of the SOS paradigm [22] towards open (e.g., incomplete) systems. In fact, in our example, such a semantics is required since the model in Fig. 1 is incomplete, i.e., it does not specify the source of the call events run and stop needed in order to trigger the machine's transitions.

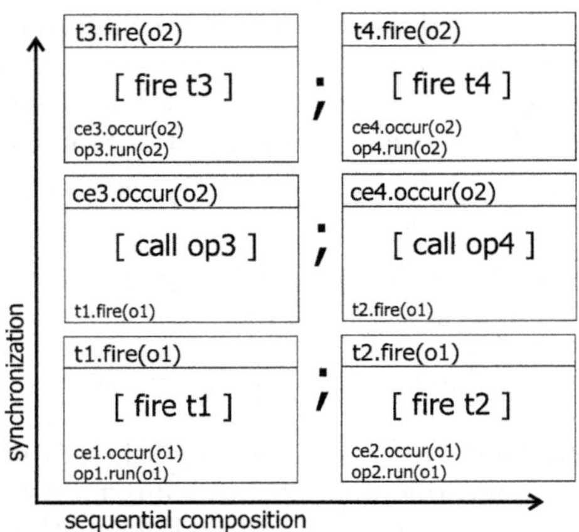

Fig. 9. Composing a run of the sample model

Figure 10 shows an expanded version of the iconized diagram *[fire t3]* in the top left of Fig. 9. It originates from an application of the operation trans.fire(o) in the context of an additional transition.[3] The diagrams *[fire t4]* to the right of *[fire t3]* as well as *[fire t1]* and *[fire t2]* in the bottom are expanded analogously.

Figure 11 details the icon labeled *[call op3]*. It shows the invocation of several operations realizing the navigation of the method call along the monitor link as specified by the target expression, and the issuing of the call event. A similar diagram could be drawn for *[call op4]*.

Finally, in Fig. 12 the composite computation is shown covering the complete scenario depicted in Fig. 1. It can be derived from the components in Fig. 9 in two different ways: by first synchronizing the single transitions (vertical dimension)

[3] In general, contextualization of rules has to be specified explicitly in our model (in this we follow the philosophy of the SOS and the tile framework [22,12]). In the present specification, however, we can safely allow to add any context but for the current links which ensure the coordinated behavior of the different statechart diagrams.

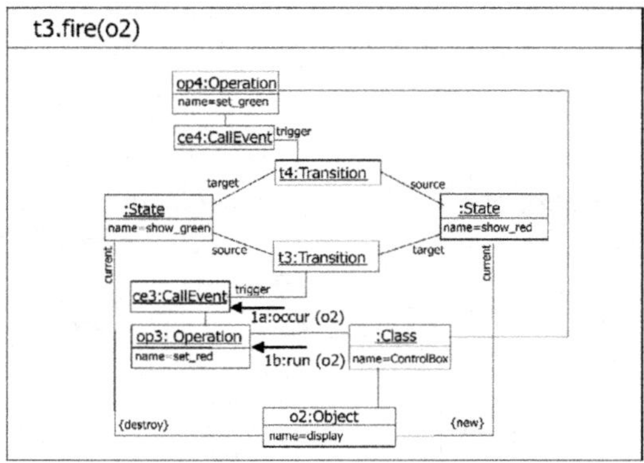

Fig. 10. Operation trans.fire(o) in context

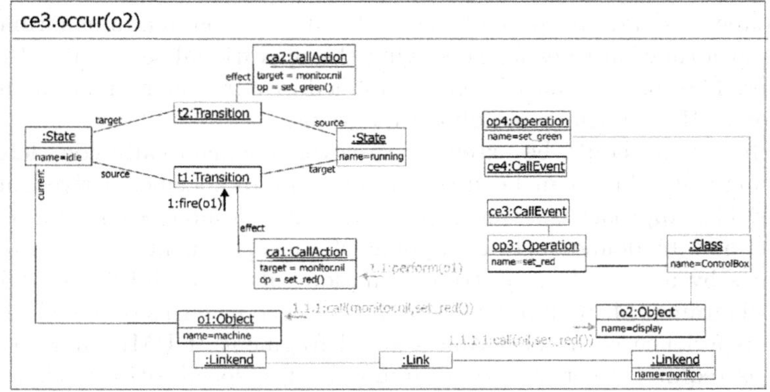

Fig. 11. Navigation of the method call

and then sequentially composing the two steps (horizontal dimension), or first building local two-step sequences (horizontal dimension) and then synchronizing them (vertical dimension).

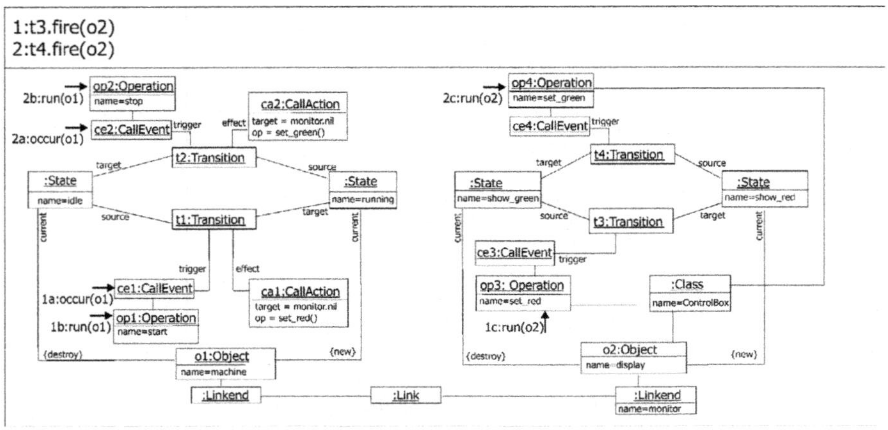

Fig. 12. Composite rule for the scenario in Fig. 1

6 Conclusion

In this paper, we have proposed the use of collaboration diagrams formalized as graph transformation rules for specifying the operational semantics of diagram languages. The concepts have been exemplified by a fragment of a dynamic meta model for UML statechart and object diagrams.

The fragment should be extended to cover a semantically complete kernel of the language which can be used to define more specific, derived modeling concepts. This approach is advocated by the *pUML* group (see e.g., [9]). Concrete examples how to define such a mapping of concepts include the flattening of statecharts by means of graph transformation rules [13] and the simplification of class diagrams [14] by implementing inheritance in terms of associations.

Our experience with specifying a small fragment of UML shows that tool support is required for testing and animating the specification. While the implementation of flat collaboration diagrams is reasonably well understood (see, e.g., [8,10]), the animation of the results of an execution on the level of concrete syntax is still under investigation. It requires a well-defined mapping between the concrete and the abstract syntax of the modeling language. One possible solution is to complement the graph representing the abstract syntax by a *spatial relationship graph*, and to realize the mapping by a graphical parser specified by a graph grammar [2].

A related problem is the integration of model execution and animation in existing UML tools. Rather than hard-coding the semantics into the tools, our approach provides the opportunity to allow for *user-defined semantics*, e.g., in the context of domain-specific profiles. Such a profile, which extends the UML standard by stereotypes, tagged values, and constraints [19], could also be used to implement the extensions to the static meta model that are necessary in order to define the operational semantics (e.g., the current links specifying the control states of objects could be realized as tagged values).

On the more theoretical side, the connection of dynamic meta modeling with proof-oriented semantics following the SOS paradigm allows the transfer of concepts of the theory of concurrent languages, like bisimulation, action refinement, type systems, etc. Like in the GOS approach [4], the theory of graph transformation can provide the necessary formal technology for transferring these concepts from textual to diagram languages.

References

1. M. Andries, G. Engels, A. Habel, B. Hoffmann, H.-J. Kreowski, S. Kuske, D. Plump, A. Schürr, and G. Taentzer. Graph transformation for specification and programming. *Science of Computer Programming*, 34:1–54, 1999. 324
2. R. Bardohl, G. Taentzer, M. Minas, and A. Schürr. Application of graph transformation to visual languages. In Ehrig et al. [6], pages 105–180. 335
3. R. Breu and R. Grosu. Relating events, messages, and methods of multiple threaded objects. *JOOP*, pages 8–14, January 2000. 325
4. A. Corradini, R. Heckel, and U. Montanari. Graphical operational semantics. In A. Corradini and R. Heckel, editors, *Proc. ICALP2000 Workshop on Graph Transformation and Visual Modelling Techniques, Geneva, Switzerland*, Geneva, July 2000. Carleton Scientific. 324, 330, 336
5. A. Corradini, U. Montanari, and F. Rossi. Graph processes. *Fundamenta Informaticae*, 26(3,4):241–266, 1996. 327
6. H. Ehrig, G. Engels, H.-J. Kreowski, and G. Rozenberg, editors. *Handbook of Graph Grammars and Computing by Graph Transformation, Volume 2: Applications, Languages, and Tools.* World Scientific, 1999. 324, 336
7. H. Ehrig, H.-J. Kreowski, U. Montanari, and G. Rozenberg, editors. *Handbook of Graph Grammars and Computing by Graph Transformation, Volume 3: Concurrency and Distribution.* World Scientific, 1999. 324
8. G. Engels, R. Hücking, St. Sauer, and A. Wagner. UML collaboration diagrams and their transformation to Java. In R. France and B. Rumpe, editors, *Proc. UML'99 Int. Conference, Fort Collins, CO, USA*, volume 1723 of *LNCS*, pages 473–488. Springer Verlag, October 1999. 335
9. A. Evans and S. Kent. Core meta modelling semantics of UML: The pUML approach. In France and Rumpe [11], pages 140–155. 335
10. T. Fischer, J. Niere, L. Torunski, and A. Zündorf. Story diagrams: A new graph transformation language based on UML and Java. In H. Ehrig, G. Engels, H.-J. Kreowski, and G. Rozenberg, editors, *Proc. 6th Int. Workshop on Theory and Application of Graph Transformation (TAGT'98), Paderborn, November 1998*, volume 1764 of *LNCS*. Springer Verlag, 2000. 335

11. R. France and B. Rumpe, editors. *Proc. UML'99 – Beyond the Standard*, volume 1723 of *LNCS*. Springer Verlag, 1999. 336, 337, 337
12. F. Gadducci and U. Montanari. The tile model. In G. Plotkin, C. Stirling, and M. Tofte, editors, *Proof, Language and Interaction: Essays in Honour of Robin Milner*. MIT Press, 1999. 333, 333
13. M. Gogolla and F. Parisi-Presicce. State diagrams in UML – a formal semantics using graph transformation. In *ICSE'98 Workshop on Precise Semantics of Modelling Techniques*, 1998. Tech. Rep. TUM-I9803, TU München. 335
14. M. Gogolla and M. Richters. Equivalence rules for UML class diagrams. In P.-A. Muller and J. Bezivin, editors, *Proc. UML'98 Workshop*, pages 86–97. Universite de Haute-Alsace, Mulhouse, 1998. 335
15. A. Knapp. A formal semantics of UML interactions. In France and Rumpe [11], pages 116–130. 324
16. M. Korff. Single pushout transformations of equationally defined graph structures with applications to actor systems. In *Proc. Graph Grammar Workshop, Dagstuhl, 1993*, volume 776 of *LNCS*, pages 234–247. Springer Verlag, 1994. 332
17. J. Lillius and I. Paltor. Formalising UML state machines for model checking. In France and Rumpe [11], pages 430–445. 324
18. Object Management Group. Action semantics for the UML, November 1998. `http://www.omg.org/pub/docs/ad/98-11-01.pdf`. 329
19. Object Management Group. Analysis and design platform task force – white paper on the profile mechanism, April 1999. `http://www.omg.org/pub/docs/ad/99-04-07.pdf`. 336
20. Object Management Group. UML specification version 1.3, June 1999. `http://www.omg.org`. 323, 324, 326
21. G. Övergaard. Formal specification of object-oriented meta-modelling. In T. Maibaum, editor, *Fundamental Approaches to Software Engineering (FASE'00), Berlin, Germany*, number 1783 in LNCS, pages 193–207. Springer Verlag, March/April 2000. 324
22. G. Plotkin. A structural approach to operational semantics. Technical Report DAIMI FN-19, Aarhus University, Computer Science Department, 1981. 324, 331, 333, 333
23. G. Reggio, E. Astesiano, C. Choppy, and H. Hussmann. Analysing UML active classes and associated state machines – a lightweight formal approach. In T. Maibaum, editor, *Fundamental Approaches to Software Engineering (FASE'00), Berlin, Germany*, number 1783 in LNCS, pages 127–146. Springer Verlag, March/April 2000. 324
24. G. Rozenberg, editor. *Handbook of Graph Grammars and Computing by Graph Transformation, Volume 1: Foundations*. World Scientific, 1997. 324

Composing Design Models: An Extension to the UML

Siobhán Clarke

Department of Computer Science, Trinity College, Dublin 2, Ireland.[1]
Siobhan.Clarke@cs.tcd.ie

Abstract: A *structural mismatch* between the specification of requirements for software systems and the specification of object-oriented software systems happens because the units of interest during the requirements phase (for example, feature, function etc.) are different from the units of interest during the object-oriented design and implementation (for example, object, class, method etc.). The structural mismatch results in support for a single requirement being scattered across the design units and a single design unit supporting multiple requirements – this in turn results in reduced comprehensibility, traceability and reuse of design models. Subject-oriented design is a new approach to designing systems based on the object-oriented model, but extending this model by adding new decomposition capabilities. The new decomposition capabilities support a way of directly aligning design models with requirements. Composition of design models is specified with *composition relationships*. This paper describes changes required to the UML metamodel to support composition relationships.

1. Introduction

Decomposition within conventional object-oriented design models is by class, interface and method. This kind of decomposition matches well with object-oriented code, providing some traceability between object-oriented designs and code. However, it does not align with the structure of requirements specifications, which are generally described by feature/capability. There is a negative impact to this structural mismatch – support for individual requirements is scattered across the design, and support for multiple requirements is tangled in individual design units. This reduces comprehensibility, making designs difficult to develop, re-use and extend.

To support the direct alignment of design models with requirements, we extend conventional object-oriented design by adding additional decomposition capabilities. The model, called *subject-oriented design*, supports the separation of the design of different requirements into different, potentially overlapping, design models. Subsequent composition of the separated design models is specified with composition relationships. A composition relationship identifies overlapping elements in different design models (called *corresponding* elements), and specifies how they are to be integrated. For example, a composition relationship with *merge* integration might be specified to compose models that may have been designed concurrently by different teams to support different requirements of the system, or to compose different optional features of a system. Composition relationships with *override* integration might be specified to support a situation where a design model is intended to extend or change the behaviour of an existing design model because a change to requirements makes (part of) the existing design model's behaviour obsolete.

---

[1] This work was performed while the author was at Dublin City University

A. Evans, S. Kent and B. Selic (Eds.): «UML» 2000, LNCS 1939, pp. 338-352, 2000.

Decomposition based on requirements, with corresponding composition specification using composition relationships, is not part of the UML. The primary contribution of this paper is the presentation of an overview of the extensions required to the UML semantics and metamodel to support this model. First though, there is a brief section describing the motivation for this work in Section 2, and a description of the model in Section 3. Section 4 describes the extensions to the UML, and Sections 5, 6 and 7 provide a discussion, a look at related work, and some conclusions.

2. Motivation

To illustrate the problems that motivate this work, an example is presented involving the construction and evolution of a simple software engineering environment (SEE) for programs consisting of expressions. The desired SEE supports the specification of expression programs. It contains a set of tools that share a common representation of expressions. The initial tool set should include an *evaluation* capability, which determines the result of evaluating expressions; a *display* capability, which depicts expressions textually; and a *check* capability, which optionally determines whether expressions are syntactically and semantically correct. The SEE should permit optional logging of operations.

Based on these requirements, a UML design for the system is illustrated in Fig. 1. The design represents expressions as abstract syntax trees (ASTs) and defines a class for each type of AST node, where each class contains accessor methods, plus methods `evaluate()`, `display()` and `check()`, realising the required tools in a standard, object-oriented manner.[2] Logging is modelled as a separate, singleton class (`Logger`); the intent is for each AST operation to invoke `Logger.beforeInvoke()` prior to performing its action, then to invoke `Logger.afterInvoke()` just before it terminates. The Logger permits applications to turn logging on and off with its `turnLoggingOn()` and `turnLoggingOff()` methods. When logging is off, `Logger`'s `beforeInvoke()` and `afterInvoke()` methods are essentially no-ops.

<u>**Assessment:**</u> The structural differences in the specification paradigms between the requirements specification, and the object-oriented design of the SEE are central to the difficulties associated with this design. The natural outcome of the structural differences is a *scattering* and *tangling* effect across the object-oriented design - the design of a single requirement is scattered across multiple classes and operations in the object-oriented design, and design details of multiple requirements will be tangled in a single class or operation in an object-oriented design.

Scattering is apparent in the SEE, as the design of requirements is scattered across the AST classes. This means that the impact of a change to a requirement is high, because a change will necessitate multiple changes across a class hierarchy. Tangling is also present in the design of the SEE in, for example, the design of the logging capability. The protocol for logging requires interaction with each method in each AST class, tangling its support with those methods. Dealing with logging necessitates dealing with design details from multiple other requirements, making it difficult to change. Other impacts of scattering and tangling include *reduced comprehensibility* (any attempt at studying the system one part at a time will potentially result in a

---

[2] Many alternative designs are also possible. A simple one is presented here to illustrate the motivating problems.

required knowledge of the full design if the "one part" chosen is a requirement, or will potentially result in a required knowledge of all the requirements if the "one part" chosen is a class in the design), and *reuse* difficulties.

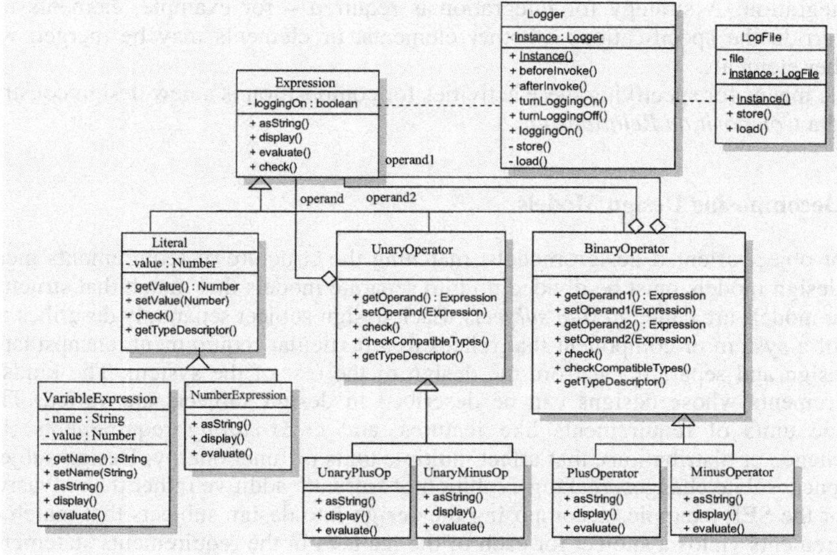

Fig. 1. SEE Design in UML

Design patterns [Gam94] prove useful in alleviating some of these problems in many cases, but their use results in the exchange of one set of problems for another. Problems with the use of design patterns are dealt with in [Cla99].

3. The Model

The approach to addressing the structural mismatch problem described here is based on providing means of further decomposing artefacts written in one paradigm so that they can align with those written in another. This suggests that it must be possible to decompose object-oriented designs in a manner that reifies the structure of requirements specifications. Requirements are generally described by feature and capability. So, this means that object-oriented designs must also decompose design models by feature and capability, thereby encapsulating and separating their designs. Since requirements are encapsulated, decomposition in this way removes the scattering of requirements across the full design. It also removes the tangling of multiple requirements in individual design units, as requirements are separated into different design models.

Decomposition in this manner requires corresponding composition support, as object-oriented designs still must be understood together as a complete design. New constructs are required for the UML to specify how design models are composed. Composing design models involves two fundamental activities:

Identification of Corresponding Elements: decomposing design models based on the structure of requirements specifications may result in overlapping parts, where there are different views of those parts in different design models. In order to successfully compose design models, those overlapping parts (called *corresponding elements*) must be identified.

Integration: A strategy for integration is required – for example, elements may override the specifications of other elements, or elements may be merged with other elements.

The means for specifying these activities for composition is a new design construct called a *Composition Relationship*.

3.1. Decomposing Design Models

For object-oriented design models, matching the structure of requirements means that design models must be divided up into separate models that match that structure. These models are called *design subjects.* Each design subject separately describes that part of a system or component that relates to a particular requirement, encapsulating its design and separating it from the design of the rest of the system. The kinds of requirements whose designs can be described in design subjects are varied. They include units of requirements like features, and *cross-cutting* requirements (like persistence or distribution), that affect multiple units of functionality. Design subjects also encapsulate changes, making evolution of software additive rather than invasive.

For the SEE example, decomposing the design into design subjects that match the requirements yields a subject for each of the features in the requirements statement – a Kernel subject for the basic expression, one each for the check, evaluate and display features, and a subject for the logging capability. Fig. 2 illustrates the designs for the subjects that work directly with expressions – Kernel, Evaluate, ChckSyntax and Display. Neither the full class models, nor the supporting collaboration diagrams, are illustrated for space reasons. This example illustrates how designs for particular features can be encapsulated, and contain the design only from the perspective of that feature, regardless of the overlap in concepts across the subjects. This is one of the strengths of the subject-oriented design model – each of the different parts of a system under design may model the same concepts in whatever way is most appropriate for that subject's view or purpose. Even in the small example of the SEE illustrated in Fig. 2, there are differences in the hierarchies specified in different subjects, and differences in naming of elements that support the same concept.

In Fig. 3, we see how a cross-cutting requirement such as logging operations can be designed separately from the operations to be logged – in this case, the operations on the expression classes. In this example, UML templates in the collaboration diagram are used to design the logging behaviour in relation to any operation to be logged. Semantics relating to merge integration of operations also influence this design, where a new operation is created to support the specification of merged behaviour. In this case, `loggedOp()` is created to define the additional logging behaviour, while `_loggedOp()` represents the re-named actual operation from a subject merged with this pattern.

Conceptually, a design subject can be written in any design language, but the focus of this paper is the UML. A UML design subject can also conceptually contain any valid UML diagrams. Scoping for this work, however, involved selecting a subset of the full set of UML diagrams, and is detailed in Section 4 "UML Metamodel

Extensions". Application of this approach to other design languages, and to all UML diagrams remain interesting issues for future research.

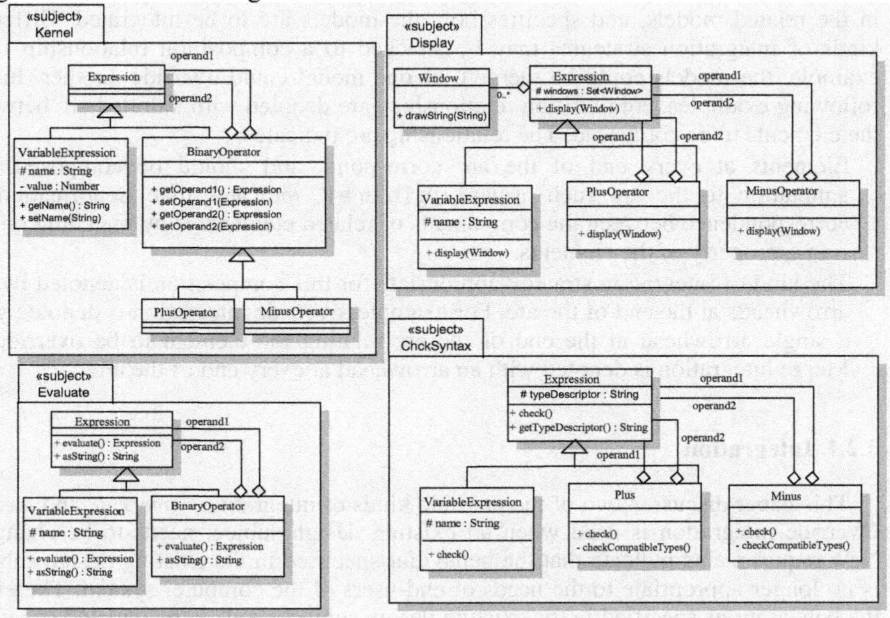

Fig. 2. Decomposing SEE design into different subjects with *differing hierarchies*

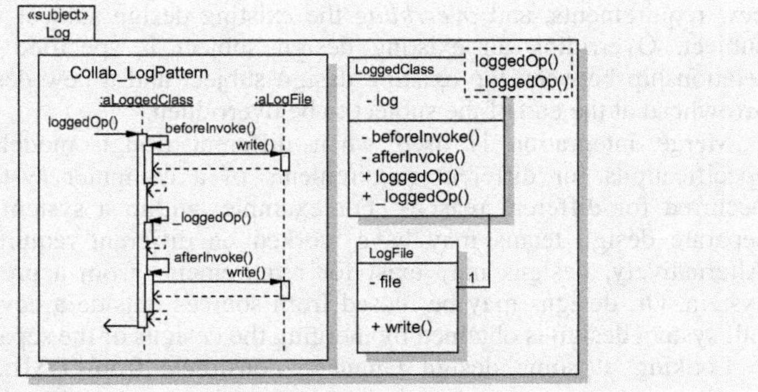

Fig. 3. Cross-Cutting Requirement as a Separate Subject

3.2. Composing Design Models

Decomposing design models brings many benefits relating to comprehensibility, traceability, evolution and reuse. However, designs that have been decomposed must also be integrated at some later stage in order to understand the design of the system as a whole. This is required for reasons such as verification, or to support a developer's full understanding of the design semantics and the impact of composition.

A composition relationship between design models specifies how those design models are to be composed. The relationship identifies corresponding design elements in the related models, and specifies how the models are to be integrated. Different kinds of integration strategies may be attached to a composition relationship - for example, the models could be merged, or one model could override another. In the following examples, composition relationships are denoted with a dotted arc between the elements to be composed. The relationship arc indicates:

Elements at every end of the arc correspond, and should be composed. An annotation to the arc such as `match[name]`, indicates that identification of correspondence between the components of related elements is by matching on the `name` property of the elements.

The kind of integration strategy appropriate for this composition is denoted by the arrowheads at the end of the arc. For example, override integration is denoted with a single arrowhead at the end of the arc relating the element to be overridden. Merge integration is denoted with an arrowhead at every end of the arc.

3.2.1. Integration

This paper discusses two of the possible kinds of integration - *override* and *merge.* Override integration is used when an existing design subject needs to be changed. New requirements indicate that the behaviour specified in the existing design subject is no longer appropriate to the needs of end-users of the computer system. Therefore the behaviour as specified in the existing design subject needs to be updated to reflect the new requirements. Changing the existing design subject is done by creating a new design subject that contains the design of the appropriate behaviour to support the new requirements, and *overriding* the existing design subject with this new design subject. Overriding an existing design subject is specified with a composition relationship between the existing design subject and a new design subject, with an arrowhead at the end of the subject to be overridden.

Merge integration is used when different design models (subjects) contain specifications for different requirements of a computer system. This may have occurred for different reasons. For example, within a system development effort, separate design teams may have worked on different requirements concurrently. Alternatively, designs may exist for requirements from a previous version of the system. Or, designs may be reused from sources outside a development effort. The full system design is obtained by merging the designs of the separate design subjects.

Looking at some design language constructs from UML, for *classifiers* and *attributes*, merge integration indicates that the composed design contains a single element, whose property values are obtained from the subjects connected by the composition relationship. Where a conflict exists between the property values of corresponding elements, reconciliation strategies may be attached to the composition relationship. Merging corresponding *operations* indicates that the specification of the (unified) operation results from the aggregation of the specifications of those operations in all of the related subjects.

In this section, we look at examples from the SEE of merging subjects that require reconciliation, the impact of merging corresponding operations, and the use of merge integration patterns for cross-cutting functionality.

3.2.1.1. Merge with Reconciliation Required

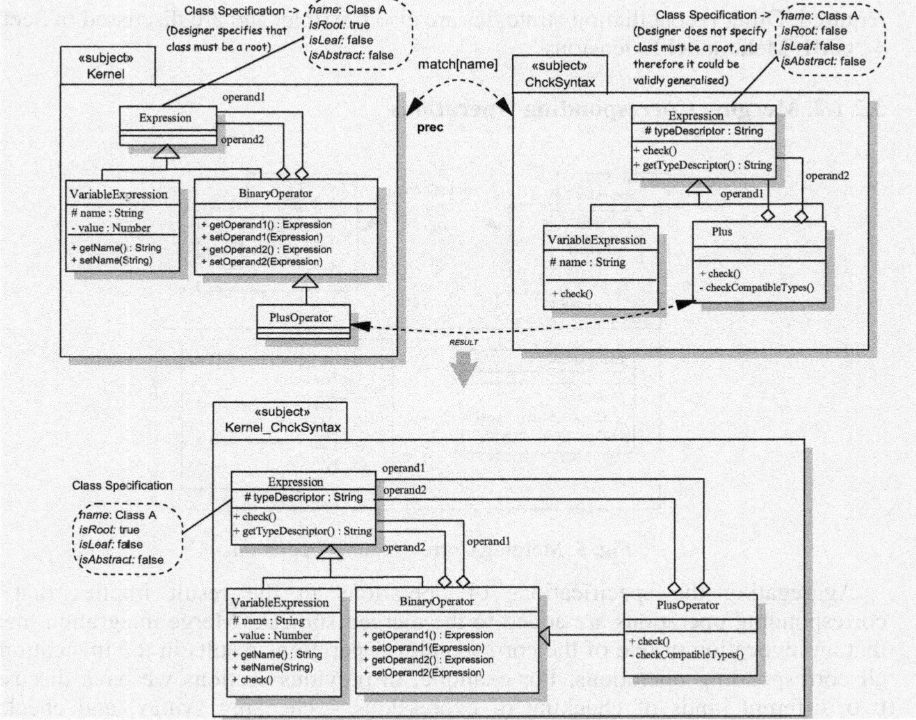

Fig. 4. Example of Merge Integration with Reconciliation

For the SEE, merging, for example, the separately designed Kernel and ChckSyntax subjects is specified with a composition relationship between the two. In Fig. 4, this is illustrated with the two-way arc relating Kernel and ChckSyntax. The `match[name]` criteria annotating the composition relationship indicates that those elements within the two subjects which have the same name are deemed to be corresponding. Further specification of corresponding elements is required in this example, as the Kernel subject named its class to handle the plus operator `PlusOperator`, but the ChckSyntax subject named it `Plus`. This is handled with an additional composition relationship between those elements.

A further look at how the designers of the subjects specified the class `Expression` indicates that the values of their properties are not the same. The impact of merge on classifiers is that a single classifier of the corresponding set of classifiers appears in the result. Since the specifications are not identical, a conflict is encountered which must be resolved. In this case, precedence has been given to the Kernel subject (indicated with the `prec` keyword at the Kernel end of the composition relationship), and so the values of the properties of `Expression` in the result are those of the specification in the Kernel subject. This reconciliation strategy also applies to the components of the related subjects, and therefore, the name of the class handling the plus operator is `PlusOperator` in the result. The composition relationship between `Plus` and `PlusOperator` could have defined its own reconciliation strategy to override the one defined by their owners if that was required. Other reconciliation strategies are also possible, and are discussed in Section 4 "UML Metamodel Extensions".

3.2.1.2. Merging Corresponding Operations

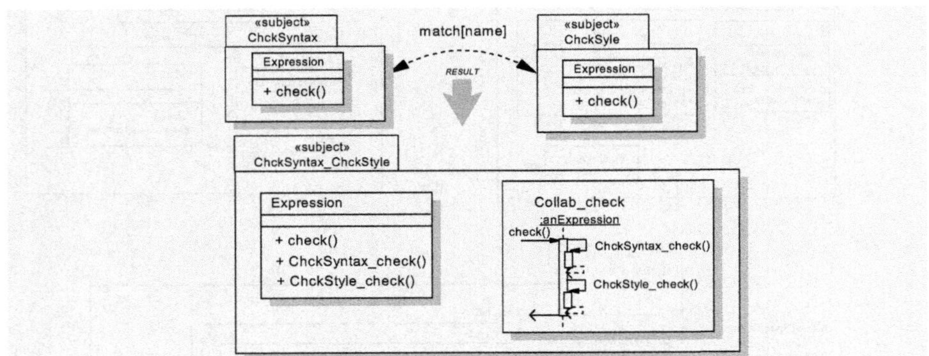

Fig. 5. Merging Corresponding Operations

Aggregating the specifications of operations in the result implies that all corresponding operations are added to the merged subject. Merge integration means that an invocation of one of the corresponding operations results in the invocation of all corresponding operations. For example, in previous sections we have discussed two different kinds of checking of expressions – checking syntax, and checking conformance with a particular style. Merging these checking subjects, as illustrated in Fig. 5, results in both kinds of checking being performed on invocation of either one. This example illustrates where renaming of actual operations occurs, together with the creation of a new operation, `check()`, used to specify the merged behaviour. Where operations have a return type, the default behaviour is that the value returned by the *last* operation run is returned. The subject-oriented programming domain also supports *summary functions* [Tar00], which synthesise the return values of each of the operations to return a value appropriate for the collaborating operations. This approach is under design for the subject-oriented design domain.

In this example, the collaboration indicating the merged behaviour of the operations is generated automatically, with the ordering of the execution of the operations set arbitrarily. Where the order of execution is important, a collaboration may be attached to the composition relationship indicating that order.

3.2.1.3. Merge Integration Patterns

For cross-cutting functionality such as logging operations, we saw how the use of templates as placeholders for elements with which the cross-cutting functionality will interact supports the independent design of such functions. In the case of logging, Fig. 3 showed operations to be logged as a template, with the logging behaviour designed around that template. Composition relationships may be used to compose such subjects with subjects that require cross-cutting functionality. The merge integration specification of the composition relationship may be defined as a pattern of integration, where the merge semantics "bind" the appropriate elements in a subject with the template elements in the cross-cutting subject.

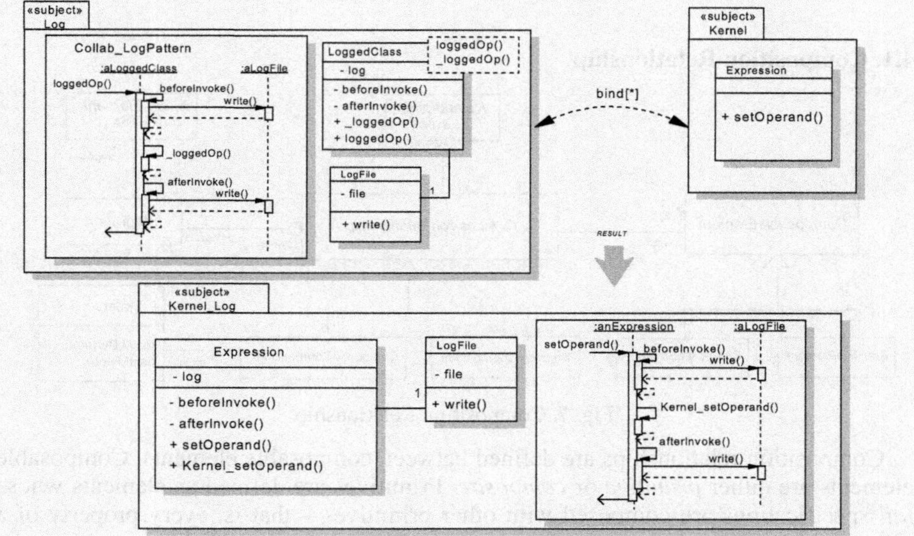

Fig. 6. Integrating Logging with Kernel

In Fig. 6, this is illustrated for the logging functionality of the SEE. In this example, the (partially illustrated) Kernel subject is merged with the Log subject containing an operation template. The "*" parameter of the `bind` annotation to the composition relationship indicates that all operations in the merging subject should (separately) replace the related pair of templates appropriately. That is, the actual operation is renamed in order to replace `_loggedOp()`, and a new operation of the same name as the actual operation is created to replace `loggedOp()`. A collaboration is added for each operation indicating the changed behaviour as a result of the merge with logging functionality – as illustrated for `setOperand()`.

4. UML Metamodel Extensions

The UML is the OMG's standard language for object-oriented analysis and design specifications [UML99]. The OMG currently defines the language using a *metamodel*. The metamodel defines the syntax and semantics of the UML, and is itself described using the UML [UML99]. The metamodel is described in a "semi-formal" [UML99] manner, using the views:

Abstract syntax: This view is a UML class diagram showing the metaclasses defining the language constructs (e.g. Class, Attribute etc.), and their relationships.

Well-formedness rules: A set of well-formedness rules, (with an informal description and an OCL definition), describes the static semantics of the metamodel, specifying constraints on instances of the metaclasses

Semantics: The meanings of the constructs are described using natural language.

In this paper, a similar style to that of the UML is used to describe syntax and semantics composition relationships. Because of space constraints, this paper contains an overview of the model. Full details and rules are in [Cla00].

4.1. Composition Relationship

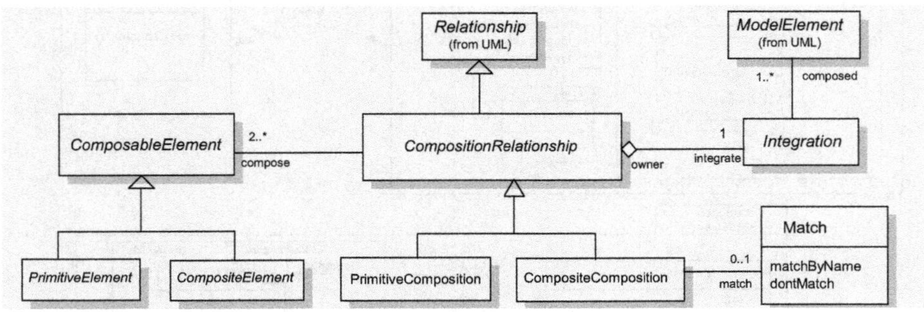

Fig. 7. Composition Relationship

Composition relationships are defined between composable elements. Composable elements are either *primitive* or *composite.* Primitives are defined as elements whose *full* specifications are composed with other primitives – that is, every property of a primitive is subject to integration semantics. For the purposes of composition, the following elements are considered to be primitives: Attributes, Operations, Associations and Interactions. There are, however, some elements that contain other elements, and cannot be considered as primitive. For example, a class contains attributes and operations, and those attributes and operations must be examined individually for correspondence matching and integration. Such elements are called *composites.* Composites are defined as elements whose components are not considered part of the full specification of the composite and therefore are considered separately for composition. Composites may contain composites and primitives, and therefore may be considered as a standard tree structure. For the purposes of composition, composites are: Subjects[3], Classifiers and Collaborations.

Elements are composed with their *corresponding* elements. Elements are said to "correspond" when they "match" for the purposes of composition, where correspondence matching specification is part of the composition relationship. A composition relationship is a new kind of relationship for the UML, and is subclassed from the Relationship metaclass (see Fig. 7).

A primitive composition relationship is a composition relationship between primitives, and a composite composition relationship is a composition relationship between composites. Composition only applies to those elements (and their components) that participate in a composition relationship. Composable elements explicitly related by a composition relationship are said to correspond, and are integrated based on the semantics of the particular integration strategy attached to the composition relationship. A more general approach to identifying corresponding elements is possible with the Match metaclass, which supports the specification of match criteria for components of composite elements related by a composition

[3] A "Subject" is defined as a stereotype of "Package"

relationship. Integration as specified in Fig. 7 is an abstract metaclass, where it is intended that it be specialised to cater for the particular integration specification required. The default semantics for integration strategies is that a composition process results in the composition of elements to new model elements, as defined by the "composed" relationship from the Integration metaclass.

Some examples of well-formedness rules for composition relationships are:

Composition relationships may only be specified between elements of the same type.

The semantics for integration specifications must specify composed elements as the same type as input elements.

Composed elements are in a different namespace from any of the input elements.

4.1.1. Semantics for Identifying Corresponding Elements

Correspondence between elements is established either directly with a primitive composition relationship, or indirectly based on matching from the specification of the relationship between their owners. Correspondence between elements is not possible where the elements are components of non-corresponding composites. Elements that participate in a composition relationship with a `dontMatch` specification do not correspond. Integration semantics are defined by subclasses of the Integration metaclass.

4.2. Override Integration

Override integration is used when an existing design subject needs to be changed. A composition relationship identifies the subject to be overridden, and the overriding subject. Override integration is subclassed from the Integration metaclass (see Fig. 8).

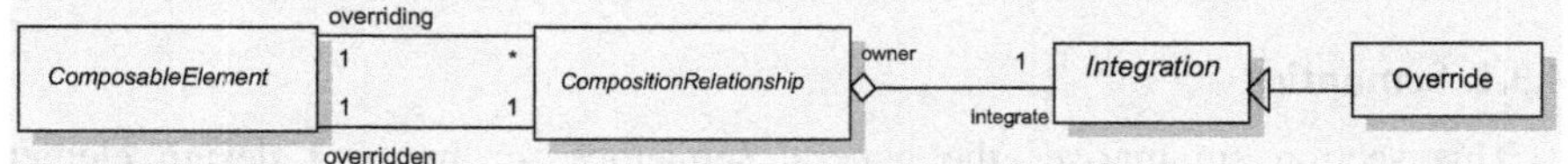

Fig. 8. Override Integration Metaclasses

4.2.1. Semantics

This section summarises the general semantics for overriding design elements that apply to each element type. Override integration is more fully defined in [Cla00]. For each element in the overridden subject, the existence of a corresponding element in the overriding subject results in the specification of the former element to be changed to that of the latter element in the composed result. Elements in an overridden composite that are not involved in a correspondence match remain unchanged, and are added to the composed result. Elements that are components of an overriding composite and are not involved in a correspondence match are added to the composed result. Overriding elements may not result in name clashes in the resulting subject. The resulting subject must conform to the well-formedness rules of the UML.

4.3. Merge Integration

Merge integration is used when different design models (subjects) contain specifications for different requirements of a computer system. Merging design subjects is done by specifying composition relationships, with merge integration, between the subjects to be merged.

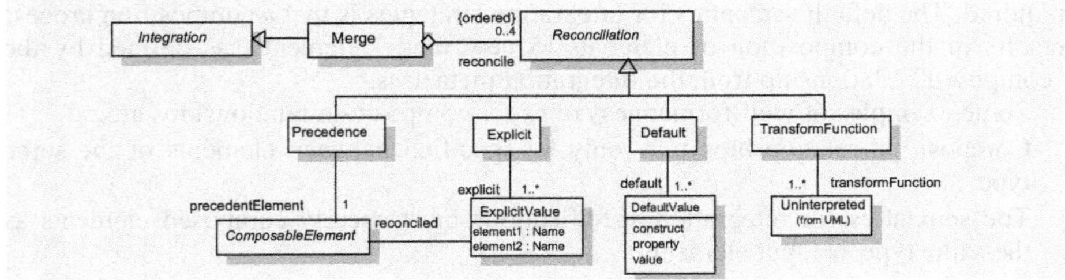

Fig. 9. Merge Integration with Reconciliation

Composition relationships identify the subjects to be merged, and the corresponding design elements within those subjects that should be merged. For many elements (for example, classifiers and attributes) this means that the corresponding elements appear once in the merged result. In cases where differences in the specifications of corresponding design elements need to be resolved, composition relationships with merge integration specify guidelines for the reconciliation. The metaclass class diagram in Fig. 9 illustrates merge integration as a subclass of the Integration metaclass attached to the composition relationship metaclass, and also illustrates the metaclasses required to support the reconciliation of elements.

When corresponding operations are merged, all of the merged operations are executed on receipt of a message that may have activated one of the operations in an input subject. Collaborations may be attached to the merge relationship to determine the order of execution, and patterns of collaborations are supported with pattern merge relationships that identify elements to replace template elements (see Fig. 10).

4.3.1. Semantics

This section summarises the general semantics for merging design elements. Merge integration is more fully defined in [Cla00].

Operations: Corresponding operations are each added to the merged subject. Where no collaboration is attached to a merge integration specification, the behaviour of the merged subject in relation to the merged operations is specified with a new collaboration specification. This collaboration specifies that invocation of one of the corresponding operations results in invocation of all corresponding operations. This is achieved by creating a new operation to specify the collaboration, and renaming the corresponding operations (see Fig. 5 for example).

When the order of execution of corresponding operations is important, a collaboration specifying this order should be attached to the merge integration. In this case, the attached collaboration is added to the merged subject as the specification of the behaviour of corresponding operations. With pattern merge integration, corresponding operations are substituted for template pairs (one operation represents the actual renamed replacing operation, and one operation whose realization is specified by the collaboration) defined in pattern collaborations. For each instance of the collaborating pattern, a collaboration is added to the merged subject that defines the execution of the actual corresponding operations. Use of templates in collaborations, together with pattern merge relationships, support the merge of *cross-*

cutting operations – that is, operations designed to supplement the behaviour of multiple operations in a subject, and therefore may be considered as a pattern.

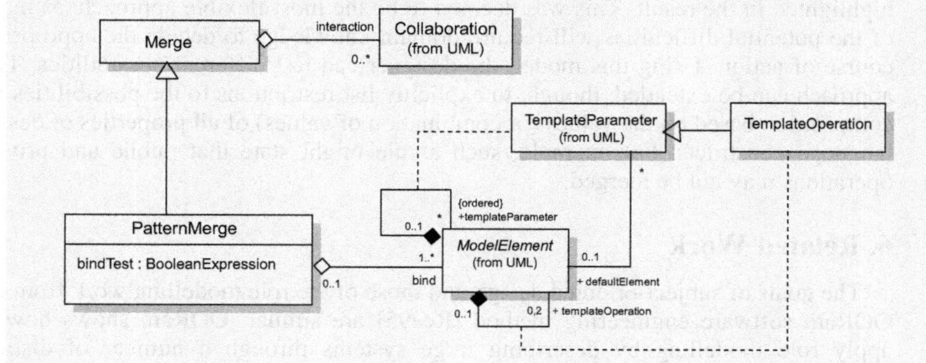

Fig. 10. Merge Integration: Collaborations and Patterns

Elements other than Operations: For all elements other than operations, corresponding elements appear once in the merged subject. Any conflicts in the specifications of corresponding elements are reconciled prior to addition to the merged subject. Reconciliation strategies may be attached to the merge integration specification as follows: One subject's specifications take precedence in the event of a conflict; A transformation function may be attached to a merge relationship that, when run against the conflicting elements, results in a reconciled element; An explicit specification of the reconciled element may be attached to a merge relationship; Default values may be specified which are to be used in the event of a conflict in specific properties of elements.

General Semantics of Merge for All Elements: Elements that are components of merging composites and are not involved in a correspondence match are added to the composed result. Merging elements may not result in name clashes in the resulting subject. The resulting subject must conform to the well-formedness rules of the UML.

5. Discussion

One of the strengths of the subject-oriented design model is its support for the design of overlapping concepts from different perspectives in different subjects. The model supports differences in the specifications of those overlapping parts, with techniques to handle conflicts. In addition, references to elements that are composed with other elements (and therefore, potentially changed in some way) are changed to refer to the composed element. For example, if an attribute has a classifier type which is integrated with another type, then the attribute's type refers to the integrated type. However, with composition of this nature, there is potential for the designer to specify a result that may not be well-formed from a UML perspective. For example, a root class with subclasses defined in one subject may be overridden with a class which is defined as a leaf class. This clearly is incorrect, and the result is ill-formed. There are many such examples across all the UML constructs. The current subject-oriented design model allows complete freedom[4] to the designer to identify corresponding elements, and compose, as desired, with breakages to the well-formedness rules highlighted in the result. This was deemed to be the most flexible approach, as many of the potential difficulties will require domain knowledge to decide the appropriate course of action. Using this model, the designer can test different possibilities. This approach can be extended, though, to explicitly list restrictions to the possibilities for composition based on the values (or combination of values) of all properties of design language constructs. For example, such a rule might state that public and private operations may not be merged.

6. Related Work

The goals of subject-oriented design and those of the role modelling work from the OORam software engineering method [Ree95] are similar. OORam shows how to apply role modelling by describing large systems through a number of distinct models. Derived models can be synthesised from base role models, as specified by *synthesis relations*. Synthesis relations can be specified both between models and between roles within the models, much like our composition relationships. The synthesis process is equivalent to the synthesis of subjects defined with a merge interaction specification. The subject-oriented design model distinguishes itself with its notion of *override* integration, and with the potential provided by composition patterns to provide for more complex possibilities for combination patterns.

Role modelling with Catalysis [Dso98] is based on UML, using *horizontal* and *vertical slices* to separate a package's contents according to concerns. Composition of artefacts is based on a definition of the UML *import* relationship, called *join*. The designer forms a new design containing the simple union of design elements, with re-naming in the event of unintended name clashes. This approach is similar to the meaning of a merge interaction specification with property matching by name. Reusable design components are supported in Catalysis with template frameworks, containing placeholders that may be imported, with appropriate substitutions, into model frameworks. This is similar to merging reusable design subjects that have no overlapping design elements, possibly using composition patterns.

The subject-oriented design model is closely related to the approach to decomposition and composition of programming models as defined by subject-oriented programming [Har93]. The composition rules governing the composition of subject programs can be derived from the composition relationships of the design model. Use of both approaches supports the alignment of requirements concerns throughout the lifecycle, as described in [Cla99]. Another programming model that has many similarities (in terms of the goals they are trying to achieve) with the subject-oriented design model is the work on aspect-oriented programming [Kic97]. Cross-cutting concerns are separated from "base programs", and are subsequently composed together in a "weaving" process. This is analogous to the separation of the design of cross-cutting concerns within the subject-oriented design model, and subsequent composition with subjects requiring such cross-cutting behaviour.

[4] The designer must conform to the well-formedness rules for composition relationships – not all of which are listed in this paper for space reasons.

7. Conclusions and Future Work

Standard object-oriented designs do not align well with requirements. Requirements are typically decomposed by function, feature or other kind of user-level concern, whereas object-oriented designs are always decomposed by class.

This misalignment results in a host of well-known problems, including weak traceability, poor comprehensibility, poor evolvability, low reuse and high impact of change. In this paper, *subject-oriented design* is described as a means of achieving alignment between requirements and object-oriented designs, and hence alleviating these problems. This alignment is possible because requirements criteria can be used to decompose subject-oriented designs into *subjects*, which can then be synthesised as specified by composition relationships. Subjects can be designed independently, even if they interact or cut across one another.

Remaining work includes defining the impact of composition on all UML design models. In addition, a formal algebra defining the rules associated with multiple compositions of multiple subjects is required. Automation of the link from subject-oriented design to subject-oriented programming is also an area worth pursuing. This includes automating the generation of subject code from subject designs, and generation of composition rules from composition relationships. Another possibility for environment support is the extent to the subject-oriented design model may be used as a design model for aspect-oriented programming. Similarities in goals between the approaches provide considerable encouragement for links between them.

Acknowledgements

Many thanks to Rob Walker and the anonymous reviewers for their comments.

References

[Cla99] S. Clarke, W. Harrison, H. Ossher, P. Tarr. *"Subject-Oriented Design: Towards Improved Alignment of Requirements, Design and Code"* In Proc. OOPSLA, 1999

[Cla00] S. Clarke. *"Composition of Object-Oriented Software Design Models"* PhD Thesis in preparation, from Dublin City University, 2000

[Dso98] D. D'Souza, A.C. Wills. *"Objects, Components and Frameworks with UML. The Catalysis Approach"* Addison-Wesley, 1998

[Gam94] E. Gamma, R. Helm, R. Johnson, J. Vlissides. *"Design Patterns. Elements of Reusable Object-Oriented Software"* Addison-Wesley 1994

[Har93] W. Harrison, H. Ossher. *"Subject-Oriented Programming (a critique of pure objects)"* In Proc. OOPSLA, 1993

[Kic97] G. Kiczales, J. Lamping, A. Mendhekar, C. Maeda, C. Lopes, J.-M. Loingtier, J. Irwin. *"Aspect-Oriented Programming"* In Proc. ECOOP, 1997

[Ree95] T. Reenskaug, P. Wold, O.A. Lehne. *"Working with Objects: The OORam Software Engineering Method".* Prentice Hall, 1995

[Tar00] P. Tarr, H. Ossher. *"Hyper/J™User and Installation Manual"* http://www.research.ibm.com/hyperspace

[UML99] *"OMG Unified Modeling Language Specification"* Version 1.3. 1999

Extreme Programming and Modelling?

Panel

Moderator:
Perdita Stevens

Panellists:
Marko Boger, Stephen Mellor, Alan Cameron Wills

1 Motivation for the Panel

Extreme Programming (XP: see `http://www.xprogramming.com`), developed by Kent Beck and others, has recently taken the OO development world by storm. It can be seen as an antidote to over-documented, inflexible development processes; by taking certain good practices (testing, iteration and code reviewing, for example) to extremes, its adherents claim to achieve better results at lower cost.

This panel aims to explore the tensions, and the possibilities for synergy, between XP and the use of UML. The obvious difficulty for such a panel at a UML event is that those present, both panellists and audience, are likely to be at least broadly favourable to the use of UML. This paper therefore includes a "Devil's Advocate" statement, in addition to more measured contributions from our panellists.

2 How to Take Part

The format of this panel will be similar to the BBC programme "Any Questions?". That is,

- questions will be submitted in advance by the audience (panellists may not themselves submit questions, but anyone may use any available means to induce others to submit questions);
- an interesting subset of these questions will be selected and ordered by the chair (but not passed to the panel in advance);
- the questioners will be invited to put their questions in person;
- each panellist will be invited to give a brief response (preferably answering the question, but the panellists in the original version are politicians, so some bending of the question is to be expected!)

To submit a question: Write it, and your name, on a piece of paper and put it in the box at conference reception – or hand it direct to me, Perdita Stevens.[1]

[1] The woman with the long plait: I apologise to any others who fit that description for any inconvenience caused.

A. Evans, S. Kent and B. Selic (Eds.): ≪UML≫ 2000, LNCS 1939, pp. 353–358, 2000.

3 Devil's Advocate Statement: Why XPers Should Eschew UML

[Disclaimer: this statement does not represent my views, and is not intended to represent the views of anyone else. It is intended to make a point by exaggeration.]

It is unnecessary, and therefore a waste of time, to develop any design documentation, let alone draw collections of UML models. The code and its tests should be all the documentation that is needed.

Worse, the perceived need to develop such diagrams may lead to design decisions being made before the information on which they depend is available; and once a design decision has been documented in a beautiful diagram (which even, or perhaps especially, with the assistance of a tool will have taken someone a considerable time), attempts to change the design will encounter resistance. Design should be developed gradually as the project progresses. Only after a problem clearly exists and can be analysed should a design solution be introduced. Don't guess: You Ain't Gonna Need It.

Design should happen between consenting adults: participants in any discussion about design should be standing around a whiteboard or similar, and should have a shared understanding of the problem and the constraints. Requiring participants to use a particular, formally defined "language" to communicate in this situation is nothing but a handicap. Anyone who has participated in such a design session knows that ad hoc notations, supplemented by gestures and verbal explanations, are perfectly adequate, and have the advantage of ultimate flexibility.

UML, with its esoteric collection of notations, is particularly likely to be a distraction from the real task. Discussion can too easily veer off into arguing over what generalisation of use cases really means, how to show complex iterations on a sequence diagram, or exactly how to define a subsystem.

4 Statement by Marko Boger

Extreme Modelling: Applying the Tenets of XP to Modelling

Extreme Modelling is a new software development process. Put simply, it is a synthesis of model-based processes and Extreme Programming (XP).

Model-based processes like the Rational Unified Process (RUP) or Catalysis usually are based on the Unified Modelling Language (UML). They have the advantage of having an expressive language for designing and communicating the architecture of object oriented software systems. But they have the disadvantage that UML models can not be tested or verified and that the gap between UML and programming languages is rather large.

XP, on the other hand, is centred around code. One of its most important corner stones are tests that are executed on the code over and over again. This provides confidence in the developed system and flexibility to change it. But it lacks an abstract notation for communicating or refactoring the design.

Extreme Modelling closes the gap between these two and combines their advantages. For this to be successful two requirements have to be met: models need to be executable and they must be testable. While the traditional way only requires a good drawing tool and XP only requires a compiler and a simple test framework, Extreme Modelling requires intensive support by an integrated tool that is able to execute UML models, test models, support the transition from model to code and keep code and model in sync. It requires intensive tool support, some of which already exist, others are still under construction.

This lays the foundation for a new development process called Extreme Modelling that allows a smooth transition from modelling to implementation phase and combines the advantage of having a modelling language with the power of XP.

About Marko Boger Marko Boger is co-founder of the company Gentleware, that develops UML tools and offers consulting and courses for Java and UML. He is author of the book Java in Distributed Systems (in German, to appear in English) and chief developer in the open-source UML-tool project ArgoUML. Marko Boger and colleagues at the University of Hamburg are authors of the Extreme Modelling synthesis.

5 Statement by Stephen Mellor

The critical assumption that underlies XP is that change is cheap.

One reason for building a model is that it's (claimed that it's) cheaper to build the model and change it, than it is to change the code. This comes about because the level of abstraction is higher and the amount of detail less. These factors remain as true as they ever were under XP.

But XP de-emphasises modelling because a model is not the code, and it is difficult and time-consuming to maintain both the model and the code, and to ensure they remain in synch. This certainly makes sense while the UML is a mere software sketching tool.

However, the UML will be executable, as soon as the semantics for actions are included. Under this set of circumstances, *the UML model is the system*, not the code.

At this point, the principles of XP apply to models, and not code. And these principles apply in pretty much the same way: some work, some are questionable, and some are a rationalisation for hacking.

About Stephen Mellor Stephen Mellor is vice-president of Project Technology, Inc., and is best known as one of the developers of the Schlaer-Mellor Method. He is active in the OMG standardisation of UML, and has recently been working on semantics for actions in UML.

6 Statement by Alan Cameron Wills

Is it consistent to believe both in the principles of eXtreme Programming, and in the usefulness of rigorous modelling? I have found it to be so. I believe the two approaches have much in common; the big difference is in where their proponents are coming from. (My ideas on rigorous modelling (RM) are represented in the D'Souza and Wills book *Objects Components and Frameworks in UML: the Catalysis approach.*)

XP says we should write tests before we code. Rigorous modelling (RM) says we should write specifications before we code. RM specifications might be in OCL (UML's language of constraints), but the motivation is to be able to build tests. Why use OCL when we'll have to code the tests anyway? Well, it's much more succinct, and this enables us to do a broad overview of the system requirements as quickly as possible, before we implement our first "spike". Going straight for writing the tests would push us into a depth-first approach. So RM and XP tell roughly the same story about testing; followers of XP may gain some benefit from outlining tests at a high level in OCL at first.

XP says we should reduce the risk of building something useless by getting feedback from the customer as early and as often as possible. RM says we should reduce the risk of building something useless by writing an unambiguous specification early on. While the customer may not understand the notation of the spec, the process of writing it yields a lot of questions arising from ambiguities and inconsistencies in the customer's initial statements. I don't believe in spending a lot of time on this, nor in getting it complete and correct and signed off before proceeding; but I have seen analysts getting value out of RM across the breadth of the requirements at a much earlier stage than they could have done by writing a spike solution; and achieving a much more consistent and complete view at an early stage than stories can provide. So the aim of both approaches is to clarify our understanding of what the customer really needs; RM offers some ways of doing this more effectively early on.

XP and most RM methods differ on whether any documentation is required that is not directly part of either the tests or the code; and whether any notation is required that isn't the programming language.

But let's be clear that this question isn't about whether or not we should draw pictures. Many programming languages have a graphical part or a graphical representation: for example, the VisualAge (etc) editors for Java Beans; many workflow languages; traditional program flowcharts. Conversely, there are modelling languages that are not pictorial – e.g. VDM and Z, widely used in the safety critical systems world. Myself, I don't think that rendering a program in pictorial terms provides any great benefit by itself: programming languages are an excellent medium for expressing and thinking about programs, and are far richer in structure than a picture. Modelling languages (like UML) are most effective for helping think about certain aspects of the program at a high level, and thus help the designers to get the details right.

For this reason, I don't find tools like Together/J very useful. This tool (like some others) keeps the code and the documentation constantly in step, and does it automatically. You're effectively programming with UML; it assumes you have nothing to say that isn't reflected directly in program code.

I find several strong reasons for writing and keeping some documentation which is not directly realised in the program code – some of it in UML. I do this in conjunction with the other practices of XP. I don't do any of these in more depth than is necessary to achieve the purpose.

- Domain models. RM provides methods of describing business processes separately from any code. When there are several systems situated within overlapping business domains, it is useful to have a common vocabulary that is independent of the particular systems. Rather than just writing a natural-language glossary, a rigorous model helps express the relationships well enough to avoid misunderstandings and inconsistent implementations.
- Enterprise integration. Defining the protocols and business rules whereby multiple applications and business departments interoperate. Such a model has to be separate from the code of any component: they may all be written in different languages, and use different internal representations of the concepts; the model is about their language of intercommunication. It is possible and desirable to write tests for conformance to such a model; but the tests can be difficult to understand and manipulate intellectually, without a succinct modelling notation. For this purpose, I would like a tool that keeps code and diagrams in step: but the code is the test software, not any of the implementations!
- Component interfaces. Same again, with a different slant on the motivation. To build very flexible software, I rely on encapsulation (separating description of externally visible behaviour from internal implementation) and pluggability (aka polymorphism: the ability of one component to work in conjunction with many others, by depending only on their external behaviour). Therefore I need a way of being precise about behaviour. Ideally, behaviour is described by tests; but I can also describe them more succinctly in UML and OCL.
- High level designs. I want to be able to refer to groups of objects as one thing, even though there may be no single corresponding object in the code; and groups of interactions as one. I want to be able to map out the concepts of my design and their interrelationships; and later introduce new classes to improve performance, flexibility etc. But I want to keep the original plan so as to make the intentions clear to maintainers.
- Design patterns. As my design develops, various patterns will emerge: common solutions to common problems across the design. Patterns should be expressed separately from the context of any specific application. They form the essentials of the architecture of the system.

The practice of rigorous modelling includes rules for the composition of partial models – used to allow requirements to be expressed from the points of view of different clients; and for the transformation of simple high-level models to more elaborate implementations. These techniques can both be realised in test code if so desired. Thus RM techniques inform XP.

To summarise:

- RM complements and provides some techniques to enhance XP;
- the combination of RM and XP is not about translating UML directly into implementation code;
- I disagree with XP only in the extremity of "no documentation"; nevertheless, documentation outside the code should be minimised, and should serve a clear purpose.

About Alan Cameron Wills Alan Cameron Wills is a consultant working with Trireme.com, which offers consultancy and training in component based and object oriented design, and on their use within a business. He has been interested in the application of formal methods to object orientation since his PhD, undertaken in Cliff Jones' group at Manchester University. He is one of the developers of the Catalysis method.

Interacting Subsystems in UML

Gunnar Övergaard[1] and Karin Palmkvist[2]

[1] Royal Institute of Technology, Stockholm, Sweden
[2] Enea Data AB, Stockholm, Sweden

Abstract. In this paper we give a description of the subsystem construct in the Unified Modeling Language, emphasizing its dynamic aspects, thus giving a detailed description of the semantics of interaction with subsystems. Depending on whether the surroundings of the subsystem make use of public elements in the subsystem or not, the subsystem is considered to be open or closed, respectively. This leads to two different ways to use the services of the subsystem: either importing it and directly accessing its public elements, or associating it and only communicating with the subsystem itself. We also discuss some implications which closed subsystems have on collaborations.

1 Introduction

The development of large systems can be done in several different ways, using a variety of techniques. Most of these techniques are either based on assembling predefined components, where the system is composed of smaller, already existing systems, or based on the principle "divide and conquer", where the system is divided into smaller parts before each part is developed using traditional techniques. If one part is still too big, it can be decomposed further into smaller parts until each part is of a size that is suitable to be developed using traditional techniques. In each case, the requirements on the overall system must be transformed into requirements on the parts, so that each part can be designed and tested separately.

The Unified Modeling Language (UML) [2] is a general-purpose modelling language which can be used in almost any object-oriented development process. The language consists of a set of constructs common to most object-oriented modelling languages, as well as constructs for more specific purposes, like modelling large systems. In UML, the main construct for modelling large systems is the subsystem construct, which is used for expressing parts of a system. How these parts are identified, and if the development process is based on a "top-down" or a "bottom-up" approach is not prescribed by UML; the subsystem construct can be used in both cases.

In this paper we focus on the dynamic aspects of subsystems, more specifically on the semantics of interaction with subsystems. We discuss different ways to communicate with subsystems, and also what implication collaborations have on the subsystem semantics. Some of these ideas originate from [1] but they have been further elaborated and formalized.

A. Evans, S. Kent and B. Selic (Eds.): ≪UML≫ 2000, LNCS 1939, pp. 359–368, 2000.

This paper is organized as follows: In the following section we start by giving a description of the subsystem construct of UML. Sections 3 and 4 describe two ways of using subsystems, as open subsystems and as closed subsystems, respectively. Section 5 discusses how the contents of a closed subsystem interact with the surroundings of the subsystem. In Section 6, we discuss closed subsystems in combination with collaborations and how this impacts on the semantics of UML, and then follow some concluding remarks.

2 Subsystems

In UML, a subsystem is used for defining one part of a (large) system. It contains a collection of elements, such as classes and associations, as well as perhaps another level of subsystems. Together, these elements constitute a realization of that part of the system. A subsystem has no behaviour of its own. All its behaviour is performed by collaborating instances of classifiers within the subsystem. Hence, the realization elements implement the functionality offered by the subsystem. Apart from these realization elements, a subsystem has a specification of its functionality. This specification describes the services which the subsystem offers to its environment. These services are performed by collaborating instances of the subsystem's realization elements. However, the specification does not reveal the internal structure of the subsystem, rather it is an abstraction of the subsystem.

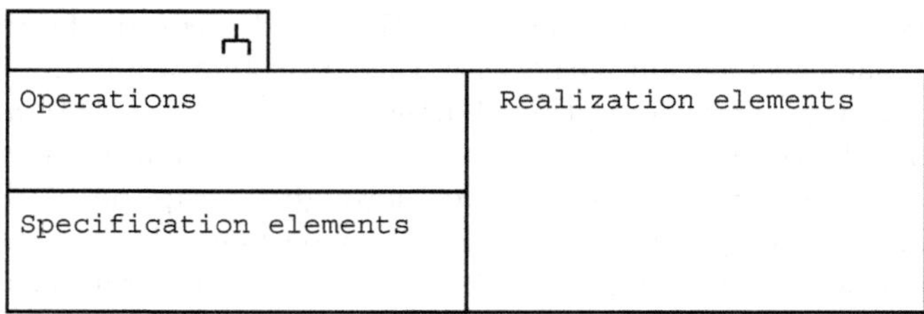

Fig. 1. A subsystem icon has two parts: one for the specification aspect of the subsystem and one for the realization aspect. The former can be expressed with operations and/or classifiers, while the latter is expressed with classifiers. The individual compartments may optionally be omitted from the diagram.

There are two advantages of having two aspects of a subsystem, i.e. a specification aspect and a realization aspect: i) it is possible to define the semantic relationship between the specification and the realization within the language rather than as only a design rule, and ii) the implementation of the subsystem is decoupled from how the subsystem is perceived by its environment. The latter implies that the realization of the subsystem can be changed without affecting the environment, as long as the realization fulfils the specification. Moreover, the subsystem's environment can be designed and implemented independently of how and when the realization of the subsystem is done, which for example reduces the timing constraints between different teams in a development project. Another implication is that the specification part of a subsystem can in fact be developed by one team as the requirement specification of the subsystem, while another team is responsible for the development of the subsystem's realization.

The specification of a subsystem can be done in a few different ways, using different kinds of constructs in UML. Most commonly, four kinds are used: *use cases*, *state machines*, *classes* and *operations*. Of course, combinations of these constructs also occur. Which one to choose depends on what kind of system/subsystem is developed. It is not within the scope of this paper to describe how to develop such a specification, nor how to develop its realization.

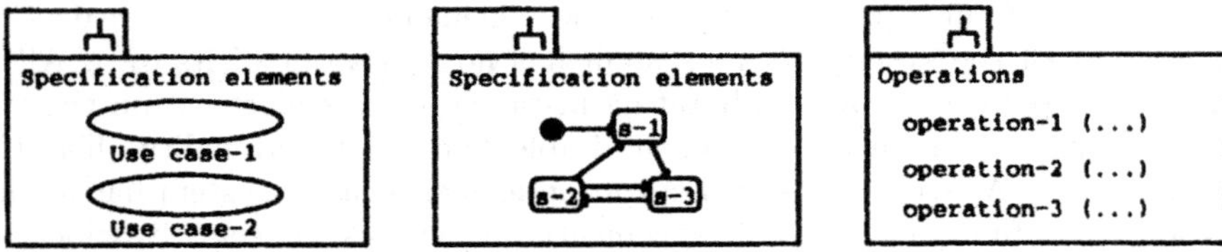

Fig. 2. A subsystem can be specified using different techniques, using e.g. use cases, state machines or operations.

There must, of course, be a mapping between the specification and the realization aspects of a subsystem. The realization must meet all the requirements expressed in the specification. Otherwise, the subsystem would not offer all the services included in its specification. Furthermore, all the functionality in the realization must originate from services in the specification, or unwanted side-effects may appear. (See [3] for a more thorough description of the mapping requirements.) The mapping between the two aspects can be expressed in a few different ways, where the realize relationship and the collaboration construct are the two most common forms. The former is suitable for stating simple mappings between a specification element and its realization, like when an operation in the specification is mapped onto an operation in one of the realization elements. Collaborations are useful for expressing more complex mappings, like how a use case is mapped onto a collection of classifiers.

Furthermore, subsystems can have relationships to each other:

- The *import* relationship implies that the namespace inside the importing subsystem is extended with the public contents of the imported subsystem (affecting the specification as well as the realization).
- An *association* between two subsystems means that they can communicate with each other, but the contents of the subsystems do not depend on each other.
- Two subsystems can have a *generalization* relationship between them, which implies that the namespace of the child subsystem is extended with the

public and the protected elements of the parent. The operations of the parent subsystem are applicable also to the child, and all relationships involving the parent are inherited by the child.

Another way of connecting one subsystem to another is to have an interface between them, offered by one of the subsystems while the other has a *use* dependency to the interface. Connecting subsystems in this way can be seen as syntactic sugar for an association between the subsystems, with the additional constraints that the association is only navigable to the subsystem offering the interface, and that only operations declared in the interface may be invoked using the association.

3 Open Subsystems

In principle, there are two ways of interacting with a subsystem. The first is to consider the subsystem to be a black box, and to have associations directly to it. In this case, the subsystem receives all incoming communications itself. The other alternative is to define associations directly to elements contained in the subsystem, which is possible only if these elements are public. We will discuss the first alternative in the next section. In this section we will focus on subsystems whose realization is (at least partially) public, allowing its surroundings to access the realization elements directly.

In general, if two instances are to communicate with each other, there must be a link between them. This link originates from an association between the classifiers of the two instances. To be able to declare this association, the two classifiers must exist in the same namespace. In this case, we have instances outside of the subsystem that communicate with instances contained in the subsystem. Hence, the contents of the subsystem must be imported into the namespace of the outside classifiers, so that the associations between the external classifiers and the internal ones can be declared.

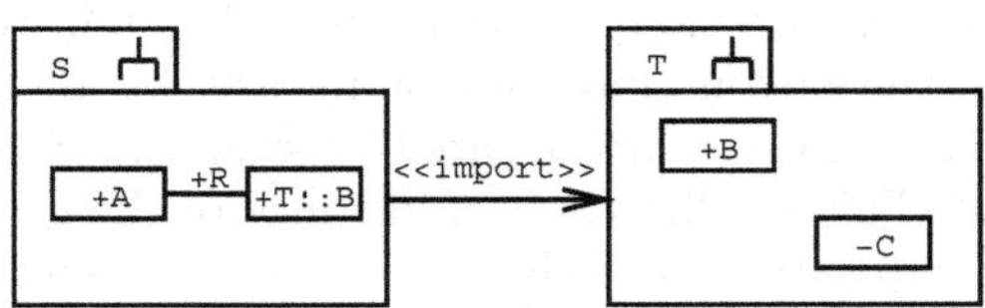

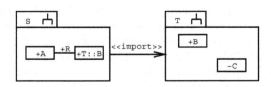

Fig. 3. The subsystem S imports the public contents of the open subsystem T. This implies that B becomes visible inside S. The association R between A and B is declared within the subsystem S.

When a subsystem is used in this way, it is referred to as an *open* subsystem, because its contents are accessed directly by the surroundings of the subsystem. Note, however, that an open subsystem may also contain private elements. Since such elements can only be used by other elements within the subsystem, the presence of private elements does not affect how the subsystem is used by its surroundings.

The specification aspect of a subsystem to be used in this way acts as a requirement specification when developing the realization, and also as a high-level specification of the services offered by the subsystem. However, to identify where a specific communication is to be sent, the public elements of the realization part of the subsystem must be examined.

4 Closed Subsystems

When all the contained elements of a subsystem are private, it is not possible to access any of these elements from the outside of the subsystem. The only way to use the services of such a subsystem is by communicating directly with the subsystem itself. A subsystem acting as a black box like this is considered to be *closed*. Note that we can consider a subsystem to be closed even if it contains public elements, by choosing to communicate only with the subsystem itself instead of importing it and directly accessing its public elements. What differs between an open and a closed subsystem is the way they are used by their surroundings. Hence one and the same subsystem may be considered open by one user of the subsystem that has an import relationship to it, but closed by another user that communicates only with the subsystem itself.

The main advantage with the closed subsystem approach is that the interior of the subsystem can be reorganized without influencing the users of the subsystem. It might even be that the realization part of the subsystem does not exist when the surroundings are designed and implemented, or that the contents of the subsystem are not available during modelling since the subsystem is implemented by a programme developed elsewhere.

For a closed subsystem, no associations are declared between external classifiers and classifiers within the realization part of the subsystem. (N.B. In this section we are focusing on communication directed *to* a closed subsystem. Communication in the other direction, i.e. *from* the subsystem to its surroundings, depends on whether the surrounding subsystems are closed or not. See Section 5 below.) Instead, all associations are declared between the external classifiers and the subsystem itself. This implies that an instance of the external classifier will have a link to the subsystem, and the communication sent from the external instance will be received by the subsystem. Therefore, a subsystem has its own unique identity which is used e.g. during communication.

Since a subsystem has no behaviour of its own, all communications sent to the subsystem are re-directed to instances inside the subsystem. How this re-direction is done is not specified within UML but is left as a semantic variation-point. (Cf. UML does not define how the method to be executed is found when a stimulus is received by an object.) Different techniques are possible, like sending all stimuli to one instance acting as a dispatcher, or sending all stimuli with a specific name to a pre-defined instance. A third alternative is to use the value of one or several of the stimulus' arguments for identifying the receiving instance. (Note, however, that an argument cannot be a pointer to an instance in the subsystem, since the instance's classifier is not visible outside the subsystem; therefore, the type of such an argument would be unknown.)

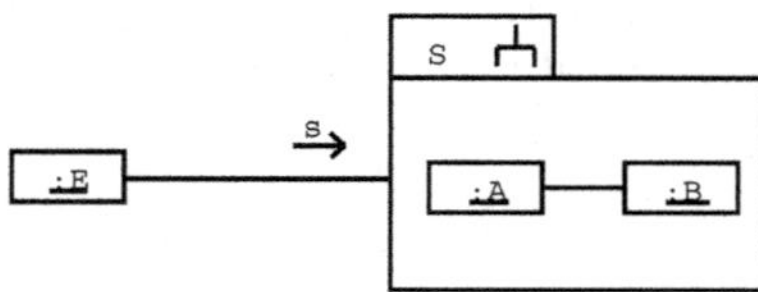

Fig. 4. An instance outside the subsystem interacts with the subsystem by sending a stimulus, *s*, via the link between the instance and the subsystem. The stimulus is re-directed inside the subsystem to an instance of a classifier within the subsystem.

When specifying the interaction with a closed subsystem, the specification of that subsystem is the only description of how to interact with the subsystem, since the realization elements are not visible outside the subsystem (cf. the operations/receptions of a class).

5 Closed Subsystem's Interaction with the Environment

Instances of classifiers declared within a closed subsystem can of course interact with each other, granted that there are links between them. Likewise, an instance in a subsystem can interact with an instance outside the subsystem, if there is a link to the external instance. Such a link can be established in a few different ways. If the classifier of the external instance exists in the namespace containing the subsystem, the classifier is visible also to the elements inside the subsystem and associations can therefore be declared between internal classifiers and external ones. The external classifier can, of course, also be imported into the subsystem if it is a public element of another, open, subsystem. Once the association is declared, links can be created between instances of the internal and the external classifiers in the usual way.

An instance inside the subsystem can also communicate with instances external to the subsystem by using the subsystem's links with its environment. These links are used when external instances communicate with the subsystem, and they can of course also be used for communication in the other direction, as long as the corresponding association is visible to the subsystem. This is due to the fact that all names visible to a subsystem, including the names of its opposite association ends, are also visible to the elements inside the subsystem. (Cf. a variable which is declared in an outer block can be used in inner blocks.) This implies that instances of the classifiers contained in the subsystem have access to the links of the subsystem as well as their own links.

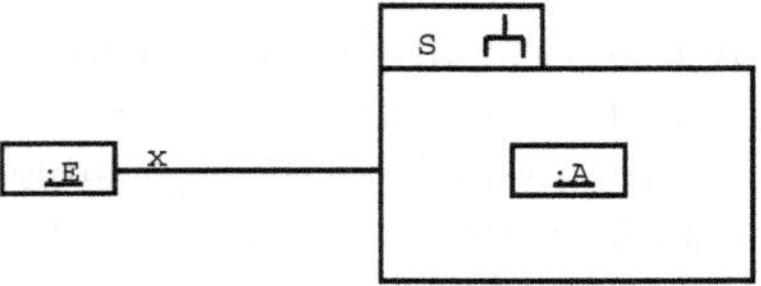

Fig. 5. The link-end x opposite to the subsystem is visible to the object A which can therefore use it to communicate with the object E.

Note that if an instance inside the subsystem needs to communicate with the subsystem itself and not with an explicit instance inside the subsystem, a link must be established between the instance and the subsystem, i.e. there must be an association between the instance's classifier and the subsystem.

6 Subsystems in Collaborations

In UML, a collaboration (including its interactions) is used for defining the roles to be played by instances, including how they interact with each other, when they jointly perform a specific task, like performing a use case. The instances are often objects, but other kinds of instances are also possible. Even (closed) subsystems can play the various roles in a collaboration. (When a subsystem is considered open, the instances of classifiers inside the subsystem are the ones taking part in the collaboration.) As was stated previously, an instance external to a closed subsystem sends its stimuli to the subsystem and it is the subsystem that re-directs these stimuli to its internal instances. Hence, it is the closed subsystem itself that plays one of the roles in the collaboration.

Note that in general when defining a collaboration, no presumption has to be made about what kind of instance will perform a specific role as long as the instance has all the features required for that role; the role can be played just as well by a closed subsystem as by an object. In the case of a closed subsystem, there are other collaborations inside the subsystem defining how instances inside the subsystem collaborate to realize the features required by the external collaboration and therefore offered by the subsystem (see Figure 6).

It should be pointed out that it is not enough that a closed subsystem re-directs the stimuli it receives to instances inside it. The stimuli must also be modified when they cross the subsystem boundary; otherwise, the stimuli will not conform to the messages in the collaborations' interactions. (A stimulus conforms to a message if the sender and the receiver of the stimulus conforms to the sender role and the receiver role, respectively, and the dispatching actions are equal.) We will explain below why this is required. We will also relax the conformance requirement of the sender of a stimulus.

Assume the following situation: there are two subsystems, S and T, both considered closed and having an association between them. The subsystem S contains one class, called A, while T contains the two classes B and C and an association between B and C. Each subsystem contains also a collaboration, CS

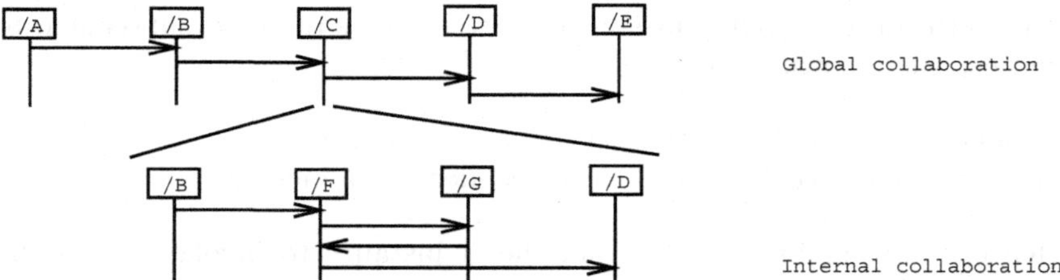

Fig. 6. A closed subsystem participating in a collaboration may have internal collaborations to define how the subsystem fulfils the features required by the external collaboration.

and CT, respectively, and there is one collaboration, CG, defined at the same level as the two subsystems.

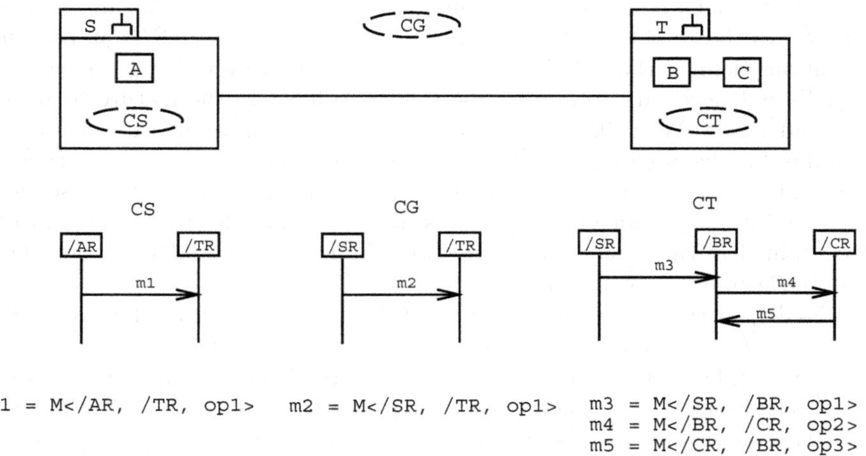

Fig. 7. The example system including its collaborations.

In Figure 7 we have included three sequence diagrams showing the interactions specified by the three collaborations. The communication taking place starts when an instance of A sends a stimulus to T to invoke the operation *op*1. The T subsystem re-directs the stimulus to an instance of B which causes the operation *op*1 to be invoked on the B instance. As a reaction, the B instance invokes the *op*2 operation on a C instance which in turn invokes the *op*3 operation on the B instance.

According to the UML specification [2, page 2-86] each stimulus has a sender and a receiver (and possibly some arguments, that we neglect here). The stimulus also states (via its call action) which operation it will invoke. A message is defined similarly, but it specifies the sender role and the receiver role instead of specific instances (the ordering of the messages is also neglected). In the subsequent text, we will use the following notation:

- $S\langle sender, receiver, operation\rangle$ denotes a stimulus
- $M\langle sender\text{-}role, receiver\text{-}role, operation\rangle$ denotes a message

Hence, the stimulus $s1$ sent from the A instance to invoke $op1$ on the T subsystem is denoted $s1 = S\langle a, t, op1\rangle$.

The sequence diagram of CS shows that a message $m1 = M\langle /AR, /TR, op1\rangle$ is defined from the $/AR$ role to the $/TR$ role. ($/AR$ is a role which has A as its base classifier, similar for the other roles in the example.) Clearly $s1$ conforms to m1 since the sender and the receiver conforms to the sender role and the receiver role, respectively, and the operations are the same.

In CG, which specifies the interaction between the two subsystems, we have the situation that s1 must conform to the message $m2 = M\langle /SR, /TR, op1\rangle$. Obviously, the receiver conforms to the receiver role, and the operations are the same, but what about the sender and the sender role? Does an instance of A conform to the $/SR$ role? No, not in the general case, since $/SR$ can have more operations defined than A. However, unlike for the receiver of a message, it is actually not necessary to require the sender to have all the features defined by the sender role. We will, at most, use the information about the sender of the stimulus for dispatching a reply. It is therefore enough to require either that the sender of the stimulus conforms to the sender role, or that the sender be contained in an instance that conforms to the sender role. Since the A instance is contained in the S subsystem which conforms to the sender role, we deduce that the stimulus $s1$ conforms to $m2$.

Finally, in the sequence diagram of CT, we can see that $s1$ must conform to $m3 = M\langle /SR, /BR, op1\rangle$. As was stated above, the A instance conforms to the sender role, and the operations are the same. What about the receiver and the receiver role? The sequence diagram shows that the $/BR$ role requires two operations: $op1$ and $op3$. Can the T subsystem conform to that role? Again, not in the general case, since the $op3$ operation could well be an internal operation used only in the interaction between instances inside the subsystem, but not by anyone outside the subsystem. Hence, the stimulus $s1$ does not conform to the message $m3$. This implies that when the subsystem re-directs a stimulus to one of its internal instances, the stimulus must be modified. This can be accomplished in two ways: either the subsystem modifies the stimulus by replacing the stimulus' receiver value with the instance that actually is going to receive the stimulus, or it dispatches a new stimulus with the correct instances. The specification of UML does not state which alternative to use; it is left as a semantic variation point. Dispatching a new stimulus implies that the conformance requirements of the stimuli to the messages are fulfilled at all times, while modifying the original stimulus only guarantees that the stimulus conforms to the messages in different collaborations in sequence; once it has conformed to a message, the stimulus might be modified so that it conforms to the message in the next collaboration. The former alternative is more intuitive, while it is easier to formally verify the latter alternative with a tool. (Of course, this does not state how the communication is performed in the implemented system. It can be implemented quite differently depending on the platform, but this is on the other hand true for all UML models.)

7 Concluding Remarks

In this paper we have given a more thorough description of the semantics of the subsystem construct than what is given in the definition of UML. We have described the two different ways to interact with a subsystem: either using public elements inside the subsystem that are imported into the communicating element's namespace, or sending the stimuli directly to the subsystem which forwards them to the correct receivers contained in the subsystem. In UML, it is not (and it should not be) defined how the subsystem identifies the internal receiver when forwarding a stimulus. Different techniques are suitable for different kinds of application areas and implementation environments.

Moreover, it should be noted that it is not stated whether a closed subsystem will modify the receiver information of a stimulus before forwarding it to the receiver contained in the subsystem, or if the subsystem dispatches a new stimulus based on the information in the old one. Other alternatives are also possible. Which alternative to choose is also left as a semantic variation point.

The semantics presented in this paper will not only increase the understanding of the subsystem construct, but also facilitate the development of tools that perform intelligent operations on models expressed in UML, like performing consistency checks, simulating a model or generating code based on a model.

In this paper we do not include the UML signal construct, which implies that operations are left as the only means for communication with subsystems. This simplification has no impact on our description as a subsystem performs no behaviour of its own but simply forwards all stimuli to instances inside it.

References

1. I. Jacobson. *Concepts for Modeling Large Real Time Systems.* PhD thesis, Royal Institute of Technology, Stockholm, Sweden, 1985. 359
2. Object Management Group, Framingham Corporate Center, 492 Old Connecticut Path, Framingham MA 01701-4568. *OMG Unified Modeling Language Specification, version 1.3*, June 1999. http://www.omg.org/cgi-bin/doc?ad/99-06-08. 359, 366
3. G. Övergaard. A Formal Approach to Collaborations in the Unified Modeling Language. In R. France and B. Rumpe, editors, *Proceedings of UML'99 – The Unified Modeling Language: Beyond the Standard, Lecture Notes in Computer Science 1723*, pages 99–115. Springer-Verlag, 1999. 361

Consistent Behaviour Representation in Activity and Sequence Diagrams

Dorina C. Petriu and Yimei Sun

Carleton University
Department of Systems and Computer Engineering
Ottawa, Canada, K1S 5B6
petriu@sce.carleton.ca

Abstract. The paper proposes a formal approach for constructing UML activity diagrams from sequence diagrams by using graph transformations. Activity diagrams are good at describing the overall flow of control in a system, as they provide support for conditional and parallel behaviour, but do not capture well object interactions. Activity diagrams are mostly used in the preliminary stages of analysis and design. As the design progresses, more detailed descriptions of object interactions become necessary, and interaction diagrams are used for this purpose. During the transition from a high level to a detailed design, the mapping between the behavior represented in activity diagrams and that described in interaction diagrams may be lost, and the two views may become inconsistent. By reconstructing the activity diagrams from sequence diagrams, consistency is re-enforced. Every activity block is cross-referenced with the corresponding sequence diagram messages, which helps designers to correlate the two views. The transformation from sequence to activity diagrams is based on PROGRES, a known visual language and environment for programming with graph rewriting systems.

1 Introduction

One of the hardest things to understand in an object-oriented system is the overall flow of control [2]. A good design has many small methods in different classes, which make it hard at times to figure out the overall sequence of system behavior. UML interaction (i.e., sequence and collaboration) diagrams help in this respect by representing the detailed sequence of behavior from object to object and from method to method [1]. However, the interaction diagrams usually represent a single scenario (i.e., an instance of a use case) or part of a scenario. It is not always clear how different scenarios are pieced together in the system execution.

UML offers another way to express the overall flow of control, this time at a higher level of abstraction, in the form of activity diagrams. Unlike most other UML features, these diagrams do not have clear origins in the previous work of Booch, Rumbaugh and Jaconson, but rather combine ideas from several techniques: the event diagram of Odell, SDL state modelling techniques, workflow modelling and Petri Nets [2]. Activity diagrams are especially useful for providing a "bird's eye" view of

A. Evans, S. Kent and B. Selic (Eds.): «UML» 2000, LNCS 1939, pp. 369-382, 2000.

the system behavior. According to many UML texts, such diagrams are mostly used in the preliminary stages of analysis and design, when classes and objects are not completely identified and their responsibilities not completely defined. As the design progresses and the need for a more detailed description of interaction among object arises, interaction diagrams become the technique of choice for modelling the way the object collaborate with each other. During the transition from a high level to a detailed design, the mapping between the behavior represented in activity diagrams and that described in interaction diagrams may be lost, and the two views often become inconsistent.

The paper proposes a method to rebuild consistent activity diagrams from a set of sequence diagrams by graph transformations, based on the graph-grammar formalism. The process will take place in two phases: one automatic, the other with the help of the designer. In the first phase, an activity diagram is built for a use case (or a set of use cases), by starting from an external stimulus and following the flow of messages in the corresponding sequence diagrams. Sequential execution, conditional branching and fork/join operations are identified in the message flow, and are translated into activity diagrams blocks. The mapping between each block and the corresponding sequence of messages will be kept for future reference. In the second phase, the designer is asked to name every activity block with a string that reflects the block's purpose. The re-constructed activity diagram will facilitate the understanding of the system by offering a high-level view consistent with the detailed description, and by providing cross-referencing between activities and the corresponding sequence diagram messages. The proposed transformation produces reasonable results for generic sequence diagrams describing systems with multiple threads of control that use iterations and/or conditional branching, but is rather meaningless for instance-level sequence diagrams without such constructs.

We are planing to work in the future on comparing a re-constructed activity diagram (which may contain more details), with the corresponding activity diagram built in the preliminary analysis stages. Such a comparison will show how the original intent was realized in the detailed design, and will point to potential inconsistencies.

Since activity diagrams are good at describing the overall flow of control for various use cases, they can be used as a basis for early performance estimations of the response time for different user requests. Previous work on converting UML models into performance models can be found in [4] and [5].

The paper also proposes to extend the UML sequence diagram notation with a "composite subsequence" block that will defer details to another diagram. This will allow breaking down a long description of object interactions into a hierarchy of sequence diagrams some at a higher level and others at a lower level of details. Similar concepts already exist in other UML diagrams, such as "composite activity" in activity diagrams [2] and "composite state" in hierarchical state diagrams [7]. Moreover, a similar concept known as "message sequence chart reference" exists in the ITU-T standard for Message Sequence Charts [3].

The paper is organized as follows. Section 2 motivates the proposed transformation from sequence to activity diagram by the means of a case study. Section 3 describes in more details the transformations form one kind to another kind of diagram. Section 4 presents the essence of the formal transformation approach based on PROGRES, a known tool for graph rewriting [8, 9, 10].

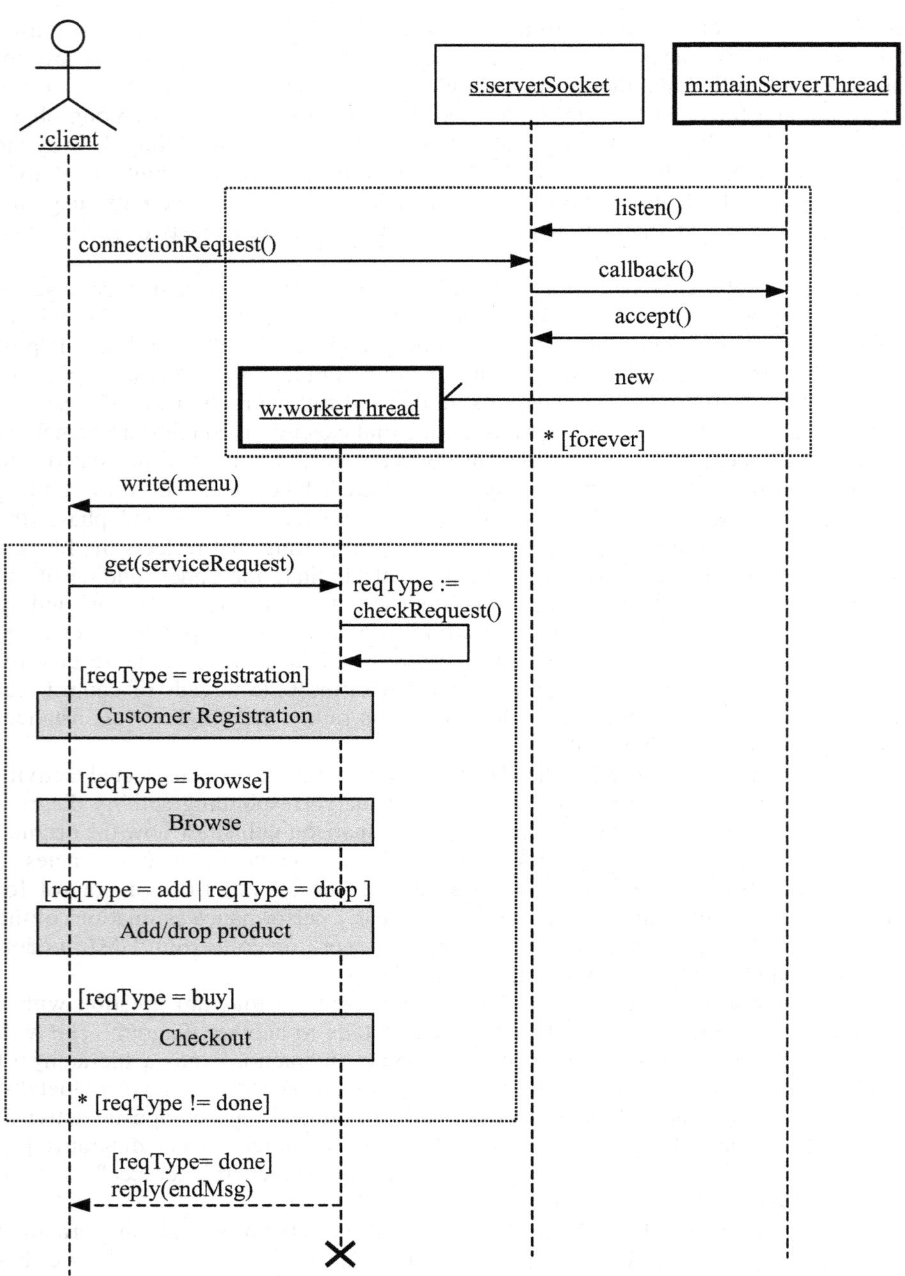

Fig. 1. Sequence diagram for e-commerce server: high-level view

2 Motivation and Case Study

The rationale for developing a formal method to reconstruct activity diagrams from sequence diagrams and for proposing an extension to the UML sequence diagram notation is best explained by the means of an example. Our case study is a simplified example of an electronic commerce server that accepts and processes request from a large number of customers. A typical customer starts his/her session by browsing through the available products and asking for more information about the products of interest. The customer may decide to add selected items to the “shopping cart”, or to drop items from the cart any time before “checking out”. When the customer decides to purchase the items from the shopping cart, he/she will proceed to "checkout”. The customer can also register with the merchant, in which case a customer account with relevant data (such as name, address, credit card information) will be created and stored in a database for later reference.

Figure 1 contains a high-level sequence diagram, which shows only the big steps of the client/server interaction: establishing the connection, creating of a worker thread dedicated to the client, looping for accepting and processing different types of client requests, and finally terminating the session and destroying the worker thread. This is a generic sequence diagram that describes all possible sequences [11]. The iteration notation, whereby “a connected set of messages may be enclosed and marked as an iteration” [7] is used twice: once for the main server thread loop (in which connection requests are accepted from the clients) and once for the repeated interaction between a client and the server. The respective iteration expressions are given at the bottom of each iteration block. The diagram also uses branches labeled by guard conditions. The extension proposed in this paper, the *composite subsequence block* is illustrated by the four shaded blocks from Figure 1, which defer the details of processing different types of request to another diagrams. A composite block suppresses details in two ways: a) by hiding messages between the objects whose lifelines cross the block, and b) by hiding other objects which may cooperate with the main protagonists. The later is similar to the way of suppression of detailed behaviour presented in [6]. The details of the block labeled `Customer registration` are given in the shaded area of Figure 2. The detailed sequence diagram shows not only the messages between the two main protagonists from Figure 1 (*i.e.,* the client and the worker thread) but also their interactions with other objects that are not specified in Figure 1. Figure 2 repeats a part of Figure 1 (the request message from the client and its type test) in order to better explain the context of the composite block.

The paper also proposes a two-phase process for constructing activity diagrams from sequence diagrams: the first phase can be automated based on formal graph transformations, whereas the second phase needs the intervention of the designer. Figure 4 illustrates the activity diagram built from the high-level sequence diagram from Figure 1 after the first transformation phase and Figure 5 after the second phase. Also, Figure 3 gives the activity diagram obtained after both phases from the sequence diagram in Figure 2.

The concept behind the first transformation phase is to follow the message flow in the sequence diagram by taking also into account the execution threads of all active objects involved in the collaboration.

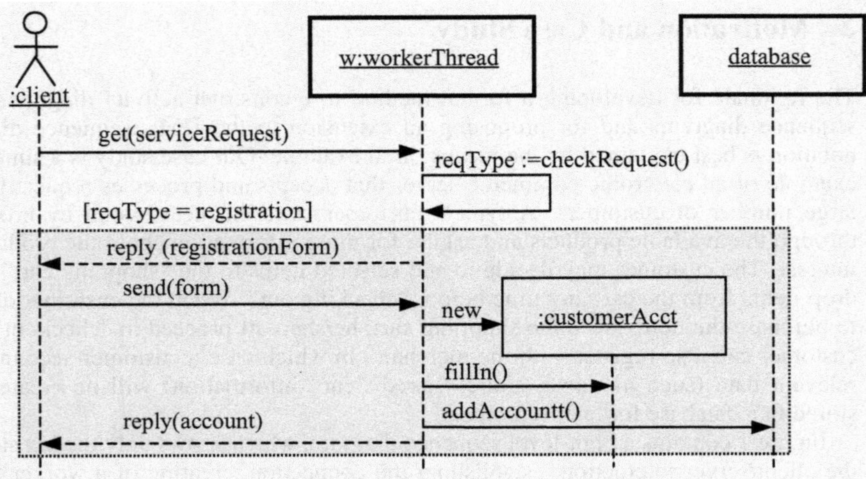

Fig. 2. Sequence diagram for customer registration

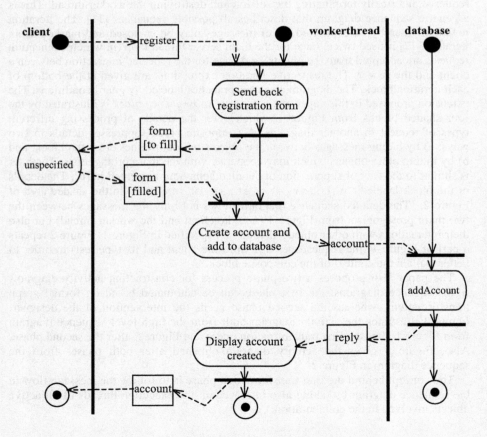

Fig. 3. Activity diagram for customer registration

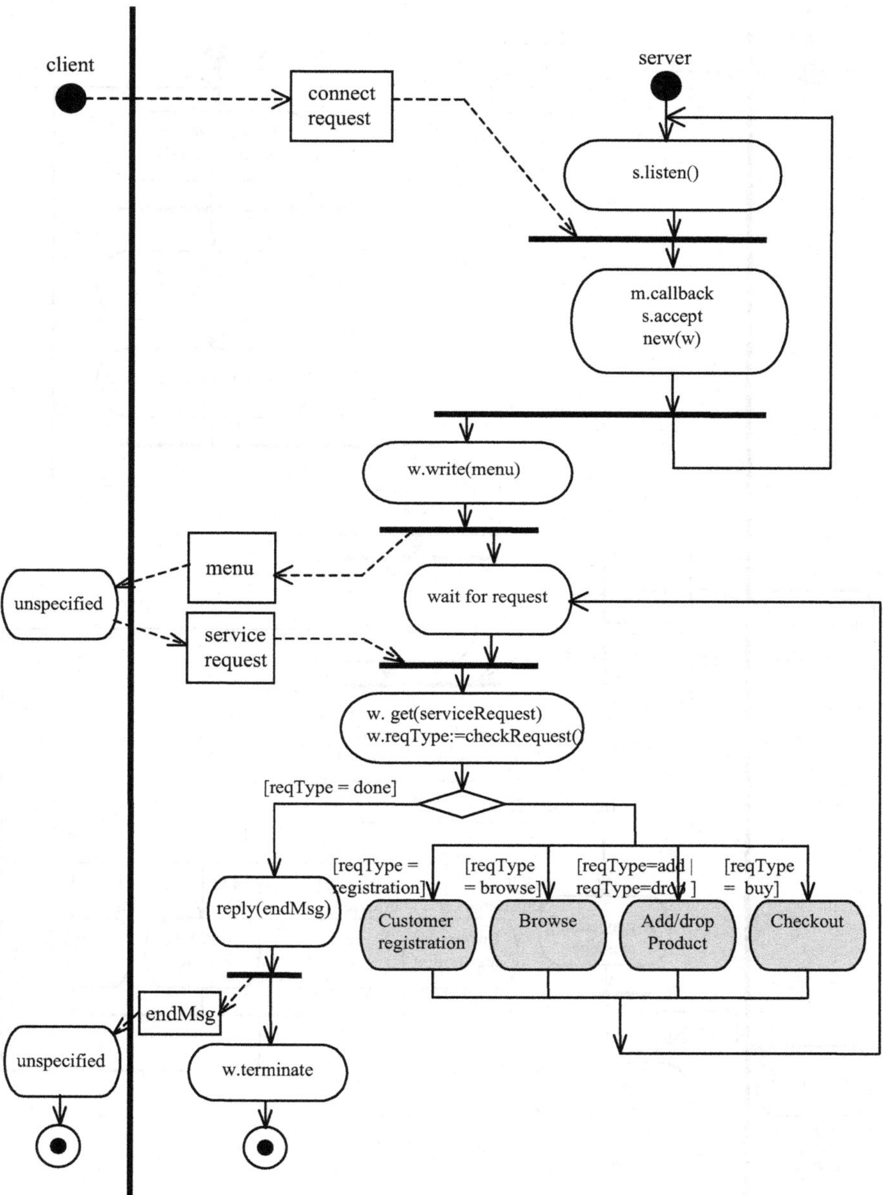

Fig. 4. Activity diagram generated from the sequence diagram from Fig. 1 (result of the first transformation phase)

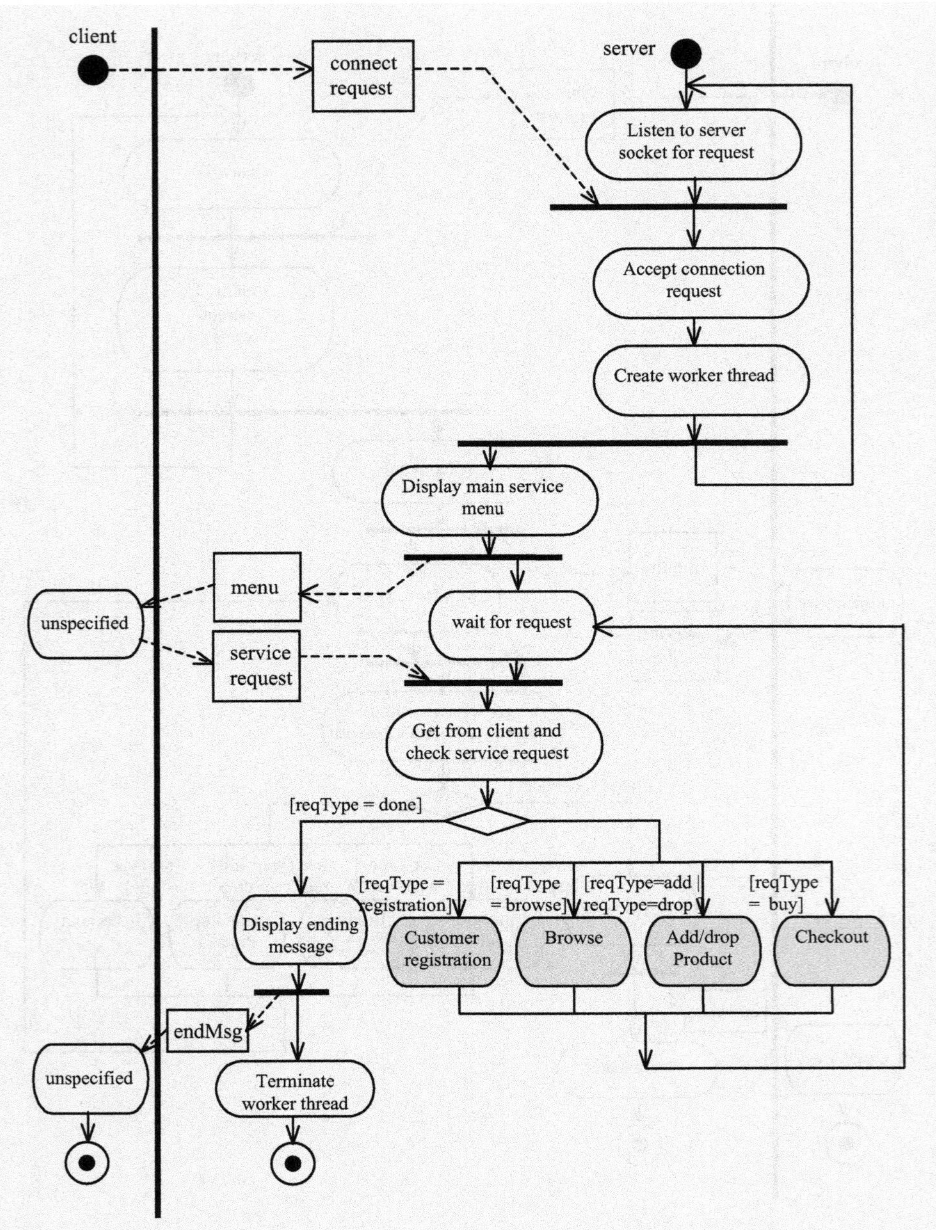

Fig. 5. Activity diagram with action names filled in by the designer (result of the second transformation phase)

The activity diagram has an initial state for each active object that exists when the diagrams starts, which is consistent with the concurrent state machine notation. For each execution thread we follow the message flow and group together in an activity block all the sequential actions executed by the receivers of consecutive messages which are sent and received in the same thread. New activity blocks are created when reaching a branching point (a new activity for every branch), after a merging point, when reaching an iteration block or a composite subsequence block. Special treatment is given to messages exchanged between different threads of control that introduce fork/join connectors in the activity diagram. For example, creating an active object is

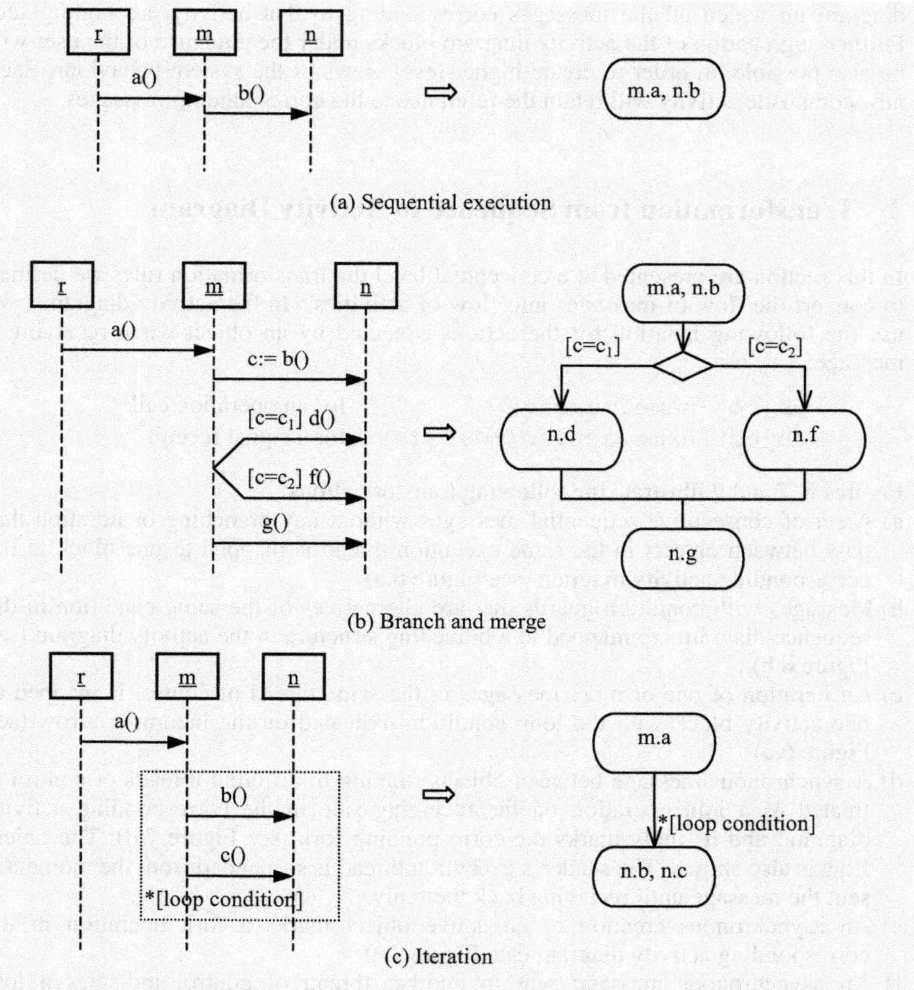

Fig.6. Transformations in the case of a single execution thread

equivalent to forking a new thread of control, sending an asynchronous signal also forks the thread, whereas the receipt of a message from another thread is equivalent to a synchronization point (*i.e.,* a join). Messages exchanged between execution threads carry objects that are represented in the activity diagram according to the notation for object flow from [11]. A more detailed description of the transformations carried out in the first phase is given in the next section.

The purpose of the second phase is to give meaningful names to each activity block, so that a reader can easily understand the activity diagram. Every block will keep a reference to all its actions and corresponding messages. When this transformation will be implemented in a UML tool, the user will have the choice to select any activity block, then open a window with the corresponding sequence diagram on which all the messages corresponding to that activity are highlighted. Further aggregation of the activity diagram blocks under the guidance of the user will be also possible, in order to create higher-level views of the system behaviour. Each new composite activity will retain the reference to the corresponding messages.

3 Transformation from Sequence to Activity Diagram

In this section are presented at a conceptual level the transformation rules we defined to convert the flow of messages into flow of activities. In the activity diagrams, we use the following notation for the actions executed by an object when receiving a message:

`object-name.message`	for an operation call
`object-name.action(message)`	for a signal receipt

Figures 6, 7 and 9 illustrate the following transformations:

a) A set of consecutive sequential messages without any branching or iteration that pass between objects in the same execution thread is mapped to one block in the corresponding activity diagram (see Figure 6.a).

b) Messages with condition guards that are alternatives of the same condition in the sequence diagram are mapped to a branching structure in the activity diagram (see Figure 6.b).

c) An iteration of one or more messages in the same thread of control is mapped to one activity block with the loop condition indicated on the incoming arrow (see Figure 6.c)

d) A synchronous message between objects running in different threads of control is treated as a join operation on the receiving side in the corresponding activity diagram, and its reply marks the corresponding fork (see Figure 7.d). The object flow is also shown. The sender's execution thread is suspended from the moment it sent the message until receiving back the reply.

e) An asynchronous creation of an active object marks a fork operation in the corresponding activity diagram (see Figure 7.e).

f) An asynchronous message sent to another thread of control indicates a join operation on the receiver side and a fork operation on the sender side in the corresponding activity diagram (see Figure 7.f). The object flow is also shown.

g) A composite subsequence block is translated into a composite activity in the corresponding activity diagram (see Figure 8).

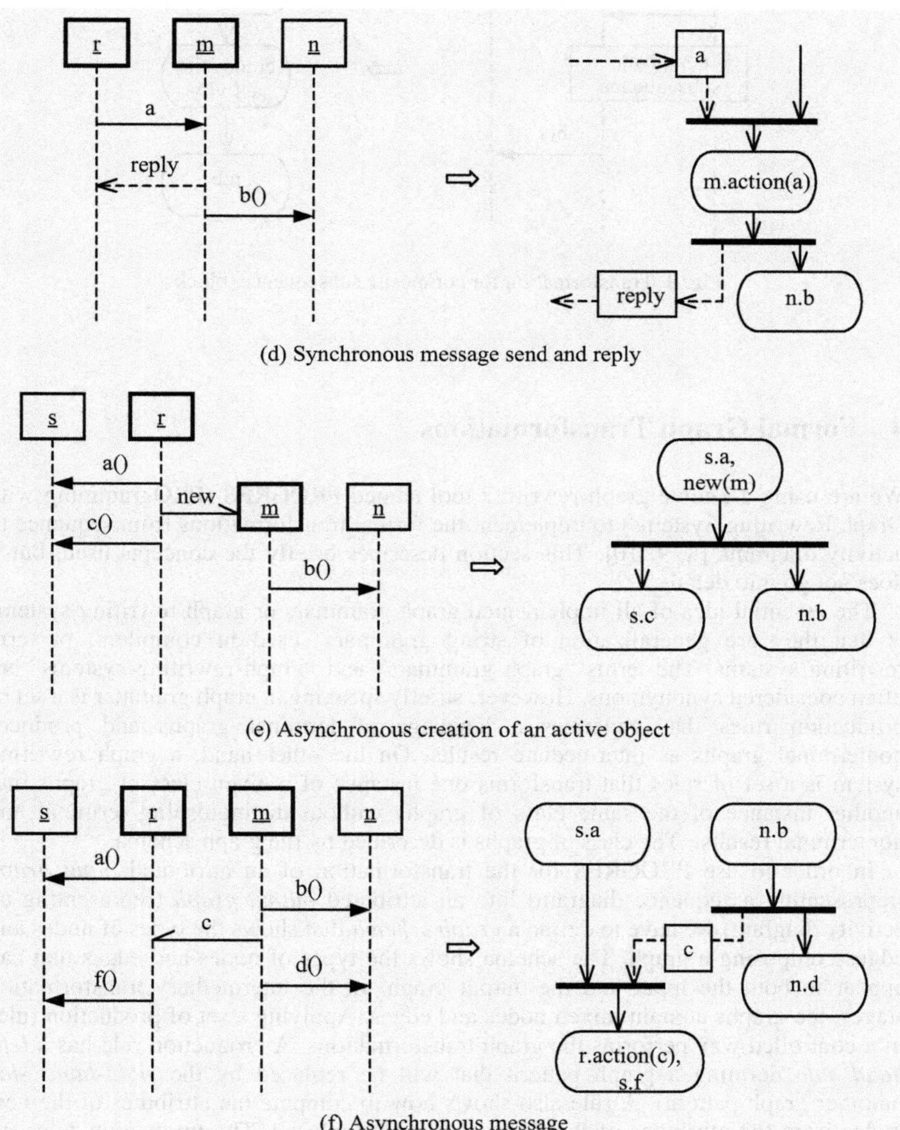

(d) Synchronous message send and reply

(e) Asynchronous creation of an active object

(f) Asynchronous message

Fig. 7. Transformations in the case of different execution threads

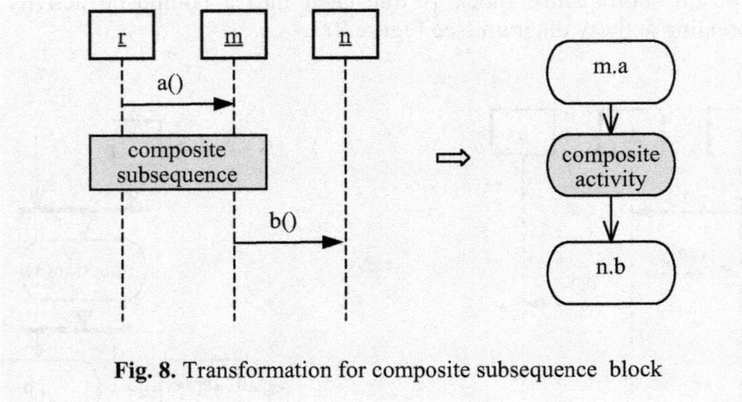

Fig. 8. Transformation for composite subsequence block

4 Formal Graph Transformations

We are using a known graph rewriting tool named PROGRES (PROgramming with Graph Rewriting Systems) to implement the formal transformations from sequence to activity diagrams [8, 9, 10]. This section describes briefly the concepts used, but it does not go into details.

The essential idea of all implemented graph grammars or graph rewriting systems is that they are generalization of string grammars (used in compilers) or term rewriting systems. The terms "graph grammars" and "graph rewriting systems" are often considered synonymous. However, strictly speaking, a graph grammar is a set of production rules that generates a language of terminal graphs and produces nonterminal graphs as intermediate results. On the other hand, a graph rewriting system is a set of rules that transforms one instance of a given class of graphs into another instance of the same class of graphs without distinguishing terminal and nonterminal results. The class of graphs is described by the graph schema.

In order to use PROGRES for the transformation of an attributed *input graph* (representing a sequence diagram) into an attributed *output graph* (representing an activity diagram) we have to define a *graph schema* that shows the types of nodes and edges composing a graph. The schema shows the types of nodes and edges that can appear in both the input and the output graph. In the intermediary transformation stages, the graphs contain mixed nodes and edges. Applying a set of production rules in a controlled way performs the graph transformations. A production rule has a *left-hand side* defining a graph pattern that will be replaced by the *right-hand side* (another graph pattern). A rule also shows how to compute the attributes of the new nodes from the attributes of the nodes that were replaced. The production rules we defined for the transformation of sequence diagrams into activity diagrams encode in the PROGRES language the rules described informally in the previous section (Figures 6, 7 and 8).

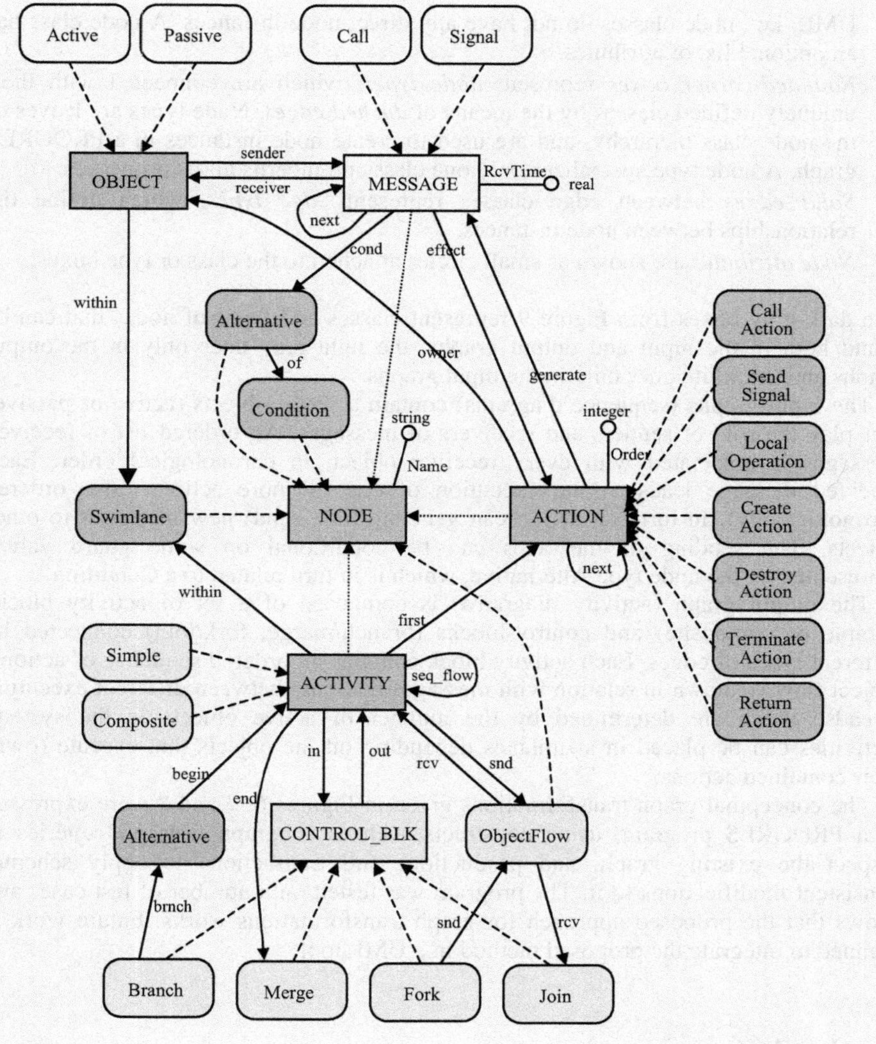

Fig. 9. PROGRES schema for sequence and activity diagrams

The schema shown in Figure 9 uses concepts from the UML meta-model [11] necessary for the description of the two types of diagrams, organized according to the following PROGRES rules:

PROGRES uses inheritance (possible multiple inheritance) to define hierarchies of node classes.

Square boxes represent *node classes*, and the inheritance relationships are represented with *dotted edges*. Node classes correspond to abstract classes in

UML, i.e., node classes do not have any direct node instances. A node class has an optional list of attributes.

Rounded-corner boxes represent *node types*, which are connected with their uniquely defined classes by the means of *dashed edges*. Node types are leaves of the node class hierarchy, and are used to create node instances in a PROGRES graph. A node type specializes only one class and inherits all its properties.

Solid edges between edge classes represent *edge types,* which define the relationships between node instances.

Node attributes are shown as small circles attached to the class or type boxes.

The dark-gray boxes from Figure 9 represent classes and types of nodes that can be found both in the input and output graphs, the light-gray ones only in the output graphs and the white ones only in the input graphs.

The input graphs (sequence diagrams) contain a set of objects (active or passive) that play the role of senders and receivers of messages. An ordered list of received messages is associated with every receiver object, in chronological order. Each received message leads to the execution of one or more actions (also ordered chronologically). In turn, an action can generate (i.e., send) new messages to other objects. The sending of messages can be conditional on some guard values represented by the node type Alternative, which is in turn related to a Condition.

The output graph (activity diagrams) is composed of a set of activity blocks (simple or composite) and control-blocks (branch/merge, fork/join) connected by different types of edges. Each activity block contains an ordered sequence of actions. Object flow is shown in relation with messages that pass between different execution threads, which are determined by the number of active objects in the system. Activities can be placed in swimlanes depending on the objects that execute (own) their contained actions.

The conceptual graph transformations given in Figures 6, 7 and 8 were expressed in a PROGRES program, using constructs such as subgraph tests and queries to inspect the existing graph, and productions and transactions to apply schema-consistent modifications to it. The program was tested on a number of test cases and shows that the proposed approach for graph transformations works. Future work is planned to integrate the proposed method in a UML tool.

5 Conclusions

The paper proposes a method to rebuild consistent activity diagrams from a set of sequence diagrams by graph transformations, based on the graph rewriting formalism. The process will take place in two phases: one automatic, the other with the help of the designer. The re-constructed activity diagrams will facilitate the understanding of the system by offering a high-level view consistent with the detailed description, and by providing cross-referencing between activities and the corresponding sequence diagram messages. Since activity diagrams are good at describing the overall flow of control for various use cases, they can be used as a basis for early performance estimations of the response time for different user requests.

The paper proposes to extend the UML sequence diagram notation with a "composite subsequence" block that will defer details to another diagram. This will allow breaking down a long description of object interactions into a hierarchy of sequence diagrams some at a higher level and others at a lower level of details. Similar concepts already exist in other UML diagrams, such as "composite activity" in activity diagrams and "composite state" in hierarchical state diagrams.

Acknowledgements

This work was partially supported by grants from the Natural Sciences and Engineering Research Council of Canada (NSERC) and Communications and Information Technology Ontario (CITO).

References

1. Booch, G., Rumbaugh, J., Jacobson, I.: The Unified Modeling Language User Guide, Addison Wesley Longman, (1999)
2. Fowler, M., Scott, K.: UML Distilled, Second Edition, Addison Wesley Longman, (2000)
3. International Telecommunication Union: Formal description techniques (FDT) – Message Sequence Chart, ITU-T Z.120 (1999)
4. Kahkipuro, P.: UML based Performance Modelling Framework for Object-Oriented Distributed Systems, Proc. of Second Int. Conference on the Unified Modeling Language, Lecture Notes in Computer Science, Vol. 1723, Springer-Verlag (1999)
5. Petriu, D.K., Wang, X.: From UML description of high-level software architecture to LQN performance models. In: Nagl, M., Schürr, A., Münch, M. (eds.): Applications of Graph Transformations with Industrial Relevance, AGTIVE'99, Lecture Notes in Computer Science, Vol. 1779. Springer-Verlag, (2000) 47-62.
6. Pooley, R., Stevens, P.: Using UML: Software Engineering with Objects and Components, Addison Wesley Longman, (1999)
7. Rumbaugh, J., Booch, G., Jacobson, I.: The Unified Modeling Language Rreference Manual, Addison Wesley Longman, (1999)
8. Schürr, A.: Introduction to PROGRES, an attributed graph grammar-based specification language, In: M. Nagl (ed): Graph-Theoretic Concepts in Computer Science, Lecture Notes in Computer Science, Vol. 411 (1990) 151-165.
9. Schürr, A.: PROGRES: A Visual Language and Environment for PROgramming with Graph Rewrite Systems, Technical Report AIB 94-11, RWTH Aachen, Germany, (1994)
10. Schürr, A.: Programmed Graph Replacement Systems, In: G. Rozenberg (ed): Handbook of Graph Grammars and Computing by Graph Transformation, (1997) 479-546.
11. OMG: Unified Modeling Language Specification, Version 1.3, (1999).

Using UML Collaboration Diagrams for Static Checking and Test Generation

Aynur Abdurazik and Jeff Offutt *

George Mason University, Fairfax VA 22030, USA

Abstract. Software testing can only be formalized and quantified when a solid basis for test generation can be defined. Tests are commonly generated from program source code, graphical models of software (such as control flow graphs), and specifications/requirements. UML collaboration diagrams represent a significant opportunity for testing because they precisely describe how the functions the software provides are connected in a form that can be easily manipulated by automated means. This paper presents novel test criteria that are based on UML collaboration diagrams. The most novel aspect of this is that tests can be generated automatically from the software design, rather than the code or the specifications. Criteria are defined for both static and dynamic testing of specification-level and instance-level collaboration diagrams. These criteria allow a formal integration tests to be based on high level design notations, which can help lead to software that is significantly more reliable.

1 Introduction

There is an increasing need for effective testing of software for safety-critical applications, such as avionics, medical, and other control systems. In addition, the growing application areas of web applications and e-commerce require software that exhibits more reliability than most traditional application areas. Without software that functions reliably, business who operate on the web will lose money, sales, and customers. This paper presents results from an ongoing project to improve the ability to test software with high reliability requirements by developing techniques for generating test cases from formal descriptions of the software. Previous work [7,8] has focused on generating tests from specifications; the current work focuses on design descriptions. Design descriptions represent a significant opportunity for testing because they precisely describe how the software functions behave in a form that can easily be manipulated by automated means.

Generating test data from high level design notations has several advantages over code-based generation. Design notations can be used as a basis for output checking, significantly reducing one of the major costs of testing. The process of generating tests from design will often help the test engineer discover

* This work is supported in part by the U.S. National Science Foundation under grant CCR-98-04111 and in part by Rockwell Collins, Inc.

A. Evans, S. Kent and B. Selic (Eds.): ≪UML≫ 2000, LNCS 1939, pp. 383–395, 2000.

problems with the design itself. If this step is done early, the problems can be eliminated early, saving time and resources. Generating tests during design also allows testing activities to be shifted to an earlier part of the development process, allowing for more effective planning and utilization of resources. Another advantage is that the test data is independent of any particular implementation of the design.

This paper presents a model for performing static analysis and generating test inputs from Unified Modeling Language (UML) collaboration diagram specifications. This work follows from previous work in developing test cases from UML statecharts [7]. Each class can have a statechart that describes the behavior of the instances of the class. The statechart models the reactions of the class to events received from the environment. The reactions to an event include sending new events to other objects and executing internal methods defined by the class. The previous paper adapted existing specification-based testing criteria [8] to UML statecharts. Our current research is focused on analyzing the behavior of a set of interacting objects. Interactions can be described using UML collaboration diagrams, and this paper presents a novel approach to generating tests data to check aspects of the software that are represented by the collaboration diagrams.

The UML is a language for specifying, constructing, visualizing, and documenting artifacts of software-intensive systems. The UML does so by providing a collection of views to capture different aspects of the system to be developed. Examples of these views include *use cases* to capture user requirements, *class diagrams* to capture the static structure of objects, *collaboration* and *sequence diagrams* to capture dynamic interactions between objects and systems, and *package* and *deployment* views that organize design elements.

This paper uses collaboration diagrams as a source for software tests. A collaboration diagram consists of objects and associations that describe how the objects communicate. An interaction occurs when two or more objects are used together to accomplish one complete task. A collaboration diagram shows an interaction organized around objects that participate in the interaction and their links to each other. Collaboration diagrams provide the following six pieces of information [3]:

1. The objects that are involved in an interaction and the structure of these objects.
2. Instances of allowable sequences of operation calls to an object.
3. The semantics of an operation.
4. The operations that are imported from other classes, thus enabling a collaboration with objects of the other class.
5. The communication pattern of objects in a collaboration (synchronous or asynchronous).
6. The execution characteristics of objects (parallel or sequential).

This information must be preserved during the transformation of a specification into an implementation. It is possible and necessary to formulate test requirements from the above points, and generate tests from the collaboration diagrams. In particular, it is suitable to consider collaboration diagrams for integration testing since collaboration diagrams specify the interactions among a set of objects.

The remainder of the paper is organized as follows. The next section gives a brief overview of software testing, and Section 3 reviews collaboration diagrams. Section 4 describes a general test case generation mechanism to generate test cases from collaboration diagrams. The paper concludes by discussing to what extent collaboration diagrams can be used in testing and suggests some future work.

2 Software Testing

Software testing includes executing a program on a set of test cases and comparing the actual results with the expected results. Testing and test design, as parts of quality assurance, should also focus on fault prevention. To the extent that testing and test design do not prevent faults, they should be able to discover symptoms caused by faults. Finally, tests should provide clear diagnoses so that faults can be easily corrected [1].

Test requirements are specific things that must be satisfied or covered during testing, for example, reaching statements are the requirements for statement coverage. *Test specifications* are specific descriptions of test cases, often associated with test requirements or criteria. For statement coverage, test specifications are the conditions necessary to reach a statement. A *testing criterion* is a rule or collection of rules that impose test requirements on a set of test cases. A *testing technique* guides the tester through the testing process by including a testing criterion and a process for creating test case values.

Test engineers measure the extent to which a criterion is satisfied in terms of *coverage*, which is the percent of requirements that are satisfied. There are various ways to classify adequacy criteria. One of the most common is by the source of information used to specify testing requirements and in the measurement of test adequacy. Hence, an adequacy criterion can be specification-based, design-based, or program-based.

A *specification-based* criterion specifies the required testing in terms of identified features of the specifications of the software, so that a test set is adequate if all the identified features have been fully exercised. Here the specifications are used to produce test cases, as well as to produce the design. A *program-based* criterion specifies testing requirements in terms of the program under test and decides if a test set is adequate according to whether the program has been thoroughly exercised. For example, if the criterion of branch testing is used, the tests are required to cover each branch in the program. A *design-based* criterion specifies the required testing in terms of design components and interactions among them, so that a test set is adequate if all the components and interactions have been exercised. Here the designs are also used to produce test cases, as well as to produce the program.

Design-based testing offers many advantages in software testing. The (formal) design of a software product can be used as a guide for designing system-level, integration-level, and class-level tests for the product. It is possible for the designer to use the design notation to precisely define fundamental aspects of the software's behavior, while more detailed and structural information is omitted. Thus, the tester has the essential information about the software's behavior without having to extract it from inessential details. This research assumes that the design is a valid representation of the system's desired behavior. The tests we generate will primarily evaluate whether the implementation correctly reflects the design.

Formal design descriptions provide a simpler, structured, and more formal approach to the development of tests than non-formal designs do. One significance of producing tests from designs is that the tests can be created earlier in the development process, and be ready for execution **before** the software is finished. Additionally, when the tests are generated, the test engineer will often find problems in the design, allowing the design to be improved before the program is implemented.

3 Collaboration Diagrams

In object-oriented software, objects interact to implement behavior. This interaction can be described in two complementary ways, one focused on individual objects and the other on a collection of cooperating objects. A state machine looks at each object individually. The collective behavior of a set of objects can be modeled in terms of how they collaborate.

A *collaboration* is a description of a collection of objects that interact to implement some behavior within a context. It contains *slots* that are filled by *objects* and *links* at run time. A collaboration slot is called a *role* because it describes the purpose of an object or link within the collaboration [6].

A Collaboration consists of *ClassifierRoles*, *AssociationRoles*, and *Interactions* [6]. A *ClassifierRole* defines a role to be played by an *Object* within a collaboration. An *AssociationRole* defines the relationships of a *ClassifierRole* to other roles. *AssociationRole* is a subset of existing *Links*. A *Link* is an individual connection among two or more objects, and is an instance of an *Association*. The objects must be direct or indirect instances of the classes at corresponding positions in an association. An *association* is a relationship among two or more specified *classifiers* that describes connections among their instances. The participating classifiers have ordered positions within the association.

An *interaction* is a behavioral specification that is composed of a sequence of communications among a set of objects within a collaboration to accomplish a specific purpose. Each interaction contains a partially ordered set of messages. A *message* is a specification of a stimulus, in other words, communication between a sender and a receiver. The message specifies the roles played by the sender object and the receiver object and it states which *operation* should be applied to the receiver by the sender. A *stimulus* is a communication between two objects that either causes an operation to be invoked or an object to be created or destroyed.

An *operation* is a specification of a transformation or query that an object may be told to execute. It has a name and a list of parameters. A *method* is a procedure that implements an operation. It has an algorithm or procedure description.

A collaboration diagram is a graphical representation of a collaboration. The objects in a collaboration diagram are instances of classes in a class diagram. Without the interaction part, a collaboration diagram is similar to a class diagram. However, they are not the same [9]. For a collaboration, there need not be an object of every class, because some classes will be irrelevant to the particular collaboration being considered. There may be two or more different objects of the same class.

A collaboration diagram has two forms. A *specification level* collaboration diagram shows *ClassifierRoles*, *AssociationRoles*, and *Messages*, where an *instance level* collaboration diagram shows *Objects*, *Links*, and *Stimuli.* The following subsection introduces *specification level* and *instance level* collaboration diagrams separately, and explores their characteristics for test case generation.

3.1 Specification and Instance Level Collaboration Diagrams

Specification level collaboration diagrams show the roles defined within a collaboration. The diagram contains a collection of class boxes and lines corresponding to *ClassifierRoles* and *AssociationRoles* in the *Collaboration.* The arrows attached to the lines map onto *Messages.* Figure 1 is a specification level collaboration diagram that is adapted from the *Unified Modeling Language Specification 1.3* [6]. Graphically, a ClassifierRole uses a class symbol, which is a rectangle. The syntax of the name of a ClassifierRole is: `'/' ClassifierRoleName ':' ClassifierName [',' ClassifierName]*`

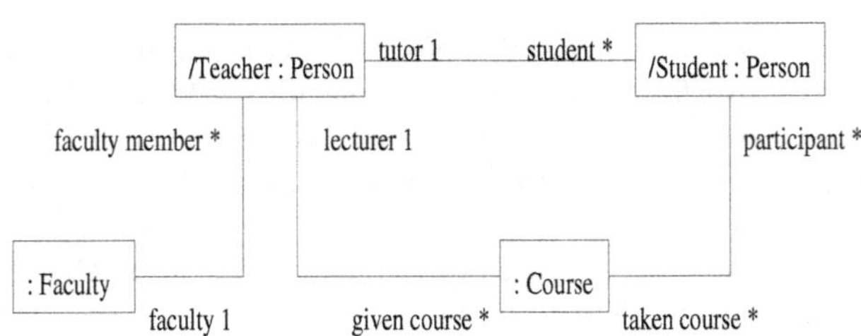

Fig. 1. Collaboration Diagram without Interaction

By examining the collaboration diagram, we can derive the following constraints: (1) `Teacher` and `Student` objects are instances of `Person` class, but they have different properties, (2) `Student` object cannot be a `Faculty`, (3) each student must have one tutor, and (4) each course must have one lecturer. The implementation can be tested according to these constraints. For example, a `Student` cannot be a `Faculty`. A `Course` cannot have more than one `Lecturer`; a `Student` should have a `Tutor`; a `Student` cannot have more than one `Tutor`, etc.

An instance level collaboration diagram shows the collaboration of the instances of *ClassifierRoles* and *AssociationRoles*. It also includes instances of *Messages* that communicate over the *AssociationRole* instances. An object playing the role defined by a *ClassifierRole* is depicted by an object box.

Figure 2 is an example of an Instance Level Specification Diagram. In this diagram, the arrows point along the line in the direction of the receiving *Object*. The arrowheads have variations that may be used to show different kind of communication. The arrowheads shown in this diagram, which are stick arrowheads, indicate flat flow of control. Each arrow show the progression to the next step in sequence. Normally all of the messages are asynchronous. Several stereotypes are attached to the links: <<parameter>> indicates method parameter; <<local>> means local variable of a method.

Specification and instance level collaboration diagrams describe the structural relationships among the participants of a collaboration and their communication patterns. A realization is a relationship between a specification and its implementation. When collaboration diagrams are used to describe the realization of use cases, they describe only the externally visible actions and their sequences. When collaboration diagrams are used to describe the realization of an operation on an object, they provide more specific information, such as (1) parameters to the operation and their usage, (2) characteristics of participating variables, e.g. local or global, (3) constraints over associations, and (4) construction and/or destruction of objects during the process.

Since collaboration diagrams include both the messages that are passed between objects and their sequences, collaboration diagrams provide both design level data flow and design level control flow information. Traditionally, data flow and control flow information are obtained from the source code. Data flow and control flow information have had significant impact on testing [5,10,11]. Hence, using collaboration diagrams in testing helps us in many ways. Obvious benefits are (1) generating test data using existing data flow and control flow testing techniques before the code generation, (2) static checking of specification itself, and (3) static checking of code.

4 Testing Criteria

Collaboration diagrams describe the structure and behavior of the system. A UML collaboration specifies what requirements must be fulfilled by the objects in a system, and what communications must take place between the objects for a specific task to be performed. UML collaboration diagrams are used at different specification abstraction levels. For example, they describe the realization of use cases, which capture high level system functionality. UML collaboration diagrams also specify the implementation of a class operation as an interaction [6,4]. Combined specifications, e.g., use cases with collaboration diagrams or class diagrams with collaboration diagrams, can be use to statically check the code and test the running application.

The following subsections explain the above idea in more detail. Subsection 4.1 gives some definitions that will be used in defining testing criteria. Subsection 4.2 analyzes the static checking opportunities within collaboration diagrams. Subsection 4.3 gives criteria for dynamic testing from collaboration diagrams.

4.1 Some Definitions

Figure 2 is a collaboration diagram for an Operation taken from a paper by Overgaard [9]. In this diagram, *processOrder(o)* is a specified operation whose implementation is modeled by the collaboration diagram. :Company is an object on which the specified operation *processOrder(o)* is called. Thus, *processOrder* belongs to the class Company. We can distinguish four types of messages in this diagram. A call to a method through an object that is defined in the calling object is a *local method invocation.* In Figure 2, `d` and `s` are local to :Company, `o` is a parameter to :Company, and `delivery` and `store` are not local. The four message types are: (1) local method invocations without return values, e.g., `deliver(d)` in Figure 2, (2) local method invocations with return values, (3) parameter object's method invocations, e.g., pNr := getpNr(), and (4) object creations, e.g. delivery(o,s). The messages, stereotypes on links, parameters, and sequence numbers that are described in the collaboration diagram are our testing objectives.

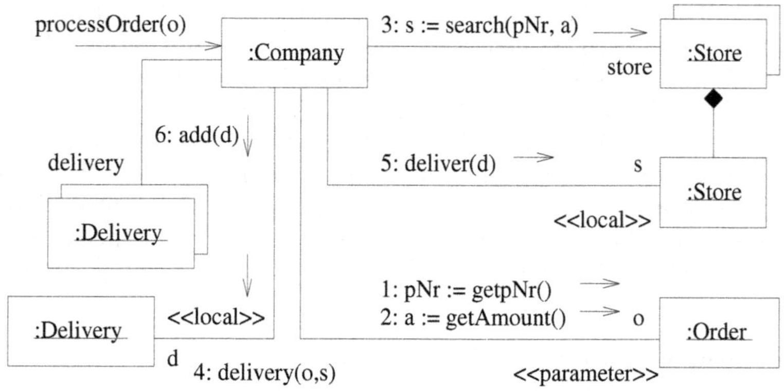

Fig. 2. A Collaboration Diagram for an Operation

The following terms will be used in the definition of testing criteria. Before defining the test criteria, we define *12* types of possible connections in collaboration diagrams. The types of connection pairs, or links, are reminiscent of data flow definitions [5], but represent data interactions that occur at a higher level (design) than traditional data flow (intra-procedural). They are classified based on information from class diagrams and collaboration diagrams, but once defined, only collaboration diagrams are needed to generate tests.

A *collaborating pair* is a pair of ClassifierRoles or AssociationRoles that are connected via a link in the collaboration diagram. The ClassifierRole part describes the type of Object with a set of required operations and attributes.

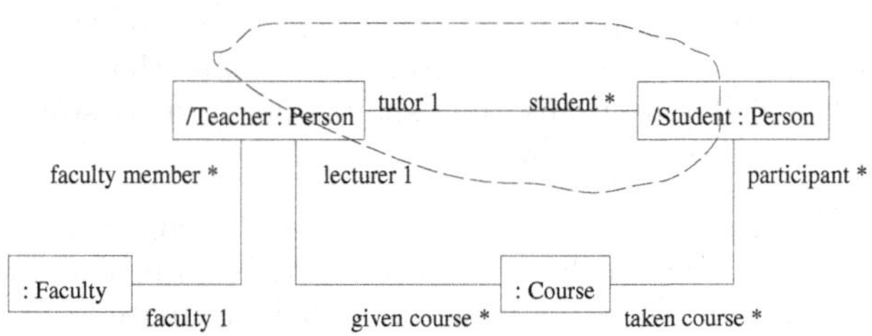

Fig. 3. Collaborating Pairs

A *variable definition link* is a link whose stimulus has a return value that is assigned to local variable. A *variable usage link* is a link whose argument-list of the stimulus includes a local variable. An *object definition link* is a stimulus that returns a reference to an object that is accessible to the target object. An *object creation link* is a link whose stimulus invokes the constructor of the class of target CollaborationRole. An *object usage link* is a link whose stimulus invokes a method (other than constructor and destructor) of a locally accessible object. An *object destruction link* is a link whose stimulus invokes the destructor of a locally accessible object.

Sometimes we are concerned with pairs of links. A *variable def-use link pair* is a pair of links in which a variable is first defined and then used. An *object def-use link pair* is a pair of links in which an object is first defined and then used. An *object creation-usage link pair* is a pair of links in which an object is first created and then used. An *object usage-destruction link pair* is a pair of links in which an object is first used and then destroyed. A *message sequence path* is a path that includes all messages in a collaboration in the order specified by the collaboration diagram.

Variable definition-usage link pairs, object creation-usage link pairs, object usage-destruction link pairs, and object creation-destruction link pairs can be used to statically check the code. Message sequence paths can be used to generate test cases. The following subsections give requirements for static checking and testing. The first subsection describes what should be checked statically. The second subsection describes test data that can be derived from a collaboration diagram.

4.2 Static Checking

Testing can be either static or dynamic. Most discussions of testing focus on dynamic testing, wherein the software is executed on some inputs. Static testing refers to checking some aspects of the software without execution, usually by evaluating the source code.

Collaboration diagrams provide constraints on a system. For example, a collaboration diagram for an operation describes specific information that is needed for this operation to be accomplished, such as return values for an invoked method during the process, parameter types, etc. The pairs that were defined in subsection 4.1 can also also be considered as constraints that cannot be violated.

We have identified four items that should be used to statically check the code. They are described as follows:

1. **ClassifierRoles:** In a collaboration, if two ClassifierRoles originate from the same base class, then they should be distinct in terms of their requested operations and values of attributes. Since they originate from the same class, it is possible that they might be mistaken for each other. For this reason, ClassifierRoles that originate from the same class should be tested to see if they have all the required attributes and operations.
2. **Collaborating Pairs:** The links on a collaboration diagram depict the structural constraints of collaborating pairs and their communication messages. The association tells if it is a one-to-one, one-to-many, or many-to-many relationship. The relationship reflects a constraint in the requirement specification. Hence, testing the structural relationship between objects can serve as verification of requirements. Each collaborating pair on the collaboration diagram should be checked or tested at least once.
3. **Message or stimulus:** Messages provide information on:
   - return value type
   - thread of control
   - operation or method name to be invoked on the target object
   - parameters to the invoked operation or method

   Testing of a message itself may reveal most integration problems. A stimulus is an instance of a message. A stimulus could be a signal, a method or operation call, or an event that causes an object to be created or destroyed. Besides carrying a specific data, messages have a direction. That is, a stimulus originates from a source object (*sender*) and resides on a target object (*receiver*). We can see that stimulus provides early information for integration testing, thus each stimulus should be used as a basis for generating test inputs.
4. **Local Variable Definition-Usage Link Pairs:** Checking variable definition-usage link pairs lets us find data flow anomalies at the design level. The following link pairs should all be checked for data flow anomalies:
   - Global Variable Definition-Use Pairs
   - Object Creation-Use Pairs
   - Object Use-Destruction Pairs
   - Object Creation-Destruction Pairs

4.3 Dynamic Testing

Collaboration diagrams provide a complete path for a use case or the realization of an operation. For the purposes of dynamic testing, this paper focuses on the collaboration diagrams for the realization of operations. We assume that there is one collaboration diagram per operation, and the implementation of an operation conforms to the collaboration. Also, collaboration diagrams provide the information necessary to test object interaction.

Test criterion: *For each collaboration diagram in the specification, there must be at least one test case t such that when the software is executed using t, the software that implements the message sequence path of the collaboration diagram must be executed.*

Each collaboration diagram represents a complete trace of messages during the execution of an operation. Therefore, a message sequence path include all variable def-use link pairs, object def-use link pairs, object creation-usage link pairs, and object usage-destruction link pairs.

We can form a *message sequence path* by using the messages and their sequence numbers. *Message sequence paths* can be traces of system level interactions or component (object) level interactions. Figure 4 shows a message sequence path that is derived from Figure 2. In this diagram, nodes represent method calls and edges represent control flow. Each node has information about the operation name and the object name that the operation is implemented in.

Criteria of this type are normally used in one of two ways. The criterion can be used as a guide for generating tests, or the criterion can be used as a metric for measuring externally created tests. This paper focuses on the measurement use of the criterion; test generation is left for future work.

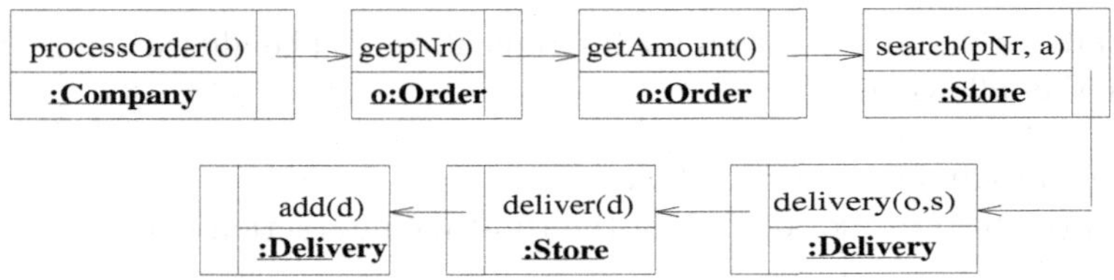

Fig. 4. A Message Sequence Path

To test that the system will produce an event trace that conforms to the message sequence path we derived from the collaboration diagram, we insert instrumentations into the original program. We assume that the type of instrumentation will not affect the performance of the application.

---

algorithm:	**Instrument (ColDiagram, Implementation)**
input:	`A collaboration diagram that models the implementation of an operation, and the implementation of the system.`
output:	`Instrumented code.`
output criteria:	`All the nodes on the message sequence path should be instrumented.`
declare:	`msgPathNode : {actionName, linkEndObjectTypeName, next}` `curNode is` **type** `msgPathNode. curNode represents the current node in the message sequence path.` `msgPath -- A linked list of` **type** `msgPathNode objects.`

```
Instrument (ColDiagram, Implementation)
BEGIN -- Algorithm Instrument
    construct a msgPathNode for each link and its link end object
    put each msgPathNode in msgPath linked list
    curNode = first node in the msgPath
    WHILE (curNode != null)
        className = curNode.linkEndObjectTypeName
        go to the actual implementation of className in the code
        actionName = curNode.actionName
        go to the actual implementation of actionName in the code
        insert instrument in actionName method
        curNode = curNode.next
    END WHILE
END Algorithm Instrument
```

Fig. 5. The Instrumentation Algorithm

Figure 5 gives an algorithm for instrumentation. The algorithm attempts to achieve the following goals:

1. insert instruments for each link
2. help the tester to keep track of the run-time interaction traces

This algorithm can be illustrated through an example. Consider the collaboration diagram in Figure 2, and its message sequence path in Figure 4. The algorithm will start with the collaboration diagram, then sort all its stimuli and their link end objects into a `msgPath` linked list. The algorithm picks the first node in the `msgPath`, {`processOrder(o)`, `Company`, *next*}. From the information contained in the `msgPath` node, the algorithm decides to insert instrumentation in the implementation of the *processOrder()* method in the *Company* class. The instrumentation should reflect the parameter type. Then, the algorithm takes the next node in `msgPath` and inserts the next instrumentation. The algorithm processes all the nodes in `msgPath` in the order of their message sequence numbers.

5 Conclusions

This paper has introduced new integration-level analysis and testing techniques that are based on design descriptions of software component interactions. There are relatively few formal testing criteria that are based on design descriptions. The techniques in this paper are innovative in that they utilize formal design descriptions as a basis, and have practical value because they can be completely automated from the widely used design notation of collaboration diagrams. Tools already exist for constructing collaboration diagrams, and tools for performing the analysis and testing described here can be built with relative ease. This paper also includes an algorithm for instrumenting a program that is implemented from collaboration diagrams. The instrumentation will ensure that tests satisfy the formal testing criteria developed in this research, and also help ensure traceability from the design artifacts to the code.

This research includes techniques to be used both statically and dynamically. The static analysis allows test engineers to find certain problems that reflect ambiguities in the design and misunderstandings on the part of the detailed designers and programmers. The dynamic technique allows test data to be generated that can assure reliability aspects of the implementation-level objects and interactions among them.

We have three major directions for the future of this work. First, we are currently carrying out an empirical evaluation of this work by implementing software that is based on collaboration diagrams, generating tests, and then using the tests to detect problems in the software. Second, we plan to implement tools to perform the static analysis on the software, and to automatically generate tests from UML collaboration diagrams. We plan to integrate these tools with Rational Software Corporation's Rational Rose tool [2]. This will allow us to carry out more extensive empirical evaluations, and to gain practical experience with using this technique. Finally, we continue to develop analysis and testing techniques that are based on the various design and specification diagrams that are part of the UML.

References

1. B. Beizer. *Software Testing Techniques.* Van Nostrand Reinhold, Inc, New York NY, 2nd edition, 1990. ISBN 0-442-20672-0. 385
2. Rational Software Corporation. *Rational Rose 98: Using Rational Rose.* Rational Rose Corporation, Cupertino CA, 1998. 394
3. Gregor Engels, L. P. J. Groenewegen, and G. Kappal. Object-oriented specification of coordinated collaboration. In *Proceedings of the IFIP World Conference on IT Tools*, pages 437–449, Canberra, Australia, September 1996. 384

4. Gregor Engels, Roland Hucking, Stefan Sauer, and Annika Wagner. Uml collaboration diagrams and their transformation to java. In *Proceedings of the Second IEEE International Conference on the Unified Modeling Language (UML99)*, pages 473–488, Fort Collins, CO, October 1999. IEEE Computer Society Press. 389
5. P. G. Frankl and E. J. Weyuker. An applicable family of data flow testing criteria. *IEEE Transactions on Software Engineering*, 14(10):1483–1498, October 1988. 388, 390
6. Object Management Group. *OMG UML Specification Version 1.3*, June 1999. Available at http://www.omg.org/uml/. 386, 386, 387, 389
7. Jeff Offutt and Aynur Abdurazik. Generating tests from UML specifications. In *Proceedings of the Second IEEE International Conference on the Unified Modeling Language (UML99)*, pages 416–429, Fort Collins, CO, October 1999. IEEE Computer Society Press. 383, 384
8. Jeff Offutt, Yiwei Xiong, and Shaoying Liu. Criteria for generating specification-based tests. In *Proceedings of the Fifth IEEE International Conference on Engineering of Complex Computer Systems (ICECCS '99)*, pages 119–131, Las Vegas, NV, October 1999. IEEE Computer Society Press. 383, 384
9. Gunnar Overgaard. A Formal Approach to Collaborations in the Unified Modeling Language. In *Proceedings of the Second IEEE International Conference on the Unified Modeling Language (UML99)*, pages 99–115, Fort Collins, CO, October 1999. IEEE Computer Society Press. 387, 389
10. A. Spillner. Control flow and data flow oriented integration testing methods. *The Journal of Software Testing, Verification, and Reliability*, 2(2):83–98, 1992. 388
11. Hong Zhu, Patrick A. V. Hall, and John H. R. May. Software unit test coverage and adequacy. *ACM Computing Surveys*, 29(4):366–427, December 1997. 388

Supporting Several Levels of Restriction in the UML

Christian Heide Damm, Klaus Marius Hansen, Michael Thomsen, Michael Tyrsted

Department of Computer Science, University of Aarhus,
Aabogade 34, 8200 Aarhus N, Denmark

{damm,marius,miksen,tyrsted}@daimi.au.dk

Abstract. The emergence of the Unified Modeling Language (UML) has provided software developers with an effective and efficient shared language. However, UML is often too restrictive in initial, informal, and creative modelling, and it is in some cases not restrictive enough, e.g., for code generation. Based on user studies, we propose that tool and meta-level support for several levels of restriction in diagrams and models is needed. We furthermore present a tool, Knight, which supports several levels of restriction as well as ways of transferring models from one level of restriction to another. This approach potentially increases the usability of the UML, and thus ultimately leads to greater quality and adoption of UML models.

1. Introduction

Modelling is an important activity in object-oriented development [18]. For visual modelling, the Unified Modelling Language (UML; [21]) has been widely accepted. Much research has focussed on extending, formalising, or refining the UML [8][9][3]. Another important research question is, however, to what extent the UML supports visual modelling as it is being carried out in actual practice? This paper seeks to answer this question, although not in a general sense, as we will mostly discuss the existing practice of initial, creative, and collaborative problem domain modelling. The question will be addressed from two perspectives: One focussing on the UML itself as a modelling language, and one focussing on the support by current tools and technologies for UML modelling.

The UML is widely used by practitioners, but our previous studies suggest that certain parts of the UML are too restrictive with respect to what can be described [5]. For example, while modelling, practitioners often draw incomplete relationships or represent concepts (classes) by illustrative freehand drawings.

Likewise, tools and technologies for UML-based modelling are in wide use. It is a striking fact, however, that Computer Aided Software Engineering (CASE) tools are not widely used and adopted [1][13][15][17]. Some of the explanations are that current CASE tools focus too much on hard aspects of software engineering, while

A. Evans, S. Kent and B. Selic (Eds.): «UML» 2000, LNCS 1939, pp. 396-409, 2000.

support for soft aspects such as collaboration, creativity, and idea generation is lacking [14].

This paper takes a closer look at the practice of initial, creative, and collaborative problem domain modelling through a number of concrete projects. Based on these, we argue for the usefulness of several levels of restriction of the UML metamodel for the usefulness of transferring a model element from one level of restriction to another. Furthermore, we present and discuss a tool, *Knight*, which illustrates the main ideas. The main characteristics of the Knight tool are: Support for a direct and fluid use, support for collaboration, and support for different levels of restriction in both model and presentation, ranging from incomplete, freehand UML diagrams to UML models close to code.

The rest of this paper is structured as follows. First, we analyse current modelling practice and its application of the UML and tools. Second, we present the Knight tool, which tries to overcome some of the problems uncovered in the analysis. Then, related and future work is discussed, followed by conclusions.

2. Current Modelling Practice

We will focus our examination of the UML's support for modelling practice on studies of two large development projects and on our own personal experience as system developers. The first project, Dragon [4], involved a research group and a large, globally distributed shipping company. The goal of the project was to implement a prototype of a global customer service system for the company. This was realised over a one and a half year period by the development of a series of successful prototypes. In this project, three of the authors participated actively and observed ongoing work.

The second project, Danfoss (`http://www.cit.dk/COT/case2-eng.html`), was concerned with implementing an embedded control system for flow meters. The project lasted a year and involved experienced developers from a research group and engineers from a private company. One of the authors participated in this project. This involved formal observations of work and active participation. Thus our approach was a mix of (ethnographic) observations and active involvement in the project studied [11].

Both projects used an iterative object-oriented approach to system development. Throughout development, UML was used on whiteboards and in CASE tools to visualise an emerging understanding of the problem and solution domains.

In order to focus the discussion, the next section presents three representative scenarios distilled from the studies. These scenarios will then subsequently be used as a basis for analysis of current modelling practice.

2.1 Scenarios

Christina and Tom are two developers working on an administrative system for a university. Lisa is a problem domain expert knowledgeable in the domain of university administration.

Scenario One: Using Incomplete and Freehand Elements. Christina and Tom have invited Lisa to a session in which they will start to model the student administration part of the administrative system. Since Christina and Tom have little knowledge of this part of the problem domain, Lisa explains her understanding of student administration. While doing this, she makes heavy use of a whiteboard, and she draws freehand diagrams of the study structure at the university. Christina and Tom, in collaboration with Lisa, then try to transform the verbal and graphical account to a class model, which contains the relevant aspects of the problem domain. Sometimes, Christina or Tom draws an incomplete association or generalisation, since it is not yet clear which classes are involved.

Scenario Two: Shifting Between Levels of Completion. Christina and Tom continue working on the diagram after the initial session with Lisa. Because they work in an iterative manner, they already have a running version of the overall administrative system, and they now want to incorporate the newly discovered student details into the system. Since the previous session was done in a flexible and creative manner, the diagram contains a lot of non-UML elements such as incomplete relationships and freehand drawings. They implement the model in code. In the process they transform the problematic parts in simple ways, e.g., by converting freehand drawings to verbal descriptions in the form of comments, and by either deleting the incomplete relationships or creating stub classes for the dangling ends. During implementation, they discover conceptual errors, which they fix in the code. For later sessions with Lisa, these changes will have to be consistent with the original diagram.

Scenario Three: Using a UML Tool. The development team uses a traditional CASE tool for various software engineering tasks such as code generation, configuration management, and documentation. Christina and Tom thus need to add the student administration model and diagram that they modelled with Lisa to their UML repository. In order to do that, they have taken photos of the whiteboard with the diagram in various stages of completion. Next, they create image files for the important freehand drawings. They then redraw the diagram in their CASE tool by hand, making sure that all parts of the model conform to the UML. References to the photos are then connected to relevant parts of the diagram.

2.2 Analysis

The three scenarios give examples of some of the obvious characteristics of practical UML modelling. This includes the use of different types of information as well as the shifts between these.

Scenario one shows that freehand drawings are used in the early phases of modelling and that sometimes open-ended modelling using, e.g., freehand drawings and incomplete relations are appropriate. At other times, a close connection to code is essential, and this puts some restrictions on the structure of the models.

During the lifetime of a model, it inevitably becomes gradually more stable and complete. Initially, the developers' knowledge of a domain is limited, and the focus is therefore on understanding the overall structures of the domain. Many issues are unclear at this point, even some of the overall structures, and it is of less importance to understand the details of the constituent parts, e.g., attributes and methods and their types and parameters. It is thus necessary to do more expressive, but less restrictive, modelling.

At some point, the model is sufficiently mature to be turned into code. It is, however, not satisfactory to have to wait until the model is complete, before turning it into code, and hence the question arises: how to turn a model with incomplete elements into code? The solution adopted in the scenarios was to fill the holes manually with default values, e.g., setting potential attributes' types to "void". By doing this, we lose information about the model, and at a following analysis/design session, the model looks different from the previous session. In the later phase, it is thus necessary to have a more restricted model, and therefore also less expressive modelling abilities.

As a project progresses, the models get more elaborated in some areas, but new areas are also investigated, like the student administration in the scenarios. This means that the same model can be stable and detailed in some areas, while being initial and containing incomplete elements in other areas.

As is evident in the scenarios, modelling is often done in collaboration, with several developers working together and often also involving domain experts. When people with different competencies work together, these people use different means to express their ideas. In scenario one, Lisa was not a computer expert, so she used the whiteboard to draw sketches. Christina and Tom, on the other hand, focused on creating a class diagram and thus used the UML notation on the whiteboard.

Also, scenario three highlighted the large gap between whiteboards and traditional UML tools. The whiteboard contained many elements that had to be modified to fit in the UML tool, and the transfer itself was manual and cumbersome. Moreover, since development was iterative, such shifts will often occur.

3. UML Tool Support for Modelling Practice

The fact that the UML metamodel disallows practices used in modelling suggests that the UML metamodel should be modified. As the analysis in section 2.2 shows, the way of expressing knowledge in a model varies. Sometimes, the flexibility to create freehand drawings and incomplete elements is needed. At other times, the model should be sufficiently restricted to allow for direct code generation.

One solution would be to make the UML metamodel more expressive so as to allow models to contain all kinds of elements needed as well as all kinds of relationships between those elements. However, in order for a model to be useful for, e.g., code generation, it is necessary that the model is restricted only to contain elements that have a straightforward translation to programming language constructs. As an example, Bunse and Atkinson propose the *Normal Object Form* (NOF) [3], which is a version of the UML metamodel that is closer to object-oriented programming languages and therefore better supports code generation from models. Thus, there *should* be support at the metamodel level for different levels of restriction.

Instead of having several more or less incidental metamodel, the UML metamodel itself could contain different *levels*. The levels of the UML metamodel should cover the range from very expressive models to models close to code. There should, at least, be the following levels:

A flexible level that supports freehand drawings, incomplete elements, etc.

A level that allows the models to be analysed (this could be the current UML metamodel)

A level, in which models are close to object-oriented programming languages, so that code generation is possible (this could be the NOF)

Ideally, the UML should support a continuum of metamodels at different levels of restriction, but, realistically, a fixed number of standardised levels should be incorporated in the UML

For each different metamodel, there will be constructs that relate to models ("meta-*model*") and constructs that relate to diagram or presentation ("meta-*presentation*"). An unrestricted meta-model will, e.g., allow attributes with no type information, and an unrestricted meta-presentation will, e.g., allow expressive freehand drawings to be used. It is interesting to consider how these varying meta-models and meta-presentations may be coupled. At times, a very restrictive meta-model and a very restrictive meta-presentation will be useful, such as when exchanging models and diagrams between organisations. At other times, there will be a need for a very expressive meta-model coupled to a very expressive meta-presentation, such as when brainstorming. Also, a coupling between a restrictive meta-model and an expressive meta-presentation is beneficial: If domain experts are involved in modelling, a presentation much like that on a whiteboard is useful.

Such a modification of the UML that supports different levels of restriction will help modelling practice. However, there is also a need for tools to support those levels. The next section describes a prototype of a tool, the *Knight tool*, which is designed to support flexible and creative modelling. We have used the Knight tool to experiment with different levels and the transition between those levels.

3.1 The Knight Tool

The Knight tool is a tool for the initial analysis and design in object-oriented software development. With a lightweight interface, it combines freehand drawings with UML diagrams. We have found that this is very important for the modelling in early phases of object-oriented software development [5]. Problems of today's Windows, Icons, Menus, and Pointers (WIMP) interfaces are many and well known [2]. The Knight tool tries to overcome such problems by basing the interaction on gestures, marking menus, and a whiteboard metaphor.

The Knight Tool is implemented in Itcl [19], an object-oriented extension of Tcl/Tk [21]. For further information on the Knight tool, refer to `http://www-.daimi.au.dk/~knight` or [5][6][7].

Interaction with Few Breakdowns. The whiteboard metaphor is the cornerstone of the Knight tool (Figure 1): The user interface is initially a blank, white surface on which the user draws strokes. These strokes are then recognised as gestures using Rubine's algorithm [24] and interpreted as commands.

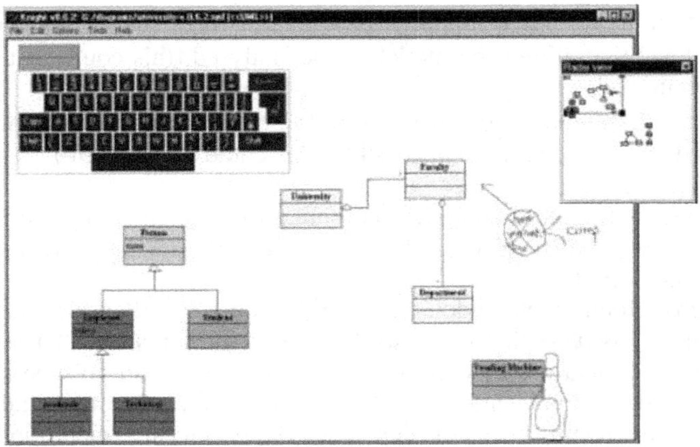

Figure 1. User interface of the Knight tool

The gestures resemble what is typically drawn on an ordinary whiteboard. For example, the gesture for drawing a class is a box, as shown in Figure 2.

Figure 2. Gesture recognition in the Knight tool.

In addition to the gestures for creating UML elements, there are also gestures for moving, editing, and deleting elements. Less common commands may be accessed through a context-sensitive pie menu, which is activated by pressing on the drawing surface for a moment.

The rationale for using gestures is to make the interaction fast and fluid: few breakdowns and focus shifts should be caused by the interaction with the tool. So far, evaluations with users have supported this claim [5].

Collaboration Support. The Knight tool may be used on an ordinary workstation with a mouse or a tablet. If used on an electronic whiteboard, collaboration between a number of developers and domain experts is supported (Figure 3).

Figure 3. Collaborating using the Knight tool on an electronic whiteboard

We have used the Knight tool on several types of electronic whiteboards, including the SMART Board (`http://www.smarttech.com`) and the Mimio (`http://-www.mimio.com`).. The SMART Board (Figure 3) is a large, touch-sensitive surface, whereas the Mimio is a small device, which can be attached to ordinary whiteboards. Given the Knight tool and a projector, both technologies gives a total interaction much like that on a whiteboard.

3.2 Knight's Support for Varying Levels of Restriction

From the analysis in the previous section, we derive that a UML tool should support metamodels with differing levels of restriction, since modelling is not done on one level of abstraction at all times. Also shifts between levels should be supported. This section discusses the current support for varying levels of restriction in the Knight tool.

Shifting Between Levels of Restriction. As identified above, there is a need for shifting between the levels of expressiveness and restriction. A user may use a tool in three ways to transform a model, so that it conforms to a certain restriction level.

Automated. The tool may automatically transform the model.

Guided. The tool may identify the elements that do not conform to the new level of restriction, and it may provide the user with advice on how each element may be transformed. The user can then decide which transformation is appropriate.

Manual. The user has to transform the model in the usual way, i.e., without any special assistance from the tool.

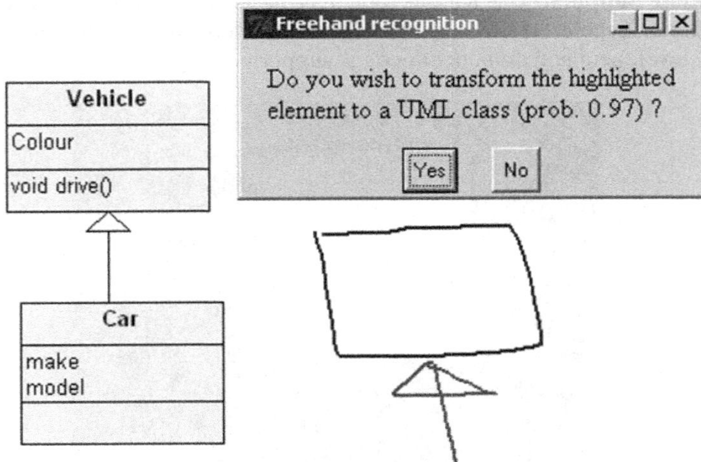

Figure 4. Guided transformation of freehand elements

The Knight tool implements all three kinds of support to varying degrees. Initially, strokes are conceptually elements in an unrestricted meta-model and -presentation. The default behaviour of Knight is to automatically transform these into UML elements. In this way, a restriction is made in the presentation as well as in the model. During integration with other CASE tools, an automated restriction is also necessary. As an example, freehand drawings are converted into comments, and incomplete elements are omitted from the restricted model. These are all examples of automated transformations.

Guided transformations are also supported in several ways. The user can ask Knight to identify the elements that are illegal in the more restricted meta-model. These will be marked graphically, and the user may then request guidance on how to transform the elements. For example, an incomplete association turns red, and in order to make it complete, the user can either delete the association or move the dangling end to a class. When the illegal elements are all removed, the model has been restricted. Furthermore, the user can ask the tool to guide a transformation where freehand elements are restricted into UML elements. The tool will then iterate through the individual marks in the drawing and present the user with a possible restriction (see Figure 4).

Figure 5 shows examples of manual transformations. In the example, a freehand drawing showing important details of the concept of a "Route" has been drawn. Depending on the context, the user may use different transformations. If the drawing is no longer significant, the user may choose to transform the drawing into a class and give it the name "Route". If it is still important to be able to refer to the drawing, the user may transform the drawing to a class and a relation to the drawing, thus using the drawing as an icon for the class. Likewise, the user may use the drawing to document a more elaborate model of a route.

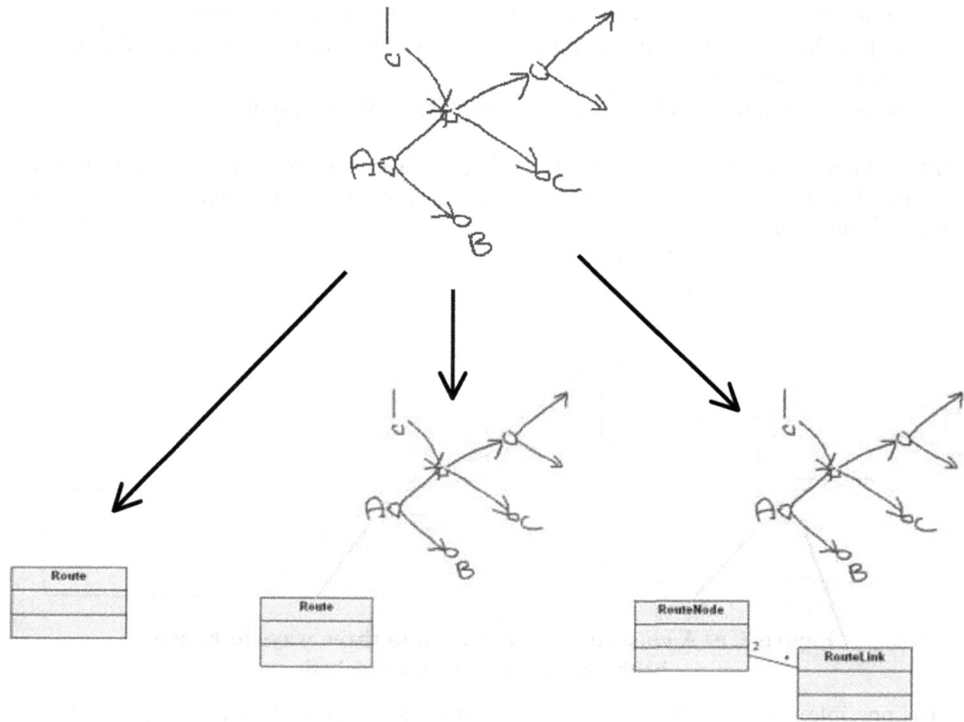

Figure 5. Restrictive transformations of a freehand drawing

Preserving the Look of Diagrams. Knight supports the creative phases of object-oriented modelling, because it allows users to create expressive models. For example, a UML class may not have a name yet, and only some of the attributes may be known and specified. However, in Knight and other UML tools, the elements often *look* finished, even when they are not (Figure 6).

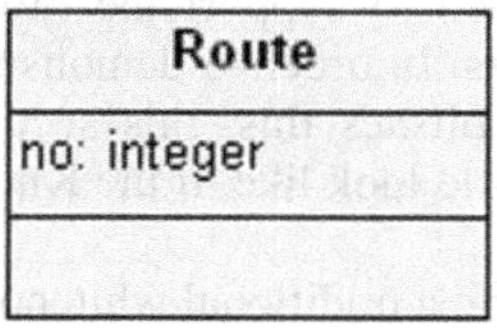

Route

no: integer

Figure 6. Unfinished elements may look finished

There is evidence that the appearance of, e.g., a diagram or a user interface influences how people perceive it [16]. A sketchy look of a diagram makes people subconsciously believe that the diagram is not finished, and hence they are more willing to suggest changes to it.b

Knight supports preservation of the look of elements. An element can be displayed in three different ways:

- it may look exactly the way it was drawn, i.e., it is not transformed,
- it may have a semi-transformed look, which is the same for all elements of the same category, or
- it may have a transformed look, e.g., the usual UML notation.

These three looks are exemplified for a UML class in Figure 7a. In Figure 7b, the Route class from Figure 6 is displayed with an untransformed look, which suggests that it is unfinished.

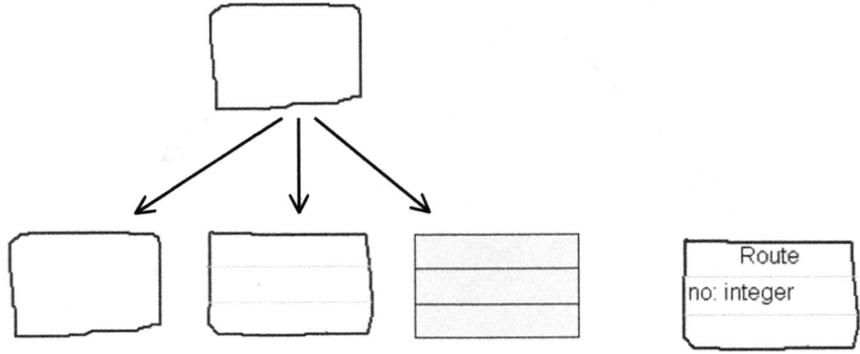

Figure 7. a) A class may be displayed in three ways in Knight, b) the Route class is not finished

It is possible for different elements in the same model to be displayed differently. In fact, as discussed in section 2.2, it is often the case that certain parts of a diagram are detailed and finished, while other parts have not yet been elaborated on. Displaying the elements corresponding to whether they are finished or not can show the situation to the users.

3.3 The Knight Tool at Work

The Knight tool was designed to support the modelling practice found in actual software development projects. In order to demonstrate *how* the use of Knight on an electronic whiteboard accomplishes this, this section will describe what the three scenarios from section 2.1 could look like, if the Knight tool was used.

Scenario One. Instead of using a traditional whiteboard, Lisa, Christina, and Tom use Knight. Because Knight supports freehand drawing, Lisa is able to illustrate the study structure directly in Knight. Christina and Tom gradually transform Lisa's freehand drawings to corresponding classes, while retaining the original drawings in the diagram.

Scenario Two. Christina and Tom have to transfer the model created together with Lisa to the overall administrative system. The model contains non-UML elements, but Christina and Tom use Knight's guidance to remedy some of the problematic elements. The rest of the non-UML elements are handled automatically by Knight, which deletes some incomplete associations and adds default types to some attributes.

Scenario Three. Because the model was created directly in Knight, there is no need to capture the contents using a camera. Freehand elements may, moreover, be connected to UML elements directly. Also, the shifts to and from ordinary whiteboards are eliminated through the use of Knight on an electronic whiteboard.

Even though the scenarios highlight the positive features of Knight, there is room for a lot of improvement. Problems and plans are discussed in the next session.

4. Related & Future Work

As mentioned in the introduction, Jarzabek and Huang [14], among others, explain the low adoption of CASE tools with that they are too concerned with software engineering aspects of development. Instead, aspects such as creativity, flexibility, and idea generation should be focussed on and more widely supported. We concur that focussing on softer aspects of system development in CASE tool development may be a way for CASE tools to gain wider acceptance. This is the very basis for our work on Knight and is what we will continue working on also in the context of other formal notations than the UML. A very important means of ensuring that Knight supports this kind of work will be to set up longitudinal studies of Knight in use. We are currently trying to do this at several Danish companies. Although many of the basic mechanisms for creative modelling are present in Knight, we suspect that further refinements are needed. For example, it should be possible to incorporate other types of media than drawing such as photographs, videos, and sound in a seamless manner. Also, the use of and transition between different levels of restrictions will have to be refined.

In [12], Haake et al. present a taxonomy for categorising information-structuring systems based on the perspectives of the user and the system. The taxonomy has two dimensions. The first dimension describes how explicitly the user specifies the types of objects. Does the user, e.g., state that a specified object is of a certain type or not? The second dimension describes how the system represents the data. Does the system, e.g., retain or discard the type information? In our default transformation when users draw UML elements by gesturing, the user does not specify that it is, e.g., a class that is drawn. However, the system infers and represents the class via type information. In this sense there is no difference between selecting a class icon from a palette and drawing a gesture for a class. In the case in which the user draws a freehand drawing and then later transforms it manually, the situation changes from one in which the user has a typed representation of an element, whereas the system does not, to a situation in which both user and system has a typed representation. We concur with Haake et al. that this provides the users with a flexibility to support the creation of objects without the overhead of deciding types immediately. The focus of this paper has been on how presentation and model in UML has been represented. This is in many ways system-centric, and one may envision a conceptualisation of levels of restriction in which cognitive aspects of users are taken into account.

In [3], Bunse and Atkinson propose the *Normal Object Form* (NOF), which is closer than UML to object-oriented programming languages. The NOF is basically a subset of UML with certain predefined extensions, and with some additional constraints on the structure of models. The authors make a distinction between *refinement* and *translation* of a UML model. The former involves adding details to the model, while remaining within the UML, and the latter is a transformation of the UML model to an object-oriented programming language. Thus, a model should be gradually *refined* until it satisfies the NOF criteria, and then it should be *translated* to code. The NOF is an example of a useful version of the UML with a specific purpose, and thus it supports our claim that there should be multiple versions of the UML. Also, models should be gradually transformed from one form (current UML, expressive) to another (NOF, restrictive), and this process could benefit from guidance or automation of a tool. The *refinement patterns* mentioned in the paper could play a role in the process, be it guidance or automation. Whereas NOF is a very restrictive version of the UML metamodel, what we propose is that the default, or lowest, level of restriction of the UML metamodel should be such that the flexible modelling described in this paper can be directly supported.

Another strand of future work is to experiment with the transportable Mimio technology, which is more lightweight than the SMART Board. A starting configuration for Knight using Mimio may be a mode, in which Mimio is used with marking pens but without projector. Strokes drawn may then either be interpreted during a session, yielding a possibility to give feedback, or be transformed to UML elements after the session using the techniques described in this paper. In-between this scenario and the one in which Mimio acts as an ordinary electronic whiteboard, a number of possibilities can be imagined. For example, UML elements may be drawn with a non-marking pen while freehand elements may be drawn with marking pens. One of our current goals is to offer a smooth transition between such scenarios.

Finally, the tool is being commercialised by Ideogramic (`http://www.ideogramic.com`). Part of this is, naturally, to support all diagram types in the UML.

5. Conclusion

The UML enables the construction of object-oriented models in a usable, visual way. However, in an object-oriented software development project – and in the process of creating a UML model – the UML is *not* sufficiently flexible, and hence it does not support all phases of object-oriented modelling. Likewise, existing tools do not support initial modelling phases in a satisfactory way.

Bunse and Atkinson [3] argue that, when coding starts, a restricted version of the UML metamodel is needed. We, on the other hand, argue that UML should support the initial phases of modelling, where incomplete diagram elements and freehand drawing are heavily used. The answer to both requests is to introduce different levels of restriction in the UML metamodel and to split it into meta-model and meta-presentation. In this way, it is possible to combine expressive or restrictive meta-presentations with expressive or restrictive meta-models.

A change in the UML metamodel should be accompanied by appropriate tool support. Modelling involves going from more or less expressive diagrams to more restricted models, and tools should support this process. This implies that tools should be aware of the different levels of restriction and be able to assist the user in going from one level to another, either automatically or semi-automatically.

In this paper, we have presented the Knight tool, which was designed to support modelling practice. The Knight tool supports collaboration in modelling, fluid modelling, and shifts between levels of restriction in modelling. Using Knight, we have demonstrated that it is in fact possible to make tool support for actual modelling practice.

Acknowledgements. This project has been partly sponsored by the Centre for Object Technology (COT, `http://www.cit.dk/COT`), which is a joint research project between Danish industry and universities. COT is sponsored by The Danish National Centre for IT Research (CIT, `http://www.cit.dk`), the Danish Ministry of Industry and University of Aarhus. Thanks to Ole Lehrmann Madsen for comments that improved this paper.

References

1. Aaen, I., Siltanen, A., Sørensen, C., & Tahvanainen, V.-P. (1992). A Tale of two Countries: CASE Experiences and Expectations. In Kendall, K.E., Lyytinen, K., & DeGross, J. (Eds.), *The impact of Computer Supported Technologies on Information Systems Development* (pp 61-93). IFIP Transactions A (Computer Science and Technology), A-8.
2. Beaduoin-Lafon, M. (2000). Instrumental Interaction: An Interaction Model for Designing Post-WIMP User Interfaces. In *Proceedings of Computer Human Interaction (CHI'2000).* The Hague, The Netherlands.
3. Bunse, C., Atkinson, C. (1999). The Normal Object Form: Bridging the Gap from Models to Code. In *Proceedings of <<UML>>'99 –The Unified Modeling L anguage*, pp. 675-690, Fort Collins, CO, USA, October.
4. Christensen, M., Crabtree, A., Damm, C.H., Hansen, K.M., Madsen, O.L., Marqvardsen, P., Mogensen, P., Sandvad, E., Sloth, L., & Thomsen, M. (1998). The M.A.D. Experience: Multiperspective Application Development in Evolutionary Prototyping. In *Proceedings of ECOOP'98*, Bruxelles, Belgium, July, Springer-Verlag, LNCS series, volume 1445.
5. Damm, C.H., Hansen, K.M., & Thomsen, M. (2000). Tool Support for Cooperative Object-Oriented Design: Gesture Based Modeling on an Electronic Whiteboard. In *Proceedings of Computer Human Interaction (CHI'2000).* The Hague, The Netherlands.
6. Damm, C.H., Hansen, K.M., Thomsen, M., & Tyrsted, M. (2000). Creative Object-Oriented Modelling: Support for Intuition, Flexibility, and Collaboration in CASE Tools. To appear in *Proceedings of ECOOP'2000.* Cannes, France.
7. Damm, C.H., Hansen, K.M., Thomsen, M., & Tyrsted, M. (2000). Tool Integration: Experiences and Issues in Using XMI and Component Technology. To appear in *Proceedings of TOOLS Europe'2000.* Brittany, France.
8. Egyed, A. & Medvidovic, N. (1999). Extending Architectural Representation in UML with View Integration. In France, R. & Rumpe, B. (Eds.) *<<UML>>'99 –The Unified*

Modelling Language. Beyond the Standard. Second International Conference. LNCS 1723, Springer Verlag.

9. Evans, A. & Kent, S. (1999). Core Meta-Modelling Semantics of UML: The pUML Approach. In France, R. & Rumpe, B. (Eds.) *<<UML>>'99 – The Unified Modelling Language. Beyond the Standard.* Second International Conference. LNCS 1723, Springer Verlag.
10. Gamma, E., Helm, R., Johnson, R., & Vlissides, J. (1995). *Design Patterns. Elements of Reusable Object/Oriented Software.* Addison-Wesley.
11. Greenbaum, J. & Kyng, M. (1991). *Design at Work: Cooperative Design of Computer Systems*. Hillsdale New Jersey: Lawrence Erlbaum Associates.
12. Haake, J.M., Neuwirth, C.M., Streitz, N.A. (1994). Coexistence and Transformation of Informal and Formal Structures: Requirements for More Flexible Hypermedia Systems. In *Proceedings of the 1994 ACM European conference on Hypermedia technology*, pp. 1-12. Edinburgh, Scotland.
13. Iivari, J. (1996). Why Are CASE Tools Not Used? In *Communications of the ACM*, 39(10).
14. Jarzabek, S. & Huang, R. (1998) The Case for User-Centered CASE Tools. In *Communications of the ACM*, 41(8).
15. Kemerer, C.F. (1992). How the Learning Curve Affects CASE Tool Adoption. In *IEEE Software,* 9(3).
16. Landay, J.A. & Myers, B.A. (1995) Interactive Sketching for the Early Stages of User Interface Design. In *Proceedings of Computer Human Interaction (CHI'95).*
17. Lending, D. & Chervany, N.L. (1998). The Use of CASE Tools. In Agarwal, R. (Eds.), *Proceedings of the 1998 ACM SIGCPR Conference*, ACM.
18. Madsen, O.L., Møller-Pedersen, B., & Nygaard, K. (1993). *Object-Oriented Programming in the BETA Programming Language*, ACM Press, Addison Wesley.
19. McLennan, M.J. (1993). [incr Tcl]: Object-Oriented Programming. In *Proceedings of the Tcl/Tk Workshop*, University of California at Berkeley, June 10-11.
20. Object Managment Group (1998). *XML Metadata Interchange* (XMI), document ad/98-07-01, July.
21. Object Managment Group (2000). *OMG Unified Modeling Language Specification*, document formal/00-03-01, March.
22. Ousterhout, J. (1994). *Tcl and the Tk Toolkit.* Addison-Wesley.
23. Rogerson, D. (1997). *Inside COM. Microsoft's Component Object Model.* Microsoft Press.
24. Rubine, D. (1991). Specifying Gestures by Example. In *Proceedings of SIGGRAPH'91*, 329-337.

A UML-Based Methodology for Hypermedia Design

Rolf Hennicker[1], Nora Koch [1,2]

[1] Institute of Computer Science
Ludwig-Maximilians University of Munich
Oettingenstr. 67, D-80538 München, Germany
{hennicke,kochn}@informatik.uni-muenchen.de

[2] F.A.S.T. Applied Software Technology GmbH
Arabellastr. 17, D-81925 München, Germany
koch@fast.de

Abstract. We propose a methodology for hypermedia design which is based on a UML profile for the hypermedia domain. Starting with a use case analysis and a conceptual model of the application we first provide guidelines for modeling the navigation space. From the navigation space model we can derive, in a next step, a navigational structure model which shows how to navigate through the navigation space using access elements like indexes, guided tours, queries and menus. Finally, a presentation model is constructed that can be directly implemented by HTML frames. The different models of the design process are represented by using a hypermedia extension of UML.

The strength of the presented methodology is given by the fact that most steps can be performed in an automatic way thus providing the basis for a generation mechanism for hypermedia design.

Keywords: Unified Modeling Language, Hypermedia System, Design Method, Systematic Development, UML Extension, Web Engineering

1 Introduction

Hypermedia development is a new and still evolving discipline. The process of learning how to develop large hypermedia applications has just begun. Hypermedia applications for the Web or CD-ROM are mostly the result of an implementation ad hoc, growing usually from small to large applications and becoming very soon difficult to maintain. Some guidelines and tools are beginning to appear assisting developers of hypermedia applications. But these current practices often fail due to inappropriate techniques, processes and methodologies.

The development of hypermedia systems differs from the developing process of traditional software in several dimensions. People with different skills are involved in the process, such as authors, layout designers, programmers, multimedia experts and marketing specialists. The role of the user is augmented and makes it more difficult to capture the requirements of the application. The non-linearity of the hyperdocuments as well as the possibility to connect easily to other hypermedia applications increments the complexity and risk of "lost in the hyperspace". Web and hypermedia

A. Evans, S. Kent and B. Selic (Eds.): «UML» 2000, LNCS 1939, pp. 410-424, 2000.

engineering has to take into account aesthetic and cognitive aspects as well that traditional software engineering environments do not support [11]. The development process tends to be more fine grained, more incremental and iterative. Maintenance is a significant part of the lifecycle of hypermedia applications in contrast to the role played in traditional systems. In addition, security is a concern of most Web applications.

If we restrict ourselves to the design steps, the main differences we can observe between design of traditional and hypermedia software are the heterogeneity of the designer group, the hypertext structure composed of nodes and links, the need of navigational assistance, the multimedia contents and the presentation of this contents e.g. for different browsers. Thus, the design is centered around three main aspects of hypermedia systems. There are the content, navigational structure and presentation. Treating this aspects separately during design will payoff in the maintenance phase.

In this work we concentrate our attention on the analysis and design workflows of an engineering process based on the Unified Process [6] adapted for hypermedia applications. We propose a design methodology which is based on a UML extension for hypermedia [1]. It consists of three steps that are performed in an iterative design process. The steps are the conceptual, navigational and presentational design. They produce the following artifacts:

conceptual model
navigation space model and navigational structure model
presentation model

The conceptual model is built taking into account the functional requirements captured with use cases. Traditional object-oriented techniques are used to construct the conceptual model, such as finding classes, defining inheritance structures and specifying constraints. It is represented by a class diagram.

Based on this conceptual model the navigation space model is constructed. It also is represented as a static class model. A set of guidelines is proposed for modeling the navigation space. A detailed specification of associations, their multiplicity and role names establishes the base for an automatic generation of the navigational structure model. In this step access structures such as indexes, guided tours, queries and menus are incorporated. The navigational structure model defines the structure of nodes and links of the hypermedia application showing how navigation is supported by the access structures. Finally, we derive from the navigational structure model and the requirements specification a presentation model based on framesets. This model can be implemented by HTML frames.

Navigational design is a critical step in the design of hypermedia application. Even simple applications with a non-deep hierarchical structure will become complex very soon by the addition of new links. Additional links improve navigability on the one hand but imply on the other hand higher risk to loose orientation. Building a navigation model not only is helpful for the documentation of the application structure, it also allows for a more structured increase of navigability.

The strength of our methodology is given by the fact that most steps can be performed in an automatic way thus providing the basis for a generation mechanism for hypermedia design.

This paper is structured as follows: Section 2 describes the starting points for the modeling process: use cases and a conceptual model. Section 3 gives guidelines to build a navigation space model based on the conceptual model. In Section 4 we present a procedure to derive the navigational structure model from the navigation space model. Section 5 shows how the presentation model is obtained from the navigational structure model. In Section 6 a brief description about related work is given. Finally, Section 7 presents some concluding remarks and an overview of future research.

2 Starting with Use Cases and a Conceptual Model

The design of hypermedia applications builds on the requirements specification in the same way as the design of software applications in general does. Following [6] we propose use cases for capturing the requirements. It is a user-centered technique that forces to define who are the users (actors) of the application and offers an intuitive way to represent the functionality an application has to fulfill for each actor.

As an example to illustrate the design process we use the Web Site of a service company. This Web site offers information about the company itself, the employees and their relationships to projects, customers and departments. We restrict ourselves in the example to these concepts although many other aspects could be included, such as information about products, documents, events, press releases and job offers. Fig. 1 shows a use case model for the project administration that is part of the use case model of the Web application. The company's, department's and employee's administration can be modeled in a similar way.

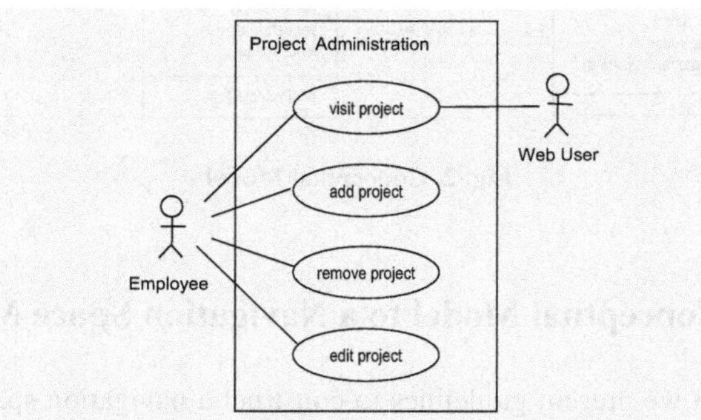

Fig. 1. Use Cases for the Project Administration

The conceptual design of the domain is based on these use cases that include the objects involved in the typical activities users will perform with the application. The conceptual design aims to build a domain model trying to take into account as little as possible of the navigation paths, presentation and interaction aspects. These aspects are postponed to the navigational and presentational steps of the design. Well-known object-oriented modeling activities are performed during the conceptual modeling, such as:

to find classes,
to specify the most relevant attributes and operations,
to determine associations between classes,
to define inheritance hierarchies,
to find dependencies,
to identify interfaces and
to define constraints.

The results of these activities is a UML class model of the problem domain. Classes are described through attributes and operations and represented graphically with UML notation [3]. The conceptual model for the Web site of a service company is shown in Fig. 2. Classes and associations defined in this step are used during navigational design to derive nodes of the hypermedia structure. Associations will be used to derive links.

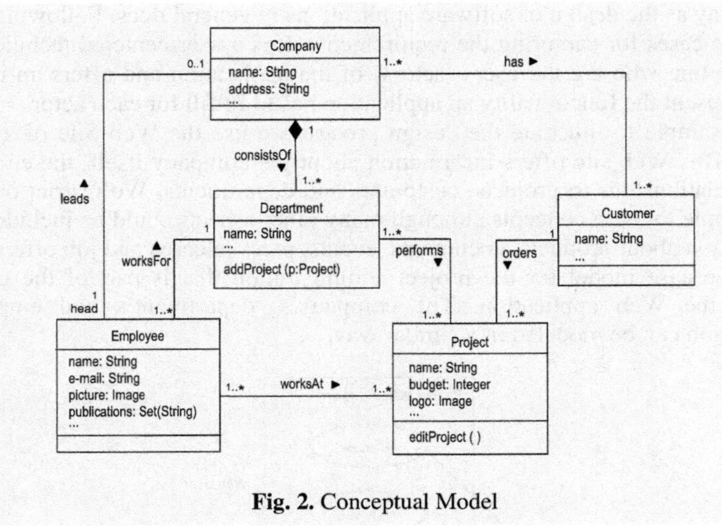

Fig. 2. Conceptual Model

3 From a Conceptual Model to a Navigation Space Model

In this section we present guidelines to construct a navigation space model from a conceptual model. The navigation space model specifies, *which* objects can be visited through navigation in the hypermedia application. *How* these objects are reached is defined by the navigational structure model that is constructed in the next section. In the process of building the navigation space model the developer takes design decisions that are crucial, such as which view of the conceptual model is needed for the application and what navigation paths are required to ensure the application's functionality. The decisions of the designer are based on the conceptual model, use case model and the navigation requirements that the application must satisfy.

3.1 Modeling Elements

For the construction of the navigation space model two modeling elements are used: navigational classes and navigation associations, which express direct navigability. They are the pendant to node and link in the hypermedia terminology.

Navigational Class. A navigational class models a class whose instances are visited by the user during navigation. Navigational classes will be given the same name as conceptual classes. For their representation we use the UML stereotype «navigational class» which is shown in Fig. 3.

Direct Navigability. Associations in the navigation space model are interpreted as direct navigability from the source navigation class to the target navigation class. Hence their semantics is different from the associations used in the conceptual model. To determine the directions of the navigation the associations of this model are directed (possibly bidirected). This is shown by an arrow that is attached to one or both ends of the association. Moreover, each directed end of an association is named with a role name and is equipped with an explicit multiplicity. If no explicit role name is given, the following convention is used: if the multiplicity is less or equal than one the target class name is used as role name; if the multiplicity is greater than one, the plural form of the target class name is used. In the following diagrams all associations with exception of composition are implicitly assumed to be stereotyped by «direct navigability».

3.2 Example

The navigation space model built with the navigational classes and navigability associations is graphically represented by a UML class diagram. Fig. 3 shows the navigation space model for the Web Site of our service company.

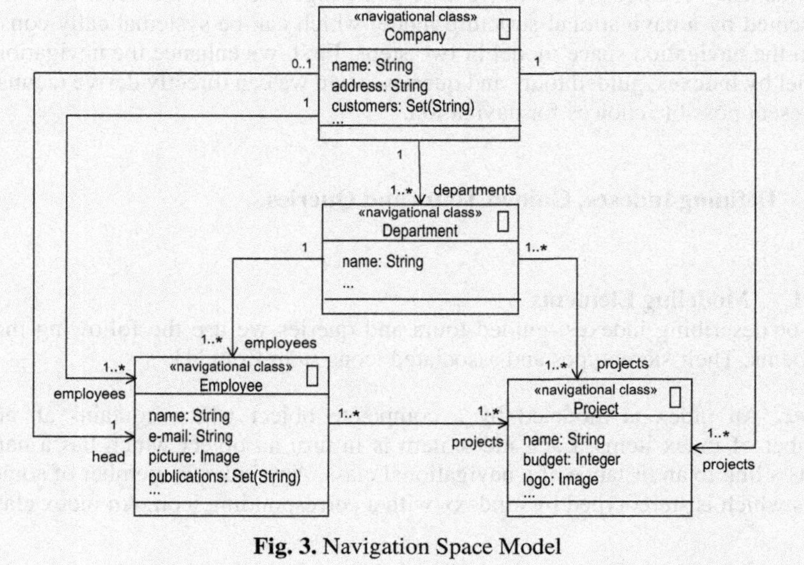

Fig. 3. Navigation Space Model

3.3 The Method

Although there is obviously no way to automate the construction of the navigation space model, there are several guidelines that can be followed by the developer:

1. Classes of the conceptual model that are relevant for the navigation are included as navigational classes in the navigation space model (i.e. navigational classes can be mapped to conceptual classes). If a conceptual class is not a visiting target in the use case model, it is irrelevant in the navigational process and therefore is omitted in the navigation space model (like the class Customer in our example).
2. Required information on the omitted classes can still be kept as attributes of other classes in the navigation space model (e.g. the newly introduced attribute customers of the navigational class Company). All other attributes of navigational classes map directly to attributes of the corresponding conceptual class. Conversely, attributes of the conceptual classes that are considered to be not relevant for the presentation are excluded in the navigation space model.
3. Often additional associations are added for direct navigation avoiding navigation paths of length greater than one. Examples are the newly introduced navigation associations between Company and Employee and between Company and Project. Scenarios described by the use case model give the input for the choice of direct navigations.

4 From a Navigation Space Model to a Navigational Structure Model

The navigation space model tells us which objects can be visited by direct navigations from other objects. In this section we proceed by describing how the navigation can be performed using access elements like indexes, guided tours, queries and menus. Technically, the navigation paths together with the access elements are presented by a navigational structure model which can be systematically constructed from the navigation space model in two steps: First, we enhance the navigation space model by indexes, guided tours and queries. Then we can directly derive menus which represent possible choices for navigation.

4.1 Defining Indexes, Guided Tours and Queries

4.1.1 Modeling Elements

For describing indexes, guided tours and queries we use the following modeling elements. Their stereotypes and associated icons stem from [1].

Index. An index is modeled by a composite object which contains an arbitrary number of index items. Each index item is in turn an object which has a name and owns a link to an instance of a navigational class. Any index is member of some index class which is stereotyped by «index» with a corresponding icon. An index class must be built conform to the composition structure of classes shown in Fig. 4. Hence the stereotype «index» is a restrictive stereotype in the sense of [2]. In practice, we will always use the shorthand notation shown in Fig. 5. Note that in the short form the association between MyIndex and MyNavigationalClass is derived from the index composition and the association between MyIndexItem and MyNavigationalClass.

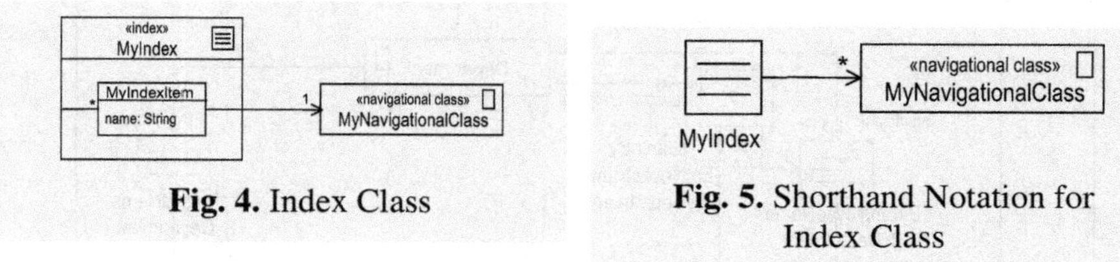

Fig. 4. Index Class

Fig. 5. Shorthand Notation for Index Class

Guided Tour. A guided tour is modeled by an object which provides sequential access to the instances of a navigational class. For classes which contain guided tour objects we use the stereotype «guidedTour» and its corresponding icon depicted in Fig. 6. As shown in Fig. 6, any guided tour class must be connected to a navigational class by a directed association which has the property {ordered}.

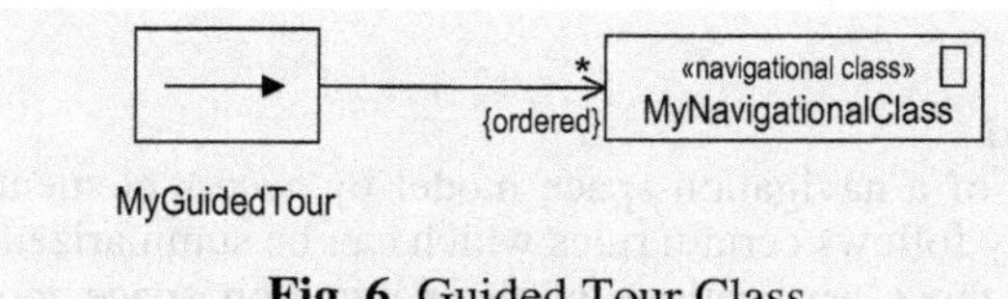

Fig. 6. Guided Tour Class

Query. A query is modeled by an object which has a query string as an attribute. (This string may be given, for instance, by an OCL select operation.) For query classes we use the stereotype «query» and the icon depicted in Fig. 7. As shown in Fig. 7, any query class is the source of two directed associations related by the constraint {or}. In this way we can model that a query with several result objects must first lead to an index which then allows to select a particular instance of a navigational class.

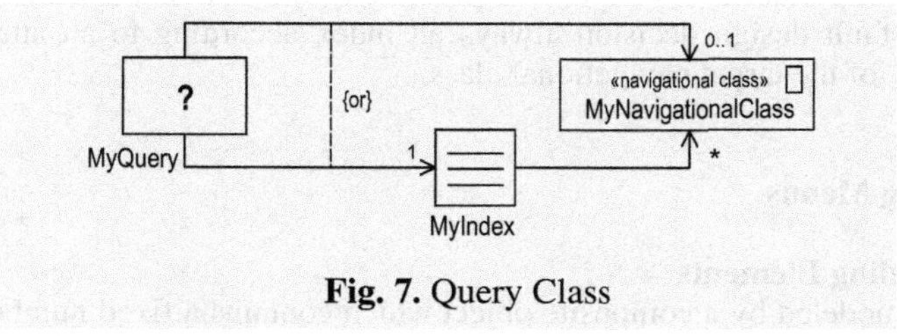

Fig. 7. Query Class

4.1.2 Example

Fig. 8 shows how the navigation space model for the Web Site of our service company can be enhanced by indexes, guided tours and queries. Note that we have included two possible ways to access the employees of a department, by an index and by a query.

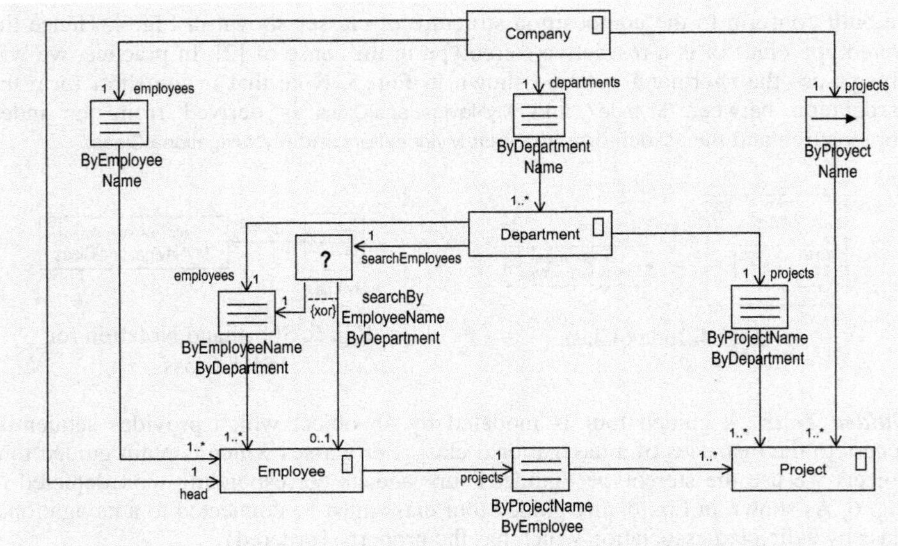

Fig. 8. Navigation Space Model enhanced with Indexes, Guided Tour and Query

4.1.3 The Method

The enhancement of a navigation space model by access elements of type index, guided tour and query follows certain rules which can be summarized as follows:

1. Consider only those associations of the navigation space model which have multiplicity greater than 1 at the directed association end.
2. For each association of this kind, choose one or more access elements to realize the navigation.
3. Enhance the navigation space model correspondingly. Thereby it is important that the roles names of the navigation in the navigation space model are now moved to the access elements (compare Fig. 3 and Fig. 8).

In step 2 it is the task of the designer to choose appropriate access elements. However, it is important to note that it is possible to fully automate also this step by taking as a default design decision always an index according to an attribute with property {key} of the target navigational class.

4.2 Defining Menus

4.2.1 Modeling Elements

A menu is modeled by a composite object which contains a fixed number of menu items. Each menu item has a constant name and owns a link either to an instance of a navigational class or to an access element. Any menu is an instance of some menu class which is stereotyped by «menu» with a corresponding icon. A menu class must be built conform to the composition structure of classes shown in Fig. 9. Hence the stereotype «menu» is again a restrictive stereotype according to the classification of stereotypes given in [2].

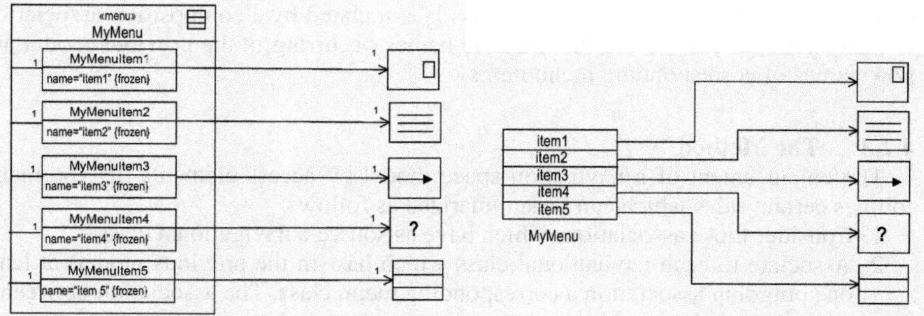

Fig. 9. Menu Class **Fig. 10.** Shorthand for Menu Class

Since menu items are assumed to have fixed names the property {frozen} is attached to each name attribute in a menu item class. Nevertheless, the same menu item class may have different instances since there may be menu items with the same name but linked to different objects. For a convenient notation of menu classes in navigational structure models we will use in the following the shorthand notation shown in Fig. 10.

4.2.2 Example

Fig. 11 shows how the navigational structure model of the previous section is

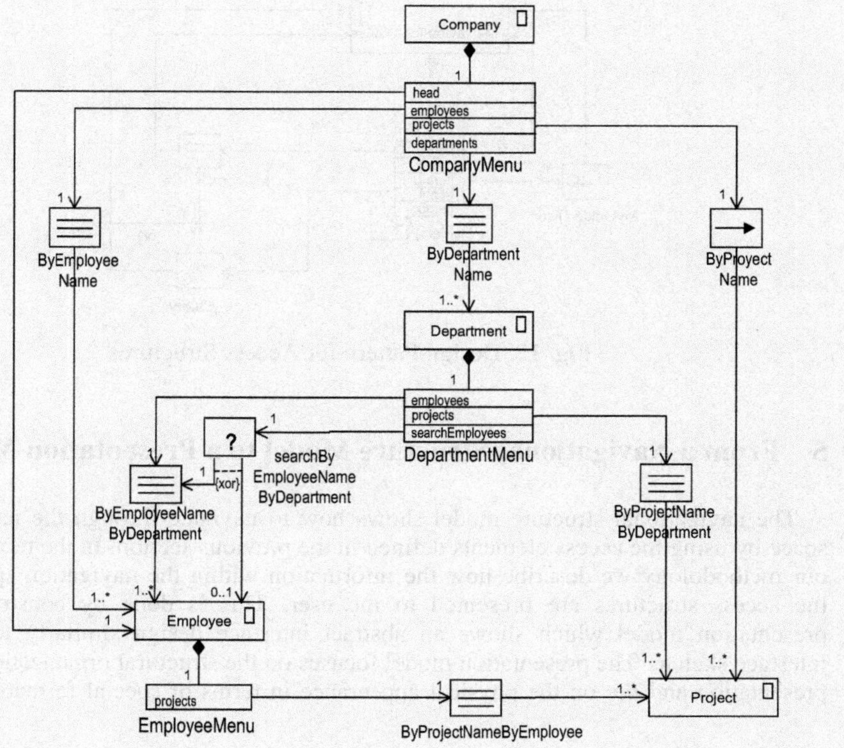

Fig. 11. Navigational Structure Model

enriched by menus where each menu class is associated by a composition association to a navigational class. Note that the role names occurring in the previous model are now names of corresponding menu items.

4.2.3 The Method

The enhancement of a navigation space model by access elements of type menu follows certain rules which can be summarized as follows:

1. Consider those associations which have as source a navigational class.
2. Associate to each navigational class which has (in the previous model) at least one outgoing association a corresponding menu class. The association between a navigational class and its corresponding menu class is a composition.
3. Introduce for each role which occurs in the previous model at the end of a directed association a corresponding menu item. By default, the role name is used as the constant name of the menu item.
4. Any association of the previous model which has as source a navigational class becomes now an association of the corresponding menu item introduced in step 3.

Note that all steps of the above method can be performed in a fully automatic way. As a result we obtain a comprehensive navigational structure model of our application. It is guaranteed by our method that this model is conform to the pattern shown in Fig. 12.

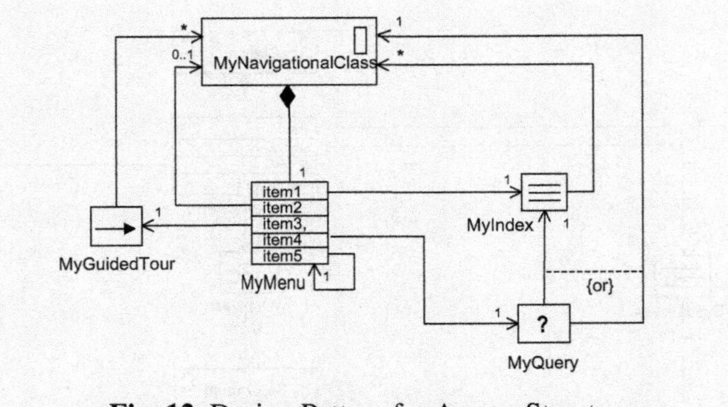

Fig. 12. Design Pattern for Access Structures

5 From a Navigational Structure Model to a Presentation Model

The navigational structure model shows how to navigate through the navigation space by using the access elements defined in the previous section. In the next step of our methodology we describe how the information within the navigation space and the access structures are presented to the user. This is done by constructing a presentation model which shows an abstract interface design similarly to a user interface sketch. The presentation model focuses on the structural organization of the presentation and *not* on the physical appearance in terms of special formats, colors, etc. Such decisions are left to the construction of user interface prototypes or to the implementation phase which is not in the scope of this paper.

5.1 Modeling Elements

For constructing a presentation model one has to decide which presentational elements will be used for the presentation of the instances of navigational classes and, on the other hand, for the presentation of the access elements. For this purpose we use several presentational modeling elements (with corresponding stereotypes). A top level element for presentation is a frameset which is modeled by a composite object that contains (lower level) presentational objects but may also contain an arbitrary number of nested framesets. A frameset is an instance of a frameset class stereotyped by «frameset» with a corresponding icon. Classes which model framesets must be built conform to the composition structure shown in Fig. 13.

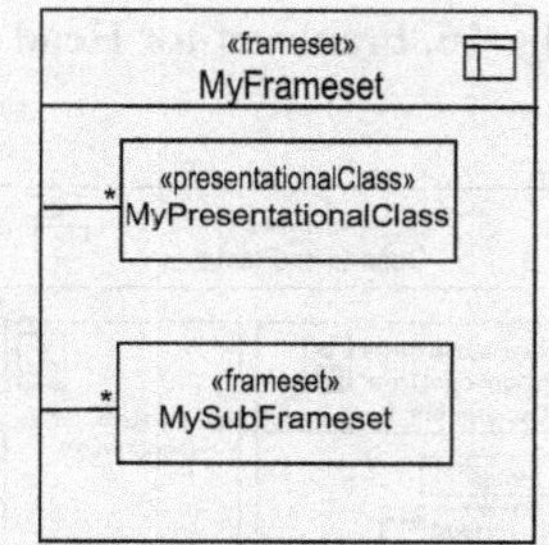

Fig. 13. Frameset

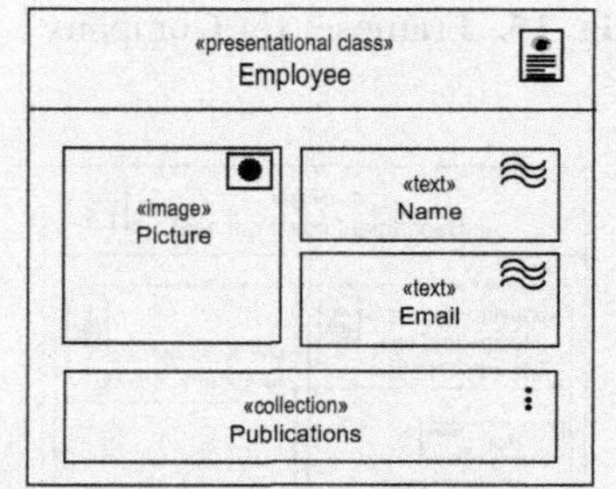

Fig. 14. Presentational Class for the Employee

Presentational objects contained in a frameset are instances of a presentational class which is stereotyped by «presentationalClass» with a corresponding icon. Such objects are containers which comprise basic presentational elements like texts, collections (i.e. lists of texts), images, anchors, anchored collections (i.e. lists of anchors) etc. The basic elements and their stereotypes are defined in [1]. Fig. 14 shows how they can be used for constructing a template for the presentation of employees.

5.2 Example

Fig. 15 to 18 show part of a presentation model for our sample application. In this example we use framesets to partition the presentation into frames, whereby the left frame shows the actual navigation tree and the right frame shows the corresponding content. How this presentation model can be systematically derived from the navigational structure model is explained in Section 5.3. For the moment it should be sufficient to point out that Fig. 15 shows the presentation of the company, Fig. 16 shows the presentation of the head of the company (after having selected Head), Fig. 17 shows the presentation of the department index by a list of anchors (after having selected Departments) and Fig. 18 shows how a selected department (for instance the i-th department Dep_i) is presented. Thereby we have not detailed the presentation class for departments which can be done similarly to the case of employees (see Fig. 14).

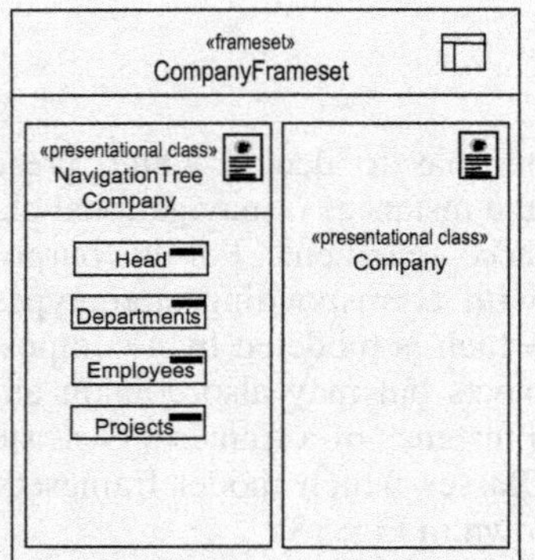

Fig. 15. Frameset for Company

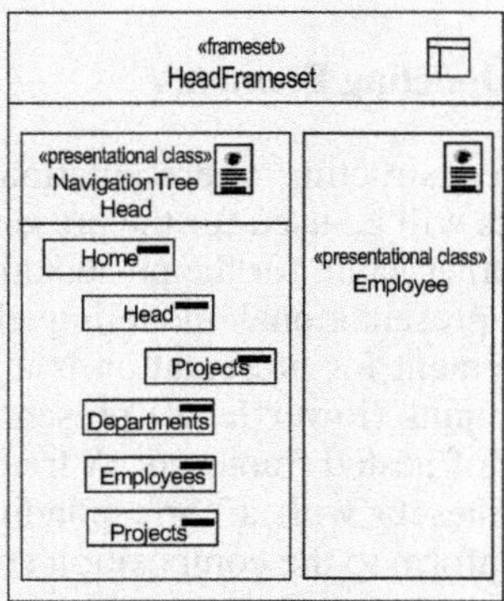

Fig. 16. Frameset for Head

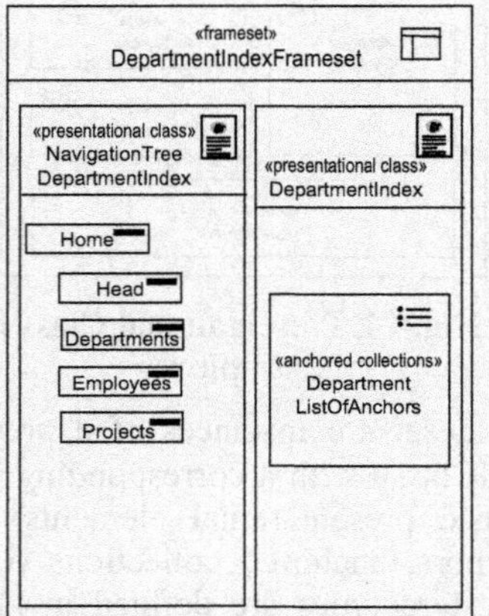

Fig. 17. Frameset for Department Index

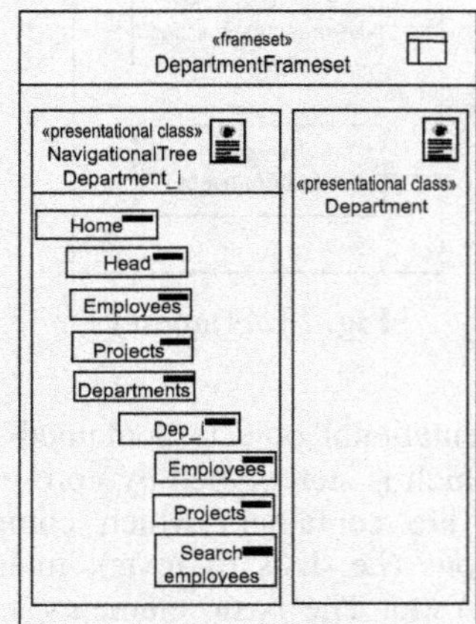

Fig. 18. Frameset for Department

5.3 The Method

Of course there are many possibilities to construct a presentation model for a given navigational structure model. In any case it is essential to define a presentation for each navigational class and one has also to support the navigation structure. The method we propose is based on the use of framesets which allow us to visualize a navigation structure. Thereby the idea is to divide a presentation always into two basic parts: One part provides a presentation of the navigation tree (showing the user's actual navigation path and hence the context of navigation) and the other part shows the corresponding content.

On this basis we define the following procedure for deriving a presentation model from a navigational structure model in an entirely systematic way.

1. Construct a presentation for each navigational class and for each index class occurring in the navigational structure model. The presentation of a navigational class has to provide a template for presenting the instances of the class which takes into account the given attributes. For instance, Fig. 14 shows a presentation for the navigational class Employee. The presentation of an index class is usually given by a list of anchors. For instance, the presentational class DepartmentIndex in the right frame of Fig. 17 defines a presentation of the index class ByDepartmentName of Fig. 11.
2. Choose one navigational class as a root for navigation. In our example we select the class Company.
3. For each navigational class and for each index class consider all possible paths (in the navigational structure model) from the root class to the actual class. For each path construct a presentation of the corresponding navigation tree.

   Let explain this step in more detail by considering our example. We start with the class Company. The corresponding navigation tree is represented by the presentational class NavigationTreeCompany in the left frame of Fig. 15. Since Company is the root of the navigation the corresponding tree is trivial and shows only the menu associated to Company.

   The presentational class NavigationTreeHead in Fig. 16 shows the navigation tree if one moves to the head of the company. Note that the root of this tree is presented by the anchor Home for going back to the company. The anchor Projects is inserted at depth 2 of the tree to present the menu associated to employees (remember that the head is indeed an employee).

   The presentational class NavigationTreeDepartmentIndex in Fig. 17 shows the navigation tree if one moves from the company to the department index and the presentational class NavigationTreeDepartment_i in Fig. 18 shows the navigation tree if one navigates further to a particular department (for instance, the i-th department Dep_i). Note that then the anchors Employees, Projects and Search Employees are inserted at depth 3 of the tree for presenting the menu associated to a department.
4. Combine the results of step 1 and step 3 accordingly to framesets. Any frameset has two parts where the right frame contains the presentation of the navigational class or index class (constructed in step 1) and the left frame represents the navigation tree (constructed in step 3) corresponding to one possible navigation to this class.

   In our example this leads to the framesets shown in Fig. 15 to 18 which of course have to be completed by taking into account all other possible navigations shown in the navigational structure model in Fig. 11. In particular, Fig. 11 contains also guided tours and queries whose presentation is not detailed here. The idea is to present a guided tour simply by two additional anchors Next and Prev (with an obvious meaning) which extend the menu of the corresponding navigational class. As a straightforward presentation of queries one will usually choose forms.

In step 3 we must ensure that there is only a finite set of navigation paths from the root class to each navigational or index class. For this purpose we assume that the given navigational structure model has no cycles, i.e. forms a directed acyclic graph.

This is not a proper restriction since anyway we provide a presentation of the navigation tree which, in particular, allows us to move backwards. Concerning the presentation of a navigation tree it is obvious that in practice the depth of the tree must be limited. For a convenient representation of such trees one may also use several frames, for instance a top frame and a left frame. In this case the left frame in Fig. 18 would be splitted into a top frame which contains the main menu and into a left frame presenting the subtree with the anchor Dep_i as a root.

Let us note that there is also a variant of the above procedure which treats the presentation of indexes differently. With this variant the department index would be included in the navigation tree on the left side while the right frame could include, for instance, some additional general information on all departments.

6 Related Work

During the last few years many methods for hypermedia and Web design have been proposed; see [10] for an overview. Most of them are not based on the UML, like RMM (Relationship Management Methodology) [5] and OOHDM (Object-Oriented Hypermedia Design Method) [13]. They utilise entity-relationship diagrams, OMT or their own notation and techniques.

Recently, some new approaches propose UML extensions for the hypermedia domain, for instance the development process of Conallen [4], the extension for multimedia applications in [12] and the UML extension of [1]. The first approach is based on the Rational Unified Process (RUP) [9] and focuses particularly on the architecture of Web applications. The second one extends UML sequence diagrams to model multimedia processes. The third one provides modeling elements for the navigational and presentational design that we have used in our methodology.

However, a guideline of activities to be performed systematically by the designer for modeling the navigation space, structure and presentation as in our approach is missing by almost all hypermedia design methods. The advantage of such a guideline is that it can be used by a Case Tool for the automatic generation of the hypermedia navigational structure and of presentation templates.

For further details on design and development methods for hypermedia systems see the comparative study of hypermedia development methods in [7].

7 Conclusions and Future Work

In this paper we have presented a methodology for hypermedia design that uses a UML profile for the hypermedia domain. The strength of our approach is given by the semi-automatic generation of the navigational structure and presentation of the application.

We describe how to build step by step:

- the navigation space model based on the conceptual model,
- the navigational structure model from the navigation space model and
- the presentation model from the navigational structure model.

The design steps presented here are part of a development process [8] based on the Unified Process [6] that covers the whole lifecycle of hypermedia applications.

The objectives of our future work are to include the modeling of the dynamic and database aspects related to hypermedia applications. The methodology will be refined and tested for the design of more complex applications, such as Web applications that require database transactions and user activities not restricted to browsing. A next step will be the construction of a Case-Tool for the semi-automatic development of hypermedia and Web applications based on our methodology.

Acknowledgement

We would like to thank Luis Mandel and Hubert Baumeister for common work related to the UML extension [1]. We thank also Andy Schürr and other participants of the GROOM 2000 Workshop for helpful suggestions and comments.

References

1. Baumeister, H., Koch, N., Mandel L.: Towards a UML extension for hypermedia design. InProceedings «UML»'99, France, R., Rumpe, B. (eds), LNCS, Vol. 1723. Springer-Verlag (1999) 614-629.
2. Berner S., Glinz M., Joos S.: A classification of stereotypes for object-oriented modeling languages. InProceedings «UML»'99, France, R., Rumpe, B. (eds), LNCS, Vol. 1723. Springer-Verlag (1999) 249-264.
3. Booch G., Rumbaugh J., Jacobson I.: The Unified Modeling Language: A User Guide. Addison Wesley (1999).
4. Conallen J.: Building Web Applications with UML. Addison-Wesley (1999).
5. Isakowitz T., Stohr E., Balasubramanian P.: A methodology for the design of structured hypermedia applications. Communications of the ACM, 8(38) (1995) 34-44.
6. Jacobson I., Booch G., Rumbaugh J.: The Unified Software Development Process. Addison Wesley (1999).
7. Koch N.: A comparative study of methods for hypermedia development. Technical Report 9901, Ludwig-Maximilians-University Munich (1999).
8. Koch N.: Hypermedia systems development based on the Unified Process. Technical Report 0003, Ludwig-Maximilians-University Munich (2000).
9. Kruchten P. *The Rational Unified Process: An Introduction.* Addison Wesley (1998).
10. Lowe D., Hall W.: Hypermedia & the Web: An engineering approach. John Wiley & Sons (1999).
11. Nanard J., Nanard M. Hypertext design environments and the hypertext design process. Communication of the ACM, August 1995, Vol 38 (8), (1995) 49-56.
12. Sauer S. and Engels G.: Extending UML for Modeling of Multimedia Applications. In Proceedings of the IEEE Symposium on Visual Languages – VL'99, IEEE Computer Society (1999) 80-87
13. Schwabe D., Rossi G.: Developing hypermedia applications using OOHDM. In Proceedings of Workshop on Hypermedia Development Process, Methods and Models, Hypertext'98 (1998).

Object Oriented Methodology Based on UML for Urban Traffic System Modeling

Michelle Chabrol and David Sarramia

Université Blaise Pascal - Clermont-Ferrand II
LIMOS. 63177 AUBIERE Cedex. FRANCE.
Tél : (33) 04 73 40 77 72, Fax : (33)04 73 40 74 44.
sarramia@iris.univ-bpclermont.fr

Abstract. This paper proposes an object-oriented modeling methodology, which is based on global and structured UTS modeling approach, using UML We show how UML diagrams are used in our methodology and why. The first part of this paper is dedicated to the domain analysis (generic) and shows which diagram to use. In the second part, we deal with system dedicated analysis. We then present a real case study we have dealt with.

1 Introduction

The complexity of problems arising from Urban Traffic Systems (UTS) forces the designers to use modeling approaches in order to design their system, and define and implement traffic management strategies. As a result, an urban traffic planning tool incorporating a holistic UTS view that covers all aspects of UTS is required for successful design planning and management.

However, required models are usually large and complex since they implement a global description of UTS. They must take into account several types of flows interacting within very different time scales. In order to increase the level of success of UTS modeling studies, we propose an object-oriented modeling methodology, which is based on a global and structured UTS modeling approach, using UML. This methodology exploits an original UTS systemic view and relies on a modeling process which promotes the development of a global communicative model of an UTS creating a descriptive model (estimation of the current state of a UTS using historical information) and/or a prescriptive one (generation of prediction-based information for a given time horizon). The communicative model comprises a structural model and a functional model built with urban planning experts thanks to an object-oriented modeling methodology. In order to fully support the analysis of UTS performance from several perspectives and objectives, and for each level of decision (strategic, tactical and operational), the proposed methodology which will be implemented in a software environment, is based on an UTS generic object-oriented conceptual model. This model provides a set of UTS concepts and views in order to easily build macroscopic, mesoscopic and microscopic models. We propose to use UML models and diagrams, and we show how they can be used in our methodology.

A. Evans, S. Kent and B. Selic (Eds.): «UML» 2000, LNCS 1939, pp. 425-439, 2000.

This paper describes the elaboration of this UTS generic object-oriented conceptual model as well as the application of the methodology for the modeling of a case study including roundabouts, traffic lights and road-train junctions.

1.1 UTS Definition

An UTS is built to ensure the travel from origin to destination of every traveler, this according to security and time criteria. These systems furnish only services and not goods as industrial manufacturing systems do. Moreover, UTS functioning is human related because its state depends on people behavior at a time. UTS managers act on the strategic level by applying long term decisions (such as political ones), on a tactical level for middle term decisions (such as infrastructure changing) and on an operational level (by changing phasing plan). Due to traffic increase, UTS are more complex and sophisticated because of the management systems used. The use of real time systems is now very common but the knowledge of UTS functioning is sometimes not sharp enough. In fact, only a few global management systems are working. The complexity of an urban management system is related to the dynamic behavior of the entities moving through the UTS.

In an UTS, there exist three types of flows : vehicle flow, information flow and decision flow.

A vehicle flow exists because vehicles need to go from an origin to a destination (OD pairs), using a deterministic routing or not. Also, a trip is a set of OD pairs describing the trip along the network.

An information flow is related to data exchange in a UTS. Information can be data on system state or decision. Information can be an top-down one (following a hierarchical process) or can be an exchange between entities (for local management system).

A decision flow is used to manage and control the system in order to achieve objectives. Decisions are of strategic, tactical or operational level.

UTS designers require a methodology during analysis and specification phases in which communication problems between urban experts are to be solved. This methodology must also propose a general framework to get and use system knowledge for management aims. In order to model UTS and solve former problems, we propose a modeling and simulation methodology, using UML as a modeling language all along the process.

2 Object Oriented Methodology

Our modeling methodology is based on a modeling process which separates the specification phase of a model from its exploitation [8]. This approach proposes the building of two models called respectively knowledge model and action model.

The knowledge model describes the structure and the working of the system in a natural or in a graphic language. If the system exists, the knowledge model comprises knowledge from observations of the system. If the system is to be built, the knowledge model contains the specifications of the future system. The action model is a translation of the knowledge model into a mathematical formalism or a programming language (for example a simulation language) and gives the performance criteria of the system. The consecutive exploitation of these two models is called modeling process. It is usually an iterative process.

The knowledge model building should be made in collaboration with the UTS experts. It should stay coherent throughout time, whatever the detail level. Once a knowledge model has been developed, the next task consists in deducing the action model. We advocate in favor of the development of a global knowledge model of a UTS prior to creating any action model. The knowledge model comprises, on the one hand, a structural model, built using a hierarchical decomposition through an top-down model definition, and, on the other hand, a decision model, built using a structured decision specification method and a flow model using a traffic flow specification method. The UTS object-oriented modeling methodology proposed in this paper should make it possible to reach the following goals:

- building a global generic object-oriented model of an UTS, this model being composed of a structural model, a decision model and a traffic flow model,
- improving the control over a modeling study and increasing its level of success by persuading urban planning experts to fully cooperate and to be responsible for the adequacy and quality of the information they provide with regard to their objectives,
- ensuring the reusability and adaptability of the generic kn owledge model,
- systematically deriving simulation models from this knowledge model, that is quasi-automatically generating simulation codes,
- facilitating the definition of interfaces for accessing other decision aid techniques (such as Operation Research [10][13] or Artificial Intelligence).

Building a generic knowledge model for the studied domain is done identifying similarities and differences between systems belonging to the domain. Generic model enhancement could be necessary when new functionalities or new entities have to be taken into account for an existing system or not. In the proposed methodology, specification and design steps follow the domain analysis. Design and implementation steps concern the action model (see fig.1). The development of the models mentioned above is carried out using the ASDI process which integrates the following stages: Analysis and Specification and Design and Implementation.

In order to better control the complexity of traffic systems, we propose a systematic decomposition of any UTS into three subsystems that are complementary, communicating and mutually disconnected. These three subsystems are the *logical* subsystem (LSS), the *physical* subsystem(PSS) and the *decision* subsystem (DSS).

Such a decomposition had been successfully used for the manufacturing system class [4][7] and has led to the building of modeling and simulation software environment. Let us now detail this decomposition for UTS.

The logical subsystem contains the moving entities of the system that are generating the flow : vehicles (with various possible kinds) and pedestrians. A vehicle has its own behavior which include reactions versus current system state (information exchange with the decision subsystem).

The physical subsystem gathers the entities that are building the physical structure. For example, the set of road structures are present. Geometric characteristics and working rules (such as priority) to be used will be described here.

The decision subsystem contains functioning rules (for example, the highway code). Speed management, road blocking, routing algorithms (static or dynamic) of vehicles and control algorithms (traffic light phases, Variable Message Sign) are also present. Any information related to the system functioning (message type, entry variables,...) must be declared here.

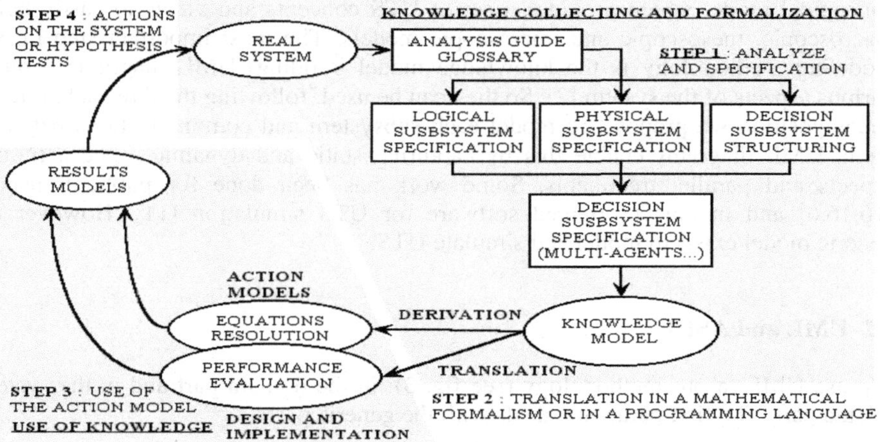

Fig. 1. Modeling methodology process

These three subsystems are communicating (see fig. 2). Using a system domain analysis instead of a system analysis, the decomposition must be done as precisely as possible in order to describe and analyze any UTS. The same knowledge can be used for studies with different levels of details .

Such a framework is then interesting from the tactical, operational, planning point of view.

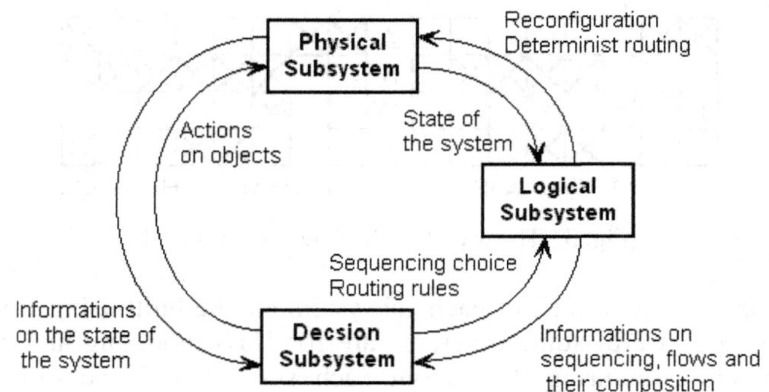

Fig. 2. Subsystems communication

3 Using UML

3.1 Introduction

In order to fully support the analysis of UTS performance from several perspectives and objectives the proposed methodology is based on an UTS generic object-oriented conceptual model which provides a set of UTS concepts and views to easily build macroscopic, mesoscopic and microscopic models. The most important step in our modeling methodology is the knowledge model building. UML diagrams capture various aspects of the system [2]. So they can be used, following the three subsystems decomposition we propose, to model each subsystem and communications between them. UML diagrams enable this by capturing static and dynamic aspects, timing aspects and parallel treatments. Some work has been done for public transport [16,16,6] and in object oriented software for UTS simulation [11]. However no generic model exists to model and simulate UTS.

3.2 UML and ASDI

We use UML in our methodology (see fig. 3): in the domain part and in the system related part. The first paragraph deals with the generic part.

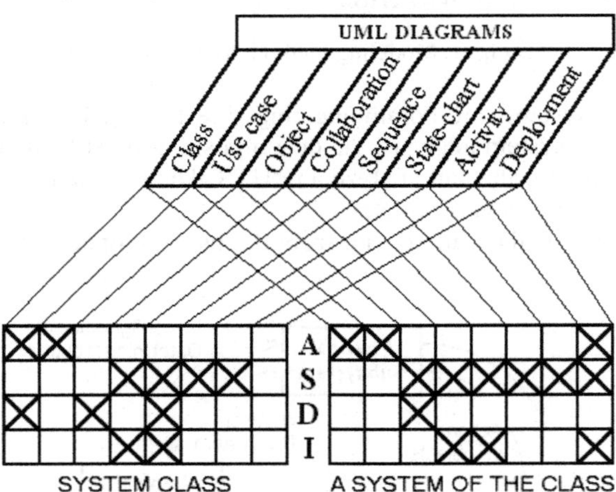

Fig. 3. The use of UML diagrams in ASDI

A generic knowledge model of each subsystem can be built using UML diagrams and we show how useful some diagrams are for UTS modeling and specification. Representing and structuring data about each subsystem is possible using class diagrams (as we do using E-R model [3]).

The decision subsystem is the most complex of all. Because of its dynamic nature, it needs more diagrams for its generic modeling. In addition to class diagrams, the use-case diagrams provide a functional view of this subsystem (describing decision processes), sequence and activity diagrams explain hierarchical decision process. To formalize the various states in which the decision subsystem can be, state chart diagrams are used. A collaboration or a sequence diagram explains data exchanges between subsystems.

Now, if we consider the dedicated system part of ASDI, additional diagrams are needed. In particular, generic class diagrams must be filtered to obtain the studied system class model. Because each case study is specific, object attributes must be filled and abstract methods must be written.

The entities of the logical subsystem have a behavior. Thus an activity diagram is necessary to precise it. We explain with this the dynamic part of flow entities (such as vehicle), and we explain how they react to local situations.

The physical parts of logical and decision entities need to be placed and inter-related. A deployment diagram is well suited to represent this.

For instance, the decision subsystem has been modeled in a generic way. As we now talk about a system, its functioning can be specified. A deployment diagram shows where and how the decision centers are placed. The management process of this system is specified by sequence, collaboration and activity diagrams: the global process has been described later on, we now describe a particular case.

Table 1 summarizes which diagrams are used to model each subsystem.

	LSS	PSS	DSS
Class	G / A	G / A	G / A
Use Case			G-D / A-S
Object	D / A	D / S	D / S
Collaboration			G-D / S
Sequence			G-D / S
State chart			G-D / S
Activity	D / S		G-D / S
Deployment		G-D / A-S	G-D / A-S

Table 1. UML diagrams (G-D : Generic-Dedicated / A-S : Analysis-Specification)

We now present UTS generic models according to our methodology.

4 Generic Models: The Three Subsystems

According to the modeling process (see fig. 1) and Table 1, we have built generic models. They have been realized and validated during different studies on various UTS [12,5]. Problems associated to UTS are generally network related problems. Urban engineers are facing vehicle flows going through the system according to various criteria (travel time, departure time ...). A continuous approach is somewhat natural. However, a discrete approach, based on entity, enables us to use any kind of representation of the system (going from a discrete one to a continuous one and vice versa is possible).

4.1 The Logical Subsystem

The logical subsystem (see fig.4) is composed of flow entities and trips. A flow entity can be a vehicle flow, an information flow or a decision flow. A trip is composed of an origin, a destination and checkpoints. To each vehicle flow is assigned a trip (OD pair), but several routings are possible. The logical subsystem communicates with the other two, supplying them data on the current system state.

According to our current preoccupations [1], a knowledge model must support the building of any kind of action model (which corresponds to the study aims: tactical, strategic or operational). This has a great importance considering the fact that any action model as well as any level of details (microscopic, macroscopic or mesoscopic) should stay coherent with the knowledge model. In order to be consistent with this and with the reality, our generic model is a discrete one: it is based on the flow entity. Thus, any kind of action model can be derived or translated from the generic knowledge model. A flow entity has attributes (such as direction, trip) and methods.

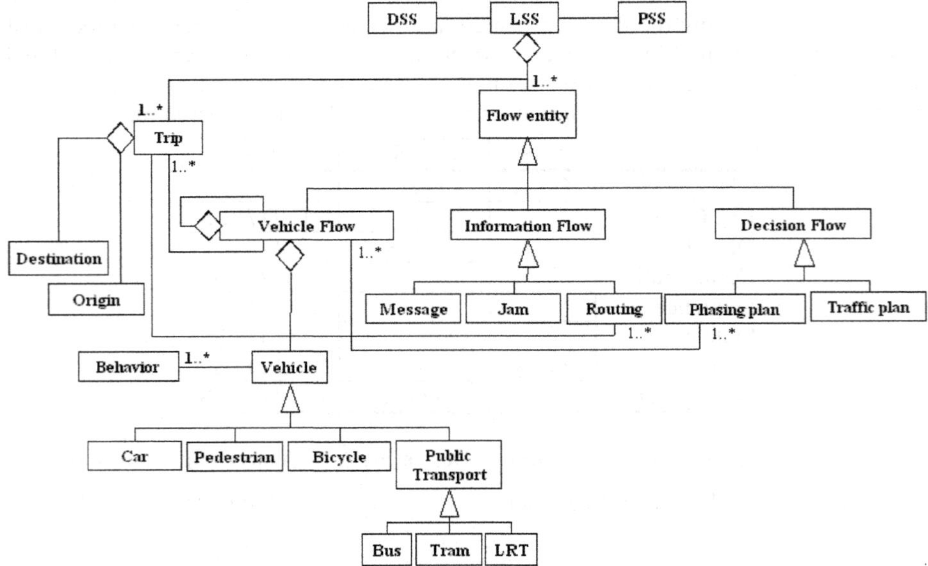

Fig. 4. Logical Subsystem Class diagram

4.2 The Physical Subsystem

The physical subsystem is quite complex in UTS. A hierarchical decomposition is necessary to obtain a sufficient level of details (see fig. 5). The physical subsystem of an UTS is composed of a networks set which will support flows. A network contains roads and highways (to keep interactions between urban and downtown areas). Here, we only give details for the urban part of it, but at this level in the modeling process we have decided that it was important to keep highway entities for intra and extra urban studies. Roads are connected by junctions. An urban network is then composed of a roadway and junctions. Various kinds of junctions are represented (roundabouts, cross junctions...). They can be described using lane decomposition. A junction is a set of lanes, that are grouped, managed, organized in a logical and repetitive manner.

Management policies are the more stable part in junctions. It is for reuse convenience that junctions are present in the knowledge model as particular entities. A junction can be considered as a subsystem having the same characteristics of a global system. Some tools [9] are dedicated to junction studies and analysis.

There are four types of lanes, namely storage lane, normal lane, exit lane and entry lane and can be dedicated to one particular vehicle type. Lanes are connected by simple and multiple forks (see fig. 6 and fig 7) in order to ease model various situations. Dynamic and static signals can be placed all along lanes and parking areas are also connected to lanes. To establish and to allow the management and the control of network and traffic, the physical part of management system and unit traffic control (UTC) is present in the physical subsystem. They will be able to control, manage and optimize the flow of vehicles having interaction with the network. This will be done using various traffic signals (traffic lights, Variable Message Signs). They can be controlled by dynamic or static policies. A partial view of the physical subsystem is given.

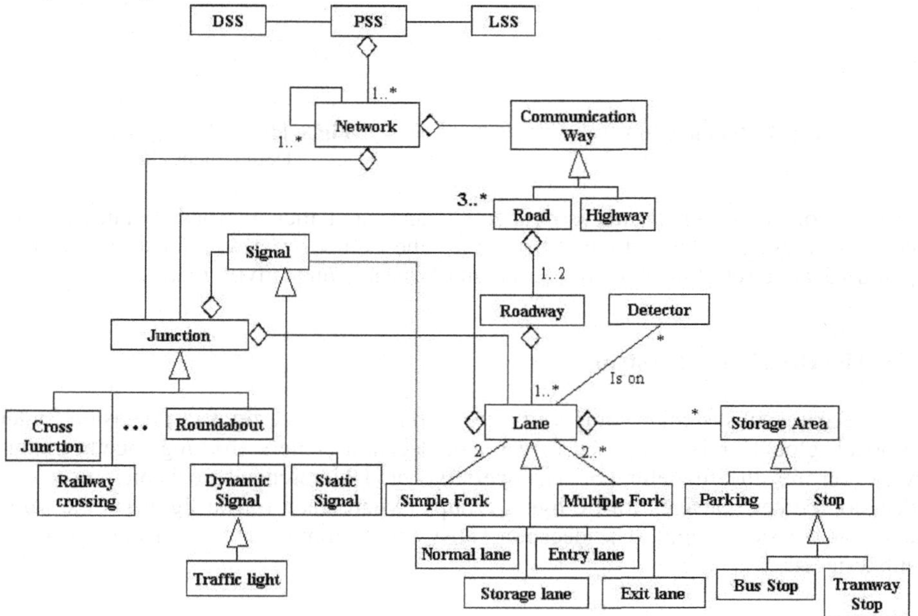

Fig. 5. Physical Subsystem Class diagram

To simplify the reading and understanding of network components connections, we have built a deployment diagram (see fig. 8) that shows spatial connectivity (note that a graph notation is also very explicit).

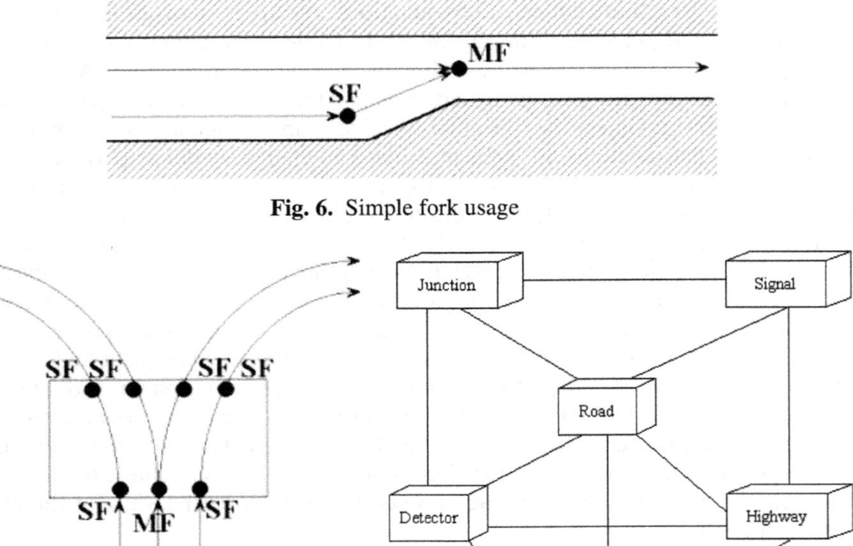

Fig. 6. Simple fork usage

Fig. 7. Multiple fork usage

Fig.8. Physical Subsystem Deployment Diagram

Detectors and signals are associated to lanes and then to roads. Lanes can be connected even if they do not belong to the same street-way-junction, because junctions are a set of lanes with internal and external connectivity matrix.

4.3 The Decision Subsystem

The decision subsystem is composed of decision centers (see fig. 9). A decision center is local, global or is composed of a set of decision centers working together. This view permits the modeling of a cooperative or a hierarchical decision process. A decision center manages traffic lights groups (where each traffic light has the same color at the same time). The decision subsystem communicates with the two other subsystems.

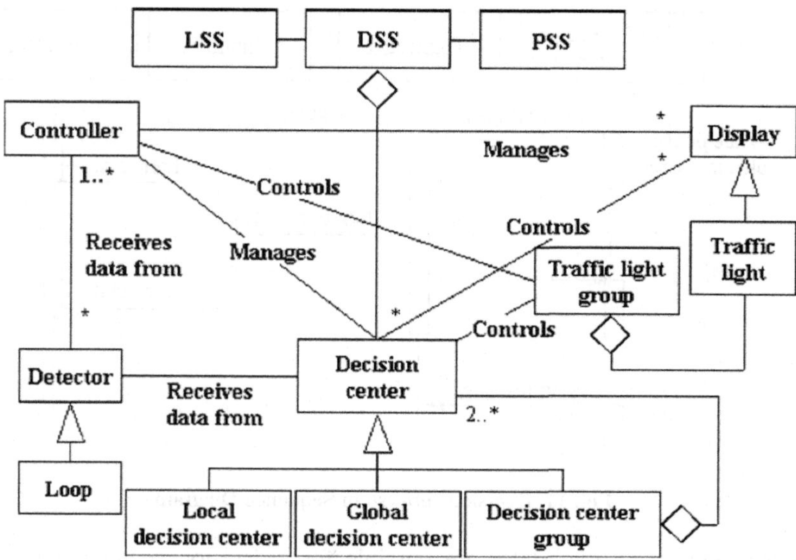

Fig. 9. Decision Subsystem Class diagram

The decision center is in charge of several decisions and management functions (see fig. 10). Such decisions are to apply phasing and traffic plans, to change the phasing plan and to supervise the whole network.

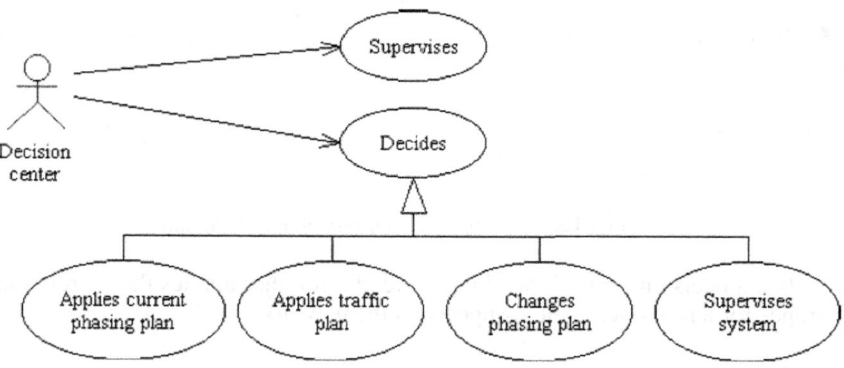

Fig. 10. Decision Subsystem Use Case diagram

The decision center manages the phasing plan on the roads and junctions it controls. A phasing plan is modified when the density becomes too high or when a time event happens (a new period of the day) (see fig. 11). For example, the lights phases can be computed having new information concerning the system state. This new sequence will be sent to the traffic light or to the corresponding unit traffic controller.

The structuring of this subsystem can be done using several methods. This can be done using a multi-agent approach [13,14].

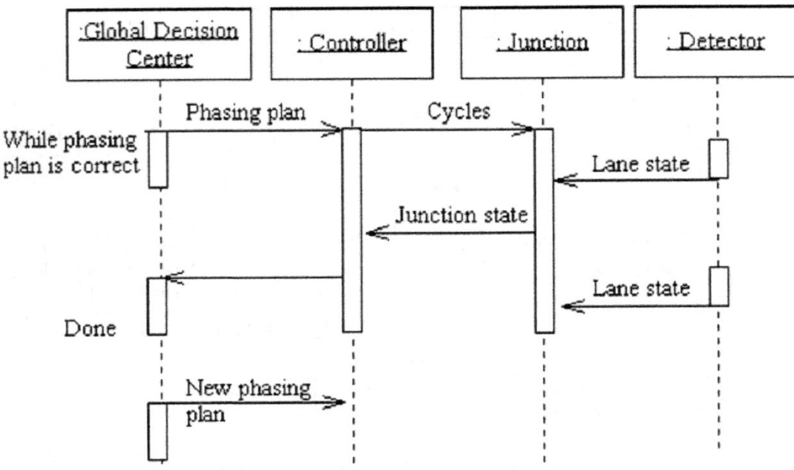

Fig. 11. Decision subsystem Sequence Diagram

In a generic way, two states are possible for a decision center : it is working correctly or not (see fig. 12). The functioning of a traffic light is described in a generic way, demonstrating two states (proper working and breakdown).

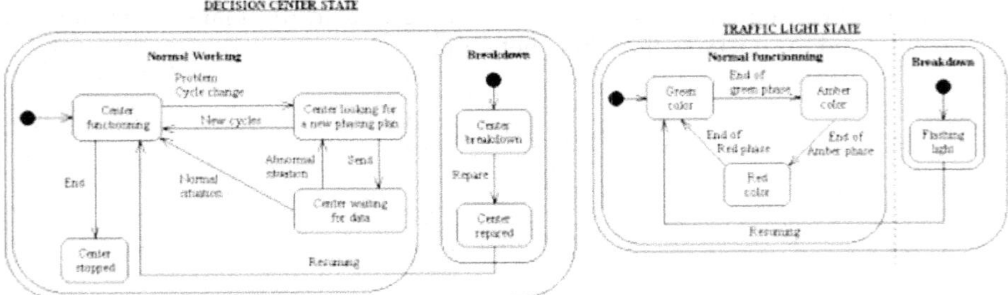

Fig. 12. Decision subsystem state-chart Diagrams

When a decision center is working correctly, it either applies the current plan or it searches for a new one, while it supervises the network.

4.4 Subsystems Communication

The three subsystems are communicating. In order to represent this, data exchange between them is explained in a collaboration or a sequence diagram at the subsystem level (see fig. 13).

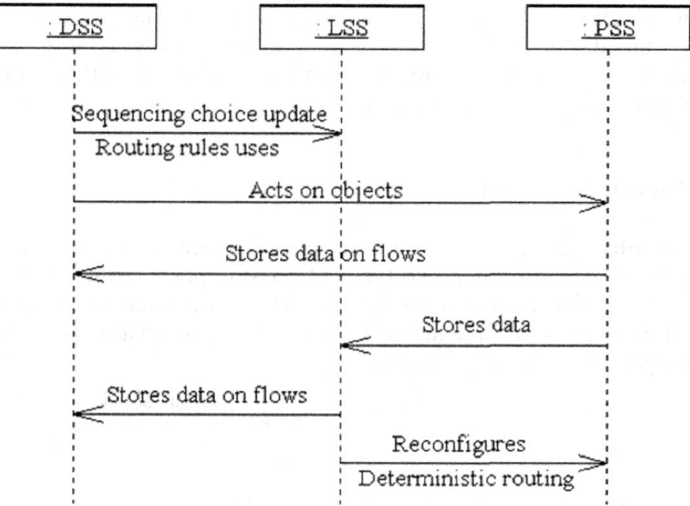

Fig. 13. Subsystem Communication

After having presented the whole set of models for our methodology, we deal with a case study.

5 A Case Study

We now present the system analysis for the Brighton case study. This system (see fig. 14) is composed of three main problems : a roundabout, a railway crossing, merging and splitting lanes, and a simple traffic light system.

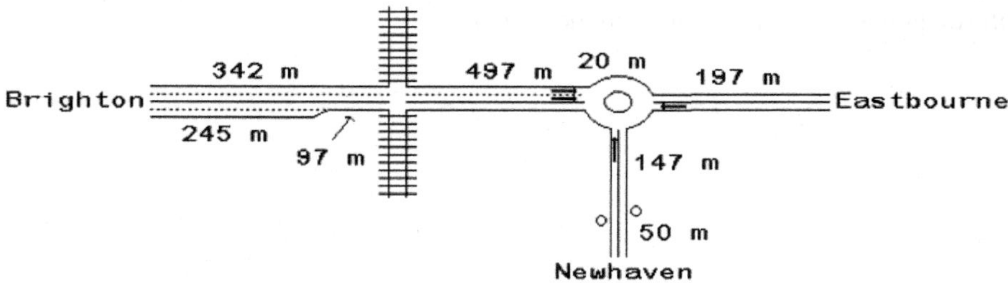

Fig. 14. Brighton UTS

In the direction of toward Brighton, there are merging-splitting lanes : the road goes from four to three and then two lanes within a few hundred meters. We then find a railway crossing (with lights). Coming from Eastbourne, there is a roundabout to go to Brighton (railway crossing) and to Newhaven (traffic lights). The main point of study is the ferry harbor located in Newhaven. Thus, when a ferry comes, a large number of vehicles want to come out and to get in to Newhaven. At that moment, the system is jammed. The study objectives are to evaluate jams and to propose solutions in order to decrease traffic density between arrivals. We detail now the knowledge model for this system according to Table 1.

5.1 The Knowledge Model

The logical subsystem : As shown on the class diagram shows (see fig.15), this UTS contains only cars (and trains), two types of phasing plans (with and without amber) and no global traffic management system. There are three origin and destination points (exit-entry points for the network). No routing information is given to users (by variable message sign or in-car system).

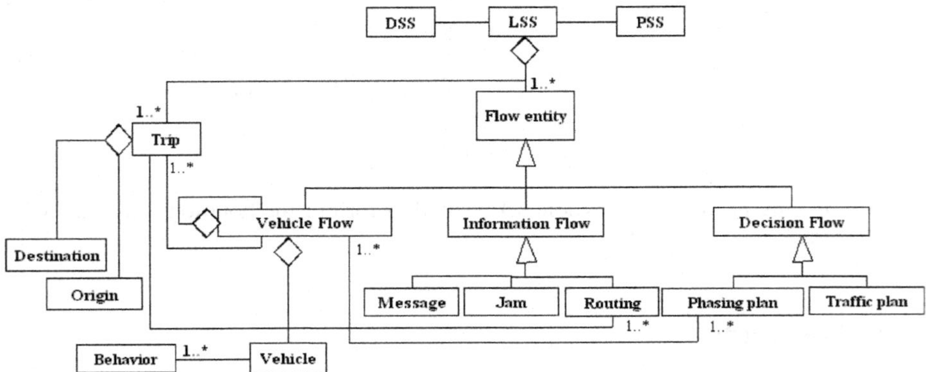

Fig. 15. Brighton Logical Subsystem Class Diagram

No activity diagram is necessary at this moment. The only one of interest would be the one related to drivers (and then to vehicle behavior).

The physical subsystem : There is a roundabout, a railway to crossing and merging lanes (see fig. 16). Layout can be shown using a deployment diagram, providing information about flows existing in the system.

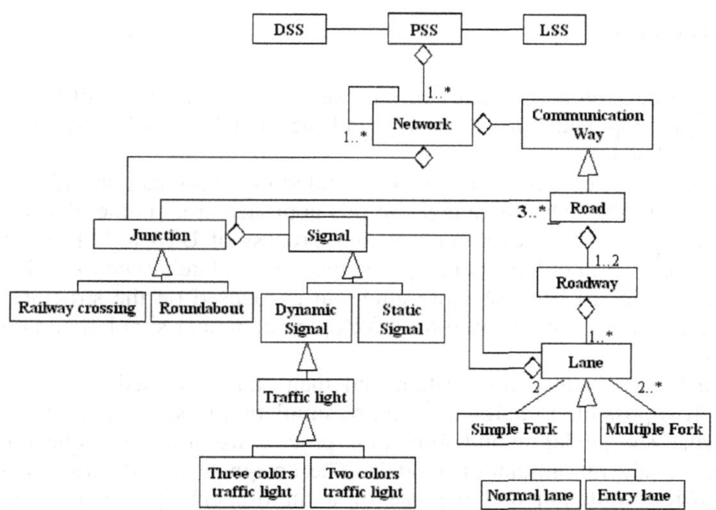

Fig. 16. Physical subsystem class diagram for Brighton

The decision subsystem : The system contains two different traffic light controllers (see fig. 17): one associated to the railway crossing, the other related to the ferry. There is no communication between them, and there is no global decision center (it is a decentralized system).

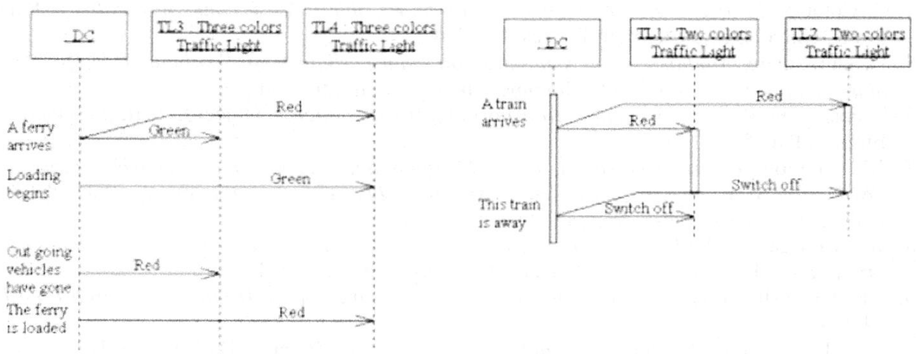

Fig. 17. Sequence Diagram for railway crossing and for ferry traffic lights

When a train arrives, traffic lights are set to red and are switched off when the train has left. When a ferry arrives, the traffic light controlling the roundabout direction is set to green while the other is set to red. When all cars have left the ferry, this traffic light is set to green, and the other to red. These two light plans are fixed.

Simulation models for this case study, discrete time and microscopic ones, have been built using these knowledge models. The simulation language used was GPSS/H. Various topologies like having two lanes everywhere even in the roundabout have been tested. According to simulation results, modifications on the real system have been decided.

6 Conclusion

When various solutions are tested, they are using a major part of the former code. Thus, the development time is shorter, and the models need less validation because they use validated parts.

This paper has described how object-oriented modeling can provide a new way of thinking about UTS. The advantages of this approach are: (1) the object is the single unifying concept in the developing models process of UTS at both operational and strategic level; (2) interdependency problems are less likely when small changes in a model occur and (3) because more attention is focused on the structure of the real world objects, a more stable base for developing computer simulation models of UTS is achieved.

Software parts related are written and then can be reused by developing class libraries. It is possible to build any kind of simulation model whatever its detail level and its type. The modeling and simulation process we propose has been used for the designing of several simulation models. The design of a software environment for urban traffic simulation and the use of a multi-agent approach for the decision subsystem structuring are scheduled.

References

1. *Traffic Flow Theory : A monograph.* Transportation Research Board, TRB185, 1996.
2. Jacobson I. Booch, G. and J. Rumbaugh. *VML Notation Guide (version 1.1).* Rational Corporation, Santa-Clara, 1997.
3. P.P. Chen. *The entity-relation ship model, towards a unified view of data.* 1(1) :9 –36, 1976.
4. C. Combes. *Méhodologie de modéisation orientée objets des systèmes hospitaliers.* PhD thesis, Université de Clermont-Ferrand II, 1994.
5. C. Durandiere. *Modéisation et simulation du trafic urbain pour l'évaluation des performances d'infrastructures*, 1995. diplôme d'ingénieur en Informatique.
6. T. Foster and L. Zhao. *Modelling transport object with patterns.* Object Expert, presented at EuroPlo P96, 5(2), 1997.
7. J.Y. Goujon. *Un environnement de modéisation multi-agents pour la spécification et l'évaluation des performances des sy stèmes industriels de production.* PhD thesis, Université de Clermont-Ferrand II, 1997.
8. M. Gourgand. *Outils Logiciels pour l'évaluation de s performances des systèmes in formatiques.* PhD thesis, Université de Clermont-Ferrand II, 1984.
9. B.D. Greenshield. A study of trafic capacity. *Proceedings of the Highway Research Board,* 14:448 – 477, 1935.
10. C.R. Larson and A.R. Odoni. *Urban Operation Research.* Prentice-Hall, VJ, 1981.
11. R.J.F. Rossetti and S. Bampi. *A software environment to integrate urban traffic simulation tasks.* JGIDA, 3(1) :56-63, 1999.
12. S. Ruch. *Un environnement de modéisation multi-domaine des systèmes àflux discrets.* PhD Thesis, Université Blaise Pascal - Clermont-Ferrand II, 1994.
13. Ph. Toint. *Transport modelling and operations research : a fruitful connection.* Technical Report 97 7, Faculté de Namur, Belgium, 1997.
14. Qi Yang. *A simulation laboratory for evaluation of dynamic traffic management systems.* Doctor of philosophy in transportation, Massachussets Institute of Technology, 1997.
15. L. Zhao and T. Foster. *Driver duty : a pattern for public transport systems.* JOOP,11(4), 1997
16. L. Zhao and T. Foster. *Cascade : A pattern language of transport systems (point and route).* JOOP, in Pattern Language and programming design 3, 12(1) 1999.

Extending OCL to Include Actions

Anneke Kleppe[1], Jos Warmer[2]

Klasse Objecten, The Netherlands, www.klasse.nl
[1]A.Kleppe@klasse.nl
[2]J.Warmer@klasse.nl

Abstract. The UML's Object Constraint Language provides the modeller of object-oriented systems with ways to express the semantics of a model in a precise and declarative manner. The constraints which can be expressed in this language, all state requirements on the static aspects of the system. The Object Constraint Language currently lacks a way to express that events have happened or will happen, that signals are or will be send, or that operations are or will be called.

This paper introduces an extension to OCL to solve the above problem: the so-called action clause. We describe how this extension is integrated with the UML semantics to avoid semantics overlap. It also shows that a modeler can use it to specify dynamic requirements declaratively on an abstract level, without the need to use full operational dynamic diagrams.

Keywords. UML, OCL, constraints, pre- and postconditions, invariants, actions, operations, dynamic semantics.

1 Introduction

The Unified Modeling Language [1], the standard set by the Object Management Group for object-oriented modeling and design, has rapidly gained acceptance amongst system analysts and designers. The Object Constraint Language is a language that has been defined as part of the UML. It provides the modeller of object-oriented systems with ways to express the semantics of an object-oriented model in a very precise manner. These semantics can be expressed in invariants, and pre- and post-conditions, which are all forms of constraints.

However, the constraints which can be expressed in the OCL, all state requirements on the static aspects of the system. Even pre- and postconditions that express the semantics of a dynamic operation, do so by comparing the system state before and after the execution. The Object Constraint Language currently lacks ways to express that events have happened or will happen, that signals are or will be send, or that operations are or will be called.

When doing business modeling, as in Eriksson and Penker [2], business rules can be written using OCL, but stimulus/response rules can not be expressed. This is certainly a shortcoming of the language that needs to be overcome. Another need for expanding the OCL to include more dynamics, is that when building components, the specification of outgoing events is very important. The expectation is that the OCL will be much used

A. Evans, S. Kent and B. Selic (Eds.): «UML» 2000, LNCS 1939, pp. 440-450, 2000.

for specifying components, therefore the language needs some manner of expressing these outgoing events.

This paper introduces a new type of constraint to the OCL, the action clause, which gives semantics to a model by stating dynamic requirements. The proposed action clause is meant to be of use for modellers that use the realtime interpretation of UML, as well as modellers that use the sequential programming interpretation. The rest of this paper is organised as follows. Section 2 explains the difficulties of integrating different views on dynamic semantics. Sections 3 and 4 introduce the action clause, its concrete and abstract syntax, and its semantics. It shows the use in the context of an operation, a classifier or a component. The next two sections (5 and 6) show how the action clause in the OCL can be used to model business rules and to specify the behavior of components. Finally, section 7 summarises this paper and draws some conclusions.

2 Issues Concerning the Dynamic Semantics of UML

Extending OCL with a construct that specifies which actions have been performed is far from straightforward. Actions are defined in the UML 1.3 meta-model and any definition in OCL needs to be properly integrated with this definition.

One of the problems we encountered is that the dynamic concepts in the UML do not have one well-defined semantics yet. (Currently, there is an effort undertaken within the OMG to set a standard for the dynamic semantics of the UML, called the action semantics.) The largest problem is that there seems to be a breach of understanding between people that interpret all dynamic information in a UML model in a realtime fashion, and people that interpret the dynamics in a more direct, sequential programming style. This breach is clearly visible in the interpretation of the event concept, defined in the UML as "a specification of a type of observable occurrence". Events can be viewed either as synchronous operation calls, or as asynchronous realtime events. The UML definition itself [1] is written towards the realtime interpretation, and makes a sequential interpretation of statecharts difficult.

In a sequential interpretation of statecharts, an event on a transition is mapped onto an operation of the class for which the statechart has been defined. The condition, if present, will be mapped onto an if-statement, or a precondition. Any actions coupled to the transition are translated to a skeleton of the method of the operation. This interpretation of statechart is also called 'protocol statecharts' in the UML. The meaning of the statechart in Figure 1 would be translated into the following piece of Java code.

```
void use() {
  if ( inState(stored) ) {
    if ( condition == good ) {
      peel(); pan.open(); setState(cooking);
    }
    if ( condition == bad ) {
      dustbin.open(); setState(thrown-out);
    }
  }
}
```

In a realtime interpretation of statecharts, an event is the reception of a signal. The signal is, either virtually, or in reality, put on an input queue when it is received by the instance modelled by the statechart; the event occurs when the signal is taken out of the input queue and processed. The meaning of the statechart in Figure 1 would then be translated to roughly the following piece of Java code.

```
void eternalLoop() {
  while ( true ) do {
    Event e = takeEventFromQueue();
    if ( e == use and inState(stored) ) {
      if ( condition == good ) {
        peel(); pan.open(); setState(cooking);
      }
      if ( condition == bad ) {
        dustbin.open(); setState(thrown-out);
      }
    }
  }
}
```

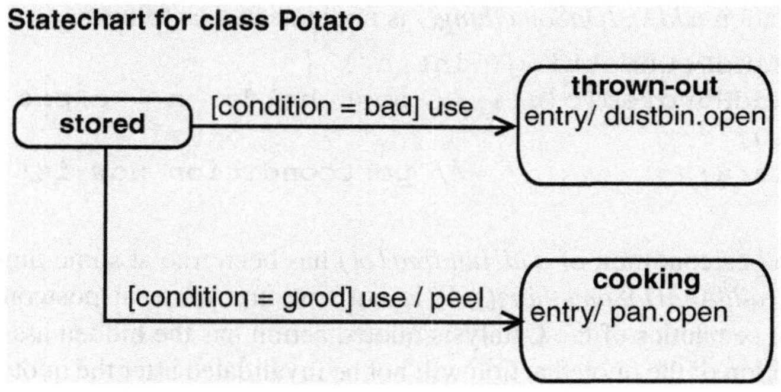

Figure 1 Example statechart

Catalysis [3] is a UML based system development method that uses constraints extensively. The Catalysis creators have clearly realized the need for specifying dynamic semantics. In Catalysis one can specify that actions have taken place as a side-effect of other actions. A Catalysis postcondition of an action specification may include a "quote" of another action specification, as in

```
action Scheduler::cancel_session( s: Session)
post: s.confirmed ==> [[ unassign_instructor( s ) ]]
```

The included action is shown between the double square brackets ([[ ]]). The inclusion means that all postconditions of the included action (in the example: *unassign_instructor*) are true at the time the postcondition for the current action (in the example: *cancel_session*) is evaluated. Another option that can be expressed is the actual sending of an operation call in a synchronous manner. In that case the postcondition of the called action must still be true at the time the postcondition for the current action is evaluated. Note that the term 'action' in Catalysis is not identical to 'action' in UML. For our purposes we can view a Catalysis 'action' as a UML 'operation'.

The Catalysis use of quoted actions implies a sequential interpretation. Because the quoted actions postcondition is true, the implication is that the quoted action must be finished before the current action may finish. Otherwise the postcondition of the quoted action will not be true at the end of the current action.

This sequential programming view on system dynamics, can not simply be used to express dynamic semantics in the OCL. The realtime interpretation needs to be supported as well. What's more, there are some hidden assumptions in the Catalysis approach. Even if a quoted action is called and finished, its postcondition will not neccesarily still be true at the time the postcondition for the current action is evaluated. This is clearly shown in the next example. The actions *addAndDoSomething()* and *addHundredTo()* are specified as follows:

```
action SomeClass::addAndDoSomething(int a)
post: [[ addHundredTo( a ) ]]

action SomeClass::addHundredTo(int a)
post: a = a@pre + 100
```

And the operation *addAndDoSomething()* is implemented as follows:

```
int addAndDoSomething( int a ) {
  a:= addHundredTo(a); // post holds: a = a@pre + 100
  a:= 10;
  return a;            // postcondition now is: a = 10
}
```

Although the postcondition of *addHundredTo()* has been true at some time during the execution of *addAndDoSomething()*, it is not true any more at postcondition time. Therefore the semantics of the Catalysis quoted action has the hidden assumption that the postcondition of the quoted action will not be invalidated after the quoted action has finished.

Catalysis defines a variant of the quoted action to specify that anothed action has been invoked asynchroneously. For this the keyword *sent* is used. The semantics states that the sent action is scheduled for execution at a later time. This definition needs to be weakened to apply to the most generic case. The scheduled action could potentially already be finished before the current action finishes.

The Syntropy [4] method includes the notion of generated events to specify that events are sent from an object. Syntropy shows generated events in state diagrams. The need to use state diagrams for this purpose only might lead to overspecification.

The examples above clearly show the requirements on the new type of constraint we want to define. In the OCL we need a mechanism for specifying outgoing messages that takes into account the various interpretations of system dynamics, and a notion of time. But if the semantics of the UML are to be strictly followed there should be no specific hidden assumptions.

3 The Action Clause

3.1 Abstract Syntax and Semantics

We propose to introduce in the OCL the concept 'action clause'. An action clause contains three parts:

1. the set of target instances to which the event (or events) is send, called targetSet,
2. the set of events that has been send to this targetSet, called eventSet,
3. a condition, which is optional.

In order to explain the semantics of our extension we need to introduce two virtual event queues for each instance (either object, or component instance). One is an input queue, one is an output queue. Naturally in object oriented systems, an operation is always executed by an instance. Operations are never stand-alone. This assumption is vital to our semantics. Whenever an operation sends an event, for every target in the targetset, a <target, event> pair is put in the virtual outputqueue of its instance (where target is the instance to which the event is send). An underlying transport mechanism will transport each event in the virtual output queue to the specified target. The notion of a transport mechanism is taken from the UML, section 2.12.4 and not further specified here.

This notion of virtual in- and outputqueues can be used in both interpretations of dynamic semantics. In the case of a synchronous operation call the transport will take no time. In the realtime interpretation the virtual inputqueue will be real, and the transport mechanism can be defined having the preferred semantics. Note that the notion of a virtual input-queue is already described in the state machine section of the UML semantics.

There is a need to be specific on the topic of time, because there are a number of issues in defining the action clause concerned with timing. For the purpose of specifying software systems, time can be viewed as a sequence of points in time, which in the remainder of this paper will be called time-points. A time-point is a moment in time that has no duration.Time-points have a monotonous ordering. If a time-point T1 is not before a time-point T2, and not after T2, then it is equal to T2. The fundamental timing issues are the following. (As a shorthand for "the time-point at which the postcondition is evaluated", we use the notation "@post".) Assume we have an action, where we want to specify that, as a result of the action, some events has been sent.

- We can not guarantee that an event that was send by the action to a certain target, was received by that target @post (asynchronous messages). The transport mechanism might take a long time.
- We can not guarantee that an event that was send by the action to a certain target, and was received by that target, is still in the inputqueue of that target at action@post. It may be dispatched or removed in some other way (a pure realtime view on dynamic semantics).
- We can not guarantee that the postcondition of an operation called (taking the operation call view on dynamic semantics) by the action is still true at action@post. Attribute and other values could have been changed in a number of ways after the called operation, as is shown in the example in section 2.
- We can not guarantee that an event that was send by the action is still in the outputqueue of the action@post.

Concluding, we may say that the only thing that can reasonably be guaranteed @post, is that an outgoing event has been in the virtual outputqueue during the execution of the operation.Therefore our definition of an action clause is:

> *An action clause evaluates to true if, and only if, whenever the condition holds, the virtual outputqueue of the instance that executes the operation has contained at some point in time during execution of the operation, all <target, event> pairs that are specified by the combination (Carthesian product) of the targetSet and the eventSet.*

This definition fits remarkably well in an object oriented view. An object can only guarantee its own behavior, but cannot guarantee the behavior of other objects.

3.2 Concrete Syntax

As concrete syntax for an action clause we propose the following (there are several other concrete syntaxes possible, we are open for discussion on this point):

```
action: if <condition> to <targetSet> send <eventSet>
```

The targetSet is a list of objects reachable from the executing object (pathName in the grammar in Warmer and Kleppe [5]), separated by comma's. The eventSet is a list of names with parameters between brackets (featureCall in the grammar), also separated by comma's. The condition can be any OCL expression of Boolean type. An example of the usage of an action clause with an operation is:

```
context CustomerCard::invalidate()
pre    : none
post   : valid = false
action: if customer.special to customer
                               send politeInvalidLetter()
action: if not customer.special to customer
                                   send invalidLetter()
```

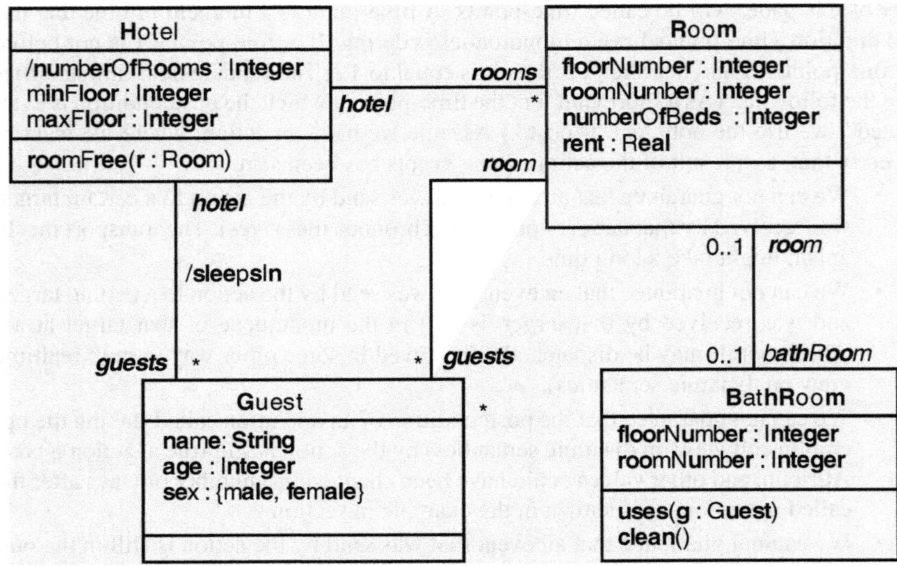

Figure 2 example class diagram

An action clause for a classifier will look similar:

```
context CustomerCard
inv    : validFrom.isBefore(goodThru)
action: if goodThru.isAfter(Date.now) to self
                                       send invalidate()
```

Section 4 will explain in more detail the use of the action clause in both circumstances.

4 Use of the Action Clause

4.1 Action Clause in an Operation Specification

Action clauses can be used to specify an operation, as shown in the example in section 3 There remains one question to be answered: when should the condition be evaluated, at precondition time or at postcondition time, or at some time-point in between? The option of some time-point in between is too vague to be a real option. The argument for evaluation at precondition time is that a client of this operation has a complete specification of the operation and can at forehand determine whether or not the events will be send. But preconditions are always conditions on the use of the operation, they state the responsibilities of the caller instance, not of the instance that executes the operation.

The action clause does not state a responsibility of the caller, neither does it restrict the use of the operation. Therefore the condition will be evaluated at postcondition time. Postconditions define what has been achieved by the operation, and so does the action clause. To be able to reference values as they were at precondition time, the @pre-construct that can be used in postconditions, can be used in the condition of the action clause too, as in the following example.

```
context BathRoom::uses(g : Guest)
pre    : if room->isEmpty then g.room = self.room
                  else g.room.floorNumber = self.floorNumber
post   : usage = usage@pre + 1
action: if usage > 10 to self send clean()
```

The meaning of the action clause is that the event *clean* will be send to the bathroom object itself, whenever the attribute *usage* is greater than ten at postcondition time.

Although we intend not to prescribe how to use the OCL, some notes on the pragmatics of the action clause are needed. In our opinion only events generated by the current operation should be specified in an action clause of an operation specification. Events send by operations called by the current one should not be included. They will be defined in the called operations. Tools can try to deduce the complete set of all events generated by the operation, by combining the action clauses.

4.2 Action Clause with a Classifier

Another part of a system specification where the action clause is useful, is the invariant of a classifier (e.g. a class, interface, or component). Currently, an invariant states what should be true “at all times” for an instance of that classifier. In practice, violation of invariants will happen. Some of these violations could be fatal, that is, the system can not function correctly if the invariant does not hold. Other violations may be acceptable and only need some "mending" of the instance for the system to function properly again. There is a need to specify what should happen when such an invariant fails. The current invariants can still be used to specify the fatal invariants, the action clause can be used to specify the less fatal invariants. We call this type of invariant action-invariant. The meaning of the action-invariant is that at the moment the condition becomes true, the event (or eventSet) is send to the target (or targetSet). Example:

```
context Room
inv    : numberOfBeds >= 1
action: if guests->isEmpty to hotel send roomFree(self)
```

Another reason to use action clauses on classifiers, is to simply specify outgoing events. For instance, when an object should notify others in certain conditions, as in the Observer pattern. Up to now all descriptions of external behavior were inevitably using notations like sequence diagrams, as in Gamma et al. [6]. Using the action clause of OCL we can write:

```
context Subject
action: if changed to self.observers send notify()
```

This means that as soon as the *changed* attribute becomes true, *notify()* will be send to all observers. This is a much more abstract specification of the behavior of the *Subject*. And what's more, the above specification is correct, both for synchronous/sequential interpretation, and for the realtime interpretation of *notify()*. When we use an interaction diagram to specify this, we are forced to make the choice between both interpretations.

Of course the Observer pattern can also be described using an operation *changed*() with an action clause, instead of an attribute. It will then look like:

```
context Subject::changed()
post: to self.observers send notify()
```

As with other invariants it is up to the implementor to decide when and how to check this action-invariant. It could be checked as part of every pre- or/and postcondition, or on a regular basis, or whenever attribute values change, or as a database trigger, etc.

5 Business Rules

One place were the OCL has apparent use is in business modeling. When using UML for business modeling, as done by Eriksson and Penker in [2], constraints are used to capture business rules. Eriksson uses the categorisation of business rules as defined by Martin and Odell [7]. They distinguish five main categories:

An *inference rule* specifies a conclusion which can be made when certain conditions are true. In OCL this can be specified using an invariant with the implies construct:

```
context Room
inv: self.bathRoom->notEmpty implies rent > 200
```

A *computational rule* calculates its result through some algorithm. In OCL these rules can be specified as an invariant of the form of an equation: "attribute = <expression>"

```
context Hotel
inv: numberOfRooms = rooms->size
```

A *structural rule* specifies conditions on classifiers and their associations, which should not be violated. These rules are specified in OCL through invariants on attributes and associations.

```
context Hotel
inv: rooms->includesAll(guests.room)
inv: minFloor <= maxFloor
```

An *operational/behavioral rule* defines conditions that must hold before and after an operation is performed. In OCL these are specified using preconditions and postconditions.

```
context BathRoom::uses(g : Guest)
pre : if room->isEmpty then g.room = room
               else g.room.floorNumber = self.floorNumber
post: usage = usage@pre + 1
```

A *stimulus response rule* specifies that certain actions should be performed when certain conditions are or become true. As mentioned by Eriksson, it is not possible to specify stimulus response rules in the current OCL 1.3. Using the action clause, we can specify stimulus response rules as follows:

```
context BathRoom
action: if usage > 10 to self send clean()
```

A modeler doing high level business modeling can use the OCL 1.3 to specify all of the required business rules, except for the stimulus response. Eriksson mentions that this is not possible in the OCL because of the declarative nature of the OCL. Using the action clause, stimulus response rules can readily be specified, while keeping the OCL fully declarative. With the action clause extension the OCL is capable of supporting all types of business rules.

6 Component Specification

Another place were the OCL has apparent use is in component modeling. Components can be described by interfaces, that specify all operations for the component. Each operation can be specified precisely by using pre- and postconditions written in OCL. This however, is not enough to grasp the full semantics of a component. One aspect, which cannot easily be described in OCL, is the fact that components also have outgoing events. The idea of Software-ICs [8] shows components to have inputs and outputs. Component models like Java Beans have put this into practice.

In UML one can describe outgoing events or operation calls using one of the dynamic diagrams. In general, interaction diagrams, state diagrams, and activity diagrams can all be used to describe outgoing traffic in one or another way. All of these diagrams focus on combinations of events or messages, their relative order, their choice points, etc., and thus they describe the behavior by stating *how* an object works internally. For example, when a collaboration is used to describe the behavior of an operation, the exact internal order of processing must be specified. The same holds when an activity diagram is used for the same purpose.

UML currently lacks a way to describe outgoing traffic at a higher level by stating *what* should be outgoing. Especially when specifying the external visible behavior of components, there is a strong need to hide the internals, but still one needs to be able to specify the outgoing events. The extension to OCL that we define in this paper, allows one to do exactly this. This is perfectly in line with the use of OCL for pre- and postconditions, where the OCL specification also states *what* should be true, and not *how* it should be achieved.

7 Conclusion

This paper introduces dynamic semantics in the OCL by adding an action clause to the language. We consider inclusion of the action clause to be a major step forward in the OCL. For the proposal in this paper we have looked at various Uml variants that already include a similar type of action clause. Each variant takes a specific view and is applicable in certain circumstances only. Therefore we could not use their semantics directly for a generic UML semantics. The extension described in this paper is generic and conforms to the 1.3 version of the UML semantics. The definition of the action clause in OCL integrates well with the rest of the UML semantics in several ways:

- The semantics of the action clauses is very generic. However, it follows the restrictions that can be laid down in a UML profile:
  - if the action clause is used within a 'sequential modeling' profile, where all actions are call actions, the semantics of the action clause in a postcondition guarantees that all actions are operations calls and that all the operations calls have finished at postcondition time.
  - if the action clause is used in a real-time profile, its semantics will follow the real-time semantics.
- An action clause with an operation is a restriction on its implementation and therefore on it puts restrictions on a dynamic diagram for the operation. Somewhere in the dynamic diagram, the specified action has to be performed.

Extending OCL with the action clause is an important change to the OCL and seems a logical extension to OCL in the forthcoming version 2.0 of the UML standard. Therefore we find it important to discuss this topic in an international forum. This paper is one of the ways we use to peform this discussion.

As far as we are able to check, it conforms to the proposed action semantics too. If the latter is not the case, we are in favour of changing our proposal to conform to that semantics.

References

[1] OMG Unified Modeling Language Specification, Version 1.3, June 1999

[2] Hans-Erik Eriksson and Magnus Penker, *Business Modeling with UML, Business Patterns at Work*, 2000, Wiley

[3] Desmond D'Souza and Alan Wills, *Objects, Components and Frameworks with UML, The Catalysis Approach*, 1999, Addison-Wesley

[4] Steve Cook and John daniels, *Designing Object Systems: Object-oriented modeling with Syntropy*, 1994, Prentice-Hall

[5] Jos Warmer and Anneke Kleppe, *The Object Constraint Language, Precise Modeling with UML*, 1999, Addison-Wesley

[6] Erich Gamma, Richard Helm, Ralph Johnson, and John Vlissides, *Design Patterns, Elements of Reusable Object-Oriented Software*, 1995, Addison-Wesley

[7] James Martin and James J. Odell, *Object-Oriented Methods, A Foundation*, 1998, Prentice-Hall

[8] Brad Cox, *Superdistribution: Objects As Property on the Electronic Frontier*, 1996, Addison-Wesley

A Structured Approach to Develop Concurrent Programs in UML *

Masaaki Mizuno, Gurdip Singh, and Mitchell Neilsen

Department of Computing and Information Sciences
234 Nichols Hall
Kansas State University
Manhattan, Kansas 66506

Abstract. This paper presents a methodology to develop synchronization code based on the global invariant (GI) approach in the context of the Unified Process in UML. This approach has the following advantages: (1) it is a formal approach that enables formal verification of programs being developed, (2) the most important activity in the programming process lies at a high level; namely, specification of GIs, (3) GIs are platform independent, and (4) existing GIs may be composed to produce GIs for more complex synchronization. We provide a set of useful GIs which work as basic patterns. Programmers can compose these GIs to produce appropriate GIs for specific applications.

1 Introduction

The Unified Process [6] in the Unified Modeling Language (UML) [3] is the de facto standard of the object oriented programming development process. Its use-case driven approach provides an effective way to develop code that describes a sequence of actions on classes and objects. At run-time, this code is executed by threads. Even though there have been several proposals [4], the current Unified Process does not provide a standard methodology to develop synchronization among such threads.

In this paper, we propose a methodology to develop synchronization code in the context of the Unified Process[1]. We consider the development process in the framework of *aspect oriented programming* [7]. In this framework, properties that must be implemented are classified into the following two types:

- a *component* which can be clearly encapsulated in a generalized procedure (*i.e.*, object, method, procedure, etc.), and
- an *aspect* which cannot be clearly encapsulated in a generalized procedure; this type includes memory access patterns and synchronization of concurrent objects.

* This research was supported in part by the DARPA PCES Project and NSF CRCD Grant Number 9980321.

[1] Issues related to specific UML notation are not addressed. Rather, the focus is on fundamental issues related to the development process.

A. Evans, S. Kent and B. Selic (Eds.): ≪UML≫ 2000, LNCS 1939, pp. 451–465, 2000.

In our methodology, the component code is developed by the Unified Process and synchronization code is developed as aspect code which is later woven into the component code to produce complete object-oriented programs in languages and/or platforms based on semaphores, general monitors (such as C++ in POSIX pthreads), Java synchronized blocks, and active monitors. The entire design process is shown below in Figure 1.

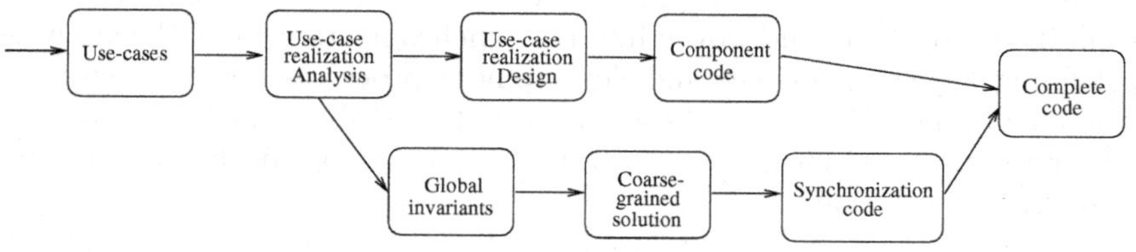

Fig. 1. Design processes and artifacts.

Our aspect language is based on Andrews' global invariant approach [1,2]. In this approach, a programmer first specifies a *global invariant* that implies the safety property for a given synchronization specification[2]. Then, a so-called *coarse-grained solution* is developed from the global invariant. The process of developing a coarse grained solution is based on Programming Logic and is strictly mechanical. The resulting coarse-grained solution preserves the global invariant. Next, the coarse-grained solution is mechanically translated to *fine-grained* synchronization code. Translations exist from coarse-grained solutions to fine-grained programs in semaphores, general monitors, active monitors in message passing systems[1], and JAVA synchronized blocks[8]. The translations preserve the global invariant; therefore, the resulting programs are guaranteed to satisfy the safety property of the synchronization specification.

The global invariant approach has many advantages.

1. It is a formal approach that enables formal verification of programs being developed.
2. The most important activity in the programming process lies at a high level; namely, specification of global invariants. Once appropriate global invariants are specified, the translation process to produce final fine-grained programs is mechanical; that is, compilers/translators can be easily constructed for translation.
3. Global invariants are platform (synchronization primitive) independent. For example, if the platform is switched from a semaphore-based to a monitor-based system, we only need to translate the coarse-grained solution to monitor-based fine-grained synchronization code.

One possible drawback of the global invariant approach is the difficulty to identify appropriate global invariants that correctly and accurately imply the safety

[2] The safety property asserts that the program never enters a bad state.

property of the synchronization specification for the system. To cope with this problem, we provide a set of useful global invariants. These invariants work as basic patterns and can be composed to produce global invariants for more complex synchronization. We will demonstrate the effectiveness of invariant composition. With this approach, we are able to solve a wide variety of synchronization problems found in [1,5].

Note that global invariants only specify safety properties. Other aspects of synchronization, such as priority, scheduling, and real-time constraints, need to be specified separately and woven into the synchronization code. We are working on defining aspect languages and development processes for these issues. Our initial results show that some of these aspects (*i.e.*, FIFO scheduling and various preferences of the readers/writers problem [1]) can be nicely incorporated in coarse grained solutions.

The rest of the paper is organized as follows: Section 2 reviews the Unified Process in UML and introduces an example problem which is used throughout the paper. Section 3 presents our methodology to develop synchronization code in the Unified Process. Section 4 presents some basic global invariants and invariant composition techniques.

2 UML and the Unified Process

The core of the Unified Process in UML is the use-case driven process. In this methodology, the development of a system starts with the identification of *actors* who interact with the system by sending stimuli and receiving responses. Use cases are used to specify the way actors interact with the system.

In the next step, we consider how the use-cases are realized by (1) identifying the necessary classes and the relationships between those classes (Class Model) and (2) describing use-case realizations which describe the collaborations between instances of the classes. Sequence diagrams, collaboration diagrams, and scenarios are often used to describe use-case realizations.

The classes and use-case realizations make up the analysis and design models. We start with the analysis model. The analysis model identifies three types of classes: boundary, entity, and control classes. Boundary objects interact with actors. Entity objects store long-lived or persistent data. Control classes represent classes that are not boundary or entity. They handle coordination, sequencing, and control of other objects. A control class is often associated with a specific use-case; a control object is created when the use case starts and terminates when the use case ends.

The design model refines the analysis model by considering the execution environment. In the design model, all (or most of) the necessary classes are identified, and the corresponding use-case realizations describe detail interactions of instances of such classes; therefore, use-case realizations can be mechanically mapped to fine-grained programs.

To explain our methodology to develop synchronization code in UML in Section 3, we consider the following telephone controller system as an example.

Example:[3] *Design a call distributor system which controls M external telephone lines and N operator telephones. When an external call arrives, the system connects the call to a free operator by ringing the operator's telephone. If all N operators are busy, the external call must wait (pending external call). In a similar way, if an operator is free but there is no pending external call, the operator must wait. When both the operator and the external call hang up, the communication is considered to have completed. When the communication completes, the system logs the following information: (1) external telephone arrival time, (2) external line id (3) connection time, (4) operator telephone id, (5) external call hang up time, (6) operator telephone hang up time, and (7) communication completion time.*

The actors of the system are operator telephones and external lines. For each actor, the following use-cases may be considered:

External Line:

1. Initiate Call: An external call arrives.
2. Disconnect Call: An external call hangs up.

Operator:

1. Become Free: The operator becomes free (the operator just came to work or completed the previous communication).
2. Pick Up Telephone: The operator picks up the telephone.
3. Hang Up Telephone: The operator hangs up the telephone.

Note that it is possible to define use-cases differently. For example, it is possible to combine 1 and 2 of the "External Line" use-cases and consider it as one long use-case.

Actors and use-cases should describe the complete specification of the system. Therefore, [6] recommends description of each use-case by a state diagram. However, since our interest is in the development of synchronization code, we do not elaborate complete use-cases.

We identify the following classes to implement our example system:

- Boundary (I/O) classes: operator telephone, external line
- Entity class: log database
- Control class: "call" object to store information about each connection

Using the above classes, we describe realizations[4]. Since our focus is on the synchronization aspect of the program, we do not describe detailed realizations. The following descriptions lie somewhere between use-cases and use-case realizations:

External Line:

[3] The example is an excerpt and revision of an exercise problem found in [9]. The exercise focuses on identification of classes and does not cover the synchronization aspect, whereas we focus only on synchronization issues of the problem.

[4] Since an operator (actor) interacts with the system through a boundary class operator telephone, terms "operator" and "operator telephone" are used interchangeably.

1. Initiate Call:
   (a) It creates a call object and records the external line id and arrival time in it, and then waits for a free operator (*i.e.*, operator telephone) to become available (R_{E1}).
   (b) When a free operator telephone is found, it informs the operator telephone of the call object.
2. Disconnect Call:
   It logs the external line hang up time in the call object and waits for the operator telephone to terminate the call (R_{E2}).

Operator Telephone:

1. Become Free:
   (a) It waits for an external call (R_{O1}).
   (b) If a pending call exists or an external call arrives, it is informed of the call object from the connected external line, records the operator telephone id, and rings the bell.
2. Pick Up Telephone:
   It records the connection time in the call object.
3. Hang Up Telephone:
   (a) It records the operator hang up time in the call object and then waits for the external line to terminate the call (R_{O2}).
   (b) When the external line terminates the call, it records the communication-termination time in the call object, logs the call object, and destroys the call object.

Each use-case realization is translated into a (sequentially executable) program which is executed by multiple threads. One way to implement such a system is to design each instance of the boundary classes (*i.e.*, M external line objects and M operator telephone objects, each controls one external line or one telephone, respectively) as an active object (which can instantiate a thread) and to instantiate one thread for each actor instance of the use-case. For example, when an external call arrives at an external line object, the system instantiates a new thread. The thread executes the program obtained for the use-case realization described in steps 1(a) and 1(b) and terminates. Later, when the call hangs up, a new thread is instantiated. The thread executes the code for the realization described in step 2 and terminates. Necessary information, such as the call object, can be passed from the former thread to the later thread using instance attributes of the external line object. This type of implementation is suitable for a system running on event-driven foundation classes, such as MFC and JFC.

3 Aspect Programming for Synchronization for the Unified Process

The Unified Process provides an effective methodology to capture a sequence of activities, which are executed by threads. In a use-case realization, sometimes its behavior depends on the states of other threads. For example, the External Line use-case realization waits for a free operator, and the Operator use-case realization waits for an external call. The current Unified Process does not have a standard methodology to develop code to handle such synchronization. We present a methodology to develop aspect code for such synchronization. We have adapted and extended the global invariant approach [1,2] to our aspect language. Resulting synchronization code is woven to the component code developed from use-case realizations. By nature of synchronization, the aspect program deals with collaboration among use-case realizations, whereas the component language (use-case realizations) focuses on collaboration among objects and classes.

The following steps describe the process of developing synchronization code and weaving it to the component code.

[Step 1] Identify synchronization regions:

The first step in our methodology is to identify *synchronization regions* in use-case realizations. A synchronization region is a segment in a use-case realization

1. in which a thread waits for some event to occur or some condition to hold (such as waiting for another thread to enter a particular segment or waiting for the number of threads in a particular segment to reach some bound), and
2. in which a thread may trigger an event or change a condition for which a thread at a synchronization region is waiting.

We define relation $\mathcal{R}$ on synchronization regions as follows: Let R_1 and R_2 be synchronization regions. If a thread at R_1 waits for an event or a condition that is triggered or changed by a thread executing R_2, then $R_1 \mathcal{R} R_2$. We consider the reflexive transitive closure of $\mathcal{R}$, denoted by $\mathcal{R}^+$. Then, equivalence classes (partitions) of synchronization regions are formed with respect to $\mathcal{R}^+$. These equivalence classes are called *synchronization clusters* or simply *clusters*. [4] has developed graphical notation for specifying interactions between two or more use case maps. A similar graphical notation can be developed for identifying synchronization regions and associating invariants with them.

Example: In the call distribution system, there are two synchronization regions in the External Line use-case realizations (R_{E1} and R_{E2}, refer to the realizations in Section 2) and two regions in the Operator Telephone use-case realizations (R_{O1} and R_{O2}). As shown in Figure 2, these synchronization regions are divided into two clusters, (R_{E1}, R_{O1}) and (R_{E2}, R_{O2}).

[Step 2] Declare synchronization counters:

For each synchronization region, R_E, we define two counters (called *synchronization counters*), an in-counter In_E and an out-counter Out_E, which are incremented when a thread enters and leaves the region, respectively. These counters represent the execution history of threads passing the region. They are used to trigger other waiting computations and check wait conditions.

We define the following two types of synchronization:

1. **anonymous synchronization:** If the synchronization is among anonymous threads that execute regions in a cluster (*i.e.*, any thread executing can

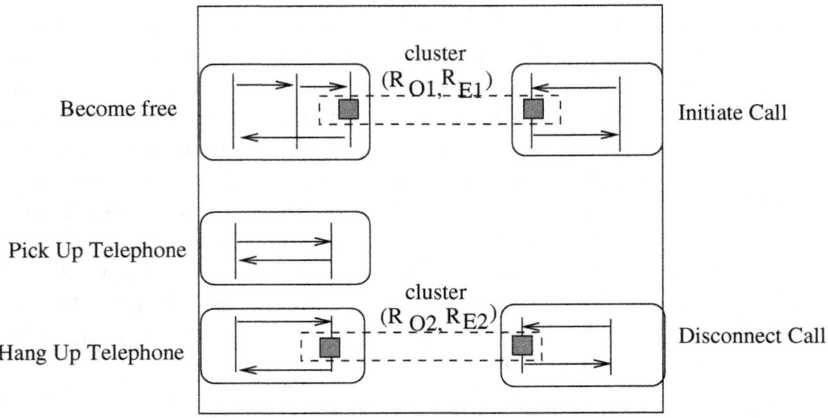

Fig. 2. Use-case realizations.

synchronize with any other threads in the cluster), one in-counter In_E and one out-counter Out_E are defined for each region R_E in the cluster. Any thread entering R_E increments In_E and any thread leaving R_E increments Out_E.

2. **specific synchronization:** If the synchronization is among a set of specific threads executing regions in a cluster, one in-counter and one out-counter are defined for each thread executing each synchronization region R_E in the cluster. The set of specific threads is said to form a *group*. For example, we can define arrays of counters $In_E[1..N]$ and $Out_E[1..N]$ for threads $T_E[i]$, $1 \leq i \leq N$ that pass through region R_E. When thread $T_E[i]$ enters and leaves R_E, it increments $In_E[i]$ and $Out_E[i]$, respectively. When a new group is formed, the synchronization counters of the threads in the group need to be initialized to zero.

Note that in the final program, synchronization counters appear only in the aspect programs and do not appear in the component programs.

Example: In the call distributor system, synchronization in cluster (R_{E1}, R_{O1}) is anonymous because any operator can serve for any external call. Therefore, four synchronization counters, In_{E1}, Out_{E1}, In_{O1}, and Out_{O1}, are defined for (R_{E1}, R_{O1}).

On the other hand, synchronization in cluster (R_{E2}, R_{O2}) is specific because only External Line threads and Operator threads that communicate with each other must synchronize. Thus, $In_{E2}[1..M]$ and $Out_{E2}[1..M]$ are defined for R_{E2}, and $In_{O2}[1..N]$ and $Out_{O2}[1..N]$ are defined for R_{O2}. The ith External Line thread $T_E[i]$ (instantiated by the ith External Line object) increments $In_{E2}[i]$ and $Out_{E2}[i]$ when it passes R_{E2}. Similarly, the jth Operator Telephone thread

$T_O[j]$ (instantiated by the jth Operator Telephone object) increments $In_{O2}[j]$ and $Out_{O2}[j]$ when it passes R_{O2}.

[Step 3] Specify global invariants:

The next step in our methodology is to identify a synchronization specification for each cluster and to specify a global invariant that implies a safety property for the specification. A global invariant is defined with connectives $\vee$, $\wedge$, and $\neg$ over terms involving the synchronization counters associated with the synchronization regions in the cluster.

Since it is often hard to identify an appropriate global invariant for a given synchronization specification, we provide a repository of reusable global invariants that describe common synchronization patterns. Programmers can describe a wide variety of synchronization specifications by composing such predefined global invariant patterns. This issue is discussed in Section 4.

Example: Cluster (R_{E1}, R_{O1}) forms anonymous "simple barrier" synchronization, in which the kth thread to enter R_{E1} and the kth thread to enter R_{O1} meet at their respective synchronization regions and leave together. As discussed in Section 4, the global invariant for simple barrier synchronization is "$Out_{E1} \leq In_{O1} \wedge Out_{O1} \leq In_{E1}$."

Note that threads that meet at R_{E1} and R_{O1} need to exchange their thread identifiers for the later synchronization at cluster (R_{E2}, R_{O2}) and the call object. The global invariant that allows such threads to exchange information is given in Section 4. For simplicity in explaining our methodology, we use the simple barrier synchronization invariant for cluster (R_{E1}, R_{O1}) in this section.

Cluster (R_{E2}, R_{O2}) also forms "simple barrier" synchronization. However, the synchronization is between specific threads. Assume that External Line thread $T_E[i]$ and Operator Telephone thread $T_O[j]$ communicate with each other. Then, the global invariant is "$Out_{E2}[i] \leq In_{O2}[j] \wedge Out_{O2}[j] \leq In_{E2}[i]$." Note that when a new group, $T_E[i]$ and $T_O[j]$, is formed in regions R_{E1} and R_{O1}, the counters, $Out_{E2}[i]$, $In_{O2}[j]$, $Out_{O2}[j]$, and $In_{E2}[i]$, must be reset to zero to synchronize correctly in cluster (R_{E2}, R_{O2}). Thus, in the above global invariant, each counter only contains a value of either 0 or 1.

[Step 4] Develop coarse-grained solutions:[5]

For each cluster, we obtain a coarse-grained solution that increments the in and out counters defined in the cluster. Let B be a Boolean expression (called a guard) and S be a sequence of statements. The following two types of synchronization constructs are used in a coarse-grained solution[1]:

1. $\langle S \rangle$: This statement specifies atomic execution of S.
2. $\langle \textbf{await}\, B \rightarrow S \rangle$: This statement specifies that the executing process is delayed until B is true; at which point, S is executed atomically. No interleaving occurs between the final evaluation of B and the execution of S.
   The formal semantics is given by the following inference rule [1]:
   Await Rule: $\frac{\{P \wedge B\} S \{Q\}}{\{P\} < \textbf{await}\, B \rightarrow S > \{Q\}}$

[5] Steps 4 and 5 are described in more detail elsewhere [1].

The coarse-grained solution for synchronization region R_E is obtained as follows: Let GI be the global invariant for the cluster containing R_E. Let S_c be an assignment statement associated with synchronization counter c for R_E (*i.e.*, c is either In_E or Out_E) such that c is referred to in GI. First, S_c is transformed into $\langle \textbf{await}\, B \rightarrow S_c \rangle$.

Since triple $\{GI\}\langle \textbf{await}\, B \rightarrow S_c\rangle\{GI\}$ must always hold, B is mechanically obtained as the weakest condition that satisfies triple $\{GI \wedge B\}\, S_c\{GI\}$ (from the Await Rule). If B is true, the statement $\langle S_c \rangle$ is used instead. Note that it is not necessary to form a coarse grained solution for synchronization counter c that is not referred to in GI.

Example: For regions R_{E1} and R_{O1}, the following coarse-grained solution is obtained:

- Region R_{E1}:

$$\langle In_{E1}++\rangle$$
$$\langle \textbf{await}\, Out_{E1} < In_{O1} \rightarrow Out_{E1}++\rangle$$

- Region R_{O1}:

$$\langle In_{O1}++\rangle$$
$$\langle \textbf{await}\, Out_{O1} < In_{E1} \rightarrow Out_{O1}++\rangle$$

For regions R_{E2} and R_{O2}, the following coarse-grained solution is obtained for each communicating pair of the threads $T_E[i]$ and $T_O[j]$:

- Region R_{E2}:

$$\langle In_{E2}[i]++\rangle$$
$$\langle \textbf{await}\, Out_{E2}[i] < In_{O2}[j] \rightarrow Out_{E2}[i]++\rangle$$

- Region R_{O2}:

$$\langle In_{O2}[j]++\rangle$$
$$\langle \textbf{await}\, Out_{O2}[j] < In_{E2}[i] \rightarrow Out_{O2}[j]++\rangle$$

[Step 5] Obtain synchronization code:

In this step, we translate the coarse-grained solution to fine-grained synchronization code in a target programming language or platform. Andrews presents algorithms to map coarse-grained solutions to programs based on semaphore, monitors, and active monitors [1]. We have developed an algorithm to obtain solutions based on Java synchronized blocks [8].

For example, the translation to the monitor with the Signal and Continue discipline[6] and a broadcast signal statement (**signal_all**()) is described as follows: We define one monitor for each cluster. Each construct $\langle \ldots \rangle$ in the coarse-grained solution becomes a separate procedure within the monitor. One condition variable is declared for each guard B in an **await** statement in the coarse-grained

[6] The Signal and Continue discipline means that a signaling thread continues and an awoken thread waits [1].

solution. Construct $\langle \textbf{await} B \rightarrow S \rangle$ is translated to a procedure with the following body:

$$\textbf{while not } B \textbf{ do } c_B.\textbf{wait}() \textbf{ od}; \ S;$$

where c_B is a condition variable associated with guard B. Construct $\langle S \rangle$ is translated to a procedure with body S.

Finally, in each procedure, if execution of any statement may potentially change some guard B to true, we add c_B.**signal**() or c_B.**signal_all**() after the statement, where c_B is a condition variable associated with guard B. If more than one thread may leave the **await** construct when B becomes true, **signal_all**() must be issued; otherwise, **signal**() should be issued.

A coarse-grained solution for specific synchronization, where synchronization counters are indexed by the thread identifier, requires the thread identifiers to be passed as parameters. All threads executing the same synchronization region wait on the same condition variable. Therefore, **signal_all()** must be issued on the condition variable to wake up even a single thread.
Example: The synchronization code for cluster (R_{E1}, R_{O1}) in monitor[7] is:

```
monitor R_E1_O1
    var
        CO1, CE1: cond;
        In_O1, Out_O1, In_E1, Out_E1 : int = 0;
    procedure IncInO1 ()
        In_O1 ++; CE1.signal();
    end
    procedure IncOutO1 ()
        while ¬ (Out_O1 < In_E1) do CO1.wait(); od
        Out_O1 ++;
    end
    procedure IncInE1 ()
        In_E1 ++; CO1.signal();
    end
    procedure IncOutE1 ()
        while ¬ (Out_E1 < In_O1) do CE1.wait(); od
        Out_E1 ++;
    end
end
```

The synchronization code for cluster (R_{E2}, R_{O2}) is:

```
monitor R_E2_O2
    var
        CE2, CO2: cond;
        In_E2 : int[1..M];
        In_O2 : int[1..N];
    procedure IncInE2 (int Eid, int Oid)
```

[7] The syntax of the monitor is a slight variation of the one defined in [1].

```
            In_E2[Eid] + +; CO2.signal_all();
        end
        procedure IncOutE2 (int Eid, int Oid)
            while ¬(Out_E2[Eid] < In_O2[Oid]) do CE2.wait(); od
            Out_E2[Eid] + +;
        end
        procedure IncInO2 (int Eid, int Oid)
            In_O2[Oid] + +; CE2.signal_all();
        end
        procedure IncOutO2 (int Eid, int Oid)
            while ¬ (Out_O2[Oid] < In_E2[Eid]) do CO2.wait(); od
            Out_O2[Oid] + +;
        end
    end
```

Note that the monitor R_{E2_O2} must provide procedures to clear its counters.

[Step 6] Weave code:

The task of the code weaver is to integrate the component code developed from the use-case realizations and the synchronization code developed in the above steps. This is done by (1) instantiating one monitor object for each monitor and (2) adding a call to the associated monitor procedure in the component code corresponding to the entry and the exit of each synchronization region.

Example: For cluster (R_{E1}, R_{O1}), let object M_{E1_O1} be an instance of monitor R_{O1_E2}. Then, "M_{O1_E1}.IncInE1();" and "M_{O1_E1}.IncOutE1();" are inserted at the entry and the exit, respectively, of the component code segment associated with R_{E1} in the use-case realization. Similarly, "M_{E1_O1}.IncInO1();" and "M_{E1_O1}.IncOutO1();" are inserted to the entry and the exit of the code segment associated with R_{O1}, respectively.

For cluster (R_{E2}, R_{O2}), let object M_{E2_O2} be an instance of monitor R_{E2_O2}. Let *Eid* and *Oid* be the identifiers of communicating threads executing an External Line object an Operator Telephone object, respectively. Then, "M_{E2_O2}.IncInE2(Eid, Oid)" and "M_{E2_O2}.IncOutE2(Eid, Oid);" are inserted at the entry and the exit of the code segment associated with R_{E2}. Similarly, "M_{E2_O2}.IncInO2(Eid, Oid)" and "M_{E2_O2}.IncOutO2(Eid, Oid);" are inserted at the entry and the exit of the code segment associated with R_{O2}, respectively.

4 Global Invariants

4.1 Invariant Patterns

Defining global invariants to match the safety property of a given synchronization specification is a non-trivial task. In order to simplify this task, we provide a repository of global invariants patterns that may be used as building blocks to compose invariants for complex synchronization requirements. The following are some example global invariant patterns:

1. Bound: the synchronization specification is that at most n threads can be in synchronization region R_B at any point in time.

The number of threads in R_B is given by $(In_B - Out_B)$. Therefore, the global invariant, $Bound(R_B, n)$, is $(In_B - Out_B \leq n)$.

2. Exclusion: at any point in time, threads can be in at most one synchronization region out of n synchronization regions $R_1, R_2, \cdots, R_n$.

The state in which no thread is in region R_i is represented by $(In_i == Out_i)$. The state in which threads are only in region R_i is represented by

$$(In_1 == Out_1) \wedge (In_2 == Out_2) \wedge \cdots \wedge (In_{i-1} == Out_{i-1}) \wedge \\ (In_{i+1} == Out_{i+1}) \wedge \cdots \wedge (In_n == Out_n)$$

Let $Comb(n, n-1)$ denote the collection of combinations of $n-1$ out of n from the set $\{1, 2, \cdots, n\}$. The global invariant, $Exclusion(R_1, R_2, \cdots, R_n)$, is

$$\vee_{C \in Comb(n,n-1)} (\wedge_{i \in C} (In_i == Out_i)).$$

For example, if $n = 3$, $Comb(3, 2)$ is $\{\{1, 2\}, \{1, 3\}, \{2, 3\}\}$. Therefore,

$Exclusion(R_1, R_2, R_3)$ is

$$((In_1 == Out_1) \wedge (In_2 == Out_2)) \vee ((In_1 == Out_1) \wedge (In_3 == Out_3)) \vee \\ ((In_2 == Out_2) \wedge (In_3 == Out_3))).$$

3. Resource management: initially, there are n resource items. A resource item is produced (or returned) and consumed (or borrowed) when a thread executes synchronization regions R_P and R_C, respectively. A thread enters R_C and waits if no resource item is available.

The global invariant, $Resource(R_P, R_C, n)$, is $(In_C \leq n + Out_P)$.

4. Simple barrier: the kth thread to enter R_1 and the kth thread to enter R_2 meet at their respective synchronization regions and leave together.

The global invariant, $SimpleBarrier(R_1, R_2)$, is $(Out_1 \leq In_2) \wedge (Out_2 \leq In_1)$. This says that threads cannot pass region R_1 any more times than threads have arrived at R_2, and vice versa.

We have extended the simple barrier synchronization to the following more general barrier synchronization:

5. General barrier: the specification is extended to synchronize threads executing in n regions, $R_1, \cdots, R_n$, where N_i threads in $R_i (1 \leq i \leq n)$ meet, form a group, and leave the barrier together.

For example, let $n = 3$, $N_1 = 2$, $N_2 = 3$, and $N_3 = 4$. Then, 2 threads in R_1 and 3 threads in R_2 and 4 threads in R_3 form a group and leave together.

The global invariant, $Barrier((R_1, N_1), (R_2, N_2), \cdots, (R_n, N_n))$, is given by

$\wedge_{1 \leq i \leq n} (\wedge_{1 \leq j \leq n} (Out_i \leq (In_j / N_j) * N_i)$, where '/' is an integer division.

The global invariant is reasoned about in the following manner: Threads entering in each section are normalized by the necessary number to form a group. That is, the N_i threads in R_i form one unit. The kth unit of threads in R_i may leave the section when the kth unit of threads have entered in every section R_j, $1 \leq j \leq n$; that is, $(Out_i \leq (In_j / N_j) * N_i))$ for $1 \leq j \leq n$. Note that in order for N_i threads to leave R_i together, it is necessary to include $(Out_i \leq (In_i/N_i) * N_i)$ in the invariant.

For example, $Barrier((R_1, 2), (R_2, 3), (R_3, 4))$ is

$$((Out_1 \leq (In_1/2) * 2) \wedge (Out_1 \leq (In_2/3) * 2) \wedge (Out_1 \leq (In_3/4) * 2)) \wedge$$
$$((Out_2 \leq (In_1/2) * 3) \wedge (Out_2 \leq (In_2/3) * 3) \wedge (Out_2 \leq (In_3/4) * 3)) \wedge$$
$$((Out_3 \leq (In_1/2) * 4) \wedge (Out_3 \leq (In_2/3) * 4) \wedge (Out_3 \leq (In_3/4) * 4)).$$

4.2 Composition

The invariant patterns can be combined in a modular fashion to build invariants for more complex synchronization problems. In composition, logical conjunctions may be used to combine several global invariants. In addition, the invariant may be augmented by the **where** clause. This allows a programmer to map several synchronization counters into a single counter using the $\equiv$ operator. For example, $Out_E \equiv In_O$ specifies that Out_E and In_O are mapped into the same counter.

The following are some examples of composition of invariants:

1. General mutual exclusion problem: there are n synchronization regions, $R_1, \cdots, R_n$. At any point in time, threads may be in at most one synchronization region, and at most N_i threads may be in region R_i for $1 \leq i \leq n$.
The global invariant is $(\wedge_{1 \leq i \leq n} Bound(R_i, N_i)) \wedge Exclusion(R_1, \cdots, R_n)$.

For example, the readers/writers problem[1] is a special case of this problem. Its global invariant is $(Bound(R_W, 1) \wedge Exclusion(R_R, R_W))$, where reader threads read in region R_R and writer threads write in R_W.

2. Barrier with information exchange: this is a variation of barrier synchronization, in which all threads leaving together need to exchange information, such as thread identifiers, with one another.

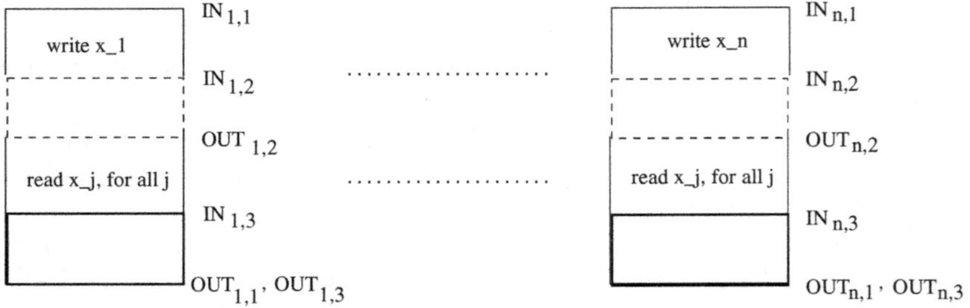

Fig. 3. Barrier with information exchange.

In many cases, we may need to construct multi-stage synchronization code. That is, we may need to define several subregions and link these subregions via the synchronization specification. This is an example of such multi-stage synchronization.

Each region R_i consists of three sub-regions as shown in Figure 3: $R_{i,1}, R_{i,2}$, and $R_{i,3}$. Region $R_{i,1}$ form bound, and $R_{i,2}$ and $R_{i,3}$ form barrier. Barrier $R_{i,2}$ is enclosed in bound $R_{i,1}$, and barrier $R_{i,3}$ overlaps the exit of bound $R_{i,1}$. A thread that has entered $R_{i,1}$ writes its information in a shared variable and then enters $R_{i,2}$. A thread that has left $R_{i,2}$ reads information written by all other threads and then enters $R_{i,3}$.

The global invariant is

$$\begin{aligned}&Bound(R_{1,1}, N_1) \wedge Bound(R_{2,1}, N_2) \wedge \cdots \wedge Bound(R_{n,i}, N_n) \wedge\\ &Barrier((R_{1,2}, N_1), (R_{2,2}, N_2), \cdots, (R_{n,2}, N_n)) \wedge\\ &Barrier((R_{1,3}, N_1), (R_{2,3}, N_2), \cdots, (R_{n,3}, N_n)),\\ &\quad \textbf{where } ((Out_{i,1} \equiv Out_{i,3}) \text{ for } 1 \le i \le n.\end{aligned}$$

The safety property is reasoned about in the following way: When a thread has entered sub-region $R_{i,1}$, it is certain that the thread is in the group. Therefore, the thread writes its information. When a thread passes the first barrier $R_{i,2}$, it it certain that all threads in the same group have written their information. Therefore, the thread reads information written by the other threads. When a thread leaves the second barrier $R_{i,3}$, it is certain that all other threads in the group have read the information. Therefore, a thread leaving $R_{i,3}$ also leaves bound $R_{i,1}$ to allow threads in the next group to enter the region.

The application of the barrier with information exchange is found in many synchronization problems. For example, the call distributor system requires that the external line thread and the operator phone thread that meet at cluster (R_{E1}, R_{O1}) to exchange the call object and their thread identifiers to synchronize at cluster (R_{E2}, R_{O2}). Therefore, cluster (R_{E1}, R_{O1}) should be the barrier with information exchange. The corresponding invariant is

$$\begin{aligned}&Bound(R_{E1,1}, 1) \wedge Bound(R_{O1,1}, 1) \wedge\\ &Barrier(R_{E1,2}, R_{O1,2}) \wedge Barrier(R_{E1,3}, R_{O1,3}),\\ &\quad \textbf{where } (Out_{E1,1} \equiv Out_{E1,3}) \wedge (Out_{O1,1} \equiv Out_{O1,3}).\end{aligned}$$

Let $T_E[i]$ and $T_O[j]$ be an External Line and Operator Telephone threads that communicate with each other. $T_E[i]$ writes the call object and its identifier between incrementing $In_{E1,1}$ and $In_{E1,2}$. It reads the identifier of the Operator Telephone thread (j) and clears $In_{E2}[i]$ and $Out_{E2}[i]$ between incrementing $Out_{E1,2}$ and $In_{E1,3}$. Similarly, $T_O[j]$ writes its identifier between incrementing $In_{O1,1}$ and $In_{O1,2}$. It obtains the call object, reads the identifier of the External Line thread (i), and clears $In_{O2}[j]$ and $Out_{O2}[j]$ between incrementing $Out_{O1,2}$ and $In_{O1,3}$.

Using our basic invariant patterns and composition techniques, we have successfully solved a wide variety of problems found in [1,5] that do not impose any special scheduling requirements.

5 Conclusion

In this paper, we have presented a methodology to develop synchronization code in UML. In this approach, the designer specifies synchronization regions and global invariants in the use-case realizations. Then, the synchronization code is mechanically obtained and woven into the component code developed from the use-case realizations.

We have demonstrated effectiveness of predefined global invariant patterns and composition of such invariants. This feature contributes to high re-usability. With our methodology, developing synchronization code in the Unified Process essentially becomes identification and composition of global invariant patterns.

We restrict global invariants to specify only the safety properties of synchronization specifications for synchronization regions. In this regard, two types of counters, In and Out are sufficient to solve a large class of problems. However, we are open to use other variables in global invariants.

We consider other issues of synchronization, such as scheduling, liveness issues, and real-time restrictions, to be other *aspects* and will handle them separately. We are working on defining aspect languages and development process for these issues. Our initial results show that some of these aspects (*e.g.*, FIFO scheduling and various preferences of the readers/writers problem [1]) can be nicely incorporated in coarse grained solutions.

References

1. G.R. Andrews. *Concurrent Programming, Principles and Practice.* Benjamin/-Cummings Publishing Co., 1991. 452, 452, 453, 453, 456, 458, 458, 458, 459, 459, 460, 463, 464, 465
2. A.J. Bernstein and P.M. Lewis. *Distributed Operating Systems and Algorithms.* Jones and Bartlett, 1993. 452, 456
3. G. Booch, J. Rumbaugh, and I. Jacobson. *The Unified Modeling Language User Guide.* Addison Wesley, 1999. 451
4. F. Bordeleau and R.J.A. Buhr. The UCM-ROOM design method: from Use Case Maps to communicating finite state machines. In *Proceedings of the Conference on the Engineering of Computer-Based Systems*, 1997. 451, 456
5. S.J. Hartley. *Concurrent Programming - The Java Programming Language.* Oxford University Press, 1998. 453, 464
6. I. Jacobson, G. Booch, and J. Rumbaugh. *The Unified Software Development Process.* Addison Wesley, 1999. 451, 454
7. G. Kiczales, J. Lampoing, A. Mendhekar, C. Maeda, C. Lopez, J. Loingtier, and J. Irwin. Aspect-oriented programming. In *Proceedings of the European Conference on Object-Oriented Programming (ECOOP), LNCS 1241*, 1997. 451
8. M. Mizuno. A structured approach for developing concurrent programs in java. *Information Processing Letters*, 69(5):232–238, 1999. 452, 459
9. S. Smith. *Object Oriented Analysis and Design (Course 323).* Learning Tree International, 1999. 454

Describing AI Analysis Patterns with UML

Simon Pickin[1], Ángeles Manjarrés[2]

[1] LPSI, E.U. Informática, Universidad Politécnica de Madrid,
Ctra. Valencia km.7, 28031 Madrid, Spain.
spickin@eui.upm.es
[2] DIA, Universidad Nacional de Educación a Distancia,
Senda del Rey s/n, 28040 Madrid, Spain
amanja@dia.uned.es

Abstract. We discuss the use of the UML to describe "Analysis Patterns" in AI, an area where OAD techniques are not widely used, in spite of the fact that some of the inspiration for the object approach can be traced to developments in this area. We study the relation between the notion of analysis pattern in the context of OO software development methods, and that of Generic Task in AI software development methods such as CommonKADS. Our interest is motivated by the belief that in the analysis and design of certain AI applications, particularly in Distributed AI, OO style patterns may be more appropriate than Generic Tasks. To illustrate the relation between these concepts, we provide a UML description of the heuristic multiattribute decision pattern, a corresponding Generic Task having already been proposed in the literature. We illustrate the wide applicability of this pattern by specialising it to obtain a therapy decision pattern. We discuss the suitability of the UML, together with OCL, for describing this and other analysis patterns arising in AI.

1 Introduction

In order to discuss the applicability of analysis patterns in AI and their relation to the notion of generic task we first attempt to arrive at a definition of analysis pattern.

O-O Analysis Patterns

The notion of software pattern is generally considered to be one of the main advances in OO design in the 1990s. The extent to which these ideas derive from those of Alexander concerning design in the fields of architecture and urban development [1] is disputed, though few would deny the usefulness of the architecture analogy. Patterns are usually defined as recurrent practical solutions to common problems, design elements which capture domain expertise and in so doing provide a form of reuse - of commonalities of different designs - at the design level. It is claimed that making the patterns which constitute a system explicit can not only reduce its development time but can also make it more flexible and easier to maintain.

Alexander´s definition of a pattern is "a recurring solution to a common problem in a given context and system of forces". Any presentation of such a recurring solution usually includes a description of the problem addressed, the elements of which the

A. Evans, S. Kent and B. Selic (Eds.): «UML» 2000, LNCS 1939, pp. 466-481, 2000.

solution is composed and the relations between them, the trade-offs made in its definition, the circumstances in which it is applicable and the constraints on its use. Again following Alexander, a pattern language is defined to be a collection of patterns together with a set of rules or guidelines for combining them in order to solve larger problems.

The analogy with architecture is more natural in the design phase of software development, and it is also in this phase that the identification of recurrent solutions is more readily accomplished. For these reasons, most of the work on patterns has concentrated to date on design phase patterns, the most widely-known catalogue of such patterns being that of [14], who define design patterns as "descriptions of communicating objects and classes that are customised to solve a general design problem in a particular context. A design pattern names, abstracts, and identifies the key aspects of a common design structure that make it useful for creating a reusable object-oriented design".

Some authors such as [6] or [4] make a classification of different patterns based on scale, large-scale patterns being referred to as "architectural patterns" or "frameworks" [10]. However, definitions often do not agree between different authors and some even dispute that these latter entities should be called patterns at all. These are concepts which are difficult to pin down and some of the definitions are inevitably rather nebulous.

On the other hand, the notion of "idioms" or "coding/programming patterns" of, for example, [6] relates more to a classification based on abstraction level. [24] extend such a classification, identifying three types of patterns: "conceptual patterns", "design patterns" and "programming patterns". According to these authors, "conceptual patterns" are described in terms of concepts from an application domain, "design patterns" in terms of software design constructs and "programming patterns" in terms of programming language constructs. These conceptual patterns roughly correspond to the analysis patterns of [13], a notable exception to the relative lack of literature on analysis patterns. Our interest is focused on this, less well-accepted type of patterns, which we will understand to be high-level abstractions commonly occurring across a large or small range of domains. The more well-known design patterns should be discernable on extension and specialisation of analysis patterns in the particular application domain.

AI Analysis Patterns?

Of course, the search for recurrent abstractions is common to scientific and philosophical enquiry in general, while recurrent solutions and the economy obtained from their reuse have long been observed to be one of the primary features of all living organisms, being the inspiration for pattern-like concepts in diverse fields.

It should therefore come as no surprise that in many areas of computer science pattern-like concepts arise so that, as stated in [7], software patterns are not an essentially OO notion. Among these concepts, in this paper we are interested in that of Generic Task used in Artificial Intelligence methodologies such as CommonKADS [25]. The Generic Task (GT) is the basic element of the expertise model, this model playing a crucial role in software development in the AI area.

We assert that OO methodologies constitute a more appropriate means of analysing and designing certain types of AI software than the usual AI methodologies, in which a predominantly functional perspective is generally taken. We therefore make the correspondence between the high-level expertise model of the usual AI methodologies and the OO analysis model, whereupon it is natural to make the correspondence between AI generic tasks and OO analysis patterns. Our approach, then, is to describe AI generic tasks as analysis patterns in a suitable OO Analysis and Design Language, for which purpose we have chosen to use the UML.

Structure of This Article

To motivate the work presented in this article, in Section 2 we compare AI Generic Tasks and OO Analysis Patterns. Then, in Section 3 we present the decision task, the basis of the analysis pattern of this article. In Sections 4 and 5 we describe in UML first the decision pattern and then its specialisation in a therapy decision pattern. Finally, in Section 6 we draw some conclusions.

2. Comparing AI Generic Tasks with OO Analysis Patterns

Considerable effort has been put into the definition of software development methodologies in the AI area, with particular emphasis being placed on the high-level analysis. Given the nature of the applications in this area, the usual requirements capture and modelling phase is interpreted to consist basically of the reproduction of the knowledge models, in the sense of Newell [21], which human experts supposedly use to carry out the intelligent tasks that are to be implemented, these tasks usually being of a scientific or technical nature.

The most common methodological perspective, that of the well-known KADS and CommonKADS [25] expertise model, is based on the separation of the models into two parts. The first contains the specification of the task being analysed and its recursive decomposition into subtasks through the application of Problem Solving Methods (PSM) until a level of directly implementable primitives is obtained. The second contains the domain model specific to the application, the elements of which are to be identified with the abstract entities, known as domain roles, which the tasks described in the first part manipulate. Any dependencies of the task part on the domain part are treated in the so-called “assumptions”.

Work in this area has thus concentrated on looking for recurrent abstractions with which to construct libraries of Generic Tasks (GTs), PSMs, as well as method and domain ontologies, to be used as building blocks in the construction of the knowledge models used to solve a wide range of AI problems [5][2].

From the software engineering perspective, several objections could be made to this approach:

Firstly, the clear separation between functionality and application domain entities characterises a predominantly functional perspective on modelling expert knowledge. Though these methodologies defend the complete autonomy of analysis with respect to later stages of the development cycle, claiming total independence of programming language and other implementation requirements, in reality the complete separation of system functionality and domain data, coupled with the use of a separate control structure means that this type of approach is fundamentally oriented towards traditional procedural programming.

Secondly, in spite of the fact that notations have been defined to support the process of defining, refining, verifying and validating models in the context of these methodologies, the most widely-used are too informal [26] and the resulting models are consequently rather ambiguous and imprecise. Many benefits can be obtained from appropriate use of more formal notations, especially when these are accompanied by an operational semantics and the possibility of incremental refinement. This well-known argument has been put forward by some KADS researchers [19][11], but to date has not had wide acceptance.

From the modelling perspective, the inadequacy of the functional paradigm for much of the modelling of expert human knowledge can be argued on the following principles:

Firstly, it identifies human reasoning with a process of data transformation and information flow between processes, ignoring well-established models which are closer to the principals of cerebral dynamics underlying neural net approaches. Minsky´s metaphor of the mind as a society of cooperative agents constitutes the essence of these models [20], in which the reasoning emerges from the interaction between communicating processes / knowledge sources. Many paradigms of recognised interest, such as intelligent agents, blackboard architectures and other Distributed AI (DAI) models, share this basic perspective. The integration, which these models assume, of functionality and data in autonomous entities fits well with the OAD. In many AI applications with complex dynamic behaviour, e.g. interactive systems such as decision support systems or intelligent tutoring systems and perhaps also strongly reactive systems such as robots (typically event-driven systems), the OO paradigm is seen to be more suitable than the functional one.

Secondly, the OO perspective has provided the backdrop for recent developments in the areas of reflection and metaprogramming [28], which can in turn provide a basis for the modelling of learning tasks, the most characteristic of AI. This approach to learning is particularly apt for showing its self-organising and structural character and was already present to a certain extent in the work on frame languages in the 70s.

Finally, on a more general note, the OO paradigm is widely recognised to promote better understanding of requirements, lead to clearer and better-structured models and to more easily maintainable applications, and facilitate component reuse. OAD techniques have been widely used in other areas of software engineering and at the present time constitute an adequate compromise between formality and flexibility.

The above arguments present a case for the use of other methodological perspectives on the modelling of AI tasks. Among the OAD techniques available, we have chosen to work with the UML, firstly since it is de facto standard and secondly since a certain amount of rigour has been introduced into its formulation, so that its semantics is more well-defined than that of its predecessors. It thus permits a greater degree of precision particularly when used jointly with its associated constraint language OCL. In addition, it facilitates the use of different levels of abstraction and in our opinion promotes incremental development better than the notations used for the usual AI functional paradigm.

As a first step towards the development of a "pattern language" for AI applications (by analogy with the libraries of GTs), we have defined the UML specification of the pattern corresponding to the heuristic multi-attribute decision GT as it is defined in [18]. As well as being a relatively novel area in which to apply the UML, this specification has enabled us to make some observations about its suitability for specifying the high levels of abstraction required.

3. The Decision Task

In this article we present a generic UML decision pattern in accordance with the Heuristic Multi-Attribute (HM) PSM, presented in [15] (though not, of course, in KADS form). The decision task is not found in the usual KADS libraries of Analysis, Modification and Synthesis tasks [5], nor is the HM method found in the libraries of PSMs [5][2], although both have been treated in the literature [12][18].

The decision task is of well-known applicability in fields such as economics or medicine, though our main interest in defining a decision pattern is that it constitutes the basic task of an "intelligent agent", the reference for many computational paradigms and currently the focus of much of attention in AI research [27].

Agent theories were inspired by Newell's study of the "interaction of intentional agents on the knowledge level", in which the concept of "intelligent agent" is identified with the description of intelligent behaviour linked to the principle of rationality [21]. This concept arises from the synthesis of diverse theories of intelligent behaviour, basically utilitarism, behaviouralism and cognitive psychology. The objective of defining an associated computational model lies at the origins of Computer Science and of AI [23][8][17]. The main mathematical background for the theory of intelligent agents is to be found in Decision Theory. This theory – combining probability and utility theory – establishes the connection between the probabalistic reasoning and the action taken, providing the theoretical basis for the design of rational agents operating in uncertain worlds. The existence of this well-defined basis constitutes another reason for choosing this particular task.

In the intelligent agent pattern described in this article, the agent's knowledge of its environment translates into knowledge about the available resources (and restrictions on their use), which determine the decision alternatives (the courses of action which can be chosen), and into a decision model, which enables the consequences associated to these alternatives to be predicted. In the HM decision method, the decision model defines a set of objectives and the means to predict their degree of satisfaction on choosing any of the alternatives as the decision. A rational decision depends on both the relative importance of the different objectives and on the probability or the degree to which they can be achieved through the available alternative actions. The performance measure of an agent is an assessment carried out on the basis of the value of its state. A rational agent will choose an alternative which, in principle, leads it to an acceptable state. It can receive feedback from its environment enabling it to assess its performance and, through its reflective capabilities, modify its own decision model (learn).

In a multiagent system, the agents also reason about the objectives of other agents and communicate with each other in order to coordinate their actions in the pursuit of common objectives. There has been a recent upsurge of interest in multiagent systems with the advent of more advanced internet and telecom services, due to their possible uses in large-scale distributed systems. This provides additional motivation for the development of the decision pattern, which could constitute an essential part of a multiagent system pattern.

Task description

The purpose of a decision task is to select a means of reaching a target state from a problem state. The selection is made from a set of alternatives which are either already available or which are to be identified as viable, in function of some available resources, subjected to certain usage restrictions, in a possibly non-deterministic environment. The concept of viable alternative can be instantiated as a course of action, a physical object, a message, a property, etc.

Given a problem identified as a decision task, the heuristic decision method comprises the design and subsequent systematic assessment of a set of alternatives, in a possibly non-deterministic environment. This assessment is carried out by weighing up any preferences among the possible consequences of the choice of alternatives (based on measures - via "attributes" - of the degree of satisfaction of a set of previously-prioritised objectives) against judgements about the uncertainty of these consequences, with the aim of selecting an ideal alternative (decision result). The assessment of the decisions adopted (or simulated) enables the continual revision of the decision model used.

A consequence is defined as a prediction about the set of implications of adopting a certain decision. A consequence is "certain" when its connection to an alternative is deterministic and is "uncertain" when it is part of a set of consequences, each with a certain occurrence probability, associated to a particular alternative. A consequence is multiattribute if it is characterised by the satisfaction measure(s) of multiple objectives. In spite of the fact that we are ignoring the analysis of uncertainty (determinism) the multi-attribute case reported on here is still complex.

The solution method we describe is adapted to those decision problems where the decision is made by a single individual and where the consequences of an action can be described in terms of cost and benefit measures, such as: decisions involving analysis of cost-benefit for the individual in question (in the choice of a job, a house, a car, a medical treatment etc.), decisions which affect the costs and benefits of other individuals or of organisations (public health, urban planning, etc.), and decisions involving economic or market analyses of the cost-effectiveness and cost-benefit, etc.

4 The HM Decision Pattern

The presentation of the pattern of this article does not conform to any of the commonly-used pattern forms. According to [24], the best way to describe a pattern depends on the intended usage and in this respect, analysis patterns and design patterns are quite distinct; it is not clear which, if any, of the more well-known forms is the most suitable here. Nevertheless, the previous section can be viewed as the presentation of the "context" and the "problem" and this section as that of the "solution". As regards the trade-offs in its definition concerning, for example, the restriction to determinism or the KADS-style assumptions, these are treated in both this and the previous section.

In this section we briefly comment on some of the modelling decisions adopted, illustrating them with the main parts of our proposed decision pattern. This analysis pattern describes a structure of classes and abstract parameterisable and extendible collaborations for the modelling of decision problems in diverse domains. The classes of the pattern being abstract, none of them can have real instances. The objects of these abstract classes which figure in the interaction diagrams therefore represent no more than prototypical instances of their subclasses. Neither has any implementation method been indicated for the operations, as these are considered to be specific to the different decision domains; child classes are needed to provide implementations. In particular, once the decision pattern has been instantiated in a specific domain, distinct child classes of a particular class, with different solution methods defined for their operations, can coexist.

Among the UML notations, we judge the class, activity and interaction diagrams to be the most useful for describing the decision pattern. We have not included any state diagrams since the dynamic behaviour of the system specified is not significant at this abstraction level (dynamic creation of links is specified in OCL).

Class diagrams

While the KADS-CommonKADS description of the HM method referred to in the literature [18] emphasizes the distinction between the task and method part, on the one hand, and the domain part, on the other, the UML model places emphasis on the ontologies of a decision domain and on their structural relations, from where the distribution of responsibilidades (attributes and operations), and the potential collaborations which implement the functionality, derive. The operations of the classes *DesignModel* and *DecisionModel* of Figures 1 and 2 correspond to the tasks of the first level decomposition of the basic inference diagram of the decision task described in [18], while the operations of the rest of the classes (subcontracted by them) are identified with subtasks resulting from further decompositions of these tasks. A progressive refinement of these classes, in the context of a concrete decision problem concludes with the appearance of implementation classes. The operations of these classes will in both cases be identified with primitive inferences of the expert models in methodologies such as KADS-CommonKADS.

It is of particular interest to comment the presence of the classes stereotyped <<*Metaclass*>> (see Figure 4) which reveal the reflective character of the proposed architecture. In AI development methodologies such as KADS-CommonKADS, the so-called "support knowledge" refers to the domain entities which play a role in the reasoning process which solves a task without being affected by it. This knowledge, which can be understood to "parameterise" the tasks, is usually considered implicit in the solution methods and is not made explicit in the analysis, unless it can be modified by a learning task. If a perspective of learning as a reflective task which modifies a self model is taken, such knowledge is modified from a metalevel where the solution model of the task is reified.

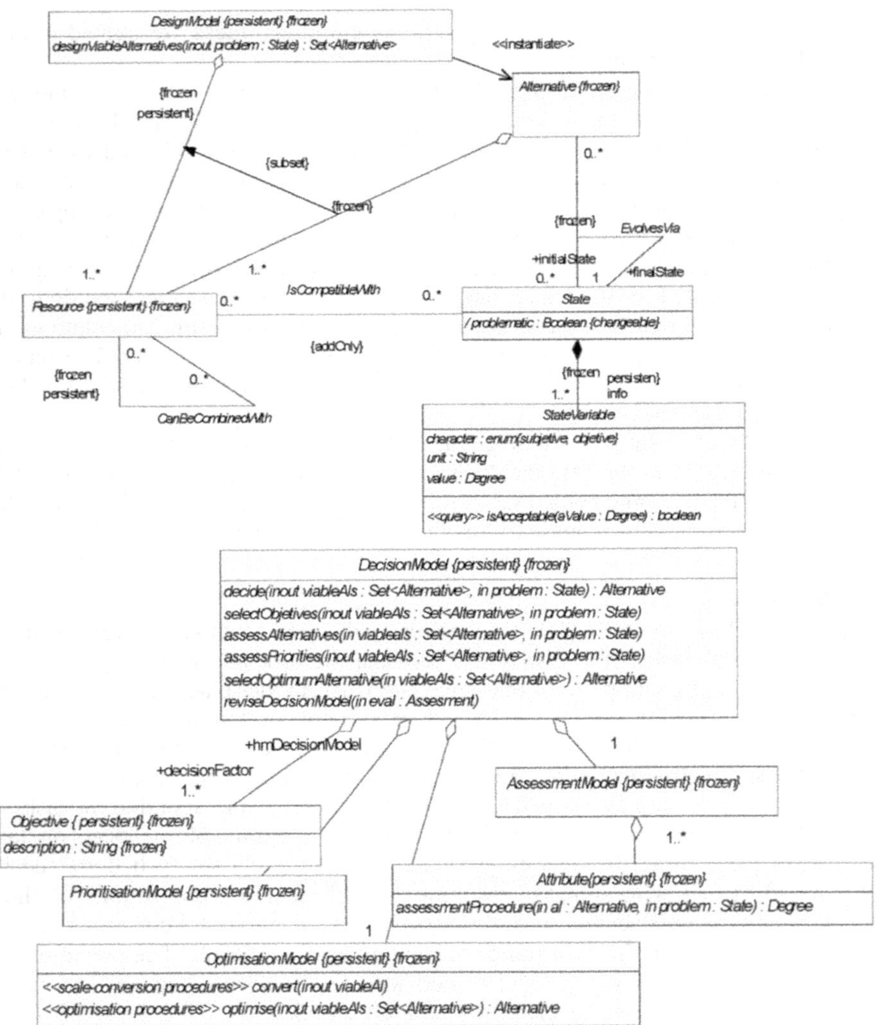

Fig. 1. Design and decision class diagrams

In the decision pattern, this perspective implies a metalevel architecture where learning is translated as modification of some of the objects involved in the decision model and of their structural relations; the classes associated to these objects have been stereotyped *{persistent}*. They have also been stereotyped *{frozen}* in order to emphasize the fact that their objects can only be modified via their associated metaclasses, by mediation of a metaobject protocol which we have specialised in the class "learning protocol". In this way, the structural character of the learning tasks of AI is brought to the fore. This modelling decision is illustrated in Figure 4, where the user of the decision system (a person or another software system) is shown as an actor who assumes the responsibility of evaluating the adopted decision, providing feedback for the (supervised) learning. The constraint "frozen" is usually applied to attributes and relations; its application to abstract classes (to denote stereotyping of all possible attributes of possible subclasses) is non-standard.

The elements of the *DecisionModel* susceptible to be modified by learning effects thus appear reified in the form of metaclasses. These elements will generally be the solution methods of the operations *decide*, *selectObjectives*, *assessAlternatives*, *assessPriorities*, *selectOptimumAlternative*, *optimise*, *scaleValues*, and *evaluationProcedure*, as well as some relations which involve objectives (not illustrated), namely the aggregation relations and relations such as *IsRelevantfor*, *InfluencesInThePriorityOf*, *CooperatesWith*, *CompetesWith* and *IsPreferableTo*.

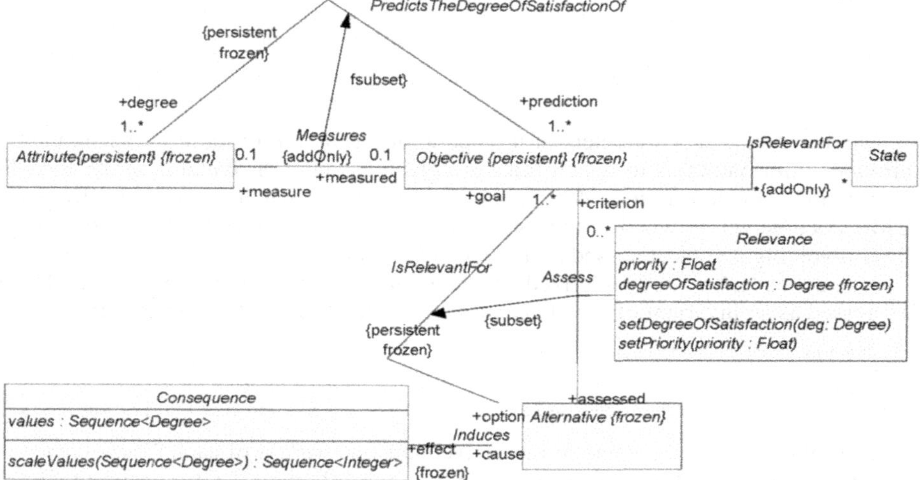

Fig. 2. Alternative class diagram (Note: "Attribute" is standard decision theory terminology)

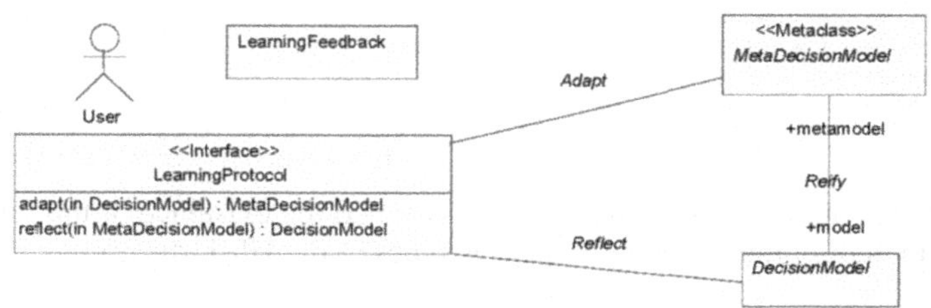

Fig. 3. Learning class diagram

As commented previously, at this level of abstraction the operations have been specified exclusively through their signatures, in some cases adding stereotypes (e.g. *scale conversion procedures*) to characterise them, or pre- and post- conditions to describe some aspects of their functionality. Thus, for example, for the operation *designViableAlternatives*, the following constraints have been specified in OCL[1]:

```
-- The operation assumes: current state problematic, resources compatible with it
-- unknown, viable alternatives not calculated.
```

[1] Note that part of the postcondition could be written as a class invariant of the class *Alternative* since this operation creates and returns all such objects which will exist in the system.

```
-- The operation calculates the compatibility relation between the input state and
-- the resources (non-empty) and returns all the alternatives (non-empty) that can
-- be designed from the resources which compose the decision model satisfying:
--  * they only use resources which are compatible with the input state
--  * they only use resources that can be combined with each other
--  * they are applicable to the input state
--  * on application to this state, they cause it to evolve to an acceptable state
-- (a,b).c is our shorthand for a.c->intersection(b.c) (ternary relation)
context DesignModel::designViableAlternatives(initial:State): Set<Alternative>
pre:      initial.problematic = true
     and initial.resource->isEmpty
     and Alternative.allInstances->isEmpty
post:     initial.resource->notEmpty
     and self.resource.alternative->notEmpty
     and result = self.resource.alternative->asSet->select( al |
                        initial.resource->includesAll(al.resource)
                  and al.resource->forAll(r1,r2|r1.canbeCombinedWith->includes(r2))
                  and al.initialState->includes(problem)
                  and (problem,al).finalState.problematic = false )
```

Characterising the parameters of the operations as *in*, *out* or *inout* in the signatures provides information as to which roles are given as static or dynamic in the KADS-CommonKADS description. We mention at this point that it is not clear from the UML documentation whether the use of these terms also depends on the creation of links involving an object passed as a parameter, as we assume.

The dependency of the derived attribute *problematic* on the state variables is expressed as an invariant of the *State* class via the following OCL constraint:

```
-- The value of the attribute "problematic" of a state is true according to
-- whether the value of one of the state variables is not acceptable.
context State inv
self.problematic=self.StateVariable->exists(var|var.isAcceptable(var.value)=false)
```

The calculation of the value of the derived attribute *values* of each *Consequence* of the class diagram of Figure 3, is expressed via the following OCL constraint (in the absence of tuples in OCL, we have to assume an iteration order):

```
-- The attribute "values" of the consequence of an alt is the sequence of values
-- of degrees of satisfaction, one for each of the obs used to assess that alt.
context Consequence inv
self.values = self.cause.relevance->iterate( rel:Relevance ;
                                            vals: Sequence(Degree) = Sequence{} |
                                            vals->append(rel.degreeOfSatisfaction) )
```

As a final comment, note that we have assumed the existence of the primitive types of OCL, including the collection types, as types in the UML diagrams.

Interaction and Activity Diagrams

In Figure 5 the functional perspective of the solution of the decision task is shown using an activity diagram. Figure 6 shows one of the collaboration diagrams.

Some pre- and post- conditions reflect the use of the relations for navigation:

```
-- The operation assumes that, for each alt viable in the current state, the objs
-- to be used to assess it have been chosen but that the conseqs. of choosing it
-- have not been calculated. The operation calculates these conseq.
context DecisionModel::AssessAlternatives(viableAls:Set<Alternative>,init:State)
pre:  viableAls->forAll(al | al->criterion->notEmpty and al->effect->isEmpty)
post: viableAls->forAll(al | al->effect->notEmpty)
```

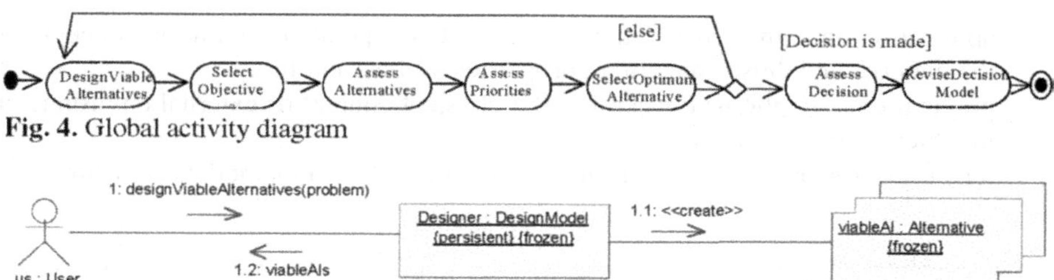

Fig. 4. Global activity diagram

Fig. 5. Design of decision alternatives collaboration diagram

The specification also includes predefined and non modifiable relations (stereotyped as *{persistent, frozen}*). We have used the constraint *{implicit}* for 'conceptual relations', that is, relations which are not used by the solution method but which may be useful for checking purposes (for instance, there is a relation *CooperateWith* between two objectives which implies that their evaluations are positively correlated.

In the case of the sequence diagrams (e.g. Figure 7) the graphical notation for messages which involve subcontracting of tasks has been used (filled arrowheads), to express that the flow of control is procedural. We have not judged it pertinent to consider "active objects", since in our case there is only one flow of control. The nesting of the message invocations corresponds, roughly speaking, to the functional decomposition of a functional analysis methodology. We have used the usual convention of locating on the left the objects which initiate the interactions, and on the right the most subordinate objects. The messages represent operation invocations (call), values returned by operations (return) and the creation of objects (create); no signals (send) are involved in this specification.

To express an iteration condition in the sending of messages, a particular use has been made of the OCL, though note that it is not possible to use the iteration construct of OCL in this context.

Finally, we have supposed that the task assessing the adopted decision is undertaken by the user actor of the system. The result of this evaluation is thus communicated as feedback for the learning (supervised learning) in the message *reviseDecisionModel* which, on invoking the operation of the same name in the *DecisionModel*, results in the modification of the metamodel. The appropriate modifications are carried out with the mediation of the *LearningProtocol*, which accesses the *DecisionMetaModel* navigating through the Reify relation, which connects each model with its metamodel. The way in which the modifications of a metamodel are reflected in the corresponding model depends on the particular design chosen for the reflective architecture, for which reason, it should not be represented at the analysis level.

Other Modelling Elements

In the KADS-CommonKADS methodologies, the information which completes the modelling tasks, denominated assumptions, is structured into different types:

epistemological assumptions: concerning the knowledge required by the solution method and divided into those concerning the availability of entities, in the application domain, which can be placed in correspondence with the concepts of the method, and those concerning properties of these entities,

pragmatic assumptions: concerning the physical context or external environment in which the system operates,

teleologic assumptions: concerning the goal the solution method has to achieve.

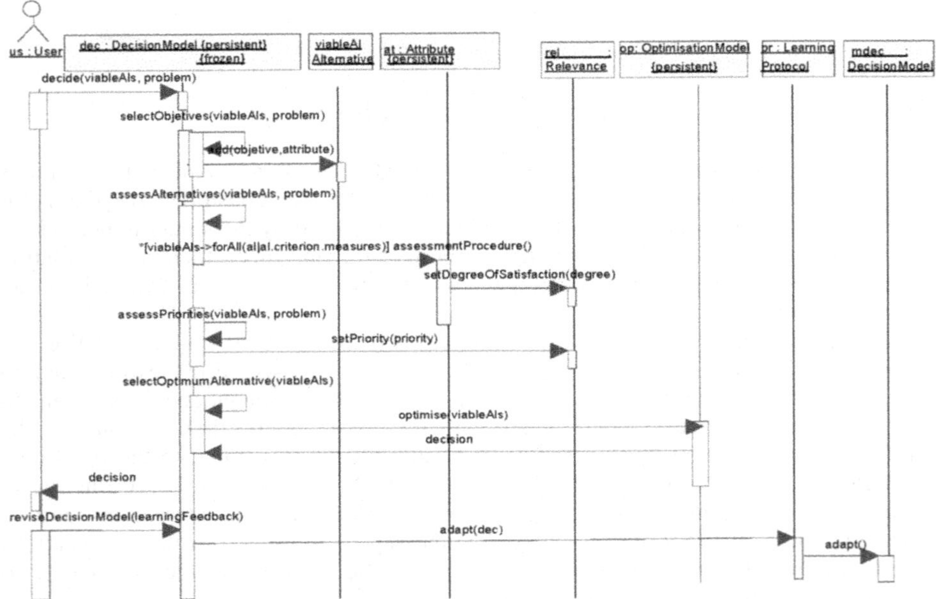

Fig. 6. Decision sequence diagram

With respect to the availability assumptions, they make no sense in an object-oriented model, in which the domain entities and the functionality are integrated.

Some of the so-called property assumptions are implicit in the class model itself, for example, the measurable character of the objectives and the possibility of measuring them using different attributes is implicit in the multiplicity of the roles of the relation *PredictsTheDegreeOfSatisfactionOf*. Other property assumptions can be included in the pattern by formalising them as OCL constraints, e.g. in the context of the operation *designViableAlternatives*, the assumptions about the mutual exclusion of the alternatives designed - no other intermediate or combined design is possible - (`problem.resource->includesAll(al.resource)`), about the existence of at least one valid alternative (`self.resource.alternative->notEmpty`) and about the compatibility of the resources used by an alternative (`self.resource->forAll(r1,r2 | r1.canBeCombinedWith ->includes(r2)`) are expressed in the OCL presented previously. The possibility of assessing each alternative with respect to at least one of the prespecified objectives through some attribute is specified in the context of the operation *SelectObjectives*:

```
-- The operation assumes that the objectives to be used to assess each alt have
-- not been selected and consequently neither have the attributes which will be
-- used to measure each of these objectives for each of these alternatives, though
-- there are known to be one or many attributes which can be used to predict the
-- degree of satisfaction of any one of them, either directly, or indirectly
-- (proxies). It also assumes that the current state is problematic.
```

```
-- The operation selects for each alt those objs of the decision model satisfying:
--    * they are relevant for that alt
--    * there is at least one attribute that can be used to assess them
--    * they are relevant for the problem state
-- and creates the links "Assess" between each alternative and the objectives
-- selected for it and the links "Measures" between each selected objective for
-- each alternative and an attribute chosen to measure it.
context DecisionModel::selectObjectives(viableAls :set<Alternative>, init :State)
pre: self.decisionFactor->forAll(ob| ob.measure->isEmpty and ob.assessed->isEmpty)
     and init.problematic = true
post: viableAls->forAll( al | (al.criterion->notEmpty) and
                  ( self.decisionFactor->select(ob | al.criterion->includes(ob)
                                                and ob.measure->notEmpty) )     =
                  ( self.decisionFactor->select(ob | al.goal->includes(ob)
                                                and ob.degree->notEmpty
                                                and ob.State->includes(initial)) )
```

5 The Therapy Decision Pattern

The importance of the decision task in the medical domain is evident from the growing interest in "clinical decision analysis", increasingly considered to be a tool of great value in clinical practice [22]. The use of decision rules, defined in a systematic and operational framework, introduces rigour in the decision process and eliminates the influence of extraneous factors. In spite of this, the clinical use of decision analysis has yet to be widely accepted. The availability of tools which aid clinical personnel to perform their own analyses should increase the acceptance of decision analysis as observed some time ago [9]. In this context, the interest in developing computational systems for supporting clinical decision analysis is clear [3].

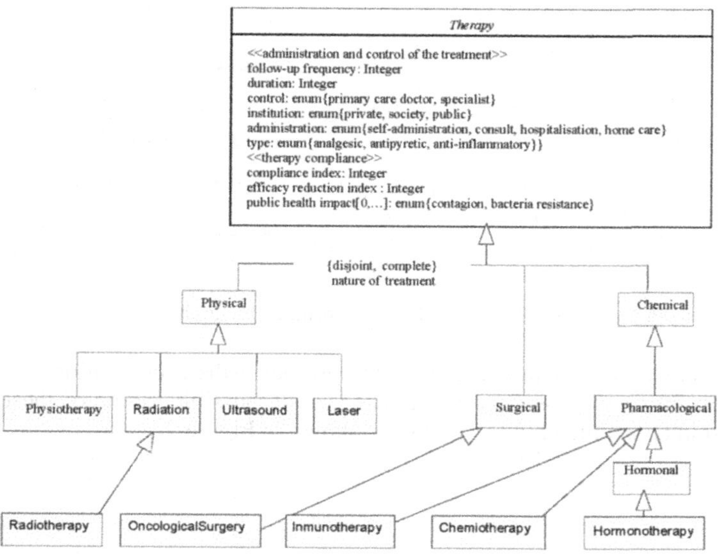

Fig. 7. Therapy class diagram

Taking into account the concrete characteristics of a patient and the set of alternative therapies a priori applicable to his or her clinical profile, the goal of the therapy decision task is to identify the ideal therapy, in accordance with a set of objectives of diverse nature - among them, quality-of-life objectives - which constitute a wide-ranging and generic assessment framework. The satisfaction of the set of therapy objectives is a function not only of objectively measurable parameters, associated to the patient, to the therapy itself and to the circumstances in which it is applied (patient age, pharmaceutical costs,...), but also of less reliably measurable parameters (side-effects, psychological attitude, quality of life during treatment,...).

The first step in defining a therapy decision pattern consists of the specialisation of the generic decision pattern abstract classes in the therapy domain. Thus, as an example, the classes *DesignModel*, *Alternative*, *Resource*, *State* and *Consequence* are specialised, respectively in the subclasses *TherapyDesignModel*, *Therapy*, *HealthResource*, *PatientState*, and *TherapyEffects* & *TherapyCosts*. The definition of these subclasses gives rise to new classes and relations, as illustrated in Figures 8 and 9. Note that the therapy decision pattern is still highly generic so that most of these classes are again abstract classes. We mention here that the need for explicit support in the UML for renaming is already felt at this high level.

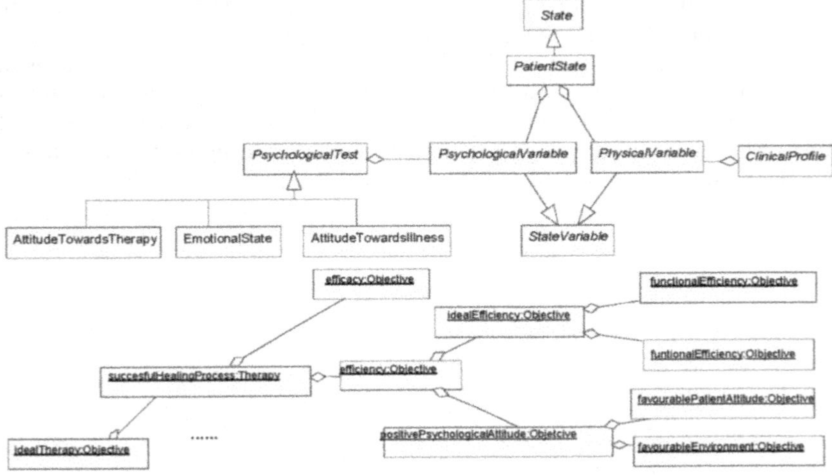

Fig. 8. Patient state class diagram and (part of an) objective instance hierarchy

With respect to the *Objective* class, at this abstraction level the specification of a set of instances relevant for any therapy domain, is already possible. Some of these instances, organised in an aggregation hierarchy are shown in Figure 9.

6 Conclusions

In this article, we define a notion of analysis pattern in AI as a counterpart to the Generic Tasks of the commonly-used AI software development methods. Our interest in defining such a correspondence is to support our contention that the OO paradigm provides an adequate framework for expertise models in certain areas of AI, and to indicate the suitability of OAD methods and techniques such as the UML for defining analysis models in these areas. We have illustrated this correspondence using the decision task, and the associated Heuristic Multi-attribute solution method, presented as a KADS-style generic task in [18]. The resulting decision pattern specified in UML is perhaps rather more complex than is usual for analysis and design patterns, in particular, concerning the use we make of the OCL to constrain the implementation of the specified operations. However, we view this extra precision which our use of UML/OCL provides, with respect to the corresponding Generic Task specification, as an advantage of our approach.

Generally speaking, we found the combination UML/OCL a powerful language for specifying AI analysis patterns. Among the advantages, apart from the extra precision mentioned above, we cite the relatively smooth transition towards implementation and the use of the metaclass stereotype for representing the learning task. Among the shortfalls felt we cite the lack of tuples in OCL and the lack of explicit support in the UML for the renaming of operations and relations, as well as for the redefining of operations. There is also a lack of clarity with respect to many issues; among those which were important in this work we cite the fate of stereotypes, tagged values and assertions across generalisation relations, the details of the specialisation of several of the UML diagram types, the inability to distinguish between different options for the sending of messages to collections of objects in the interaction diagrams and the use of constraints in interaction diagrams. There are also cases where we found that the UML is too close to implementation, and even too close to a certain type of implementation, for analysis, such as in the use of the "add" operation in sequence diagrams recommended in [4] to indicate creation of a link. The upcoming Action Semantics Language should remove any need to define UML features with, albeit oblique, references to implementation concepts.

References

1. Alexander, C., Ishikawa, S., Silverstein, M.: A Pattern Language. Oxford Univ. Press (1977)
2. Benjamins V.R.: Problem-solving methods for diagnosis and their role in knowledge acquisition. Int. J. Expert Systems: Research and Applications, **8**(2), (1995) 93-120.
3. Bleichrodt, H., Johannesson, M.,: The validity of QALYs: An experimental test of constant proportional tradeoff and utility independence. Medical Decision Making **17**(1) (1996)21-32
4. Booch, G., Rumbaugh J., Jacobson, I.: The Unified Modeling Language User Guide. Addison-Wesley (1998)
5. Breuker, J. & van de Velde, W.: CommonKADS Library for Expertise Modelling. Reusable Problem Solving Components. IOS Press, Amsterdam (1994).
6. Buschmann, F., Meunier, R., Rohnert, H., Sommerlad, P., Stal, M.: Pattern-Oriented Software Architecture: A System of Patterns. John Wiley and Sons (1996)
7. Coplien, J.: Broadening beyond objects to patterns and to other paradigms. ACM Computing Surveys **28A**(4) (1996) http://www.acm.org/surveys/1996/ObjectsAndBeyond
8. Dennet, D.C.: Content and Consciousness. Routledge and Kegan Paul, London. (1969)
9. Deyo, R.A., Patrick, L.P., (1989). Barriers to the use of health status measures in clinical investigation, patient care, and policy research. Medical Care **27** (1989)

10. Fayad, M, Schmidt, D.C.: Object-Oriented Application Frameworks. Communications of the ACM **40**(10) (1997)
11. Fensel, D., Van Harmelen, F.: A comparison of languages which operationalise and formalise KADS models of expertise. Knowledge Engineering Review, **9**, (1994) 105-146
12. Fox, R., Ochoa, G.: Routine decision making using Generic Tasks. Expert Systems with Applications **12** (1997) 109-117.
13. Fowler, M.: Analysis Patterns: Reusable Object Models. Addison-Wesley (1997)
14. Gamma, E., Helm, R., Johnson, R., Vlissides, J.: Design Patterns: Elements of Reusable Object-Oriented Software Addison-Wesley (1995)
15. Keeney, R. L. & Raiffa, H.: Decisions with Multiple Objectives. Preferences and Value Trade-offs. Wiley series in probability and mathematical statistics (1976)
17. McCarthy, J., Hayes, P.J.: (1969). Some philosophical problems from the standpoint of Artificial Intelligence. In: Meltzer, B., Michie, D., & Swann, M. (eds.): Machine Intelligence, **4**. Edinburgh University Press, Edinburgh, Scotland (1969) 463-502
18. Manjarrés, A., Martinez, R., Mira, J.: A new task for expert systems analysis libraries: the decision task and the HM method. Expert Systems with Applications **16** (1999) 325-341
19. Meseguer, P., Preece, A.: Assessing the role of formal specifications in verification and validation of knowledge -based systems. In: Proc. 3rd IFIP Int. Conf. on "Achieving Quality in Software" (AQuIS'96). Chapman and Hall (1996) 317-328.
20. Minksy, M.: The Society of Mind. Simon and Schuster, New York (1986)
21. Newell, A. (1982): The knowledge level. Artificial Intelligence, **18** (1982) 87-127
22. Neumann, P.J., Zinner, D.E., Wright, J.C.: Are methods for estimating Qualys in cost-effectiveness analyses improving? Medical Decision Making **17** (1997) 402-408.
23. Putnam, H.: Minds and Machines. In: Hook, S. (ed.): Dimensions of Mind. Macmillan, London. (1960) 138-164
24. Riehle, D., Zullighoven, H.: Understanding and Using Patterns in Software Development. Theory and Practice of Object Systems **2**, 1 (1996)
25. Schreiber, A.T., Wielinga, B., de Hoog, R., Akkermans, H., van de Velde, W.: CommonKADS: A Comprehensive Methodology for KBS Development. IEEE Expert, **12**, (1994) 28-36
26. Schreiber, A.T., Wielinga, B., de Hoog, R., Akkermans, J.M., van de Velde, W., Anjewierden, A.: CML: The CommonKADS conceptual modelling language. In: Steels, L., Schreiber, A.T., van de Velde, W. (eds.): Proc. European Knowledge Acquisition Workshop (EKAW'94). Lecture Notes in Artificial Intelligence, **867**. Springer-Verlag, Berlin Heidelberg: (1994) 1-25
27. Stuart, R., Norvig, P.: Artificial Intelligence. A modern approach. Englewood Cliffs, NY: Prentice-Hall International Editions (1995)
28. Zimmerman, C. (ed.): Advances in Object-Oriented Metalevel Architectures and Reflection. CRC Press (1996)

Precise Modeling of Design Patterns

Alain Le Guennec, Gerson Sunyé, and Jean-Marc Jézéquel

IRISA/CNRS, Campus de Beaulieu, F-35042 Rennes Cedex, FRANCE
email: aleguenn,sunye,jezequel@irisa.fr

Abstract. Design Patterns are now widely accepted as a useful concept for guiding and documenting the design of object-oriented software systems. Still the UML is ill-equipped for precisely representing design patterns. It is true that some graphical annotations related to parameterized collaborations can be drawn on a UML model, but even the most classical GoF patterns, such as Observer, Composite or Visitor cannot be modeled precisely this way. We thus propose a minimal set of modifications to the UML 1.3 meta-model to make it possible to model design patterns and represent their occurrences in UML, opening the way for some automatic processing of pattern applications within CASE tools. We illustrate our proposal by showing how the Visitor and Observer patterns can be precisely modeled and combined together using our UMLAUT tool. We conclude on the generality of our approach, as well as its perspectives in the context of the definition of UML 2.0.

1 Introduction

From the designer point of view, a modeling construct allowing design pattern [8] participant classes to be explicitly pointed out in a UML class diagram can be very useful. Besides the direct advantage of a better documentation and the subsequent better understandability of a model, pointing out an occurrence of a design pattern allows designers to abstract known design details (e.g. associations, methods) and concentrate on more important tasks.

We can also foresee tool support for design patterns in UML as a help to designers in overcoming some adversities [2][7][15]. More precisely, a tool can ensure that pattern constraints are respected, relieve the designer of some implementation burdens, and even recognize pattern occurrences within source code, preventing them from getting lost after they are implemented. In this context, we are not attempting to detect the need of a design pattern application but to help designers to explicitly manifest this need and therefore abstract intricate details. Neither are we trying to discover which implementation variant is the most adequate to a particular situation, but we would like to discharge programmers from the implementation of recurrent trivial operations introduced by design patterns. According to James Coplien [3] p. 30 - *patterns should not, can not and will not replace programmers* - , our goal is not to replace programmers nor designers but to support them.

But in its current incarnation as of version 1.3 from the OMG, the UML is ill-equipped for precisely representing design patterns. It is true that some graphical

A. Evans, S. Kent and B. Selic (Eds.): ≪UML≫ 2000, LNCS 1939, pp. 482–496, 2000.

annotations related to parameterized collaborations can be drawn on a UML model, but even the most classical GoF patterns, such as Observer, Composite or Visitor cannot be modeled precisely this way (see Sect. 1.1). Ideas to overcome the shortcomings of collaborations are sketched in Sect. 1.2, providing some guidelines to model the "essence" of design patterns more accurately. An example showing how the Visitor and Observer patterns can be precisely modeled and combined together using our UMLAUT tool is presented in Sect. 2. Related approaches are then discussed in Sect. 4. We then conclude with a discussion of the generality of our approach, as well as its perspectives in the context of the definition of UML 2.0. To alleviate the reading of the paper, we have moved to an appendix some complementary support material needed to understand the extensions to UML that we propose.

1.1 Problem Outline

The current official proposal for representing design patterns in the Unified Modeling Language is to use the *collaboration* design construct. Indeed, the two conceptual levels provided by collaborations (i.e. parameterized collaboration and collaboration usage) seem to be appropriate to model design patterns.

At the general level, a parameterized collaboration is able to represent the structure of the solution proposed by a pattern, which is enounced in generic terms. Here patterns are represented in terms of classifier and association roles. The application of this solution, i.e. the terminology and structure specification into a particular context (so called instance or occurrence of a pattern) are represented by expansions of template collaborations. This design construct allows designers to explicitly point out participant classes of a pattern occurrence.

Parameterized collaborations are rendered in UML in a way similar to template classes [1], p.384. Thus, roles represented in theses collaborations are actually template parameters to other classifiers. More precisely, each role has an associated *base*, which serves as the actual template parameter (the template parameter and the argument of a binding must be of the same kind [14] p.2-46.)

However, there are severe limitations for modeling design patterns as parameterized collaborations:

First, the use of generic templates is not fully adapted to represent the associations between pattern roles and participant classes. More precisely, as each classifier role (actually its base class) is used as a template parameter, it can be bound to at most one participant class. Therefore, design patterns having a variable number of participant classes (e.g. Visitor, Composite) cannot be precisely bound. Also, if the use of base classes in a template collaboration is necessary to allow the binding (bindings can only be done between elements having the same meta-type), its utility and its underlying representation are unclear.

Second, some constraints inherent to design patterns cannot be represented by collaborations, since they involve concepts that cannot be directly included as OCL constraints. For instance, in the Visitor [8] pattern, the number of visit methods defined by the visitor class must be equal to the number of concrete element classes. This constraint can not be written in OCL unless an access to the UML meta-model is provided.

Third, collaborations provide no support for feature roles. In design patterns, an operation (or an attribute) is not necessarily a real operation. It defines a behavior that must be accomplished by one or more actual operations. This kind of role cannot be defined in a collaboration, nor is it possible to describe behavioral constraints (e.g. operation A should call operation B).

These limitations were extensively discussed in previous work by the authors [16]. In this paper, we propose some solutions to overcome these problems.

A misunderstanding with the term *role* might be a possible source of the present inadequacy of collaborations to model design patterns. In a UML collaboration, roles represent placeholders for *objects* of the running system.

However, in the design pattern literature, the term role is often associated to participant *classes* and not only objects in a design model. There can also be roles for associations and inheritance relationships. In other words, pattern roles refer to an upper level. This subtle difference can be noted when binding a parameterized collaboration to represent an occurrence of a pattern: it is impossible to assign a single role to more than one class.

This difference is also observable when writing OCL constraints to better model a design pattern: frequently, this kind of constraints needs access to meta-level concepts, that cannot be directly accessed by OCL.

1.2 Patterns as Sets of Constraints: Leitmotiv in UML

Design patterns are described using a common template, which is organized in a set of sections, each one relating a particular aspect of the pattern. Before extending this description of how to model design patterns in UML, let us dispel some possible misunderstanding concerning the modeling of design patterns.

It is not our intention to model every aspect of design patterns, since some aspects are rather informal an cannot be modeled. We are interested in a particular facet of patterns, which is called *Leitmotiv* by Amnon Eden [5]: the generic solution indicated by a design pattern, which involves a set of participants and their collaborations.

Our intention is to model the leitmotiv of design patterns using structural and behavioral constraints. The goal of this approach is to provide a precise description of how pattern participants should collaborate, instead of specifying a common fixed solution. Design patterns can be expressed as constraints among various entities, such as classifiers, structural and behavioral features, instances of the respective classifiers, generalization relationships between classifiers, generalization relationships between behavioral features, etc.

All those entities are modeling constructs of the UML notation. That is, they can be thought of as instances of meta-classes from the UML meta-model. This suggests that patterns can be expressed with meta-level constraints.

The parameters of the constraints together form the *context* of the pattern, i.e. the set of participants collaborating in the pattern. Since the UML meta-model is defined using a UML class diagram, we can make the reasonable assumption that it is not different than any other UML model.

Therefore, we propose to use meta-level collaborations to specify design patterns. However, to avoid any ambiguity in the sequel, we will explicitly use "M2" if necessary when referring to the UML meta-model and "M1" when referring to an ordinary UML model, following the conventions of the classical 4-layer metamodel architecture. The material presented in appendix explains in details how collaborations and OCL constraints can be used together in a complementary way, and we apply this principle to specify the structural constraints of patterns in Sect. 2. A different approach is needed to specify the behavioral properties associated with a pattern, and Sect. 2.4 presents how temporal logic could be used to that purpose. Finally, Sect. 3 shows how an appropriate redefinition of the mapping of dashed-ellipses permits to keep that familiar notation to represent occurrences of design patterns.

2 Modeling Design Patterns in Action

2.1 Presentation of the Visitor and Observer Patterns

Figure 1 shows the participants in the Visitor design pattern represented as a meta-level collaboration. It consists of a hierarchy of class representing concrete nodes of the structure to be visited, and a visitor class (or possibly a hierarchy thereof). Each element class should have an accept() routine with the right signature, for which there should be a corresponding visitElement() routine in the visitor class.

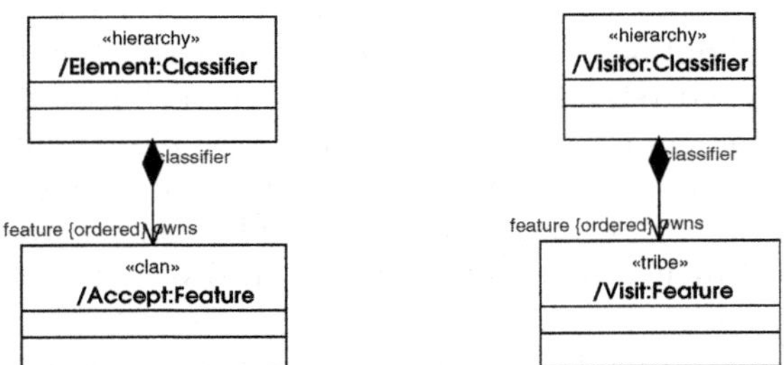

Fig. 1. Meta-level collaboration of the Visitor design pattern

Figure 2 shows a collaboration representing the participants in the Observer design pattern. It consists of a subject class (or hierarchy thereof) whose instances represent observed nodes, and a class (or hieararchy thereof) whose instances represent observers. The subject class should offer routines to attach or detach an observer object, and a routine to notify observer objects whenever the state of the subject changes. The observer class should offer an update() routine for notification purpose.

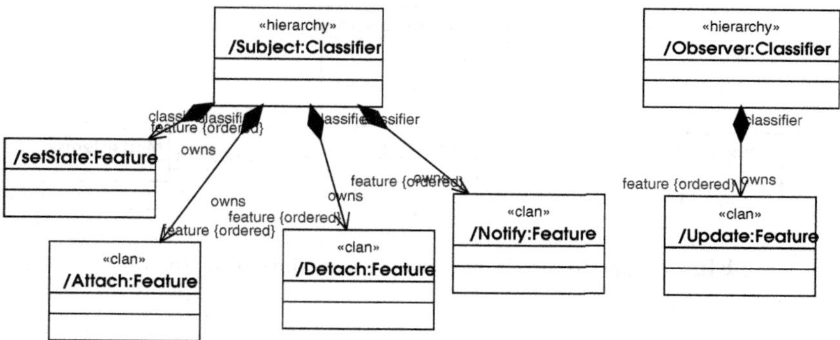

Fig. 2. Meta-level collaboration of the Observer design pattern

2.2 Structural Constraints

When a behavioral (or a structural) feature appears in the specification of a design pattern, this does not mean that there must be an identical feature in a pattern occurrence. Actually, the specification describes *roles* that can be played by one or more features in the model. Using meta-level collaborations clears this possible confusion.

An example of a *feature role* is the Attach() feature of the Observer pattern. It represents a simple behavioral feature that adds an observer into a list. This does not mean that this feature cannot perform other actions, nor that it should be named "Attach" and have exactly the same parameters.

Some feature roles are more complex than the above example is, since they represent the use of dynamic dispatch by a family of behavior features. An example of this is the Accept() feature role of the Visitor design pattern. It represents a feature that should be implemented by concrete elements. Such a family of features is named a *Clan* by Eden [5] (p.60).

Finally, some other feature roles represent a set of clans, i.e. a set of features that should be redefined in a class hierarchy. The feature role Visit() of the Visitor design pattern is an example of this particular role. It designates a set of features (one for each concrete element) that should be implemented by concrete visitors. Such a family of features is named a *Tribe* by Eden [5] (p.61).

2.3 Factoring Recurring Constraints with Stereotypes

These kinds of structural constraints among features and classes are recurring in pattern specifications, and factoring them would significantly ease the pattern designer's task.

The natural means provided by the UML to group a set of constraints for later reuse is the *stereotype* construct. Figure 3 recalls how constraints can be attached to a stereotype. These constraints will later transitively apply to any elements to which the stereotype is applied (OCL rule number 3, page 2-71 of the UML1.3 documentation [14]).

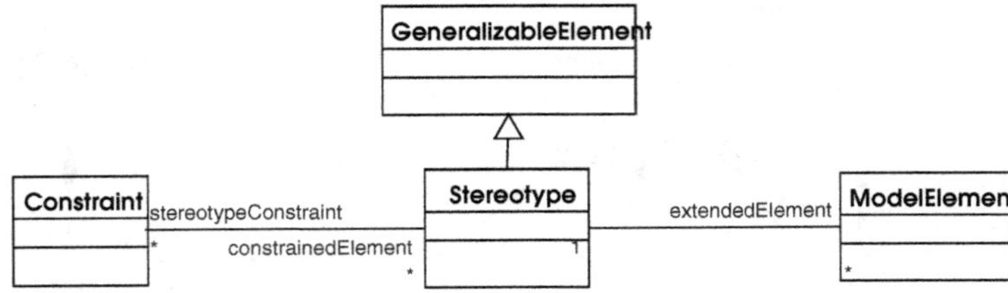

Fig. 3. How to attach recurring constraints to a stereotype

Clans The first stereotype presented here is called <<Clan>>. A clan is a set of behavioral features that share a same signature and are defined by different classes of a same hierarchy. In OCL, clans are defined as follows:

```
isClan(head      : BehaviorFeature,
       features  : Sequence(BehaviorFeature)) inv:
features->forAll(f | f.sameSignature(head))
```

Other examples of clans are the AlgorithmInterface() feature role of the Strategy pattern or the notify() feature role of the Observer pattern (see Fig.2).

Tribes The second stereotype is called <<Tribe>> and is somewhat similar to the first one. A tribe is set of behavioral features that consists of other sets of behavioral features each of which is a clan. A tribe is defined in OCL as follows:

```
isTribe(heads,features:Sequence(BehaviorFeature)) inv:
features->forAll(f|heads->exists(head| head.sameSignature(f)))
```

Elements of a tribe do not necessarily have the same signature, as elements of a clan do. Other examples of tribes are the setState() feature role of the Observer pattern (see Fig. 2) or the Handle() feature role of the State pattern.

Auxiliary Operations The above OCL constraints both use an operation that compares behavioral feature signatures. Two features share the same signature if they have the same set of parameters (including the "return" parameter):

```
sameSignature(featA, featB : BehaviorFeature) : boolean;

sameSignature =
        featA.parameter()->collect(par | par.type()) =
        featB.parameter()->collect(par | par.type())
```

2.4 Behavioral Properties and Temporal Logic

Behavioral Properties of the Visitor Pattern

[1] A given call of anElement.accept(aVisitor) is always followed by a call of aVisitor.visitAnElement(anElement). If we want the call to visit to be synchronous ("nested flow of control"), we need a second constraint:
[2] A given call of aVisitor.visitAnElement(anElement) always preceeds the return of a call of anElement.accept(aVisitor).

Behavioral Properties of the Observer Pattern

[1] After a given call of aSubject.attach(anObserver), and before any subsequent call of aSubject.notify() or of aSubject.detach(anObserver), the set of observers known by aSubject must contain anObserver.
[2] A given call of aSubject.detach(anObserver) if any must follow a corresponding call of aSubject.attach() and no other call of aSubject.attach(anObserver) should appear in between.
[3] After a given call of aSubject.detach(anObserver), and before any subsequent call of aSubject.notify() or of aSubject.attach(anObserver), the set of observers known by aSubject must not contain anObserver.
[4] A given call of aSubject.notify() must be followed by calls of observers.update(), and all these calls must precede any subsequent call of aSubject. attach(anObserver), of aSubject.detach(anObserver) or of aSubject.notify(). Note that we do not require the notification to be synchronous, just that all the observers which are known when notification starts will be eventually notified. We could allow for collapsing of pending notification events by allowing another call of aSubject.notify() before all calls of update: pending calls would then not have to occur twice to satisfy the constraints (this can be very useful in GUI design notably, to improve rendering speed).

Using Temporal Logic Note how general and declarative the constraints are. For instance, it is not written down that update() shall contain a loop calling notify(), because the pattern *does not have* to be implemented like that. We do not want to proscribe correct alternative solutions. The constraints just ensure that some events shall occur if some others do, and prevent erroneous orders.

A form of temporal logic would provide the right level of abstraction to express the behavioral properties expected of all pattern occurrences. Some recent research efforts [12,4] have begun to investigate the integration of temporal operators within OCL, reusing the current part of OCL for atoms of temporal logic formulas. Although this work is very valuable and necessary, we cannot reuse it directly in our context, because the resulting OCL expressions belong to the model level (M1): They lack quantification over modeling elements and therefore cannot capture the "essence" of a pattern's behavior.

Behavioral properties do rely on quantification over operations, their target, their parameters, and various other entities which will later be bound to elements of the M1 level. This suggests that they are at the same level as the OCL expressions we used to specify the structural constraints of patterns. However, OCL is not really appropriate to formally specify the behavioral properties of a pattern: such OCL expressions would have to express very complex properties on a model of all possible execution traces (such a "runtime model" is actually under work at the OMG.) Making these OCL expressions completely explicit would amount to building a model checker: A simulator would produce execution traces following the rules of a semantics, and the OCL expressions would represent the properties to be checked. However, special OCL operations could be defined to simplify complex OCL expressions. To the extent that the designer could use these predefined operations to completely abstract away from the actual details of the runtime model, they would provide a formal definition for a set of OCL temporal operators.

Another interesting topic for future research is how to adapt UML sequence diagrams so that they could describe behavioral constraints at the more general level needed for design patterns.

3 Representing Pattern Occurrences

3.1 Bridging the Gap between the Two Levels of Modelisation

An occurrence of a pattern can be represented by a collaboration occurrence (see more details in the appendix) at the meta-model level (M2) connecting (meta-level) roles in the collaboration with instances *representing* modeling elements of the M1 model (instances in M2 represent modeling elements of M1). The bindings would belong to the M2 model, not to the M1 model. They link instances in M2 that are *representations* of modeling elements of M1.

The problem is similar to expressing that a class in a given (M1) model is an "instance" of a <<meta>> class of the same model. Normally the "is an instance of" dependency is between an Instance and a Classifier, and not between a Classifier and another Classifier. So this dependency would appear in the model of the model, where the normal class would appear as an instance while the <<meta>> class would appear as a classifier.

The standard <<meta>> stereotype acts as an inter-level "bridge", making up for the fact that UML is not a fully reflexive language and therefore avoiding a very significant extension. Using <<meta>> allows for representing or *transposing* M2 entities into M1. An appropriate M1 dependency can then be used to relate M1 entities to entities "transposed" from M2.

Now we can define a pattern using a M2 collaboration and still represent it and access it from an ordinary M1 model by using the <<meta>> stereotype. A pattern occurrence is then represented by a composite dependency between arbitrary model elements and classifier roles of the collaboration transposed from M2 (see Fig. 4), in a way similar to a CollaborationOccurrence (see Fig. 6 in appendix), except for the fact that a real collaboration occurrence connects instances to classifier roles, while a pattern occurrence connects any model elements to classifier roles of a <<meta>> collaboration.

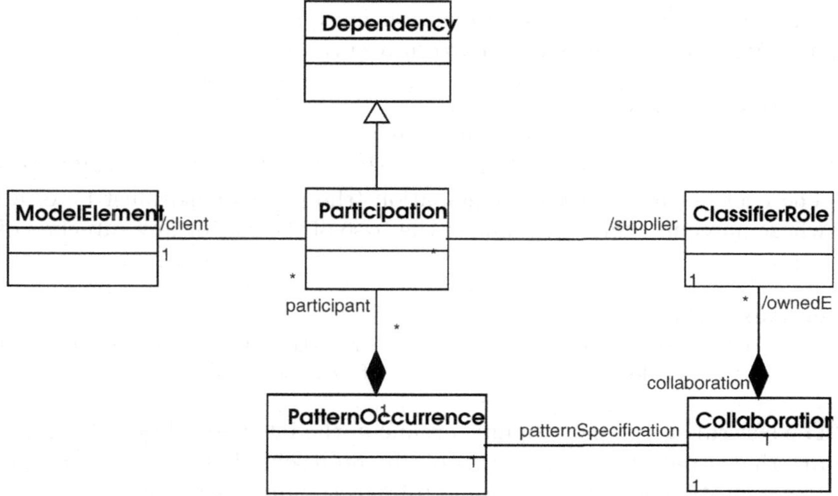

Fig. 4. Meta-model extensions to represent pattern occurrences

Additional Well-Formedness Rules Aassociated to Pattern Occurrences

[1] The pattern specification of the pattern occurrence must be a <<meta>> collaboration.

```
context PatternOccurrence inv:
        self.patternSpecification.stereotype->
            exists(s | s.name = 'meta')
```

[2] The number of participants must not violate multiplicity constraints of the roles in the <<meta>> collaboration.

```
context PatternOccurrence inv:
    (self.patternSpecification.ownedElement->
        select(cr | cr.oclIsKindOf(ClassifierRole)))
    ->forall(cr : ClassifierRole |
        let nbOfParticipants =
            cr.supplierDependency->select(p |
            p.oclIsKindOf(Participation))->size()
        in (cr.multiplicity.ranges->forall(r |
            r.lower <= nbOfParticipants
                        and nbOfParticipants <= r.upper)))
```

Additional Well-Formedness Rules Associated to Participations

[1] The supplier must be a classifier role.

```
context Participation inv:
        self.supplier.oclIsKindOf(ClassifierRole)
```

[2] The supplier role of the participation must be a role of the collaboration specifying the corresponding pattern occurrence.

```
context Participation inv:
        self.supplier.namespace
              = self.patternOccurrence.patternSpecification
```

[3] The client element of the participation (the participant) must be of a kind whose name matches the name of the base of the role or any sub-class of the base.

```
context Participation inv:
     supplier.oclAsType(ClassifierRole).base.allSubtypes()->
        exists(c | c.name = self.client.type.name)
```

The last rule is the most significant one in the inter-level bridging context. It ensures that a pattern occurrence could be represented at the M2 level directly by a collaboration occurrence binding roles to *conforming* instances representing modeling elements of M1. Note that the type cast realized with oclAsType is always valid because of rule [1].

3.2 Graphical Representation of Pattern Occurrences

Figure 5 presents a class diagram in which two pattern occurrences are used (we assume that all visit() operations call the markNode() operation, whose effect is in turn notified to the observer that can count marked nodes).

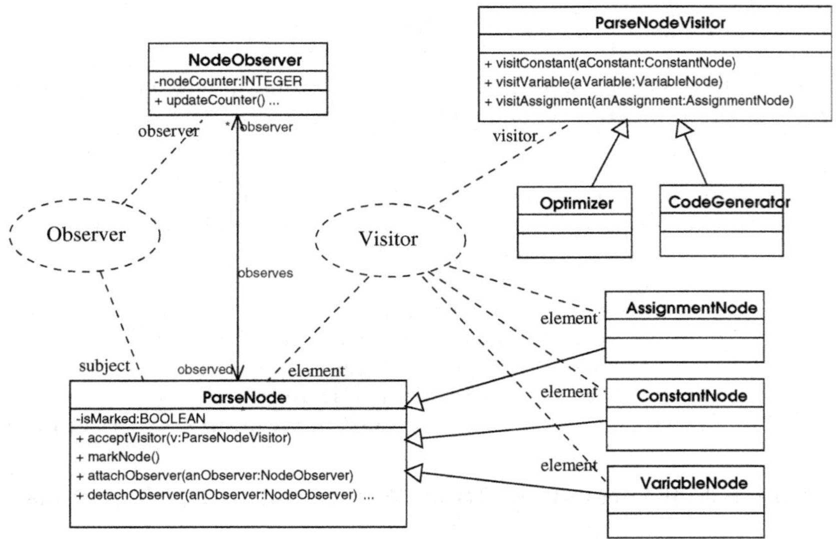

Fig. 5. A model combining two pattern occurrences

We chose to keep the familiar ellipse notation to represent both pattern occurrences as defined in the previous section and collaboration occurrences as defined in the appendix, in order not to disrupt designers accustomed to the current UML notation for design patterns.

Note that Fig. 5 does not show all participation relationships, because this would clutter the diagram for no good reason since there is no ambiguities. For the same reason, neither does it represent the relationships between pattern occurrences and the corresponding <<meta>> collaborations. However, a tool should provide the option of showing all participations, even those involving behavioral features or generalizations, possibly using dialog boxes. Also, as there may be many behavioral features participating in a pattern such as the observer (potentially all those that change the state of the subject), a good tool should also propose a default list of matching participants to ease the designer's task.

4 Conclusion and Related Work

4.1 Related Work

PatternWizard is one of the most extensive projects of design pattern specification, and has influenced our research work in several points. PatternWizard proposes LePUS [6] a declarative, higher order language, designed to represent the generic solution, or *leitmotif*, indicated by design patterns. Our work differs from PatternWizard in two aspects. First, we use UML and OCL to specify patterns. We believe that a UML collaboration and OCL rules can be easier to understand than LePUS formulae and the associated visual notation. Second, PatternWizard works at the code level and is not integrated to any design model.

An approach to the validation of design patterns through their precise representation is proposed by Görel Hedin [9]. She uses attribute grammars to precisely model a pattern and explicit markers in a program to distinguish a pattern occurrence and validate it. Patterns are represented as a set of class, attribute and method roles, related by *rules* which have the same goal as the OCL constraints in our proposal. Using attribute extension is a way to extend the static semantics with new rules, while leaving the original syntax unchanged.

In [11], a dedicated logic called MMM for "Model and MetaModel logic" is used to express constraints and patterns. This logic can express *causal obligations* and can manipulate entities from both M1 and M2, but it is not based on OCL. The authors give a MMM specification of a Subject/Observer cooperation that includes both structural and behavioral aspects. However, the notion of role does not seem to be supported. Without roles, the generic form of a pattern cannot be completely represented, limiting this interesting approach to the specification of particular occurrences of design patterns.

Another research effort in precise representation of design patterns was presented by Tommi Mikkonen [10]. He proposes to formalize temporal behaviors of patterns using a specification method named DisCo. An interesting aspect of his work is that its formalism allows pattern occurrences to be combined through refinements between pattern definitions.

4.2 Conclusion

The use of meta-level collaborations and constraints, instead of the suggested parameterized collaborations, allows a more precise representation of design pattern structural and behavioral constraints. However, one may argue that this approach is not appropriate since we accomplish changes in the UML meta-model which is supposed to be standardized and static. Although this observation is true, it is also true that our approach does not change the UML abstract syntax. This is because the representation of a design pattern as a meta-model collaboration does not add new modeling constructs to UML. It only adds a way to enforce particular constraints among existing constructs.

Our approach also fits quite well with the Profile mechanism. A collection of design patterns, modeled with meta-level collaborations, could be provided as a Profile to a UML CASE tool which could reuse the pattern definitions.

In its current incarnation at the OMG, the UML is ill-equipped for precisely representing design patterns: even the most classical GoF patterns, such as Observer, Composite or Visitor cannot be modeled precisely with parameterized collaborations in UML 1.3. In this paper, we have proposed a minimal set of modifications to the UML 1.3 meta-model to make it possible to model design patterns and represent their occurrences in UML, opening the way for some automatic processing of pattern applications within CASE tools.

We are implementing these ideas in the UMLAUT tool (freely available from `http://www.irisa.fr/pampa/UMLAUT/`) in order to better document the occurrences of design patterns in UML models, as well as to help the designer to abstract away from the gory details of pattern application. Because in our proposal the "essence" of design patterns can be represented at the meta-level with sets of constraints, we can also foresee the availability of design pattern libraries that could be imported into UML tools for application into the designer's UML models. We are starting to build such a library as an open source initiative.

References

1. Grady Booch, James Rumbaugh, and Ivar Jacobson. *The Unified Modeling Language User Guide*. Addison-Wesley, 1998. 483
2. Jan Bosch. Language support for design patterns. In *TOOLS Europe'96*, pages 197–210. Prentice-Hall, 1996. 482
3. James O. Coplien. *Software Patterns*. SIGS Management Briefings. SIGS Books & Multimedia, 1996. 482
4. Dino Distefano, J.-P. Katoen, and Arend Rensink. On a temporal logic for object-based systems. Technical report CTIT 00-06, University of Twente, 2000. 488
5. Amnom H. Eden. *Precise Specification of Design Patterns and Tool Support in Their Application*. PhD thesis, University of Tel Aviv, 1999. 484, 486, 486
6. Amnon H. Eden, Amiram Yehudai, and Joseph Gil. Patterns of the agenda. In *LSDF97: Workshop in conjunction with ECOOP'97*, 1997. 492
7. Gert Florijn, Marco Meijers, and Pieter van Winsen. Tool support for object-oriented patterns. In *ECOOP'97*, volume 1241 of *LNCS*, pages 472–495. Springer-Verlag, Jyväskylä, Finland, June 1997. 482

8. Erich Gamma, Richard Helm, Ralph Johnson, and John Vlissides. *Design Patterns: Elements of Reusable Object-Oriented Software.* Professional Computing Series. Addison-Wesley, Reading, MA, 1995. 482, 483
9. Grel Hedin. Language support for design patterns using attribute extension. In *Workshop on Language Support for Design Patterns and Object Oriented Frameworks (LSDF), ECOOP'97*, pages 209–231, 1997. 492
10. Tommi Mikkonen. Formalizing design patterns. In *ICSE'98*, pages 115–124. IEEE CS Press, 1998. 492
11. Claudia Pons, Gabriel Baum, and Miguel Felder. Integrating object-oriented model with object-oriented metamodel into a single formalism. In *Proceedings Second ECOOP Workshop on Precise Behavioral Semantics (with an Emphasis on OO Business Specifications)*, pages 155–167. TUM-I9813, 1998. 492
12. Sita Ramakrishnan and John McGregor. Extending OCL to support temporal operators. In *Proceedings of the 21st International Conference on Software Engineering (ICSE99) Workshop on Testing Distributed Component-Based Systems, LA, May 16 - 22, 1999*, 1999. 488
13. Trygve Reenskaug. UML collaboration and OOram semantics, November 1999. http://www.ifi.uio.no/~trygver/documents/991108-UML/uml-collaboration.ps. 495
14. UML RTF. *OMG Unified Modeling Language Specification, Version 1.3, UML RTF proposed final revision.* OMG, June 1999. 483, 486, 494, 495
15. Jiri Soukup. Implementing patterns. In *Pattern Languages of Program Design*, pages 395–412. Addison-Wesley, Reading, MA, 1995. 482
16. G. Sunyé, A. Le Guennec, and J.-M. Jézéquel. Design pattern application in UML. In E. Bertino, editor, *ECOOP'2000 proceedings*, number 1850, pages 44–62. Lecture Notes in Computer Science, Springer Verlag, June 2000. 484

A Appendix: Defining the *Context* of OCL Expressions with Collaborations

A.1 Collaborations as Context for Reusable OCL Expressions

Section 7.3 of the UML documentation [14] defines what the *context* of an OCL expression is. The context specifies how the expression is "connected" to the UML model, that is, it declares the names that can be used within the expression.

UML proposes two kinds of context for OCL constraints:

Classifiers to which an <<invariant>> can be attached. The OCL expression can refer to "self" and to all subexpressions reachable from "self" using the navigation rules defined in Sect. 7.5.

Behavioral Features (Operations or Methods) to which a <<precondition>> and/or a <<postcondition>> can be attached. The OCL expression can refer to "self" and to all formal parameters of the behavioral feature. Note that although OCL postconditions can express that a new object has been created (using oclIsNew()), the context does not provide any way to declare a local variable that will denote the newly created object.

A Collaboration can also be attached to a Classifier or to a Behavioral Feature. The collaboration can described how the behavioral feature is realized, in terms of roles played by "self" and the various parameters. One can also use the predefined stereotypes <<self>>, <<parameter>>, <<local>>, or <<global>> to make the roles more explicit within the collaboration.

Note that a given role can sometimes be played by several instances in a collaboration occurrence, in the limits imposed by the multiplicy of the role, and is then represented with a "multi-object" box, resembling stacked objects.

This suggests that Collaborations could well be used systematically as a precise graphical representation of the context of a OCL expression. Each parameter maps to a role having the parameter's type as base. A parameter which would be an OCL sequence of objects of a given type would map to a role with a multiplicity greater than one. Auxiliary variables introduced by "let expressions" (see 7.4.3 of [14]) can also be represented by corresponding roles in the collaboration.

A.2 Binding a Parameterized OCL Expression to the Model

The way particular instances are attached to the respective roles is not very clear in the UML documentation: When a behavioral feature is called, the target of the call action and its effective arguments are supposed to be bound to the corresponding roles, but this is left implicit.

UML is apparently missing a construct to *bind* an instance to a role. The UML notation describes "instance level collaborations" (see Fig. 3-52 p314) as object diagrams representing snapshots of the system, where the roles of the objects are indicated in the object-box. But the mapping onto the UML abstract syntax is not described: how are Instances bound to ClassifierRoles?

Without further information, the only plausible mapping we found is to add the ClassifierRole (which is a kind of Classifier) to the set of current types of the Instance playing this role. Although this correctly reflects the dynamic nature of roles, this mapping explicitly relies on multiple and dynamic classification, which might be deemed too sophisticated, and is not well-defined in the UML context. Another disadvantage of this mapping is that it is too fine-grained: There is no way to *group* individual bindings together and say that they all belong to the same collaboration. This can cause confusion if a snapshot presents a set of instances participating in more than one collaboration at the same time.

Note also that the existing Binding construction of UML relates to generic template instantiations (see Sect. 1.1), which is a completely different matter altogether. We suggest that it be renamed as TemplateExpansion, which would better reflect its semantics, and reserve the name Binding for a new construct whose purpose is to bind an instance to a role, with a semantics equivalent to the dynamic classification alternative presented above. Note that it is desirable that individual Bindings be grouped together to form the whole effective context of a collaboration occurrence. UML1.1 offered the possibility to have *composite dependencies*, but this valuable capability has apparently been removed during the transition to UML1.3. We propose that it be brought back in.

A very similar approach is proposed in [13]: an InstanceCollaboration construct is used to group a set of Instances, while the relation between role and instance is expressed using classification instead of an explicit dependency.

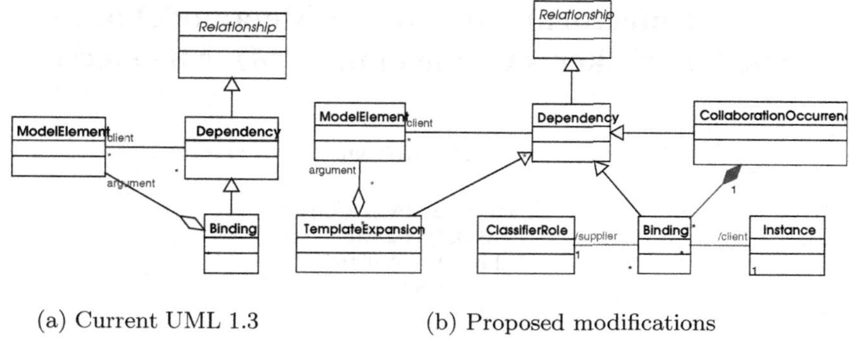

(a) Current UML 1.3 (b) Proposed modifications

Fig. 6. Meta-model modifications for collaboration occurrences

Additional Well-Formedness Rules Associated to Roles and Bindings

[1] The number of instances playing a given role must not violate the multiplicity constraint of the role.

```
context ClassifierRole inv:
        let nbOfInstances =
                self.supplierDependency->select(b |
                        b.oclIsKindOf(Binding))->size()
        in (self.multiplicity.ranges->forall(r |
                        r.lower <= nbOfInstances
                        and nbOfInstances <= r.upper))
```

A.3 Graphical Representation of Bindings

There could be several ways of representing bindings between instances and roles.

1. Using the "instance level collaboration" idea of putting the role in the object-box. This solution is appropriate in some circumstances and is already known, and so is worth keeping.
2. Using a dependency arrow with a <<bind>> stereotype connecting the instance on the object diagram and the role on the collaboration diagram. This solution is not very attractive because it is too fine-grained and also requires both diagrams to be present together.
3. Reusing the dashed-ellipse notation originally proposed to represent instantiations of template collaborations, while changing the mapping of the ellipse onto the abstract syntax: The ellipse would represent the composition of all individual bindings, while each line going out of the ellipse would map to an individual binding dependency between the instance at the end of the line and the role whose name is given by the line label. This notation actually is generalizable to any composite dependency.

Architectural Patterns for Metamodeling: The Hitchhiker's Guide to the UML Metaverse

Cris Kobryn

InLine Software Corp.
P.O. Box 2320
Fallbrook, CA 92028
USA
ckobryn@acm.org

Abstract. Metamodels are playing an increasingly important role in the specification of distributed object and component architectures, such as CORBA, CORBA Component Model, Enterprise JavaBeans and DCOM/COM+. By recursively abstracting the details associated with implementation, metamodels improve rigor and facilitate system integration and interoperability. The uses of metamodels range from specifying modeling languages and metadata repositories to defining data interchange formats and software processes (methods).

The OMG Unified Modeling Language (UML) has proven an effective and popular choice for specifying metamodels. The OMG is using the UML to specify a comprehensive metadata architecture that includes metamodels (UML, Meta Object Facility, Common Warehouse Metamodel) and an XML-based metadata interchange format (XMI). Many other organizations are also using the UML to specify metamodels, such as the Meta Data Coalition's Open Information Model.

Despite these successful applications of UML metamodels, many modelers still struggle with the relationships between models and metamodels, especially when they are specifying multiple-layer or multiple-viewpoint metamodel architectures, or when they are defining UML profiles or other language extensions. Metamodeling is still a nascent technique, and there is a lack of consensus regarding when and how it should be applied.

This presentation explores the issues that modelers face when specifying UML metamodels and profiles, and summarizes the lessons learned from defining the UML, the Meta-Object Facility and UML profiles using a 4-layer metamodel architectural pattern. It specifies the structure of the architectural pattern using a UML parameterized collaboration, and shows how it can be extended to provide better support for round-trip engineering. The presentation concludes with recommendations to improve the rigor and the efficiency of the metamodel specifications for the UML and the Meta Object Facility that are relevant to the next major revisions of these industry standards.

A. Evans, S. Kent and B. Selic (Eds.): «UML» 2000, LNCS 1939, p. 497, 2000.

Reconciling the Needs of Architectural Description with Object-Modeling Notations

David Garlan and Andrew J. Kompanek

Carnegie Mellon University
Pittsburgh, PA 15213 USA
{garlan, kompanek}@cs.cmu.edu

Abstract. Complex software systems require expressive notations for representing their software architectures. Two competing paths have emerged. One is to use a specialized notation for architecture – or architecture description language (ADL). The other is to adapt a general-purpose modeling notation, such as UML. The latter has a number of benefits, including familiarity to developers, close mapping to implementations, and commercial tool support. However, it remains an open question as to how best to use object-oriented notations for architectural description, and, indeed, whether they are sufficiently expressive, as currently defined. In this paper we take a systematic look at these questions, examining the space of possible mappings from ADLs into object notations. Specifically, we describe (a) the principle strategies for representing architectural structure in UML; (b) the benefits and limitations of each strategy; and (c) aspects of architectural description that are intrinsically difficult to model in UML using the strategies.

1 Introduction

A critical level of abstraction in the description of a complex system is its software architecture. At an architectural level one describes the principal system components and their pathways of interaction. Architectural descriptions are typically used to provide an intellectually tractable, birds-eye view of a system, and to permit design-time reasoning about system-level concerns, such as performance, reliability, portability, and conformance to external standards and architectural styles.

In practice most architectural descriptions are informal documents. They are usually centered on box-and-line diagrams, with explanatory prose. Visual conventions are idiosyncratic, and usually project-specific. As a result, architectural descriptions are only vaguely understood by developers, they cannot be analyzed for consistency or completeness, they are only hypothetically related to implementations, their properties cannot be enforced as a system evolves, and they cannot be supported by tools to help software architects with their tasks.

To improve the situation a number of people have suggested the use of more standardized and formal notations for architectural description. Viewed broadly, there are two main sources of such recommendations. One is from the software architecture research community, which has proposed a number of "architecture description languages" (ADLs) specifically designed to represent software and system architectures [17]. These languages have matured over the past five years. Most come with tool sets that support many aspects of architectural design and analysis, such as graphical editing, code generation, run-time monitoring, anomaly detection, and performance analysis.

A. Evans, S. Kent and B. Selic (Eds.): «UML» 2000, LNCS 1939, pp. 498-512, 2000.

The other source is from the object-oriented community. Object modeling notations have had considerable success, both as domain-modeling and implementation-modeling notations. For the former, object-oriented entity-relation diagrams (and related notations) have provided a natural mechanism to represent domain entities and their relations. In the latter case, for systems that are to be implemented in an object-oriented fashion, object-modeling notations provide a natural way to represent class structures, relationships between those classes, and certain aspects of class/system behavior.

But are object-oriented notations also appropriate as architectural descriptions? A number of authors have argued yes, claiming that the current capabilities are precisely what is needed [3, 13]. Moreover, recently there have been proposals that attempt to show how ADL concepts can be mapped directly into a notation like UML [11,16,18].

Unfortunately, each proposal is different, and each covers only *some* aspects of architectural description. We believe that what is needed is more systematic view of the problem, one that clarifies what needs to be modeled at an architectural level, identifies candidate constructs in an object modeling language, and examines the strengths and weaknesses of adopting a particular modeling strategy. Practitioners could then decide more rationally which, if any, of the possible techniques is most appropriate.

In this paper we attempt to do that for the *structural* aspects of software architecture. We start by examining the needs for architectural description—based on what is now done informally in practice and what features are captured by ADLs. Then we consider a number of strategies for representing architectures in UML, contrasting the advantages and drawbacks of each. Finally, we summarize the key lessons from this activity.

2 Related Work

A number of authors have examined ways to model architectures using object notations. Among the earliest of these were purveyors of object-oriented methods, who attempted to provide a uniform path from requirements to implementations using only object notations. In these treatments architecture is usually not specifically called out as a representation in need of special treatment, but viewed as a form of high-level object-oriented design.

The lack of explicit treatment of architectures in those methods prompted several authors to take a more careful look at the needs of architectural modeling. Kruchten [13] for example, proposes a set of (4+1) views to capture the various aspects of architectural information. Other authors have examined the use of object-oriented notations for modeling architectural styles and patterns [3]. Finally, profiles have been proposed within the UML standards community for commercial modeling languages that include explicit architectural concepts, including a profile for Corba [23] and real-time systems [28].

Recently, there have been a number of attempts to understand more broadly how to *map* architectural models as expressed in an architecture description language into object notations [11,16,18,19]. As we noted earlier, each of these proposes a particular form of modeling that exploits the constraints of the particular architectural domain or language. Unlike this paper, they have not attempted to consider systematically the *space* of possible embeddings, or enumerate the situations under which *alternative* embeddings might be desirable – although they do serve as relevant data points. On the other hand, for specific mapping strategies many of these efforts go beyond our paper by also considering mappings of non-structural aspects to UML, such as architectural behavior.

3 Architectural Description

The software architecture of a system defines its high-level structure, exposing its gross organization as a collection of interacting components. Currently there is considerable diversity in the ways that practitioners represent architectures, although most depend on informal box-and-line diagrams.

In an effort to put architectural description on a more solid notational and semantic footing, over the past decade a number of architecture description languages have been proposed [1,2,6,9,14,15,18,20,29]. While these languages (and their associated tool sets) differ in many details, there has emerged a general consensus about the main ingredients of architectural description. Focusing on architectural structure, we take that core set of concepts as the starting point for this paper[1]. In this shared ontology there are five basic concepts: components, connectors, systems, properties, and styles.

Components represent the computational elements and data stores of a system. Intuitively, they correspond to the boxes in box-and-line descriptions of software architectures. Typical examples of components include clients, servers, filters, blackboards, and databases. Components may have multiple interfaces (which we will call *ports*), each interface defining a point of interaction between a component and its environment. A component may have several ports of the same type (e.g., a server may have several active http connections).

Connectors represent interactions among components. They provide the "glue" for architectural designs, and correspond to the lines in box-and-line descriptions. From a run-time perspective, connectors mediate the communication and coordination activities among components. Examples include simple forms of interaction, such as pipes, procedure call, and event broadcast. Connectors may also represent complex interactions, such as a client-server protocol or a SQL link between a database and an application. Connectors have interfaces that define the *roles* played by the participants in the interaction.

Systems represent graphs of components and connectors. In general, systems may be hierarchical: components and connectors may represent subsystems that have *internal* architectures. We will refer to these as *representations.* When a system or part of a system has a representation, it is also necessary to explain the mapping between the internal and external interfaces. We will refer to the elements of this mapping as *bindings.*

Properties represent additional information (beyond structure) about the parts of an architectural description. Although the properties that can be expressed by different ADLs vary considerably, typically they are used to represent anticipated or required extra-functional aspects of an architectural design. For example, some ADLs allow one to calculate system throughput and latency based on performance estimates of the constituent components and connectors [30]. In general, it is desirable to be able to associate properties with any architectural element in a description (components, connectors, systems, and their interfaces). For example, an interface (port or role) may describe an interaction protocol.

Types and Styles represent families of related systems. An architectural *style* typically defines a vocabulary of design element types as a set of component, connector, port, role, binding, and property types, together with rules for composing instances of the types [10].

[1] These concepts are largely those in found in Acme [7].

Examples include data-flow architectures based on graphs of pipes and filters, blackboard architectures, and layered systems.

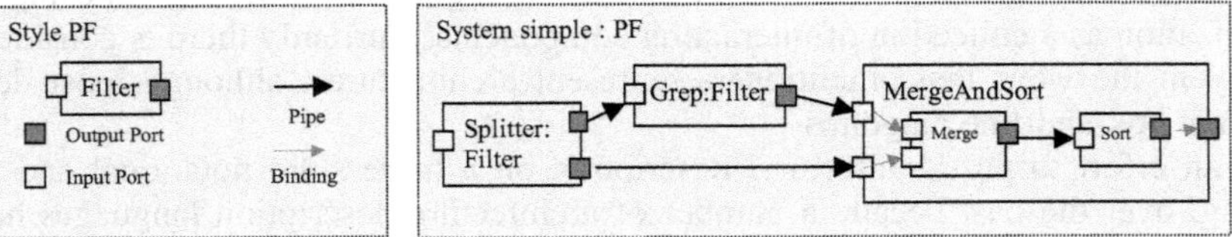

Fig. 1. A system in the Pipes and Filters style

To illustrate the use of these concepts, consider the simple example shown in Figure 1, which we will use throughout the paper. The system defines a simple string-processing application that extracts and sorts text. The system is described in a pipe-filter style, which provides a design vocabulary consisting of a filter component type and pipe connector type, input and output port types, and a port-port binding type. In addition, there would likely be constraints (not shown) that ensure, for example, that the reader/writer roles of the pipe are associated with appropriate (input/output) ports. The system is described hierarchically: *MergeAndSort* is defined by a representation that is itself a pipe-filter system. Properties of the components and connectors (not illustrated) might list, for example, performance characteristics used by a tool to calculate overall system throughput.

4 UML Background

UML unifies a number of object modeling notations in a common framework and is quickly becoming a standard object notation for industry [4,5,26,27]. While a detailed description of UML is beyond the scope of this paper, we summarize its principal constructs (known as model *elements*) that can be used to model software architectures:

Classes, Interfaces and Objects: Classes are the primary construct for describing the logical view of a system. Classes have properties in the form of *attributes*, provide abstract services in the form of *operations,* and can be logically related to one another using *associations*. Classes may expose their functionality through a set of supported *interfaces*, collections of related operations. Classes have instances called *objects*, which are used in models called *collaborations* to depict behavior under particular scenarios.[2]

Component and Component Instances: Components are used to describe the physical, deployable pieces of a system. Like classes, components in UML expose their functionality through interfaces. Components are typically related to each other using dependency relationships. The deployment of a system on a set of hardware is described by associating components with hardware *nodes*.

Packages: UML provides a grouping mechanism that is used to partition large UML models into manageable chunks called *packages*. UML also defines a type of grouping element called a *subsystem,* which is typically used to encapsulate the object models that define a coarse-grained module in a system.

Relationships: Model elements are related to one another with *associations* and *dependencies*. Dependency is the most generic relationship in UML, indicating that an element depends in some way on the definition of another element. Association is a richer

[2] In the UML meta-model, the prototypical "objects" in collaborations are referred to as collaboration *roles*.

relationship that describes an abstract relationship between classes and the roles the classes play in the relationship.

Stereotypes: To allow the extension of UML with domain-specific concepts, UML provides a mechanism for associating constraints with elements of a model, using a constraint language, *OCL* [25]. These constraints can be grouped and named using a construct called a *stereotype*. UML also includes a set of standard stereotypes.

The above constructs can be composed in various ways in a UML model and visualized in diagrams. Textual *annotations* may be associated with any of them. Frequently, these annotations are in the form of *tagged values:* arbitrary attribute-value pairs.

UML also defines a set of models for describing the dynamic behavior of a system, including collaboration diagrams that specify system behavior using event-based *interaction scenarios*, descriptions based on *state machines*, and *use cases*.

5 Strategies & Evaluation Criteria

We now consider five strategies for modeling architectural structure (as expressible in ADLs) using UML. We will organize the presentations of alternatives around the choices for representing component types and instances, since the components are typically the central design elements of an architectural description. For each choice we then consider sub-alternatives for the other architectural elements (connectors, styles, etc.). Of the five strategies, the first three consider ways to use classes and objects to model components. The fourth is based on UML components, and the fifth on UML subsystems.

However, before considering those strategies, we need to be clear about the criteria for evaluation. Ideally we would like a mapping strategy to exhibit three characteristics:

1. *Semantic Match:* It should respect documented UML semantics and the intuitions of UML modelers. The interpretation of UML model should be close to the interpretation of the original ADL description so the model is intelligible to both designers and UML-based tools. In addition, the mapping should produce legal UML models.
2. *Legibility:* The resulting architectural descriptions in UML should bring conceptual clarity to a system design, avoid visual clutter, and highlight key design details.
3. *Completeness:* The architectural concepts identified in Section 3 should be representable in the UML model.

6 Classes & Objects – Types as Classes, Instances as Objects

Perhaps the most natural candidate for representing component and connector types in UML is the class concept. Classes describe the conceptual vocabulary of a system just as component and connector types form the conceptual vocabulary of an architectural description in a particular style. Additionally, the relation between classes and instances is similar to the relationship between architectural types and their instances. The mapping described for the C2 architectural style in [16] is a variation on this approach.

Figure 2 illustrates the general idea. Here we characterize the filter architectural type as the UML class "filter." Instances of filters, such as "split" are represented as corresponding objects in an object (instance) diagram. We now take a closer look at this strategy by examining how the concepts in Section 3 can be described in UML.

6.1 Components

As noted, the type/instance relationship in architectural descriptions is a close match to the class/object relationship in a UML model. In UML, classes, like component types in architectural descriptions, are first-class entities and are the richest structures available for capturing software abstractions. The full set of UML descriptive mechanisms are

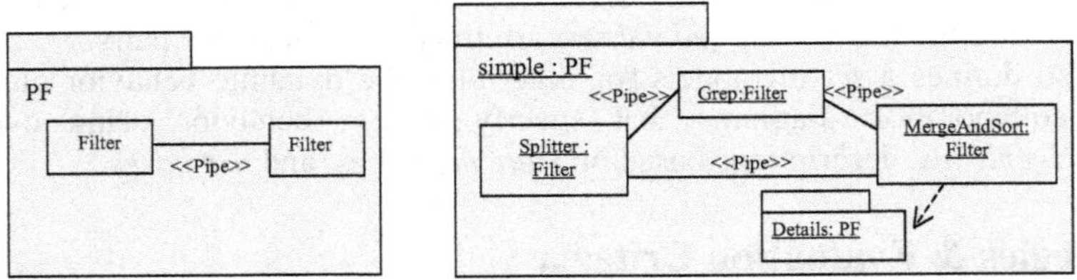

Fig. 2. Types as classes, instances as objects.

available to describe the structure, properties, and behavior of a class, making this a good choice for depicting detail and doing analysis using UML-based analysis tools.

Properties of architectural components can be represented as class attributes or with associations; behavior can be described using UML behavioral models; and generalization can be used to relate a set of component types. The semantics of an instance or type can also be elaborated by attaching one of the standard stereotypes (e.g., indicating that a component runs as a separate process with the <<process>> stereotype).

However, the match between component types and classes, and component instances and objects, is not perfect. In architectural descriptions a component instance often has additional structure not required by the component's type. For example, a component instance might define additional ports not required by its type, or associate an implementation in the form of additional structure that is not part of its type's definition. However, in UML an object cannot include parts that its class does not also define.

6.2 Ports (Component Interfaces)

There are six reasonable ways to represent ports.

Option 1: No explicit representation. We can leave ports out of the model entirely. This leads to the simplest diagrams, but suffers from the obvious problem that there is no way to characterize the names or properties of the ports. However, this might be a reasonable choice in certain situations, such as when components have only a single port, or when the ports can be inferred from the system topology.

Option 2: Ports as Annotations. We can represent ports as annotations. This approach provides a home for information about ports, although annotations have no semantic value in UML and hence cannot be used as a basis for analysis. Again, if the detailed properties of a port are not of concern this might be a reasonable approach.

Option 3: Ports as Class/Object Attributes. Ports can be treated as attributes of a class/object. In this approach ports are part of the formal structural model, but they can have only a very simple representation in a class diagram – essentially a name and type.

Option 4: Ports as Interfaces. Describing port types as UML interfaces has three advantages. First, the interface and port concepts have a similar intent: they both characterize aspects of the ways in which an entity can interact with its environment. Second, the UML "lollipop" notation provides a compact description of a port in a class diagram depicting a component type. In an instance diagram, a UML association role (corresponding to a port instance) qualified by the interface name (the port type) provides a compact way to designate that a component instance is interacting through a particular port instance. Finally, this approach provides visually distinct depictions of components and ports, in which ports can clearly be seen as subservient to components.

However, while the interface and port concepts are similar, they are not identical. An interface exposes a set of operations that can be invoked by the environment of a component. In contrast, the description of a port in an ADL often includes both the services *provided* by the component, as well as those it *requires* from its environment. Furthermore, it is meaningful for a component type to have several instances of the same port type, while it is not meaningful to say that a class realizes several versions of the same. For example, there is no easy way to define a "splitter" filter type that has two output ports of the same "type" using this technique. Finally, unlike classes, interfaces do not have attributes or substructure.

Option 5: Ports as Classes. Another alternative is to describe ports as classes contained by a component type. This is essentially the approach taken in the UML Real-Time Profile [22,28]. This overcomes a certain lack of expressiveness in UML interface descriptions: we can now represent port substructure and indicate that a component type has several ports of the same type. A component instance is modeled as an object containing a set of port objects. Unfortunately, this approach also suffers from problems: by representing ports as classes, we not only clutter the diagram, but we also lose clear discrimination between ports and components. It is possible to make the diagram more suggestive using a notational variation on this scheme in which the ports are contained classes. But then indicating points of interaction is counterintuitive, as containment usually indicates that a class owns other classes whose instances may or *may not* be accessible through instances of the parent class.

Option 6: Ports as UML Classes that realize interfaces. The final option is a combination of options 4 and 5: represent ports as classes which themselves expose interfaces. This option is more expressive than the previous two techniques, but suffers from the semantic mismatch problem of both options. It is also the least visually appealing. Unless ports are discriminated from components visually, the added clutter in a diagram would mask the overall topology of components, defeating one of the main purposes of architectural description. It also makes interpretation more difficult because a reader is expected to understand that a pair of objects stands for a single object in the original model.

6.3 Connectors

Option 1: Types as Associations; Connectors as Links. In an architectural box-and-line diagram of a system, the lines between components are connectors. One tempting way to represent connectors in UML is as associations between classes or links between objects. The approach is visually simple, provides a clear distinction between components and connectors, and makes use of the most familiar relationship in UML class diagrams: association. Moreover, associations can be labeled, and when a direction is associated with the connector it can be indicated with an arrow in UML.

Unfortunately, although the identification between connectors and associations is visually appealing, connectors have a different meaning than associations. A system in an architectural description is built-up by choosing components with behavior exposed through their ports and connecting them with connectors that coordinate their behaviors. A system's behavior is defined as the collective behavior of a set of components whose interaction is defined and limited by the connections between them. In contrast, while an association or link in UML represents a potential for interaction between the elements it relates, the association mechanism is primarily a way of describing a conceptual relationship between two concepts.

Using an association to represent architectural connection has other problems. Since associations are relationships *between* UML elements, an association cannot stand on its own in a UML model. Consequently, there is no way to represent a connector type in isolation. To have any notion of a connector type within this scheme, one must resort to naming conventions or the use of stereotypes whose meaning is captured by an OCL description. Also, the approach does not allow one to specify the interfaces to the connector (i.e., its roles).

Option 2: Types as Association Classes. One solution to the lack of expressiveness is to qualify the association with a class that represents the connector type. This way the attributes of a connector type or connector can be captured as attributes of a class or object. Unfortunately, this technique still does not provide any way of explicitly representing connector roles. The approach is similar to the one taken in the UML Real-time Profile, in which association endpoints are identified with roles in a collaboration [28].

Option 3: Types as Classes; Connectors as Objects. One way to define roles in UML is to represent a connector as a class that is associated with model elements representing roles. We have the same options for representing roles as we had for ports: as interfaces realized by a class, as "child" classes contained by a connector class or as child classes that realize interfaces. Given a scheme for representing ports and roles, an attachment (between a port and a role) may be represented as an association or a dependency.

6.4 Systems

Option 1: Systems as UML Subsystems. The primary mechanism in UML for grouping related elements is the package. In fact, UML defines a standard package stereotype, called <<subsystem>>, to group UML models that represent a logical part of a system. The choice of subsystems is appropriate for *any* choice of mappings of components and connectors and works particularly well for grouping classes.

Unfortunately, subsystems have different semantics than systems in an architectural description. In a model, a package represents set of elements that may be imported into another context, but not a structure per se. In contrast, a system in architectural design is a structure with sub-parts in the form of its components and connectors. Unlike classes, packages also lack attributes for defining system level properties.

Option 2: Systems as Objects. A second option is to use objects to represent systems. If architectural instances are represented as objects, we can introduce an explicit system class whose instances contain the component and connector objects that make up the system. Then we can capture richer semantics using attributes and associations/links. Unfortunately, this approach has the drawback that by representing a system in the same way as a component or connector we lose the semantic distinction between a system as a configuration of elements. It is also introduces visual clutter.

Option 3: Systems as Subsystems Containing a System Object. This alternative is a combination of the first two techniques. It combines the expressiveness of Option 2 with the visual advantages of Option 1. However, we still have the basic semantic mismatch and the additional clutter complicates a diagram.

Option 4: Systems as Collaborations. A set of communicating objects (connected by links) is described in UML using a collaboration. If we represent components as objects, we can use collaborations to represent systems. While this is a natural way to describe run-time structures, unfortunately this leaves no way to explicitly represent system-level properties. There is also a semantic mismatch – a collaboration describes a representative interaction between objects that provides a partial description, whereas an architectural configuration is meant to capture a complete description at some level of abstraction.

There are of course many variations on Options 2 and 3, corresponding to the same variations on the use of classes, objects and stereotypes to describe components which we described in the last section and in the next.

6.5 Representations

A representation is just a system that is related to a component or connector and includes bindings that describe the relationship between the element and (one of) its representations. If systems are represented as packages, an element can be related to its representations through dependency, possibly with an annotation indicating the name of the representation. There are a number of options for representing bindings: (1) as annotations (a weak depiction); (2) as dependency between an outer element and inner element (only possible with techniques in which ports and roles are explicitly represented); (3) as set of elements with attributes that describe binding (visually cluttered). Alternatively, if systems are represented as classes, representations can be associated with their parent element using associations and links.

7 Classes & Objects – Types as Stereotypes, Instances as Classes

The second major alternative for modeling a component type in UML is to define a stereotype. In this way, we can describe the meaning of our architectural vocabulary in a way that distinguishes an architectural element type from the UML class concept. A component instance is then represented as a class with a stereotype. Using this approach, architectural concepts become distinct from the built-in UML concepts, and in principal, a UML-based modeling environment can be extended to support the visualization and analysis of new architectural types within a style and enforce design constraints captured in OCL. This is essentially the approach taken in [18].

In Figure 3, the Filter Type is defined by a set of constraints expressed in OCL that are identified with the <<Filter>> Stereotype. Filter instances (e.g., splitter) are represented as classes that bear the Filter stereotype. We now examine this approach in more detail.

7.1 Components

Representing instances as classes has a number of advantages. For example, we can capture a set of possible run-time configurations (e.g., one-to-many relationships) in a single diagram. By using classes, we also allow component instances to include structure in addition to the structure defined by their types, overcoming a limitation of the class/instance approach.

Unfortunately, the approach has a number of disadvantages. Stereotypes are not first class, so we can't define structure, attributes, or behavior except by writing OCL constraints. Furthermore, there is no way to visualize stereotypes in diagrams, unless, in the future, there is support in UML environments for manipulating, visualizing and analyzing extensions to the UML meta-model. There is also currently no way to express sub-typing relationships between stereotypes. Among other consequences, this means that we can't take advantage of analysis capabilities offered by UML tools to analyze architectural types, or associate behavioral models with types.

Furthermore, a class may have only one stereotype. Consequently, we can't use any the other built-in stereotypes to add meaning to a component that already has a stereotype. Arguably, using a *class* to represent an architectural *instance* is also not intuitive.

There are a number of options for representing ports. The ports defined by a component type would be represented as OCL expressions that state what structure a class standing for a component of this type should have. We can represent a component instance's ports in the same ways we modeled a component type's ports in last approach.

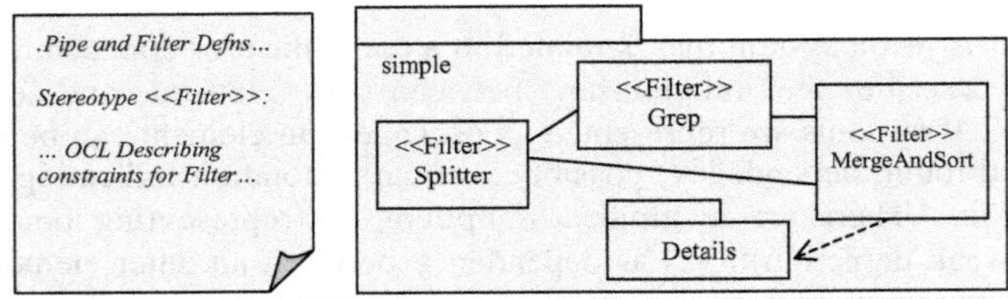

Fig. 3. Types as stereotypes, instances as stereotyped classes.

7.2 Connectors, Systems, Representations, and Styles

The options for representing connectors are similar to the options we had for representing connector types in the last approach. The same options exist for describing overall systems and for indicating representations as for the first variation, although in this we represent system instances as represented styles in the previous approach. In this case, there can be no explicit representation of a style using UML model elements. Instead, the style is embodied in a set of stereotypes.

8 Classes & Objects – Types as classes, Instances as Classes

The third class-based approach is to represent component types as classes (like the first approach) and component instances as classes (like the second). The observations we made in the previous two sections about the suitability of the classes to represent component types and instances apply here as well: by representing both component types and instances as classes, we have the full set of UML features to describe both component types and instances. We can also capture patterns at both the type (as part of a description of an architectural style) and instance level, supporting the description of a dynamic architecture whose structure evolves at run-time.

Figure 4 illustrates this approach, defining both the "filter" type and instances of filters (e.g., "splitter") as classes. We now examine this approach in light of the previous two class-based approaches.

8.1 Components

Although, the approach has many of the strengths of the previous two approaches, it suffers from a number of problems. Unlike the second approach, we no longer explicitly distinguish architectural vocabulary and the UML class concept. Representing both types and instances as classes also blurs the distinction between type and instance, although stereotypes may be used to reinforce this distinction.

There are two viable options for relating a component type to its instances within this scheme: generalization and dependency. Generalization captures the structural relationship between a type and instance (namely, the instance "subclass" must be substitutable for the type) but it blurs the type-instance distinction. The other option is to represent this

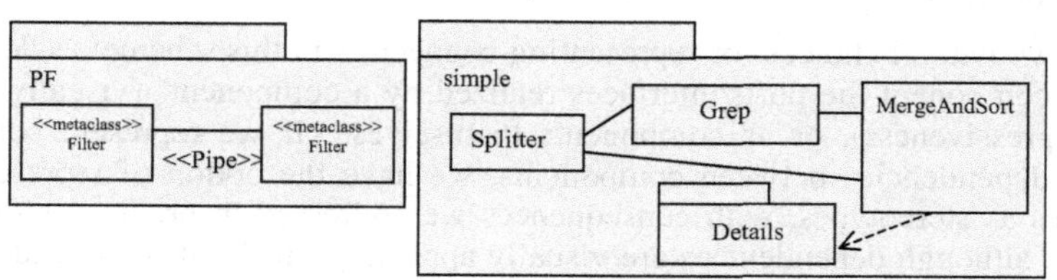

Fig. 4. Types & instances as classes.

relationship as a (perhaps stereotyped) dependency, which is semantically weaker but carries less semantic baggage than the generalization relationship.

8.2 Connectors

The same issues arise when describing connections. For a full discussion of options for describing connections in terms of classes, see variation #1.

8.3 Systems, Representations and Styles

The options for representing systems and styles are similar to those in the two previous approaches using (a) packages, or (b) classes and objects.

9 Using UML Components

UML includes a "component" modeling element, which is used to describe *implementation* artifacts of a system and their deployment. A component diagram is often used to depict the topology of a system at a high level of granularity and plays a similar function, although at the implementation level, as an architectural description of a system. In Figure 5 we represent the "filter" type as a UML component and instances (e.g., "splitter") as instances of this UML component.

9.1 Components

UML components are a natural candidate for representing architectural components. Components have interfaces, may be deployed on hardware, and commonly carry a stereotype and are depicted with a custom visualization. UML components are often used as part of diagrams that depict an overall topology, and just as it is natural to talk about mapping architectural components to hardware, components are assigned to nodes in UML deployment diagrams. For some architectural styles, the identification of abstract components with implementation-level components is a reasonable choice.

Unfortunately, in UML components are defined as concrete "chunks" of implementation (e.g., executables, or dynamic link libraries) that realize abstract interfaces – unlike the more abstract notion of components found in ADLs, which frequently have only an indirect relationship to deployable piece of a system. Nonetheless, the concepts share more than a name. Components expose interfaces (as with classes) and can be used to represent the ports exposed by a component, just as they were used in the strategy based on classes and objects.

However, the rich set of class associations available to relate classes are not available for components, limiting how we can describe ports, represent patterns, and indicate connection. (Moreover, UML behavioral models cannot reference components.)

9.2 Connectors

There are two natural choices for representing connectors in this scheme: as dependencies between a component the ports/interfaces realized by a component (visually simple but lacking expressiveness), or as components themselves. If we represent connector instances as dependencies between components, we have the option of representing connector types as stereotypes, with consequences we addressed in previous sections. Unfortunately, although dependencies are visually appealing, the built-in dependency notion in UML does not adequately capture the idea of architectural connection or provide an explicit descriptive capability. Representing a connector as a UML component addresses

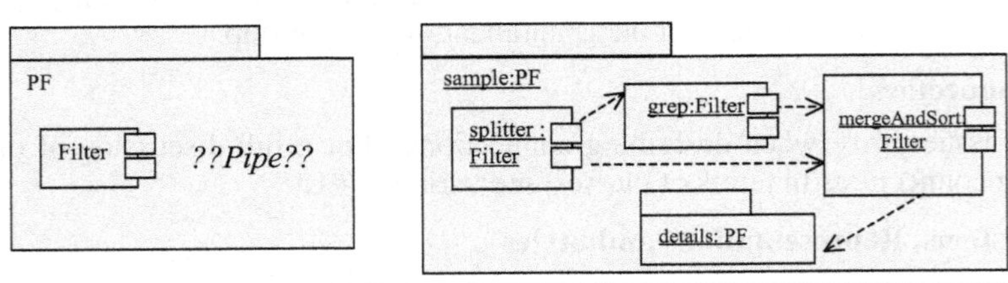

Fig. 5. Components as UML components.

this problem, but unfortunately blurs the distinction between components and connectors.

10 Using Subsystems

We now describe how a subsystem (a stereotyped UML package) can be used to describe the components in a system and the component types in a style. This approach has the appeal that packages are an ideal way to describe coarse-grained elements as a set of UML models. Also, the package construct is already familiar to UML modelers, and to those extending UML, as a way of bundling large pieces or views of a system.

In Figure 6, we describe the "filter" type as a package and filter instances as package instances (e.g., "splitter").

10.1 Components

The subsystem construct is used in UML to group or encapsulate a set of model elements that describe some logical piece of a system, similar to components in architectural descriptions. Subsystems (indeed, any package) can include structures based on any of the UML models. This has an advantage over describing components and connectors as classes – by identifying a component or connector with a package, we can not only include structure as classes (or objects), we can also include behavioral models. There are many options for describing component or connector substructure. This approach also has a visual appeal – substructure can be depicted as "embedded" in the package. Component and Component types would be modeled in essentially the same way, although one could also take advantage of the UML template mechanism when defining a type.

Although visually appealing, this approach suffers from a number of problems. In UML, a package is (semantically speaking) little more than a folder in which related models and elements can be stored. One does not talk about a package having interfaces; instead a package makes its elements (e.g., classes) available to other packages through export. Representing substructure (like ports) as elements contained by a package is also counterintuitive. The fact that certain elements correspond to ports, others to properties, others to reps, is misleading. Expressing the behavior of a component would also be awkward, since packages themselves do not have dynamic behavior in UML. Packages may only be related by dependence, which restricts how connection/attachment can be depicted. It also blurs the distinction between a system and a component in a system.

10.2 Connectors

There are two natural choices for representing connectors in this scheme: dependencies (visually simple but lacking expressiveness), or packages themselves. While dependencies have visual appeal, the dependency notion does not fully capture the notion architectural connection. As we've noted before, a package does not have to describe of connector properties and structure. As with components, we could include behavioral description of the connector within the package, although relating it meaningfully to the package itself is difficult, as it was for components.

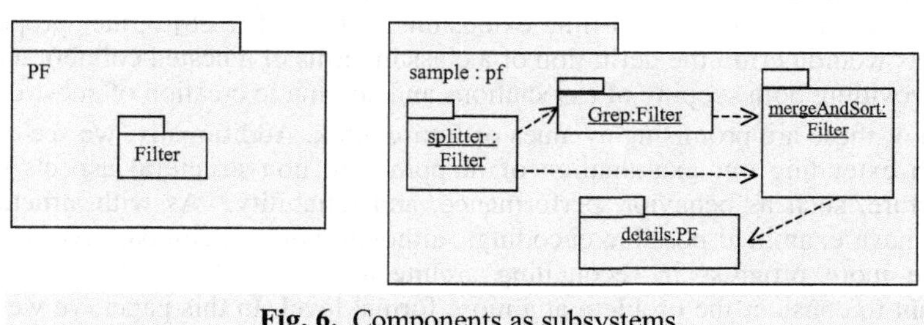

Fig. 6. Components as subsystems.

11 Discussion and Conclusions

We have briefly examined five strategies for encoding in UML the representations of architectural structure expressible using modern ADLs: for each of these we considered a number of variations and considered the strategies with respect to completeness, legibility, and semantic match. What are the lessons to be gained from this?

First, *there is no single best way to encode ADLs in UML.* Each of the strategies has strengths and weaknesses, depending on how well they support the evaluation criteria. With respect to completeness and legibility there is a typically a tradeoff: encodings that emphasize completeness (by providing a semantic home for all of the aspects of architectural design) tend to be verbose, while graphically appealing encodings tend to be incomplete. Hence, the best strategy will depend on what aspects of architectural design needed to be represented. In restricted situations (for example, if there is only one type of connector) it may be preferable to use an incomplete, but visually appealing, encoding.

Second, *all of the encodings exhibit some form of semantic mismatch.* UML's vocabulary of classes, objects, packages, components, associations, etc., while varied and rich, is ultimately designed to support an object-oriented view of software design. As such, UML does not provide a completely adequate foundation for architecture-based description of systems. In this paper, we illustrated a number of specific examples of mismatch, including the following: (a) neither the class, subsystem or component concept is a perfect match to the ADL component concept; (b) unlike objects, architectural instances may need to define additional structure not defined by their types; (c) the port concept has no good analog in UML, since unlike interfaces, a port should be able to define both provided and *required* services, and a component might have multiple instantiations of a particular port type; (d) there is no satisfactory way to fully describe a connector and its roles; and (e) although the ADL type and instance concepts are very similar to the class and object concepts of UML, neither class diagrams nor collaboration diagrams are wholly appropriate for describing architectural configurations.

Given these observations, one might well ask whether there are reasonable alternatives to direct encoding of architecture in ADL. We see two plausible alternative paths:

1. Continue to use ADLs, but map to OO implementations. In this approach architecture description retains its own notations, but tools are provided to convert those descriptions to *lower-level* object notations in situations where the implementation is done in an object-oriented fashion.
2. Extend UML to include additional concepts for architectural modeling. This could be done by extending the UML meta-model, or by defining a profile for architectural design. Indeed, we can already see the inclusion of architectural notions, such as ports, in proposals for real-time extensions to UML [22,28]. Other proposed extensions would permit the definition of a class in terms of a nested collaboration diagram – providing both scoping of associations and automatic creation of substructure.

Both of these are promising avenues of future work. Additionally, we see considerable value in extending our examination of mappings to non-structural aspects of software architecture, such as behavior, performance, and reliability. As with structure, several authors have examined possible encodings, although not in a comparative study. Finally, to make more progress in reconciling architecture description with UML it will be important to consider the problem at a more formal level. In this paper we were forced to appeal to intuition regarding issues of semantic similarity. It would be desirable to have a more precise foundation on which to base this comparison.

12 Acknowledgements

We acknowledge the contributions of the members of the ABLE group at Carnegie Mellon, of the SEI Product Line Systems Program, and the members of the UML standards community who are working toward a proposal for architectural description in UML. We give special thanks to Bran Selic for guiding us in the UML standardization process and to Pedro Pinto for his work on encoding architectural descriptions in UML.

References

1. Allen, R.; Garlan, A. Formalizing Architectural Connection. *Proceedings of the 16th Intl. Conf. on SW Eng.*, 1994.
2. Binns, P.; and Vestal, S. Formal Real-Time Architecture Specification and Analysis. *Proceedings of 10th IEEE Wkshp on Real-Time OS and Sw*, May 1993.

3. Buschmann, F; Meunier, R.; Rohnert, H.; Sommerlad, P. and Stal, M. *Pattern-Oriented Software Architecture, A System of Patterns*. John Wiley & Sons, 1996.
4. Booch, G.; Rumbaugh, J and Jacobson, I. *The UML User Guide*. Addison-Wesley.
5. Booch, G.; Rumbaugh, J and Jacobson, I. *The UML Reference Manual.* Addison-Wesley.
6. Coglianese, L. and R. Szymanski. DSSA-ADAGE: An Environment for Architecture-based Avionics Development. *In Proceedings of AGARD'93*, May 1993.
7. Garlan, D; Monroe, Robert T. and Wile, D. Acme: Architectural Description of Component-Based Systems. *Foundations of Component-Based Systems*, Cambridge University Press, 2000.
8. Garlan, D.; Monroe, R.T. and Wile, D. *Acme Reference Guide*. Available from http://www.cs.cmu.edu/~acme.
9. Garlan, D.; Allen, R.; and Ockerbloom, J. (1994), Exploiting Style in Architectural Design Environments. *SIGSOFT'94.*
10. Garlan, D. and Shaw, M. *Software Architecture: Perspectives on an Emerging Discipline.* Prentice Hall, 1996.
11. Hofmeister, C., Nord, R.L. and Soni, D.. Describing Software Architecture with UML. *Proceedings of the TC2 1st Working IFIP Conf. on Sw Architecture (WICSA1)* 1999.
12. Kobryn, C. Modeling Enterprise Software Architectures Using UML. *In 1998 Proceedings International Enterprise Distributed Object Computing Workshop*, IEEE, 1998.
13. Kruchten, P.B. The 4+1 View Model of Architecture. *IEEE Software*, pp. 42-50, Nov. 1995.
14. Luckham, D.; Augustin, L.M.; Kenney, J.J.; Vera, J.; Bryan, D.; Mann, W. (1995) Specification and Analysis of System architecture using Rapide. *IEEE Trans on Software Eng.*
15. Magee, J.; Dulay, N.; Eisenbach, S. and Kramer, J. *Specifying Distributed Software Architectures. Proceedings of the 5th European Software Eng. Conf.*, 1995.
16. Medvidovic, N. and Rosenblum, S. Assessing the Suitability of a Standard Design Method for Modeling Software Architectures. *Proc. of the TC2 1st Working IFIP Conf. on Sw. Arch. (WICSA1),* 1999.
17. Medvidovic, N. and Taylor, R.N (1997), A Framework for Classifying and Comparing Architecture Description Languages. *In Proceedings of the 6th European Software Engineering Conference together with with FSE4* .
18. Medvidovic, N.; Oreizy, P.; Robbins, J.E. and Taylor, R.N. (1996), Using object-oriented typing to support architectural design in the C2 style. *Proceedings of ACM SIGSOFT'96: 4th Symp. on the Found. of Software Eng. (FSE4).*
19. Monroe, R.T.; Kompanek, A; Melton, R. and Garlan, D. Architectural Style, Design Patterns, and Objects. *IEEE Software*, January 1997.
20. Moriconi, M.; Qian, X.; and Riemenschneider, R. (1995), Correct Architecture Refinement. *IEEE Transactions on Software Engineering*, pp. 356-372 (April).
21. Object Management Group (OMG), Analysis and Design Platform Task Force. White Paper on the Profile mechanism Version 1.0. OMG Document ad/99-04-97, April 1999.
22. OMG. UML Profile for Performance, Scheduling and Time. OMG Document ad/99-93-13.
23. OMG. UML Profile for Corba. RFP. OMG Document ad/99-03-11.
24. Robbins, R.E.; Medvidovic, D.F.; Redmiles, D.F. and Rosenblum, D.S. Integrating Architecture Description Languages with a Standard Design Method. *In Proceedings of the 20th Intl. Conf. on Software Eng. (ICSE'98).*
25. Rational Software Corporation and IBM (1997), OCL specification. OMG document ad/97-8-08. Available from http://www.omg.org/docs/ad.
26. UML Semantics. OMG ad/97-08-04. http://www.omg.org/docs/ad/97-08-04.pdf .
27. UML Notation Guide. OMG ad/97-08-05. http://www.omg.org/docs/ad/97-08-05.pdf
28. Selic, B; Rumbaugh, J. Using UML for Modeling Complex Real-Time Systems. White Paper.
29. Shaw, M.; DeLine, R.; Klein, D.; Ross, T; Young, D.; and Zelesnik, G. Abstractions for Software Architecture and Tools to Support Them. *IEEE Trans. on Software Eng*, 1995.
30. Spitznagel, B and Garlan, D. Architecture-Based Performance Analysis. *Proceedings of the 10th Intl. Conf. on Software Eng. and Knowledge Eng. (SEKE'98)*, 1998

Towards a UML Profile for Software Architecture Descriptions

Mohamed Mancona Kandé and Alfred Strohmeier
Swiss Federal Institute of Technology Lausanne
Software Engineering Laboratory, CH-1015 Lausanne EPFL, Switzerland
{mohamed.kande, alfred.strohmeier}@epfl.ch

Abstract. To formally describe architectures of software systems, specific languages called Architecture Description Languages (ADLs) have been developed by academic institutions and research labs. However, more and more research and industrial projects are using the standard Unified Modeling Language (UML) for representing software architectures of systems. In this paper, we focus on how to extend the UML by incorporating some key abstractions found in current ADLs, such as connectors, components and configurations, and how the UML can be used for modeling architectural viewpoints. Our approach is demonstrated by the software architecture of a video surveillance system. It is therefore the purpose of the paper to show that a UML profile for software architecture abstractions is needed.
Keywords: Software architecture abstractions, software architecture description, architectural modeling, architectural viewpoint, architectural view, ADL, UML, connector, component, configuration.

1 Introduction

Because the number of organizations using software infrastructures to run their core business grows, society is becoming increasingly dependent on long-running and large software-intensive systems. To facilitate the development of such systems and support their evolution, we need tools for explicitly supporting formal representations of the software architecture of a system. This is one of the goals of research in software architecture [1,2]. A formal software architecture representation provides the ability to understand, communicate and reason about high-level properties of software-intensive systems from different perspectives or viewpoints.

Current notations for modeling software architectures are either formal, i.e., based on a special modeling language, called an Architecture Description Language (ADL), or they are just informal and ad hoc, e.g. the whiteboard approach. Because of their roots in formal methods, existing ADLs are generally hard to understand and do not integrate well with current software development practices. Moreover, existing ADLs often take into account only a single particular perspective, from which the architect has to model all key aspects of the software system.

In contrast, the standard Unified Modeling Language (UML) is a general tool that provides advanced techniques and notations supporting the full life cycle of system modeling, from requirements analysis to implementation. Furthermore, the UML supports multiple views. The UML concepts and constructs can therefore be divided into different subsets, corresponding to various aspects of the system [3,4,5]. However, as a general-purpose language, the UML does not directly provide constructs

A. Evans, S. Kent and B. Selic (Eds.): «UML» 2000, LNCS 1939, pp. 513-527, 2000.

related to software architecture modeling, such as architectural configurations, connectors, and styles. For instance, specifying a connector requires the definition of a concept that allows us to localize component interactions. Therefore, we need to separate communication concerns (e.g., patterns of object interactions) from computation concerns (e.g., objects). In UML, however, there is no direct support for such a separation of concerns. This point is further discussed in subsection 4.2.1. Moreover, a UML component diagram can be used to describe the organization of a software system in terms of its components and interconnections at specification level. However, when describing an architectural configuration (i.e., a collection of instances of component and connector types), it is unclear 1) how to instantiate component interfaces and dependency relationships; 2) how to associate interaction protocols with component dependencies.

Integrating the UML with some existing ADLs has already been addressed [14]. One approach is to define rules for translating architectural descriptions from a particular ADL into UML. Another approach is to add key constructs needed by software architecture modeling to the standard UML. However, using this second approach will result in a large and complex language, hard to understand and to use.

In this paper, we propose a third approach which is based on extending UML in a standard way, i.e., by using only standard extension mechanisms of the UML, resulting in a "Profile for Software Architecture Descriptions". It might be worth noting that several kinds of profiles are under consideration by the Object Management Group, e.g., the "Profile for Enterprise Distributed Object Computing".

This paper is organized as follows: section 2 briefly presents different trends in software architecture research. Section 3 gives some examples of what should be defined in a UML profile for software architecture descriptions. Section 4 presents some extensions to the UML for supporting the modeling of software architectures; and finally section 5 summarizes the paper and proposes some future work.

2 Software Architecture Trends

First of all, we have to admit that there is no standard definition of what is called software architecture and that there is no single, accepted framework for codifying architectural concepts. This lack of a standard does not facilitate the emergence of common practices in software architecture and their controlled evolution [13]. The diversity in the realm of software architecture stems from the variety of issues that reflect the concerns of the authors.

One community in software architecture research, following the academic trend, is driven by formality [1,7]. As stated by M. Shaw and D. Garlan, two pioneers in software architecture research, an ADL is necessary to have precise descriptions of software components and their interconnections [1], without giving any implementation details of the system to be constructed.

Work on ADLs has concentrated on improving analysis and system-generating capabilities of the languages [6,8,9]. Unfortunately, current ADLs do not integrate well with common software development methodologies and tools. Although the concept of multiple views is generally recognized as very important [18, 16], no single ADL provides a means for modeling multiple views and checking their completeness and coherence [17].

Another community, following the trend of industry, is driven by the applicability of software architecture methodologies and the notations used for their description [4]. It uses the UML for representing and documenting architectural designs. On one hand, using the standard UML for architectural modeling is a convenient way to integrate architectural designs with various other software design models. On the other hand, UML lacks adequate notations and the corresponding semantics for modeling key constructs found in most existing ADLs, such as components, connectors, configurations, and architectural styles. Also, in order to be able to capitalize on the effort spent in elaborating a software architecture description, e.g. by analyzing and verifying it, standard UML tools should provide more powerful analysis capabilities.

Despite the controversies about the definition of software architecture, we adopt in the remainder of this paper the definition given by L. Bass, P. Clemens and R. Kazman [2]: "The software architecture of a program or computing system is the structure or structures of the system, which comprise software components, the externally visible properties of those components, and the relationships among them".

3 What Is Needed to Define a UML Profile for Software Architecture Descriptions?

In order to define a profile for Software Architecture Descriptions in UML, one needs to identify the key concepts that are required for software architecture descriptions and understand how those concepts are related. In the following, we present an example that introduces the architecture of a simple Video Surveillance System and highlights some software architecture elements.

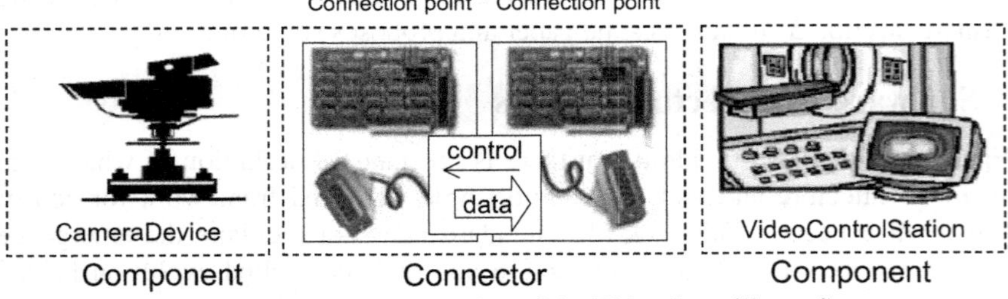

Figure 1: Architectural Illustration of the Video Surveillance System

Figure 1 shows a very informal representation of the architecture of the Video Surveillance System (VSS). VSS consists of a set of video cameras that interact with a control station over a communication platform. The example illustrates two kinds of software architecture constructs: the *components* of the system and their interconnection realized by a *connector*. The boxes are used as graphical symbols for both kinds of constructs. They visually encapsulate their realizations, i.e., the pictures contained in the boxes.

The CameraDevice component abstracts a set of geographically distributed video cameras, whereas the VideoControlStation component abstracts the part of the system that remotely controls the cameras and continuously receives the video streams.

The connector is an abstraction for the communication platform. It consists of two kinds of nested boxes that represent *connection points* and the *protocol of interactions* between these connection points, respectively. A connection point represents an interface to the connector a component can use. In order to be able to participate in a communication mediated by a connector, a component must implement this interface. The implementation might be in software or in hardware. For instance, in Figure 1, two circuit boards implement the interfaces with the camera device and the video control station.

The protocol of interaction describes the way communication between connection points is performed. The cable in Figure1 shows the hardware part and the control/data box shows the software part of the implementation of the protocol of interaction.

To distinguish between a software architecture, describing a family of similar systems, and one of its instantiations, i.e. an individual system architecture, we need the concept of *architectural configuration*. In our example, an architectural configuration is created by interconnecting specific instances of CameraDevice with a specific instance of a VideoControlStation.

In addition, many authors [1,2,8,9,10] have advocated the use of patterns in software architecture descriptions. For example, in configurations of the Video Surveillance System, the instances of VideoControlStation and CameraDevice will have to behave like "sink" or "client", and "source" or "server", respectively, when they consume and produce video streams, or provide and require services from each other. The software architecture of the Video Surveillance System is hence using the *architectural styles* known as client-server and pipe-and-filter styles [1,10].

All elements mentioned so far for describing software architectures are provided by current ADLs [6,8,9], but the resulting models do not integrate well with other artifacts resulting from the software development process. Because UML is a widely used notation in software development, the definition and use of a UML Profile for Software Architecture would yield software architecture models that integrate much better with other development artifacts. In addition to current ADLs, the UML Profile should also provide support for identifying and describing *architectural viewpoints* [13]. Unlike current ADLs, the UML Profile should be able to deal with various *architectural views*, a concept slightly different from a view as defined in standard UML.

All the architectural terms introduced above are explained in the next section.

4 UML Extensions for Modeling Architectures

The goal of this section is to present some extensions to the UML that define the software architecture abstractions introduced in the previous section. Therefore, we propose a notation and precise semantics for these abstractions, applying two mechanisms proposed by the OMG [12], which are referred to as "*lightweight extension mechanism*" and "*heavyweight extension mechanism*". A lightweight extension mechanism allows one to adapt the UML semantics without changing the UML metamodel. It is supported by the UML through the provision of built-in extension mechanisms known as Tagged Values, Stereotypes, and Constraints. In contrast, a heavyweight extension mechanism allows one to adapt the UML semantics by extending the standard metamodel.

In the following subsections, we make use of both extension mechanisms to propose a UML Profile for Software Architecture. A profile is "... a consistent definition context for elements such as, but not limited to, well formedness rules, tagged values, stereotypes, constraints, semantics expressed in natural language, extensions to the standard metamodel and transformation rules" [12].

First, we present our interpretation of the concepts of architectural viewpoints and architectural views proposed by the IEEE's Recommended Practice for Architectural Description (P1471) [13], then we apply a heavyweight extension mechanism for incorporating these concepts into the UML metamodel. Second, we use some lightweight extension mechanisms for specifying connectors, components, architectural patterns, and configurations of software architectures.

4.1 Architectural Viewpoints

The software architecture definition given in this paper, as well as the results of a large amount of research on ADLs, have been based on the assumption that software architecture is focussed on reasoning about structural issues at system-level [1,2,6,7,8,9]. We believe that focusing just on the structural issues does not cover all concerns of software architecture, since it is difficult or even impossible to cover all concerns of the stakeholders from just one perspective. Different stakeholders have different concerns relative to a system under development, and these concerns affect the system's operation as well as its architectural qualities such as scalability, persistence, security, reliability, distribution and performance.

Software architecture must address all the significant system-level properties or any desired combination of these properties that is of interest to any stakeholder. To achieve this, new mechanisms are needed to separate all architecturally important concerns. One way to separate architectural concerns is to describe software architecture from different perspectives or viewpoints. The concept of multiple viewpoints allows us to group different stakeholders' concerns into different sets of related kinds of concerns; each set represents a certain aspect of the system that can be "viewed" from a particular viewpoint. The notions of architectural views and viewpoints have been used in reference models such as the "4+1 View Model"[1] [16] and the ISO's Reference Model for Open Distributed Processing (RM-ODP) [19]. Both reference models have a limited fixed number of views and viewpoints and do not permit creating new ones. We believe that such a fixed number of views and viewpoints is not sufficient for covering all aspects of software architecture.

We use the terms architectural view and viewpoint as defined in the IEEE's P1471. According to the P1471, an architectural viewpoint is "a specification of the conventions for constructing and using a view. A viewpoint acts as a pattern or template from which to develop individual views by establishing the purposes and audience for a view and the techniques for its creation and analysis". In what follows, we propose an interpretation of this definition providing a UML-based conceptual frame-

[1] Rational Software Corporation is using the "4+1 View Model" as a reference model for their development methods, but it is not standardized.

work for architectural descriptions, which does not prescribe a limited number of architectural viewpoints and views. In this interpretation, an architectural viewpoint defines a particular perspective of a software architecture representation that allows the establishment of rules, notations and a main view by which one or more architectural views are created, depicted, analyzed and managed. In a viewpoint definition, the *rules* determine the manner in which the concerns of the architect[2] are represented in architectural views. These rules are expressed by means of notations that involve techniques for depicting architectural elements in a view, and they also describe the conventions that guide a projection of the main view onto particular views. The *notations* of a viewpoint describe the language elements that are needed for appropriately representing all the concerns of the software architect from the perspective defined by that viewpoint. The *main view* represents the primary focus of the architect from the particular perspective defined by that viewpoint. By convention, the name of the main view corresponds to the name of its viewpoint. Note that sometimes the model of the main view (most abstract model) can not be graphically described, e.g., a quality management viewpoint [21] will not have a corresponding model in the main view.

Using the main view as the most abstract architectural view to be referred to for projections allows one to structure the system from a particular angle, yet focus on specific concerns.

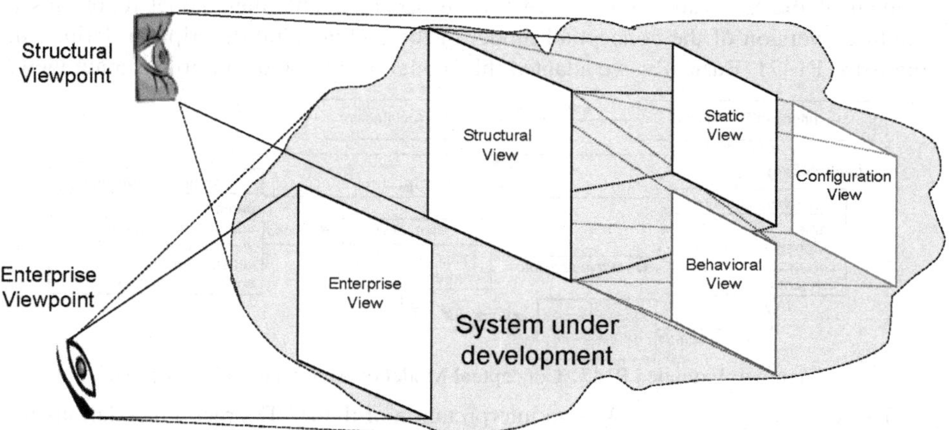

Figure 2: Example of the Relationship between Viewpoints and Views

Figure 2 presents an example of the relationship between architectural viewpoints and views. In this Figure, we distinguish between two architectural viewpoints, the structural viewpoint and enterprise viewpoint. Each of them represents an abstraction mechanism allowing the system under development to be "viewed" from a particular angle. Each viewpoint defines a main view illustrating the primary focus of the architect in that viewpoint. To describe distinct aspects of software architecture, the main view of a viewpoint needs to be projected onto different architectural views.

[2] In this UML-based conceptual framework, the concerns of the software architect from a specific viewpoint represent the concerns of the system's stakeholders involved in that viewpoint.

This is shown by projecting the main view of the system from the *structural viewpoint* onto the *static view*, *behavioral view* and *configuration view* (more details in section 4.2). Note that main views, e.g. the enterprise view and the structural view, might overlap, and the same holds for architectural views.

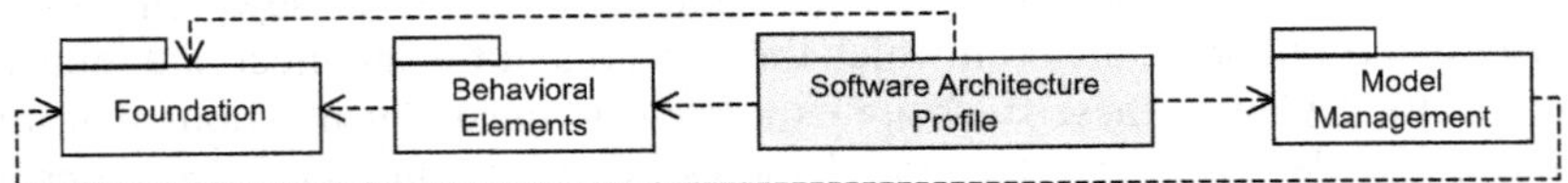

Figure 3: Dependencies between the Software Architecture Profile and the UML Metamodel

To specify the software architecture profile, we use a heavyweight extension mechanism by adapting the UML metamodel. Figure 3 illustrates the relationships between the software architecture profile and the standard metamodel of the UML. The software architecture profile is represented by a UML package that defines the elements for describing software architectures explicitly. The Software Architecture Profile package depends on the Behavioral Elements package because it needs to extend, for example, the UML notion of collaboration to define complex connectors. Its dependence on the Model Management package is justified by using, for example, the subsystem concept that is required to define the general notion of a component.

Figure 4 depicts a metamodel in terms of a UML class diagram that introduces the content of the Software Architecture Profile package. This metamodel represents a modified version of the conceptual model of the architectural description defined in the IEEE P1471. Basically, we adapted this model by adding the notion of main view.

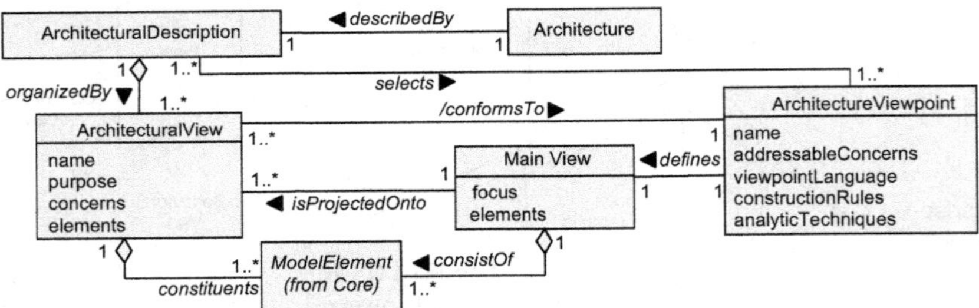

Figure 4: Extended P1471 Conceptual Model of Architectural Description

This conceptual framework is an interpretation of the IEEE's recommendations for software architecture descriptions within a UML-based context. UML provides already a general notion of view, and discusses possible connections between views, i.e., the consistency of the elements used in different views [4]. R. Hilliard and others have stated that there are problems related to the use of multiple views in the field of software architecture [20,17]. The connection between UML models that describe different views helps to solve some of these problems.

In this profile, the concepts of viewpoints and views are considered to be first-class citizens. We now present some examples of architectural viewpoints, showing how to describe the main view of a viewpoint in a concrete way. A typical example of an architectural viewpoint is the *structural viewpoint* that is addressed by almost every ADL. Other possibilities for architectural viewpoints are, e.g., *ODP viewpoints* [19], *requirements engineering viewpoint*, *quality management viewpoint* [21], etc.

Figure 5 shows the model of the structural view[3] for the Video Surveillance System. This model reflects the main focus of the software architect when considering the system from the structural perspective. In this example, the model of the structural view is presented in terms of components and connectors, and constraints on these components and connectors. Thus, the structural view consists of two component types, CameraDevice and VideoControlStation, which are interconnected by the connector, VSConnector. For brevity we omit the discussion of architectural constraints.

Figure 5: Model of the Structural View for the Video Surveillance System.

A component type is defined by the UML stereotype «archComponent». Such a component type, similar to that defined by Miller et al. [23], is a subsystem, which has the properties of both a UML Class and a UML Package.

The connector type is represented by a stereotype of Collaboration that contains a connector icon, shown by the black and white connected circles, in the upper right hand corner.

As this connector type serves as the description of numerous kinds of component interactions (as mentioned in section 3), the VSConnector is considered to be a higher-order (or complex) connector. The notations and semantics of connectors, including higher-order connectors, are described in subsection 4.2.1.

4.2 Architectural Views

An architectural view is an abstraction mechanism. It is a particular way of looking at an architectural description that illustrates some concerns of the software architect from a specific perspective and suppresses details of implementation, algorithm, and data representation. According to our conceptual framework, an architectural view represents a projection of the main view of a system from a particular viewpoint. Such a projection allows the software architect to concentrate on the description of the system, taking into account some of the stakeholders' concerns and ignoring others. The above definition of the notion of architectural view is compatible with the UML notion of view. However, the latter is more general and does not distinguish between different levels of abstraction. For example, the UML static view can, on one hand, describe a conceptual analysis class model, with a class representing a domain concept, and on the other hand describe an implementation class model, with a class representing code.

To give examples of architectural views, we will project the structural view of the Video Surveillance System. The result is three kinds of architectural views that describe the static structure, dynamic structure and configuration structure of the software architecture of the system.

---

[3] According to the naming convention, the *structural view* is the main view of the *structural viewpoint*.

4.2.1 Static View

To describe the static structure of the system, the software architect projects the structural view onto the static view. The elements in the model describing the static view are presented in terms of *component types* and *connector types* in the system, and constraints on these components and interconnections.

In this view, a component represents an encapsulation unit for data and computation, called a *computational component*. Its stereotype is represented by the keyword «computational». A *component type* encapsulates the static structure of a computational component. It is specified as a set of *interface elements* that together define the *component interface*. A computational component communicates with other components through its interface. Thus, each interface element defines a logical interaction point between the component and its environment.

The concept of computational component used in this paper is similar to "computational objects" defined by the RM-ODP [19]. However, the approach we propose for specifying this concept is principally based on the notion of "capsule" introduced by B. Selic and J. Rumbaugh [11]. Like a capsule class, a computational component type defines additional class compartments that are labeled with the keywords operational, signal and stream. These compartments are used for the declaration of the interface elements. The keywords operational, signal and stream indicate the kinds of interface elements that can be supported or required by a computational component. Semantically, an interface element type is not equivalent to a UML interface, as it can be instantiated at runtime (as in ROOM [22]).

Another alternative to represent a computational component consists in placing a computational icon (see icon on CameraDevice) in the upper right hand corner of the class name compartment. For the sake of clarity, we show both the stereotype and the icon on the elements in Figure 6.

The type of an interface element is either *operational*, *signal* or *stream*. An operational interface element type describes a set of operations that can be required or provided by a specific component, whereas a signal interface element type specifies a set of signals that can be sent or received by a specific component. A stream interface element type specifies a set of quality of services to be guaranteed by data flow connections, as well as a collection of streams that can be consumed or produced by a specific component.

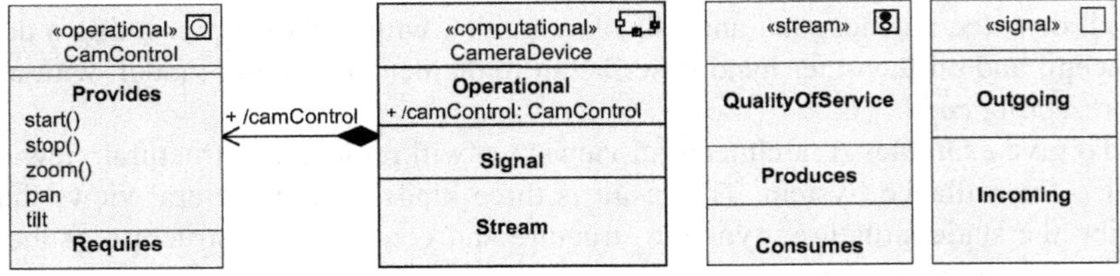

Figure 6: Static structure of the computational component type CameraDevice.

Figure 6 shows an example of the static structure of a computational component type, called CameraDevice. The interface of the CameraDevice is specified by the CamControl, which is an interface element of type «operational». Accordingly, the CameraDevice provides a set of operations (such as start, zoom, and stop) that allows the control station to remotely control a video camera implementing the CamControl. The composition relationship between CameraDevice and CamControl indicates that the interface element is an externally visible part of the component. The label (camControl) on the association end represents the public classifier role to be fulfilled by an instance of the CamControl, which is referred to as a port in the configuration view (see 4.2.3). The other two unnamed interface element types are not used in the example but show the graphical notations for stream and signal interface element types.

A *connector* is an abstraction that explicitly represents a locus of definition for component interconnections and communication responsibilities. A connector type defines a pattern of interactions between two or more components. Like a connector type, a Collaboration in UML describes a pattern of interaction among a set of participants, which are usually instances of classes or data types. The structure of a Collaboration is defined by a collection of roles, called *Classifier roles* and *Association roles*. A Classifier role is a slot that describes the role played by a participant in the Collaboration, whereas an Association role describes the connection between two Classifier roles within the Collaboration [4]. The description of Collaboration often depends on the participants (objects and/or classes). However, in software architecture, it is important to be able to specify a connector independently of any of the components that may use it to communicate. To enable connector modeling in UML, we propose a stereotype of a Collaboration that allows us to separate the specification of connectors from that of the components. We define therefore the stereotype «connector» that specializes the Collaboration concept by hiding Classifier roles and introducing the notion of *Connection role* and *Connection point*.

A connection role is a stereotype of an association role, a particular association, which describes the connection between two compatible connection points. A connection role extends an association role by defining some constraints (restrictions or semantic conditions) to be applied on the connection. These constraints should be fulfilled in any interaction mediated between the connection points. A connection role also allows one to describe a protocol of interactions, as shown in the behavioral view. A connection point is a concept that represents a connector interface. It is a kind of "association end role" that defines the participation of a component in a connector type. A connection point is specified in terms of messages or data flows that a participant component can exchange with others in interactions mediated by the connector.

The benefit of this approach is that 1) it allows one to specify simple connector types and higher-order connector types using the same notation; 2) a simple connector type can define some architectural styles implicitly; 3) a higher-order connector type can be specified as a composition of simple connector types.

The static structure of a simple connector type consists of two connection points and a connection role. A simple connector type can only mediate interactions between two components. For instance, one connection point could be seen as defining the participation of the client component, while the other defines the participation of the server component. In this case, a connector role defines the protocol of interactions between the client and the server and the constraints that are applied to both participants. The same reasoning could be used in the case of the pipe-and-filter style, with the difference that the connection role would define the properties of the pipe, whereas the connection points would represent the participation of the filter components.

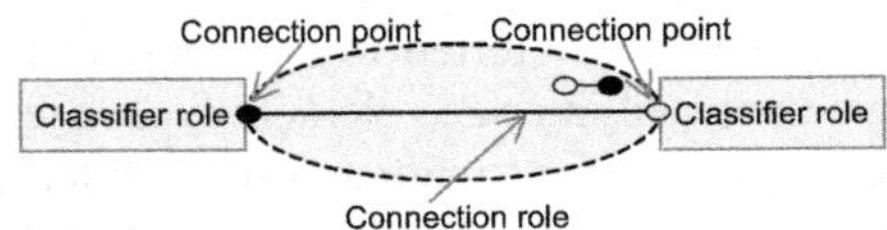

Figure 7: Static Structure of a Simple Connector type.

Figure 7 gives an overview of the static structure of a simple connector type. The white and the black circles are two connection points, conjugates of one another. We took the concept of "conjugated" elements from B. Selic et al. in [11] and [22]. Conjugated connection points are two connection points that are compatible but one is the inverse of the other.

A higher-level connector type is a composition of two or more simple connector types. Figure 8 presents an example of the static structure of a higher-order connector type, the VSConnector. The labeled white circles on the border of the collaboration symbol represent the simple connector types that are combined to define the specification of the higher-order connector. In other words, each white circle is a shorthand representation of two conjugated connection points and one connection role. Accordingly, the VSConnector is presented as a composition of the following five simple connector types: VirtualDevice, StreamController, StreamEndPoint, VideoStream and StreamEndPointSignaling.

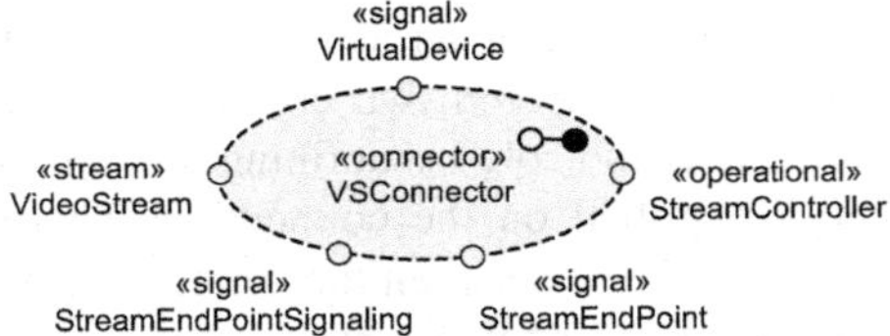

Figure 8: Static Structure of the VSConnector.

VirtualDevice defines all configuration related interactions that can take place between two compatible multimedia devices. It describes the sequence of alternating configuration signals that are exchanged between the interacting parties. StreamController mediates the interactions for initiating and finishing the negotiation procedure in point-to-point multimedia connections. It describes how to control and coordinate the connection activities that are particular to stream connections between multimedia devices. StreamEndPoint determines the interactions related to the control of individual flow endpoints composing a stream endpoint. It describes how to control and manage flow connections between multimedia devices. VideoStream defines a set of data flows, where each flow represents a continuous sequence of objects in a specific direction. It defines the continuous media transfer between components and describes the quality of service constraints that are related to it. StreamEndPointSignaling is needed to mediate a set of signals for the establishment and release of stream connections (in a non-sophisticated environment).

An elaborated description of these five simple connector types is shown in Figure 9. In this figure, the keyword "Connector" and the scope operator "::" preceding the name of the connection point type indicate that the connection point is defined within the scope of a connector. This allows one to differentiate between interface elements of components and connection points in connectors at the configuration level.

A connection point can be a signal, a stream or an operational connection point. The form of communication supported by a simple connector type corresponds to the type of its connection points. Similarly, the higher-order connector type supports all the kinds of communication that are supported by its constituents. In Figure 8, for instance, the form of communication supported by the simple connector type VirtualDevice is signal. This is indicated by the corresponding stereotype «signal». Thus, we can see that the higher-order connector type VSConnector supports the mediation of streams, signals and operations.

Like other constructs in the UML, the Object Constraint Language (OCL) can be used in the static view to define constraints on the components and connectors.

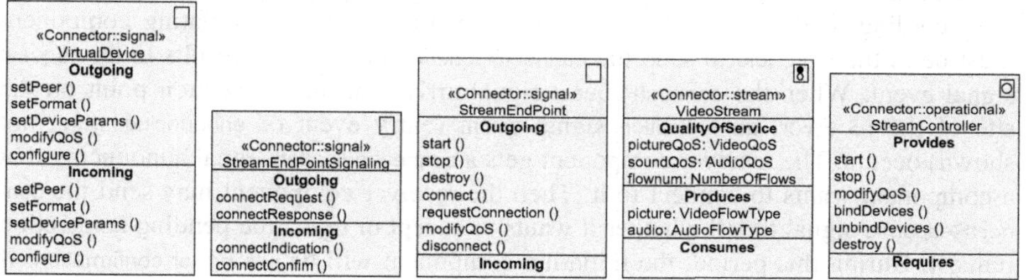

Figure 9: Elaborated Simple Connector types composing the VSConnector.

4.2.2 Behavioral View

The purpose of the behavioral view is to provide the part of the software architecture description that focuses on behavioral (or dynamic) properties of a system under development. To describe the behavioral structure of the system, the software architect makes a projection of the structural view onto the behavioral view. This projection allows the architect to separate the behavioral concerns of the system from all the others. The behavioral properties of the system are defined by the behavior of its computational *component types* and *connector types* and the constraints on the elements describing that behavior.

The behavioral structure of a computational component is defined by the specification of its interface protocol, the *component interface protocol (CIP)*. The component interface protocol describes the allowable sequence of data flows, call events and signal events that a given component may be engaged in. A component interface protocol can be modeled as a composite state machine that contains the entire set of the protocol state machines of all the interface elements. An approach that can be used to specify operational interface elements has been proposed in [15].

As for components, the behavioral structure of a connector is defined by using protocol state machines. To describe the behavior of a simple connector type, we specify the protocol of interactions of the connection role using a UML protocol state machine.

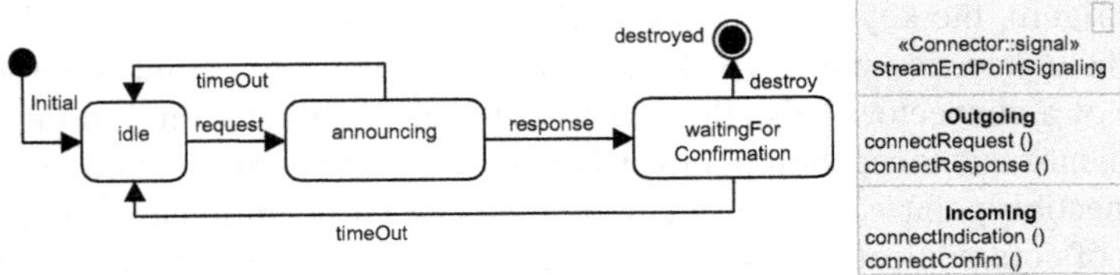

Figure 10: Representation of the StreamEndPointSignaling in the behavioral and static views.

In the case of a higher-order connector type, a composite state machine will be used that contains the protocol state machines of each of the simple connector types composing it. Figure 10 shows an example of a protocol state machine that describes the behavior of the simple connector type StreamEndPointSignaling. It describes the allowable sequences of signal events that are related to the establishment and release of stream connections between two communicating components.

According to the protocol that is shown in Figure 10, the initiating component must be in the state idle to send the connectRequest signal, which results in the request signal event. When the connectRequest signal arrives at the connection point on the site of the receiver, an indication signal event (entry event of announcing state, not shown) occurs. The receiver component gets a connectIndication signal announcing that a component wants to connect to it. Then the receiver component may send the connectResponse signal to tell whether it wants to accept or reject the pending connection request. During this period, the initiating component will be waiting for confirmation. If the connection request is accepted, the response signal event occurs at the connection point on the site of the initiating component. This results in the arrival of the connectConfirm signal at the interface of the component issuing the connection request. In both the announcing and waitingForConfirmation states, it is possible that the process restarts when the timeOut signal event occurs. In the waitingForConfirmation state, the connection is deleted when the destroy signal event occurs.

Figure 10 also illustrates that views can be interdependent, e.g., the state machine models the behavior of the StreamEndPointSignaling connection point.

4.2.3 Configuration View

The purpose of the configuration view is to offer a partial description of the software architecture of a system under development that focuses on a set of instances of the component and connector types defined in the previous architectural views. As in the other views, this projection allows the software architect to separate the configuration issues from all the other kinds of concerns. The elements that define the configuration structure are *instances* of computational component types and connector types, together with the constraints on these elements.

A simple configuration structure can be described by using only simple connectors and two components, whereas a complex configuration structure requires the instantiation of a higher-level connector type and several component types. Thus, the interconnection of components using a composition of many simple connectors may be used to define the configuration structure of a complex system. To get different configurations of the same architecture, a higher-order connector type is instantiated in different ways. In this case, some kind of configuration script may be needed for each particular configuration. The script defines which of the simple connector types of a higher-order connector type would be instantiated in a specific configuration.

The instance of a simple connector type has two categories of elements: *dynamic ports* and a *link* between these ports, where each (base) port has a corresponding conjugate (symbolized by a '~'). A dynamic port is an instance of a connection point that is dynamically created (as part of the connector type instance) and attached to a component. To attach a dynamic port to a component means that the component has to provide a realization of the connection point. The link between the ports represents an instance of the connection role defined by the connector type.

When a component type is instantiated, all of its interface element types are also instantiated. The instances of the interface element types are, in contrast to dynamic ports, called *static ports*. To differentiate dynamic ports from static ports, the stereotype of the connector type is prefixed with the keyword "Connector" («Connector::portname»), indicating that the port is an instance of a connection point.

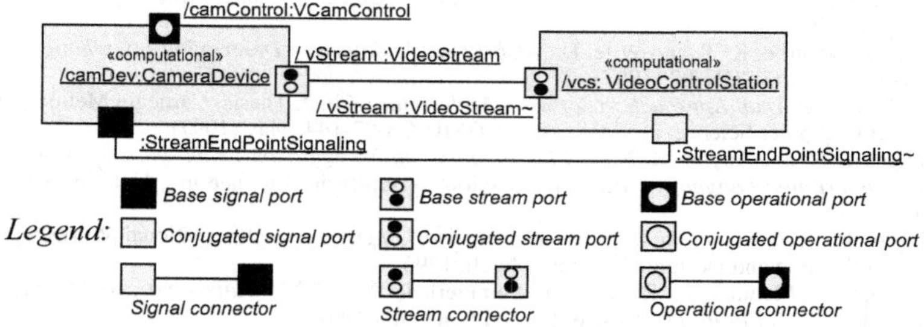

Figure 11: Simple Configuration of the Video Surveillance System

Figure 11 presents an example of configuration of the VSS that shows an instance of the VSConnector, CameraDevice and VideoControlStation. The stream port (black and white circles within a box) indicates that the stream communication is bi-directional.

According to the configuration script used for this example, the instantiation of the VSConnector shown contains only the simple connector type instances StreamEndPoint-Signaling and VideoStream.

5 Summary and Future Work

In this paper, we have argued for a UML profile for software architecture descriptions which extends the standard UML by incorporating some key constructs found in current ADLs. For this purpose, we focused on a set of software architecture concepts, such as viewpoints, views, connectors, components and configurations. We illustrated also how they can be combined to describe different views that may represent together the software architecture of a system in UML.

The resulting approach is an interpretation of the IEEE's Recommended Practice for Architectural Description (P1471). We demonstrated it on a video surveillance system, which in particular highlighted the ability to describe the combination of three different types of communication: signal, operational and streaming protocols.

Furthermore, we proposed an approach how to specify simple and complex connectors.

Though there are still many open issues, we hope that this paper is a first step in the right direction towards a UML profile for software architecture descriptions.

In future work, we will refine the proposed UML profile, apply it to other examples and address some issues related to the support of Multi-Dimensional Separation of Concerns (MDSOC) in software architecture. Also, we will investigate the usefulness of Aspect-Oriented Programming techniques for implementing higher-order connectors. Finally, we will explore different ways to describe configuration scripts, and define constraints between simple connectors composing a complex connector.

6 References

1. Shaw, M., Garlan, D.: *Software Architecture - Perspectives on an Emerging Discipline*. Prentice-Hall, New Jersey (1996).
2. Bass, L., Clements, P., Kazman, R.: *Software Architecture in Practice*. Addison-Wesley (1998).
3. Booch, G., et al.: *The Unified Modeling Language User Guide*. Addison-Wesley (1998).
4. Rumbaugh, J., et al.: *The Unified Modeling Language Reference Manual*. Addison-Wesley (1999).
5. *The Unified Modeling Language Specification*. Object Management Group (On-line at http://www.omg.org).
6. Garlan, D., Monroe, R. T. and Wile, D.: *ACME: An Architecture Description Interchange Language*. Proceedings of CASCON '97 (1997).
7. Allen, R. J.: *A Formal Approach to Software Architecture*. Ph.D. Thesis, Carnegie Mellon University, School of Computer Science, available as TR# CMU-CS-97-144, May (1997).
8. Medvidovic, N. and Taylor, R. N.: *A Classification and Comparison Framework for Software Architecture Description Languages*. IEEE Transactions on Software Engineering, Vol. 26, No.1, January 2000.
9. Clements, P.: *A Survey of Architecture Description Languages*. 8th International Workshop on Software Specification and Design, Germany, March, 1996.
10. Buschmann, F., Meunier, R., Rohnert, H., Sommerlad, P., Stal M.: *Pattern-Oriented Software Architecture –A System of Patterns* . John Wiley and Sons Ltd (1996).
11. Selic, B., Rumbaugh, J.: *Using UML for Modeling Complex Real-Time Systems*. ObjecTime, (1998).
12. Object Management Group: *Analysis and Design Platform Task Force White Paper on the Profile mechanism*. Version 1.0. OMG Document ad/99-04-07, URL: www.omg.org.
13. IEEE Architecture Working Group: *Draft Recommended Practice for Architectural Description* (Version 5). October (1999).
14. Robbins, J. E., et al.: *Integrating Architecture Description Languages with a Standard Design Method*. In Proc. of the 20th Intl. Conf. on Software Engineering (ICSE'98), pp. 209-218 (1998).
15. Sendall, S., Strohmeier, A.: *From Use Case to System Operation Specifications*. To be published in the UML'2000 Conf. Proc., Stuart Kent and Andy Evans (Ed.), LNCS (2000).
16. Kruchten, P. B: *The 4+1 view model of architecture*. IEEE Software, 12(6):42-50, (1995).
17. Le Métayer, D. and Périn M.: *Multiple Views in Software Architecture*. Position paper from the First Working IFIP Conference on Software Architecture WICSA1, San Antonio, (1999).
18. Perry, D. E. and Wolf, A. L.: *Foundations for the Study of Software Architecture*. ACM SIGSOFT Software Engineering Notes, 17:4 (October 1992).
19. ISO/IEC 10746-1/2/3. *Reference Model for Open Distributed Processing –Part 1: Overview/Part2: Foundations/Part3: Archictecture*. ISO/IEC (1995).
20. Hilliard R.: *Views and Viewpoints in Software Systems Architecture*. Position paper from the First Working IFIP Conference on Software Architecture WICSA1, San Antonio, (1999).
21. Sommerville et al. *Managing Process Inconsistency Using Viewpoints*. IEEE Transactions on Software Engineering, Vol. 25, No.6, November/December 1999.
22. Selic, B., Gullekson, G., Ward, P. T.: *Real-Time Object-Oriented Modeling*. Wiley, (1994).
23. Miller, J., Wirfs-Brock, R.: *How Can a Subsystem Be Both a Package and a Classfier?* 2nd International Conference UML '99, The Unified Modeling Language: Beyond the Standard, USA, 1999.

Rewrite Rules and Operational Semantics for Model Checking UML Statecharts

Gihwon Kwon

Department of Computer Science, Kyonggi University
Suwon-si, Kyonggi-do, Korea
khkwon@kuic.kyonggi.ac.kr

Abstract. Model checking of UML statecharts is the main concern of this paper. To model check it, however, its description has to be translated into the input language of the model checker SMV. For the purpose of translating UML statecharts as closely as possible into SMV, we use rewrite rules and its operational semantics.

1 Introduction

Model checking is well known and most widely used techniques in industry for formal verification on hardware systems in the last two decades [1]. There has been also a growing tendency to apply model checking techniques to formal verification of software systems such as specifications [2], source codes[3], and embedded software [4]. In this paper, model checking statecharts is the main concern under the conviction that model checking techniques has a great potential of formal verification on statecharts. We choose SMV [5] as the target model checker for the following reasons. First, SMV deals well with both synchronous systems and asynchronous ones. Additionally, it covers a wide spectrum of systems from abstract systems to concrete ones as well as from deterministic systems to non-deterministic ones. Finally, it can handle large state spaces up to 10^{100} states using symbolic model checking techniques with the help of BDD representations.

To model check statecharts, however, a description has to be translated into the SMV input language. The aim of this paper is to describe how statecharts can be translated as closely as possible into the SMV input language to allow for branching time temporal logic model checking of statecharts. The translation presented here is based on conditional term rewriting systems. Major components of statecharts are active states and transition labels. In our translation, a set of active states is encoded as a *term* and transition labels as *conditional rewrite rules*. A term rewrites to another one if conditions hold and there exists a match between a term and rewrite rules. Because term rewriting closely corresponds to state transitions of statecharts as well as transition relations on Kripke structures, it can be served as a bridge to connect them. The translation was guided by the operational semantics of conditional term

A. Evans, S. Kent and B. Selic (Eds.): «UML» 2000, LNCS 1939, pp. 528-540, 2000.

rewriting systems and it covers advanced constructs such as history states and conflict resolutions, etc.

In our translation, however, hierarchical structures of statecharts is not respected with the following reasons. First, interlevel transitions which violates the clean structure of hierarchy just as goto statements in programming languages are widely used in statecharts; not rarely used. Additionally, the scope rule of state names is global. For instance, it can be referenced in anywhere with the construct `in(s)`, which determines whether the state `s` is active or not. Finally, we have to resolve conflicts between enabling transitions, in case conflicts are occurs. However, conflict resolutions need a global analysis because transitions are often in conflict with another located at a distance. However, there are some research on exploiting hierarchical structures to reduce the state explosion problems [6,7]. It seems to us there will be strong debates on hierarchical model checking statecharts.

The present paper is organized as follows: in Section 2 related works on model checking Harel's statecharts and UML statecharts are given. in Section 3 preliminaries such term, rewrite rules and rewriting relation are introduced. And its operational semantics is given in Section 4. The translation of statecharts to SMV is described in Section 5. Finally conclusion is given in Section 6.

2 Previous Works on Model Checking Statecharts

Harel's statecharts have become a successful specification method for describing dynamic aspects of object behaviors [8]. This success is mainly due to the fact that statecharts form a highly expressive language because they extend traditional state transition diagrams with a rich set of notions such as hierarchy and parallelism. Therefore research community has paid much attention to formal verification of statecharts. Summary of previous works on model checking Harel's statecharts is given in Table 1.

Table 1. Related works on model checking Harel's statecharts

Author	Model checker	Formalism	Input	Hierarchy
Day, 1993 [9]	Voss	Higher-order logic	Subset	No
Mikk, 1998 [10]	SPIN	Hierarchical automata	Subset	No
Damm, 1998 [11]	SIEMENS AG	Asynchronous transition diagram	Full	No
Heinle, 2000 [12]	SMV	Extended temporal logic	Subset	Yes

These efforts make formal verification of statecharts real [13]. As a result related tools will be available in the near future within commercial CASE tools.

Compared to Harel's statecharts, however, there was not much research on model checking UML statecharts. Table 2 gives a list of related works done recently. Latella [14] and Gnesi [15] represent UML statecharts as extended hierarchical automata [17]

for easy translation. But they deal with only basic subset of UML statecharts. On the other hand, Lilius [16] represents UML statehcrats as rewrite rules in. His works is closed to ours, but there was no mention of how to translate it into the input language of the model checker. These motivate us to study on this topic.

Table 2. Related works on model checking UML statecharts

Author	Model checker	Formalism	Input	Hierarchy
Latella, 1999 [14]	SPIN	Hierachical automata	Subset	No
Gnesi, 1999 [15]	JACK	Hierachical automata	Subset	No
Lilius, 1999 [16]	SPIN	Rewrite rules	Full	No

3 Preliminaries

Normalization: Statecharts allow for hierarchical decomposition in the sense that every state may contain whole statecharts. Such an inner chart is referred to as a sub-chart. Whereas *or*-states may have at most one chart, *and*-states have at least two charts. All charts of an *and*-state are supposed to operate in parallel, so all of them are simultaneously active as long as that *and*-state is active. An *and*-state just can be treated as a collection of independent *or*-states, each of which contains a nonempty chart. This idea leads to some normalization, one can assume that charts are always contained in an *or*-state. Even toplevel state may be included in a single chart. We extend that normalization to all statecharts. As a result, we get normalized statecharts with the following properties:

Every chart has a name,
Every state should belong to a chart.

The main reason why we take normalized statecharts as an input is that it makes the term pattern regular which will be explained in the following.

Terms: According to the UML specifications [18] a configuration is defined as a maximal set of states that are currently active. In this paper, a configuration is encoded as a term from the fact that states can be regarded as a function which take subcharts as its arguments, if any [16]. Therefore *and*-state is an *n*-ary function because it takes *n* subcharts as its children. On the other hands, *or*-state is a unary function because it takes only a subchart. Every chart is regarded as a unary function because its type is the *or*-type. Since basic state does not take any subcharts, it is regarded as a nullary function so called *constant*. Definition of a term is as follows:

Individual variables are terms,
Individual constants are terms,
For an *n*-ary funtion symbol f and terms $t_1,\ldots,t_n$, $f(t_1,\ldots,t_n)$ is a term.

As described in the previous section, normalized statecharts makes the term pattern regular such that a chart is always followed by a state and a term starts with a chart and end with a state. We found this term pattern useful when we formalize statecharts.

Every chart has a default transition label which is enabled in the same step the chart is active. The function *default*: $_c$ $_s$ takes a chart and returns a target state of a default transition label in that chart, where $_c$ and $_s$ is a set of charts and a set of states, respectively. State hierarchies is encoded as a refinement function : $_c$ **P**($_c$) which makes a chart is decomposed into a set of subcharts. Let * and $^+$ denote reflexive transitive closure and transitive closure of , respectively. At the start time, there are some active states and charts. The function *initial*: $_c$ T takes a chart and returns an initial term that denotes which charts and states are active at initial time. Its definitions

initial(*c*) =
  if (*default*(*c*))=
  then *c*(*default*(*c*))
  else if (*default*(*c*))={c_1,…,c_n}
    then *c*(*default*(*c*) (*initial*(c_1),…,*initial*(c_n)))
  end

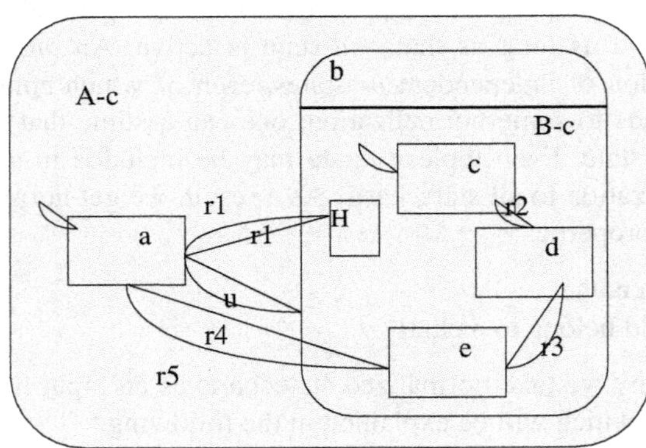

Fig.1. An example of statecharts

Rewrite rules: A transition label consists of 5-tuple (*src*, *evt*, *con*, *act*, *tgt*), where *src* is a source state, *evt* the trigger event, *con* the condition, *act* the action, *tgt* the target state. Transitions are enabled under the following conditions come to be true: *src* belongs to the current configuration, *evt* happens, and *con* holds. Enabled transitions are finally executed if conflicts does not occur. As consequences of executing transitions, the action *act* is performed and the target state *tgt* belongs to the next configuration while the source state *src* does not active in the next configuration any longer. This paper encodes transition labels as conditional rewrite rules {*trg*} *lhs* *rhs* {*act*}, where *trg* = *evt* *con* is a boolean expression, *lhs* and *rhs* is a term built from *src* and *tgt*, respectively. And *act* is an action. Two parts, *trg* and *lhs*, of the rewrite rule is responsible for the enabling transition: if the trigger *trg* evaluates to true and the left hand side *lhs* evaluates to true with respect to the current configuration, then it is enabled. For example, there are some rewrite rules from Fig.1

r_2: [] $B\text{-}c(c)$ $B\text{-}c(d)$ {}
r_3: [] $B\text{-}c(d)$ $B\text{-}c(e)$ {}
r_4: [u] $A\text{-}c(b(B\text{-}c(X))$ $A\text{-}c(a)$ {}
r_5: [] $A\text{-}c(b(B\text{-}c(e))$ $A\text{-}c(a)$ {}

Labels such as r_2 is only used for the sake of conveniences for referencing rewrite rules.

Rewriting relations: Consider the rewriting sequence t_0 … t_i t_j …, where $j=i+1$ and j is the next step of i. We use the subscripts 0, i and j denote *initial*, *current*, and *next*, respectively. Statecharts always starts from an initial configuration t_0 (Appendix gives the algorithm how to get t_0). And then the current term t_i is changed to the next term t_j whenever rewrite rules are executed. Terms t_i and t_j has a rewriting relation, in symbols, t_i t_j iff a term t_i rewrites to t_j. Let $t_i[u]$ denote a term t_i which contains an occurrence of the subterm u and $t_i[u/v]$ the term t_i where the subterm occurrence u has been replaced by v. A term t_i rewrites to t_j iff there exists a rewrite rule {*trg*} *lhs* *rhs* {*act*} and a substitution such that $u=lhs$ and condition c holds and $t_j = t_i[u/(rhs\ )]$.

We define three rules for rewriting relations. First, the *subterm rewrite rule* is applied only to the subterm u when there exists a rewrite rule to be matched with u. When it is applied to u, there is a subterm rewriting u rhs . On the other hand, statecharts allows parallel decomposition in the sense that several components can be executed without interfering with each other. So there is the possibility of being enabled several rewrite rules lhs_1 rhs_1,…, lhs_n rhs_n to match with subterms u_1,…,u_n. In this case, we apply the subterm rewrite rule to each subterms: u_1 $(rhs_1\ _1)$,…,u_n $(rhs_n\ _n)$. We get the next configuration by composing each subterm rewritings: $t_j = t_i[u_1/(rhs_1\ _1),\ldots, u_n/(rhs_n\ _n)]$. For this reason it is referred to as the *whole term rewrite rule*. In addition, there is another possibility that no rules are enabled. In this case, the *stuttering* rule $t_j = t_i$ is applied, which means there is no change [10].

4 Operational Semantics

A behavior of statecharts is defined as a set of runs which is a sequence of status. A *status* consists of three components:

Configuration,
Event queue,
Data values.

To keep the point simple, we rule out detailed language constructs provided in UML statecharts. Instead, we will concentrate on states which are represented with a map data structures [19]. In the following, we describe a gentle introduction to a map structure and its operations before going any further steps.

Map: A mapping from type A to a type B is an association of some objects of type A to some objects of tpye B, and can be thought of as a finite set of ordered pairs of the form $\{a \quad b\}$ which is called a *maplet*, with the restriction that no two pairs in a mapping have the same first component. If a mapping, m, contains the maplet $x \quad y$, then it is said that 'm maps x to y'. The following symbols are used in the rest of the paper:

{} denotes the empty map,
$m(a)$ denotes the object to which a is mapped by the map m. Undefined if a is not in the domain of m
dom m denotes the set of elements to which the map m can be applied,
rng m denotes the set containing the second component of all the maplet in m,
$S - m$ denotes the domain restriction of m by a set S,
$m_1 + m_2$ denotes the map m_1 overwrites by the map m_2.

Structures: The Kripke structure is chosen as semantics for conditional term rewriting. It consists of three components (M, m_0,). First, $M = \quad \cdot$ is a states spaces of Kripke structure, where

: $_c$ $_s$ is a map from a chart to its state.
: **seq**($_e$) is an event queue consisted of a sequence of events, where $_e$ is a set of events.

The elements of M are also called *status* which are formed simply by enclosing the components in brackets ($_i$, $_i$). And $m_0 \quad M$ is the initial status, where $m_0 = (\ _0, \ _0)$. And $M \cdot M$ is the step relation of Kripke structures. When the enabling conditions hold, a maximal non-conflicting set of rewrite rules may be executed which constitutes a transition in Kripke structures. We refer to it as a step which will be explained later.

We need a function to get a meaning given a term which denote a syntactical object. The function $||t||$: $T \quad \{c \quad s \mid c \quad _c$ and $s \quad _s\}$ takes a term and returns a set of maplet $c \quad s$ which means a chart c takes a state s, where T is a set of terms. Its inductive definition:

$||c(X)|| = \{sc \quad (sc) \mid sc \quad ^*(c)\}$

$||c(s)|| = \{c \quad s\}$

$||c(s(u_1,\ldots,u_n))|| = ||u_1|| \quad \ldots \quad ||u_n|| \quad ||c(s)||$

where X is a variable and u_i a subterm. If a chart c contains a variable X, then we get all subchart configurations under the chart c.

Semantics for enabling rewrite rules: A rewrite rule is enabled if and only if the trigger *trg* evaluates to true and the *lhs* to true with respect to the current status. To keep it as simple as possible, we will focus on states and events. *trg* evaluates to true if the following condition holds:

$(\ _i, \ _i) \mid$ []	iff	a tautology
$(\ _i, \ _i) \mid$ `[e]`	iff	`e = dequeue(` $_i$`)`
$(\ _i, \ _i) \mid$ **`en(s)`**	iff	$c \quad _{i-1}(c) \quad$ `s` $\quad _i(c) =$ `s`
$(\ _i, \ _i) \mid$ **`ex(s)`**	iff	$c \quad _{i-1}(c) =$ `s` $\quad _{i-1}(c) \quad$ `s`
$(\ _i, \ _i) \mid$ **`in(s)`**	iff	$c \quad _i(c) =$ `s`

where `e` $\quad _e$ and `s` $\quad _s$ denotes a event variable and a state variable, respectively. And `dequeue(` $_i$`)` fetches the last entered event from $\ _i$. The *lhs* of a rewrite rule evaluates true if and only if every chart of *lhs* belongs to the current state map:

$(\ _i, \ _i) \mid \ lhs$ iff c **dom** $\|lhs\| \quad \|lhs\|(c) = \ _i(c)$

Rewrite rules are enabled if and only if both the *trg* and the *lhs* evaluates to true with respect to the current status:

$(\ _i, \ _i) \mid \{trg\}\ lhs \quad rhs\ \{act\} \quad R$ iff $\quad (\ _i, \ _i) \mid \ trg \quad (\ _i, \ _i) \mid \ lhs$

where R is a set of rewrite rules.

Step relation: When the triggers occur and the conditions hold, a maximal non-conflicting set of rewrite rules may be executed which constitutes a step transition in Kripke structures. In our semantics, a step can be defined with composing of several micro steps such as:

$t_i \quad t_{j1} \quad \ldots \quad t_{in} \quad t_{jn}$

$t_i \quad t_j$

Consider the step sequence $(\ _0, \ _0) \quad \ldots \quad (\ _i, \ _i) \quad (\ _j, \ _j) \quad \ldots$ which starts from the initial status $(\ _0, \ _0)$. In the beginning, there are no active events. So the initial status is $(\|t_0\|$, nil).

A step is defined in terms of three rules: *subterm*, *whole term*, and *stuttering*. The *subterm* rewrite rule applies to the subterm u when there is a term rewriting $u \quad rhs$. Its meaning is defined as follows:

$$\frac{(\ _i, \ _i) \mid [trg]\, lhs \quad rhs\ \{\}}{(\text{dom} \| lhs \|, \| rhs \|, \text{nil})}$$

$$\frac{(\ _i, \ _i) \mid [trg]\, lhs \quad rhs\ \{/e\}}{(\text{dom} \| lhs \|, \| rhs \|, < e >)}$$

Suppose there is a term $t_i[u_1,\ldots,u_n]$ and there are rewrite rules $lhs_1 \quad rhs_1, \ldots, lhs_n \quad rhs_n$ to match with subterms $u_1,\ldots,u_n$. After the *subterm* rule is applied to $u_1,\ldots,u_n$ of the t_i, we get n subtrem rewriting relations $u_1 \quad (rhs_1 \ _1),\ldots,u_n \quad (rhs_n \ _n)$. As the result of composing them, we get the next configuration $t_j = t_i[u_1/(rhs_1 \ _1),\ldots, u_n/(rhs_n \ _n)]$. Its meaning of a *whole term* rewriting is defined:

$$\frac{\dfrac{(\ _i,\ _i) \mid [trg_1]lhs_1 \quad rhs_1\,\{act_1\}}{(a_{j1}, b_{j1}, c_{j1})} \qquad \dfrac{(\ _i,\ _i) \mid [trg_n]lhs_n \quad rhs_n\,\{act_n\}}{(a_{jn}, b_{jn}, c_{jn})}}{(\ _i, <e>^{\wedge}\ _i) \quad ((a_{j1} \quad a_{jn}) - \ _i + b_{j1} + \quad + b_{jn}, <c_{j1}> \quad <c_{jn}> \quad _i)}$$

where ^ denotes a sequence concatenation. Finally, the meaning of the *stuttering* rule applied if and only if there is no rewrite rules matched to a subterm u:

$$\frac{\leftarrow ((\ _i, <e>^{\wedge}\ _i) \mid [trg]lhs \quad rhs\,\{act\} \quad R)}{(\ _i, <e>^{\wedge}\ _i) \quad (\ _i,\ _i)}$$

Whereas congisuration is not changed, event has just consumed.

5 Translation of Statechart to SMV

Charts: Let c be a chart containing a set of states $\{s_1,\ldots,s_n\}$. A chart must be in one and one of these states at any given time because its type is *or*. The states of each chart are modeled with an enumeration-type like construction. For every chart $c \quad _c$, the following code is inserted into the translated SMV program

```
VAR
  c:{s1,...,sn};
```

Activation of charts: Let s be a state of the chart c and $sc_1,\ldots,sc_n$ immediate subcharts of the state s. On the same time when the control of c reaches s, its subcharts $sc_1,\ldots,sc_n$ becomes active. On the contrary, $sc_1,\ldots,sc_n$ is not active any longer on the same time when c leaves s. It goes without saying that the topchart say tc is always active. Subchart activity is defined by the formula:

$active(tc) = true$

$active(sc_1) = active(c) \quad c = s$

...

$active(sc_n) = active(c) \quad c = s$

We get the following SMV conditions:

```
DEFINE
  tc-active:= 1;
  sc1-active:= c-active & c=s;
  ...
  scn-active:= c-active & c=s;
```

Initializations: According to the semantics, statecharts starts with a initial status ($_0$,nil). Suppose $_0 = \{c_1 \quad s_1,\ldots,c_n \quad s_n\}$. Then we get the following condition for initialization.

```
INIT
 c1=s1 & ... & cn=sn
INIT
 eq[1]=nil & . .. & eq[m]=nil
```

Enabling rewrite rules: According to the semantics, rewrite rules are enabled if and only if the trigger *trg* evaluates to true and the *lhs* to true with respect to the current status. In general, enabling rewrite rule *r* is defined by the following formula

lhs *trg* *r*

But with respect to the efficiency we consider only the innermost part of a term. The function *innermost* takes a left-hand side *lhs* of rewrite rules and returns a set of predicates for the innermost part. Its definitions:

innermost(*c*(*X*)) = {*c-active*}
innermost(*c*(*s*)) = {*c-active* & *c* = *s*}
innermost(*c*(*s*(u_1,…,u_n))) = *innermost*(u_1) & … & *innermost*(u_n)

Suppose *innermost*(*lhs*)={ec_1,…,ec_n}. Then we get the following SMV code for enabling rewrite rules:

```
DEFINE
 r:= ec1 & □ & ecn & trg
```

Term rewriting: When a rewrite rule *r*: *lhs* *rhs* *R* is executed, the set of charts and states affected by *r* is ||*rhs*||. We collect all charts and states affected by rewrite rules by the generalized union.

$$= \bigcup_{i=1}^{n} \{(r: c \quad s) \mid r \quad R, c \quad s \quad \|rhs_i\|\}$$

SMV does not allow multiple assignments to a variable. To avoid this problem, we can order the set with respect to a chart. As a result, we get

' = {(*c*, *r*: *s*)}

Suppose ' = {(c_1, r_1:s_1), (c_1, r_2:s_2), … , (c_1, r_n:s_n), … }. Then we get the following SMV conditions for state transitions for a chart c_1:

```
ASSIGN
 next(c1):= case
  r1 : s1;
  r2 : s2;
  ...
  rn : sn;
  1  : c1;
 esac;
```

On the other hand, there is a case that a chart has a only one state but it served as a default state. In this case, no transition labels goes out from this state. It only keeps a default state when it is active. So the following code is inserted into the translated SMV program:

```
ASSIGN
 next(Top-c):= case
  Top-c-active : Top-c;
  1            : Top-c;
 esac;
```

History states: A history state allows a chart to remember the last state that was active in it prior to the transition from it. In our translation, we introduce a variable say *HB* for each chart containing a history state to indicate whether or not the chart was visited last time. For example, we consider two cases for the transition label r_1 in Fig.1. whether or not it has a history. Modified rewrite rules are:

r_{11}: $[HB = 0]\ A\text{-}c(a) \quad A\text{-}c(b(B\text{-}c(c)))\ \{\}$
r_{12}: $[HB \quad 0]\ A\text{-}c(a) \quad A\text{-}c(b(B\text{-}c(B\text{-}c)))\ \{\}$
r_4: $[u]\ A\text{-}c(b(B\text{-}c(X)) \quad A\text{-}c(a)\ \{HB = 1\}$
r_5: $[]\ A\text{-}c(b(B\text{-}c(e)) \quad A\text{-}c(a)\ \{HB = 1\}$

For transitions r_4 and r_5, we have to set the flag for *HB* before leaving the chart. Fragments of the translated SMV code:

```
VAR
 HB: boolean;
INIT
 HB = 0
DEFINE
 r11:= A-c=a & !HB;
 r12:= A-c=a & HB;
ASSIGN
next(B-c):=
 case
  r11 : c;
  r12 : B-c;
 esac;
```

Definitely the target state of transition label r_1 is dependent upon the variable *HB*. If it has a history then its target states is the last state active. Otherwise its target state is a default state. There is one action related to the history state: **hc! (***c***)**, which means first enter the chart *c* and clear its history. Suppose *HB* is the history state for *c*. The formal semantics of the history clear action is:

$$\frac{(\ _i,\ _i)\mid\ [trg]\,lhs \quad rhs\,\{/\mathrm{hc!}(c)\}}{HB = 0}$$

Conflicts resolution: There are two kinds of conflicts in Fig 1. For the one case, r_2 is in conflict with r_4 and r_3 in conflict with r_4, because they both exit the same state. As for the other case, r_4 is in conflict with r_5. The former can be resolved by **priority**, and the latter resolved by **nondeterminism** according to the UML specifications [18]. To determine conflicts we need to have a function *exit*(*lhs*) = **P**($_s$) take a left hand side of a rule and returns a set of exit states:

$exit(lhs) = \mathbf{rng}\ \|lhs\|$

So two rewrite rules are in conflict with each other if and only if the intersection of the set of states they exit is non-empty:

$conflict(r_1,r_2) = (exit(r_1) \quad exit(r_2) \quad\quad)$

The function $topchart(lhs) = \quad_c$ takes a left hand side of rewrite rules and returns a topchart. We can order two rules with respect to the top chart of rewrite rules with the help of *. Two rules can be ordered if there is a reflective transitive relation between them. So r_1 has a priority over r_2:

$r_1 \frown r_2$ if and only if $^*(topchart(r_1)) = topchart(r_2)$

In case the ordering exists between them, we can resolve conflicts in terms of **priority**. If r_1 has a priority over r_2, then r_2 is only enabled as long as r_1 is disabled. This derives the following formula:

$conflict(r_1,r_2) \quad r_1 \frown r_2 \quad\quad \leftarrow r_1 \quad r_2$

This formula is reflected in the following SMV condition:

```
DEFINE
 cr2:= !r1 & r2;
```

where *cr* stands for conflict-free rewrite rule.

On the other hand, there is a case that there is no ordering between conflicting rewrite rules. Suppose there are *n* conflict transitions $r_1,\ldots,r_n$.

$r_i,r_j \quad \{r_1,\ldots,r_n\} \quad r_i \;/\; r_j \quad r_i \not\frown r_j$

In this case conflicts are solved by **nondeterminism** which takes an active transition nondeterministically and the others are disabled. We get the following formula.

$(r_1 \quad \leftarrow r_2 \quad \ldots \quad \leftarrow r_n)$

$(\leftarrow r_1 \quad r_2 \quad \ldots \quad \leftarrow r_n)$

...

$(\leftarrow r_1 \quad \leftarrow r_2 \; \ldots \quad r_n)$

Only one of them is executed, and the others are not enabled. In SMV, we the auxiliary variable *nd* whose range 1 to *n* to choose a rewrite rule nondeterminitically.

```
VAR
 nd: 1..n;
DEFINE
 cr1:=(r1 & !r2 &□& !rn)|(r1 &□& rn & nd=1)
 cr2:=(!r1 & r2 &□& !rn)|(r1 &□& rn & nd=2)
 ...
 crn:=(!r1 & !r2 &□& rn)|(r1 &□& rn & nd=n)
```

The following fragments show how to deal with conflicts by nondeterminism in our approach.

```
VAR
 nd: boolean;
DEFINE
 cr4:= (r4 & !r5) | (r4 & r5 & nd=0);
 cr5:= (!r4 & r5) | (r4 & r5 & nd=1);
```

Either r_4 or r_5 is chosen, but not both. In most CASE tools, nondeterminism is implemented by making user select one from conflicting transitions. This is not truly nondeterminism.

6 Conclusions

Recently some works [14,15,16] on model checking UML statecharts has done under the conviction that model checking techniques has a great potential of formal verification on statecharts. For allowing linear time model checking of UML ststecharts, Latella [14] encoded statecharts as extended hierarchical automata which was proposed by Mikk [17]. Gnesi [15] also transformed statecharts to extended hierarchical automata for branching time model checking. However, they only deal with basic constructs of UML statecharts. Lilius [16] has proposed for linear time model checking of UML statecharts. He encoded statecharts in terms of rewrite rules. But our works is different from his works with respect to the following points: First, we considered the normalized statecharts as an input. Additionally, we give a operational semantics to rewrite rules. Finally, we describe the translation of statecharts to SMV

In summary, we described the translation of UML statecharts to the SMV input language for allowing branching time model checking based on rewrite rules.

References

1. J.R. Burch, E.M. Clarke, D.E. Long, K.L. McMillan, D.L. Dill, "Symbolic Model Checking for Sequential Circuit Verification," IEEE Trans. on Computer-Aided Design of Integrated Circuits and Systems, Vol.13, No.4, pp.401-424, 1994.
2. W. Chan, R.J. Anderson, P. Beame, S. Burns, F. Modugno, D. Notkin, J. D. Reese, "Model checking large software specifications," IEEE Trans. on Software Engineering, Vol.24, No.7, pp.498-520, 1998.
3. K. Havelund, T. Pressburger, "Model Checking Java Programs Using Java PathFinder," To appear in International Journal on Software Tools for Technology Transfer, available at http://ase.arc.nasa.gov/havelund.
4. J. Staunstrup, et. al., "Practical Verification of Embedded Software," IEEE Computer, Vol. 33, No. 5, 2000
5. K.L. McMillan, "Symbolic Model Checking: An approach to the state explosion problem," PhD thesis, Department of Computer Science, Carnegie Mellon University, 1992.
6. R. Alur and M. Yannakakis, "Model checking of hierarchical state machines," Proceedings of ACM Symposium on the Foundations of Software Engineering, pp.175-188, 1998
7. G. Behrmann, et. al., "Verification of hierarchical state/event systems using reusability and compositionality," Proceedings of TACAS/ETAPS'99, LNCS 1579, pp.163-177, 1999
8. D. Harel, A. Naamad, "The STATEMATE semantics of statecharts," ACM Trans. on Software Engineering and Methodology, Vol.5, No.4, pp.293-333, 1996.
9. N. Day, "A Model Checker for Statecharts," Master thesis, Department of Computer Science, University of British Columbia, 1993

10. E. Mikk, Y. Lakhnech, M. Siegel, G.J. Holzmann, "Implementing Statecharts in Promela/SPIN," Proceedings of the IEEE Workshop on Industrial-Strength Formal Specification Techniques, 1999
11. W. Damm, B. Josko, H. Hungar, and A. Pnueli, "A compositional real-time semantics of STATEMATE designs," Proceedings of COMPOS'97, LNCS 1536, pp. 186-238, 1998
12. W. Heinle, E. Clarke, "STP: translation of statecharts to SMV," in preparation, 2000
13. T. Bienmueller, W. Damm, and H. Wittke, The STATEMATE Verification Environment - Making it real," Proceedings of CAV'00, LNCS 1855, 2000
14. D. Latella, I. Majzik and M. Massink, "Towards a formal operational semantics of UML statechart diagrams," The 3rd International Conference on Formal Methods for Open Object-Oriented Distributed Systems, Kluwer Academic Publishers, 1999.
15. S. Gnesi, D. Latella, M. Massink, "Model checking UML satetchart diagrams using JACK," Proceedings of the IEEE International Symposium on High Assurance Systems Engineering, 1999.
16. J. Lilius and I.P. Paltor, "The Semantics of UML State Machines," Proceedings of <<UML>>'99 – The Unified Modeling Language, Lecture Notes in Computer Science 1723, 1999.
17. E. Mikk, Y. Lakhnech, M. Siegel, "Hierarchical automata as model for statecharts," Proceedings of Asian Computing Science Conference ASIAN'97, Lecture Notes in Computer Science 1345, 1997
18. OMG Unified Modeling Language Specification, Version 1.3, June 1999, available at http://www.rational.com/uml/resources/documentation/index.jtmpl
19. C.B. Jones, Systematic Software Development Using VDM, Prentice-Hall, 1986

Part-Whole Statecharts for the Explicit Representation of Compound Behaviours

Luca Pazzi

University of Modena and Reggio Emilia
via Campi 213/B
I-41100 Modena, Italy
pazzi@unimo.it

Abstract. Although very effective, the adoption of Statecharts in object-oriented software development methods poses many problems, since their way to compose behavioral abstractions can be framed in the general context of implicit composition. In particular, the need to embed references from one behavioral description to other ones has mayor drawbacks since the description of a single entity behaviour is not self-contained, and the global behaviour results implicitly defined by following references from one entity to the other. In other words, both single and global behaviors are difficult to understand, modify and reuse. The paper proposes to overcome most of such problems by adopting Part-Whole Statecharts, whose primary policy for controlling complexity strictly enforces distinct layers for wholes and their parts. Since wholes may become parts of other aggregations, a recursive syntax and semantics can be given straightforwardly.

1 Introduction

The object-oriented programming paradigm ignores (among other things) the *distinction* between two broad kinds of relational knowledge.

- *part-to-part relationships* that link entities to entities in an arbitrary way;
- *part-to-whole relationships* that bind part entities to whole entities and induce decreasing complexity between the related entities.

Consequently, most object-oriented development methodologies (e.g., *Object Modelling Technique* methodology OMT [13]) and database conceptual models (e.g., Kim's *composite objects* [9]) adopted special notations and semantics to distinguish part-of associations, aimed at enforcing (vertical) constraints of exclusiveness and lifetime dependence between the whole and its parts.

An even more elusive conceptual problem relates to the acknowledgement of a *correlation* between part-to-part (horizontal) relationships and part-to-whole (vertical) relationships. A whole can be indeed defined as a complex aggregate entity, whose *component parts* are bound both together by part-to-part (horizontal) relationships and to the whole by (vertical) part-of relationships. Further, a whole presents *emergent features* [14] and *coordinate behaviour* among the parts.

A. Evans, S. Kent and B. Selic (Eds.): ≪UML≫ 2000, LNCS 1939, pp. 541–555, 2000.

Depending on whether or not a correlation among associative and part-of knowledge is acknowledged within a modelling paradigm, two approaches are feasible when modelling the structure of a whole:

Explicit approach The *structure* of a *whole* is modeled through an *object type* of the modelling paradigm which contains part-of relationships to the component objects and encapsulates (horizontal) relationships of dependence among them.

Implicit approach The *structure* of a *whole* is realized through a web of references by which the relationships of dependence among the component objects are modeled. In this way, *associative knowledge* between component objects is modeled *directly*, without resorting to a specific *object type* of the modelling paradigm.

At the conceptual level, missing wholes has major drawbacks on the overall quality of software design. Explicit modelling policy allows to *reuse* object types for the parts and the whole, as well as to *extend* and to *understand* the whole without having to onsider many scattered objects. The Smalltalk-like object-oriented programming paradigm [4] is strongly committed towards implicit modelling due to its imperative flavour and the lack of a specific construct for modelling associative knowledge as a whole. Inter-object horizontal knowledge (like dynamic dependencies and relationships) is thus modelled directly by implementation-level constructs (like message passing and references). Such a naive tendency tends to be corrected by most of the object-oriented methodologies. Rumbaugh argued in such sense for an extended object-oriented model called *object-relationship* model [12], where *the explicit modelling of relationships is aimed at preserving conceptual information concerning aggregation that may get lost in the implementation phase.* Following such guidelines, OMT [13] recognizes that *associations* (i.e., part-to-part relationships, by the OMT jargon) may have properties and that association types may be attached to associations. A similar approach was subsequently followed, among others, by Fusion [3], Syntropy [1] and, finally, is part of the OMT heritage in the *Unified Modeling Language* (UML) [5]. Besides, UML aims at supporting directly the concept of *whole* by a bunch of higher-level development concepts such as collaborations, frameworks, patterns, and subsystems. However, despite the abundancy of whole-related concepts, UML is not fully committed to the explicit modelling approach since it lacks constructs for specifying behaviour of aggregations of objects as explicit wholes. For example, the dynamics of subsystems, as defined by collaborations and specified by state machines, has to resort to an implicit specification of the whole behaviour, as discussed in the rest of the paper. Moreover, introducing wholes into the UML requires to revise part of the current methodology in order to achieve *structural continuity* [2], that is the ability to link behavioral and structural information as a whole, from analysis through the following phases of the design.

In this paper we propose to adopt Part-Whole Statecharts [11], a modelling construct for the *explicit* representation of compound behaviors. Traditional

Statecharts [6][7] were adopted by OMT [13] to specify allowable sequences of changes to object classes, due to the great capability of Statecharts to tame the complexity of the domain. It is only with Syntropy [1] that another level of encapsulation is introduced, by hosting the behaviour of object types into special states, called *states of existence*, which embed an entity's behaviour. Statecharts can be thus used, straightforwardly, to *compose* the states of existence of (component) entities into the state of existence of a (compound) entity. However, as discussed in the next Section, this way of composing behaviors is *implicit* composition. For example, it is not possible to refer to the state of an aggregation (subsystem) as a whole, rather it is necessary to refer to the single states of the single state machines which describe the behaviour of the components.

The main objective of Part-Whole Statecharts is to *shift* the implicit semantics of composition through mutual references to an explicit semantics of composition representing the behaviour of the composition as a whole. The semantics is directly enforced by the specification of a "higher level" state machine whose events and states correspond, respectively, to sequences of events and tuples of states taken from the component state machines.

This paper is organized as follows: in Section 2 we present the traditional approach to Statecharts composition and, at the same time, we introduce the compound state machines (labelled transition systems) which are behaviorally-equivalent to AND composed Statecharts, discussing the ways by which the semantics of compositionality is enforced. Section 3 presents the Part-Whole Statecharts graphical formalism, together with a formal syntax and semantics. Additional formal definitions are reported in appendix A.

2 From Statecharts to Compound State Machines

The adoption of state-based formalisms in Software Engineering Methods allowed to specify the behaviour of complex systems in a way that is, at the same time, clear, realistic, formal and rigorous [8]. A clear notion of the system being modelled can be, in fact, given by the complementary static and dynamic information represented by *states* as ÒsnapshotÓ of the situation at a given point in time, and by *events* labelling the transitions among the different states, that is the changes among the different situations. In the rest of the paper we adopt labelled transition systems as a model of finite state automata:

Definition 1. *A labelled transition system (lts) is a four-tuple* $\langle Q, E, q_0, T\rangle$, *where* Q *is a set of states,* E *is an alphabet of events,* $q_0 \in Q$ *is the initial state and* $T \subseteq Q \times E \times Q$ *is the transition relation. We write* $p \overset{e}{\rightsquigarrow} q$ *for* $(p, e, q) \in T$.

State transitions can, additionally, specify both a pre-condition C and a post-condition A directly in the diagram notation. If $(r, e, s) \in T$ is a transition, then labelling $e[C]/A$ the arc linking state r to s means that, once the event e is detected and the system is in state r, then, if the (guard) pre-condition C holds then the system moves to state s and the (action) post-condition A holds after the transition.

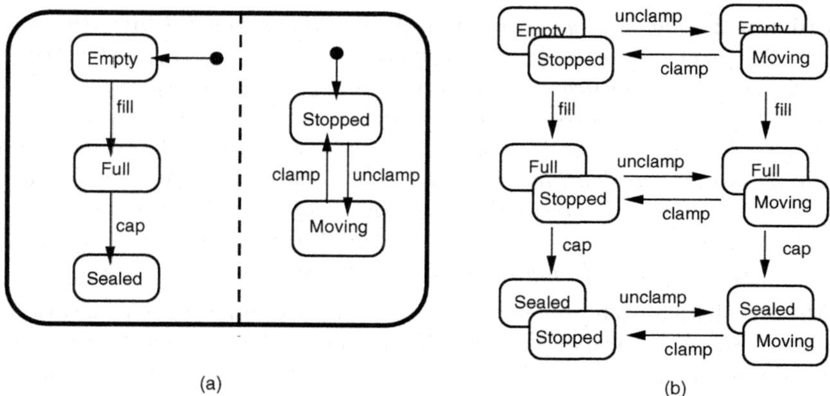

Fig. 1. The state of a bottle in a bottling plant (a) is given by the two parallel substates separated by the dotted line which is equivalent (b) to a cartesian product automaton.

2.1 The State Explosion Problem and Its (Partial) Solution

The problem with state based representation is that, as either the dimension of the problem or the level of detail increases, state transition diagrams become exponentially unmanageable. If we have n different entities each having an average number of states k, then we have to deal with a potential number of states of the order of k^n (state explosion problem).

Statecharts provide a solution by two basic state decomposition mechanisms: the *parallel* (AND) mechanism, by which a system entering an AND decomposed state is, *at the same time*, in all of its substates, and the *nested state* (XOR) mechanism, by which a system entering an XOR decomposed state is *exactly* in one of its substates. This allows to *factorize* huge state machine diagrams in terms of concurrent, smaller ones, thus reducing the number of states to kn.

Observe the example of Figure 1 (a), adapted from [1], which depicts the joint behaviour of a *bottle* and a *vacuum operated clamp* in a bottling plant. An instance of this Statechart is, at all times, in one state of the state machine on the left (the bottle) and in one state of the state machine on the right (the clamp). We hypothesize an asynchronous model of joint behaviour, that is we allow the Statechart to take either a state transition from the left *or* a a state transition from the right, but not to take both simultaneously. In other words, Statechart semantics is given by the compound state machine depicted in Figure 1 (b).

The general model of asynchronous composition of $m \geq 1$ labelled transition systems, where each component takes *exactly one* of its basic transitions at each step, is called the *cartesian product* of labelled transition systems. Compound states and labels of the resulting compound labelled transition system are given, respectively, by the cartesian product of the set of states and by the tagged union of the set of labels of the components. The transition relation of the cartesian product of labelled transition system is finally given by the *union* of the transition relations of the component automata.

Definition 2. *The m-ary* cartesian product *of the m labelled transition systems $\mathcal{L}_1, \ldots, \mathcal{L}_m$ given the m-tuple of identifiers $I =_{def} (n_1, \ldots, n_m)$, denoted $(\mathcal{L}_1 \otimes \cdots \otimes \mathcal{L}_m)_I$, is the labelled transition system $\mathcal{L}_u = \langle \bar{Q}, E_u, \mathbf{q}_0, T_u \rangle$ where $\bar{Q} = Q_1 \times \cdots \times Q_m$ is the cartesian product of the set of states of the components, $E_u = \bigcup_{i=1}^{m} E_i \times \{n_i\}$ is the the tagged union of the component alphabets of labels (where n_i is the i-th identifier in I), and $\mathbf{q}_0 = (q_{01}, \ldots, q_{0m})$ is the intial state. Finally the transition relation $T_u \subseteq \bar{Q} \times E_u \times \bar{Q}$ is in turn defined by letting, for any state $\mathbf{p} = (p_1, \ldots, p_i, \ldots, p_m) \in \bar{Q}$ and any* tagged *event $(e, n_i) \in E_u$, $(\mathbf{p}, (e, n_i), \mathbf{q}) \in T_u$ if and only if $(p_i, e, q_i) \in T_i$, with $\mathbf{q} = (q_1, \ldots, q_i, \ldots, q_m)$.*

More realistically, however, we need to express some synchronisation constraints among the parallel parts making up a complex behaviour. For example, a logical requirement is that the bottle has to be clamped before being filled and sealed. In other words, it can not be filled or sealed when moving.

Synchronisation between the different parts of an AND-decomposed state may be achieved in different ways. One way is through preconditions on state transitions, in the literature referred to as *mutual condition testing*. For example, in Figure 2 (a), the guard predicate in(Stopped) in both the fill and cap state transitions requires the bottle to be stopped (that is to be in the Stopped state) in order to be filled and sealed. This achieves the result to cross out two state transitions on the cartesian product automaton as shown in Figure 2 (b).

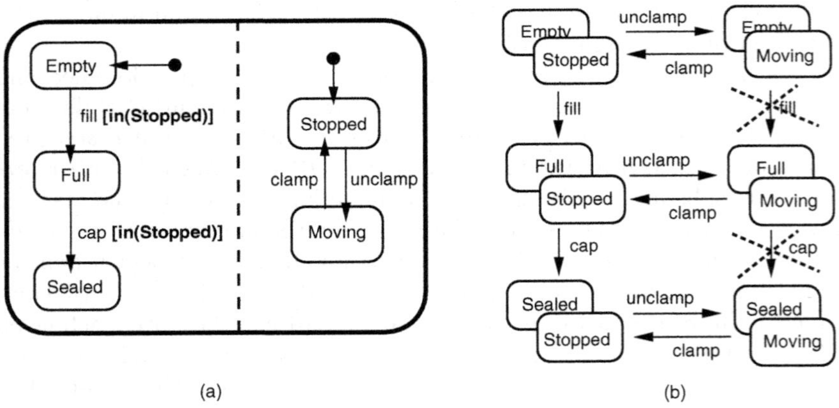

Fig. 2. We have to clamp the bottle before filling and sealing it!

Another way of specifying an additional behavioral semantics among the concurrent parts consists in grouping together different state transitions through the *event broadcast* mechanism. When the action part of the transition contains the name of an event, this is immediately broadcast towards the parallel parts of the Statechart and is regarded as the occurrence of a new event. Such a new event occurence may trigger additional state transitions, which, on their turn, may propagate other events, and so on in a *chain reaction* fashion. Suppose that the bottle of the example is filled with a poisonous liquid, so that it is necessary to release the filled bottle immediately in order to seal it as soon as possible. We may specify that the action unclamp has to follow the event fill by specifying the former in the action part of the state transition labelled by fill. Figure 3 shows how the addition of an action clause to the fill transition on the left part of the Statechart (a) achieves the effect of grouping two transitions on the cartesian automaton (b).

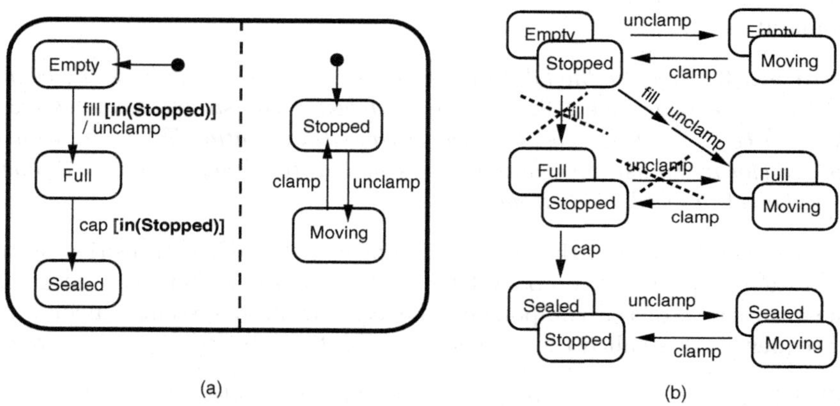

Fig. 3. Danger! The liquid is toxic: seal the bottle as soon as possible!

In order to build a suitable semantics domain for Statecharts, we have therefore to take into account the whole set of state transition sequences that may be expressed within a composition. We start by defining the set of sequences (words) that can be originated from an alphabet of events and the operation of concatenation among its elements.

Definition 3. *Let E be an alphabet of labels. The set of (not empty) finite sequences (words) over E is defined as $E^+ = \{\langle e_1 e_2 \dots e_m \rangle \mid m > 0, \forall i \in 1 \dots m : e_i \in E\}$. Let $\Lambda = \langle\rangle$ denote the* empty *sequence (word). We additionally define $E^0 = \{\Lambda\}$, $E^1 = \{\langle e \rangle \mid e \in E\}$ and $E^* = E^0 \cup E^+$.*

Definition 4. *Let $w = \langle e_1 e_2 \dots e_m \rangle$ and $w' = \langle e'_1 e'_2 \dots e'_n \rangle$ be finite event sequences of length m and n respectively. The* concatenation *ww' of the two sequences is the sequence $\langle e_1 e_2 \dots e_m e'_1 e'_2 \dots e'_n \rangle$ of length $m + n$. We have moreover that $w\Lambda = \Lambda w = w$ for all $w \in E^*$, that is Λ is the idempotent element for concatenation.*

The subsequent (and crucial) step consists in defining a transition relation whose labels are words of labels taken from a given transition relation.

Definition 5. *Let the transition relation $T \subseteq Q \times E \times Q$ be associated with the labelled transition system $\mathcal{L} = \langle Q, E, q_0, T \rangle$. We define $T^1 \subseteq Q \times E^1 \times Q$ such* *that* $(p, \langle e \rangle, q) \in T^1$ *iff* $(p, e, q) \in T$. *We define* $T^* \subseteq Q \times E^* \times Q$ *be the* transitive reflexive transition relation *correspondent to* T *such that*

1. *For all* $q \in Q$ *we have that* (q, Λ, q) *is in* T^*.
2. $T^1 \subseteq T^*$;
3. *If* (p, e, q) *and* (q, f, r) *are in* T^*, *then* (p, ef, r) *is in* T^*, *where* ef *is the concatenation of the label sequences* e *and* f.

It is useful to have a * (star) operator to build transitive reflexive closure automata:

Definition 6. *Suppose the labelled transition system* $\mathcal{L} = \langle Q, E, q_0, T \rangle$ *be given. We define the* transitive reflexive closure *labelled transition system associated with* $\mathcal{L}$ *to be* $\mathcal{L}^* = \langle Q, E^*, q_0, T^* \rangle$ *whose transition relation* T^* *is the transitive reflexive closure transition relation correspondent to* T *and whose event alphabet* E^* *is the set of words built from* E.

The general model of the composition of $m \geq 1$ labelled transition systems, where each step of the compound labelled transition system is a *sequence* of basic transitions of the component labelled transition systems (including the null sequence Λ) is called the *sequence produuct* of labelled transition systems.

Definition 7. *The* m*-ary sequence composition of* m *labelled transition systems* $\mathcal{L}_1 \ldots \mathcal{L}_m$ *given the* m*-tuple of identifiers* $I = \{n_1, \ldots, n_m\}$, *denoted* $(\mathcal{L}_1 \oplus \cdots \oplus \mathcal{L}_m)_I$ *is built by first taking the cartesian product* $\mathcal{L}_u = (\mathcal{L}_1 \otimes \cdots \otimes \mathcal{L}_m)_I$ *of the component labelled transition systems, and then taking its transitive reflexive closure* $\mathcal{L}_u^*$.

2.2 The Quest for Modularity

Statecharts reduce the complexity of traditional state diagrams by both state decomposition and broadcast mechanisms. As observed in the introduction, the Statecharts XOR decomposition mechanism can be used to host state machines representing the behaviour of *object types* within special states, called *states of existence* [1]. It is clear that an object is, at each time, in *one and only one* of its basic states. Moreover, in order to localise an object's behaviour, it seems natural not to have state transitions that cross such a boundary.

A further step towards modularization consists in adopting the AND (decomposition) mechanism for aggregating the behaviour of object types into more complex behaviors. Consider the AND composition of the behaviors of a nozzle and a bottle in the bottling plant. Such a *pouring process* may be viewed as the synchronization of two entities and as such represented by the complex behaviour of Figure 4. Achieving synchronization through the direct communication of events requires to specify context-exogenous details within parallel subsystems and clearly means looking ahead to the composition of the whole system. Consider for example the case of Figure 4. Synchronyzed behaviour is achieved by both broadcasting events and mutual testing of conditions from

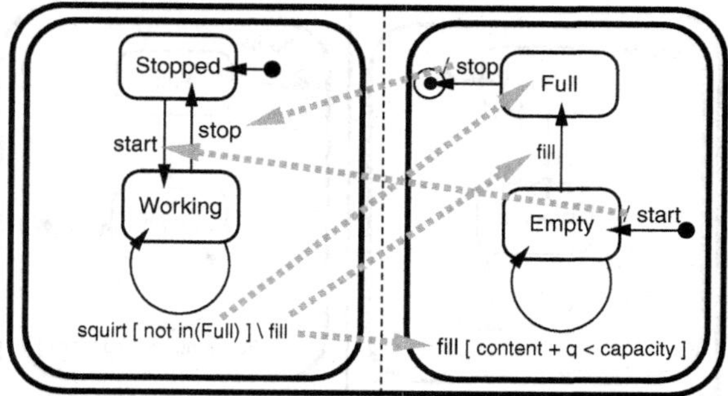

Fig. 4. The AND composition of the two statecharts represents the compound behaviour of a nozzle filling a bottle. The grey arrows emphasize the *horizontal* mutual dependencies which enforce synchronization but hamper reusability (observe that the component state machines are *not* self-contained)

Nozzle to Bottle subsystem and vice versa (see the grey arrows in the picture). Nozzle Statechart does not represent the behaviour of a standalone nozzle, rather the behaviour of a "nozzle which squirts into a bottle". The same can be observed for bottle behaviour. It "opens" the nozzle when it is empty and "closes" it when full. In the next Section we present a state-based formalism which allows to compose the essential behaviour of the entities and therefore overcomes such difficulties.

3 Part-Whole Statecharts

Part-Whole Statecharts (referred to as either PW Statecharts or PWS in the rest of the paper) are a state-based formalism designed with the objective to avoid implicit binding of behavioral abstractions. By forbidding direct event communication, the modeler is forced towards high-level modelling of synchronization aspects by defining a suitable state machine in the whole section. Observe the PW Statechart of Figure 5, where the line separating parallel parts is no longer a *dashed* line, but rather is drawn as *solid* in order to suggest graphically that no direct communication is allowed between the concurrent parts. Instead a dashed line separates concurrent parts from the *whole* section, suggesting that components are allowed to communicate with the whole-section automaton. This achieves two complementary results:

1. Parts are cleared from mutual synchronization details, thus allowing a *black-box*, context-independent, reuse of component Statecharts.
2. The whole semantics of aggregation is gathered within the whole-section automaton, which explicitly represents the behavioral composition by:
   - *explicit states* which are mapped to the compound states belonging to the cartesian product of the set of states of the component state machines.

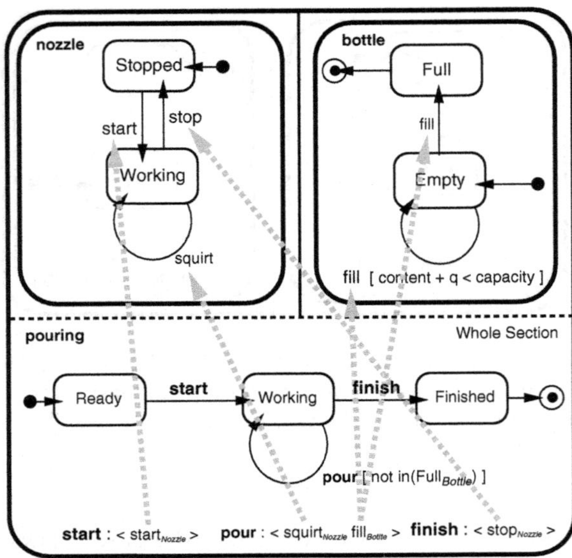

Fig. 5. Explicit composition of the two Statecharts of Figure 4. The grey arrows emphasize the *vertical* dependencies which enforce synchronization without hampering reusability (observe that the component state machines are now self-contained). The last row shows the way events of the whole sections map to event sequences drawn from the component event alphabets. The quantity of liquid squirted each time by the nozzle is represented by q.

- *explicit state transitions* labelled by high-level events, which are mapped to event sequences drawn from the basic alphabets of the component state machines.

By prohibiting any communication and mutual knowledge among the different parts, *self-containment* and *encapsulation* are enforced, since the parts ignore each other, thus allowing their reuse in different contexts. Moreover, the whole section provides an additional context for reuse and extendibility, with obvious advantages in terms of software quality factors. A behavioral layer constituted by the alphabet of high-level events is also provided, which represents the only interface needed in order to deal with the interacting entities as a whole, thus achieving additional benefits in terms of overall *information hiding*. The intuitive semantics may be thus thought of as propagating events *to* and *from* the component state machines and the whole-section state machine (observe, however, that in this paper we do not propose any event propagation model).

3.1 Syntax

A formal syntax can be given (as in [10] for traditional Statecharts) by considering PW Statecharts as elements of an inductively-defined algebra P of terms. A

PWS term is a tree, whose leaves have the form $s = [n : (), W]$ and the generic nodes have the form $s = [n : (s_1, \ldots, s_k), W, \phi]$, where $n \in \mathcal{N}$ is an identifier, $s_1, \ldots, s_k$ are PWS terms and $W = \langle Q, E, q_0, T \rangle$ is a labelled transition system as in Definition 1. The behavioral relationships among the different levels of the tree are essentially encoded by the mapping $\phi : Q \times E \rightarrow \mathsf{E}^*$, where $\mathsf{E} = \bigcup_{i=1}^{k} E_i \times \{n_i\}$ is the *tagged* union set of the alphabets of events of the component terms, with E_i and n_i being, respectively, the alphabet of events and the identifier of the i-th component s_i. We write more compactly $\mathbf{e} : \langle e_1 e_2 \ldots e_m \rangle$ instead of $\phi(p, e) = \langle e_1 e_2 \ldots e_m \rangle$ when we label an outgoing state transition from a state p. Moreover, we write e_{n_i} for the tagged event (e, n_i). In other word, an event e belonging to a root node s is univokely associated to a sequence of events drawn from the transitive reflexive closure of the tagged union of the alphabets of events of its *child* terms. For example, let $n_1 = \mathit{nozzle}$ and $n_2 = \mathit{bottle}$ be the child terms of the compound PWS *pouring* of Figure 5. We have that $E_1 = \{\mathit{start}, \mathit{stop}, \mathit{squirt}\}$ and $E_2 = \{\mathit{fill}\}$. We build then the tagged union set $\mathsf{E} = \{\mathit{start}_{\mathit{nozzle}}, \mathit{stop}_{\mathit{nozzle}}, \mathit{squirt}_{\mathit{nozzle}}, \mathit{fill}_{\mathit{bottle}}\}$ of events, which is the basic set by which event sequences will be built. Such a mapping can be depicted in the state diagram as suggested by Figure 5. Finally let the function $\mathsf{name} : P \rightarrow \mathcal{N}$ be defined by $\mathsf{name}([n : (s_1, \ldots, s_k), W, \phi]) = n$ and $\mathsf{name}([n : (), W]) = n$, denote the identifier of a PWS term. We require finally that, for every term $s = [n : (s_1, \ldots, s_k), W]$, for $i = 1 \ldots k$, $\mathsf{name}(s_i) \neq n$: in that case the term is said to be *well-formed* if $s_1, \ldots, s_k$ are also well-formed terms (leaf terms are trivially well-formed).

3.2 Semantics

As shown by way of example in Section 2.1, giving a semantics to a parallel composition of labelled transition systems means *restricting* – i.e. taking a suitable subautomaton of – the labelled transition system containing the complete set of compound behaviors of the component Statecharts. In the case of Part-Whole Statecharts such a *complete* automaton has a nested structure reflecting the syntactic structure of the term. We call it the *full* labelled transition system $\mathsf{lts}(s)$ associated to a term s of P, defined inductively along the structure of the term s as follows:

1. $\mathsf{lts}([n : (), W]) = W^1$
2. $\mathsf{lts}([n : (s_1, \ldots, s_k), W, \phi]) = (\mathsf{lts}(s_1) \oplus \cdots \oplus \mathsf{lts}(s_k))_{(\mathsf{name}(s_1), \ldots, \mathsf{name}(s_k))}$

where $W^1 = \langle Q, E^1, q_0, T^1 \rangle$ if $W = \langle Q, E, q_0, T \rangle$, that is, the full labelled transition system associated to a *leaf* term is the sequence automaton having state transition sequences of lenght 1 corresponding to the state transitions of W and the full labelled transition system associated to a *root* term is the *sequence product* lts (Definition 7) of the full ltss associated to the components of the term. Finally, let the semantic domain $\mathsf{LTS} = \{\mathcal{L} \subseteq_{lts} \mathsf{lts}(s) \mid s \in P\}$ be the set of subautomata of the full ltss associated with the (well-formed) terms of the language. For example, suppose we want to build the full lts associated to the PWS of Figure 5. We have:

$$\begin{aligned}\mathsf{lts}([pouring : (s_1, s_2), W, \phi]) &= (\mathsf{lts}(s_1) \oplus \mathsf{lts}(s_2))_{(\mathsf{name}(s_1),\mathsf{name}(s_2))} \\ &= (W_1^1 \oplus W_2^1)_{(nozzle,bottle)}\end{aligned}$$

and consequently, the behaviour of *pouring* is one of the subautomaton in such a sequence product lts. Due to the recursive structure of the full lts, the restriction can be easily achieved recursively. At each level of the tree, we check whether a lts homomorphism (Section 9) can be established (through the mapping ϕ) between the whole-section lts W and the sequence product of the semantics of the component subtrees. In the affirmative case, the term is said to be *correctly specified* and the semantics is simply the homomorphic image induced.

Let $\Psi : P \to \mathsf{LTS}$ be the semantic function which assigns a labelled transition system to a PWS term. There are two cases:

Leaf terms. The semantics of the term is the lts itself, except that it contains single-event sequences instead of single events. In symbols, if $s = [n : (), W]$ then

$$\Psi(s) = W^1 \tag{1}$$

Compound terms. Let $\Psi(s_1), \ldots, \Psi(s_k)$ be the semantics of the root term components $s = [n : (s_1, \ldots, s_k), W, \phi]$. We first make the sequence product lts of the semantics of the component subtrees, that is $\Psi_u^*(s) = (\Psi(s_1) \oplus \cdots \oplus \Psi(s_k))_I$, with $I =_{def} (\mathsf{name}(s_1), \ldots, \mathsf{name}(s_k))$. Consider the mapping $h = (h_Q, h_{QE})$ from $W = \langle Q, E, q_0, T\rangle$ to $\Psi_u^*(s) = \langle \bar{Q}, E_u^*, \mathbf{q}_0, T_u^*\rangle$ characterized by the function ϕ and by the specification of the initial state q_0 of W as follows:

1. Let $h_Q(q_0) = \mathbf{q}_0$.
2. If $h_Q(p) = \mathbf{p}$ and $(p, e, q) \in T$ then let $h_{QE}(p, e) = \phi(p, e)$ and let $h_Q(q) = \mathbf{q}$, where $\mathbf{q}$ is the state resulting from the application of the sequence $\phi(p, e)$ to $\mathbf{p}$.

Then, if for all $(p, e, q) \in T$ the condition $(h_Q(p), h_{QE}(p, e), h_Q(q)) \in T_u^*$ holds, then h is a lts homomorphism and the PWS term is said to be *correctly specified*. In that case, if $s_1, \ldots, s_k$ are also correctly specified (terms of the form $s = [n : (), W]$ are trivially correctly specified), the semantics of the term s is given by the *homomorphic image* induced by h on $\Psi_u^*(s)$:

$$\Psi(s) = \check{h}(\Psi_u^*(s)) \subseteq_{lts} \Psi_u^*(s) \tag{2}$$

For example, suppose to check whether the Statechart of Figure 5 is correctly specified. We start by letting the initial state of W, Ready, correspond, trough the mapping h_Q, to the initial state of the product, that is (Stopped, Empty). At this point there is an outgoing transition in W from Ready to Working, labelled by start. By applying the event sequence corresponding to start, that is $\phi(\mathsf{start}) = \langle \mathsf{start}_{Nozzle}\rangle$, to (Stopped, Empty) we obtain the state (Working, Empty). As a consequence we let Working and (Working, Empty) correspond through h_Q and we add the transition

$$\text{(Stopped, Empty)} \overset{\langle \text{start}_{Nozzle} \rangle}{\rightsquigarrow} \text{(Working, Empty)}$$

to the homomorphic image. The self state transition in W from Working to itself, labelled by pour, has to correspond to a self state transition from the corresponding state in the homomorphic image to itself, labelled by the sequence $\langle \text{squirt}_{Nozzle}, \text{fill}_{Bottle} \rangle$. We then add

$$\text{(Working, Empty)} \overset{\langle \text{squirt}_{Nozzle} \text{fill}_{Bottle} \rangle}{\rightsquigarrow} \text{(Working, Empty)}$$

to the homorphic image. As soon as the guard condition $[\texttt{content} + \texttt{q} < \texttt{capacity}]$ does not hold, we have

$$\text{(Working, Empty)} \overset{\langle \text{squirt}_{Nozzle} \text{fill}_{Bottle} \rangle}{\rightsquigarrow} \text{(Working, Full)}$$

At this point, no additional pour labelled state transitions can be taken in W, since it is guarded by $[\texttt{not in}(\text{Full})]$. The only allowed state transition is then finish, that is we complete the homomorphic image lts by

$$\text{(Working, Full)} \overset{\langle \text{stop}_{Nozzle} \rangle}{\rightsquigarrow} \text{(Stopped, Full)}$$

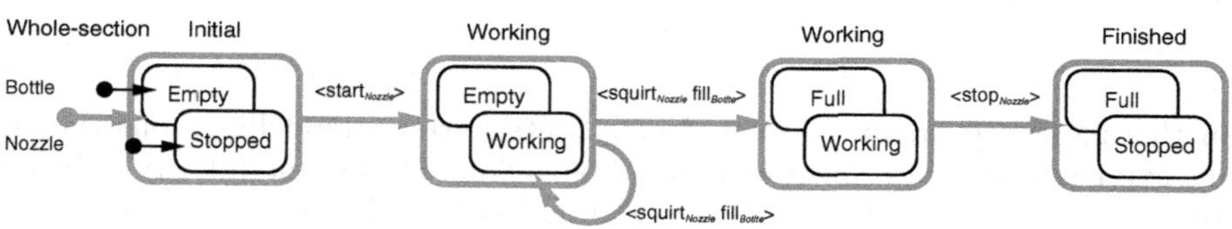

Fig. 6. The homomorphic image induced by W and ϕ.

3.3 Extendibilty and Reusability

The advantage of having an explict state machine representing behavioral aggregation can be better understood when extending the global behaviour and/or adding additional entites. For example, in Figure 7, we simply extend the state machine in the whole-section as shown in Figure 7, in order to extend the global behaviour of the plant. In Figure 8 it is suggested how to add a second nozzle to the bottling example. Observe that it is allowed to use the same high-level event pour in different contexts, since the resulting sequences are identified univocally, through mapping ϕ, by both the starting state of the transition and by the event name. Observe that both the pictures suggest a *black-box* (re)use of component Statecharts. It may be discussed, finally, whether to leave some form of visibility to the states in the main state machine of the components: alternatively, the guard condition $\text{in}(\text{Full}_{Bottle})$ of Figure 5 could be handled by raising a suitable exception, which is triggered when entering the state.

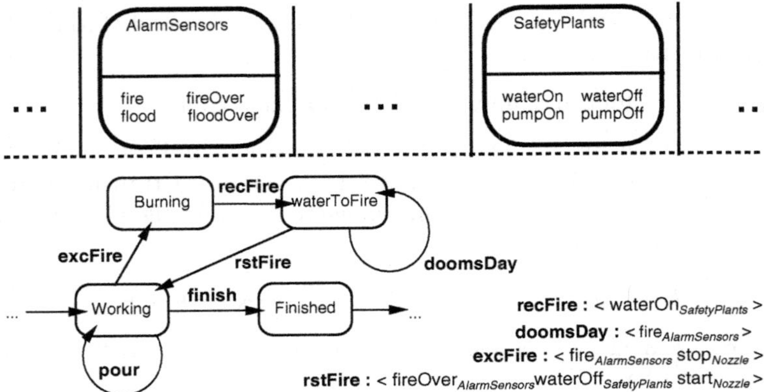

Fig. 7. Suppose we have to take into account different exceptional cases that may occur in the bottling plant (fire, floodings, etc.), such that any exceptional case requires a different response from the components of the system. Observe how this can be simply achieved by adding more components as well as states and state transitions in the whole-section.

4 Conclusions

In this paper we presented Part-Whole Statecharts, a modelling construct for the explicit representation of compound behaviors. Lack of modularity of behavioral semantics contrasts with the overall philosophy of object-oriented systems, depicting objects as behavioral units. The paper proposes to shift the semantics of aggregation from an implicitly defined web of references to an explicit state machine, which represent the dynamics of the aggregation between entities.

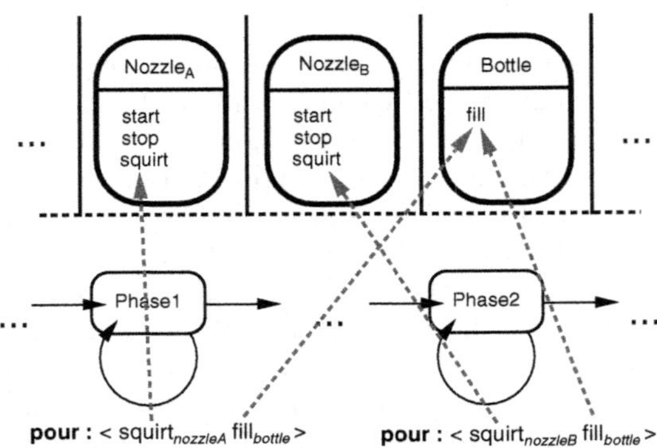

Fig. 8. Extending the bottling example by adding a second nozzle.

By using objects not only to represent structure, but also to localise behaviour, the object-oriented paradigm requires a *one-to-one* correspondence between behavioral and static abstractions. The explicit behavioral *aggregation* proposed in the paper represents a further step in that direction. We discuss in conclusion some interesting consequences that can be drawn.

The basic assumption inherent in object-oriented modelling is that static aspects are to be considered *primitive* knowledge and, as a consequence, elicited *separately* and *independently* from dynamic aspects. By the OMT approach, for example, a system is analyzed *first* by its static structure (*object modelling phase*), that is the structure of its objects and their relationship to each other at a single moment in time, *then* changes to the objects and their relationships over time (dynamic modelling phase). The common approach considers thus the *static layer* as prioritary. This fact coerces the subsequent design (that is, find the objects first, then model behaviour by using the objects found in the first place). The UML case confirms this tendency. As observed in the paper, dynamic information plays instead a critical role in determining the static structure, since very often only the observation of dynamic aspects calls for introducing wholes. This calls for revising the basis of the overall modelling philosophy which can be built on top of the instruments of the Unified Modelling Language.

References

1. S. Cook and J. Daniels. *Designing Object Systems - Object-Oriented Modelling with Syntropy.* Prentice-Hall, 1994. 542, 543, 544, 547
2. D. Champeaux (de), D. Lea, and P. Faure. The process of object-oriented design. In *OOPSLA92 Proceedings*, 1992. 542
3. D. Coleman et al. *Object-Oriented Development The Fusion Method.* Prentice-Hall, 1994. 542
4. A. Goldberg and D. Robson. *Smaltalk-80: The Language and its Implementation.* Addison-Wesley, Reading, MA, 1983. 542
5. The UML Group. Omg unified modeling language specification (draft), version 1.3 alpha r5. Technical report, Object Management Group, Inc., 1999. 542
6. D. Harel. Statecharts: A visual formalism for complex systems. *Science of Computer Programming*, 8:231–274, 1987. 543
7. D. Harel. On visual formalisms. *Communications of the ACM*, 31, 1988. 543
8. D. Harel and Gery E. Executable object modeling with statecharts. In *ICSE18*, 1994. 543
9. W. Kim. *Introduction to object-oriented databases.* The MIT Press, 1990. 541
10. Gerald Luettgen, Michael von der Beeck, and Rance Cleaveland. Statecharts via process algebra. Technical Report TR-99-42, Institute for Computer Applications in Science and Engineering, October 1999. 549
11. L. Pazzi. Extending statecharts for representing parts and wholes. In *Proceedings of the EuroMicro-97 Conference, Budapest, Hungary*, 1997. 542
12. J. Rumbaugh. Relations as semantic constructs in an object-oriented language. In *OOPSLA Proceedings*, 1987. 542
13. J. Rumbaugh, M. Blaha, W. Premerlani, F. Eddy, and W. Lorensen. *Object-Oriented Modeling and Design.* Prentice Hall, 1991. 541, 542, 543
14. R. Weber. *Ontological Foundations of Information Systems*, chapter 6. Coopers & Lybrand, 1997. 541

A Appendix

A.1 Labelled Transition System Inclusion and Equality

Definition 8. *A labelled transition system* $\mathcal{S} = \langle Q', q_0', E', T' \rangle$ *is a* subautomaton *of the labelled transition system* $\mathcal{T} = \langle Q, q_0, E, T \rangle$ *(in symbols* $\mathcal{S} \subseteq_{lts} \mathcal{T}$*) if and only if* $Q' \subseteq Q$, $q_0' = q_0$, $E' \subseteq E$ *and* $T' \subseteq T$.

A.2 Labelled Transition System Homomorphism

Definition 9. *If* $\mathcal{L}_1 = \langle Q_1, E_1, q_{01}, T_1 \rangle$ *and* $\mathcal{L}_2 = \langle Q_2, E_2, q_{02}, T_2 \rangle$ *are labelled transition systems, a* labelled transition system homorphism *from* $\mathcal{L}_1$ *to* $\mathcal{L}_2$ *is a pair* $h = (h_Q, h_{QE}) : Q_1 \times E_1 \to Q_2 \times E_2$ *of* onto *functions* $h_Q : Q_1 \to Q_2$ *and* $h_{QE} : Q_1 \times E_1 \to E_2$ *such that* $h_Q(q_{01}) = q_{02}$ *and* $(p_1, e_1, q_1) \in T_1 \Rightarrow (h_Q(p_1), h_{QE}(p_1, e_1), h_Q(q_1)) \in T_2$ *hold for all* $(p_1, e_1, q_1) \in T_1$. *Finally, let*

$$\check{h}(\mathcal{L}_2) = \langle Q, E, q_0, T \rangle \subseteq_{lts} \mathcal{L}_2$$

be the homomorphic image induced by *the homorphism* onto $\mathcal{L}_2$, *where*

- $Q = \{h_Q(q) \mid q \in Q_1\}$
- $E = \{h_{QE}(q, e) \mid (q, e) \in Q_1 \times E_1\}$
- $q_0 = h_Q(q_{01})$
- $T = \{(h_Q(p), h_{QE}(p, e), h_Q(q)) \mid (p, e, q) \in T_1\}$

Modeling of Architectures with UML
Panel

Moderator:
Thomas Weigert[1]

Panellists:
David Garlan[2], John Knapman[3], Birger Møller-Pedersen[4], Bran Selic[5]

[1] Motorola, Schaumburg, IL, U.S.A.
thomas.weigert@motorola.com
[2] Carnegie Mellon University, Pittsburgh, PA, U.S.A
garlan@sei.cmu.edu
[3] IBM, Winchester, U.K.
knapman@uk.ibm.com
[4] Ericsson AS, 1375 Billingstad, Norway
Birger.Moller-Pedersen@eto.ericsson.se
[5] Rational Software Inc., Kanata, Canada
bran@objectime.com

Abstract. A critical level of abstraction in the modeling of a large, complex system is its architecture. At an architectural level one models the principal system elements and their interaction. Architectural models are typically used to provide an intellectually tractable, birds-eye view of a system and to permit design-time reasoning about system-level concerns such as performance, reliability, portability, and conformance to external standards and architectural styles.

In practice most architectural descriptions are informal documents. They are usually centered on box-and-line diagrams, with explanatory prose. Visual conventions are idiosyncratic, and usually project specific. As a result, architectural descriptions are only vaguely understood by developers, they cannot be analyzed for consistency or completeness, they are only hypothetically related to implementations, their properties cannot be enforced as a system evolves, and they cannot be supported by tools to help software architects with their tasks.

There exist several architecture description languages, but we are interested in the use of UML. We aim to identify requirements on architectural modeling and how different modeling concepts of UML meet these requirements. This paper is not intended as a critique of the UML but as a discussion of approaches to modeling architectures that have been tried, more or less successfully.

This paper was influenced by discussions with Steve Mellor and Ed Seidewitz, whose comments and feedback are greatly appreciated.

A. Evans, S. Kent and B. Selic (Eds.): «UML» 2000, LNCS 1939, pp. 556-569, 2000.

1 What Does UML Say about Architecture?

We begin by examining how UML treats architecture. (We shall focus on the current version of UML, which is 1.3.)

The modeling glossary of the UML specification provides the following definition of *architecture.*

> The organizational structure and associated behavior of a system. An architecture can be recursively decomposed into parts that interact through interfaces, relationships that connect parts, and constraints for assembling parts. Parts that interact through interfaces include classes, components and subsystems. [1, p. B-3]

The *UML Reference Manual* provides a similar but somewhat refined definition.

> The organizational structure of a system, including its decomposition into parts, their connectivity, interaction mechanisms, and the guiding principles that inform the design of a system. [2, p. 150]

Common to both these definitions are the consideration of the following primary architectural facets.

> Architecture is concerned with the *decomposition* of a system into parts,
> the *connections* between these parts, and
> the *interaction* of the parts of the system required for the functioning of the system.

Further, these definitions are for the architecture of a *system.* The *UML Reference Manual* offers a definition of *system* that is largely the counterpart of the definition of *architecture.*

> A collection of connected units organized to accomplish a purpose. A system can be described by one or more models, possibly from different viewpoints. The system is the "complete model." [2, p.467]

Again we can note two important aspects to this definition.

> A system has a well-defined *purpose.*
> A system is *complete* in the sense that it is the totality of what is being modeled to realize this purpose.

We have established that architecture has to do with the decomposition of systems. The next question is, therefore, what systems consist of (i.e. what the parts constituting the architecture of a system are). A System and its corresponding specification is defined in UML as follows:

> A model describes possible states of a system consisting of objects, values and links.

We read this as stating that architecture is concerned with structuring of systems in terms of instances at run-time (since the definition is referring to the possible states of a system).

> The *architecture* defines the high-level structure and behavior of the system during execution.

Note that this does not refer to the run-time of an implementation based upon a UML model but to a conceptual "UML run-time." Some parts of the run-time architecture are present in the structuring of the corresponding specification while others, such as the partitioning into packages have more to do with managing large specifications. A system may require many specification elements (e.g. many classes), but have a simple run-time architecture. (A system is large and complex because it has many and complex instances, not because its specification has many elements.)

The above definition of architecture is general; just like the UML it should apply to all application domains. Specific approaches and languages, e.g., the UML profiles based on ROOM (UML-RT [3]) or SDL [4], or the generic architectural description language ACME [6], all appear to rely on a view of architecture that is in line with the above UML view. They each have introduced their own facilities and vocabulary for describing system structures (see Table 1).

As an example of an even more specific approach to architecture, the recent Request for Proposal for a UML profile for Event-based Architectures in Enterprise Application Integration (EAI) [5] defines:

> Application Architecture: A constrained description [...] of the principal objects that comprise a collection of IT systems (a superordinate system in UML terms) together with their interactions. [...] An application architecture may include high-level descriptions of objects provided in infrastructure products and other vendor-supplied packages.

> Event-based architecture: An application architecture based on the central importance of business events. Business events are represented as messages to and from IT systems, which may give rise to other messages between and within IT systems in a timely manner.

We can summarize all these definitions of architecture in UML terms along the following lines:

The architecture of a system is composed of instances of various kinds (subsystems, classifier instances, objects, components) and their interactions.

So far the terms *architecture* and *system* have been identified, and it is established that the parts of a system are *instances* of various kinds. In the cited definitions, it is also important that these parts *interact* with each other, and that a system *interacts* with the environment.

Finally, the introduction to and the definition of Interaction describes what it means for parts of a system to interact:

> An *interaction* specifies the communication between *instances* performing a specific task. Each interaction is defined in the context of a collaboration [1, 2-107].

> The purpose of an *interaction* is to specify the communication between a set of *interacting instances* performing a specific task. An interaction is defined within a collaboration, i.e. the collaboration defines the context in which the interaction takes place. The *instances* performing the communication specified by the *interaction* conform to the classifier roles of the collaboration [1, 2-114].

The important statement in these passages is that

the parts of a system that interact are *instances.*

A system can be, and usually is, described by some or all of the following viewpoints, or models. The *requirements model* defines the required capabilities of the system relative to its environment. The *analysis model* defines an implementation-independent realization of the requirements of the system. The *logical model* defines the design for realizing the requirements of the system taking into account implementation issues, but without considering issues of physical packaging, distribution and deployment. The *physical model* defines the residence of elements of the logical model in various physical components, the deployment of those components on physical nodes and the physical connections between those components and nodes. In light of the above, we consider architecture as applying to analysis models and logical models.

2 Requirements on Architectural Modeling

Architectural modelers commonly agree that the architecture of a system, in particular a large-scale system, is best described by the hierarchical decomposition of its instance structure (see [6, 7]). This instance structure is one of connected instances. It describes how the parts of a system interact to carry out the functionality of the whole. For the modeling of large-scale systems it is important to support the representation of the system in terms of what instances it is composed of, how these instances are encapsulated in higher-level instances, how these instances are connected, and what communication between these instances is possible.

In the spirit of UML, these requirements aim at providing a generic model for describing system structure that is independent of a particular engineering domain (e.g., real-time systems) or the choice of component integration technology (e.g., CORBA).

Beyond the representation of structure, architectural modeling also has a behavioral component, as has been touched upon earlier. There are requirements on behavior modeling corresponding to the requirements on the modeling of structure (e.g., regarding the decomposition of Interactions), as well as requirements of its own (e.g., regarding the decomposition of state machines). Space limitations have forced us to restrict this discussion to the modeling of structure.

2.1 Composition and Connection of Instances

Architecture is about composition of instances. Class Composition makes it possible to define classes of objects that have a number of "contained" objects, but it must also be possible to specify the connections between the instances of an architecture. Links could be used as they connect instances. However, object diagrams are intended for describing snapshots of (parts of) a system, not for prescribing the contents of, e.g., a composite class.

> Connections must *connect instances* or at least "instance placeholders," so connections are not associations between classifiers.

The specification of an architecture must include the *initial instantiations*, which come into existence when the system itself is instantiated. The initial instantiation includes the initial instances and their connections.

Connectors must do more than connect instances. At a minimum, they specify allowed communication and possible interactions. Beyond representing mere conduits of communication, they may themselves capture the key communication relationship between two architectural elements. As such, they may impose constraints on the elements that could potentially be connected through them. Connections must allow the definition of complex transactions, and they may need to maintain information about the state of these transactions.

Connections must be able to specify the expectations they place on the instances they connect, both in terms of the functional capabilities these instances must support and the interaction sequences that these instances must participate in.

Transactions between architectural elements are examples of structured collaborations that follow a precisely specified pattern of behavior (often referred to as *protocols*). Specifying these patterns of behavior is key to successful architectures since it eliminates one major source of integration problems. In addition, if such specifications are defined independently of any particular structural context, they can become reusable components.

2.2 Abstraction

It must be possible to refine abstract architectures into more detailed ones. This is needed not only for top-down design but also to derive different variations from a common abstract architecture. One of the most effective ways of achieving such refinement is to use inheritance. (Using inheritance, one could, e.g., describe product families by generating different subclasses from a common abstract architecture.) Hence we need to support inheritance of architectural specifications, both of the structure and the behavior.

In order to define subclasses of architectures, we have to be able to define classifiers of architectures. That is, it should be possible to define the specification of a classifier to be its contained instances and their connections.

Inheritance realizes one type of genericity, whereby a single abstract specification captures the essential features of a number of different variations. However, there are other forms of genericity, such as polymorphism, which are equally useful that should also be supported in architectural modeling.

It must be possible to define classifiers of architectures so that architectures can be created dynamically and so that an architecture specification can be inherited.

Consequentially, it will be possible to add, supersede, or replace objects and connect them to the architecture, as well as to add new connections between existing objects in the inherited architecture. Similarly, it will be possible to create elements of the architecture dynamically, to establish connections between objects dynamically, and to reconfigure the assembly of connections dynamically.

2.3 Interaction Points and Encapsulation

In order to make objects of an architecture as independent as possible from each other, it should be possible to specify–as part of a classifier–the possible interaction points along with their allowed communication.

This goes beyond mere association by trying to achieve "plug-substitutability" of the architectural structure. Plug-substitutability needs additional mechanisms to establish *interaction points* where architectural elements are connected and through which they interact.

Architectural elements are typically involved in multiple collaborations with diverse other architectural elements. This indicates a need for the ability to present multiple specialized interaction points such that each element sees only those capabilities of the architectural element that are required for its specific purposes. This is analogous to the distinct sockets that we typically see on hardware elements.

Interaction points are not just object interfaces: in addition to simple message calls and receptions, they must include outputs and the definition of complex transactions. Because each interaction point may be involved in a different transaction, it is not sufficient to support multiple interaction points of different types, but we also need to support the possibility of multiple interaction point instances of the same type on the same architectural element.

> Interaction points must be able to specify both a *required* and a *provided* interface, both in terms of signals and operations. In other words, interaction points must specify the requirements a system places on its environment, in addition to the services the system offers to its environment.
>
> It must be possible to define the interaction points as parts of classifiers, independently of the structural context of instances of the classifiers.

In order to describe the *allowed communication* at an interaction point it must be possible to specify the incoming and outgoing messages of an architectural element independently of any knowledge of where this element will be used. Requiring knowledge about the other end of a communication breaks encapsulation and is undesirable for architectural modeling.

2.4 Scalability

There is a strong need to support the notion of architecture at many different levels of granularity. A system may be decomposed into parts, each of which may have its own architecture. Depending on the complexity of the system at hand, we may need to do this down to an arbitrary depth. Similarly, but in the opposite direction, we need to allow existing architectures to be composed simply and directly into yet greater architectures.

> Architecture mechanisms must *scale*, so they must be *recursive.* Instances may in turn have architecture in terms of instances and their connections. Applying recursion the other way implies that a system is a special, outermost instance.

3 Architectural Modeling Using the UML

In the following, we investigate four different structuring concepts of the UML: Subsystems, Composition, Attributes, and Collaboration. They have been applied to an example architecture (see Fig. 1) to illustrate applying these structuring concepts to the representation of the architecture of this simple system.

As we shall see, none of these approaches will prove completely satisfactory. Their limitations could be overcome by defining special stereotypes of generic UML elements to introduce constraints as was done in the case of the UML-RT [3] and SDL [4] profiles. However, the ability to model architectures is a common requirement for most software domains and, consequently, should be part of the core modeling capabilities of UML rather than being limited to a profile.

Fig. 1 shows the kind of picture one will typically find in architecture specification documents, i.e., it is not UML.

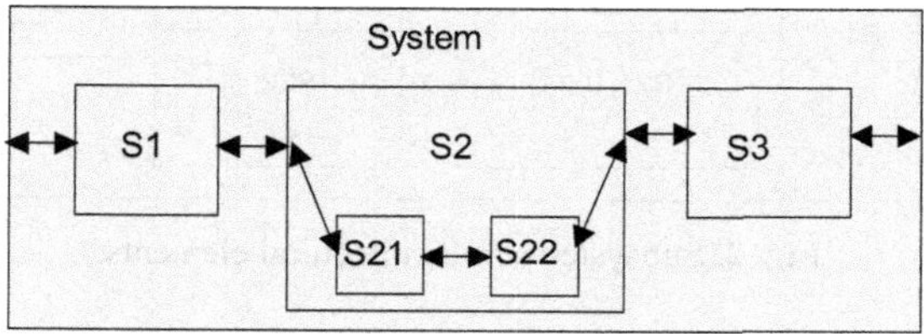

Fig. 1. Example architecture

The boxes represent the instances as part of the system. The lines represent connections, and these will have properties as described above. The text in each box gives the names of the parts. A property not specified in the figure is that *S1* and *S3* have the same definition as if, e.g., they were of the same class, say *S*. *S2* is specified "in-line," but it must be possible to have its content either abstracted away or specified in a separate diagram, so that *S2* would have the same appearance as *S1* and *S3*.

Finally, we examine whether the concept of Interface satisfies the requirements placed on the encapsulation boundaries.

3.1 Subsystems

Instantiable subsystems, primarily considered as classifiers, meet the requirement of abstraction and scalability in that different subsystems (instances) of the same system can be of the same subsystem classifier. Subsystems can contain subsystems to any depth, and each of these can be specified by separate (static structure) diagrams.

Although the concept of Subsystem would seem to be the obvious choice of UML mechanism for specifying architectures, there are several reasons why subsystems do not meet our requirements (see Fig. 2):

Subsystems do not support encapsulation. The interfaces are really interfaces of objects within the subsystem. Similarly, subsystems cannot be connected: Any association connected to a subsystem specifies a link to an instance of a class that it contains.

It is not possible to identify subsystems, so it is not possible to interact with a subsystem without knowing some objects within the subsystem.

Subsystems do not have interaction points. In order to show that *S1* interacts with *S21* and *S3* with *S22* in Fig. 2, we have to make associations crossing the boundary of *S2*. Subsystems may have interfaces, but interfaces do not provide a complete, reified interaction point concept. This is somewhat ameliorated for subsystems by the use of boundary classes within subsystems.

The two occurrences of *S* in Fig. 2 really represent the same subsystem *S*. There is nothing stated in Fig. 2 that ensures that there will be two instances of *S* that are part of *System*.

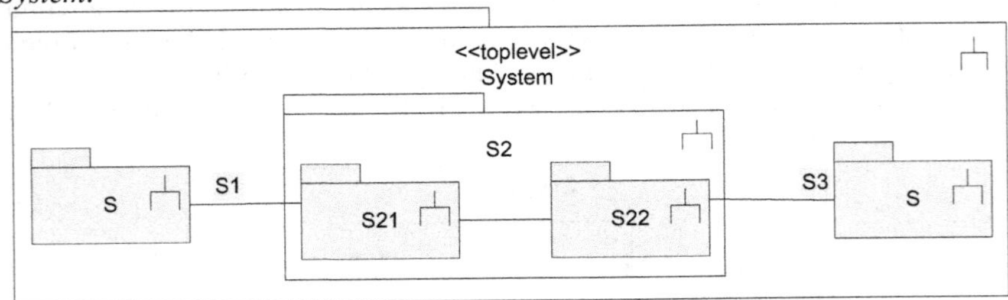

Fig. 2. Subsystems as architectural elements.

If *S2* is defined by a separate diagram (for scalability reasons), then it would *not* be possible to specify that *S1* is associated with *S21* and that *S3* is associated with *S22*. Interfaces on *S2* would not help, as it is not possible to connect these with the contained subsystems. A separate diagram for *S2* would appear as in Fig. 3.

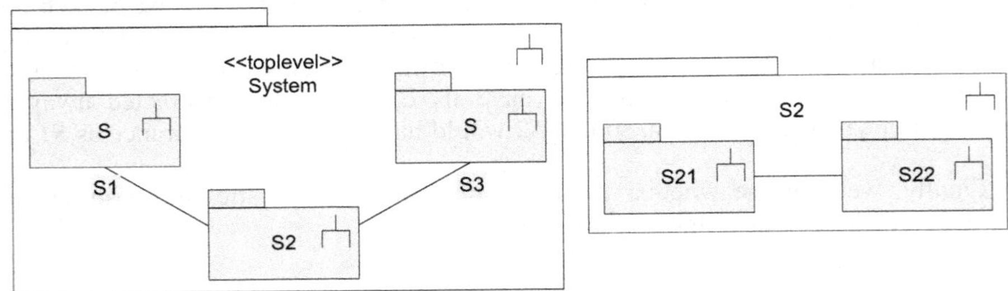

Fig. 3. Subsystem *S2* as a separate package diagram.

Here it is not possible to specify that the contained subsystems will be associated with subsystems outside *S2*. It is not even possible to specify that they will be connected via interaction points of the enclosing *S2*. Note that this is not a fundamental problem, but a problem with the UML notation. In state machines, for example, tricks like stub states get around a similar issue. Another way of getting around this problem would be to use boundary objects.

The instances of the subsystem are instances of the classes of the subsystem. These have to be created as the result of some *create* actions, and as the subsystem does not have any behavior, these *create* actions must be performed by instances of the classes of the subsystem.

3.2 Composition

The mechanism chosen by most users is class composition, possibly augmented with stereotyped classes. This approach is well supported by tools, and class diagrams are among the best-understood and most used part of the UML. The notation provided in the Notation Guide (see [1, p. 3-74] and Fig. 4), but supported by few tools, conveys the architecture better than the alternative representation relying on class symbols together with composition associations.

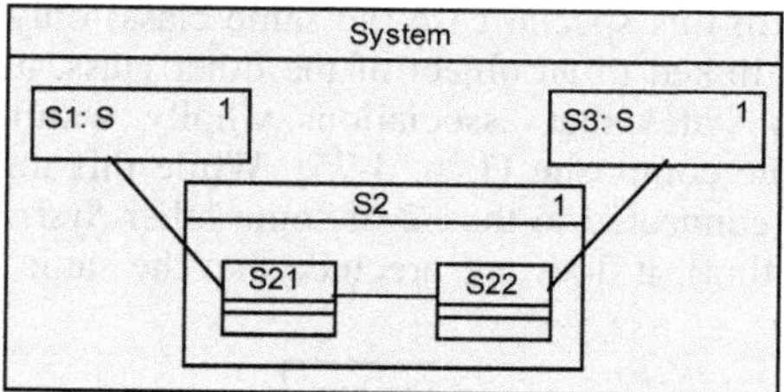

Fig. 4. Composite classes as architectural elements.

On this approach, architecture specifications can benefit from features of classes that have to do with architecture (encapsulation, interfaces) as well as features of classes that make it possible to dynamically create an architectural element and to apply, e.g., specialization to architecture patterns defined by classes.

It is also straightforward to specify that two parts of an architecture have the same specification, simply by making them objects of the same class. If we use bounded multiplicities as shown in Fig. 4, this approach also provides us with initial instances.

However, there are also problems with this approach: Classes in a composition can be associated, but composition does not allow the expression of relationships between specific instances in the context of a particular composite.

Although encapsulation is supported better than with subsystems (for example, the interfaces are interfaces of the composite object) classes do not have interaction points.

The lack of an interaction point concept makes it impossible to specify (in Fig. 5) that the contained classes of *S2* will be associated with classes outside of *S2*. It is not even possible to specify that they will be connected via some kind of interface of the enclosing *S2*.

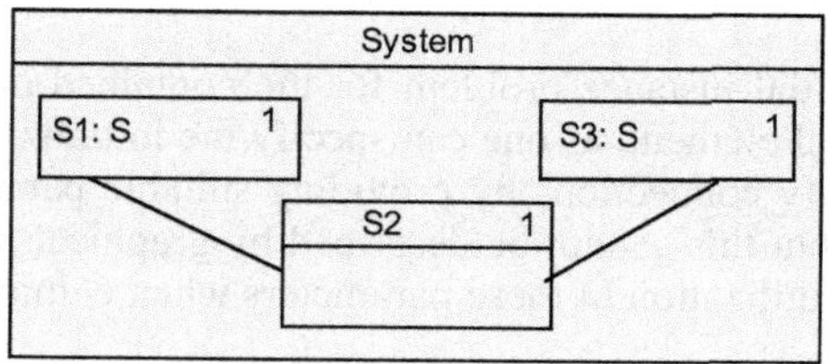

Fig. 5. Composite class view.

In general, a class diagram is not able to specify the topology of an architecture of specific instances because classes and associations are abstractions. Classes define properties of potential instances, and associations define constraints on potential links, but neither can specify specific instances or links. This point is best illustrated by the well-known car example [8] that is concerned with specifying connections without introducing special classes for this purpose. In terms of our running example, the specification in Fig. 5 may look like a specification of a class of *System* objects with two *S* objects connected to an instance of *S2*.

This is, however, not the case. Fig. 5 is more or less equivalent to the specification in Fig. 6, which only says that an *S2* object may have two links to an *S* object, but it does not state that it will be linked to two distinct *S* objects. Specifying an association between two classes (in this special case the same class) only specifies that a given object of this class is linked to an object of the other class, not a specific object. In addition, Fig. 5 also states that associations wholly within the composite class symbols are part of the composite [1, p. 3-75]. While this may preclude that in the *System* object an *S* is connected to the *S2* of some other *System* (at least not through this particular association), it does not preclude that the same *S* is connected by two links to *S2*.

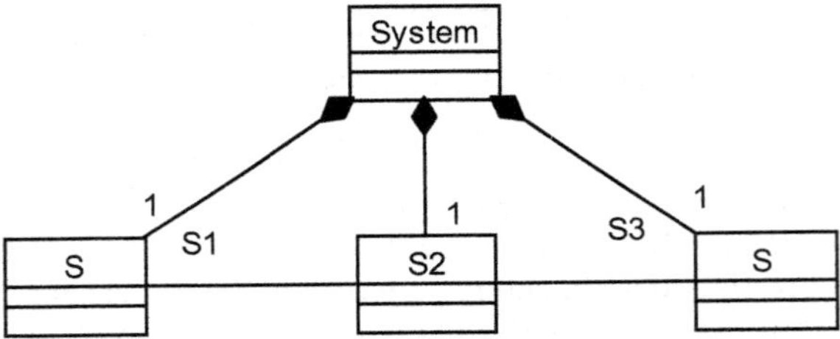

Fig. 6. Composite association view.

The problem here is that composition cannot limit associations between contained parts to the context of the whole without constraining how instances of the aggregated classes are associated or attributed in other contexts.

3.3 Attributes

The Notation Guide (see [1, p.3-75]) describes attributes as a kind of composition between a classifier and the classifier of the attribute. Specification of architecture by means of attributes relies also on the fact that attribute links may denote objects (and not only values).

This solves the initial instance problem for the contained objects, but not for the outermost architectural element, as one can specify the initialization of attributes. It is also possible to specify connections by providing suitable parameters to the creation of the initial values, but this cannot be described by graphical means and needs to be matched by a careful utilization of these parameters when communicating.

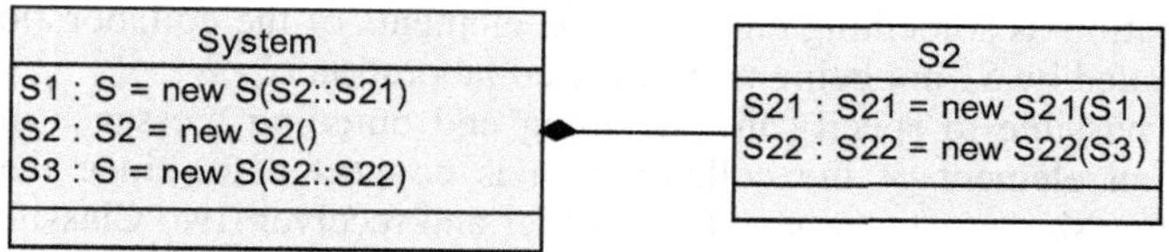

Fig. 7. Attributes as architectural elements.

Regarding encapsulation, this approach has the same problem as subsystems and composition: It is not possible to specify that the connections to *S2* should also be connections to the parts of *S2*.

3.4 Collaboration

A well-known alternative is to use a combination of composition (or attributes) and collaboration. The composition introduces the composite class, while an associated collaboration (with the represented classifier being the composite class) defines the structure of objects and their communication constituting the architecture.

Contrary to the earlier approaches, the associated collaboration also allows the specification of the communication between the connected instances by attaching Interactions to the collaboration. These interactions comprise the sequence of Messages that are interchanged between the connected instances.

In effect, if we model connectors and architectural elements as features of the containing class, then the collaboration can be interpreted as a constraint on these features. This is illustrated in Fig. 8. The collaboration diagram to the right represents the content of the collaboration *C*, shown on the left as realizing the system. (Note that Fig. 8 does not correspond to the way collaborations are utilized to model structure in the UML-RT [3] profile.)

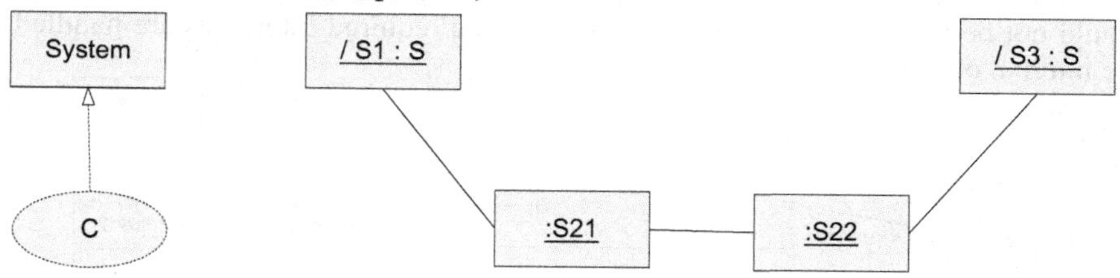

Fig. 8. Collaboration representing the structure of a class.

In addition to the difficulties already described for composition (or attributes), this alternative has the following problems:

A collaboration does not define a structure that may be instantiated. Instead, it is a way of describing how the parts, once instantiated, may interact.

The elements of a collaboration are not really objects but roles. This means that, for example, in Fig. 8 the same object could be playing both the *S1* and *S3* role, contrary to the architecture we are trying to specify.

It is not possible to specify that the elements of the collaboration interact through interfaces of the composite class. In fact the composite class does not even appear in the collaboration as something enclosing the elements of the collaboration. In Fig. 8, this is illustrated by *S2* not being part of the collaboration *C*.

It is not possible to specify the incoming and outgoing messages independently from what an element of the collaboration is connected to, since the metamodel requires that a Message must have both sender and receiver (two ClassifierRoles). As a consequence, to specify the allowed communication of a composite requires knowledge of the identity of the recipient of outbound messages or senders of incoming messages.

3.5 Interfaces

A classifier may have relationships to an interface of *provided* functional capabilities, and a separate interface of *required* functional capabilities. The way this is specified in UML is shown in Fig. 9: The classes, however, are not specifications of one single interaction point and the connections are obtained by two different mechanisms (generalization and dependency).

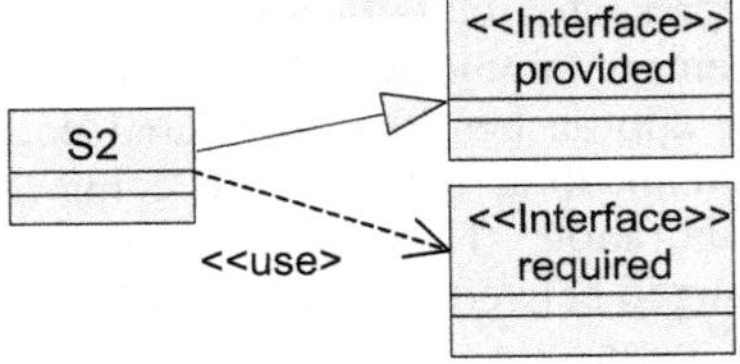

Fig. 9. Provided and required interfaces.

This needs two interfaces, but they do not define any interaction points for the connection of external and internal objects. If *S2* is defined to be a composition of *S21* and *S22*, and this has to be specified in a separate diagram (see Fig. 10), then it would not be possible to specify that the provided/required interfaces are handled by the internal objects.

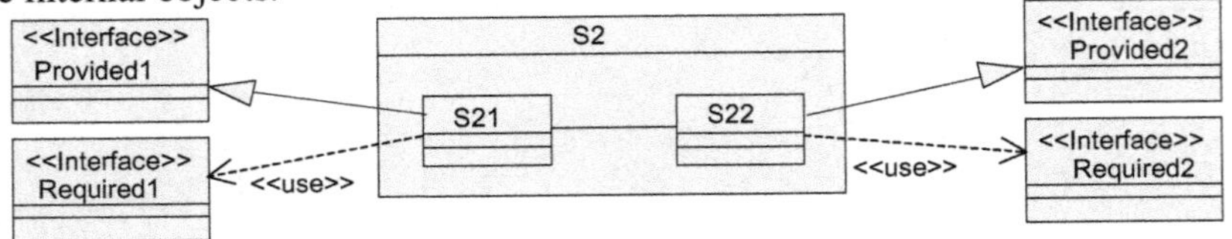

Fig. 10. An architectural element with its interfaces.

Further, if the allowed signals need to be specified, then interfaces cannot be used, as they only cover operations. The notion of reception is supposed to cover that, but the metamodel does not support the association of receptions with a class. Reception is a specialization of BehavioralFeature and classifiers can have features in general, but for BehavioralFeature the specializations Operation and Method are explicitly part of the metamodel, while Reception is not.

4 Conclusion

The specifications of run-time architectures discussed in this paper concern the structure of systems. By structure we mean a specification of instances of architectural elements and their relationships. Structural relationships that need to be modeled are:

Communication relationships. Two or more architectural elements interact with each other using one or more explicit communication facilities. The semantics of these facilities varies and includes broadcast and multicast as well as point-to-point.

Containment relationships. These provide encapsulation in the form of composition and aggregation, with their standard UML meaning.

Layering relationships. Here a layer of software hides an underlying realization and provides more complex and/or more specialized capabilities to architectural elements in higher layers.

The vocabulary of the UML, while varied and rich, is ultimately designed to support an object-oriented view of software design. That view emphasizes composition of systems from parts that provide certain services and depend on the services of other parts. As discussed here, architecture takes a broader view, particularly with respect to the interaction of parts. Another key concern is the way that objects and classes are mixed in the specification of architectures.

UML currently does not provide a satisfactory solution to the modeling of architectures. However, the familiarity of UML to many designers and developers provides a strong incentive to try to overcome these obstacles. The most promising approach is to extend the UML to include an explicit architectural vocabulary. This could be done by extending the UML metamodel, or by defining a profile for architectural modeling. Indeed, several profiles that include architectural notions [3, 4, 5] have already been defined or are under development.

References

1. OMG Unified Modeling Language Specification, Version 1.3, OMG Document ad/99-06-08, June 1999.
2. J. Rumbaugh, I. Jacobson and G. Booch, *Unified Modeling Language Reference Manual*, Addison Wesley, 1999, p. 150.
3. B. Selic, UML-RT: A Profile for Modeling Complex Real-Time Architectures, Technical Report, ObjecTime Ltd., 1999.
4. SDL Combined with UML, Recommendation Z.109, International Telecommunications Union, 1999.
5. UML Profile for Event Based Architectures in Enterprise Application Integration (EAI) Request for Proposal, OMG document ad/00-03-07, March 2000.
6. D. Garlan, R. Monroe, D. Wile, *ACME Reference Guide*. Available from the URL http://www.cs.cmu.edu/~acme
7. N. Medvidocic and R. Taylor, "A Framework for Classifying and Comparing Architecture Description Languages", *Proc. 6th European Software Engineering Conference*, 1997.
8. C. Bock and J. Odell, "A Foundation for Composition", *Journal Of Object-Oriented Programming*, Vol 7, No 6, 1994.

ACME	ROOM / UML-RT	SDL
Component: The primary computational elements and data stores of a system. Intuitively, they correspond to the boxes in box-and-line descriptions of software architectures.	***Capsule:*** A capsule models a complex active object that may have multiple ports through which it interacts with its environment.	***Agent:*** An agent represents an active object or a set of active objects that interact(s) with its environment through gates.
Connector: Represents interactions among components. Connectors mediate the communication among components.	***Connector:*** A connector is a communication object that conveys messages between ports attached to its end. The message exchange conforms to the protocol associated with the port.	***Channel:*** A channel connects two (sets of) agents by their gates and represents the possibility of communication between these. Any communication has to obey the constraints imposed by the interfaces associated with the ports.
System: Represents configurations of components and connectors.	*Nothing directly matching, but the outermost capsule takes this role.*	***System:*** The outermost agent.
Port: Component interfaces are defined by a set of ports. Each port identifies a point of interaction between the component and its environment. A component may provide multiple interfaces by using different types of ports.	***Port:*** A port serves as an interaction point for capsules. Ports can receive signals and synchronous calls and can also be the source of signals and calls.	***Gate:*** A gate serves as an interaction point between an agent and its environment. Gates can send and receive signals, exceptions, and synchronous calls.
Role: Connectors also have interfaces that are defined by a set of roles. Each role of a connector defines a participant of the interaction represented by the connector.	***Protocol role and Protocol:*** Protocol roles specify one party in a protocol. A protocol is a generic specification of a closed group of participants that interact in specific ways to achieve one or more desired objectives.	***Interface:*** An interface specifies constraints on the communication between agents. It specifies the type of information an agent may offer to the environment as well as the type of information an agent may receive from the environment.

Table. 1. Comparison of several modeling notations supporting architectures (quoted from various presentations).

Author Index

Lecture Notes in Computer Science

For information about Vols. 1–1856
please contact your bookseller or Springer-Verlag

Vol. 1857: J. Kittler, F. Roli (Eds.), Multiple Classifier Systems. Proceedings, 2000. XII, 404 pages. 2000.

Vol. 1858: D.-Z. Du, P. Eades, V. Estivill-Castro, X. Lin, A. Sharma (Eds.), Computing and Combinatorics. Proceedings, 2000. XII, 478 pages. 2000.

Vol. 1860: M. Klusch, L. Kerschberg (Eds.), Cooperative Information Agents IV. Proceedings, 2000. XI, 285 pages. 2000. (Subseries LNAI).

Vol. 1861: J. Lloyd, V. Dahl, U. Furbach, M. Kerber, K.-K. Lau, C. Palamidessi, L. Moniz Pereira, Y. Sagiv, P.J. Stuckey (Eds.), Computational Logic – CL 2000. Proceedings, 2000. XIX, 1379 pages. (Subseries LNAI).

Vol. 1862: P.G. Clote, H. Schwichtenberg (Eds.), Computer Science Logic. Proceedings, 2000. XIII, 543 pages. 2000.

Vol. 1863: L. Carter, J. Ferrante (Eds.), Languages and Compilers for Parallel Computing. Proceedings, 1999. XII, 500 pages. 2000.

Vol. 1864: B. Y. Choueiry, T. Walsh (Eds.), Abstraction, Reformulation, and Approximation. Proceedings, 2000. XI, 333 pages. 2000. (Subseries LNAI).

Vol. 1865: K.R. Apt, A.C. Kakas, E. Monfroy, F. Rossi (Eds.), New Trends Constraints. Proceedings, 1999. X, 339 pages. 2000. (Subseries LNAI).

Vol. 1866: J. Cussens, A. Frisch (Eds.), Inductive Logic Programming. Proceedings, 2000. X, 265 pages. 2000. (Subseries LNAI).

Vol. 1867: B. Ganter, G.W. Mineau (Eds.), Conceptual Structures: Logical, Linguistic, and Computational Issues. Proceedings, 2000. XI, 569 pages. 2000. (Subseries LNAI).

Vol. 1868: P. Koopman, C. Clack (Eds.), Implementation of Functional Languages. Proceedings, 1999. IX, 199 pages. 2000.

Vol. 1869: M. Aagaard, J. Harrison (Eds.), Theorem Proving in Higher Order Logics. Proceedings, 2000. IX, 535 pages. 2000.

Vol. 1870: P. Deransart, M. Hermenegildo, J. Małuszynski (Eds.), Analysis and Visualization Tools for Constraint Programming. XXI, 363 pages. 2000.

Vol. 1872: J. van Leeuwen, O. Watanabe, M. Hagiya, P.D. Mosses, T. Ito (Eds.), Theoretical Computer Science. Proceedings, 2000. XV, 630 pages. 2000.

Vol. 1873: M. Ibrahim, J. Küng, N. Revell (Eds.), Database and Expert Systems Applications. Proceedings, 2000. XIX, 1005 pages. 2000.

Vol. 1874: Y. Kambayashi, M. Mohania, A M. Tjoa (Eds.), Data Warehousing and Knowledge Discovery. Proceedings, 2000. XII, 438 pages. 2000.

Vol. 1875: K. Bauknecht, S.K. Madria, G. Pernul (Eds.), Electronic Commerce and Web Technologies. Proceedings, 2000. XII, 488 pages. 2000.

Vol. 1876: F. J. Ferri, J.M. Iñesta, A. Amin, P. Pudil (Eds.), Advances in Pattern Recognition. Proceedings, 2000. XVIII, 901 pages. 2000.

Vol. 1877: C. Palamidessi (Ed.), CONCUR 2000 – Concurrency Theory. Proceedings, 2000. XI, 612 pages. 2000.

Vol. 1878: J.P. Bowen, S. Dunne, A. Galloway, S. King (Eds.), ZB 2000: Formal Specification and Development in Z and B. Proceedings, 2000. XIV, 511 pages. 2000.

Vol. 1879: M. Paterson (Ed.), Algorithms – ESA 2000. Proceedings, 2000. IX, 450 pages. 2000.

Vol. 1880: M. Bellare (Ed.), Advances in Cryptology – CRYPTO 2000. Proceedings, 2000. XI, 545 pages. 2000.

Vol. 1881: C. Zhang, V.-W. Soo (Eds.), Design and Applications of Intelligent Agents. Proceedings, 2000. X, 183 pages. 2000. (Subseries LNAI).

Vol. 1882: D. Kotz, F. Mattern (Eds.), Agent Systems, Mobile Agents, and Applications. Proceedings, 2000. XII, 275 pages. 2000.

Vol. 1883: B. Triggs, A. Zisserman, R. Szeliski (Eds.), Vision Algorithms: Theory and Practice. Proceedings, 1999. X, 383 pages. 2000.

Vol. 1884: J. Štuller, J. Pokorný, B. Thalheim, Y. Masunaga (Eds.), Current Issues in Databases and Information Systems. Proceedings, 2000. XIII, 396 pages. 2000.

Vol. 1885: K. Havelund, J. Penix, W. Visser (Eds.), SPIN Model Checking and Software Verification. Proceedings, 2000. X, 343 pages. 2000.

Vol. 1886: R. Mizoguchi, J. Slaney /Eds.), PRICAI 2000: Topics in Artificial Intelligence. Proceedings, 2000. XX, 835 pages. 2000. (Subseries LNAI).

Vol. 1888: G. Sommer, Y.Y. Zeevi (Eds.), Algebraic Frames for the Perception-Action Cycle. Proceedings, 2000. X, 349 pages. 2000.

Vol. 1889: M. Anderson, P. Cheng, V. Haarslev (Eds.), Theory and Application of Diagrams. Proceedings, 2000. XII, 504 pages. 2000. (Subseries LNAI).

Vol. 1890: C Linnhoff-Popien, H.-G. Hegering (Eds.), Trends in Distributed Systems: Towards a Universal Service Market. Proceedings, 2000. XI, 341 pages. 2000.

Vol. 1891: A.L. Oliveira (Ed.), Grammatical Inference: Algorithms and Applications. Proceedings, 2000. VIII, 313 pages. 2000. (Subseries LNAI).

Vol. 1892: P. Brusilovsky, O. Stock, C. Strapparava (Eds.), Adaptive Hypermedia and Adaptive Web-Based Systems. Proceedings, 2000. XIII, 422 pages. 2000.

Vol. 1893: M. Nielsen, B. Rovan (Eds.), Mathematical Foundations of Computer Science 2000. Proceedings, 2000. XIII, 710 pages. 2000.

Vol. 1894: R. Dechter (Ed.), Principles and Practice of Constraint Programming – CP 2000. Proceedings, 2000. XII, 556 pages. 2000.

Vol. 1895: F. Cuppens, Y. Deswarte, D. Gollmann, M. Waidner (Eds.), Computer Security – ESORICS 2000. Proceedings, 2000. X, 325 pages. 2000.

Vol. 1896: R. W. Hartenstein, H. Grünbacher (Eds.), Field-Programmable Logic and Applications. Proceedings, 2000. XVII, 856 pages. 2000.

Vol. 1897: J. Gutknecht, W. Weck (Eds.), Modular Programming Languages. Proceedings, 2000. XII, 299 pages. 2000.

Vol. 1898: E. Blanzieri, L. Portinale (Eds.), Advances in Case-Based Reasoning. Proceedings, 2000. XII, 530 pages. 2000. (Subseries LNAI).

Vol. 1899: H.-H. Nagel, F.J. Perales López (Eds.), Articulated Motion and Deformable Objects. Proceedings, 2000. X, 183 pages. 2000.

Vol. 1900: A. Bode, T. Ludwig, W. Karl, R. Wismüller (Eds.), Euro-Par 2000 Parallel Processing. Proceedings, 2000. XXXV, 1368 pages. 2000.

Vol. 1901: O. Etzion, P. Scheuermann (Eds.), Cooperative Information Systems. Proceedings, 2000. XI, 336 pages. 2000.

Vol. 1902: P. Sojka, I. Kopeček, K. Pala (Eds.), Text, Speech and Dialogue. Proceedings, 2000. XIII, 463 pages. 2000. (Subseries LNAI).

Vol. 1903: S. Reich, K.M. Anderson (Eds.), Open Hypermedia Systems and Structural Computing. Proceedings, 2000. VIII, 187 pages. 2000.

Vol. 1904: S.A. Cerri, D. Dochev (Eds.), Artificial Intelligence: Methodology, Systems, and Applications. Proceedings, 2000. XII, 366 pages. 2000. (Subseries LNAI).

Vol. 1905: H. Scholten, M.J. van Sinderen (Eds.), Interactive Distributed Multimedia Systems and Telecommunication Services. Proceedings, 2000. XI, 306 pages. 2000.

Vol. 1906: A. Porto, G.-C. Roman (Eds.), Coordination Languages and Models. Proceedings, 2000. IX, 353 pages. 2000.

Vol. 1907: H. Debar, L. Mé, S.F. Wu (Eds.), Recent Advances in Intrusion Detection. Proceedings, 2000. X, 227 pages. 2000.

Vol. 1908: J. Dongarra, P. Kacsuk, N. Podhorszki (Eds.), Recent Advances in Parallel Virtual Machine and Message Passing Interface. Proceedings, 2000. XV, 364 pages. 2000.

Vol. 1910: D.A. Zighed, J. Komorowski, J. Żytkow (Eds.), Principles of Data Mining and Knowledge Discovery. Proceedings, 2000. XV, 701 pages. 2000. (Subseries LNAI).

Vol. 1912: Y. Gurevich, P.W. Kutter, M. Odersky, L. Thiele (Eds.), Abstract State Machines. Proceedings, 2000. X, 381 pages. 2000.

Vol. 1913: K. Jansen, S. Khuller (Eds.), Approximation Algorithms for Combinatorial Optimization. Proceedings, 2000. IX, 275 pages. 2000.

Vol. 1914: M. Herlihy (Ed.), Distributed Computing. Proceedings, 2000. VIII, 389 pages. 2000.

Vol. 1917: M. Schoenauer, K. Deb, G. Rudolph, X. Yao, E. Lutton, J.J. Merelo, H.-P. Schwefel (Eds.), Parallel Problem Solving from Nature – PPSN VI. Proceedings, 2000. XXI, 914 pages. 2000.

Vol. 1918: D. Soudris, P. Pirsch, E. Barke (Eds.), Integrated Circuit Design. Proceedings, 2000. XII, 338 pages. 2000.

Vol. 1919: M. Ojeda-Aciego, I.P. de Guzman, G. Brewka, L. Moniz Pereira (Eds.), Logics in Artificial Intelligence. Proceedings, 2000. XI, 407 pages. 2000. (Subseries LNAI).

Vol. 1920: A.H.F. Laender, S.W. Liddle, V.C. Storey (Eds.), Conceptual Modeling – ER 2000. Proceedings, 2000. XV, 588 pages. 2000.

Vol. 1921: S.W. Liddle, H.C. Mayr, B. Thalheim (Eds.), Conceptual Modeling for E-Business and the Web. Proceedings, 2000. X, 179 pages. 2000.

Vol. 1922: J. Crowcroft, J. Roberts, M.I. Smirnov (Eds.), Quality of Future Internet Services. Proceedings, 2000. XI, 368 pages. 2000.

Vol. 1923: J. Borbinha, T. Baker (Eds.), Research and Advanced Technology for Digital Libraries. Proceedings, 2000. XVII, 513 pages. 2000.

Vol. 1924: W. Taha (Ed.), Semantics, Applications, and Implementation of Program Generation. Proceedings, 2000. VIII, 231 pages. 2000.

Vol. 1925: J. Cussens, S. Džeroski (Eds.), Learning Language in Logic. X, 301 pages 2000. (Subseries LNAI).

Vol. 1926: M. Joseph (Ed.), Formal Techniques in Real-Time and Fault-Tolerant Systems. Proceedings, 2000. X, 305 pages. 2000.

Vol. 1927: P. Thomas, H.W. Gellersen, (Eds.), Handheld and Ubiquitous Computing. Proceedings, 2000. X, 249 pages. 2000.

Vol. 1931: E. Horlait (Ed.), Mobile Agents for Telecommunication Applications. Proceedings, 2000. IX, 271 pages. 2000.

Vol. 1766: M. Jazayeri, R.G.K. Loos, D.R. Musser (Eds.), Generic Programming. Proceedings, 1998. X, 269 pages. 2000.

Vol. 1791: D. Fensel, Problem-Solving Methods. XII, 153 pages. 2000. (Subseries LNAI).

Vol. 1932: Z.W. Raś, S. Ohsuga (Eds.), Foundations of Intelligent Systems. Proceedings, 2000. XII, 646 pages. (Subseries LNAI).

Vol. 1933: R.W. Brause, E. Hanisch (Eds.), Medical Data Analysis. Proceedings, 2000. XI, 316 pages. 2000.

Vol. 1934: J.S. White (Ed.), Envisioning Machine Translation in the Information Future. Proceedings, 2000. XV, 254 pages. 2000. (Subseries LNAI).

Vol. 1937: R. Dieng, O. Corby (Eds.), Knowledge Engineering and Knowledge Management. Proceedings, 2000. XIII, 457 pages. 2000. (Subseries LNAI).

Vol. 1938: S.Rao, K.I. Sletta (Eds.), Next Generation Networks. Proceedings, 2000. XI, 392 pages. 2000.

Vol. 1939: A. Evans, S. Kent, B. Selic (Eds.), «UML» – The Unified Modeling Language. Proceedings, 2000. XIV, 572 pages. 2000.